Human Communication

THIRD EDITION

Human Communication

THIRD EDITION

Judy C. Pearson
North Dakota State University

Paul E. Nelson
North Dakota State University

Scott Titsworth
Ohio University

Lynn Harter
Ohio University

**McGraw-Hill
Higher Education**

Boston   Burr Ridge, IL   Dubuque, IA   New York   San Francisco   St. Louis
Bangkok   Bogotá   Caracas   Kuala Lumpur   Lisbon   London   Madrid   Mexico City
Milan   Montreal   New Delhi   Santiago   Seoul   Singapore   Sydney   Taipei   Toronto

The *McGraw·Hill* Companies

Mc Graw Hill **Higher Education**

Published by McGraw-Hill, an imprint of The McGraw-Hill Companies, Inc., 1221 Avenue of the Americas, New York, NY 10020. Copyright © 2008, 2006, 2003. All rights reserved. No part of this publication may be reproduced or distributed in any form or by any means, or stored in a database or retrieval system, without the prior written consent of The McGraw-Hill Companies, Inc., including, but not limited to, in any network or other electronic storage or transmission, or broadcast for distance learning.

This book is printed on acid-free paper.

4 5 6 7 8 9 0 WCK/WCK 0 9

ISBN : 978-0-07-338501-3 (student edition)
MHID: 0-07-338501-8

ISBN : 978-0-07-332883-6 (annotated instructor's edition)
MHID: 0-07-332883-9

Editor in Chief: *Mike Byan*
Publisher: *Frank Mortimer*
Sponsoring Editor: *Suzanne Earth*
Marketing Manager: *Leslie Oberhuber*
Director of Development: *Rhona Robbin*
Senior Development Editor: *Jennie Katsaros*
Editorial Assistant: *Erika Lake*
Associate Production Editor: *Alison Meier*
Art Director: *Jeanne M. Schreiber*
Design Manager: *Preston Thomas*
Text Designer: *Kay Lieberherr*
Cover Designers: *Kim Menning and DiAnna VanEycke*
Art Editor: *Ayelet Arbel*
Photo Research Coordinator: *Natalia Peschiera*

Photo Researcher: *David Tietz, Editorial Image, LLC*
Production Supervisor: *Tandra Jorgensen*
Composition: *10.5/12 Goudy by Aptara, Inc.*
Printing: *45# PubMatte, Quebecor World, Inc.*
Front cover, left to right: © *Bill Sykes Images,* © *Ryan McVay/Getty Images,* © *Brand X Pictures/PunchStock,* © *Dynamic Graphics, Inc. All rights reserved./Jupiterimages,* © *Purestock/Punch-Stock,* © *Corbis/PictureQuest*
Back Cover, left to right: © *Getty Images,* © *Beathan/Corbis,* © *Dave & Les Jacobs/SuperStock,* © *BananaStock/PictureQuest,* © *Burke/Triolo Productions/Jupiterimages*

Credits: The credits section for this book begins on page C-1 and is considered an extension of the copyright page.

Library of Congress Cataloging-in-Publication Data

Human communication / Judy C. Pearson . . . [et al.]. — 3rd ed.
    p. cm.
  Includes bibliographical references and index.
  ISBN-13: 978-0-07-338501-3
  ISBN-10: 0-07-338501-8
  1. Communication. I. Pearson, Judy C.
P90.H745 2008
302.2—dc22   2007018061

The Internet addresses listed in the text were accurate at the time of publication. The inclusion of a website does not indicate an endorsement by the authors or McGraw-Hill, and McGraw-Hill does not guarantee the accuracy of the information presented at these sites.

www.mhhe.com

dedication

We dedicate this book to our children Emma, Rebekah, Benjamin, Kathryn, Christopher, Chip, and Dana.

brief contents

BRIEF CONTENTS

ONLINE UNIT: *Mediated Communication and Media Literacy:* This section is found on the book's *Online Learning Center* website at www.mhhe.com/pearson3

contents

C O N T E N T S

P A R T   T W O   Communication Contexts

P A R T T H R E E Fundamentals of Public Speaking:
Preparation and Delivery

from the authors

FROM THE AUTHORS

Dear Colleagues:

This communication text was written by four teachers with extensive backgrounds in communication fundamentals. One married couple—Pearson and Nelson—has written many editions of communication texts for almost four decades, and they have served as basic course directors and introductory course teachers at a number of private and public universities. The other married couple—Titsworth and Harter—is much younger but equally involved in introductory courses. Together, this foursome wrote an earlier edition of this textbook. Their common love of communication studies, undergraduate instruction, and translation of complex research into useful application drove this enterprise.

(left to right) Judy Pearson, Paul Nelson, Lynn Harter, and Scott Titsworth

Human Communication is an introductory college textbook designed to make communication studies immediate and relevant to students. Some communication textbooks rest on rhetorical traditions that extend back over two millennia. Other textbooks mainly cite experimental studies, the results of social science research over the last 45 years. This textbook embraces both approaches: It respects the field's rich rhetorical traditions and practices, and it uses the results of current social science research to enlighten students about how communication works in personal relationships, interviews, work teams, and public forums.

Because the beginning course is often the only communication course many students take, instructors have ambitious goals for their students. Students are expected to learn about how communication operates in their minds (intrapersonal communication), how communication works on the job (interviews, organizational communication, and work teams), how communication works in dating, courtship, and marriage (interpersonal communication), and how communication works in the one-to-many context (public speaking). While no student will emerge from the course with expertise in these areas, they will learn the fundamentals of human communication, giving them a basis from which to grow and develop into more fully functioning communicators.

Judy C. Pearson   Paul E. Nelson   Scott Titsworth   Lynn Harter

preface

As communication professors we have spent many days in the classroom. Our commitment to the discipline, belief in the essential importance of communication in meeting twenty-first-century challenges, and interest in extending our knowledge to others motivated us to co-author this text. We hope that our book will enhance learning and add to the excitement and fulfillment that people experience when they study communication.

Written for the basic course, *Human Communication* is a hybrid text that teaches principles and skills in interpersonal communication, small-group communication, public communication, organizational communication, and mediated communication. With its distinctive student-friendly voice, the text coaches students in the fundamentals of human communication and places relevant skills, engaging theory, and energizing pedagogy at the forefront of the book.

Key Elements

Human Communication introduces students to the main contexts of human communication following these key themes:

- **A Student-Centered Approach**—We simplify complex ideas without significant distortion and provide examples so that students can understand and apply communication studies to their lives.
- **Cooperative and Collaborative Learning**—Students are encouraged to think about concepts, share their ideas with classmates, and reveal their thinking to the class when invited to do so.
- **Critical Thinking**—We challenge students to think intelligently and critically about communication concepts, issues, and practices.
- **Practical Application**—Throughout the text we emphasize practical knowledge, useful applications, and everyday skills.
- **Finding and Evaluating Information**—The text guides students through the trials of finding and evaluating information so that they will become educated individuals who can critically assess content, weigh arguments and evidence, and judge the value of information and ideas.
- **Communicating Ethically**—We encourage responsible, moral, and ethical communication practices.
- **Understanding Diversity**—In their personal and professional lives, students will meet people from a variety of cultural backgrounds. We encourage cultural competence by addressing diversity issues throughout the book, especially in chapter 7, "Intercultural Communication."
- **Using Technology**—We teach students to critically assess web-based resources.
- **Using Visualization**—A substantial video series was developed and produced specifically for this text (see page xix for details).

Signature Features

Innovative and practical chapter features include the following:

- **Skill Builder** and **Try This** boxes that call on students to practice communication competencies
- **Culture Notes** that encourage sensitivity to diversity
- **Think, Pair, Share** exercises that stimulate critical thinking
- **E-Notes** that highlight technology
- **Myths, Metaphors, and Misunderstandings** boxes that encourage students to think about the influence of cultural values on our understanding of communication and communication behaviors

New to This Edition

Chapter Organization and Content

This third edition of *Human Communication* has been thoroughly updated. Throughout, readers will find coverage of new topics and expansion of other important concepts. These include a discussion of the communication skills that employers seek (chapter 1), a discussion of ethnic, racial, and social influences on language (chapter 3), multicultural examples of nonverbal communication (chapter 4), research on gender/sex differences in listening (chapter 5), a section on the nature of friendships including Rawlins's theory (chapter 6), a discussion of how to respond to illegal and inappropriate job interview questions (chapter 8), and new student presentations with explanatory side notes in informative (chapter 14) and persuasive (chapter 15) speaking.

"Interviewing" and "Communicating at Work," separate chapters in the previous edition, have been combined as chapter 8, "Workplace Communication"; the new chapter focuses on the practical skills students will need as they transition from college to the workplace.

"Mediated Communication and Media Literacy" (formerly chapter 11) is now on the book's *Online Learning Center*, www.mhhe.com/pearson3.

New features

New **chapter-opening vignettes** deal with contemporary issues that will appeal to students. Topics include the controversy over the use of Native American and other racially linked mascots; how Dan Brown's *Da Vinci Code*, an icon of popular culture, challenges the traditional meanings we give to everyday symbols; the controversy surrounding Michael J. Fox's commercials about stem cell research; and how social networking websites like MySpace and Facebook raise questions related to friendship and interpersonal communication issues.

The new **ESL** feature reflects our changing cultural landscape. The diverse population of the United States means that multilingual communication encounters are, in many parts of the country, the norm rather than the exception. Each chapter provides a number of tips to help students bridge language and cultural barriers. Topics include ways ESL speakers can adapt their nonverbal behaviors, cross-cultural friendships and romantic relationships, cross-cultural skills in the workplace, cultural differences and group dynamics, and topic selection for ESL speakers.

The new end-of-chapter **Review and Study Guide** includes 10 multiple-choice and two critical thinking questions for each chapter to help students test their understanding of the key chapter concepts.

Resources for Instructors and Students

The *Human Communication* website, the *Online Learning Center* at www.mhhe.com/pearson3, provides instructors and students with creative and effective tools that make teaching and learning easier and more engaging. These include:

- Updated **Instructor's Manual, Resource Integrator, and Test Bank.** This provides a wealth of teaching strategies, activities, and resources for instructors and students.
- **Video, *Communicating Everyday.*** Each of the nine episodes of this video series runs approximately seven minutes. With consistent characters and plotlines, these stories illustrate key communication concepts by applying them to scenarios involving family, friends, colleagues, and instructors—in the home, at school, and at work. Icons throughout the text indicate connections to the ***Communicating Everyday*** video series.
- **Video, *Public Speaking.*** There are 11 full-length speeches and 18 speech excerpts in all. Four of the full-length speeches will give students a clear sense of the differences between speeches that have problems in their content and delivery and those that could be considered "model" speeches. Thus, students can view informative and persuasive speeches that need improvement, followed respectively by their "improved versions."
- **Self-quizzes with feedback.** To prepare for exams, students can take a practice test for each chapter consisting of 15 multiple-choice and five true/false questions. When students choose an incorrect answer, they are given an immediate explanation of their mistake and invited to try again.
- **Key Term Flashcards with sound.** Some students prepare for quizzes and examinations by reviewing chapter glossaries. The Key Term Flashcards program manages the text glossary by chapter and allows students to create "decks" of key terms that they can read and/or listen to.

Print Resource for Instructors

Annotated Instructor's Edition. The AIE has marginal notes that provide teaching ideas, examples, and suggestions for class discussions and activities.

acknowledgments

ACKNOWLEDGMENTS

The authors are grateful to colleagues across the country who reviewed the book and recommended improvements. Because of their detailed and insightful comments, a much better book emerged for the benefit of our adopters and their students. A warm thank you to each of you!

Teleconference Reviewers

Mary Albert Darling
Spring Arbor University

Karen Anderson
University of North Texas

James Gray
Montgomery College

Laura Guerrero
Arizona State University

Linda Long
North Lake College

Patricia Spence
Richland College

Written Reviewers

Patricia Amason
University of Arkansas

Diane Bifano
Palm Beach Community College

Irene Canel-Petersen
Miami Dade College

Laura Jo Fox Cashmer
Joliet Junior College

Jean M. Kapinsky
Northcentral Technical College

Betty Jane Lawrence
Bradley University

Nancy R. Levin
Palm Beach Community College

Yvette Lujan
Miami Dade College

Jim Lyle
Clarion University

Mischelle L. McIntosh
Cedarville University

Robert E. Mild Jr.
Fairmont State University

Donna Munde
Mercer County Community College

Lori Norin
University of Arkansas-Fort Smith

Trudi Peterson
Monmouth College

Rebecca Robideaux
Boise State University

Theresa Rogers
Baltimore City Community College

Barbara J. Schmidt
Des Moines Area Community College

Barbara Tucker
Dalton State College

Vivian Van Donk
Joliet Junior College

Bill Wallace
Northeastern State University

Visual Preview: A Guided Tour

Human Communication presents a practical balance of definitive content and everyday applications with innovative features that encourage discussion of real-world issues.

Controversy over the use of Native American mascots.

Controversy over Michael J. Fox's television commercials.

NEW chapter-opening vignettes encourage critical thinking through discussion of contemporary issues.

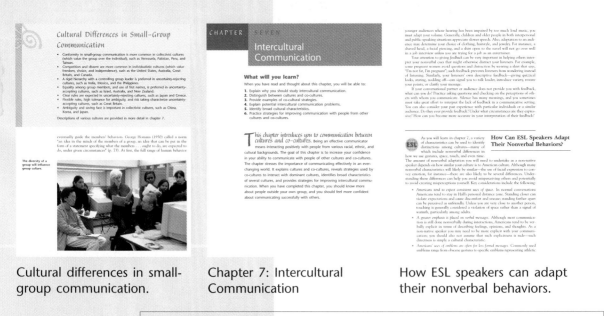

Cultural differences in small-group communication.

Chapter 7: Intercultural Communication

How ESL speakers can adapt their nonverbal behaviors.

The text encourages cultural competence and understanding by exploring issues of diversity throughout the book.

Offers Distinctive Pedagogy That Promotes Active Learning

Skill Builder and Try This boxes help students apply their skills to communication issues.

Skill Builder

Try This

Think, Pair, Share boxes provide exercises that stimulate critical thinking and collaboration.

Think, Pair, Share

Provides End-of-Chapter Features for Easy Review

Chapter summaries, key terms, and study questions allow students to test their comprehension of core information presented in the chapters.

Offers Two Original Communication Video Programs for Analysis and Discussion

The videos, found on the *Online Learning Center* at www.mhhe.com/pearson3, the website for *Human Communication*, are related and connect to the content in the textbook.

Communicating Everyday: Written in the style of a contemporary television drama, this nine-part video series illustrates many of the concepts discussed in the text in an entertaining and thought-provoking way.

Public Speaking: Eleven full speech videos and 18 video excerpts by student speakers illustrate the various presentation techniques and elements of a speech. Included are two sets of *model* and *needs improvement* speeches.

Videos

Communicating Everyday

- Sam's Graduation Party
- The Right Kind of Care
- Where There's Smoke
- On the Air with Campus Community Connection
- You Look Great
- Opposites Attract
- Reporting for KTNT: Susan Elliott
- Senior Seminar
- Pulling the Weight at Work

Public Speaking Videos

FULL SPEECHES

1. Passionate about Risks (Self-Introduction)
2. Motorcycle Club (Tribute)
3. Cell Phones as Communication Tools (Informative: Needs Improvement)
4. Cell Phones as Communication Tools (Informative: Improved Version)
5. Mad Cow Disease (Informative)
6. Competitive Sports (Informative)
7. How to Play the Drums (Demonstration)
8. Sharks: The Misunderstood Monster (Persuasive: Needs Improvement)
9. Sharks: The Misunderstood Monster (Persuasive: Improved Version)
10. Supporting Stem Cell Research (Persuasive)
11. I'll Take the Cow over the Chemicals (Persuasive)

VIDEO CLIPS

1. Conveying the Central Idea
2. Appealing to Motivations
3. Using an Example
4. Making a Contrast
5. Using an Analogy
6. Using Testimony
7. Using Statistics
8. Introductions: Relating a Story
9. Introductions: Citing a Quote
10. Introductions: Arousing Curiosity
11. Conclusions: Citing a Quotation
12. Conclusions: Giving an Illustration
13. Using Internet Graphics
14. Presenting a PowerPoint "Build"
15. Using a Vivid Image
16. Relating a Speech to the Listeners' Self-Interest
17. Using Deductive Reasoning
18. Using Inductive Reasoning

CHAPTER ONE

Introduction to Human Communication

What will you learn?

When you have read and thought about this chapter, you will be able to:

1. State reasons why the study of communication is essential.
2. Define communication.
3. Name the components of communication.
4. Explain some principles of communication.
5. Explain the ways in which intrapersonal, interpersonal, public, and mass communication differ from each other.
6. Define communication competence.
7. Name some of the tenets of the National Communication Association Credo on Ethics.

In this chapter you will be introduced to communication, including some of the fundamental concepts and terms you will need to know for the remainder of this text. You will learn why it is important to study communication and how communication is defined. This chapter will show you how communication begins with you and extends to other people, and it will identify the components of communication. Finally, you will learn about the characteristics of the various communication contexts.

"**T**alk and change the world." This is the slogan of a group of female U.S. senators who have been meeting for over a decade. The group is composed of both Democrats and Republicans. It has had some notable success in helping U.S. women achieve economic, social, and political equality. For instance, the women in the group have supported providing retirement funds for homemakers and medical trials include more women.

After the 2006 elections, the group expanded to 16 women, the largest number of women in the Senate in the history of the country. Diane Sawyer of *Good Morning America* took note of this historic moment by interviewing the group soon after the elections. Several of the senators stressed the importance of communication in advancing various causes, whether it be enhancing national security or creating economic opportunity.

Today's political culture more often than not involves vicious party battles. In contrast, Senator Olympia Snow of Maine described the group of female senators as "a zone of civility where members disagree without being disagreeable." Several senators noted they are "agents of change," serving as a model for "a new chapter in American politics." They claimed to be "fresh voices" in bringing diverse people together to find common ground. As the interview progressed, the group of 16 Democrats and Republicans pledged to build consensus to solve the many problems facing the country. (For more information about this interview, go to goodmorningamerica.com.)

This story is meaningful on several levels. For one thing, it shows the potential for change based on an approach in which both parties work together. For another, it indicates that women are gradually cracking the gender barrier in U.S. politics. Perhaps most important, however, it shows the many roles that communication plays in the group's efforts. Through communication of their vision, these women persuaded voters to elect them. Through communication, they were able to find common ground, cutting across deeply divided party lines. Through communication, they staked out an agenda to advance the causes, not just of other women, but of the entire country.

Both their individual and collective stories teach us one thing: Communication is the foundation on which personal and social success is built. In this chapter you will learn about communication on a deeper level, including the terms, processes, and contexts of communication.

Communication Is Essential

Studying communication is essential for you. Communication is central to your life. Effective communication can help you solve problems in your professional life and improve relationships in your personal life. Communication experts believe that poor communication is at the root of many problems and that effective communication is one solution to these problems.

Communication is consequential. Understanding the theory, research, and application of communication will make a significant difference in your life and in the lives of people around the world. The world changed on September 11, 2001, and people became far more aware of the importance of communication principles—particularly intercultural communication principles. Communication principles and practices can resolve disputes among nations as well as among friends and family. Effective communication may not solve all the world's problems, but better communication practices can help us solve or avoid many problems.

Communication is ubiquitous. You cannot avoid communication, and you will engage in communication nearly every minute of every day of your life. Communication plays a major role in nearly every aspect of your life.

Regardless of your interests and goals, the ability to communicate effectively will enhance and enrich your life. But learning *how* to communicate is just as important as learning *about* communication. Studying communication comprehensively offers at least seven advantages:

1. *Studying communication can improve the way you see yourself.* Communication is "vital to the development of the whole person" (Morreale, Osborn, & Pearson, 2000, p. 4). As we will see in chapter 2, most of our self-knowledge comes from the communicative experience. As we engage in thought (*intra*personal communication) and in interactions with significant other people (*inter*personal communication), we learn about ourselves. People who are naive about the communication process and the development of self-awareness, self-concept, and self-efficacy may not see themselves accurately or may be unaware of their own self-development. Knowing how communication affects self-perception can lead to greater awareness and appreciation of the self.

Learning communication skills can improve the way you see yourself in a second way. As you learn how to communicate effectively in a variety of situations—from interpersonal relationships to public speeches—your self-confidence will increase. In a study based on the responses from 344 students at a large public university, students who completed a communication course perceived their communication competence to be greater in the classroom, at work, and in social settings. Most dramatic were their perceived improvements in feeling confident about themselves, feeling comfortable with others' perceptions of them, reasoning with people, and using language appropriately (Ford & Wolvin, 1993). In short, your success in interacting with other people in social situations and your achievements in professional settings will lead to more positive feelings about yourself.

2. *Studying communication can improve the way others see you.* In chapter 2 we will discuss self-presentation, image management, and locus of control. You will learn that you can to a considerable extent control your own behavior, which will lead to positive outcomes with others. You will find that your interactions can be smoother and that you can achieve your goals more easily as you manage the impression you make on others.

You can improve the way others see you a second way. Generally, people like communicating with others who can communicate well. Compare your interactions with someone who stumbles over words, falls silent, interrupts, and uses inappropriate language to express thoughts to your interactions with someone who has a good vocabulary, listens when you speak, reveals appropriate personal information, and smoothly exchanges talk turns with you. Which person do you prefer? Most of us prefer competent communicators. As you become increasingly competent, you will find that others seek you out for conversations, for assistance, and for advice.

3. *Studying communication can increase what you know about human relationships.* The field of communication includes learning about how people relate to each other and about what type of communication is appropriate for a given situation. Most people value human relationships and find great comfort in friendships, family relationships, and community relationships. Within these relationships we learn about trust, intimacy, and reciprocity.

Human relationships are vital to each of us. Human babies thrive when they are touched and when they hear sounds; similarly, adults who engage in human relationships appear to be more successful and satisfied than do those who are isolated. Human relationships serve a variety of functions. They provide us with affection (receiving and providing warmth and friendliness), inclusion (experiencing feelings that we belong and providing others with messages that they belong), pleasure (sharing happiness and fun), escape (providing diversion), and control (managing our lives and influencing others) (Rubin, Perse, & Barbato, 1988).

We learn about the complexity of human relationships as we study communication. We learn, first, that other people in relationships are vastly different from each other. We learn that they may be receptive or dismissive toward us. We learn that they may behave as if they are superior or inferior to us. We learn that they might be approachable or highly formal. People are clearly not interchangeable with each other.

We also learn that our interactions with others may be helpful or harmful. Communicators can share personal information that builds trust and rapport. The same personal information can be used outside the relationship to humiliate or shame the other person. While some relationships enhance social support, others are riddled with deception and conflict. Interactions are not neutral.

To see how interpersonal communication and conflict are related, view the "Opposites Attract" video clip on the *Online Learning Center* at www.mhhe.com/pearson3.

We learn that people coconstruct the reality of the relationship. Families, for example, love to tell stories of experiences they have had when on vacation, when moving across the country, or when some particularly positive or negative event occurred. Indeed, they often take turns "telling the story." Couples, too, create and tell stories of their lives. Couples' stories may be positive as the couple emphasizes their feelings of belongingness and their identity as a couple. On the other end of the spectrum, stories may be highly negative as people deceive others with information that allows them to cover up criminal acts such as drug use, child abuse, or murder.

Human relationships are complex. As you study communication, you will clarify the variables involved in relationships—the people, the verbal and nonverbal cues provided, the effect of time, the nature of the relationship, and the goals of the participants. You will be far better equipped to engage in relationships with an understanding of the communication process.

People who have communication skills also experience greater relational satisfaction (Egeci & Gencoz, 2006). If you receive training in communication skills, you are more likely to report greater relationship satisfaction than do those who do not receive such training (Ireland, Sanders, & Markie-Dodds, 2003). The link between communication skills and life satisfaction is strong. The connection holds true in health contexts (Dutta-Bergman, 2005), including situations in which family members are experiencing life-threatening illnesses (Manne et al., 2006).

Open Public Discourse

Does public discourse today operate in an open forum in which a variety of perspectives can be offered on important issues? After you have considered this question and offered arguments for both sides, share your responses with a classmate. How do you agree? How do you disagree? For advanced reading on methods of mapping the universe of discourse, see Anderson and Prelli (2001).

4. *Studying communication can teach you important life skills.* Studying communication involves learning important skills that everyone will use at some point in his or her life, such as critical thinking, problem solving, decision making, conflict resolution, team building, media literacy, and public speaking. Allen, Berkowitz, Hunt, and Louden (1999) analyzed dozens of studies and concluded that "communication instruction improves the critical thinking ability of the participants." Our visual literacy is improved as we understand the technical and artistic aspects of the visual communication medium (Metallinos, 1992).

Studying communication early in your college career can enhance your success throughout college. Consider the centrality of oral communication to all of your college classes. You regularly are called on to answer questions in class, to provide reports, to offer explanations, and to make presentations. In addition, your oral and written work both depend on your ability to think critically and creatively, to solve problems, and to make decisions. Most likely, you will be engaged in group projects in which skills such as team building and conflict resolution will be central. These same skills will be essential throughout your life.

5. *Studying communication can help you exercise your constitutionally guaranteed freedom of speech.* Few nations have a bill of rights that invites people to convey their opinions and ideas, yet freedom of speech is essential to a democratic form of government. Being a practicing citizen in a democratic society means knowing about current issues and being able to speak about them in conversations, in speeches, and through the mass media; it also involves being able to critically examine messages from others.

Our understanding of communication shapes our political lives. Mass communication and communication technology have sharply altered the political process. Today many more people have the opportunity to receive information than ever before. Through the mass media, people in remote locations are as well informed as those in large urban centers. The public agenda is largely set through the media. Pressing problems are given immediate attention. Blumer (1983) notes, "At a time when so many forces—volatility, apathy, skepticism, a sense of powerlessness, and intensified group hostility—appear to be undermining political stability, media organizations have become pivotal to the conduct of human affairs."

While some people may feel more enfranchised by the common denominator of the media, others feel more alienated as they become increasingly passive in the process. Whereas face-to-face town meetings were the focus of democratic decision making in times past, today people receive answers to questions, solutions to problems, and decisions about important matters from the media. Many feel powerless and anonymous.

In the wake of the terrorist attacks of September 11, 2001, Americans began to rediscover and recognize the value of a democratic form of government. At the same time, they recognized how vulnerable they were to people who did not endorse basic democratic principles. Americans also learned that terrorist dictators could use the media as easily as could those who came from more reasonable and more democratic ideologies.

The study and understanding of communication processes is profoundly political. Hart (1993) opines that "those who teach public address and media studies teach that social power can be shifted and public visions exalted if people learn to think well and speak well" (p. 102). Paraphrasing the ancient Greek rhetorician Isocrates, Hart notes, "To become eloquent is to activate one's humanity, to apply the imagination, and to solve the practical problems of human living" (p. 101). Freedom goes to the articulate.

You have the opportunity to be a fully functioning member of a democratic society. You also have the additional burden of understanding the media and other information technologies. Studying communication will help you learn how to speak effectively, analyze arguments, synthesize large quantities of information, and critically consume information from a variety of sources. The future of our society depends on such mastery.

6. *Studying communication can help you succeed professionally.* A look at the job postings in any newspaper will give you an immediate understanding of the importance of improving your knowledge and practice of communication. The employment section of *The Washington Post* provides some examples (Today's Employment, 1998):

   - "We need a results-oriented, seasoned professional who is a good communicator and innovator" reads one ad for a marketing manager.

   - Another ad, this one for a marketing analyst, reads, "You should be creative, inquisitive, and a good communicator both in writing and orally."

   - An ad for a training specialist calls for "excellent presentation, verbal, and written communication skills, with ability to interact with all levels within organization."

As a person educated in communication, you will be able to gain a more desirable job (Bardwell, 1997; Cockrum, 1994; Peterson, 1997; Ugbah & Evuleocha, 1992). You may believe that some professions are enhanced by communication skills but that many are not. Professionals in fields such as accounting, auditing, banking, counseling, engineering, industrial hygiene, information science, public relations, and sales have all written about the importance of oral communication skills (Hanzevack & McKean, 1991; Horton & Brown, 1990; LaBar, 1994; Messmer, 1997; Nisberg, 1996; Ridley, 1996; Simkin, 1996). More recently, professionals in the computer industry (Coopersmith, 2006; Glen, 2006), genetics and science (Bubela, 2006), farming and ranching (Harper, 2006), education (Lavin Colky & Young, 2006), and midwifery (Nicholls & Webb, 2006) have stressed the importance of communication skills to potential employees. The variety of these careers suggests that communication skills are important across the board.

Communication skills are important in your first contact with a prospective employer. By studying communication, your interviewing skills will be enhanced. Further, personnel interviewers note that oral communication skills, in general, significantly affect hiring decisions (Peterson, 1997). One survey showed that personnel managers identified effective speaking and listening as the most important factors in hiring people (Curtis, Winsor, & Stephens, 1989). In another survey, employers identified the most important skills for college graduates as oral communication, interpersonal skills, teamwork, and analytical abilities (Collins & Oberman, 1994).

Employers view your written and oral communication competencies and your ability to listen and analyze messages as essential job skills (Bubela, 2006; Coopersmith, 2006; Glen, 2006; Harper, 2006; Lavin Colky & Young, 2006; Maes, Weldy, & Icenogle, 1997; Nicholls & Webb, 2006; Parnell, 1996; Winsor, Curtis, & Stephens, 1997). Similarly, college graduates perceive communication coursework as essential (Pearson, Sorenson, & Nelson, 1981). In short, communication competence is important.

Communication skills are important not only at the beginning of your career but throughout the work life span. Dauphinais (1997) observes that communication skills can increase upward mobility in one's career. Business executives note the importance of communication competence (Argenti & Forman, 1998; Reinsch & Shelby, 1996). Finally, communication skills are among the top priorities for entrepreneurs.

Communication skills have become even more critical to employers over time (Johnson & Johnson, 1995). What communication skills are employers seeking? Clearly, listening skills are one of the most important components of communication (Edwards, Peterson, & Davies, 2006; Mlynek, 2006; Nichols, 2006), and you will learn about listening in chapter 5. Speaking clearly, succinctly, and persuasively is crucial to many jobs including sales jobs (Nichols, 2006), and we cover these topics in chapters 3, 13, and 16. An ability to work in teams or groups is vital (Cano & Cano, 2006; Houssami & Sainsbury, 2006; Miller, 2006), and you will learn about this in chapter 9. Employers are also seeking interpersonal skills (Johnson & Johnson, 1995), which we will consider in chapter 6. Public speaking skills, covered in chapters 10–15, are important in most professions because of the requirement that employees give talks and presentations (Bates, 2004). Finally, employers seek employees with strong written communication skills (Gray, Emerson, & MacKay, 2005). You will have an opportunity to improve your writing skills as you prepare outlines and manuscripts for public speeches, which we also cover in chapters 10–15.

7. *Studying communication can help you navigate an increasingly diverse world.* As you stroll through a mall, deposit money in a bank, go to a movie, or work at your job, odds are that about one in every five people you come into contact with will speak English as a second language. According to the 2005 American Community Survey, conducted by the U.S. Census Bureau, nearly 20% of respondents speak a language other than English in their home. The increasingly diverse population of the United States means that multilingual communication encounters are, for most of us, the norm rather than the exception. Learning how to communicate in today's world, whether English is your first language or not, requires an understanding of communication and culture and how those two concepts are related.

 As you develop an understanding of basic communication concepts and learn how to apply those concepts in everyday interactions, you will be better equipped to bridge language and cultural barriers. As you progress through this book, you will learn a number of specific skills that promote effective interpersonal relationships, teamwork, and online communication. Most chapters include advice on how you can adapt specific skills during interactions with people whose first language is not English.

Communication: The Process of Using Messages to Generate Meaning

Now that you have considered why learning about communication is important, you need to know exactly what the term means. Over the years, scholars have created hundreds of definitions of communication. How they define the term can limit or expand the study of the subject. In this text, the definition is simple and broad—simple enough to allow understanding and broad enough to include many contexts.

Communication comes from the Latin word *communicare*, which means "to make common" or "to share." The root definition is consistent with our definition of communication. In this book, **communication** is defined as the process of using messages to generate meaning. Communication is considered a **process** because it is an activity, an exchange, or a set of behaviors—not an unchanging product. Communication is not an object you can hold in your hands—it is an activity in which you participate. David Berlo (1960), a pioneer in the field of communication, probably provided the clearest statement about communication as a process:

> If we accept the concept of process, we view events and relationships as dynamic, ongoing, ever changing, continuous. When we label something as a process, we also mean that it does not have a beginning, an end, a fixed sequence of events. It is not static, at rest. It is moving. The ingredients within a process interact; each affects all the others.

What is an example of how process works in everyday communication? Picture three students meeting on the sidewalk between classes and exchanging a few sentences. This "snapshot" does not begin and end with the students' first words and last sentence. Since they all stopped to chat with each other, you might assume that their relationship began before this encounter. Since they all seem to have a common understanding of what is being said, you might assume that they share experiences that similarly shape their perceptions. You also might assume that this brief encounter does not end when the students go their ways, but rather that they think about their conversation later in the day or that it leads to another meeting

communication

The process of using messages to generate meaning.

process

An activity, exchange, or set of behaviors that occurs over time.

Understanding emerges from shared meanings.

later in the week. In other words, a snapshot cannot capture all that occurs during communication, a process that starts before the words begin and ends long after the words end.

Messages include verbal and nonverbal symbols, signs, and behaviors. When you smile at another person, you are sending a message. When a radio announcer chooses language to emphasize the seriousness of a recent event, she is creating a message. The public speaker might spend days choosing just the right words and considering his bodily movements, gestures, and facial expression.

People hope to generate common meanings through the messages they provide. **Meaning** is the understanding of the message. You know that all of the messages you generate are not shared by others with whom you try to communicate. You try to flirt with someone you meet in class, but the other person seems oblivious to your subtle nonverbal signals. College professors are generally very knowledgeable about a subject matter, but they vary greatly in their ability to convey shared meanings.

Understanding the meaning of another person's message does not occur unless the two communicators can elicit common meanings for words, phrases, and nonverbal codes. When you use language, meaning facilitates an appropriate response that indicates that the message was understood. For example, suppose you ask a friend for a sheet of paper. She says nothing and gives you one sheet of paper. You and your friend share the same meaning of the message exchanged. But a message can be interpreted in more than one way, especially if the people involved have little shared experience. In such a case, a more accurate understanding of the intended meaning can be discerned by *negotiating,* that is, by asking questions.

meaning

The understanding of the message.

◀ **SKILL** BUILDER ▶

While you may believe that you accurately interpret the meaning that others are trying to convey, you probably do not. On at least six different occasions in the next week, ask a person with whom you are communicating if you can paraphrase the meaning of his or her message. Write down how well you did in each of these instances. How could you improve your understanding of others' messages?

Components of Communication

In this section you will learn how communication in action really works. The components of communication are people, messages, codes, channels, feedback, encoding and decoding, and noise.

People

People are involved in the human communication process in two roles—as both the sources and the receivers of messages. A **source** initiates a message, and a **receiver** is the intended target of the message. Individuals do not perform these two roles independently. Instead, they are the sources and the receivers of messages simultaneously and continually.

People do not respond uniformly to all messages, nor do they always provide the same messages in exactly the same way. Individual characteristics, including race, sex, age, culture, values, and attitudes, affect the ways people send and receive messages. (Throughout this text you will find discussions about the ways in which culture and sex affect communication.)

The Message

The **message** is the verbal and nonverbal form of the idea, thought, or feeling that one person (the source) wishes to communicate to another person or group of people (the receivers). The message is the content of the interaction. The message includes the symbols (words and phrases) you use to communicate your ideas, as well as your facial expressions, bodily movements, gestures, physical contact, tone of voice, and other nonverbal codes. The message may be relatively brief and easy to understand or long and complex. Some experts believe that real communication stems only from messages that are intentional, or have a purpose. However, since intent is sometimes difficult to prove in a communication situation, the authors of this text believe that real communication can occur through either intentional or unintentional messages.

The Channel

The **channel** is the means by which a message moves from the source to the receiver of the message. A message moves from one place to another, from one person to another, by traveling through a medium, or channel. Airwaves, sound waves, twisted copper wires, glass fibers, and cable are all communication channels. Airwaves and cable are two of the various channels through which you receive television messages. Radio messages move through sound waves. Computer images (and sound, if there is any) travel through light waves, and sometimes both light and sound waves. In person-to-person communication, you send your messages through a channel of sound waves and light waves that enable receivers to see and hear you.

Feedback

Feedback is the receiver's verbal and nonverbal response to the source's message. Ideally, you respond to another person's messages by providing feedback so that the source knows the message was received as intended. Feedback is part of any communication situation. Even no response, or silence, is feedback, as are restless behavior and quizzical looks from students in a lecture hall. Suppose you're in a building you've never been in before, looking for a restroom. You ask a person quickly passing by, "Excuse me, can you tell me . . . ," but the person keeps on going without acknowledging you. In this case, the intended receiver did not

source

A message initiator.

receiver

A message target.

message

The verbal or nonverbal form of the idea, thought, or feeling that one person (the source) wishes to communicate to another person or group of people (the receivers).

channel

The means by which a message moves from the source to the receiver of the message.

feedback

The receiver's verbal and nonverbal response to the source's message.

What's in a Name?

Americans name their children after relatives, entertainers, famous people, and biblical figures. Many Spanish-speaking males are named after Jesus, and thousands of Muslim males are named after Mohammed. In China, too, names have meanings that can influence how a person feels about him- or herself. Wen Shu Lee (1998), a professor originally from Taiwan, published an article about the names of women in China. She claims that naming practices often reflect gender- and class-based oppression. The name *Zhao Di,* for example, "commands a daughter to bring to the family a younger brother, while 'expelling' more younger sisters." The name reflects a higher value on male children. Does your name influence what you think of yourself? Does your name affect how, when, and with whom you communicate? What's in a name?

respond, yet even the lack of a response provides you with some feedback. You may surmise that perhaps the receiver didn't hear you or was in too much of a hurry to stop.

Code

A computer carries messages via binary code on cable, wire, or fiber; similarly, you converse with others by using a code called "language." A **code** is a systematic arrangement of symbols used to create meanings in the mind of another person or persons. Words, phrases, and sentences become "symbols" that are used to evoke images, thoughts, and ideas in the mind of others. If someone yells "Stop" as you approach the street, the word *stop* has become a symbol that you are likely to interpret as a warning of danger.

Verbal and nonverbal codes are the two types of code used in communication. **Verbal codes** consist of symbols and their grammatical arrangement. All languages are codes. **Nonverbal codes** consist of all symbols that are not words, including bodily movements, use of space and time, clothing and other adornments, and sounds other than words. *Nonverbal* codes should not be confused with *nonoral* codes. All nonoral codes, such as bodily movement, are nonverbal codes. However, nonverbal codes also include oral codes, such as pitch, duration, rate of speech, and sounds like "eh" and "ah."

Encoding and Decoding

If communication involves the use of codes, the process of communicating can be viewed as one of encoding and decoding. **Encoding** is defined as the process of translating an idea or a thought into a code. **Decoding** is the process of assigning meaning to that idea or thought. For instance, suppose you are interested in purchasing a new car. You are trying to describe a compact model to your father, who wants to help you with your purchase. You might be visualizing the car with the black interior, sporty design, and red exterior that belongs to your best friend. Putting this vision into words, you tell your father you are interested in a car that is "small and

code
A systematic arrangement of symbols used to create meanings in the mind of another person or persons.

verbal codes
Symbols and their grammatical arrangement, such as languages.

nonverbal codes
All symbols that are not words, including bodily movements, use of space and time, clothing and adornments, and sounds other than words.

encoding
The process of translating an idea or thought into a code.

decoding
The process of assigning meaning to the idea or thought in a code.

well designed." You encode your perceptions of a particular car into words that describe the model. Your father, on hearing this, decodes your words and develops his own mental image. But his love of larger cars affects this process, and as a result, he envisions a sedan. As you can see, misunderstanding often occurs because of the limitations of language and the inadequacy of descriptions. Nonetheless, encoding and decoding are essential in sharing your thoughts, ideas, and feelings with others.

Noise

In the communication process, **noise** is any interference in the encoding and decoding processes that reduces the clarity of a message. Noise can be physical, such as loud sounds; distracting sights, such as a piece of food between someone's front teeth; or an unusual behavior, such as someone standing too close for comfort. Noise can be mental, psychological, or semantic, such as daydreams about a loved one, worry about the bills, pain from a tooth, or uncertainty about what the other person's words mean. Noise can be anything that interferes with receiving, interpreting, or providing feedback about a message.

noise

Any interference in the encoding and decoding processes that reduces message clarity.

Communication Principles

A definition of communication may be insufficient to clarify the nature of communication. To explain communication in more detail, we consider here some principles that guide our understanding of communication.

Communication Begins with the Self

How you see yourself can make a great difference in how you communicate. Carl Rogers (1951) wrote, "Every individual exists in a continually changing world of experience of which he [or she] is the center" (p. 483). For instance, when people are treated as though they are inferior, or intelligent, or gifted, or unattractive, they will often begin acting accordingly. Many communication scholars and social scientists believe that people are products of how others treat them and of the messages others send them.

As persons, our understanding of the world is limited by our experiences with it. Shotter (2000) suggests that we cannot understand communication through external, abstract, and systematic processes. Instead, he describes communication as a "ceaseless flow of speech-entwined, dialogically structured, social activity" (p. 119). In other words, communication is participatory; we are actively involved and relationally responsive in our use of communication. Shotter would contrast his perspective of a participatory-holistic view of communication with one that is abstract and systematic.

To apply this perspective, let us consider an example. Suppose you have a roommate who is from another country. The roommate's religion, belief system, and daily habits challenge your perspective of communication, derived from interacting primarily with people in the United States who hold Western and Christian values. To the extent that you each try to impose your own preconceptions on the communication you share, you may be dissatisfied and experience conflict. By preimposing "rules" of communication derived from your earlier experiences in two distinctive cultures, you are bound to fail in this new relationship. If you are able to move beyond such a view and allow your perception of your communication to become a product of your interactions, you may be able to communicate in interesting and effective ways.

Every day we experience the centrality of ourselves in communication. As a participant in communication, you are limited by your own view of the situation. A student, for instance, may describe a conflict with an instructor as unfair treatment: "I know my instructor doesn't like the fact that I don't agree with his opinions, and that's why he gave me such a poor grade in that class." The instructor might counter, "That student doesn't understand all the factors that go into a final grade." Each person may believe that he or she is correct and that the other person's view is wrong. As you study communication, you will learn ways to better manage such conflict.

Communication Involves Others

George Herbert Mead (1967) said that the self originates in communication. Through verbal and nonverbal symbols, a child learns to accept roles in response to the expectations of others. For example, Dominique Moceanu, a successful Olympic gymnast, was influenced quite early in life by what others wanted her to be. Both her parents had been gymnasts, and apparently her father told her for years that her destiny was to be a world-class gymnast (Hamilton, 1998). Most likely she had an inherent ability to be a good one, but she may not have become a medal-winning gymnast without the early messages she received from her parents and trainers. Like Moceanu, you establish self-image, the sort of person you believe you are, by the ways others categorize you. Positive, negative, and neutral messages that you receive from others all play a role in determining who you are.

Communication itself is probably best understood as a dialogic process. A **dialogue** is simply the act of taking part in a conversation, discussion, or negotiation. When we describe and explain our communicative exchanges with others, we are doing so

dialogue

The act of taking part in a conversation, discussion, or negotiation.

Understanding can emerge from dialogue.

from a perspective of self and from a perspective derived from interacting with others. Our understanding of communication occurs not in a vacuum but in light of our interactions with other people. (For further reading, see Czubaroff, 2000.)

In a more obvious way, communication involves others in the sense that a competent communicator considers the other person's needs and expectations when selecting messages to share. The competent communicator understands that a large number of messages can be shared at any time, but sensitivity and responsiveness to the other communicators are essential. In short, communication begins with the self, as defined largely by others, and involves others, as defined largely by the self.

Communication Has Both a Content and a Relational Dimension

All messages have both a content and a relational dimension. Messages provide substance and suggest a relationship among communicators. Another way to think about this distinction is that the content of the message describes the behavior that is expected, while the relational message suggests how it should be interpreted. For example, if I assert, "Sit down," the content of the brief message is a request for you to be seated. Relationally, I am suggesting that I have the authority to tell you to be seated. Consider the difference between "Sit down!" and "Would you care to be seated?" While the content is essentially the same, the relational aspect seems far different. Generally, the content of the message is less ambiguous than is the relational message.

Communication Is Complicated

Communication, some believe, is a simple matter of passing information from one source to another. In a sense, communication defined in this way would occur whenever you accessed information on the web. However, you know that even in this most basic case, communication does not necessarily occur. For example, if you access a homepage written in a language you do not understand, no communication occurs. If the material is highly complex, you might not understand its message. Similarly, you might be able to repeat what someone else says to you, but with absolutely no understanding of the intent, or the content, of the message.

The potential complexity of communication can be observed by carefully analyzing and discussing the video clip "Sam's Graduation Party" on the *Online Learning Center.*

Communication is far more than simple information transmission. Communication involves choices about the multiple aspects of the message—the verbal, nonverbal, and behavioral aspects; the choices surrounding the transmission channels used; the characteristics of the speaker; the relationship between the speaker and the audience; the characteristics of the audience; and the situation in which the communication occurs. A change in any one of these variables affects the entire communication process.

Communication Quantity Does Not Increase Communication Quality

You might believe that a textbook on communication would stake claims on the importance of increased communication. You may have heard counselors or therapists encouraging people to communicate more: "What we need is more communication." However, greater amounts of communication do not necessarily lead to more harmony or more accurate and shared meanings. Sometimes people disagree, and the more they talk, the more they learn that they are in conflict. Other times people have very poor listening or empathy skills and misunderstand vast quantities of information. Communication, defined simply as verbiage, does not necessarily lead to positive outcomes.

Communication Is Inevitable, Irreversible, and Unrepeatable

Although communication is complicated, and more communication is not necessarily better communication, communication occurs almost every minute of your life. If you are not communicating with yourself (thinking, planning, reacting to the world around you), you are observing others and drawing inferences from their behavior. Even if others did not intend messages for you, you gather observations and draw specific conclusions. A person yawns, and you believe that he is bored with your message. A second person looks away, and you conclude that she is not listening to you. A third person smiles (perhaps because of a memory of a joke he heard recently), and you believe that he is attracted to you. We are continually gleaning meanings from others' behaviors, and we are constantly behaving in ways that have communicative value for them.

Communication Cannot Be Reversed

Have you ever insulted someone accidentally? You may have tried to explain that you did not intend to insult anybody, or said you were sorry for your statement, or made a joke out of your misstatement. Nonetheless, your comment lingers both in the mind of the other person and in your own mind. As you understand the irreversibility of communication, you may become more careful in your conversations with others, and you may take more time preparing public speeches. We cannot go back in time and erase our messages to others.

Communication Cannot Be Repeated

Have you ever had an incredible evening with someone and remarked, "Let's do this again." But when you tried to re-create the ambience, the conversation, and the setting, nothing seemed right. Your second experience with a similar setting and person yielded far different results. Just as you cannot repeat an experience, you cannot repeat communication.

What Are Communication Contexts?

Communication occurs in a **context**—a set of circumstances or a situation. Communication occurs between two friends, among five business acquaintances in a small-group setting, and between a lecturer and an audience that fills an auditorium. At many colleges and universities, the communication courses are arranged by context: interpersonal communication, interviewing, small-group communication, public speaking, and mass communication. The number of people involved in communication affects

context

A set of circumstances or a situation.

the kind of communication that occurs. You may communicate with yourself, with another person, or with many others. The differences among these situations affect your choices of the most appropriate verbal and nonverbal codes.

Intrapersonal Communication

Intrapersonal communication is the process of using messages to generate meaning within the self. Intrapersonal communication is the communication that occurs within your own mind. For example, suppose you and the person you've been dating for two years share the same attitude toward education and a future career. After the two of you finish your undergraduate degrees, you plan to attend graduate school together and then to run your own business. But one day your partner informs you that he or she has decided to work in the family's business immediately after graduating. In your opinion this action changes everything, including you and your partner's future together. When you begin to share your feelings with your partner, he or she becomes angry and says your attitude is just another example of your inflexibility. You tell your partner that you can't discuss the issue now and that you need to think things over for a while. You leave, thinking about what has just happened and what the future holds for the two of you. You are engaged in intrapersonal communication.

Intrapersonal communication occurs, as this example suggests, when you evaluate or examine the interaction that occurs between yourself and others, but it is not limited to such situations. This form of communication occurs before and during other forms of communication as well. For instance, you might argue with yourself during a conversation in which someone asks you to do something you don't really want to do: Before you accept or decline, you mull over the alternatives in your mind.

Intrapersonal communication also includes such activities as solving problems internally, resolving internal conflict, planning for the future, and evaluating yourself and your relationships with others.

intrapersonal communication

The process of using messages to generate meaning within the self.

Intrapersonal communication occurs in our reflections.

18

Intrapersonal communication—the basis for all other communication—involves only the self.

Each one of us is continually engaged in intrapersonal communication. Although you might become more easily absorbed in talking to yourself when you are alone (while walking to class, driving to work, or taking a shower, for instance), you are likely to be involved in this form of communication in crowded circumstances as well (such as during a lecture, at a party, or with friends). Think about the last time you looked at yourself in a mirror. What were your thoughts? Although intrapersonal communication is almost continuous, people seldom focus on this form of communication.

Indeed, not all communication experts believe that intrapersonal communication should be examined within communication studies. The naysayers argue that communication requires two or more receivers of a message, and since there are no receivers in intrapersonal communication, no communication actually occurs. They reason that intrapersonal communication should be studied in a discipline such as psychology or neurology—some field in which experts study the mind or the brain. Nonetheless, intrapersonal communication is recognized by most scholars within the discipline as one context of communication.

Interpersonal Communications

When you move from intrapersonal to interpersonal communication, you move from communication that occurs within your own mind to communication that involves one or more other persons. **Interpersonal communication** is the process of using messages to generate meaning between at least two people in a situation that allows mutual opportunities for both speaking and listening. Like intrapersonal communication, interpersonal communication occurs for a variety of reasons: to solve problems, to resolve conflicts, to share information, to improve perceptions of oneself, or to fulfill social needs, such as the need to belong or to be loved. Through our interpersonal communication, we are able to establish relationships with others that include friendships and romantic relationships.

Dyadic and small-group communication are two subsets of interpersonal communication. **Dyadic communication** is simply two-person communication, such as interviews with an employer or a teacher; talks with a parent, spouse, or child; and interactions among strangers, acquaintances, and friends. **Small-group communication** is the process of using messages to generate meaning in a small group of people (Brilhart & Galanes, 1998). Small-group communication occurs in families, work groups, support groups, religious groups, and study groups. Communication experts agree that two people are a dyad and that more than two people are a small group if they have a common purpose, goal, or mission. However, disagreement emerges about the maximum number of participants in a small group. Technology also poses questions for communication scholars to debate: Does a small group have to meet face-to-face? That teleconferences can involve small-group communication is uncontroversial, but what about discussions in chat rooms on the Internet? Small-group communication is discussed in greater detail later in this text.

Public Communication

Public communication is the process of using messages to generate meanings in a situation in which a single source transmits a message to a number of receivers, who give

interpersonal communication

The process of using messages to generate meaning between at least two people in a situation that allows mutual opportunities for both speaking and listening.

dyadic communication

Two-person communication.

small-group communication

The process of using messages to generate meaning in a small group of people.

public communication

The process of using messages to generate meanings in a situation in which a single source transmits a message to a number of receivers.

nonverbal and, sometimes, question-and-answer feedback. In public communication the source adapts the message to the audience in an attempt to achieve maximum understanding. Sometimes virtually everyone in the audience understands the speaker's message; other times many people fail to understand.

Public communication, or public speaking, is recognized by its formality, structure, and planning. You probably are frequently a receiver of public communication in lecture classes, at convocations, and at religious services. Occasionally, you also may be a source: when you speak in a group, when you try to convince other voters of the merits of a particular candidate for office, or when you introduce a guest speaker to a large audience. Public communication most often informs or persuades, but it can also entertain, introduce, announce, welcome, or pay tribute.

Mass Communication

mass communication

The process of using messages to generate meanings in a mediated system, between a source and a large number of unseen receivers.

Mass communication—the process of using messages to generate meanings in a mediated system, between a source and a large number of unseen receivers—always has some transmission system (mediator) between the sender and the receiver. When you watch your favorite TV show, the signals are going from a broadcast studio to a satellite or cable system and then from that system to your TV set: The mediator is the channel, the method of distribution. This type of communication is called "mass" because the message goes to newspaper and magazine readers, TV viewers, and radio listeners. Mass communication is often taught in a college's or university's department of mass communication, radio and television, or journalism.

Computer-Mediated Communication

Computer-mediated communication (CMC) includes human communication and information shared through communication networks. CMC requires digital literacy, which is the ability to find, evaluate, and use information that is available via computer. The e-mail messages, discussion group threads, newsgroup notes, instant messages, and web page constructions serve as the message while humans continue to serve as the source or receiver of those messages.

How is CMC unique as a communication context? Messages can be sent and received asynchronously (at different times). People can prestructure messages to which they give a great deal of thought, or they can quickly dash off a message with no thought at all. CMC occurs over a single channel although people have cleverly added emoticons (which we will define and discuss in chapter 4) to lend another dimension to CMC. CMC may allow equality among people as demographic features and social status are removed. But CMC can also encourage racism, sexism, and other bias by the nature of the messages that are created and provided to literally millions of people.

The various communication contexts can be determined by several factors: the number of people involved, the level of formality or intimacy, the opportunities for feedback, the need for restructuring messages, and the degree of stability of the roles of speaker and listener. Table 1.1 compares the contexts on the basis of these factors.

TABLE 1.1 DIFFERENCES AMONG COMMUNICATION CONTEXTS

Contexts	Intrapersonal Communication	Interpersonal Communication		Public Communication	Mass Communication	Computer-Mediated Communication
		Dyadic Communication	Small-Group Communication			
Number of People	1	2	Usually 3 to 10; maybe more	Usually more than 10	Usually thousands	2 to billions
Degree of Formality or Intimacy	Most intimate	Generally intimate; interview is formal	Intimate or formal	Generally formal	Generally formal	Intimate or formal
Opportunities for Feedback	Complete feedback	A great deal of feedback	Less than in intrapersonal communication but more than in public communication	Less than in small-group communication but more than in mass communication	Usually none	None to a great deal
Need for Prestructuring Messages	None	Some	Some	A great deal	Almost totally scripted	None to totally scripted
Degree of Stability of the Roles of Speaker and Listener	Highly unstable; the individual as both speaker and listener	Unstable; speaker and listener alternate	Unstable; speakers and listeners alternate	Highly stable; one speaker with many listeners	Highly stable; on-air speakers, invisible listeners	Unstable to highly stable

Communication Myths, Metaphors, and Misunderstandings

metaphors

A means to understanding and experiencing one thing in terms of another.

Throughout this text we challenge you to think about common communication myths, metaphors, and misunderstandings in various contexts including interpersonal relationships, workplace interactions, the delivery of health care, and even the learning that takes place in classrooms. At the most basic level, Lakoff and Johnson (1980) describe **metaphors** as a means to understanding and experiencing one thing in terms of another. Communication scholars argue that our way of knowing about the world, based on language and nonverbal communication, is largely metaphorical. We talk, think, and act in ways that structure our worldview in metaphorical ways. Metaphors can take on mythic, larger-than-life qualities and can lead to misunderstandings.

For example, Americans tend to approach "arguments as war" (Tannen, 1998). This metaphor is evident in such statements as "she *attacked* and *shot down* all of my arguments," "your claims are *indefensible*," and "to win this argument, we must act *strategically*." As a consequence, we usually experience an argument as something that we can win or lose. With the selection of a new metaphor, we could view and experience arguments in different ways. Take a moment to reflect about how the metaphor of "argument as dance" changes the way you think about arguments, participants, the process of arguing, and potential outcomes. Participants could be viewed as actors engaged in balanced, harmonious, and aesthetically pleasing performances rather than as warriors engaged in a battle. There are times when it is necessary and right to fight and defend yourself or your country. However, when all, or even most, arguments are approached from a warlike mentality, we limit our creativity and imagination for solving problems.

We encourage you to think deeply about how cultural values are reflected in common communication myths and metaphors of everyday life, and how misunderstandings can result. Today, more than ever, you will interact with people from other cultures. Intercultural communication may be viewed as the exchange of information between individuals who are unalike culturally; it will be covered in detail in chapter 7. And throughout the book we integrate examples of intercultural communication. As we present the various myths, metaphors, and misunderstandings, you will continue to see the importance of intercultural communication. You will also understand that human communication is complex, captivating, and consequential.

What Are the Goals of Communication Study?

You learned the importance of studying communication at the beginning of this chapter. You will derive many benefits: You can improve the way you see yourself and the ways others see you; you can increase what you know about human relationships; you can learn important life skills; you can better exercise your constitutionally guaranteed freedom of speech; and you can increase your chances of succeeding professionally. How will you achieve these outcomes? To the extent that you become a more effective and ethical communicator, you will enhance the likelihood of these positive results.

Effective Communication

communication competence

The ability to effectively exchange meaning through a common system of symbols, signs, or behavior.

Effective communication is also known as communication competence. **Communication competence** is defined simply as the ability to effectively exchange meaning through a common system of symbols, signs, or behavior. As you will learn in this book, communication competence is not necessarily easy to achieve. Communication competence can be difficult because your goals and others' goals may be discrepant. Similarly, you and those with whom you communicate may have a different understanding of your relationship. Cultural differences may cause you to view the world and other people differently. Indeed, different perspectives about communication may themselves create problems in your interactions with others. As you read this text, you will learn about the multiple variables involved in communication, and you will become more competent in your communication.

You need to recognize now that while communication competence is the goal, the complexity of communication should encourage you to be a student of communication over your lifetime. In this course you will begin to learn the terminology and the multiple variables comprised in communication. Although you will not emerge from the course as totally effective, you should see significant changes in your communication abilities. The professional public speaker or comedian, the glib TV reporter, and the highly satisfied spouse in a long-term marriage make communication look easy. However, as you will learn, their skills are complex and interwoven with multiple layers of understanding.

Ethical Communication: The NCA Credo

A second goal in studying communication lies in its ethical dimension. **Ethics** may be defined as a set of moral principles or values. Ethical standards may vary from one discipline to another just as they differ from one culture to another. Within the communication discipline, a set of ethics has been adopted. In 1999 the National Communication Association created the following set of ethics:

> Questions of right and wrong arise whenever people communicate. Ethical communication is fundamental to responsible thinking, decision making, and the development of relationships and communities within and across contexts, cultures, channels, and media. Moreover, ethical communication enhances human worth and dignity by fostering truthfulness, fairness, responsibility, personal integrity, and respect for self and others. We believe that unethical communication threatens the quality of all communication and consequently the well-being of individuals and the society in which we live. Therefore we, the members of the National Communication Association, endorse and are committed to practicing the following principles of ethical communication:
>
> > We advocate truthfulness, accuracy, honesty, and reason as essential to the integrity of communication.
> >
> > We endorse freedom of expression, diversity of perspective, and tolerance of dissent to achieve the informed and responsible decision making fundamental to a civil society.
> >
> > We strive to understand and respect other communicators before evaluating and responding to their messages.
> >
> > We promote access to communication resources and opportunities as necessary to fulfill human potential and contribute to the well-being of families, communities, and society.
> >
> > We promote communication climates of caring and mutual understanding that respect the unique needs and characteristics of individual communicators.
> >
> > We condemn communication that degrades individuals and humanity through distortion, intimidation, coercion, and violence, and through the expression of intolerance and hatred.

ethics

A set of moral principles or values.

To analyze and discuss applications of the NCA Credo on Communication Ethics, view the "You Look Great" and "Pulling Your Own Weight" video clips on the *Online Learning Center.*

We are committed to the courageous expression of personal convictions in pursuit of fairness and justice.

We advocate sharing information, opinions, and feelings when facing significant choices while also respecting privacy and confidentiality.

We accept responsibility for the short- and long-term consequences of our own communication and expect the same of others.

These "Nine Commandments" are actually quite straightforward. They suggest that we should be open, honest, and reasonable. They affirm our belief in the First Amendment to the Constitution of the United States of America. They affirm that respect for other people and their messages is essential. They acknowledge the need for access to information and to people. Finally, they identify responsibility for our behavior as important.

These ideals are derived from Western conceptions of communication and a belief in democratic decision making. They also reflect ideologies of people within the communication discipline. We acknowledge that these standards might not be consistent with other cultures, belief systems, religions, or even academic disciplines. Murray (2000), for example, would suggest that we more properly should derive ethical standards in dialogue with others, combining our own perspective with others' ethical standards.

While we hold the NCA Credo as the best set of ethical conventions guiding communication, we recognize that others might not view these ideals as appropriate for all of us or appropriate at all times. In any case, throughout this text, we will consider the importance of ethics and will make reference to this credo.

TRY ◆ THIS

Our communication, and that of others, is not always effective or ethical. Identify an experience in which communication between you and another person was not effective. Identify another experience in which it was not ethical.

Chapter Review & Study Guide

SUMMARY

In this chapter you learned the following:

▶ Communication is essential because:
- Understanding communication can improve the way people view themselves and the way others view them.
- People learn more about human relationships as they study communication and learn important life skills.
- Studying communication can help people exercise their constitutionally guaranteed freedom of speech.
- An understanding of communication can help people succeed professionally.

▶ The components of communication are people, messages, channels, feedback, codes, encoding and decoding, and noise.

▶ Communication is the process of using messages to exchange meaning.

- Communication begins with the self and involves others.
- Communication has both a content and relational dimension.
- Communication is complicated.
- Increased quantity of communication does not necessarily increase the quality of communication.
- Communication is inevitable, irreversible, and unrepeatable.

▶ Communication occurs in intrapersonal, interpersonal, public, mass, and computer-mediated contexts. The number of people involved, the degree of formality or intimacy, the opportunities for feedback, the need for prestructuring messages, and the degree of stability of the roles of speaker and listener all vary with the communication context.

▶ Communication behavior should be effective and ethical.

KEY TERMS

Go to the *Online Learning Center* at **www.mhhe.com/pearson3** to further your understanding of the following terminology.

Channel
Code
Communication
Communication competence
Context
Decoding
Dialogue
Dyadic communication
Encoding

Ethics
Feedback
Interpersonal communication
Intrapersonal communication
Mass communication
Meaning
Message
Metaphors
Noise

Nonverbal codes
Process
Public communication
Receiver
Small-group communication
Source
Verbal codes

STUDY QUESTIONS

1. Communication is considered a process of using messages to generate meaning because it is
   a. an activity or exchange instead of an unchanging product
   b. a tangible object
   c. something with a beginning, middle, and end
   d. static

2. Understanding another person's messages does not occur unless
   a. the speaker uses nonverbal messages
   b. common meanings for words, phrases, and nonverbal codes are elicited
   c. the listener asks questions
   d. both parties use verbal and nonverbal symbols

3. People, messages, codes, channels, feedback, encoding, decoding, and noise are components of
   a. audience
   b. meaning
   c. communication
   d. context

4. Which communication principle considers variables such as verbal, nonverbal, and behavioral aspects, channel used, and audience characteristics?
   a. Communication has a content and relational dimension.
   b. Communication begins with the self.
   c. Communication involves others.
   d. Communication is complicated.

5. Intrapersonal communication is communication _____, and interpersonal communication is communication _____.
   a. between two or more people; within the self
   b. between two or more people; with a large number of people
   c. within the self; between two or more people
   d. within the self; within a small group of people

6. A main difference between public communication and mass communication is that
   a. mass communication is unstable
   b. public communication is mediated by television
   c. public communication allows for feedback from the listeners
   d. mass communication is generally informal and public communication is formal

7. Which of the following terms is defined as the ability to effectively exchange meaning through a common system of symbols, signs, or behavior?
   a. dyadic communication
   b. communication competence
   c. message
   d. feedback

8. Ethical standards within the communication discipline have been created by the
   a. National Communication Association
   b. American Communication Association
   c. Communication Administration
   d. Public Speaking Administration

9. According to the text, studying communication is essential because it can
   a. improve the way you see yourself and the way others see you
   b. teach you important life skills
   c. help you succeed professionally
   d. all of the above

10. When you respond to a speaker with a verbal or nonverbal cue, you are
    a. giving feedback
    b. not communicating
    c. an example of noise
    d. using a metaphor

Answers:

1. (a); 2. (b); 3. (c); 4. (d); 5. (c); 6. (c); 7. (b); 8. (a); 9. (d); 10. (a)

CRITICAL THINKING

1. In the beginning of the chapter, six advantages to studying communication are discussed. Explain how these benefits apply to you in your chosen area of study.

2. Think of your own computer use. How do you use computer-mediated communication (CMC) in your daily life (that is, for school, personal use, or work)? Do you use one kind of CMC more than the other?

SELF-QUIZ

For further review, try the chapter self-quiz on the *Online Learning Center* at **www.mhhe.com/pearson3.**

REFERENCES

Allen, M., Berkowitz, S., Hunt, S., & Louden, A. (1999). A meta-analysis of the impact of forensics and communication education on critical thinking. *Communication Education, 48,* 18–30.

Anderson, F. D., & Prelli, L. J. (2001). Pentadic cartography: Mapping the universe of discourse. *Quarterly Journal of Speech, 87,* 73–95.

Argenti, P. A., & Forman, J. (1998). Should business schools teach Aristotle? *Strategy & Business.* Retrieved from *www.strategy-business.com/briefs/98312.*

Bardwell, C. B. (1997). Standing out in the crowd. *Black Collegian, 28,* 71–79.

Bates, J. (2004, December 15). Unaccustomed as I am . . . *Nursing Standard, 19*(14–16), 25.

Berlo, D. (1960). *The process of communication.* New York: Holt, Rinehart & Winston.

Bigge, R. (2006, October 2). Wearing the digital dunce cap. *Maclean's, 119*(39), 64.

Blumer, J. G. (1983). Communication and democracy: The crisis beyond and the ferment within. *Journal of Communication, 33,* 166–173.

Brilhart, J. K., & Galanes, G. J. (1998). *Effective group discussion* (9th ed.). New York: McGraw-Hill.

Bubela, T. (2006). Science communication in transition: Genomics hype, public engagement, education and commercialization pressures. *Clinical Genetics, 70,* 445–450.

Cano, C. P., & Cano, P. Q. (2006). Human resources management and its impact on innovation performance in companies. *International Journal of Technology Management, 35,* 11–27.

Cockrum, K. V. (1994). Role-playing the interview. *Vocational Education Journal, 69,* 15–16.

Collins, M., & Oberman, D. (1994). What's the job outlook for '94? *Journal of Career Planning and Employment, 54,* 57–58.

Coopersmith, J. (2006). The dog that did not bark during the night. *Technology and Culture, 47,* 623–637.

Curtis, D. B., Winsor, J. L., & Stephens, R. D. (1989). National preferences in business and communication education. *Communication Education, 38,* 6–14.

Czubaroff, J. (2000). Dialogical rhetoric: An application of Martin Buber's philosophy of dialogue. *Quarterly Journal of Speech, 86,* 168–189.

Dauphinais, W. (1997). Forging the path to power. *Security Management, 41,* 21–23.

Dutta-Bergman, M. J. (2005). The relation between health-orientation, provider-patient communication, and satisfaction: An individual-difference approach. *Health Communication, 18,* 291–303.

Edwards, N., Peterson, W. E., & Davies, B. L. (2006, October). Evaluation of a multiple component intervention to support the implementation of a "therapeutic relationships" best practice guideline on nurses' communication skills. *Patient Education and Counseling, 63* (1/2), 3–11.

Egeci, I., & Gencoz, T. (2006). Factors associated with relationship satisfaction: Importance of communication skills. *Contemporary Family Therapy: An International Journal, 28,* 383–391.

Ford, W. S. Z., & Wolvin, A. D. (1993). The differential impact of a basic communication course on perceived communication competencies in class, work, and social contexts. *Communication Education, 42,* 215–233.

Glen, P. (2006, October 2). How indispensable should you be? *Computerworld, 40*(40), 50.

Gray, F., Emerson, L., & MacKay, B. (2005). Meeting the demands of the workplace: Science students and written skills. *Journal of Science Education and Technology, 14*(4), 425–435.

Hamilton, K. (1998, November 2). A very ugly gym suit. *Newsweek,* 52.

Hanzevack, E. L., & McKean, R. A. (1991). Teaching effective oral presentations as part of the senior design course. *Chemical Engineering Education, 25,* 28–32.

Harper, B. (2006, August 25). Communication is crucial. *Farmer's Weekly, 145*(8), 2.

Hart, R. P. (1993). Why communication? Why education? Toward a politics of teaching. *Communication Education, 42,* 97–105.

Horton, G. E., & Brown, D. (1990). The importance of interpersonal skills in consultee-centered consultation: A review. *Journal of Counseling and Development, 68,* 423–426.

Houssami, N., & Sainsbury, R. (2006). Breast cancer: Multidisciplinary care and clinical outcomes. *European Journal of Cancer, 42,* 2480–2491.

Ireland, J. L., Sanders, M. R., & Markie-Dodds, C. (2003). The impact of parent training on marital functioning: A comparison of two group versions of the triple-p positive parenting program for parents of children with early-onset conduct problems. *Behavioural and Cognitive Psychotherapy, 31,* 127–142.

Johnson, L. M., & Johnson, V. E. (1995, January/February). Help wanted—accountant: What the classifieds say about employer expectations. *Journal of Education for Business, 70*(3), 130–134.

LaBar, G. (1994). Putting together the complete hygienist. *Occupational Hazards, 56,* 63–66.

Lakoff, G., & Johnson, M. (1980). *Metaphors we live by.* Chicago: University of Chicago Press.

Lavin Colky, D., & Young, W. H. (2006). Mentoring in the virtual organization: Keys to building successful schools and businesses. *Mentoring and Tutoring: Partnership in Learning, 14,* 433–447

Lee, W. S. (1998). In the names of Chinese women. *Quarterly Journal of Speech, 84,* 283–302.

Maes, J. D., Weldy, T. G., & Icenogle, M. L. (1997). A managerial perspective: Oral communication competency is most important for business students in the workplace. *Journal of Business Communication, 34,* 67–80.

Manne, S. L., Ostroff, J. S., Norton, T. R., Fox, K., Goldstein, L., & Grana, G. (2006). Cancer-related relationship communication in couples coping with early stage breast cancer. *Psycho-Oncology, 15,* 234–247.

Mead, G. H. (1967). *Mind, self, and society from the standpoint of a social behaviorist.* Charles W. Morris (ed.). Chicago: University of Chicago Press.

Messmer, M. (1997, August). Career strategies for accounting graduates. *Management Accounting,* 4–10.

Metallinos, N. (1992, September–October). *Cognitive factors in the study of visual image recognition standards.* Paper presented to the Annual Conference of the International Visual Literacy Association, Pittsburgh. (ERIC Document Reproduction Service No. ED 352936).

Miller, J. F. (2006). Opportunities and obstacles for good work in nursing. *Nursing Ethics, 13,* 471–487.

Mlynek, A. (2006, September 11). Say goodbye to shy. *Canadian Business, 79*(18), 125–128.

Murray, J. W. (2000). Bakhtinian answerability and Levinasian responsibility: Forging a fuller dialogical communicative ethics. *Southern Communication Journal, 65,* 133–150.

National Communication Association, Washington, DC. Reprinted by permission of NCA.

Nicholls, L., & Webb, C. (2006). What makes a good midwife? An integrative review of methodologically-diverse research. *Journal of Advanced Nursing, 56,* 414–429.

Nichols, M. (2006, September 15). Listen up for better sales. *Business Week Online,* 12.

Nisberg, J. N. (1996). Communication: What we hear, what we say vs. what they hear, what they say. *The National Public Accountant, 41,* 34–38.

Pascopella, A. (2006, June). Shared pain and payoffs. *University Business, 9*(6), 96–100.

Pearson, J. C., Sorenson, R. L., & Nelson, P. E. (1981). How students and alumni perceive the basic course. *Communication Education, 30,* 296–299.

Peterson, M. S. (1997). Personnel interviewers' perceptions of the importance and adequacy of applicants' communication skills. *Communication Education, 46,* 287–291.

Reinsch, L., & Shelby, A. N. (1996). Communication challenges and needs: Perceptions of MBA students. *Business Communication Quarterly, 59,* 36–52.

Ridley, A. J. (1996). A profession for the twenty-first century. *Internal Auditor, 53,* 20–25.

Rogers, C. (1951). *Client-centered therapy.* Boston: Houghton Mifflin.

Rubin, R. B., Perse, E. M., & Barbato, C. A. (1988). Conceptualization and measurement of interpersonal communication motives. *Human Communication Research, 14,* 602–628.

Shotter, J. (2000). Inside dialogical realities: From an abstract-systematic to a participatory-wholistic understanding of communication. *Southern Communication Journal, 65,* 119–132.

Simkin, M. G. (1996). The importance of good communication skills on "IS" career paths. *Journal of Technical Writing & Communication, 26,* 69–78.

Tannen, D. (1998). *The argument culture: Moving from debate to dialogue.* New York: Random House.

Today's Employment. (1998, October 18). *The Washington Post,* pp. K33, K49.

Ugbah, S. D., & Evuleocha, S. U. (1992). The importance of written, verbal, and nonverbal communication factors in employment interview decisions. *Journal of Employment Counseling, 29,* 128–137.

Wirbel, L. (2006, October 9). Civic duty applies to all. *Electronic Engineering Times, 1444,* 4.

Perception, Self, and Communication

What will you learn?

When you have read and thought about this chapter, you will be able to:

1. Explain some of the reasons why differences in perception occur.
2. Describe how selection, organization, and interpretation occur during perception.
3. Differentiate among figure and ground, proximity, closure, and similarity in communication examples.
4. Identify errors you might make when you perceive others.
5. Understand how your view of yourself is related to communication.
6. Differentiate among self-fulfilling prophecies, self-image, and self-esteem.
7. Provide examples of confirmation, rejection, and disconfirmation.
8. List steps you can take to improve your self-concept.
9. Define identity management and explain the component parts of actors, performance, and face.

This chapter introduces you to the role of perception and the role of the self in communication. The chapter opens by explaining what perception is; then it describes why differences in perception occur and what occurs during perception. Next, the chapter moves to our perceptions of others, including errors we occasionally make in those perceptions. A discussion of the role of the self in communication completes the chapter. After you read this chapter, you will have a better understanding of the communicative importance of how you see yourself and how you see others.

In Shakespeare's *Romeo and Juliet,* Juliet innocently asks, "What's in a name?" She was implying that a mere name could not affect her love for Romeo (of the rival Montague family). But for some people today, names do matter, especially when applied to sports teams and mascots. Of particular sensitivity are names and symbols that seem to mock or demean Native Americans, such as "Savages" and tomahawk-wielding mascots.

In 2005 the National Collegiate Athletic Association (NCAA) adopted a new policy to prohibit the display of abusive racial or ethnic names, mascots, or imagery at any of the 88 NCAA championships. Some 18 colleges and university teams felt the impact of the policy, ranging from the Florida State Seminoles to the Southeast Oklahoma University Savages.

Designed to promote cultural respect, the policy soon ran into trouble. Some people objected that the ruling prohibited even positive names like Warriors and Chieftains just because they referred to Native Americans. At the same time, similar names that referred to other groups, such as Trojans and Aztecs, were tolerated. As one editorial writer put it, that sends "a message that Native Americans are sensitive in a way that other groups are not" (*The Boston Globe,* June 5, 2005). Others argued that the policy did not go far enough in ridding sports of insulting references. This controversy is likely to linger in political and legal circles for years and spark endless debate.

The controversy over the use of Native American and other racially linked names and mascots illustrates how perception influences our views of the world and our communication with others. For some, Native American names and mascots represent a way of honoring a group; for others, that same use represents racism. In this chapter you will learn how the difference between these two views stems from individual perspectives and perceptions.

What Is Perception?

In this chapter we focus on perception, the self, and communication. Differences in perception affect the way we understand events, others, and ourselves. Consequently, perception affects self-concept, self-efficacy, and our presentation of self. In turn, perception influences, our experience and assessment of others and our communication with them. The way you sense the world—the way you see, hear, smell, touch, and taste—is subjective, uniquely your own. Nobody else sees the world the way you do, and nobody experiences events exactly as you do. The uniqueness of human experience is based largely on differences in **perception**—"the process of becoming aware of objects and events from the senses" (DeVito, 1986). Since our perceptions are unique, communication between and among people becomes complicated.

At one time experts tended to see perception as passive. Passive perception means that, like video recorders, people are simply recorders of stimuli. Today perception is considered to be more active. **Active perception** means that your mind selects, organizes, and interprets that which you sense. So each person is a different video camera, and each person aims the camera at different things; each person's

perception

The process of becoming aware of objects and events from the senses.

active perception

Perception in which your mind selects, organizes, and interprets that which you sense.

lens is different; each person sees different colors; and each person's audio picks up different sounds. Perception is subjective in that you interpret what you sense; you make it your own, and you add to and subtract from what you see, hear, smell, and touch. **Subjective perception** is your uniquely constructed meaning attributed to sensed stimuli.

Consider how much your inner state affects your perceptions. If you have a bad headache, the pain probably will affect the way you treat your children, the way you respond to a pop quiz, and even the way you see yourself in the mirror. Consider also how complicated communication becomes when you know that everyone has his or her own view, uniquely developed and varying according to what is happening both outside and inside the mind. Perception is just one of the many factors that complicate communication.

How do you see the world around you? Perhaps comparing the way your mind works to the way a computer works will help you answer this. Think of your conscious experiences as the images that appear on your computer monitor. Think of what you sense with your eyes, nose, tongue, ears, and fingertips as that which is read off your computer disk. The picture you see on the screen is not the same as the bits on the disk; instead, an image is generated from the bits to create something you can see. "What we perceive in the world around us is not a direct and faithful representation of that world itself, but rather a 'computer enhanced' version based upon very limited data from that world" according to Wright (1994).

> *We promote communication climates of caring and mutual understanding that respect the unique needs and characteristics of individual communicators.*
>
> NCA Ethics
> Credo

subjective perception

Your uniquely constructed meaning attributed to sensed stimuli.

Why Do Differences in Perception Occur?

Perception is subjective, active, and creative. Differences in perception may be the result of physiological factors, people's past experiences and roles, their cultures and co-cultures, and their present feelings and circumstances.

TRY ◆ THIS

Think of an event that recently occurred in your life in which your perception of what happened might be quite different from the perceptions of others.

Physiological Factors

You are not physiologically identical to anyone else. People differ from each other in sex, height, weight, body type, and senses. You may be tall or short, have poor eyesight, or have impaired hearing; you may be particularly sensitive to smells; or your body temperature may be colder than the rest of your family's body temperatures.

Sex is another physiological factor that may lead to perceptual differences. Some authors have suggested that hemispheric differences in the cerebral cortex of the brain are sex-linked. These differences account for females' language facility and fine hand control and for males' spatial and mathematical abilities, as well as their increased likelihood of dyslexia, stuttering, delayed speech, autism, and hyperactivity (Restak, 1984). Regardless of these findings, experts have found no conclusive evidence establishing an anatomical difference between the brain structures of human females and males.

Differences in perception also may arise from temporary conditions. A headache, fatigue, or a pulled muscle can cause you to perceive a critical comment when a friendly one is being offered. You may not see a stop sign if your thoughts are elsewhere. Similarly, if you are tired, you may perceive stimuli differently than when you are well rested. Other physiological needs, such as hunger and thirst, may also affect your perceptive skills.

Past Experiences and Roles

Just as your size, sex, and senses can affect your perceptions, so can your past experiences and your various roles.

The concept that best explains the influence of your past experiences on your perceptions is **perceptual constancy**—the idea that your past experiences lead you to see the world in a way that is difficult to change; your initial perceptions persist. What happened to you in the past influences your current perceptions. A bad experience in a given situation may cause you to avoid that situation in the future. Your experiences affect how you respond to professors, police, politicians, and lawyers.

Roles also influence perceptions. A **role** is "the part an individual plays in a group; an individual's function or expected behavior" (DeVito, 1986, p. 269). You may be a student, a single mother or father, a political leader, or a business major. Your roles affect your communication: whom you talk to, how you talk to them, what language you use, and how you respond to feedback. A good example of how perceptual constancy and role are related involves parents' treatment of their children. Even after some people become adults, their parents treat them as they did when they were growing up. Roles also tend to change with context: in your parents' home you are a son or daughter; in your own home you may be a roommate or a mother or father; in the classroom you are a student; and at work you may be an editor or a manager.

Culture and Co-culture

The ways people greet each other, position themselves when they talk, and even eat and sleep are all influenced by culture. **Culture** can be defined as a system of shared beliefs, values, customs, behaviors, and artifacts that the members of a society use to cope with one another and with their world. Marshall R. Singer (1982), an intercultural communication researcher, maintains that what people see, hear, taste, touch, and smell is conditioned by their culture. He says that people's perceptions are largely learned; the greater the experiential differences among people, the greater the disparity in their perceptions. Conversely, the more similar their backgrounds, the more similarly they perceive the world.

People from different cultures and different countries perceive communication differently. American speakers who are accustomed to a certain level of feedback might find audiences in Finland and Norway to be inexpressive. Interpersonal communication behaviors also vary as a result of cultural differences. Lu (1997), for

---

The relationship between perception and communication can be analyzed in the video clip "Where There's Smoke" on the *Online Learning Center* at www.mhhe.com/pearson3.

perceptual constancy

The idea that your past experiences lead you to see the world in a way that is difficult to change; your initial perceptions persist.

role

The part an individual plays in a group; an individual's function or expected behavior.

culture

A system of shared beliefs, values, customs, behaviors, and artifacts that the members of a society use to cope with one another and with their world.

example, found that Chinese teachers use different techniques to alter students' behavior in the classroom than do American teachers. Chinese teachers prefer punishment-oriented or antisocial strategies such as "I'll give you an F if you don't do this assignment."

As the United States becomes increasingly diverse, people in service industries need to rethink their communication practices. Differences in perception are plentiful. For example, physicians and other health care workers at Bailey's Health Center in Falls Church, Virginia, were concerned with a large number of "no shows." People made follow-up appointments that they never kept. In talking with the patients, who were primarily from Central America, they learned that refusing an appointment time would be viewed as rude. That is, knowing that they could not keep a new appointment was not cause to refuse it (Levine, 2006).

Differences in perception that are created by cultural differences can be overcome in our interaction with others.

To complicate matters further, your co-culture also affects your perceptions of the world. A **co-culture** is "a group whose beliefs or behaviors distinguish it from the larger culture of which it is a part and with which it shares numerous similarities" (DeVito, 1986). Four of the more common co-cultures in the United States today are Latinos, African Americans, women, and gays and lesbians (Samovar, Porter, & Stefani, 1998). Women and men, for example, tend to see the world differently, to communicate about it differently, and even to practice and perceive communication itself differently. Women tend to see talk as relational, as a way to share and understand feelings, whereas men tend to see talk as instrumental, as a way to achieve a task (Pearson, 1995). Culture and co-culture are discussed in greater detail in chapter 7.

co-culture

A group whose beliefs or behaviors distinguish it from the larger culture of which it is a part and with which it shares numerous similarities.

Present Feelings and Circumstances

Your daily, monthly, or yearly cycle may affect how you perceive stimuli. If you are an "evening person," you might not be able to discriminate among multiple-choice answers on an exam at 8:00 a.m. as well as you could later in the day. If you are having a bad week, you might be offended by the humor of one of your friends; later in the month, you might find the same remark very funny. You might perceive stimuli more acutely in the cooler months of winter than you do in the warmer summer months.

If you have ever spent a night alone in a large house, a deserted dormitory, or an unfamiliar residence, you probably understand that perceptions are altered by circumstances. Most people experience a remarkable change in their hearing at night when they are alone. They hear creaking, whining, scraping, cracking sounds at night but not during the day. The lack of other stimuli—including light, other sounds, and people with whom to talk—coupled with a slight feeling of anxiety provides circumstances that result in more acute hearing.

What Occurs in Perception?

You engage in three separate activities during perception: selection, organization, and interpretation. No one is aware of these separate processes because they occur quickly and almost simultaneously. Nonetheless, each activity plays a discrete role in perception.

Selection

No one perceives all the stimuli in his or her environment. Through selection, you neglect some stimuli in your environment and focus on other stimuli. For example, when you drive or walk to your classes, you are probably bombarded with sights, sounds, smells, and other sensations. At the time, you elect to perceive some of the stimuli and to disregard others. You smell steak cooking as you walk by a restaurant, but you ignore the dimness of the evening. Afterward, it's likely you will recall the stimuli you perceived but will have forgotten the other stimuli.

You also select the messages to which you attend. You might not hear one of your parents admonishing you, but you do hear the much softer sound of your name being called from a distance. You may "tune out" one of your professors while you listen to the hard rainfall outside the classroom window. You might listen to the criticism a friend offers you, but not the corresponding praise.

Four types of selectivity are selective exposure, selective attention, selective perception, and selective retention. In **selective exposure** you expose yourself to information that reinforces, rather than contradicts, your beliefs or opinions (Wilson & Wilson, 1998). In other words, conservative Republicans are more likely than liberal Democrats to listen to Rush Limbaugh and Oliver North on the radio and to read editorials by George Will. Liberal Democrats, on the other hand, are more likely to avoid these sources of information and listen to sources that support their beliefs.

In **selective attention,** even when you do expose yourself to information and ideas, you focus on certain cues and ignore others. In class, you might notice the new outfit your friend is wearing but not the earring worn by the man three seats in front of you. At a buffet table, you might be drawn to the smells and the foods that you recognize and select only those. In an elevator, you may notice the conversation between the two other people in the elevator but not the music that's being piped in overhead.

In communication, we do not treat all sounds, words, phrases, and sentences equally. We might attend to a sound that is similar to our names because of familiarity. We might hear a word that we view as obscene or novel because of its nature. We might focus on an unfamiliar comparison or a humorous cliché. We might

selective exposure

The tendency to expose yourself to information that reinforces, rather than contradicts, your beliefs or opinions.

selective attention

The tendency, when you expose yourself to information and ideas, to focus on certain cues and ignore others.

Think, Pair, Share

Similar or Different?

To whom do you listen and to what do you direct your attention? You might believe that your classmates make choices that are similar to yours. By yourself, list the type of music you prefer and three of the top musical groups you enjoy. Identify your favorite reading material. What television programs do you normally watch? What is your favorite website? What is the primary purpose for your use of the Internet? If you were going to spend time conversing with one other person, whom would you choose? If you were going to participate in a discussion, which three people would you prefer to communicate with? After you have compiled your individual answers, pair up with a classmate and share your answers. Consider similarities and differences in your responses. Are you surprised by some of the differences? How do you account for the similarities?

attend to a sentence that is striking or provocative. Selective attention is as central to communication as it is to other perceived entities.

After you expose yourself to a message and then select it for further attention, you see that message through your own special lens. **Selective perception** is the tendency to see, hear, and believe only what you want to see, hear, and believe (Wilson & Wilson, 1998). Suppose someone accused your trustworthy, law-abiding friend of 20 years of stealing; would you believe that person? You may not listen to the accusations, or even look at the evidence, because you believe it simply is not possible that your friend would ever do such a thing.

 One example of selective perception involves how teachers observe signs of confusion or frustration from students. In a study exploring how different types of teachers respond to the unique needs of people who speak English as a second language (ESL), it was found that different types of teachers are more adept at perceiving nonverbal signals of confusion from ESL students (Curtin, 2005). Teachers who tend to use more interaction and dialogue in their classroom are quick to observe nonverbal behaviors signaling a lack of understanding; in contrast, teachers who rely more on lecture tend to miss such signals. These findings illustrate how selective perception, perhaps driven by past experiences and roles, can cause some teachers to selectively perceive and react to such nonverbal signs while others do not. While these findings point to the need for all teachers to be more observant of students' nonverbal behaviors, they may also suggest that ESL students need to be more active in telling teachers when they have difficulty in understanding specific terms or ideas.

Finally, you select the stimuli you will recall or remember. **Selective retention** is the tendency to remember better the things that reinforce your beliefs rather than those that oppose them (Wilson & Wilson, 1998). For example, make a list of some of the bad qualities of someone you dislike and a list of some of the bad qualities of someone you admire. Compare your lists. Usually, people can easily think of the negative qualities of someone they dislike, but they often find it difficult to think of an admirable person's negative qualities (Wilson & Wilson, 1998).

All of us can recall conversations we had with other people. Over time, those recollections are probably affected by selective retention. We recall critical comments that someone made about our abilities when we later proved them to be wrong. We remember (and perhaps even exaggerate) honorific remarks that were

selective perception

The tendency to see, hear, and believe only what you want to see, hear, and believe.

selective retention

The tendency to remember better the things that reinforce your beliefs rather than those that oppose them.

made. We enjoy retelling conversations that paint a picture that is consistent with our beliefs about ourselves and others.

Selection is the first process that occurs during perception; the next is organization.

Organization

Each person organizes the stimuli in his or her environment. Organization is the grouping of stimuli into meaningful units or wholes. You organize stimuli in a number of ways, such as through figure and ground, closure, proximity, and similarity.

Figure and Ground

One organization method is to distinguish between figure and ground. **Figure** is the focal point of your attention, and **ground** is the background against which your focused attention occurs. When looking at Figure 2.1, some people might perceive a vase or a candlestick, whereas others perceive twins facing each other. People who see a vase identify the center of the drawing as the figure and the area on the right and left as the ground (or background). Conversely, people who see twins facing each other identify the center as the ground and the area on the right and left as the figure.

How do figure and ground work in communication encounters? In your verbal and nonverbal exchanges, you perform a similar feat of focusing on some parts (figure) and distancing yourself from others (ground). When you hear your name in a noisy room, your name becomes figure and the rest becomes ground; on a posted grade list, your student ID number becomes figure and the other numbers become ground. Here's another example: During a job evaluation your employer may talk about your weaknesses and strengths, but the so-called weaknesses may make you so angry that you don't even remember the strengths. The messages about weaknesses are figure, and the ones about strengths are ground. Because of who and what you are, and because of your own unique perceptual processes, your attention focuses and fades, and you choose the figure or ground of what you see, hear, smell, touch, and taste.

Closure

Another way of organizing stimuli is **closure,** the tendency to fill in missing information in order to complete an otherwise incomplete figure or statement. If someone were to show you Figure 2.2 and ask you what you see, you might say it is a

Figure 2.1   An example of figure and ground: a vase or twins?

Figure 2.2   An example of closure: ink blobs or a cat?

---

figure

The focal point of your attention.

ground

The background against which your focused attention occurs.

closure

The tendency to fill in missing information in order to complete an otherwise incomplete figure or statement.

picture of a cat. But as you can see, the figure is incomplete. You see a cat only if you are willing to fill in the blank areas.

Closure also functions in your communication interactions. You see two people standing face-to-face and gazing deeply into each other's eyes, and you "fill in" your inference that they are lovers. A public speaker says, "We need to preserve our neighborhoods," and you assume she is against the proposed low-income housing. Visual closure might involve completing the circle or seeing the cat, but mental closure means filling in the meaning of what you hear and observe.

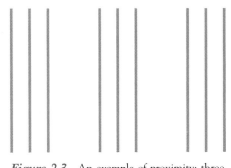

Figure 2.3   An example of proximity: three groups of lines or nine separate lines?

Proximity

You also organize stimuli on the basis of their proximity. According to the principle of **proximity,** objects physically close to each other will be perceived as a unit or group (DeVito, 1986). This principle is at work in Figure 2.3. You are most likely to perceive three groups of three lines, rather than nine separate lines.

Proximity works verbally and nonverbally in communication. Nonverbal examples include thinking that the person standing next to the cash register is the cashier and assuming that the two people entering the room at the same time are together. And here is a verbal example: Suppose your boss announces that due to an economic downturn he is forced to lay off 25 employees, and one hour later he calls you into his office—the proximity of the messages leads you to believe that you will be laid off.

proximity

The principle that objects physically close to each other will be perceived as a unit or group.

Similarity

Similarity is probably one of the simplest means of organizing stimuli. On the basis of the principle of **similarity,** elements are grouped together because they resemble each other in size, color, shape, or other attributes. The saying "Birds of a feather flock together" can hold true as well for human groups, who often organize by ethnicity, religion, political leaning, or interests. In Figure 2.4 you probably perceive circles and squares, rather than a group of geometric shapes, because of the principle of similarity.

similarity

The principle that elements are grouped together because they share attributes such as size, color, or shape.

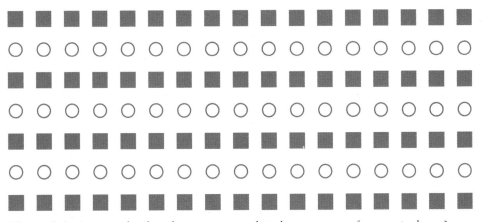

Figure 2.4   An example of similarity: squares and circles or a group of geometric shapes?

How does similarity work in our relationships and our interactions? Generally, we seek friends, work partners, and roommates based on similarity. We choose to interact with those who are similar, on some dimension, to ourselves. Because our perceptions are egocentric, we choose to communicate with those we believe are similar to us. In other words, our friends tend to represent some part of our self (Leary, 2002). We reject, or certainly are less interested in interacting with, people who are highly different from the way we see ourselves.

To understand the relationship between the organization of stimuli and communication, think about a classroom setting. When you enter the room, your tendency is to organize the stimuli, or people there, into specific groups. Your primary focus is on acquaintances and friends—the *figure*—rather than on the strangers, who function as the *ground*. You talk to friends sitting near the doorway as you enter, due to their *proximity*. You then seat yourself near a group of students you perceive as having interests identical to yours, thus illustrating *similarity*. Lastly, you see your instructor arrive with another professor of communication; they are laughing, smiling, and conversing enthusiastically. *Closure* is a result of your assumption that they have a social relationship outside the classroom.

Interpretation

interpretive perception

Perception that involves a blend of internal states and external stimuli.

The third activity you engage in during perception is interpretation, the assignment of meaning to stimuli. **Interpretive perception,** then, is a blend of internal states and external stimuli. The more ambiguous the stimuli, the more room for interpretation. The basis for the well-known inkblot test lies in the principle of interpretation of stimuli. Figure 2.5 shows three inkblots that a psychologist might ask you to interpret. The ambiguity of the figures is typical.

When interpreting stimuli, people frequently rely on the context in which the stimuli are perceived, or they compare the stimuli to other stimuli (Figure 2.6). Sometimes context helps, but other times it can create confusion in interpretation.

You can become so accustomed to seeing people, places, and situations in a certain way that your senses do not pick up on the obvious. Many people who read the following sentence will overlook the problem with it:

The cop saw the man standing on the the street corner.

Figure 2.5   An example of interpretation: the inkblot.

We achieve closure on the sentence and interpret its meaning without being conscious of the details, so the repeated *the* is overlooked. Context provides cues for how an action, an object, or a situation is to be interpreted or perceived. Not seeing the double *the* in the sentence would be no problem for a reader trying to comprehend meaning, but a proofreader's job would be in jeopardy if such an error was missed often.

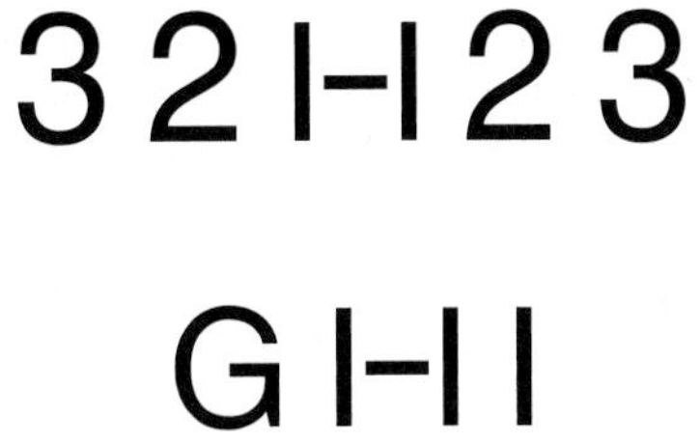

3 2 H 2 3

G H I

Figure 2.6   An example of the usefulness of context in the interpretation of stimuli.

How does interpretation work in our interactions with others? Imagine that you are working in a group in one of your classes. One member of the group always comes prepared and seems to dominate the group interaction and to dictate the direction the project is taking. Another member of the group frequently misses agreed-upon group meeting times, arrives late when he does come, and is never prepared. How do you interpret the behavior of these two people?

Suppose you are more like the first person than the second. You might feel that the first person is challenging your leadership in the group. On the other hand, you consider the enormous contributions she makes by bringing a great deal of research and planning each time. You dismiss the second person as lazy, unmotivated, and a poor student. You are worried that he will bring the group grade down.

Now suppose you are more like the second person than the first. You, too, miss meetings, arrive late, and do virtually nothing to prepare. You might interpret the first person's behavior as showing off, but, at the same time, you are glad that she is going to lead the group to a good grade. You see the second person as laid-back and fun. In fact, you decide you would like to hang out with him.

How Do You Perceive Others?

Once we understand the active nature of perception and recognize that people hold unique perceptions as a consequence, we can see that we might make errors when we perceive other people. Attribution, in general, is the ascribing of something to somebody or something. When we consider our perceptions of others, **attribution** refers to the assignment of meaning to their behavior. Attributions may vary based on our relationship with the other person (Manusov, Trees, Reddick, Rowe, & Easley, 1998). In this section we will consider some of the common attributions that we make in understanding other people that may lead us to make perceptual errors—errors that are a result of the processes of perception discussed earlier in this chapter.

attribution

The assignment of meaning to people's behavior.

Attribution Errors

Attribution errors occur when people mistakenly explain their own behavior or the behavior of others.

Fundamental Attribution Error

The **fundamental attribution error** occurs when we make judgments about other people's successes and failures: When other people fail, we assume it is because of their personal failure; when they succeed, we assume it is because of the situation in which they find themselves. Imagine that a friend of yours loses a state beauty contest. Most likely you would conclude that it is a result of her physical features, weight, personality, or other characteristics. On the other hand, her success would not be based on these same qualities. Instead, you might conclude that she was lucky, that few contestants competed this year, or that some other circumstance accounts for her success.

Self-Serving Bias

Although other people's successes are often viewed as situational, and their failures as personal failures, we attribute our own successes and failures in exactly the opposite way. The **self-serving bias** maintains that our successes are due to our personal qualities—intelligence, wit, political savvy—and our failures occur because of our circumstances (for example, the teacher did not like me, no one received grades of A, the class was too difficult for undergraduate students, my adviser did not explain that I needed a prerequisite, the departmental chair is a bigot).

Perceptual Errors

Many perceptual errors exist. We will consider only two of the most common errors: stereotyping and first impressions.

Stereotyping

Stereotyping occurs when we offer an oversimplified or standardized image of a person because of her or his group membership. How does stereotyping work? First, we categorize other people into groups based on a variety of criteria—age, sex, race, sexual orientation, occupation, region of the country, or physical abilities. Next, we infer that everyone within that group has the same characteristics. For instance, we might conclude that all lesbians are masculine, that people on the East Coast are fast-talking, or that older people are conservative.

Our expectations and our interpretations of the behavior of others are then guided by these perceptions. When we observe people from other groups, we exaggerate, or overestimate, how frequently they engage in the stereotypic behaviors we believe they hold. We ignore, or underestimate, how frequently they engage in the behaviors that we do not believe they engage in.

The influence of perception on stereotyping can be observed in the video clip "The Right Kind of Care" on the *Online Learning Center*.

Unfortunately, our stereotypes of people from different groups are often negative (Hendrix, 2002). If you are a man, you might hold some negative views of women. If you are white, you might believe that black people are not as qualified for higher education as you are. If you are able-bodied, you might not empathize with someone in a wheelchair. Hughes and Baldwin (2002) found that these negative stereotypes created different communication patterns when white and black individuals, for example, interacted. They suggest that "macrolevel interpretations between interracial speakers may be problematic" (p. 113).

Attributional Style

What kinds of attributions do you make? Do you believe that you have control over your fate, or do you think that others control your successes and failures? To learn more about yourself, complete the Locus of Control and Attribution Style Test at **www.queendom.com/tests/personality.** The test is scored online in a matter of seconds.

Our explanations for the expected and unexpected behaviors are frequently in error as we assume situational reasons for unexpected outcomes and personal reasons for expected outcomes. For example, if we believe that teenagers are foolhardy and high risk takers, we explain the behavior of a careful and conservative teenager by concluding that this is her "public behavior" and that she actually behaves differently in private.

Finally, we differentiate ourselves from people whom we stereotype. The woman who has some African-American heritage but does not identify with it might view other black people as possessing qualities that are different from her own. The man who has only the slightest Hispanic background but is proud of this heritage may see Caucasians as boring and too prudent.

First Impressions

Each of us seeks to form a first impression of others—an initial opinion about people upon meeting them. Frequently, these "first impressions" are based on other people's appearance and may occur in as little as 3 seconds (Sterling, 2006). The nonverbal cues they offer are particularly powerful. We notice their clothing, their height and weight, their physical attractiveness, and their interaction skills and make a snap judgment.

As people make their first impressions, they also compare the new person to themselves. According to Sterling (2006), we make certain comparisons and draw certain conclusions in a business setting. For example, if the person appears to be of a comparable business or social level, we decide that they are worthy of further interaction. If they appear to be of a higher level, we admire them and cultivate them as a valuable contact. If they appear to be of lower status, we tolerate them but keep them at arm's length.

Our first impressions are powerful, and sometimes they lead to errors in our assessment of others. Imagine a businessperson who has traveled all day and arrives late for a meeting. Her flight was delayed, her luggage was lost on route, and she is disheveled and harried. New business acquaintances might dismiss her simply on the grounds of her appearance.

First impressions may be affected by specific situations or circumstances that the other person is experiencing, making our initial assessment inaccurate. Just the same, we tend to cling to these impressions in future interactions. Rather than altering our opinion, we filter out new information that disputes our original appraisal.

Imagine that you met a friend's mother on a holiday. Your friend's mother drank a great deal and was highly gregarious. You conclude that she enjoys parties and is very friendly. On your next encounters with the friend's mother, she seems quiet and businesslike. Nonetheless, you adhere to your original conclusion that she is a fun-loving and talkative individual.

Understanding that our perceptions of others rest on a subjective, active, and creative perceptual process is important. Our perceptions of others are unique, and individuals are perceived in multiple ways by multiple interactants. We can more fairly appraise others and their behavior by understanding common attribution and perceptual errors and the extent to which we are engaged in them.

Another important skill is perceptual checking, a process that helps us understand another person and her or his message more accurately. Perceptual checking has three steps. First, you describe to the other person the behavior—including the verbal and nonverbal cues—that you observed. Second, you suggest plausible interpretations. Third, you seek clarification, explanation, or amplification.

For example, imagine that you are assigned a group project in one of your classes. Another member of the group asks you to produce all of your primary sources for the research project. You presented this source material weeks ago. You respond by saying, "I understand that you want me to give you my primary sources" (describe the behavior or the message). "I have a feeling that you do not trust me" (first interpretation). "Or maybe you just want to create the bibliography for the whole group" (second interpretation). "Can you explain why you want my primary sources" (request for clarification)?

Perceptual checking may be even more important in our personal or romantic relationships. Suppose a platonic friend provides you with a very romantic birthday present. You begin by describing the behavior: "The gift you gave me was very romantic." You then suggest alternative interpretations: "Perhaps you want to change the nature of our relationship" (first interpretation)? "Maybe this gift was for someone else" (second interpretation)? "Maybe you don't view the gift as romantic" (third interpretation)? "Can you tell me what you intended?"

On the *Online Learning Center* at www.mhhe. com/pearson3, view the video segment titled "Opposites Attract" to analyze the use of perceptual checking during interpersonal conflict.

In perceptual checking, you must suggest interpretations that do not cause the other person to be defensive. In the first instance, imagine that you offered as one explanation, "Maybe you want my primary sources so you can claim that you did all of the research." The other person is most likely to become defensive. In the second instance, you could have offered, "Maybe you don't realize that I don't want a romantic relationship with you." Most likely, embarrassment and a loss of face would follow.

As another example, recall the situation in Falls Church, Virginia, at the medical clinic where patients from Central America did not keep their appointments. The health care workers had to do some follow-up to learn about the cultural differences. They needed to describe the behavior, suggest an interpretation, but then allow the patients to explain the practice.

Perceptual checks were also necessary when physicians learned that they could not look directly at a Hmong man and that breast self-exam programs for Muslim women needed to be conducted before regular hours so no men were on the property. Women from other countries report being surprised by the directness and invasiveness of male physicians' questions and sometimes do not answer these questions truthfully or fully (Levine, 2006). Health care workers must continue to do perceptual checks to ensure that the women are receiving the best medical care possible.

◄ **SKILL** BUILDER ►

Bring an object to class that means a great deal to you. With a partner, explain the significance of this object. The partner should listen carefully to you. When you are finished, the partner should ask questions about the object. When the partner is satisfied that she or he understands your relationship to the object, she or he should try a perceptual check (first, describing your message; then suggesting some alternative interpretations; and finally, concluding by asking for the correct interpretation). When you are satisfied that the partner understands your message, reverse roles.

Who Are You?

The discussion of perception naturally leads to a look at self-perception. How you perceive yourself plays a central role in communication, regardless of whether the communication is in a daydream, in a journal, in a small group, or at a podium. An early step in considering yourself a communicator is to contemplate who you are. In chapter 6 we present the Johari window, which will help you understand the self-disclosure process. The Johari window serves as a reminder that you may know some things about yourself but that you do not know everything. You might have some habits in the way you communicate to others but be unaware of them. Perhaps you use verbal fillers such as "and then" or nonverbal fluencies such as "um" when you give a presentation in class. Perhaps you report stories that are offensive to some of your friends. These are your communicative behaviors, but you are unaware of them.

What you know about yourself includes your past, present, and future. Your past goes all the way back to how you were reared, or how your family taught you to think, believe, and behave. You began as a spontaneous creature who cried when hungry or frustrated, lashed out when angry, and giggled and beamed when happy. Over time, adults took away some of your spontaneity until you behaved like a little adult—until you ate at mealtimes, held your anger in check with your teachers, laughed when appropriate, and cried little if at all. Your emotions, as well as your physical responses, were altered to make you responsible for your own behavior.

Determining who you are is not a matter of simply adding up your past experiences, however. Philosophers and psychologists have debated the nature of personal identity for centuries. John Locke, for example, felt that an individual's personal identity was founded on consciousness rather than in terms of his or her body or soul. The *Stanford Encyclopedia of Philosophy* (available at http://plato.stanford.edu/entries/identity-personal/) identifies a number of issues that personal identity introduces. For example, if people change over time, which parts of their personal identity are persistent? How are we similar to others and how are we different?

These same questions are studied today in social scientific research. People's personal identities influence their perceptions of others (Seta, Schmidt, & Bookhout, 2006). Personal identities appear to have some stability and some fragmentation; in other words, they are not necessarily either intrinsically stable or fragmented (Day, Kington, Stobart, & Sammons, 2006).

Personal identities can be changed, and people can improve their behavior as a result. For example, some low-income and minority teens who had low academic attainment were taught strategies that allowed the development of a "new academic possible self." These students achieved higher grades, scored higher on standardized tests, and showed greater academic initiative. At the same time, their levels of depression, absenteeism, and in-school misbehavior declined (Oyserman, Bybee, & Terry, 2006).

How can personal identity research be applied to communication? When a speaker creates a message that points up shared values with listeners, the listeners perceive a personal identity match and are more likely to be persuaded. Other factors may interfere with this cause-effect relationship, however. For example, if the shared values are unexpected because of someone's political party membership or other social group affiliations, the message may be rejected and the persuasive attempt may fail (Nelson & Garst, 2005).

Your awareness of who you are develops in your communication with yourself, that is, your intrapersonal communication. Shedletsky (1989) writes that intrapersonal communication includes "our perceptions, memories, experiences, feelings, interpretations, inferences, evaluations, attitudes, opinions, ideas, strategies, images, and states of consciousness." Intrapersonal communication may be viewed as "talking to ourselves"; it is also synonymous with thinking. Intrapersonal communication appears to be the most common context of communication, the foundation for the other contexts.

Your awareness of who you are also develops in your communication with others. Once you mastered language, symbolic interactionism shaped you in ways that made you what you are today. **Symbolic interactionism** refers to the process of development of the self through the messages and feedback received from others (Mead, 1934). You may have been punished for acting up in class, rewarded for athletic skill, or ignored for saying too little. The result is the person you see in the mirror today.

symbolic interactionism

The process in which the self develops through the messages and feedback received from others.

Self-Fulfilling Prophecy

An aspect of symbolic interactionism is the **self-fulfilling prophecy**—the idea that you behave and see yourself in ways that are consistent with how others see you (Wood, 1997, p. 383). Through a number of studies on academic performance, Rosenthal and Jacobson (1968) found that students who were expected to do well actually performed better than students who were not expected to perform well. In other words, "We learn to see ourselves in terms of the labels others apply to us. Those labels shape our self-concepts and behaviors" (Wood, 1997, p. 128).

Indeed, your concept of yourself originated in the responses you received when you were young, and to some extent, self-fulfilling prophecies help maintain your self-concept. In many ways, individuals attempt to behave in ways consistent with other people's expectations, regardless of whether those expectations are positive or negative. But the self-fulfilling prophecy is not a simple, straightforward concept: Individuals do not simply and routinely behave in the ways other people expect them to. For you it may be that other people's expectations play a more important role than your own or, conversely, that you see your own expectations as more relevant. In either case, however, others' observations about who and what you are can have a powerful influence on the self.

The self-fulfilling prophecy has had interesting applications. Indeed, a good body of work has centered on demonstrating how stereotyping others in negative ways may lead to their underperformance (Maass & Cadinu, 2003). Some people

self-fulfilling prophecy

The idea that you behave and see yourself in ways that are consistent with how others see you.

are more susceptible to being negatively stereotyped than are others. The characteristics of those who are vulnerable include anxiety, intrusive thoughts, and shifts toward caution.

Learning More About Yourself

Perhaps you now understand why the ancients said, "Know thyself." They, like people today, believed that self-awareness is a discovery worth making. It tells you which choices are open to you and which ones are not. If you hate chemistry, you should not become a physician or pharmacist. If you like to write and are good at it, you may have a future as a writer. If you are skillful at athletics, perhaps you can exploit that talent with scholarships, varsity sports, and even professional sports. What you have learned about yourself in the past, and what you learn about yourself today, will affect your future.

In the here-and-now, you should be aware of what kind of person you are. Are you timid, shy, and unassertive? Are you healthy, vigorous, and energetic? Do you welcome change, adventure, and risk? Do you see yourself as capable, unstoppable, and hard-driving? The answers to these and many other questions are the key to your self-awareness. As Will Schutz (1982) notes, "Given a complete knowledge of myself, I can determine my life; lacking that mastery, I am controlled in ways that are often undesirable, unproductive, worrisome, and confusing" (p. 1).

Joseph O'Connor was a high school junior when he spent two weeks in the Sierra Nevada mountain range of northeastern California—a challenge that changed his level of self-awareness. Rain poured, hail pelted, and the beauty of dawn at 13,000 feet entranced him. Writing about his self-awareness in an article titled "A View from Mount Ritter: Two Weeks in the Sierras Changed My Attitude Toward Life and What It Takes to Succeed," O'Connor (1998) states:

> The wonder of all I'd experienced made me think seriously about what comes next. "Life after high school," I said to myself. "Uh-oh." What had I been doing the last three years? I was so caught up in defying the advice of my parents and teachers to study and play by the rules that I hadn't considered the effects my actions would have on me. (p. 17)

O'Connor's experience changed his self-awareness, and he went from being a D student to one who made the honor roll.

You don't have to go to the mountains to come to a new awareness of yourself. If you want to learn more about yourself, you can take several steps to achieve that goal. If you want to learn more about your physical self, you should get an annual physical. You can also talk to your relatives about the causes of death of older people in your family. What health ailments do your parents and grandparents face? Are these problems inherited?

If you want to learn more about your personality and how others perceive you, you can talk with relatives, friends, co-workers, bosses, and even your children if you are a parent. Consider other features of your life that will suggest how you are perceived. Do people seek you out as a relational

New experiences may lead to increased self-knowledge.

partner? Do others ask you to participate in social events? Do friends ask you for advice? Also consider the number of friends you have.

What kind of worker are you? Do you like to work alone or with others? What kinds of jobs have you held? Have you been given increasing amounts of responsibility in those jobs, or have you frequently lost jobs? Do your grades indicate that you are motivated and disciplined or that you are not living up to your potential? Do others seek you out to partner with them on work- or school-related projects?

Are you skillful in communication? Do you enjoy public speaking and receive invitations to talk to civic and church groups? Can you listen to others uncritically and empathize with them? Are you adept at problem solving or conflict resolution? Are you an effective and adaptive leader? Are you apprehensive about communication? Are you argumentative? You can learn about your communication skills or deficits through a number of research methods. For example, the latter three concepts can be found on the web by typing "Leader Effectiveness and Adaptability," "Personal Report of Communication Apprehension," and "Argumentativeness Scale," respectively, into a search engine. Many valid and reliable instruments measuring communication constructs can be found online, in communication journals, and in resource books.

Self-Actualization

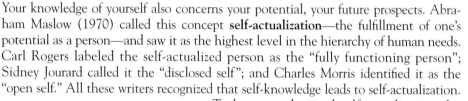

self-actualization

According to Maslow, the fulfillment of one's potential as a person.

Your knowledge of yourself also concerns your potential, your future prospects. Abraham Maslow (1970) called this concept **self-actualization**—the fulfillment of one's potential as a person—and saw it as the highest level in the hierarchy of human needs. Carl Rogers labeled the self-actualized person as the "fully functioning person"; Sidney Jourard called it the "disclosed self"; and Charles Morris identified it as the "open self." All these writers recognized that self-knowledge leads to self-actualization.

To better understand self-actualization, let us consider Maslow's work. Maslow probably began his theoretical work on self-actualization when he met Kurt Goldstein in 1951. Earlier, working with Harry Harlow, Maslow observed how baby rhesus monkeys formed attachments with each other. No doubt, Maslow began to consider how primates order their needs during this earlier time (http://www.ship.edu/~cgboeree/maslow.html).

Maslow arranged the needs that people have in a triangle known as the hierarchy of needs. The triangle is depicted in Figure 2.7.

Physiological needs include our needs for food and water, rest, pain avoidance, and sexual activity. Safety needs include our needs for stability, protection, and some sorts of structure. Among our love and belonging needs are our needs for friends, family, and community. Esteem needs include feeling respected, having a good reputation, being confident, and having certain levels of mastery. These bottom four levels of needs are grouped together as deficit needs, or D-needs.

Figure 2.7 Maslow's hierarchy of needs.
SOURCE: Maslow and Lowery, 1998.

Cultural Differences In Memory

Research by Qi Wang and her associates (Han, Leichtman, & Wang, 1998; Wang & Leichtman, 2000; Wang, Leichtman, & Davies, 2000; Wang, Leichtman, & White, 1998) shows that American adults and preschool children recall their personal memories differently than do indigenous Chinese. Since our self-concept is dependent on our self-awareness, these cultural differences are important.

"Americans often report lengthy, specific, emotionally elaborate memories that focus on the self as a central character," says Wang. "Chinese tend to give brief accounts of general routine events that center on collective activities and are often emotionally neutral. These individual-focused vs. group-oriented styles characterize the mainstream values in American and Chinese cultures, respectively" (www.news. cornell.edu/Chronicles/6.28.01/memory-culture.html).

Wang and Leichtman (2000) also investigated the stories and personal experiences of American and Chinese 6-year-olds. They found that Chinese children were more concerned with moral correctness and authority and American children had a greater sense of independence in their narratives. Cultural values and differences were obvious. "These findings indicate that cultural differences in autobiographical memory are apparently set by early preschool years and persist into adulthood. They are formed both in the larger cultural context that defines the meaning of the self and in the immediate family environment," Wang concludes. "The self and autobiographical memory are intertwined not only within an individual but also in the overarching cultural system" (www.news.cornell.edu/Chronicles/6.28.01/memory-culture.html).

By that, Maslow suggested that if we do not have one of these needs met, we feel a deficit. If we do have the need met, we do not notice it.

Self-actualization is given a different status (as illustrated on the triangle). Self-actualization is a "being need," or a B-need. If we are self-actualized, we continue to feel the need to be self-actualized. Unlike the D-needs, being fulfilled in self-actualization does not mean that we do not feel the desire to have more. Instead, the more self-actualized we become, the more we want to be even stronger.

At the same time, we cannot begin to become self-actualized if we have unmet D-needs. If we are dehydrated, we seek water. If we do not feel safe, we are alert and on guard. If we have no one to love us, we seek people to care for us. Low self-esteem may lead to defensiveness. These needs must first be met if we are to move to a position where we can become self-actualized.

People are at their very best when they are self-actualized. Indeed, self-actualization almost suggests a "spiritual" height. People who are self-actualized seek a number of other qualities. For example, they seek truth and eschew dishonesty. They desire justice and order rather than injustice and lawlessness. They are playful rather than stern and staid. They seek goodness, beauty, unity, and uniqueness (http://www.deepermind.com/20maslow.htm; http://www.ship.edu/~cgboeree/maslow. html; Maslow & Lowery, 1998).

How can you become more self-actualized? The obvious first steps are to organize your life in a way that your lower-order needs are fulfilled. You may find that you need more education so you can earn sufficient money to feel safe and secure. Maybe you do not feel that you have enough people in your life and must invest time in reaching out to others. After you have managed your lower-order needs, you can begin to travel toward self-actualization.

How Do You Evaluate Yourself?

In addition to knowing who you are, you need to consider how you feel about yourself. Your self-appraisal develops from words and actions (symbolic interactionism), from what others say to you and do with you (self-fulfilling prophecies), and from the way you perceive yourself. The self is socially constructed through communication; that is, your self is a result of how others speak to you and treat you and how you see yourself. Your evaluation of yourself is composed of two parts: self-image and self-esteem.

Self-Image

self-image

The picture you have of yourself; the sort of person you believe you are.

Self-image is the picture you have of yourself, the sort of person you believe you are. Included in your self-image are the categories in which you place yourself, the roles you play, and other, similar descriptors you use to identify yourself. If you tell an acquaintance you are a grandfather who recently lost his wife and who does volunteer work on weekends, several elements of your self-image are brought to light—the roles of grandparent, widower, and conscientious citizen.

But self-image is more than how you picture yourself; it also involves how others see you. Michael Argyle (1969) notes that self-image is originally based on characterizations by others and that others characterize us most often by family roles, followed by occupation, marital status, and religious affiliation.

Three types of feedback from others are indicative of how they see us: confirmation, rejection, and disconfirmation (Watzlawick, Beavin, & Jackson, 1967).

confirmation

Feedback in which others treat you in a manner consistent with who you believe you are.

Confirmation occurs when others treat you in a manner consistent with who you believe you are. You see yourself as intelligent, and your parents praise you for your excellent grades in school; you believe you have leadership abilities, and your boss puts you in charge of a new work team. Confirmation can occur through humor or even teasing (Heisterkamp & Alberts, 2000).

rejection

Feedback in which others treat you in a manner that is inconsistent with your self-definition.

On the other hand, **rejection** occurs when others treat you in a manner that is inconsistent with your self-definition. Gerald R. Ford was the first vice-president to succeed a U.S. president when he took the oath of office in 1974. While Ford had been a popular member of Congress for many years, he was appointed, not elected, to the office of president. In 1976 Ford won the Republican nomination for President, but he was defeated in the general election to Democrat Jimmy Carter. Ford probably believed that he was a good public official but his loss to Carter suggested that the voters thought otherwise. The popular vote was inconsistent with Ford's self-concept.

disconfirmation

Feedback in which others fail to respond to your notion of self by responding neutrally.

The third type of feedback is **disconfirmation,** which occurs when others fail to respond to your notion of self by responding neutrally. A small child repeatedly tries to get a parent to look at something he has drawn, but the parent gives it only a cursory glance and buries her head back in her newspaper. A student writes what he thinks is an excellent composition, but the teacher offers no encouraging remarks. Rather than relying on how others classify you, consider how you identify yourself. The way in which you identify yourself is the best reflection of your self-image.

MYTHS, METAPHORS, & MISUNDERSTANDINGS

When learning about concepts associated with the "self," it is tempting to assume that each of us has one self that guides our communication. In fact, scholars from various fields suggest that the "one true self" assumption is becoming a myth. Kenneth Gergen (2000), for instance, suggests that we no longer have single or even stable senses of self because we have become "saturated" with social situations requiring the use of different personas. Think about how you act one way with your friends at school and change back to another self when you are at home. Have you gotten into trouble because your school self emerged at the family dinner table? This is exactly the type of complex system of selves that Gergen says we are all developing.

Self-Esteem

The second part of self-concept is **self-esteem**—how you feel about yourself, how well you like and value yourself. Self-esteem is usually based on perceptions of your successes or failures. Think of self-esteem as the plus or minus you place on your self-perception. If you have an unfavorable perception of yourself, you are said to have low self-esteem; if you have a favorable perception of yourself, you have high self-esteem.

But perception and communication are affected regardless of whether self-esteem is high or low. For example, Baumgardner and Levy (1988) found that people with high self-esteem tend to view others who are motivated as bright people and those who are not motivated as less bright. In other words, they think people who put forth effort also have great ability. People with low self-esteem do not make this distinction. This lack of discrimination may prevent people with low self-esteem from understanding the behaviors necessary for succeeding.

Although self-esteem is important, some critics believe educators have spent too much time and effort trying to get young people to feel good about themselves and too little time and effort trying to get them to earn the right to those good feelings. For example, Shaw (1994) showed that although self-esteem rose among young people to all-time highs, test scores plummeted to new lows.

You communicate in a variety of ways whether or not you value yourself. At the same time, what other people say about you can affect your self-esteem.

self-esteem

The feeling you have about your self-concept; that is, how well you like and value yourself.

Improving Self-Concept

Numerous people have made dramatic changes in their lifestyle, their behavior, and, in turn, their self-concept. The news is filled with stories of former convicts who become responsible members of the community, alcoholics who are able to abstain from drinking, and highly paid TV, movie, and rock stars who are able to overcome their fame and have fairly normal family lives. Dramatic changes occur in people. Although you might not choose to follow the paths of those in the news, their stories do provide evidence that people can change.

Usually, people want to change their self-concept when it is inhibiting their development as an individual, as an upwardly mobile employee, or as a member of a family. Perhaps you have never been comfortable in conversations with strangers;

as a result, you often feel inadequate at receptions, parties, and business socials. Maybe you have never worked well in groups and thus have a hard time picturing yourself as part of a work team. Your inability to work with others can be regarded as a detriment to professional advancement. Or perhaps you bicker often with your spouse or partner, and you worry about how your argumentative style affects your relationship not only with that person but with others as well. A sensed need to change is what inspires people to improve their self-concept.

If you wish to change your self-concept in order to improve your ability to communicate with others, several steps will provide assistance along the way. First, you must *have a goal or objective*. For example, you might decide that you want to quit drinking caffeinated beverages. Today you drink several cups of coffee and a number of soft drinks containing caffeine. The goal of abstaining from caffeine must be identified, recognized, and shared with others. You might want to write it down in a journal in which you track your success in this behavioral change.

Second, you need to *make your goal realistic*. Perhaps quitting caffeine "cold turkey" is not realistic. Instead, you decide to modify the goal to go from 12 caffeinated beverages a day to two cups of coffee in the morning. This more realistic goal will allow you to decrease your intake without being unmanageable, at least in the short-term. You can modify your goal after you have achieved this first objective.

Third, you need to *find information about how to achieve your goal*. Maybe you have gained 20 pounds since starting college and your clothes no longer fit properly. What do you do? You might talk to friends who are slender to learn their strategies for maintaining their weight. You might investigate what your college or university offers in the way of exercise programs and on-campus weight management courses. You might go online to find low-fat recipes, self-help groups, and exercises you can do at home or in your room. Again, tracking your progress can provide help along the way.

Fourth, you need to *exercise control and restraint*. If you have spent 10 years of your life smoking cigarettes, you are probably not going to quit overnight. On the other hand, deciding that you will quit smoking only to begin again the next day will not move you closer to your goal. How can you avoid old behaviors and substitute new ones? Spending time with people who share your goal is one way. Do not spend time with others who smoke if you are trying to quit; do not go to bars if you are attempting to abstain from alcohol; and stay away from coffeehouses if caffeine is your enemy. Try to give yourself every advantage in achieving your goal.

Fifth, you need to *gain support from friends and family members*. If you are dieting, you do not want to visit your parents only to find that they have made several of your calorie-laden "special treats." You need to enlist the help of others. Let your friends and family know that you are dieting and how they can be helpful in the process. People in a support group might become new friends and associates. They share your goal, and you can often be more successful when you are working together.

Finally, you need to *accept yourself*. You have practiced poor health habits or had less-than-desirable relationships in the past. You have made a commitment to change. The pathway will probably not be smooth and straight, however. You will encounter problems and barriers from time to time; remember that your goal is worthy of your time and attention to it. Accept yourself as you are—imperfect, but with a will to make essential changes.

Barriers to Improving Self-Concept

Altering your self-concept is not a simple matter. One of the factors that makes change difficult is that people who know you expect you to behave in a certain way. In fact, they helped create and maintain your self-concept. These people may continue to insist that you maintain a particular self-concept, even when you are attempting to change.

Sometimes people work against themselves when they try to change their self-concept. For example, you might label yourself "passive"; that is, even when others voice opinions contrary to yours or attack values you hold, you say nothing in defense. This passivity may be consistent with other aspects of your self-concept, such as "open-minded" and "nonargumentative." You can alter one aspect of your self-concept only to the extent that it does not contradict other aspects. If your passivity fits with your self-concept of being warm toward and supportive of others, you may find that becoming more assertive is difficult unless you are also willing to be less supportive on some occasions.

How Do You Present Yourself?

In this chapter we have shown the relationship between perception, self-perception, and communication. Communication and perception influence each other. Communication is largely responsible for our self-perceptions. Communication can also be used to change the perceptions that others have of us. We attempt to influence others' perceptions of ourselves through self-presentation.

In our daily interactions we present ourselves to people, both consciously and unconsciously. Self-presentation may be defined as the way we portray ourselves to others. Generally, our self-presentation is consistent with an ideal self-image, allows us to enact an appropriate role, influences others' view of us, permits us to define the situation in our terms, and/or influences the progress of an interaction.

Erving Goffman (1959, 1974, 1981) first described the process of self-presentation. Goffman adopted the symbolic interactionist perspective described earlier. He described everyday interactions through a dramaturgical, or theater arts, viewpoint. His theory embraces individual identity, group relationships, the context or situation, and the interactive meaning of information. Individuals are viewed as "actors," and interaction is seen as a "performance" shaped by the context and situation and constructed to provide others with "impressions" consistent with the desired goals of the actor. **Identity management** is thus defined as the control (or lack of control) of the communication of information through a performance. In identity management people try to present an "idealized" version of themselves in order to reach desired ends.

identity management

The control (or lack of control) of the communication of information through a performance.

You may believe that you do not engage in identity management. However, a number of research studies illustrate that people act differently when they are being viewed than when they are not. For example, people speaking on a telephone who are expressing empathy or shared emotions do not engage in facial responsiveness, whereas people expressing the same sentiments in face-to-face encounters do (Chovil, 1991). Investigations in this area suggest that people generally do engage in identity management in their face-to-face interactions.

Electronic Self-Presentation

Although Goffman's work centered on face-to-face interaction, electronic communication allows us to consider applications of his theory beyond interpersonal communication. The World Wide Web has developed quickly and has revolutionized communication between people. Today many people have their own home pages in which they present themselves to others with new resources. Stone (1998) has discussed the nature of our "electronic selves." What do home pages communicate? Find five web pages and analyze the differences among them. What impressions do you have about the person who created the web page?

high self-monitors

Individuals who are highly aware of their identity management behavior.

low self-monitors

Individuals who communicate with others with little attention to the responses to their messages.

face

The socially approved and presented identity of an individual.

facework

Verbal and nonverbal strategies that are used to present your own varying images to others and to help them maintain their own images.

politeness

Our efforts to save face for others.

Why might you believe that you do not engage in identity management? You have engaged in this behavior for your entire life. You were rewarded for it when you performed in it and were punished when you deviated from it. At this point, identity management may be unconscious and second nature. **High self-monitors** are those individuals who are highly aware of their identity management behavior (Snyder, 1979).

On the other hand, we know that some people are unaware of the importance of identity management. They have little idea about how others perceive them, and they know even less about how to interact with others. These **low self-monitors** communicate with others with little attention to the responses to their messages. Still others believe that identity management is somehow unethical or deceptive. To understand the importance of identity management, we return to the theory.

In addition to the concepts of actors and performance, Goffman introduced the notion of **face,** as the socially approved and presented identity of an individual. Each of us has several "faces" that we present, depending on the group in which we interact and the context or situation in which we find ourselves. You may see yourself as a part-time worker, a full-time student, a dancer, an athlete, a scholar, and a poet. You engage in **facework**—verbal and nonverbal strategies used to present these varying images to others and to help them maintain their own images.

Penelope Brown and Stephen C. Levinson (1987) extended the ideas of Goffman in their contribution of "politeness theory." Politeness theory states that we have an interest in positive face—the desire to be liked and respected—and negative face—the desire to be free from constraint and imposition. Positive face is threatened when we let someone else know—directly or indirectly—that we do not approve of them or their behavior. Negative face is threatened when we order other people to do things or when we ask people to give up freedoms that they would normally hold. Generally, people try to support both the positive and negative face of others because they do not want them to feel embarrassed. When we witness one person causing a second person to lose face, we feel embarrassed for the second person, and we might take action against the first. **Politeness,** then, is composed of our efforts to save face for others.

William L. Benoit (1995) made an important contribution when he offered a "theory of image restoration." Benoit observed that people encounter damage to their reputation because of their own actual or suspected wrongdoing. He suggests that people engage in "communicative behavior designed to reduce, redress, or avoid damage to their reputation (or face or image)" (p. vii). Upon reflection, Benoit

TABLE 2.1   IMAGE REPAIR STRATEGIES

STRATEGY/TACTIC	KEY CHARACTERISTIC	EXAMPLE
DENIAL		
Simple denial	Did not act (or act did not occur)	"I did not have an accident with the car."
Shift blame	Another did act	"If the car has a huge dent in it, someone else hit me."
EVADE RESPONSIBILITY		
Provocation	Act was a response to another's offense	"I was threatened by a large truck and I had no choice but to go off the road."
Defeasibility	Lack of information or ability	"I did not know that the brakes would not hold."
Accident	Act was a mishap	"No one could have prevented the accident; it was, after all, an accident."
Good intentions	Act was meant well	"I tried to do the best thing and consider the safety of all of the drivers."
REDUCE OFFENSIVENESS		
Bolster	Stress good traits	"You know that I am a good driver."
Minimize	Act not serious	"The dent on the car can be easily fixed."
Differentiate	Act less serious than similar ones	"Remember that Sarah totaled her car last year."
Transcend	More important considerations	"The most important thing to remember is that no one was injured."
Attack accuser	Reduce credibility of attacker	"You had two fender-benders last year; this is my first one."
Compensate	Reimburse victims	"I'll pay for the damages out of my own allowance."
CORRECTIVE ACTION	Plan to solve or to prevent recurrence	"I promise I will drive slower and more carefully in the future."
MORTIFICATION	Apology	"I am really sorry that I put the car in the ditch and dented the fender."

SOURCE: Benoit, 1997.

renamed the theory "image repair" because restoration suggests that the image may have been restored to its prior state (Benoit, 2000; Burns & Bruner, 2000). Table 2.1 summarizes the five general strategies and accompanying tactics that Benoit discovered.

Identity management is important, then, because it helps us avoid embarrassment—for ourselves and others. In addition, identity management allows us to achieve our goals through our communicative behavior. When we use language appropriate for the occasion, when we demonstrate empathy through facial expression and bodily movement, when we use self-disclosure appropriately, and when we wear clothing that is within appropriate guidelines, we increase the likelihood that we will be viewed as credible and achieve our goals.

In the next two chapters you will learn more about verbal and nonverbal communication. Your understanding of these symbolic means of communicating will be enhanced by your understanding of identity management. Wiggins, Wiggins, and Vander Zanden (1993) suggest that three essential types of communication are used to manage impressions: manner, appearance, and setting. Manner includes both verbal and nonverbal codes. Your manner might be seen as brusque, silly, businesslike, immature, friendly, warm, or gracious. Your appearance may suggest a role that you are playing (lab assistant), a value that you hold (concern for the environment), your personality (relaxed), or your view of the communication setting (unimportant). The setting includes your immediate environment (the space in which you communicate) as well as other public displays of who you are (the kind of home in which you live, the type of automobile you drive).

Chapter Review & Study Guide

SUMMARY

In this chapter you learned the following:

▶ Perception is important in communication because perception affects the way we understand events, others, and ourselves.

▶ Our perceptions are unique because of physiological factors, past experiences, culture and co-culture, and present feelings and circumstances.

▶ During perception, three separate activities are occurring: selection, organization, and interpretation.
- Through selection you neglect some stimuli in your environment and focus on others. Four types of selectivity are selective exposure, selective attention, selective perception, and selective retention.
- The stimuli you focus on are organized in a number of ways—through figure and ground, closure, proximity, and similarity.

▶ We often make errors in our perceptions of others.
- We make attributional errors, including the fundamental attribution error and the self-serving bias.
- We engage in perceptual errors such as stereotyping and first impressions.

▶ How you perceive yourself plays a central role in communication.
- Understanding yourself includes understanding your attitudes, values, beliefs, strengths, and weaknesses.

- Symbolic interactionism, self-fulfilling prophecy, and self-actualization are all related to understanding yourself.
- A person's evaluation of him- or herself consists of self-image and self-esteem.
- Self-image is the picture you have of yourself and involves how others see you.
- Three types of feedback from others indicate how they see you: confirmation, rejection, and disconfirmation.
- Self-esteem is how you feel about yourself.
- You can improve your self-concept.

▶ Identity management is the control (or lack of control) of the communication of information through a performance.
- People who are high self-monitors are well aware of their identity management behavior, whereas people who are low self-monitors communicate with others with little attention to the responses to their messages.
- Face is the socially approved identity an individual presents.
- Facework includes the verbal and nonverbal strategies people use to present their own varying images to others and to help them maintain their own images.
- Our positive face is the desire to be liked and respected; our negative face is our desire to be free from constraint and imposition. Politeness is defined as our efforts to save face for others.

KEY TERMS

Go to the *Online Learning Center* at **www.mhhe.com/pearson3** to further your understanding of the following terminology.

Active perception	High self-monitors	Selective exposure
Attribution	Identity management	Selective perception
Closure	Interpretive perception	Selective retention
Co-culture	Low self-monitors	Self-actualization
Confirmation	Perception	Self-esteem
Culture	Perceptual constancy	Self-fulfilling prophecy
Disconfirmation	Politeness	Self-image
Face	Proximity	Self-serving bias
Facework	Rejection	Similarity
Figure	Role	Subjective perception
Fundamental attribution error	Selective attention	Symbolic interactionism
Ground		

STUDY QUESTIONS

1. Which of the following may be the result of physiological factors, past experiences and roles, cultures, and present conditions?
   a. selection
   b. similarity
   c. self-serving bias
   d. differences in perception

2. By neglecting some stimuli and focusing on other stimuli, you are engaging in which process of perception?
   a. organization
   b. selection
   c. classification
   d. interpretation

3. _____ is an organizational method whereby missing information is filled in to create the appearance of a complete unit, and _____ is another organizational technique whereby elements are grouped based on their similarities in size, color, and shape.
   a. Closure; similarity
   b. Proximity; figure and ground
   c. Similarity; proximity
   d. Closure; proximity

4. The more ambiguous the stimuli,
   a. the less room for confusion
   b. the more room for interpretation
   c. the less room for interpretation
   d. the less you rely on context

5. Which type of error occurs when assigning meaning to a behavior?
   a. perceptual
   b. self-fulfilling prophesy
   c. attribution
   d. stereotyping

6. The idea that you behave and see yourself in ways that are consistent with how others view you is
   a. self-image
   b. symbolic interactionism
   c. self-fulfilling prophesy
   d. perception

7. The picture you have of yourself and the sort of person you believe yourself to be is your
   a. self-esteem
   b. self-fulfilling prophesy
   c. self-image
   d. self-monitor

8. If an individual thinks he or she is a good leader and is subsequently chosen as captain of the basketball team, this is an example of
   a. self-concept
   b. rejection
   c. disconfirmation
   d. confirmation

9. When people seek to present an ideal version of themselves, they are engaging in
   a. identity management
   b. confirmation
   c. attribution
   d. selection

10. Which of the following statements is true?
    a. Politeness is saving face for yourself.
    b. Face is the socially approved and presented identity of an individual.
    c. High self-monitors are individuals who communicate with little attention to feedback.
    d. Low self-monitors are individuals who are highly aware of their identity management behavior.

Answers:
1. (d); 2. (b); 3. (a); 4. (b); 5. (c); 6. (c); 7. (c); 8. (d); 9. (a); 10. (b)

CRITICAL THINKING

1. Singer states that people's perceptions are largely learned because what people see, hear, taste, touch, and smell is conditioned by their culture. What parts of your culture are key factors in how you perceive events in day-to-day life?

2. Using the book's steps to improving self-concept as a guide, describe some ways in which you can improve your self-concept. What difficulties do you anticipate?

SELF-QUIZ

For further review, try the chapter self-quiz on the *Online Learning Center* at www.mhhe.com/pearson3.

REFERENCES

Argyle, M. (1969). *Social interaction*. New York: Atherton.

Baumgardner, A. H., & Levy, P. E. (1988). Role of self-esteem in perceptions of ability and effort: Illogic or insight? *Personality and Social Psychology Bulletin, 14,* 429–438.

Benoit, W. L. (1995). *Accounts, excuses, and apologies: A theory of image restoration discourse*. Albany: State University of New York Press.

Benoit, W. L. (2000). Another visit to the theory of image restoration strategies. *Communication Quarterly, 48,* 40–44.

Brown, P., & Levinson, S. C. (1987). *Politeness: Some universals in language usage*. Cambridge: Cambridge University Press.

Burns, J. P., & Bruner, M. S. (2000). Revisiting the theory of image restoration strategies. *Communication Quarterly, 48,* 27–39.

Chovil, N. (1991). Social determinants of facial displays. *Journal of Nonverbal Behavior, 15,* 141–154.

Curtin, E. (2005). Instructional styles used by regular classroom teachers while teaching recently mainstreamed ESL students: Six urban middle school teachers share their experiences and perceptions. *Multicultural Education, 12*(4), 36–42.

Day, C., Kington, A., Stobart, G., & Sammons, P. (2006). The personal and professional selves of teachers: Stable and unstable identities. *British Educational Research Journal, 32,* 601–616.

DeVito, J. A. (1986). *The communication handbook: A dictionary*. New York: Harper & Row.

Gergen, K. (2000). *The saturated self: Dilemmas of identity in contemporary life*. New York: Basic Books.

Goffman, E. (1959). *The presentation of self in everyday life*. New York: Doubleday Anchor.

Goffman, E. (1974). *Frame analysis: An essay on the organization of experience*. New York: Harper & Row.

Goffman, E. (1981). *Forms of talk*. Oxford: Basil Blackwell.

Han, J. J., Leichtman, M. D., & Wang, Q. (1998). Autobiographical memory in Korean, Chinese, and American children. *Developmental Psychology, 34*(4), 701–713.

Heisterkamp, B. L., & Alberts, J. K. (2000). Control and desire: Identity formation through teasing among gay men and lesbians. *Communication Studies, 51,* 388–403.

Hendrix, K. G. (2002). "Did being Black introduce bias into your study?" Attempting to mute the race-related research of black scholars. *Howard Journal of Communication, 13,* 153–171.

Hughes, P. C., & Baldwin, J. R. (2002). Communication and stereotypical impressions. *Howard Journal of Communication, 13,* 113–128.

Leary, M. (2002). The self as a source of relational difficulties. *Self and Identity, 1,* 137–142.

Levine, S. (2006, March 20–26). Culturally sensitive medicine: Doctors learn to adapt to immigrant patients' ethnic and religious customs. *The Washington Post National Weekly Edition, 23*(22), p. 31.

Lu, S. (1997). Culture and compliance gaining in the classroom: A preliminary investigation of Chinese college teachers. *Communication Education, 46,* 10–29.

Maass, A., & Cadinu, M. (2003). Stereotype threat: When minority members underperform. *European Review of Social Psychology, 14,* 243–275.

Manusov, V., Trees, A. R., Reddick, L. A., Rowe, A. M. C., & Easley, J. M. (1998). Explanations and impressions: Investigating attributions and their effects on judgments for friends and strangers. *Communication Studies, 49,* 209–223.

Maslow, A. H. (1970). *Motivation and personality* (2nd ed., pp. 35–72). New York: Harper & Row.

Maslow, A., & Lowery, R. (Ed.) (1998). *Toward a psychology of being* (3rd ed.). New York: Wiley.

Mead, G. H. (1934). *Mind, self, and society*. Chicago: University of Chicago Press.

Nelson, T. E., & Garst, J. (2005). Values-based political messages and persuasion: Relationships among speaker, recipient, and evoked values. *Political Psychology, 26,* 489–515.

O'Connor, J. T. (1998, May 25). A view from Mount Ritter: Two weeks in the Sierras changed my attitude toward life and what it takes to succeed. From *Newsweek*, May 25, 1998, p. 17. © 1998 Newsweek, Inc. All rights reserved. Reprinted by permission.

Oyserman, D., Bybee, D., & Terry, K. (2006). Possible selves and academic outcomes: How and when possible selves impel action. *Journal of Personality and Social Psychology, 91,* 188–204.

Restak, R. (1984). *The brain*. New York: Bantam Books.

Rosenthal, R., & Jacobson, L. (1968). *Pygmalion in the classroom*. New York: Holt, Rinehart & Winston.

Samovar, L. A., Porter, R. E., & Stefani, L. (1998). *Communication between cultures*. Belmont, CA: Wadsworth.

Schutz, W. (1982). *Here comes everyone* (2nd ed.). New York: Irvington.

Seta, C. E., Schmidt, S., & Bookhout, C. M. (2006). Social identity orientation and social role attributions: Explaining behavior through the lens of self. *Self and Identity, 5*, 355–364.

Shaw, P. (1994, Summer). Self-esteem rises to all-time high; test scores hit new lows. *Antioch Review*, 467–474.

Shedletsky, L. J. (1989). The mind at work. In L. J. Shedletsky (Ed.), *Meaning and mind: An intrapersonal approach to human communication*. ERIC and the Speech Communication Association.

Singer, M. R. (1982). Culture: A perceptual approach. In L. A. Samovar & R. E. Porter (Eds.), *Intercultural communication: A reader* (3rd ed., pp. 54–61). Belmont, CA: Wadsworth.

Snyder, M. (1979). Self-monitoring processes. In L. Berkowitz (Ed.), *Advances in experimental social psychology*. New York: Academic Press.

Sterling, M. (2006). Do you make your first impression your best impression? Retrieved October 22, 2006, from http://entrepreneurs.about.com/cs/marketing/a/uc051603a.htm.

Stone, A. R. (1998). *The war of desire and technology at the close of the mechanical age*. Cambridge, MA: MIT Press.

Wang, Q., & Leichtman, M. D. (2000). Same beginnings, different stories: A comparison of American and Chinese children's narratives. *Child Development, 71*(5), 1329–1346.

Wang, Q., Leichtman, M. D., & Davies, K. I. (2000). Sharing memories and telling stories: American and Chinese mothers and their 3-year-olds. *Memory, 8*(3), 159–177.

Wang, Q., Leichtman, M. D., & White, S. H. (1998). Childhood memory and self-description in young Chinese adults: The impact of growing up an only child. *Cognition, 69*(1), 73–103.

Watzlawick, P., Beavin, J. H., & Jackson, D. D. (1967). *Pragmatics of human communication: A study of interactional patterns, pathologies, and paradoxes*. New York: Norton.

Wiggins, J. A., Wiggins, B. B., & Vander Zanden, J. (1993). *Social psychology* (4th ed.). New York: McGraw-Hill.

Wilson, J., & Wilson, S. (Eds.). (1998). *Mass media/mass culture*. New York: McGraw-Hill.

Wood, J. T. (1997). *Communication theories in action*. Belmont, CA: Wadsworth.

Wright, R. (1994, July–August). That never really happened. *The Humanist*, 30–31.

CHAPTER THREE

Language and Meaning

What will you learn?

When you have read and thought about this chapter, you will be able to:

1. Define language and state several of its characteristics.
2. Identify three sets of rules that govern language use.
3. Explain how language and culture are intertwined.
4. Describe the various forms of unique language and how they can provide both beauty in and barriers to communication.
5. Use specific techniques, like paraphrasing and dating, to demonstrate your verbal communication skills.

This chapter is about the importance of language and how language functions in communication.

In this chapter you will learn about the world of language, including the definition of language and its many characteristics. You will learn that language can be both an enhancement and an obstacle to communication. Finally, specific suggestions are provided for improving your verbal skills.

ollowing its publication in 2003, *The Da Vinci Code* by Dan Brown became one of the best-selling books of all time. It has sold more than 60 million copies worldwide, in over 40 languages. A major motion picture based on the book was a big hit. What brought all this attention to *The Da Vinci Code*? It presents a provocative religious theory and exposes a conspiracy within a religious community to protect long-held secrets.

What makes the story so fascinating is that the author embeds this mystery in a web of symbols, word puzzles, and secret brotherhoods, dating from the time of early Christianity, to the works of Renaissance artist Leonardo da Vinci, to the present. As the story unfolds, Brown literally redefines the meaning of many Christian symbols and images to give an unconventional interpretation of Christianity. Some discount Brown's thesis as pure fiction or outright blasphemy, while others have used his book to entirely reframe their religious views.

Regardless of how one views Brown's novel, the book itself is firmly rooted in today's popular culture. Brown whipped up a public frenzy by directly challenging the traditional meanings given to everyday symbols.

Although Brown was mostly concerned with religious symbolism, the meaning of any symbol can be contested. In this chapter you will learn about a specific type of symbol—the words that we use to communicate with one another. And you will see how language is used and misused as we try to share meaning with other people.

What Is Language?

language

A collection of symbols, letters, or words with arbitrary meanings that are governed by rules and used to communicate.

decode

The process of assigning meaning to others' words in order to translate them into thoughts of your own.

Language is a collection of symbols, letters, or words with arbitrary meanings that are governed by rules and used to communicate. Language consists of words or symbols that represent things without being those things. The word *automobile* is a symbol for a vehicle that runs on gasoline, but the symbol is not the vehicle itself. When you listen to others' verbal communication, you **decode,** or assign meaning to, their words in order to translate them into thoughts of your own. Because language is an imperfect means of transmission, the thoughts expressed by one person never exactly match what is decoded by another.

Verbal communication is essential in virtually all of our endeavors, from the very private to the most public. Both writing and speaking rely on the use of language. Verbal communication represents one of the two major codes of communication; the other is nonverbal communication, which we will discuss in the next chapter. In Chapter 4 we will consider the similarities and differences of these two codes.

Our definition tells you that language consists of words or symbols, has rules, and is arbitrary, but the definition does not reveal some of the other important characteristics of language. Language is also abstract, is intertwined with culture, and organizes and classifies reality. In this section we take a closer look at each of these characteristics.

Language Has Rules

Language has multiple rules. Three sets of rules are relevant to our discussion: semantic rules, syntactic rules, and pragmatic rules. **Semantics** is the study of the way humans use language to evoke meaning in others. Semantics focuses on individual words and their meaning. Semanticists—people who study semantics—are interested in how language and its meaning change over time.

While semantics focuses on the definition of specific words, **syntax** is the way in which words are arranged to form phrases and sentences. For example, in the English language the subject is usually placed before the verb, and the object after the verb. Other languages have different rules of syntax, including reading from right to left. You **encode** by translating your thoughts into words. Syntax changes the meaning of the same set of words. For example, the declarative statement "I am going tomorrow" uses syntax to signal that someone is leaving the next day. If you change the word arrangement to "Am I going tomorrow?" the statement becomes a question and acquires a different meaning.

Pragmatics is the study of language as it is used in a social context, including its effect on the communicators. Messages are variable, depending on the situation. Ambiguous messages such as "How are you?" "What's new?" and "You're looking good" have different meanings, depending on the context. For example, many people use such phrases as **phatic communication**—communication that is used to establish a mood of sociability rather than to communicate information or ideas. Indeed, they would be surprised if someone offered a serious or thoughtful answer to such questions or statements. On the other hand, if you are visiting your grandmother who has been ill, your questions about how she is feeling are sincere and designed to elicit information. Similarly, you might genuinely be complimenting another person's new haircut, new tattoo, or new tongue bolt when you tell him he is looking good. Pragmatic rules help us interpret meaning in specific contexts.

Language and Culture Are Intertwined

Although we will talk about the role of intercultural communication in a later chapter, it is important to note the relationship between language and culture here. **Culture** may be defined as all of the socially transmitted behavior patterns, beliefs, attitudes, and values of a particular period, class, community, or population. We often think of the culture of a country (Greek culture), institution (the culture of higher education), organization (the IBM culture), or group of people (the Hispanic culture). Culture and language are thus related as the transmission of culture occurs through language.

The relationship between culture and language is not as simple as it might first appear, however. Let us take the example of women and men and communication. Several years ago, books and articles were written on the differences between women and men in their communicative practices. As this research further developed, gender was expanded to refer to a complex social construct rather than simple biological sex. Some authors argued that gender was just as important as social class in understanding variations in communication (Schilling-Estes, 2002).

Language and culture are related in a second way. Culture creates a lens through which we perceive the world and create shared meaning. Language thus develops in response to the needs of the culture or to the perceptions of the world. Edward Sapir and Benjamin Lee Whorf were among the first to discuss the relationship

semantics

The study of the way humans use language to evoke meaning in others.

syntax

The way in which words are arranged to form phrases and sentences.

encode

The process of translating your thoughts into words.

pragmatics

The study of language as it is used in a social context, including its effect on the communicators.

phatic communication

Communication that is used to establish a mood of sociability rather than to communicate information or ideas.

culture

The socially transmitted behavior patterns, beliefs, attitudes, and values of a particular period, class, community, or population.

Sapir-Whorf hypothesis

A theory that our perception of reality is determined by our thought processes and our thought processes are limited by our language and, therefore, that language shapes our reality.

between language and perception. The **Sapir-Whorf hypothesis,** as their theory has become known, states that our perception of reality is determined by our thought processes and our thought processes are limited by our language and, therefore, that language shapes our reality (Whorf, 1956). Language is the principal way that we learn about ourselves, others, and our culture (Bakhurst & Shanker, 2001; Cragan & Shields, 1995; Wood, 1997).

The Sapir-Whorf hypothesis has been illustrated in multiple cultures (Samovar & Porter, 2000; Whorf, 1956). The Hopi language serves as an early example. The Hopi people do not distinguish between nouns and verbs. In many languages, nouns are given names that suggest that they remain static over time. For example, we assume that words like *professor, physician, lamp,* and *computer* refer to people or objects that are relatively unchanging. Verbs are action words that suggest change. When we use words like *heard, rehearsed, spoke,* and *ran,* we assume alterations and movement. The Hopi, by avoiding the distinction between nouns and verbs, thus refer to people and objects in the world as always changing.

Other examples come from the terms that we use for various colors. For instance, the color spectrum allows us to understand colors as blending into each other and allowing an infinite number of colors, but leading scientists agree on only seven component colors of white light: red, orange, yellow, green, blue, indigo, and violet.

Second, people who use color in their work (artists, designers) probably use many more color terms than do those for whom color is not so important (firefighters, police officers). The first group might readily describe persimmon, puce, lavender, and fuchsia while the second group limits their vocabulary (and thus their perceptions) to orange, red, purple, and pink.

Finally, people who speak different languages also have different color terms from those who speak English. The color blue is familiar to most English speakers—both in their vocabulary and as a recognized color. English speakers use the word *blue* to refer to shades ranging from cyan to sky to navy to midnight blue. In Vietnamese and in Korean, a single word refers to blue or green. Japanese people use the word *ao* to refer to blue, but the color they are referencing is (for English speakers) actually (to us) green. Finally, Russian speakers do not have a single word for the range of colors that English speakers denote as blue; instead, they have one color for light blue and another for dark blue.

Waquet and Howe (2001) wrote an enlightening treatise on this same topic. In *Latin: A Symbol's Empire* they trace the domination of Latin in the civic and religious worlds of Europe. Its influence on the entire world followed as scholars, educational institutions, and the Roman Catholic Church adopted Latin as their official language. Latin, like any other language, affects perception and the development of culture. The domination of the language has surely shaped the cultures of many Western countries.

The Sapir-Whorf hypothesis, while complex, is not universally accepted by people who study language. For example, critics point out that Inuits may have a large number of words for snow because of their view of snow or because they actually have more varieties of snow in their world. Artists may have more color terms, and printers more words for different fonts, simply because of their work and environment. Thus, the critics note, thought and language may not be intimately related, but experience and language are. Our need to describe our environment and the items within it cause us to create language to do so.

Language And Culture

The Ojibwe band of Native Americans sponsors a website devoted to the culture, art, history, language, and people of their tribe. The site, **www.nativetech.org/shinob,** provides multiple links to help the novice understand this group of people, who live in Minnesota, Wisconsin, and Michigan. Find additional websites that provide similar information for another culture. Suggest how the language of the people you identify may affect their perceptions of the world.

Language Organizes and Classifies Reality

Because you cannot account for all the individual things in the world when you speak, you lump them into groups; thus, all four-legged pieces of furniture with seats and backs are called "chairs." Following is an example of how you might use classification when trying to identify someone in a crowd:

"See that guy over there?"

"Which one?"

"The tall one."

"The one with short brown hair?"

"No, the fat one with shoulder-length hair and glasses."

In this case language is used to classify by sex, height, weight, hair color, and adornment.

You cannot think of your own identity without words because you are symbolically created through language. Your existence emerges through language, yet language is an inadequate means of describing you. You can describe yourself as "an Italian Roman Catholic," but those words say nothing about your height, weight, age, sex, personality, IQ, ambitions, or dreams. So language creates us, without capturing our complexities.

Language Is Arbitrary

To understand language, you need to understand how words engender meaning. Words are arbitrary: They have no inherent meanings; they have only the meanings people give them. For example, in the English language, a person who has suffered from a difficult past experience is known as a "victim." This concept is illustrated by Ogden and Richards's (1923) semantic triangle, adapted in Figure 3.1. This figure illustrates the connection between people's concept of a victim, the word *victim*, and an actual victim. When many people use a word to represent an object or idea, the word is included in the dictionary. The agreed-upon meaning or dictionary meaning is called the **denotative meaning.** Including a word in the dictionary, however, neither keeps its meaning from changing nor tells you the **connotative meaning**—an individualized or personalized meaning that may be emotionally laden. Connotative meanings are meanings others have come to hold because of personal or individual

denotative meaning

The agreed-upon meaning or dictionary meaning of a word.

connotative meaning

An individualized or personalized meaning of a word, which may be emotionally laden.

View an animation of this illustration on the *Online Learning Center.*

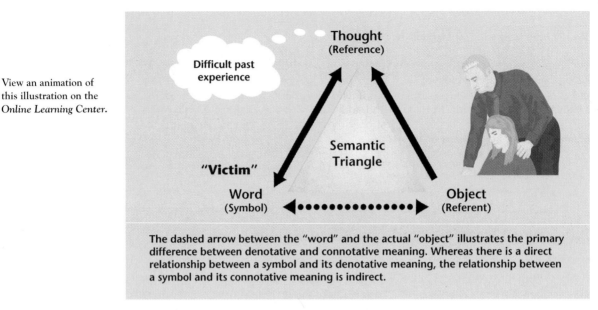

The dashed arrow between the "word" and the actual "object" illustrates the primary difference between denotative and connotative meaning. Whereas there is a direct relationship between a symbol and its denotative meaning, the relationship between a symbol and its connotative meaning is indirect.

Figure 3.1 Denotative and connotative meaning.

experience. For example, the word *love* holds vastly different meanings for people because of their unique experiences with that concept.

To understand connotative meaning further, consider the language that relational couples create. In a romantic relationship you may have pet names for each other, special terms for activities in which you participate, and unique ways to communicate private thoughts in public settings. Bruess and Pearson (1993) showed that married couples are most likely to create such terms early in their relationships and that the creation of such terms is associated with relational satisfaction.

Language is symbolic. The words we choose are arbitrary and are based on an agreed-upon connection between them and the object or idea that we are referencing. Language varies based on a variety of features of the communicators, including their relational history. When two people hold different arbitrary symbols for a concept or object, they share messages but not meanings.

Language and its meaning are personal. Each person talks, listens, and thinks in a unique language (and sometimes several) that contains slight variations of its agreed-upon meanings and that may change each minute. Your personal language varies slightly from the agreed-upon meanings. It is shaped by your culture, country, neighborhood, job, personality, education, family, friends, recreation, sex, experiences, age, and other factors. The uniqueness of each individual's language provides valuable information as people attempt to achieve common, shared meaning. But because language is so personal, it can also present some difficulties in communication.

The meanings of words also vary when someone uses the same words in different contexts and situations. For example, *glasses* might mean "drinking glasses" if you are in a housewares store but most likely would mean "eyeglasses" if you are at the optometrist's office. Semanticists say that meaning emerges from context. But in the case of language, context is more than just the situation in which the communication occurred: Context includes the communicators' histories, relationships, thoughts, and feelings.

The Importance of Context: The Gullah Mystery

White people in coastal South Carolina thought the black people in their area spoke a very strange kind of English until a linguist unlocked a 200-year-old mystery. The linguist discovered, through ancient records of slave dealers, that the Gullahs—the black people of lowland, coastal Carolina—originally came from Sierra Leone in West Africa. The reason the Gullahs' language persisted for so long when other tribal languages disappeared in America was that the Gullahs proved highly resistant to malaria, a disease that drove the slave owners inland and left the Gullahs in relative isolation.

SOURCE: *Family Across the Sea,* a public television documentary produced by Educational Television of South Carolina.

MYTHS, METAPHORS, & MISUNDERSTANDINGS

A rhetorical debate has taken place among scholars and practitioners over the labeling of individuals who experience sexual harassment (e.g., Clair, 1996, 1998). Metaphors such as "target," "victim," and "survivor" have been proposed as symbolic choices. Which do you think is most appropriate? In reflecting on this question, consider these language choices in terms of the components of Figure 3.1, the semantic triangle of meaning. What understandings (references) are constructed through the different symbolic choices (survivor, victim, target) that refer to people who have encountered sexual harassment (referents)? Are some meanings more empowering than others?

Language Is Abstract

Words are abstractions, or simplifications of what they stand for. Words stand for ideas and things, but they are not the same as those ideas and things. People who study meaning say "the word is not the thing." Semanticist S. I. Hayakawa (1978) introduced the "ladder of abstraction," which illustrates that words fall somewhere on a continuum from concrete to abstract. Figure 3.2 shows an example of a ladder of abstraction for a dog named Tina. The words used to describe her become increasingly abstract as you go up the ladder.

NCA Ethics Credo

We strive to understand and respect other communicators before evaluating and responding to their messages.

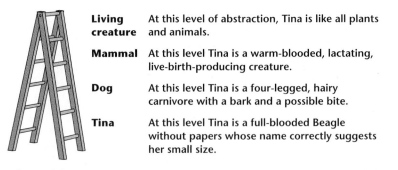

Living creature	At this level of abstraction, Tina is like all plants and animals.
Mammal	At this level Tina is a warm-blooded, lactating, live-birth-producing creature.
Dog	At this level Tina is a four-legged, hairy carnivore with a bark and a possible bite.
Tina	At this level Tina is a full-blooded Beagle without papers whose name correctly suggests her small size.

Figure 3.2   The ladder of abstraction.

SOURCE: Concept adapted from Hayakawa (1978).

How Can Language Be an Enhancement or an Obstacle to Communication?

People sometimes use language in unique or unusual ways, and communication may be helped or hindered when this occurs. For example, people sometimes break the semantic, syntactical, or pragmatic rules of a particular culture by replacing them with the language rules of another culture. Co-cultural memberships, too, may encourage one set of words over another. More personal decisions may dictate the choice and structuring of words. Finally, a person might not understand the communication context and use language that does not follow normal pragmatic rules.

You might be able to make sense of unconventional language usage in some situations; at other times, language used in a specialized way may be an obstacle to communication; and in still others, it may add beauty or a new understanding. Alternative or unconventional language includes grammatical errors and the use of colloquialisms, clichés, euphemisms, slang, profanity, jargon, regionalisms, and sexist, racist, or heterosexist language.

Grammatical Errors

Oral communication, in some situations, does not require the same attention to grammar as does written communication. For example, to hear people say, "Can I go with?" and "We're not sure which restaurant we're going to" are common, but neither of these sentences is desirable in written communication. "May I go with you?" and "We're not sure to which restaurant we're going" are correct but sound stilted because of the informal nature of these hypothetical utterances. Although we are often corrected for making grammatical errors in our writing, we are rarely corrected for speaking the same way. On the other hand, some grammatical errors are more obvious than others—for example, "I told him I ain't going to do it" or "Could you pass them there peanuts?" Communicators who make such errors may find that others form negative opinions about them. Grammatical errors are thus particularly problematic in more formal situations or when another person is assessing your competence. When you are in a classroom, a job interview, or a new relationship, grammatical errors may result in a negative outcome.

Colloquialisms

Colloquialisms are words and phrases used informally. Sometimes colloquial words and phrases are unclear, particularly to someone who is a stranger to your region. Non-native speakers and foreigners may be particularly confused by colloquialisms. Similarly, people from other co-cultures may not understand your intended meaning. On the other hand, colloquialisms may serve relational purposes. Typical examples of colloquialisms are "Have a good day," "Good to see you," "Take care now," and "See you."

Colloquialisms are frequently used in informal situations.

Clichés

A **cliché** is an expression that has lost originality and force through overuse. Common clichés include "No pain, no gain," "Beauty is only skin deep," "One for all and all for one," and "No use crying over spilled milk." So many clichés exist that avoiding them would be impossible in your day-to-day conversations, and doing so is unnecessary. Clichés can be a shorthand way to express a common thought. But clichés may be unclear to individuals who are unfamiliar with the underlying idea, and they are usually ineffective in expressing ideas in fresh ways.

Euphemisms and Doublespeak

Like clichés, euphemisms can confuse people who are unfamiliar with their meaning. A **euphemism** is a more polite, pleasant expression used in place of a socially unacceptable form (DeVito, 1986). Rothwell (1982) observes that euphemisms enter the language to "camouflage the naked truth" (p. 93). Most people use euphemisms in their everyday language. Euphemisms are frequently substituted for short, abrupt words, the names of physical functions, or the terms for some unpleasant social situations. Although euphemisms are frequently considered more polite than the words for which they are substituted, they distort reality. For example, you might hear people say "powder my nose," "see a man about a dog," "visit the little girls' room," or "go to the bathroom" instead of "urinate."

Closely related to euphemisms is **doublespeak**—any language that is purposefully constructed to disguise its actual meaning. This concept originated in the 1950s and was used initially to refer to political messages with either desirable or undesirable meanings. Some examples of doublespeak are "aerial ordinance" for bombs and missiles, "collateral damage" for the killing of innocent bystanders, "person of interest" for a suspect in a crime, and "preowned" for something that is used or second-hand.

Euphemisms and doublespeak are not necessarily to be avoided. While they can disguise the meaning a person is attempting to convey, they can also substitute for rude or obnoxious commentary. Euphemisms, especially unique euphemisms, can add interest to a conversation. They can also reinforce relational closeness as friends and colleagues regularly use similar euphemisms.

Slang

slang

A specialized language of a group of people who share a common interest or belong to a similar co-culture.

Slang is a specialized language of a group of people who share a common interest or belong to a similar co-culture. Although many people understand slang, they avoid using it in formal oral and written communication. Slang is temporary in nature. For example, in the 1950s common terms used by young women and men were *scuzz* and *zilch*. In the 1960s young people used the words *pic*, *groovy*, and *uptight*. In the 1970s young people said *turkey*, *gross*, and *queer*. You know which slang terms are popular today.

Slang helps a co-culture establish its membership and its boundaries. Recall the first time one of your parents used a slang term that was popular with you and your friends when you were in high school. Most likely you were appalled and perhaps decided that you would never use the term again. By using the slang term, your parent was "invading" your co-culture and attempting to act like a member. The purpose of slang is to keep insiders in and outsiders out.

Profanity

profanity

Language that is disrespectful of things sacred.

The word *profane* comes from a Latin word meaning "outside the temple." Thus **profanity** is language that is disrespectful of things sacred. Certainly, some people participate in groups in which profanity is normative. But when you are speaking to people outside your "group"—especially in professional interviews, work teams, or public-speaking situations—the use of profanity is unwise. Profanity, like slang,

While medical jargon may obstruct communication with patients, nonverbal cues can provide comfort.

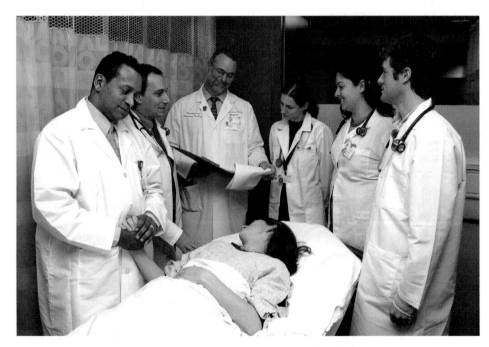

may provide a vehicle for establishing group norms or developing relational closeness in some settings.

Jargon

Jargon is the technical language developed by a professional group, such as physicians, educators, electricians, economists, or computer operators. Some examples of jargon include *CPR, InCo, brief,* and *storyboard.* Jargon can be an efficient and effective aid in communicating with those who share an understanding of the terms. However, like slang, jargon can lead to confusion when individuals who understand such terms attempt communication with those who do not. The situation in which and the group with whom you are communicating are essential variables when you are considering whether to use jargon. Most of us err in overusing it, out of habit. Unfortunately, others are more inclined to be puzzled than to ask, "What do you mean by PBL and APR?"

jargon

The technical language developed by a professional group.

TRY ◆ THIS

Make a list of the jargon used in your area of study or in a job you have or had in the past. Ask a friend to do the same. Do you know what the words on your friend's list mean? Can he or she determine what the words on your list mean?

Regionalisms

Regionalisms are words and phrases specific to a particular region or part of the country. The word *coke* in Texas has the same meaning as *soda* in New York and *pop* in Indiana. When people from different parts of the country try to talk with each other, clarity can break down. Some of us move with frequency from one region of the country to another; others tend to stay in one area. You may believe that you will never leave your home state but find that you are transferred for occupational advancement. Careful listening, which is almost always a good idea, is especially important when you move to a new region. You can fairly easily identify and learn to use language that is particular to a location. Regionalisms encourage group membership for those who use them and create divisiveness for those who are unfamiliar with the terms.

regionalisms

Words and phrases specific to a particular region or part of the country.

Sexist, Racist, and Heterosexist Language

Language can communicate prejudice, and it can silence some members of co-cultures as it privileges others (Hecht, 1998; Taylor & Hardman, 1998). **Sexist language** is language that excludes individuals on the basis of gender, **racist language** is language that insults a group because of its skin color or ethnicity, and **heterosexist language** is language that implies that everyone is heterosexual. Whereas some of the other unique language choices have both positive and negative features, language that is sexist, racist, or heterosexist has only negative consequences. Avoid generalizations and stereotypes—beliefs, based on previously formed opinions and attitudes, that all members of a group are more or less alike. For example, not all nurses are women, and not all doctors and lawyers are men. Rather than "A professor needs to read incessantly to keep up with his field," say "Professors need to read incessantly to keep up with their field." Also, avoid gender-specific compound words, like *salesman,* and

sexist language

Language that excludes individuals on the basis of gender.

racist language

Language that insults a group because of its skin color or ethnicity.

heterosexist language

Language that implies that everyone is heterosexual.

gender-specific occupational titles when the gender is irrelevant. For example, instead of "Our clergyman is a great fisherman," say "Our pastor is a great angler."

TRY ◆ THIS

Think of words you could use in place of those that are gender-specific, such as anchorman, chairman, congressman, forefathers, freshman, housewife, handyman, *and* mankind.

Most people have a good idea of what racist language is. Rather than using racist language, call people what they want to be called. White people should not decide what black people should be called, and straight people should not decide what gay and lesbian individuals should be called.

Homosexual people have always existed, in our culture and in other cultures. However, in many cultures language has masked that reality. An increasing number of gay and lesbian individuals have declared or shared their sexual orientation in recent years. At the same time, many people reject any orientation other than heterosexual in their language choices and their pairing of women and men. If you are not gay or lesbian and do not have close friends who have this orientation, you may not be sensitive to your language that privileges heterosexuality. Consider using terms like *partner, companion,* and *friend* instead of *husband, girlfriend, and spouse.*

◄ SKILL BUILDER ►

LANGUAGE QUIZ

To determine how well you understand the uses of language discussed in this section, complete the following quiz. Which of the following represent colloquialisms, clichés, euphemisms, slang, jargon, regionalisms, or sexist, racist, or heterosexist language?

1. *"Flake off!"*
2. *"Squirrel away some money."*
3. *"She's a cute chick."*
4. *"Don't add insult to injury."*
5. *"We are engaged in ethnic cleansing."*
6. *"I haven't seen you in a coon's age."*
7. *"Who is the reporting authority?"*
8. *"The missus and I will go."*
9. *To a woman: "Who's your boyfriend?"*
10. *"How much spam do you receive every day?"*
11. *"Better late than never."*
12. *"No time for a thorough cleaning, so I will just clat over the floor."*
13. *"I can really burn rubber."*
14. *"The employer is engaged in 'right-sizing.'"*

Answers:
1. Slang; 2. Colloquialism; 3. Sexist/racist/heterosexist; 4. Cliché; 5. Euphemism; 6. Regionalism; 7. Jargon; 8. Colloquialism; 9. Sexist/racist/heterosexist; 10. Jargon; 11. Cliché; 12. Regionalism; 13. Slang; 14. Euphemism.

It's important to recognize that the names for differ- **How Can Language Skills**
ent kinds of language are not mutually exclusive; **Be Improved?**
that is, a particular expression could fit in more than
one category. Can you see how the brief sentence
"How's it going?" could be a colloquialism, a cliché,
and perhaps even a regionalism? Nonetheless, these categories provide a vocabulary
you can use to describe the language you hear every day.

Words need not be obstacles to communication. You can make specific changes
in your language usage that will help you become a more effective communicator.
The changes include avoiding intentional confusion, being descriptive, being concrete, differentiating between observation and inference, and demonstrating cultural
competence. Before examining those changes, two notes of caution are in order.

First, you are limited in your language changes by factors you do not always
understand or control. Before reading this chapter, you may have been unaware of
all the influences—such as your culture, co-culture, religion, sex, and neighborhood—
on language. Even now, you may be influenced by factors of which you are unaware.
For example, earlier in the chapter, you learned that language, culture, and perception are intertwined. But the intimate relationship among them also creates
difficulties for people in changing their language and their perceptions when their
culture remains intact. For example, women were generally seen as inferior to men
in the Old Testament, and the word "helper" is used as a synonym for "woman." If
you have grown up in a family that accepts the Old Testament unconditionally, but
you view women as equal to men, you may have difficulty in avoiding using language that places women as men's helpers or as unequal to them.

Second, when experimenting with new language behavior, you should consider
the purpose of your former behavior and the purpose of your new verbal patterns.
Sometimes ambiguous, colloquial, or distorted language serves an important purpose. You may use such terminology to protect yourself—to establish a healthy self-
concept or maintain a distorted self-concept, or to deny self-knowledge or gain
time to develop self-knowledge. You may also use such forms to protect others—
to help them maintain a selective view of reality, to help them distort their world,
or to help them acknowledge successes or deny difficulties. A "gifted child" may
feel pressure to succeed. The term *sanitation specialist* changes our perception of a
"garbage man." The cliché "No pain, no gain" is verbalized to justify overstrenu-
ous exercise.

Your choice of language provides information to others about how you see yourself, how you see others, and what relationships you believe exist between yourself
and others. You may relax around friends and classmates and use language deemed
"inappropriate" by your parents or co-workers. If you are being interviewed for a job,
you may use language that is particular to your profession and may be careful to use
correct grammar. With a lover you may use words that have special meaning.
Changes in your verbal behavior must occur within the context of the situation in
which you find yourself. You must consider what you wish to share with others
through your language and how clearly you wish to be known. Your prior relationships with others and your current goals in the interactions are important considerations. Understanding and sharing are the ultimate benefits of verbal clarity; you
must decide how important these goals are to you and which ones are attainable.
With these points in mind, you are ready to consider how you can improve your
verbal skills.

Avoid Intentional Confusion

Some people's verbal patterns become so habitual that the people using them no longer realize such patterns are intentionally confusing. They begin to believe that "everyone" speaks the way they do. They take comfort in their clichés. You should strive to become increasingly sensitive to your own use of empty language, ambiguities, clichés, and euphemisms. Having someone else monitor your statements and point out problem areas is often helpful. After someone else has sensitized you to your confusing phraseology, you can "take the reins in your own hands," that is, do the job yourself.

◄ SKILL BUILDER ►

Write two descriptions. The first should be of an object with which you are familiar but with which others might not be familiar. For example, you could describe a favorite piece of art, a pet, an automobile, or a place you have visited. The second should be a description of an event that was particularly emotional for you. The event could be a wedding, the birth of a baby, graduation day, or a celebration.

Exchange these descriptions with a classmate. Have the classmate draw the object that you described in the first instance. How accurate is the drawing? Can you trace any errors to your description?

Next, ask your classmate to describe in his or her own words the event about which you wrote. Your classmate should write this description completely before sharing it with you. Did your classmate capture the feeling you experienced? Can you explain how you could have provided better language to capture your feelings?

Rewrite both descriptions based on the feedback you gained from your classmate. What did you learn in this exercise?

Use Descriptiveness

descriptiveness

The practice of describing observed behavior or phenomena instead of offering personal reactions or judgments.

Descriptiveness is the practice of describing observed behavior or phenomena instead of offering personal reactions or judgments. You can be descriptive in different ways: by checking on your perceptions, paraphrasing, using operational definitions, and defining terms.

Check Your Perceptions

One of the most common ways you can be descriptive is through simple checks on your perception. To communicate effectively with another person, you and the other person need to have a common understanding of an event that has occurred or a common definition of a particular phenomenon. You can check with another person to determine if his or her perception is the same as yours. For example, if a room feels too hot to you, you might ask, "Isn't it hot in here?" After a particularly difficult week, you might ask, "It's been a long week, hasn't it?" Or after an exam, you might ask, "Wasn't that test difficult?" Many disagreements occur because people do not stop to make these simple checks on their perception.

Paraphrase

Paraphrasing can also help you improve your use of descriptive language. **Paraphrasing** is restating another person's message by rephrasing the content or intent of the message. Paraphrasing is not simply repeating exactly what you heard. Paraphrasing allows the other person—the original speaker—to make corrections in case you misinterpreted what he or she said. The original speaker must actively listen to your paraphrase to determine whether you understood both the *content* and the *intent* of what he or she said.

Use Operational Definitions

Another kind of descriptiveness involves using **operational definitions**—that is, definitions that identify something by revealing how it works, how it is made, or what it consists of. Suppose a professor's syllabus states that students will be allowed an excused absence for illness. A student spends a sleepless night studying for an exam in another course, misses class, and claims an excused absence because of illness. The student explains that she was too tired to come to class, and the professor explains that illness is surgery, injury, vomiting, diarrhea, or a very bad headache. This operational definition of illness does not please the student, but it does clarify what the professor means by "illness." In other examples, a cake can be operationally defined by a recipe, and a job by its description. Even abstractions become understandable when they are operationalized. Saying that someone is "romantic" does not reveal much compared with saying that someone prepared a four-course dinner for you and then slow-danced with you in your living room.

Define Your Terms

Confusion can also arise when you use unusual terms or use words in a special way. If you suspect someone might misunderstand your terminology, you must define the term. In such an instance, you need to be careful not to offend the other person; simply offer a definition that clarifies the term. Similarly, you need to ask others for definitions when they use words in new or unusual ways.

You may wish to consider figures of speech in your attempts to be increasingly descriptive. Although figures of speech may lead to confusion in some instances, they can also clarify meaning. For example, a woman in her 70s learned that she had a heart problem, and her physician described the blockage in her heart valve by specifying the number of millimeters the valve was open. The woman was distressed because she did not have a frame of reference for the measurement. A nurse who overheard the conversation explained, "The valve should be the size of a water hose, but your valve has an opening that is smaller than a drinking straw." The comparison was one the woman could understand.

Be Concrete

A person whose language is **concrete** uses words and statements that are specific rather than abstract or vague. "You have interrupted me three times when I have begun to talk. I feel as though you do not consider my point of view as important as yours" is specific. In contrast, "You should consider my viewpoint, too," is vague.

Earlier in the chapter, semanticists were briefly mentioned. Count Alfred Korzybski started the field of general semantics with the noble purpose of improving human behavior through the careful use of language. The general semanticists' contribution includes the use of more precise, concrete language to facilitate the transmission and reception of symbols as accurately as possible. They encourage practices that make language more certain to engender shared meanings. Two such practices are dating and indexing.

Dating

dating

Specifying when you made an observation, since everything changes over time.

frozen evaluation

An assessment of a concept that does not change over time.

Dating is specifying when you made an observation, which is necessary because everything changes over time. Often, you view objects, people, or situations as remaining the same. You form a judgment or view of a person, an idea, or a phenomenon, and you maintain that view even though the person, idea, or phenomenon may have changed. Dating is the opposite of **frozen evaluation,** in which you do not allow your assessment to change over time. When using dating, instead of saying that something is always or universally a certain way, you state *when* you made your judgment and clarify that your perception was based on that experience.

For example, if you took a course with a particular instructor two years ago, any judgment you make about the course and the instructor must be qualified as to time. You may tell someone, "English 101 with Professor Jones is a breeze," but that judgment may no longer be true. Or suppose you went out with someone a year ago, and now your friend is thinking about going out with him. You might say that he is quiet and withdrawn, but that may no longer be accurate: Time has passed, the situation is different, and the person you knew may have changed. You can prevent communication problems by saying "English 101 with Professor Jones was a breeze for me when I took it during the spring of 2002," or "Joe seemed quiet and withdrawn when I dated him last year, but I haven't seen him since."

Indexing

indexing

Identifying the uniqueness of objects, events, and people.

Indexing is identifying the uniqueness of objects, events, and people. Indexing simply means recognizing the differences among the various members of a group. Stereotyping, which was defined earlier in the chapter, is the opposite of indexing. People often assume that the characteristics of one member of a group apply to all members of a group. For example, you might assume that because you have a good communication instructor, all instructors in the department are exceptional, but that may not be the case. Indexing can help you avoid such generalizations. You could say, "I have a great communication instructor. What is yours like?" Or, instead of saying "Hondas get good gas mileage—I know, I own one," which is a generalization about all Hondas based on only one, try "I have a Honda that uses very little gas. How does your Honda do on gas mileage?" And, rather than "Firstborn children are more responsible than their younger brothers or sisters," try using indexing: "My older brother is far more responsible than I. Is the same true of your older brother?"

Differentiate Between Observations and Inferences

Another way to improve language skills is to discern between observations and inferences. Observations are descriptions of what is sensed; inferences are conclusions drawn from observations. For example, during the day you make observations as to where objects in a room are placed. However, at night, when you walk through the room, although you cannot see where the objects are placed, you conclude that they are still where they were during the day, and you are able to walk through the room without bumping into anything. You have no problem with this kind of simple exchange of an inference for an observation—unless someone has moved the furniture or placed a new object in the room, or unless your memory is inaccurate. Even simple inferences can be wrong. Many shins have been bruised because someone relied on inference rather than observation.

The differences between observations and inferences become even more clouded when more than one culture is involved. For example, American students studying in Denmark concluded that Danish students were not very friendly. Their inference was based on their experiences attending parties that included both Danish and American undergrads. The Danes tended to arrive in groups and spend the bulk of the evening conversing with that particular group of friends. The Americans were accustomed to moving among several groups and talking with many of the people present. The Danish students were amiable, but they expressed their friendliness differently than the American students. The Americans, in this instance, confused their observation of the Danish students with an inference about their feelings toward others.

Demonstrate Cultural Competence

Our world is truly becoming a global village as increasing numbers of people travel around the globe for business and pleasure. You may well spend part of your undergraduate years in another country as a student, an intern, or a visitor. Even if you do not travel abroad, you know the significance of being able to communicate with people from other cultures.

The United States has become increasingly diverse as people from other countries are making their home here. The last official census for which results are available, in 2000, showed that nearly 47 million people who are residents of the United States speak English as a second language and speak another language in their homes. The most frequently spoken language is Spanish, but many U.S. residents are native speakers of French or Creole, German, Chinese, and Italian. Significant increases in people of Hispanic origins in the United States have occurred in recent decades (www.census.gov/prod/2003pubs/c2kbr-29.pdf).

The United States is fortunate to have a rich mixture of people of different national, ethnic, racial, religious, and individual characteristics. At the same time, differences in cultural backgrounds, as we have seen, are tied to differences in language and in perception. Nearly every day we read about conflicts between people from different ethnic, racial, religious, or national backgrounds. Intercultural conflict may be one of the truly significant problems of our time.

Cultural competence is defined as "the ability of individuals and systems to respond respectfully and effectively to people of all cultures, classes, races, ethnic backgrounds and religions in a manner that recognizes, affirms, and values the worth of individuals, families, and communities and protects and preserves the dignity of each" (www.cwla.org/programs/culturalcompetence/). Cultural competence is essential if we are to have satisfying personal, family, and community lives and if we are to be successful in the workplace.

Cultural competence can be demonstrated through communicative skills. You will learn more about cultural competence in chapter 7 on intercultural communication, as well as in other chapters. Empathic listening and critical thinking, which

View the video clip titled "The Right Kind of Care" on the *Online Learning Center* at www.mhhe.com/pearson3. Analyze whether Susan and her grandmother demonstrated cultural competence.

cultural competence

The ability of individuals and systems to respond respectfully and effectively to people of all cultures, classes, races, ethnic backgrounds, and religions in a manner that recognizes, affirms, and values the worth of individuals, families, and communities and protects and preserves the dignity of each.

you will study in chapter 5, will help you become more sensitive to differences in the verbal and nonverbal cues that others offer. Audience analysis, the topic of chapter 10, will provide you with tools that you can use to assess the characteristics of people with whom you interact. Generally, listening rather than speaking, and understanding rather than judging, will be invaluable as you become more culturally competent.

How Can ESL Speakers Improve Their Language Skills?

If you speak English as a second language, you know that language skills take time and effort to develop. Although much work still needs to be done to better understand how to help non-native speakers build their language skills, the National Teachers of English as a Second Language (www.tesol.org) provides this advice:

1. *Keep language functional.* Rather than initially learning a second language through vocabulary lists and formal rules of grammar, you should try to learn how to use language in conversation. By learning the functional rules of language, you will develop skills more quickly.

2. *Be aware of language nuances.* As you learn the English language, recognize that how it functions differs depending on who you are talking to and in what context. As with your native language, there are many nuances to the English language. As you pay attention to slight variations in how English is used, your skills in English will accumulate rapidly. Being flexible, observant, and patient is important as you learn about these differences.

3. *Recognize that language learning is long-term.* Native speakers begin learning language from infancy, so it should be no surprise that non-native speakers need time to develop skills. For many non-native speakers it may take up to 5–7 years to attain proficiency with English. You can try to speed your learning by engaging in consistent, meaningful interactions with native speakers.

4. *Develop language processes interdependently.* Old views of language acquisition assumed that language learning was linear—that you learned first to listen, then to speak, and finally to read in a second language. Newer views suggest that these processes happen at the same time. Thus, to develop your skills more quickly, you should engage in all of these activities consistently.

5. *Use your own language to help.* Your intuitive understanding of your native tongue can assist you in learning English. For example, in your native language there are probably some differences between spoken and written language. Using those differences as a guide, can you discover similar differences in English? By comparing and contrasting your language with English, you will more quickly develop an automatic understanding of how to use English appropriately in different situations.

Chapter Review & Study Guide

SUMMARY

In this chapter you learned the following:

► Language is a collection of symbols, letters, and words with arbitrary meanings that are governed by rules and are used to communicate.

► Language consists of words or symbols that represent something without being that thing. Language employs rules of semantics, syntax, and pragmatics.

► Language, perception, and culture are intertwined.

► Language is arbitrary, organizes and classifies reality, is abstract, and shapes perceptions.

► People sometimes use language in unconventional ways, which can present a barrier or a bonus to communication. Examples of unconventional language include:
  • Grammatical errors.
  • Clichés.

  • Euphemisms and doublespeak.
  • Slang.
  • Profanity.
  • Jargon.
  • Colloquialisms.
  • Regionalisms.
  • Sexist, racist, and heterosexist language.

► You can change and improve your use of language by:
  • Avoiding intentional confusion.
  • Being more descriptive.
  • Being more concrete.
  • Differentiating between observations and inferences.
  • Demonstrating communication competence in your interactions with others.

KEY TERMS

Go to the *Online Learning Center* at **www.mhhe.com/pearson3** to further your understanding of the following terminology.

Cliché
Colloquialisms
Concrete language
Connotative meaning
Cultural competence
Culture
Dating
Decode
Denotative meaning
Descriptiveness

Doublespeak
Encode
Euphemism
Frozen evaluation
Heterosexist language
Indexing
Jargon
Language
Operational definitions
Paraphrasing

Phatic communication
Pragmatics
Profanity
Racist language
Regionalisms
Sapir-Whorf hypothesis
Semantics
Sexist language
Slang
Syntax

STUDY QUESTIONS

1. Which of the following is *not* a characteristic of language?
   a. classifies reality
   b. organizes reality
   c. is intertwined with culture
   d. is concrete

2. Because massages can vary depending on the situation, it is important to examine the context of the communication. This is called

   a. syntax
   b. pragmatics
   c. semantics
   d. encoding

3. Which statement reflects the relationship between language and culture?
   a. Language does not progress in response to the needs of the culture, but culture does progress in response to language.

    b. Language is a minor way that we learn about our culture.

    c. Culture creates a lens through which we perceive the world and create shared meaning.

    d. Language and culture are not related.

4. When doctors communicate with technical language, they are using
   a. profanity
   b. euphemisms
   c. doublespeak
   d. jargon

5. One way to improve language skills is to restate the other person's message by rephrasing the content of the message, a process called
   a. defining your terms
   b. paraphrasing
   c. using concrete language
   d. dating

6. A word's dictionary definition is its _____ meaning, and an individualized or personalized definition is its _____ meaning.
   a. denotative; connotative
   b. denotative; abstract
   c. connotative; denotative
   d. concrete; connotative

7. Communication may be helped or hindered when
   a. proper grammar is used
   b. language is used in unique or unusual ways
   c. clichés are avoided
   d. sexist or racist language is utilized

8. Dating, or specifying when you made an observation, is important because
   a. you always view objects, people, or situations as remaining the same
   b. situations do not change over time
   c. you are saying that something is always or universally a certain way
   d. you clarify that your perception was based on a particular experience in a specific context

9. Which of the following terms refers to disrespectful language?
   a. profanity
   b. jargon
   c. clichés
   d. colloquialisms

10. When you describe observed behavior instead of offering personal reactions, you are
   a. avoiding intentional confusion
   b. being concrete
   c. using descriptiveness
   d. demonstrating cultural competence

Answers:

1. (d); 2. (b); 3. (c); 4. (d); 5. (b); 6. (a); 7. (b); 8. (d); 9. (a); 10. (c)

CRITICAL THINKING

1. What are some euphemisms and slang used to refer to death? To marriage? Explore where these sayings originated.

2. Choose an object and develop your variation of Hayakawa's ladder of abstraction. Include descriptions that fall in all areas of the continuum from concrete to abstract.

SELF-QUIZ

For further review, try the chapter self-quiz on the *Online Learning Center* at **www.mhhe.com/pearson3**.

REFERENCES

Bakhurst, D., & Shanker, S. G. (Eds.). (2001). *Jerome Bruner: Language, culture, and self.* Kent, UK: W. B. Saunders.

Bruess, C. J. S., & Pearson, J. C. (1993). "Sweet pea" and "pussy cat": An examination of idiom use and marital satisfaction over the life cycle. *Journal of Social and Personal Relationships, 10,* 609–615.

Clair, R. P. (1996). Discourse and disenfranchisement: Targets, victims, and survivors of sexual harassment. In E. B. Ray (Ed.), *Communication and disenfranchisement: Social health issues and implications* (pp. 313–327). Mahwah, NJ: Lawrence Erlbaum.

Clair, R. P. (1998). *Organizing silence: A world of possibilities.* New York: State University of New York Press.

Cragan, J. F., & Shields, D. C. (Eds.). (1995). *Symbolic theories in applied communication research: Bormann, Burke and Fisher.* Cresskill, NJ: Hampton Press.

Derrida, J. (1974). *Of grammatology* (G. Spivak, Trans.). Baltimore: Johns Hopkins University Press.

DeVito, J. A. (1986). *The communication handbook: A dictionary.* New York: Harper & Row.

Hayakawa, S. I. (1978). *Language in thought and action.* Orlando, FL: Harcourt Brace Jovanovich.

Hecht, M. L. (Ed.). (1998). *Communicating prejudice.* Thousand Oaks, CA: Sage.

Moore, M. P. (1996). From a government of the people, to a people of the government; irony as rhetorical strategy in presidential campaigns. *Quarterly Journal of Speech, 82,* 22–37.

Ogden, C. K., & Richards, I. A. (1923). *The meaning of meaning: A study of the influence of language upon thought and of the science of symbolism.* New York: Harcourt Brace & World.

Rothwell, J. D. (1982). *Telling it like it isn't: Language misuse and malpractice/What we can do about it.* Englewood Cliffs, NJ: Prentice-Hall.

Samovar, L. A., & Porter, R. E. (2000). *Intercultural communication: A reader* (9th ed.). Belmont, CA: Wadsworth.

Schilling-Estes, N. (2002). American English social dialect variation and gender. *Journal of English Linguistics, 30,* 122–137.

Taylor, A., & Hardman, M. J. (Eds.). (1998). *Hearing muted voices.* Cresskill, NJ: Hampton Press.

Waquet, F., & Howe, J. (2001). *Latin: A symbol's empire.* New York: Verso Books.

Whorf, B. L. (1956). Science and linguistics. In J. B. Carroll (Ed.), *Language, thought and reality* (pp. 207–219). Cambridge, MA: MIT Press.

Wood, J. T., (1997). *Communication theories in action.* Belmont, CA: Wadsworth.

CHAPTER FOUR

Nonverbal Communication

What will you learn?

When you have read and thought about this chapter, you will be able to:

1. Define nonverbal communication.
2. Describe how verbal and nonverbal codes work in conjunction.
3. Identify two problems people have in interpreting nonverbal codes.
4. Define and identify nonverbal codes.
5. Recognize the types of bodily movement in nonverbal communication.
6. Describe the role of physical attraction in communication.
7. State the factors that determine the amount of personal space you use.
8. Understand how objects are used in nonverbal communication.
9. Utilize strategies for improving your nonverbal communication.

This chapter focuses on the role of nonverbal codes in communication. The chapter first looks at the problems that can occur in interpreting nonverbal codes. Next, some of the major nonverbal codes are identified and defined, including bodily movement and facial expression, bodily appearance, space, time, touching, and vocal cues. The chapter concludes with a discussion of some solutions to the problems you might encounter in interpreting nonverbal codes.

We are all familiar with the saying "A picture is worth a thousand words." But that is perhaps an understatement in today's society, in which millions of people immediately view images on devices ranging from cell phones to high-definition plasma televisions. The actor Michael J. Fox took advantage of the use of visual imagery to give viewers an idea of the effects of Parkinson's disease, images rarely seen on television.

Fox, perhaps best known for the characters he played in the TV series *Family Ties* and in the *Back to the Future* movies, has recently traded in Hollywood scripts for political ads. He is a spokesperson for the expansion of stem cell research, which uses cells from human embryos to try to find cures for several life-threatening illnesses, including Alzheimer's and Parkinson's disease. Fox was the perfect actor for the commercials: As a 20-year-old he was diagnosed with Parkinson's disease.

His 2006 political ads were passionate calls for more federal support for stem cell research. His message took on added force from the image he presented. The tremors associated with his disease caused his arms and upper body to shake continually. Reactions to Fox's commercials were intense—both pro and con. Those who favor stem cell research considered Fox's efforts courageous and effective. But those who oppose the research because of the involvement of human fetuses were incensed. Talk show host Rush Limbaugh went so far as to imply that Fox exaggerated his tremors to influence the emotions of viewers. The dialogue and commentary that the ad generated focused mostly on the ethics of Fox's imagery and much less on the scientific and ethical questions surrounding the use of stem cells.

The controversy ignited by Fox's commercials resulted less from his message than from his nonverbal imagery as he delivered the message. The lesson is clear: Nonverbal communication heavily influences the ways others perceive us. In this chapter you will learn about the various ways that nonverbal communication can help—and hinder—effective communication.

What Is Nonverbal Communication?

This chapter focuses on nonverbal communication and the relationship between nonverbal and verbal communication. The chapter should help you make sense of the most frequently seen nonverbal codes, as well as provide you with some suggestions for improving your nonverbal communication. Let us begin with a definition of nonverbal communication and a brief discussion on its significance.

Nonverbal communication is the process of using messages that are not words to generate meaning. Nonverbal communication includes nonword vocalizations such as inflection and nonword sounds such as "ah" and "hmm." Communication is complex. We cannot quantify the relative contribution of nonverbal communication to verbal communication (Lapakko, 1997), but nonverbal communication often provides much more meaning than people realize. Indeed, when we are not certain about another person's feelings or our feeling about him or her, we may rely

nonverbal communication

The process of using messages that are not words to generate meaning.

far more on nonverbal cues and less on the words that are used (Grahe & Bernieri, 1999; Vedantam, 2006).

You know the importance of nonverbal communication in your own life. Imagine how difficult communication would be if you could not see the people with whom you are communicating, hear their voices, or sense their presence. Actually, this is what occurs when you send e-mail or instant messages or chat with others online. As electronic forms of communication have become more prevalent, people have found creative ways to communicate feeling and emotions. Emoticons are sequences of characters composed in two-dimensional written formats for the purpose of expressing emotions. The most common example of the emoticon is the "smiley" or "smiley face." Emoticons are a form of nonverbal communication, and they illustrate the importance of this means of communication, no matter the context.

How are Verbal and Nonverbal Communication Related?

In the last chapter we examined verbal communication and verbal codes. Both verbal and nonverbal communication are essential for effective interactions with others. How are the two related? Nonverbal communication works in conjunction with the words that we utter in six ways: to repeat, to emphasize, to complement, to contradict, to substitute, and to regulate. Let us consider each of these briefly.

Repetition occurs when the same message is sent verbally and nonverbally. For example, you frown at the PowerPoint presentation while you ask the speaker what he means. Or you direct a passing motorist by pointing at the next street corner and explaining where she should turn.

Emphasis is the use of nonverbal cues to strengthen your message. Hugging a friend and telling him that you really care about him is a stronger statement than using either words or bodily movement alone.

Complementation is different from repetition in that it goes beyond duplication of the message in two channels. It is also not a substitution of one channel for the other. The verbal and nonverbal codes add meaning to each other and expand the meaning of either message alone. Your tone of voice, your gestures, and your bodily movement can all indicate your feeling, which goes beyond your verbal message.

Contradiction occurs when your verbal and nonverbal messages conflict. Often this occurs accidentally. If you have ever been angry at a teacher or parent, you may have stated verbally that you were fine—but your bodily movements, facial expression, and use of space may have "leaked" your actual feelings. Contradiction occurs intentionally in humor and sarcasm. Your words provide one message, but your nonverbal delivery tells how you really feel.

Substitution occurs when nonverbal codes are used instead of verbal codes. You roll your eyes, you stick out your tongue, you gesture thumbs down, or you shrug. In most cases your intended message is fairly clear.

Regulation occurs when nonverbal codes are used to monitor and control interactions with others. For example, you look away when someone else is trying to talk and you are not finished with your thought. You walk away from someone who has hurt your feelings or made you angry. You shake your head and encourage another person to continue talking. While verbal and nonverbal codes often work in concert, they also exhibit differences that we will consider next.

repetition

The same message is sent both verbally and nonverbally.

emphasis

The use of nonverbal cues to strengthen verbal messages.

complementation

Nonverbal and verbal codes add meaning to each other and expand the meaning of either message alone.

contradiction

Verbal and nonverbal messages conflict.

substitution

Nonverbal codes are used instead of verbal codes.

regulation

Nonverbal codes are used to monitor and control interactions with others.

Why are Nonverbal Codes Difficult to Interpret?

Nonverbal communication is responsible for much of the misunderstanding that occurs during communication. Just as people have difficulty interpreting verbal symbols, so do they struggle to interpret nonverbal codes. The ambiguity of nonverbal communication occurs for two reasons: People use the same code to communicate a variety of meanings, and they use a variety of codes to communicate the same meaning.

One Code Communicates a Variety of Meanings

The ambiguity of nonverbal codes occurs in part because one code may communicate several different meanings. For example, the nonverbal code of raising your right hand may mean that you are taking an oath, you are demonstrating for a cause, you are indicating to an instructor that you would like to answer a question, a physician is examining your right side, or you want a taxi to stop for you. Also consider how you may stand close to someone because of a feeling of affection, because the room is crowded, or because you have difficulty hearing.

Although people in laboratory experiments have demonstrated some success in decoding nonverbal behavior accurately (Horgan & Smith, 2006), in actual situations receivers of nonverbal cues can only guess about the meaning of the cue (Motley & Camden, 1988). Several lay authors have been successful in selling books suggesting that observers can learn to easily and accurately distinguish meaning from specific nonverbal cues. Unfortunately, these authors have not been able to demonstrate any significant improvement among their readers. Single cues can be interpreted in multiple ways.

A Variety of Codes Communicate the Same Meaning

Nonverbal communication is not a science: Any number of codes may be used to communicate the same meaning. One example is the many nonverbal ways by which adults communicate love or affection. You may sit or stand more closely to someone you love. You might speak more softly, use a certain vocal intonation, or alter how quickly you speak when you communicate with someone with whom you are affectionate. Or perhaps you choose to dress differently when you are going to be in the company of someone you love.

Cultural differences are especially relevant when we consider that multiple cues may be used to express a similar message. How do you show respect to a speaker in a public-speaking situation? In some cultures respect is shown by listeners when they avert their eyes; in other cultures listeners show respect and attention by looking directly at the speaker. You may believe that showing your emotions is an important first step in resolving conflict, whereas a classmate may feel that emotional responses interfere with conflict resolution.

◄ SKILL BUILDER ►

You can improve your own nonverbal communication by first becoming aware of how you communicate. Using one of the multiple video technologies, record yourself when you are engaged in a conversation, group discussion, or public speech. Watch the recording with classmates, and take note of your facial expressions, gestures, posture, and other nonverbal features. How might you improve your nonverbal communication?

What Are Nonverbal Codes?

Nonverbal codes are codes of communication consisting of symbols that are not words, including nonword vocalizations. Bodily movement, facial expression, bodily appearance, the use of space, the use of time, touch, vocal cues, and clothing and other artifacts are all nonverbal codes. Let us consider these systematic arrangements of symbols that have been given arbitrary meaning and are used in communication.

Bodily Movement and Facial Expression

The study of bodily movements, including posture, gestures, and facial expressions, is called **kinesics,** a word derived from the Greek word *kinesis*, meaning "movement." Some popular books purport to teach you how to "read" nonverbal communication so that you will know, for example, who is sexually aroused, who is just kidding, and whom you should avoid. Nonverbal communication, however, is more complicated than that. Interpreting the meaning of nonverbal communication is partly a matter of assessing the other person's unique behavior and considering

nonverbal codes

Codes of communication consisting of symbols that are not words, including nonword vocalizations.

kinesics

The study of bodily movements, including posture, gestures, and facial expressions.

Greetings

Chinese, Japanese, and Koreans bow, and Thais bow their heads while holding their hands in a prayerlike position. The bumi putra, or Muslim Malaysians, have a greeting of their own: They shake hands as westerners do, but they follow up by touching their heart with their right hand to indicate that they are greeting you "from the heart."

the context. You don't just "read" another person's body language; instead, you observe, analyze, and interpret before you decide the probable meaning.

Assessing another person's unique behavior means that you need to know how that person usually acts. A quiet person might be unflappable even in an emergency situation. A person who never smiles may not be unhappy, and someone who acts happy might not actually be happy. You need to know how the person expresses emotions before you can interpret what his or her nonverbal communication means.

Considering the context means that the situation alters how you interpret nonverbal communication. Many people become talkative, candid, or belligerent when they drink alcoholic beverages. Finding someone excessively friendly at a long party might be more attributable to the proof of the drinks than to anything else. People tend to be formally polite at ceremonies, emotionally unguarded in their homes, and excessively prudent when applying for a job.

To look more deeply into interpreting nonverbal communication, let us consider the work of some experts on the subject: Albert Mehrabian, Paul Ekman, and Wallace Friesen.

Mehrabian (1971) studied nonverbal communication by examining the concepts of liking, status, and responsiveness among the participants in communication situations.

- *Liking* is expressed by forward leaning, a direct body orientation (such as standing face-to-face), close proximity, increased touching, relaxed posture, open arms and body, positive facial expression, and direct eye contact. For example, look at how a group of males acts when drinking beer and watching a game on television, or watch newly matched couples in the spring.

- *Status*, especially high status, is communicated nonverbally by bigger gestures, relaxed posture, and less eye contact. Male bosses sometimes put their feet up on their desks when talking to subordinates, but subordinates rarely act that way when talking to their boss.

- *Responsiveness* is exhibited by movement toward the other person, by spontaneous gestures, by shifts in posture and position, and by facial expressiveness. In other words, the face and body provide positive feedback to the other person.

Ekman (1993, 1997, 1999a, 1999b) and Ekman and Friesen (1969) categorized movement on the basis of its functions, origins, and meanings. Their categories include emblems, illustrators, affect displays, regulators, and adaptors.

emblems

Nonverbal movements that substitute for words and phrases.

- **Emblems** are nonverbal movements that substitute for words and phrases. Examples of emblems are a beckoning first finger to mean "come here," an open hand held up to mean "stop," and a forefinger and thumb forming a circle to mean "OK." Be wary of emblems; they may mean something else in another culture.

- **Illustrators** are nonverbal movements that accompany or reinforce verbal messages. Examples of illustrators are nodding your head when you say yes, shaking your head when you say no, stroking your stomach when you say you are hungry, and shaking your fist in the air when you say, "Get out of here." These nonverbal cues tend to be more universal than many in the other four categories of movement.

- **Affect displays** are nonverbal movements of the face and body used to show emotion. Watch people's behavior when their favorite team wins a game, listen to the door slam when an angry person leaves the room, and watch men make threatening moves when they are very upset with each other but don't really want to fight.

- **Regulators** are nonverbal movements that control the flow or pace of communication. Examples of regulators are starting to move away when you want the conversation to stop, gazing at the floor or looking away when you are not interested, and yawning and glancing at your watch when you are bored.

- **Adaptors** are nonverbal movements that you might perform fully in private but only partially in public. For example, you might rub your nose in public, but you would probably never pick it.

illustrators

Nonverbal movements that accompany or reinforce verbal messages.

affect displays

Nonverbal movements of the face and body used to show emotion.

regulators

Nonverbal movements that control the flow or pace of communication.

adaptors

Nonverbal movements that you might perform fully in private but only partially in public.

Finally, Ekman and Friesen (1967) determined that a person's facial expressions provide information to others about how he or she feels, while the person's body orientation suggests how intensely he or she feels. Put facial expression and body orientation together, and your interpretation of nonverbal messages will become more accurate.

To illustrate the importance of nonverbal communication, consider the finding that audiences who can see the speaker understand more of the message than audiences who cannot see the speaker (Macaluso, George, Dolan, Spence, & Driver, 2004; Schwartz, Berthommier, & Savariaux, 2004). Apparently, attending to bodily movements and facial expressions increases our ability to interpret meaning.

Physical Attraction

Beauty, it has been noted, is in the eye of the beholder. However, some research has suggested that particular characteristics—bright eyes, symmetrical features, and thin or medium build—are generally associated with physical attraction (Cash, 1980; Kowner, 1996). Moreover, such characteristics may not be limited to our culture but may be universal (Brody, 1994).

Although we may want to believe that physical attractiveness is irrelevant to other aspects of our lives, we cannot deny the evidence. Our culture is obsessed with the concept of beauty. The influence of physical appearance begins when we are young. By age 4, children are treated differently based on their physical appearance by their day care teachers (Cash, 1980; Langlois & Downs, 1979). When children misbehave, their behavior is viewed as an isolated, momentary aberration if they are physically attractive, but as evidence of a chronic tendency to be bad if

Physical attractiveness is an important nonverbal attribute, but the media may distort realistic views of physical attractiveness.

they are unattractive. These patterns continue throughout childhood and adolescence (Knapp & Hall, 1992).

Physical attractiveness generally leads to more social success in adulthood. Women who are attractive report a larger number of dates in college. Both women and men who are attractive are seen as more sociable and sensitive (Knapp & Hall, 1992). Attractive people receive higher initial credibility ratings than do those who are viewed as unattractive (Widgery, 1974).

Physically attractive people are generally more likely to succeed at work, too. They are more likely to be hired, and they receive higher salaries when they are hired (Knapp & Hall, 1992; Schneider, 2001). Some studies suggest that these conclusions might not be equally true for women and men. Attractive females are sometimes judged as less competent than are unattractive females. In some instances, "beauty and brains do not mix" for women. For males, either attractiveness has no link to competence or attractive men are viewed as more competent (Kaplan, 1978).

Physical attractiveness affects our assessments of others, and the media influence our assessments. For example, one study found that boys age 13–15 were affected by watching advertisements with "thin ideal" teenage girls. Afterwards, they stated a preference for a thin girlfriend. The media may be indirectly affecting girls' body images based on boys' preferences, expectations, and evaluations of them (Hargreaves & Tiggeman, 2003).

Space

proxemics

The study of the human use of space and distance.

Anthropologist Edward T. Hall (1966) introduced the concept of **proxemics**—the study of the human use of space and distance—in his book *The Hidden Dimension*. This researcher and others, such as Werner (1987), have demonstrated the role space plays in human communication. Two concepts considered essential to the study of the use of space are territoriality and personal space.

* *Territoriality* refers to your need to establish and maintain certain spaces as your own. In a shared dormitory room the items on the common desk area mark the territory. For example, you might place your notebook, pens and pencils, and PDA on the right side of the desk and your roommate might place books, a cell phone, and a laptop on the left side. While the desk is shared, you are each claiming part of the area. On a cafeteria table the placement of the plate, glass, napkin, and eating utensils marks the territory. In a neighborhood it might be fences, hedges, trees, or rocks that mark the territory. All are nonverbal indicators that signal ownership.

- *Personal space* is the personal "bubble" that moves around with you. It is the distance you maintain between yourself and others, the amount of space you claim as your own. Large people usually claim more space because of their size, and men often take more space than women. For example, in a lecture hall, observe who claims the armrests as part of their personal bubbles.

Hall (1966) was the first to define the four distances people regularly use while they communicate. His categories have been helpful in understanding the communicative behavior that might occur when two people are a particular distance from each other. Beginning with the closest contact and the least personal space, and moving to the greatest distance, Hall's categories are intimate distance, personal distance, social distance, and public distance.

- *Intimate distance* extends from you outward to 18 inches, and it is used by people who are relationally close to you. Used more often in private than in public, this intimate distance is employed to show affection, to give comfort, and to protect. Graves and Robinson (1976) and Burgoon (1978) note that use of intimate distance usually elicits a positive response because individuals tend to stand and sit close to people to whom they are attracted.

- *Personal distance* ranges from 18 inches to 4 feet, and it is the distance used by most Americans for conversation and other nonintimate exchanges.

- *Social distance* ranges from 4 to 12 feet, and it is used most often to carry out business in the workplace, especially in formal, less personal situations. The higher the status of one person, the greater the distance.

- *Public distance* exceeds 12 feet and is used most often in public speaking in such settings as lecture halls; churches, mosques, and synagogues; courtrooms; and convention halls. Professors often stand at this distance while lecturing.

Distance, then, is a nonverbal means of communicating everything from the size of your personal bubble to your relationship with the person to whom you are speaking or listening. A great deal of research has been done on proxemics (see, e.g., Andersen, Guerrero, Buller, & Jorgensen, 1998; McMurtray, 2000; Terneus & Malone, 2004). Virtual environments allow researchers to study the human use of space in relatively unobtrusive ways (Bailenson, Blascovich, Beall, & Loomis, 2001). Sex, size, and similarity seem to be among the important determiners of personal space.

Gender affects the amount of space people are given and the space in which they choose to communicate (Ro'sing, 2003). Men tend to take more space because they are often larger than women (Argyle & Dean, 1965). Women take less space, and children take and are given the least space. Women exhibit less discomfort with small space and tend to interact at closer range (Addis, 1966; Leventhal & Matturro, 1980; Snyder & Endelman, 1979). Perhaps because women are so often given little space, they come to expect it. Also, women and children in our society seem to desire more relational closeness than do men.

Your relationship to other people is related to your use of space (Guardo, 1969). You stand closer to friends and farther from enemies. You stand farther from strangers, authority figures, high-status people, physically challenged people, and people from racial groups different from your own. You stand closer to people you perceive as similar or unthreatening because closeness communicates trust.

The physical setting also can alter the use of space. People tend to stand closer together in large rooms and farther apart in small rooms (Sommer, 1962). In addition, physical obstacles and furniture arrangements can affect the use of personal space.

The use of space can be analyzed in the video clip titled "Sam's Graduation Party" on the *Online Learning Center*. You can also analyze what happens when personal space is violated by viewing "You Look Great."

The cultural background of the people communicating also must be considered in the evaluation of personal space. Hall (1963) was among the first to recognize the importance of cultural background when he was training American service personnel for service overseas. He wrote:

> Americans overseas were confronted with a variety of difficulties because of cultural differences in the handling of space. People stood "too close" during conversations, and when the Americans backed away to a comfortable conversational distance, this was taken to mean that Americans were cold, aloof, withdrawn, and disinterested in the people of the country. USA housewives muttered about "waste-space" in houses in the Middle East. In England, Americans who were used to neighborliness were hurt when they discovered that their neighbors were no more accessible or friendly than other people, and in Latin America, exsuburbanites, accustomed to unfenced yards, found that the high walls there made them feel "shut out." Even in Germany, where so many of my countrymen felt at home, radically different patterns in the use of space led to unexpected tensions. (p. 422)

Cultural background can result in great differences in the use of space and in people's interpretation of such use. As our world continues to shrink, more people will be working in multinational corporations, regularly traveling to different countries and interacting with others from a variety of backgrounds. Sensitivity to space use in different cultures and quick, appropriate responses to those variations are imperative.

Time

chronemics

Also called temporal communication; the way people organize and use time and the messages that are created because of their organization and use of it.

Temporal communication, or **chronemics,** refers to the way that people organize and use time and the messages that are created because of their organization and use of it. Time can be examined on a macro level. How do you perceive the past, future, and present? Some people value the past and collect photographs and souvenirs to remind themselves of times gone by. They emphasize how things have been. Others live in the future and are always chasing dreams or planning future events. They may be more eager when planning a vacation or party than they are when the event arrives. Still others live in the present and savor the current time. They try to live each day to its fullest and neither lament the past nor show concern for the future.

MYTHS, METAPHORS, & MISUNDERSTANDINGS

The metaphor "time is money" is central to the American way of life (Lakoff & Johnson, 1980). Time, from this perspective, is a commodity whose scarcity enhances its worth. How do students experience "time as money"? Can you think of times when you or others you know have used this metaphor? What positive outcomes and/or misunderstandings emerged from this use of imagery?

One distinction that has been drawn that helps us understand how individuals view and use time differently is the contrast between monochronic and polychronic people. *Monochronic* people view time as very serious and they complete one task at a time. Often their jobs are more important to them than anything else—perhaps even including their families. Monochronic people view privacy as important. They tend to work independently, and they rarely borrow or lend money or other items. They may appear to be secluded or even isolated. In contrast, *polychronic* people work on several tasks at a time. Time is important, but it is not revered. Interpersonal relationships are more important to them than their work. Polychronic individuals tend to be highly engaged with others.

◄ **SKILL** BUILDER ►

We become better communicators as we are able to distinguish between others' varying behaviors. In the next week, observe at least three of your friends. Describe how each of them uses time differently. Do they tend to be more monochronic or polychronic? What cues did you use to make this assessment? How can you be more effective in your communication with them if they are monochronic? If they are polychronic? Consider adaptations that you can make when you encounter a person who is more monochronic than polychronic.

Our use of time communicates several qualities. Our urgency or casualness with regard to the starting time of an event could be an indication of our personality, our status, or our culture. Relaxed, relational people may arrive and leave late, whereas highly structured, task-oriented people may arrive and leave on time or even early. People with high status are generally granted the opportunity of arriving late, whereas those with low status are expected to arrive on time. Punctuality is more important in North America than in South America. Dinner guests in eastern U.S. urban areas may view a suggested time of arrival more flexibly than do rural people in the upper Midwest.

Touching

Tactile communication is the use of touch in communication. Because touch always involves invasion of another person's personal space, it commands attention. It can be welcome, as when a crying child is held by a parent, or unwelcome, as in sexual harassment. Our need for and appreciation of tactile communication starts early in life. Schutz (1971) observed:

> The unconscious parental feelings communicated through touch or lack of touch can lead to feelings of confusion and conflict in a child. Sometimes a "modern" parent will say all the right things but not want to touch the child very much. The child's confusion comes from the inconsistency of levels: if they really approve of me so much like they say they do, why don't they touch me? (p. 16)

Insufficient touching can lead to health disorders, such as allergies and eczema, speech problems, and even death. Researchers have found that untouched babies and small children can grow increasingly ill and die (Hertenstein, 2002; Loots & Devise, 2003; Montagu, 1971).

For adults, touch is a powerful means of communication (Aguinis, Simonsen, & Pierce, 1998; Fromme et al., 1989). Usually, touch is perceived as positive, pleasurable, and reinforcing. The association of touch with the warmth and caring that began in infancy carries over into adulthood. People who are comfortable with touch are more likely to be satisfied with their past and current lives. They are self-confident, assertive, socially acceptable, and active in confronting problems.

tactile communication

The use of touch in communication.

Touch commands attention and is essential to many rituals.

TRY ◆ THIS

Think about how you use nonverbal communication. Are you comfortable touching and being touched? Do you frequently hug others or shake hands with others? Why or why not?

Touch is part of many important rituals. In baptism the practice can range from as little as a touch on the head during the ceremony to as much as a total immersion in water. Prayers in some churches are said with the pastor's hand touching the person being prayed for. In fundamentalist Christian churches, the healer might accompany the touch with a mighty shove, right into the hands of two catchers. Physician Bernie Siegel (1990) wrote the following in his book on mind–body communication:

> I'd like to see some teaching time devoted to the healing power of touch—a subject that only 12 of 169 medical schools in the English-speaking world deal with at all . . . despite the fact that touch is one of the most basic forms of communication between people. . . . We need to teach medical students how to touch people. (p. 134)

Religion and medicine are just two professions in which touch is important for ceremonial and curative purposes.

Touch varies by gender (Lee & Guerrero, 2001). The findings relating touch with gender indicate the following:

- Women value touch more than men do (Fisher, Rytting, & Heslin, 1976).
- Women are touched more than men, beginning when they are 6-month-old girls (Clay, 1968; Goldberg & Lewis, 1969).

- Women touch female children more often than they touch male children (Clay, 1968; Goldberg & Lewis, 1969).
- Men and their sons touch each other the least (Jourard & Rubin, 1968).
- Female students are touched more often and in more places than are male students (Jourard, 1966).
- Males touch others more often than females touch others (Henley, 1973–1974).
- Males may use touch to indicate power or dominance (Henley, 1973–1974).

On the last point, to observe who can touch whom among people in the workplace is interesting. Although fear of being accused of sexual harassment has eliminated a great deal of touch except for handshaking, the general nonverbal principle is that the higher-status individual gets to initiate touch, but touch is not reciprocal: The president might pat you on the back for a job well done, but in our society you don't pat back.

Further, both co-culture and culture determine the frequency and kind of nonverbal communication. People from different countries handle nonverbal communication differently—even something as simple as touch (McDaniel & Andersen, 1998). Sidney Jourard (1968) determined the rates of touch per hour among adults from various cultures. In a coffee shop, adults in San Juan, Puerto Rico, touched 180 times per hour; while those in Paris, France, touched about 110 times per hour; followed by those in Gainesville, Florida, who touched about 2 times per hour; and those in London, England, who touched only once per hour. North Americans are more frequent touchers than are the Japanese (Barnlund, 1975).

Touch sends such a powerful message that it has to be handled with responsibility. Touch may be welcomed by some in work or clinical settings, but it is equally likely that touch is undesirable or annoying. Certainly touch can be misunderstood in such settings (Kane, 2006; Lee & Guerrero, 2001; Strozier, Krizek, & Sale, 2003). When the right to touch is abused, it can result in a breach of trust, anxiety, and hostility. When touch is used to communicate concern, caring, and affection, it is welcome, desired, and appreciated.

Vocal Cues

Nonverbal communication includes some sounds, as long as they are not words. We call them **paralinguistic features**—the nonword sounds and nonword characteristics of language, such as pitch, volume, rate, and quality. The prefix *para* means "alongside" or "parallel to," so *paralinguistic* means "alongside the words or language."

The paralinguistic feature examined here is **vocal cues**—all of the oral aspects of sound except words themselves. Vocal cues include

- **Pitch:** the highness or lowness of your voice.
- **Rate:** how rapidly or slowly you speak.
- **Inflection:** the variety or changes in pitch.
- *Volume:* the loudness or softness of your voice.
- *Quality:* the unique resonance of your voice, such as huskiness, nasality, raspiness, or whininess.

paralinguistic features

The nonword sounds and nonword characteristics of language, such as pitch, volume, rate, and quality.

vocal cues

All of the oral aspects of sound except words themselves.

pitch

The highness or lowness of the speaker's voice.

rate

The pace of your speech.

inflection

The variety or changes in pitch.

- *Nonword sounds:* "mmh," "huh," "ahh," and the like, as well as pauses or the absence of sound used for effect in speaking.
- *Pronunciation:* whether or not you say a word correctly.
- *Articulation:* whether or not your mouth, tongue, and teeth coordinate to make a word understandable to others (such as a lisp).
- *Enunciation:* whether or not you combine pronunciation and articulation to produce a word with clarity and distinction so that it can be understood. A person who mumbles has an enunciation problem.
- *Silence:* the lack of sound.

These vocal cues are important because they are linked in our minds with a speaker's physical characteristics, emotional state, personality characteristics, gender characteristics, and even credibility. In addition, vocal cues, alone, have a persuasive effect for people when they are as young as 12 months (Vaish & Striano, 2004).

According to Kramer (1963), vocal cues frequently convey information about the speaker's characteristics, such as age, height, appearance, and body type. For example, people often associate a high-pitched voice with someone who is female, younger, and/or smaller. You may visualize someone who uses a loud voice as being big or someone who speaks quickly as being nervous. People who tend to speak slowly and deliberately may be perceived as being high-status individuals or as having high credibility.

A number of studies have related emotional states to specific vocal cues. Joy and hate appear to be the most accurately communicated emotions, whereas shame and love are among the most difficult to communicate accurately (Laukka, Juslin, & Bresin, 2005; Planalp, 1996). Joy and hate appear to be conveyed by fewer vocal cues, and this makes them less difficult to interpret than emotions such as shame and love, which are conveyed by complex sets of vocal cues. "Active" feelings such as joy and hate are associated with a loud voice, a high pitch, and a rapid rate. Conversely, "passive" feelings, which include affection and sadness, are communicated with a soft voice, a low pitch, and a relatively slow rate (Kramer, 1963).

Personality characteristics also have been related to vocal cues. Dominance, social adjustment, and sociability have been clearly correlated with specific vocal cues (Bateson, Jackson, Haley, & Weakland, 1956). Irony, on the other hand, cannot be determined on the basis of vocal cues alone (Bryant & Tree, 2005).

Although the personality characteristics attributed to individuals displaying particular vocal cues have not been shown to accurately portray the person, as determined by standardized personality tests, our impressions affect our interactions. In other words, although you may perceive loud-voiced, high-pitched, fast-speaking individuals as dominant, they might not be measured as dominant by a personality inventory. Nonetheless, in your interactions with such people, you may become increasingly submissive because of your perception that they are dominant. In addition, these people may begin to become more dominant because they are treated as though they have this personality characteristic.

Vocal cues can help a public speaker establish credibility with an audience and can clarify the message. Pitch and inflection can be used to make the speech sound aesthetically pleasing, to accomplish subtle changes in meaning, and to tell an audience whether you are asking a question or making a statement, being sincere or sarcastic, or being doubtful or assertive. A rapid speaking rate may indicate you are confident about speaking in public or that you are nervously attempting to conclude your speech. Variations in volume can be used to add emphasis or to create suspense. Enunciation is especially important in public speaking because of the increased size of the audience and the fewer opportunities for direct feedback. Pauses can be used in a public speech to create dramatic effect and to arouse audience interest. Vocalized pauses—"ah," "uh-huh," "um," and so on—are not desirable in public speaking and may distract the audience.

Silence is a complex behavior steeped in contradictions. To be sure, silence is far better than vocalized pauses in public speaking. Too, silence may signal respect and empathy when another person is speaking or disclosing personal information. One observer notes: "Sometimes silence is best. Words are curious things, at best approximations. And every human being is a separate language. . . . [Sometimes] silence is best" (Hardman, 1971). On the other hand, silence may signal the dark side of communication. People in power, in dominant cultures, or in positions of authority may silence others. Those with whom they come in contact may be marginalized or embarrassed and feel that they must remain silent because of sexism, racism, taboo, incidents of violence or abuse, shame, or a hostile environment (Olson, 1997).

objectics

Also called object language; the study of the human use of clothing and other artifacts as nonverbal codes.

artifacts

Ornaments or adornments you display that hold communicative potential.

TRY ◄► THIS

When you picture people you talk to on the telephone before meeting them, does your expectation of how they will look usually turn out to be accurate? What vocal cues did they use that led to your picture of how they would look?

Clothing and Other Artifacts

Objectics, or **object language,** refers to the study of the human use of clothing and other artifacts as nonverbal codes. **Artifacts** are ornaments or adornments you display that hold communicative potential, including jewelry, hairstyles, cosmetics, automobiles, canes, watches, shoes, portfolios, hats, glasses, tattoos, body piercings, and even the fillings in teeth. Your clothing and other adornments communicate your age, gender, status, role, socioeconomic class, group memberships, personality, and relation to the opposite sex. Dresses are seldom worn by men, low-cut gowns are not the choice of shy women, bright colors are avoided by reticent people, and the most recent Paris fashions are seldom seen in the small towns of America.

These cues also indicate the time in history, the time of day, the climate, and one's culture (Frith, Hong, & Ping Shaw, 2004). Clothing and artifacts provide physical and psychological protection, and they are used to spur sexual attraction and to indicate self-concept. Your clothing and artifacts clarify the sort of person you believe you are (Fisher, 1975). They permit personal expression (Boswell, 2006), and they satisfy your need for creative self-expression (Horn, 1975). A person who exhibits an

What do you conclude about this person based on her artifacts?

interest in using clothing as a means of expression may be demonstrating a high level of self-actualization (Perry, Schutz, & Rucker, 1983). For example, an actress who always dresses in expensive designer dresses may be showing everyone that she is exactly what she always wanted to be.

Many studies have established a relationship between an individual's clothing and artifacts and his or her characteristics. Conforming to current styles is correlated with an individual's desire to be accepted and liked (Taylor & Compton, 1968). In addition, individuals feel that clothing is important in forming first impressions (Henricks, Kelley, & Eicher, 1968).

Perhaps of more importance are the studies that consider the relationship between clothing and an observer's perception of that person. In an early study, clothing was shown to affect others' impressions of status and personality traits (Douty, 1963). People also seem to base their acceptance of others on their clothing and artifacts. In another early study, women who were asked to describe the most popular women they knew cited clothing as the most important characteristic (Williams & Eicher, 1966).

Clothing also communicates authority and people's roles. Physicians have historically worn a white coat to indicate their role. For many people the white coat signified healing and better health. As the white coat has begun to be phased out, however, the physician's ability to persuade patients to follow advice may have declined as well. Thus the physician may need to learn alternative symbolic means of persuasion (Panja, 2004).

What Are Some Ways to Improve Nonverbal Communication?

Sensitivity to nonverbal cues is highly variable among people (Rosenthal, Hall, Matteg, Rogers, & Archer, 1979). You can improve your understanding of nonverbal communication, though, by being sensitive to context, audience, and feedback.

The *context* includes the physical setting, the occasion, and the situation. In conversation your vocal cues are rarely a problem unless you stutter, stammer, lisp, or suffer from some speech pathology. Paralinguistic features loom large in importance in small-group communication, in which you have to adapt to the distance and to a variety of receivers. These features are perhaps most important in public speaking because you have to adjust volume and rate, you have to enunciate more clearly, and you have to introduce more vocal variety to keep the audience's attention. The strategic use of pauses and silence is also more apparent in public speaking than it is in an interpersonal context in conversations or small-group discussion.

The occasion and physical setting also affect the potential meaning of a nonverbal cue. For example, when would it be appropriate for you to wear a cap over unwashed, uncombed hair and when would it be interpreted as inappropriate? The distance at which you communicate may be different based on the setting and the occasion: You may stand farther away from people in formal situations when space allows, but closer to family members or to strangers in an elevator.

The *audience* makes a difference in your nonverbal communication, so you have to adapt. When speaking to children, you must use a simple vocabulary and careful enunciation, articulation, and pronunciation. With an older audience or with younger audiences whose hearing has been impaired by too much loud music, you must adapt your volume. Generally, children and older people in both interpersonal and public-speaking situations appreciate slower speech. Also, adaptation to an audience may determine your choice of clothing, hairstyle, and jewelry. For instance, a shaved head, a facial piercing, and a shirt open to the navel will not go over well in a job interview unless you are trying for a job as an entertainer.

Your attention to giving *feedback* can be very important in helping others interpret your nonverbal cues that might otherwise distract your listeners. For example, some pregnant women avoid questions and distraction by wearing a shirt that says, "I'm not fat, I'm pregnant"; such feedback prevents listeners from wondering instead of listening. Similarly, your listeners' own descriptive feedback—giving quizzical looks, staring, nodding off—can signal you to talk louder, introduce variety, restate your points, or clarify your message.

If your conversational partner or audience does not provide you with feedback, what can you do? Practice asking questions and checking on the perceptions of others with whom you communicate. Silence has many meanings, and you sometimes must take great effort to interpret the lack of feedback in a communicative setting. You can also consider your past experience with particular individuals or a similar audience. Do they ever provide feedback? Under what circumstances are they expressive? How can you become more accurate in your interpretation of their feedback?

How Can ESL Speakers Adapt Their Nonverbal Behaviors?

 As you will learn in chapter 7, a variety of characteristics can be used to identify distinctions among cultures—many of which include nonverbal differences in how we use gestures, space, touch, and even time. The amount of nonverbal adaptation you will need to undertake as a non-native speaker depends on how similar your culture is to American culture. Although many nonverbal characteristics will likely be similar—the use of facial expression to convey emotion, for instance—there are also likely to be several differences. Understanding those differences can help you avoid misperceiving others and potentially to avoid creating misperceptions yourself. Key considerations include the following:

- *Americans tend to expect consistent uses of space.* In normal conversations Americans tend to stay in Hall's personal distance zone. Standing closer can violate expectations and cause discomfort and unease; standing farther apart can be perceived as unfriendly. Unless you are very close to another person, touching is generally considered a violation of space rather than a signal of warmth, particularly among adults.

- *A greater emphasis is placed on verbal messages.* Although most communication is still done nonverbally during interactions, Americans tend to be verbally explicit in terms of describing feelings, opinions, and thoughts. As a non-native speaker you may need to be more explicit with your communication; you should also not assume that such explicitness is rude—such directness is simply a cultural characteristic.

- *Americans' uses of emblems are often for less formal messages.* Commonly used emblems range from obscene gestures to specific emblems representing athletic teams. Unlike emblems in other cultures, very few American emblems signify status or respect.

- *Eye contact is expected.* In nearly every communication situation, consistent eye contact is viewed positively as a signal of confidence, warmth, and attentiveness. Even in situations in which there are strong power differences, such as the communication between a supervisor and employee, eye contact is desirable; a lack of consistent eye contact can cause you to be viewed as untrustworthy or noncredible.

- *For vocal characteristics, bigger tends to be better.* Listeners tend to react positively to speakers who have strong volume, good vocal variety, and forceful projection and articulation.

As a general principle, Americans tend to be expressive with most nonverbal behaviors though such expressiveness is typically not found with respect to space and touch. There are many other cultural characteristics of American nonverbal behavior that you will notice as you gain more experience observing native speakers. Some of those differences you may integrate into your own communication repertoire; others you may dismiss. Being observant and asking native speakers about their use of various nonverbal behaviors, as well as their expectations for how others use those behaviors, will help you develop your own skills more quickly.

Mediated communication affects the importance of physical attractiveness in another way. Today many people get to know each other online. As a result, attractiveness may now be based on words and messages rather than on physical traits. People who are not perfect specimens have the opportunity to flirt and to charm. And physically attractive people can be deemed desirable on the basis of other characteristics including their intellect and their interests. Clearly, online relationships will change the nature of physical attraction in the future (Levine, 2000).

Chapter Review & Study Guide

SUMMARY

In this chapter you learned the following:

▶ Verbal and nonverbal codes work in conjunction with each other.

▶ People often have difficulty interpreting nonverbal codes because
  - They use the same code to communicate a variety of meanings.
  - They use a variety of codes to communicate the same meaning.

▶ Nonverbal codes consist of nonword symbols such as
  - Bodily movements and facial expression.
  - Bodily appearance.
  - Personal space.
  - Time.
  - Touching.
  - Vocal cues.
  - Clothing and artifacts.

▶ You can solve some of the difficulties in interpreting nonverbal codes if you
  - Consider all of the variables in each communication situation.
  - Consider all of the available verbal and nonverbal codes.
  - Use descriptive feedback to minimize misunderstandings.

KEY TERMS

Go to the *Online Learning Center* at **www.mhhe.com/pearson3** to further your understanding of the following terminology.

Adaptors	Illustrators	Proxemics
Affect displays	Inflection	Rate
Artifacts	Kinesics	Regulation
Chronemics	Nonverbal codes	Regulators
Complementation	Nonverbal communication	Repetition
Contradiction	Objectics	Substitution
Emblems	Paralinguistic features	Tactile communication
Emphasis	Pitch	Vocal cues

STUDY QUESTIONS

1. What is included in nonverbal communication?
   a. only vocalized cues
   b. only nonvocalized cues
   c. nonword vocalizations as well as nonvocalized cues
   d. vocalized words

2. Nonverbal codes work together with vocalized words to
   a. repeat and emphasize
   b. complement and regulate
   c. contradict and substitute
   d. all of the above

3. One of the difficulties of interpreting nonverbal codes is
   a. one code may communicate several different meanings

   b. no two nonverbal codes communicate the same meaning
   c. each nonverbal cue has only one perceived meaning
   d. observers can easily distinguish meaning from specific nonverbal cues

4. Bodily movement, facial expression, the use of time, and vocal cues, among other actions, are examples of
   a. kinesics
   b. complementation
   c. nonverbal codes
   d. adaptors

5. When interpreting nonverbal communication, it is important to consider
   a. context
   b. only observed behavior

c. gut instinct

d. "reading" people

6. Pointing to your wrist while asking for the time is an example of a(n)

a. adaptor

b. illustrator

c. regulator

d. emblem

7. Compared to those who are unattractive, physically attractive people

a. are treated differently as children

b. generally have more success socially

c. are more likely to succeed at work

d. all of the above

8. With regard to chronemics, Americans of high status

a. are granted the opportunity of arriving late

b. are always on time

c. work on several tasks at a time

d. view privacy as important

9. In relation to gender and tactile communication, which of the following is true?

a. Females and their daughters touch each other the least.

b. Men value touch more than women do.

c. Women are touched more than men.

d. Females touch others more often than males touch others.

10. Which of the following provide physical and psychological protection, permit personal expression, and communicate age, gender, socioeconomic class, and personality?

a. vocal cues

b. affect displays

c. illustrators

d. artifacts

Answers:

1. (c); 2. (d); 3. (a); 4. (c); 5. (a); 6. (b); 7. (d); 8. (a); 9. (c); 10. (b)

CRITICAL THINKING

1. Think back to chapter 2 on perception. Which nonverbal cues have you demonstrated that led others to make errors in perception? Which nonverbal cues have others demonstrated that led you to make errors in your perception? Why do you think these particular cues resulted in misinterpretation or confusion?

2. When you are at the library or other public place, note how people "mark their territory." Do they use their backpack or purse, books, or nothing at all? Also observe the size of people's personal space. Does one gender have a smaller space than the other? Does age make a difference? In what situations does that distance decrease?

SELF-QUIZ

For further review, try the chapter self-quiz on the *Online Learning Center* at **www.mhhe.com/pearson3**.

REFERENCES

Addis, B. R. (1966). *The relationship of physical interpersonal distance to sex, race, and age.* Unpublished master's thesis, University of Oklahoma.

Aguinis, H., Simonsen, M. M., & Pierce, C. A. (1998). Effects of nonverbal behavior on perceptions of power bases. *Journal of Social Psychology, 138*(4), 455–475.

Andersen, P. A., Guerrero, L. K., Buller, D. B., & Jorgensen, P. F. (1998). An empirical comparison of three theories of nonverbal immediacy exchange. *Human Communication Research, 24*(4), 501–536.

Argyle, M., & Dean, J. (1965). Eye-contact, distance, and affiliation. *Sociometry, 28*, 289–304.

Bailenson, J. N., Blascovich, J., Beall, A. C., & Loomis, J. M. (2001). Equilibrium theory revisited: Mutual gaze and personal space in virtual environments. *Presence: Teloperators and Virtual Environments, 10,* 583–598.

Bailey, W., Nowicki, S., & Cole, S. P. (1998). The ability to decode nonverbal information in African American, African and Afro-Caribbean, and European American adults. *Journal of Black Psychology, 24*(4), 418–432.

Barnlund, D. C. (1975). Communicative styles of two cultures: Public and private self in Japan and the United States. In A. Kendon, R. M. Harris, & M. R. Key (Eds.), *Organization of behavior in face-to-face interaction.* The Hague: Mouton.

Bateson, G., Jackson, D. D., Haley, J., & Weakland, J. H. (1956). Toward a theory of schizophrenia. *Behavioral Science, 1,* 251–264.

Boswell, R. (2006). Say what you like: Dress, identity, and heritage in Zanzibar. *International Journal of Heritage Studies, 12,* 440–457.

Brody, J. E. (1994, March 21). Notions of beauty transcends culture, new study suggests. *The New York Times,* p. A14.

Bryant, G. A., & Tree, J. E. F. (2005). Is there an ironic tone of voice? *Language and Speech, 48,* 257–277.

Burgoon, J. K. (1978). A communication model of personal space violations: Explication and an initial test. *Human Communication Research, 4,* 129–142.

Cash, T. F. (1980, July 7). If you think beautiful people hold all the cards, you're right, says a researcher. *People Weekly, 14,* 74–79.

Clay, V. S. (1968). The effect of culture on mother–child tactile communication. *Family Coordinator, 17,* 204–210.

Douty, H. I. (1963). Influence of clothing on perception of persons. *Journal of Home Economics, 55,* 197–202.

Ekman, P. (1993). Facial expression of emotion. *American Psychologist, 48,* 384–392.

Ekman, P. (1997). Should we call it expression or communication? *Innovations in Social Science Research, 10,* 333–344.

Ekman, P. (1999a). Basic emotions. In T. Dalgleish & T. Power (Eds.), *The handbook of cognition and emotion* (pp. 45–60). Sussex, UK: John Wiley.

Ekman, P. (1999b). Facial expressions. In T. Dalgleish & T. Power (Eds.), *The handbook of cognition and emotion* (pp. 301–320). Sussex, UK: John Wiley.

Ekman, P., & Friesen, W. V. (1967). Head and body cues in the judgment of emotion: A reformulation. *Perceptual and Motor Skills, 24,* 711–724.

Ekman, P., & Friesen, W. V. (1969). The repertoire of nonverbal behavior: Categories, origins, usage, and coding. *Semiotica, 1,* 49–98.

Fisher, J. D., Rytting, M., & Heslin, R. (1976). Hands touching hands: Affective and evaluative effects of interpersonal touch. *Sociometry, 3,* 416–421.

Fisher, S. (1975). Body decoration and camouflage. In L. M. Gurel & M. S. Beeson (Eds.), *Dimensions of dress and adornment: A book of readings.* Dubuque, IA: Kendall/Hunt.

Frith, K. T., Hong, C., & Ping Shaw, K. T. (2004). Race and beauty: A comparison of Asian and Western models in women's magazine advertisements. *Sex Roles, 50*(1/2), 53–61.

Fromme, D. K., Jaynes, W. E., Taylor, D. K., Hanold, E. G., Daniell, J., Rountree, J. R., & Fromme, M. L. (1989). Nonverbal behavior and attitudes toward touch. *Journal of Nonverbal Behavior, 13,* 3–14.

Goldberg, S., & Lewis, M. (1969). Play behavior in the year-old infant: Early sex differences. *Child Development, 40,* 21–31.

Grahe, J. E., & Bernieri, F. J. (1999). The importance of nonverbal cues in judging rapport. *Journal of Nonverbal Behavior, 23,* 253–269.

Graves, J. R., & Robinson, J. D. (1976). Proxemic behavior as a function of inconsistent verbal and nonverbal messages. *Journal of Counseling Psychology, 23,* 333–338.

Guardo, C. J. (1969). Personal space in children. *Child Development, 40,* 143–151.

Hall, E. T. (1963). Proxemics: The study of man's spatial relations and boundaries. In I. Galdston (Ed.), *Man's image in medicine and anthropology* (pp. 422–445). New York: International Universities Press.

Hall, E. T. (1966). *The hidden dimension.* New York: Doubleday.

Hardman, P. (1971, September). Every human being is a separate language. *The Salt Lake Tribune.*

Henley, N. (1973–1974). Power, sex, and nonverbal communication. *Berkeley Journal of Sociology, 18,* 10–11.

Henricks, S. H., Kelley, E. A., & Eicher, J. B. (1968). Senior girls' appearance and social acceptance. *Journal of Home Economics, 60,* 167–172.

Hertenstein, M. J. (2002). Touch: Its communicative functions in infancy. *Human Development, 45,* 70–95.

Horgan, T., & Smith, J. (2006). Interpersonal reasons for interpersonal perceptions: Gender-incongruent purpose goals and nonverbal judgment accuracy. *Journal of Nonverbal Behavior, 30,* 127–140.

Horn, M. J. (1975). Carrying it off in style. In L. M. Gurel & M. S. Beeson (Eds.), *Dimensions of dress and adornment: A book of readings.* Dubuque, IA: Kendall/Hunt.

Horton, R. S. (2003). Similarity and attractiveness in social perception: Differentiating between biases for the self and the beautiful. *Self and Identity, 2,* 137–152.

Jourard, S. M. (1966). An exploratory study of body accessibility. *British Journal of Social and Clinical Psychology, 5,* 221–231.

Jourard, S. M. (1968). *Disclosing man to himself*. Princeton, NJ: Van Nostrand.

Jourard, S., & Rubin, J. E. (1968). Self-disclosure and touching: A study of two modes of interpersonal encounter and their inter-relation. *Journal of Humanistic Psychology, 8*, 39–48.

Kane, M. N. (2006). Research note: Sexual misconduct, non-sexual touch, and dual relationships: Risks for priests in light of the code of pastoral conduct. *Review of Religious Research, 48*, 105–110.

Kaplan, R. M. (1978). Is beauty talent? Sex interaction in the attractiveness Halo Effect. *Sex Roles, 4*, 195–204.

Knapp, M. L., & Hall, J. A. (1992). *Nonverbal communication in human interaction* (3rd ed.). Fort Worth: Harcourt Brace Jovanovich.

Kowner, R. (1996, June). Facial asymmetry and attractiveness judgment in developmental perspective. *Journal of Experimental Psychology, 22*, 662–675.

Kramer, E. (1963). The judgment of personal characteristics and emotions from nonverbal properties of speech. *Psychological Bulletin, 60*, 408–420.

Lakoff, G., & Johnson, M. (1980). *Metaphors we live by*. Chicago: University of Chicago Press.

Langlois, J. H., & Downs, A. C. (1979). Peer relations as a function of physical attractiveness: The eye of the beholder or behavioral reality? *Child Development, 59*, 409–418.

Lapakko, D. (1997). Three cheers for language: A closer examination of a widely cited study of nonverbal communication. *Communication Education, 46*, 63–67.

Laukka, P., Juslin, P. N., & Bresin, R. (2005). A dimensional approach to vocal expression of emotion. *Cognition and Emotion 19*, 633–653.

Lee, J. W., & Guerrero, L. K. (2001). Types of touch in cross-sex relationships between coworkers: Perceptions of relational and emotional messages, inappropriateness, and sexual harassment. *Journal of Applied Communication Research, 29*, 197–220.

Leventhal, G., & Matturro, M. (1980). Differential effects of spatial crowding and sex on behavior. *Perceptual and Motor Skills, 51*, 111–119.

Levine, D. (2000). Virtual attraction: What rocks your boat. *CyberPsychology and Behavior, 3*, 565–573.

Loots, G., & Devise, I. (2003). The use of visual-tactile communication strategies by deaf and hearing fathers and mothers of deaf infants. *Journal of Deaf Studies and Deaf Education, 8*, 31–43.

Macaluso, E., George, N., Dolan, R., Spence, C., & Driver, J. (2004). Spatial and temporal factors during processing of audiovisual speech: A PET study. *NeuroImage, 21*, 725–732.

Malandro, L. A., Barker, L., & Barker, D. A. (1989). *Nonverbal communication*. New York: Random House.

McDaniel, E., & Andersen, P. A. (1998). International patterns of interpersonal tactile communication: A field study. *Journal of Nonverbal Behavior, 22*, 59–76.

McMurtray, J. W. (2000). Exploring that other space. *Ad Astra, 12*(1), 38–39.

Mehrabian, A. (1971). *Silent messages*. Belmont, CA: Wadsworth.

Montagu, A. (1971). *Touching: The human significance of the skin*. New York: Harper & Row.

Motley, M. T., & Camden, C. T. (1988). Facial expression of emotion: A comparison of posed expressions versus spontaneous expressions in an interpersonal communication setting. *Western Journal of Speech Communication, 52*, 1–22.

Olson, L. C. (1997). On the margins of rhetoric: Audre Lorde transforming silence into language and action. *The Quarterly Journal of Speech, 83*, 49–70.

Panja, A. (2004, January 3). *BMJ: British Medical Journal, 328*(7430), 57.

Perry, M. O., Schutz, H. G., & Rucker, M. H. (1983). Clothing interest, self-actualization and demographic variables. *Home Economics Research Journal, 11*, 280–288.

Planalp, S. (1996). Varieties of cues to emotion in naturally occurring situations. *Cognition and Emotion, 10*, 137–154.

Rosenthal, R., Hall, J. A., Matteg, M. R. D., Rogers, P. L., & Archer, D. (1979). *Sensitivity to nonverbal communication: The PONS Test*. Baltimore: Johns Hopkins University Press.

Ro'sing, I. (2003). The gender of space. *Philosophy and Geography, 6*, 189–211.

Schneider, D. (2001). *Attractiveness*. Retrieved from http://www.ruf.rice.edu/~sch/social%20course/Attractiveness.htm.

Schutz, W. C. (1971). *Here comes everybody*. New York: Harper & Row.

Schwartz, J. L., Berthommier, F., & Savariaux, C. (2004). Seeing to hear better: Evidence for early audio-visual interactions in speech identification. *Cognition, 93*(2), B69–B78.

Siegel, B. S. (1990). *Peace, love and healing: Bodymind communication and the path to self-healing: An exploration*. New York: Harper Perennial.

Snyder, C. R., & Endelman, J. R. (1979). Effects of degree of interpersonal similarity on physical distance and self-reinforcement theory predictions. *Journal of Personality, 47*, 492–505.

Sommer, R. (1962). The distance for comfortable conversation: A further study. *Sociometry, 25*, 111–116.

Strozier, A. L., Krizek, C., & Sale, K. (2003). Touch: Its use in psychotherapy. *Journal of Social Work Practice, 17*, 49–62.

Taylor, L. C., & Compton, N. H. (1968). Personality correlates of dress conformity. *Journal of Home Economics, 60,* 653–656.

Terneus, S. K., & Malone, Y. (2004). Proxemics and kinesics of adolescents in dual-gender groups. *Guidance and Counseling, 19,* 118–123.

Vaish, A., & Striano, T. (2004). Is visual reference necessary? Contributions of facial versus vocal cues in 12-month-olds' social referencing behavior. *Developmental Science, 7,* 261–269.

Vedantam, S. (2006, October 2–8). A mirror on reality: Research shows that neurons in the brain help us understand social cues. *The Washington Post National Weekly Edition, 23*(50), p. 35.

Werner, C. M. (1987). Home interiors: A time and place for interpersonal relationships. *Environment and Behavior, 19,* 169–179.

Widgery, R. N. (1974). Sex of receiver and physical attractiveness of source as determinants of initial credibility perception. *Western Speech, 38,* 13–17.

Williams, M. C., & Eicher, J. B. (1966). Teenagers' appearance and social acceptance. *Journal of Home Economics, 58,* 457–461.

CHAPTER FIVE

Listening and Critical Thinking

What will you learn?

When you have read and thought about this chapter, you will be able to:

1. Describe the listening process and identify the primary features that distinguish listening from hearing.
2. Discuss three reasons why listening is important in our lives.
3. Define and discuss examples of active, empathic, critical, and enjoyment listening.
4. Analyze barriers to effective listening, including internal and external noise, perceptions of others, and yourself.
5. Use strategies for critical thinking to evaluate both the communication situation and the message of the speaker.
6. Describe differences in listening behaviors between men and women.
7. Adapt general strategies for effective listening to specific situations including the workplace, the classroom, and mediated environments.
8. Engage in ethical listening behaviors.

Listening is our most frequently used and least studied communication skill. In this chapter you will learn about the listening process, some factors that can inhibit effective listening, different types of listening, and strategies for becoming a more effective listener. Our hope is that you will learn that listening, like any other communication behavior, is a skill that must be developed through forethought and practice.

Walk into any modern hospital, and you cannot help but be impressed by the wide array of medical technology, from electronic thermometers to large-scale imaging devices that can detect microscopic tumors. Such technology has undeniable benefits, but critics caution that these devices should not overwhelm the human side of medicine—the physician who *listens* to his or her patient's feelings, fears, and concerns.

Most medical schools are beginning to recognize the need to train medical professionals to be better listeners. They have created programs in which community members "play" patients in mock medical interviews. Student doctors and nurses are evaluated on their listening and other communication skills as they interact with these patients. After the sessions the patients give feedback on how well they think the students listened and reacted to their feelings.

The simulated interviews help the medical students understand the benefits of listening. They see how a dialogue between patient and practitioner can result in more insightful and quicker diagnoses, more effective treatment, and greater patient satisfaction. Perhaps most importantly, they learn that health and healing go far beyond technology.

Listening is one of the most important communication skills that we can acquire. Listening is the primary way that we understand others, enrich our own lives, and learn important, often vital, information. As the use of patient interviews in medical school shows, listening is a skill that must be developed through practice. In this chapter you will learn how to develop your own listening skills in your relationships with others, in the workplace, and in the classroom.

What Is Listening?

Have you ever had the embarrassing experience of having someone ask you a question during a conversation when you were only pretending to listen? You have no idea what the question was, so you have no idea what the answer should be. Or have you ever had someone ask you to do something that was important to that person but unimportant to you—so you forgot to do it? The sounds may go into your ears, but that does not mean that your brain interprets them; nor does it mean that your mind stores the message or that your body does what the message requested. Sometimes you hear, you listen, and you even understand the message, but you do not obey. The listening process is complicated. Much happens between the reception of sounds and an overt response by the receiver.

The first step in learning about listening is to understand the distinction between hearing and listening. **Hearing** is simply the act of receiving sound. You can close your eyes to avoid seeing, pinch your nose to avoid smelling, and shrink away to avoid touch, but your ears have no flaps to cover them. Their structure suggests that for your own protection, your ears should never be closed, even when you sleep. Because you cannot close your ears, you receive and hear sounds constantly.

hearing

The act of receiving sound.

International Listening Association

The International Listening Association (ILA) is the scholarly organization devoted to the study and teaching of listening behaviors. The ILA website has a wide variety of information about listening including quotations, bibliographies, and links to research articles. The web address for the ILA is **www.listen.org**.

However, hearing is not the same as listening. **Listening,** as defined by the ILA, is "the active process of receiving, constructing meaning from, and responding to spoken and/or nonverbal messages. It involves the ability to retain information, as well as to react empathically and/or appreciatively to spoken and/or nonverbal messages" (1995, p. 1). As you can see, listening involves more than simply hearing. Notably, listening is an active process involving the construction and retention of and reaction to meanings we assign to information.

listening

The active process of receiving, constructing meaning from, and responding to spoken and/or nonverbal messages. It involves the ability to retain information, as well as to react empathically and/or appreciatively to spoken and/or nonverbal messages.

MYTHS, METAPHORS, & MISUNDERSTANDINGS

A common myth is that listening is mostly a physical act. In fact, listening is much more of a mental act than a physical act. As you will learn in this chapter, listening requires you to actively think about and process information.

The process of listening is summarized in Figure 5.1. As the illustration shows, we receive stimuli (such as music, words, or sounds) in the ear, where the smallest bones in the body translate the vibrations into sensations registered by the brain.

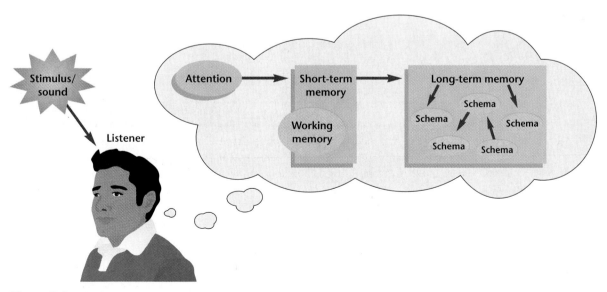

Figure 5.1 The listening process.

The brain, using what is referred to as attention and working memory, focuses on the sensations and gives them meaning. Your brain might, for example, recognize the first few bars of a favorite song, the voice of a favorite artist, or the sound of a police siren. Upon hearing these sounds, you immediately know what they mean. Your interpreted message is then stored in short-term memory for immediate use or in long-term memory for future recall (Janusik, 2005).

As we discuss later, people create many obstacles to effective listening. Not all obstacles, however, are the fault of lazy, unethical, or ineffective listeners. Because listening is a process, natural barriers present themselves at various stages. These natural barriers are explained for each major step in the listening process: attention, working memory, short-term memory, and long-term memory.

Attention

After the ear receives sound waves, the brain sorts them by importance. Think of the last time you had a conversation in the mall or cafeteria. Your brain was being bombarded by aural stimuli, or sounds, but your mind was able to block out the other sounds and focus on your friend's voice. In most circumstances this process of blocking out irrelevant stimuli and focusing on important stimuli is volitional, or voluntary. That is, we want to selectively hear what our friend has to say rather than the fragmented chatter of the adolescents ahead of us. In other situations, our attention is automatic rather than selective. We automatically focus attention in the direction of a loud bang, a siren, or the cry of a baby.

Attention can be selective or automatic. **Selective attention** is the sustained focus we give to stimuli we deem important. We selectively pay attention to our favorite television show, to our friends during conversation, and to the professors in our classes. Selective attention can be impeded by our mind's instinct to pay automatic attention to certain stimuli. **Automatic attention** is the instinctive focus we give to stimuli signaling a change in our surroundings (like a person walking into the room), stimuli that we deem important (our name being shouted from across the room), or stimuli that we perceive to signal danger (like a siren or loud bang). The problem faced by all of us is that automatic attention competes with selective attention. When we are trying to selectively pay attention to one stimulus (like our professor's lecture), other stimuli naturally draw our automatic attention.

selective attention

The sustained focus we give to stimuli we deem important.

automatic attention

The instinctive focus we give to stimuli signaling a change in our surroundings, stimuli that we deem important, or stimuli that we perceive to signal danger.

TRY ◆ THIS

In your next class, make a list of all stimuli in the communication environment that could draw your automatic attention. What strategies might you use to eliminate the potential for distraction?

---

working memory

The part of our consciousness that interprets and assigns meaning to stimuli we pay attention to.

Working Memory

Once we have paid selective attention to relevant sounds and stimuli, our brain must initially process and make sense of those stimuli. **Working memory** is the part of our consciousness that interprets and assigns meaning to stimuli we pay attention to. Our working memory looks for shortcuts when processing information. Rather than trying to interpret each letter in a word, our working memory quickly recognizes the pattern of letters and assigns meaning. Likewise, when we hear the sounds of a word, our working memory recognizes the pattern of sounds rather than trying to process each sound separately. On a larger scale, our working memory can recognize patterns of words. For instance, if you watch the game show *Wheel of Fortune*, your working memory helps you look for patterns of words combined into phrases, even when all of the letters and words are not visible.

Because the recognition of patterns is an essential function of working memory, working memory must work in conjunction with long-term memory. Although we discuss long-term memory in detail later, understand that working memory looks for connections between newly heard information and information stored in long-term memory. If your mind finds connections, patterns are more easily distinguished and listening is more efficient.

Short-Term Memory

Once interpreted in working memory, information is sent to either short-term or long-term memory. **Short-term memory** is a temporary storage place for information. All of us use short-term memory to retain thoughts that we want to use immediately but do not necessarily want to keep for future reference. You might think of short-term memory as being similar to a Post-it note. You will use the information on the note for a quick reference but will soon discard it or decide to write it down in a more secure location.

short-term memory

A temporary storage place for information.

We constantly use short-term memory, but it is the least efficient of our memory resources. Classic studies in the field of psychology have documented that short-term memory is limited in both the quantity of information stored and the length of time information is retained (Miller, 1994). In terms of quantity, short-term memory is limited to 7 ± 2 bits of information. A bit of information is any organized unit of information including sounds, letters, words, sentences, or something less concrete like ideas, depending on the ability of working memory to recognize patterns. If your short-term memory becomes overloaded (for average people more than 9 bits of information), you begin to forget. Short-term memory is also limited to about 20 seconds in duration unless some strategy like rehearsal is used. If you rehearse a phone number over and over until you reach your dorm room, you will likely remember it. However, if something breaks your concentration and you stop rehearsing, the number will likely be lost. Unfortunately, many listeners rely too much on short-term memory during the listening process. Researchers in the field of communication have found that individuals recall only 50% of a message immediately after listening to it and only 25% after a short delay (Gilbert, 1988).

Long-Term Memory

Information processed in working memory can also be stored in long-term memory for later recall. Similarly, information temporarily stored in short-term memory can be deemed important and subsequently stored in long-term memory. If short-term memory is the Post-it note in the listening process, long-term memory is the supercomputer. **Long-term memory** is our permanent storage place for information

long-term memory

Our permanent storage place for information including but not limited to past experiences; language; values; knowledge; images of people; memories of sights, sounds, and smells; and even fantasies.

including but not limited to past experiences; language; values; knowledge; images of people; memories of sights, sounds, and smells; and even fantasies. Unlike short-term memory, long-term memory has no known limitations in the quantity or duration of stored information.

Explanations of how long-term memory works are only speculative; however, researchers hypothesize that our thoughts are organized according to **schema,** which are organizational "filing systems" for thoughts held in long-term memory. We might think of schema as an interconnected web of information. Our ability to remember information in long-term memory is dependent on finding connections to the correct schema containing the particular memory, thought, idea, or image we are trying to recall.

In theory, people with normal functioning brains never lose information stored in long-term memory. How is it, then, that we often forget things we listen to? When we try to access information in long-term memory, we access schema holding needed information through the use of stimulus cues, which could be words, images, or even smells and tastes. If the cue we receive does not give us enough information to access the corresponding schema, we may be unable to recall the information. Consider, for example, a situation in which you see a person who looks familiar. In this case you recognize the person (a visual cue); however, that stimulus does not provide you with enough information to recall who it is. If you hear the person's voice or if she or he mentions a previous encounter with you, you may then have enough information to activate the correct schema and recall specific details about her or him.

Long-term memory plays a key role in the listening process. As we receive sounds, our working memory looks for patterns based on schema contained in our long-term memory. Thus our ability to use language, to recognize concepts, and to interpret meaning is based on the schema we accumulate over a lifetime. If we encounter new information that does not relate to preexisting schema, our working memory instructs our long-term memory to create new schema to hold the information. The arrows in Figure 5.1 depict this working relationship between schema and working memory.

schema

Organizational "filing systems" for thoughts held in long-term memory.

The Importance of Listening in Our Lives

Given our basic understanding of listening, it is clearly an essential skill for effective communicators. A classic study of listening showed that Americans spend more than 40% of their time listening (Rankin, 1926). Weinrauch and Swanda (1975) found that business personnel, including those with and without managerial responsibilities, spend nearly 33% of their time listening, almost 26% of their time speaking, nearly 23% of their time writing, and almost 19% of their time reading. When Werner (1975) investigated the communication activities of high school and college students, homemakers, and employees in a variety of other occupations, she determined that they spend 55% of their time listening, 13% reading, and 8% writing. Figure 5.2 shows how much time college students spend in various communication activities each day. According to these studies, you spend over half your time (53%) listening either to the mass media or to other people.

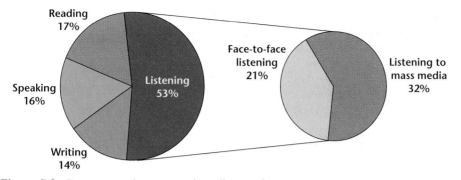

Figure 5.2 Proportions of time spent by college students in communication activities.

TRY ◆ THIS

For one week, keep a communication journal tracking what type of communication activities you engage in during your lunch break (such as talking, reading, listening face-to-face, and listening to the media). At the conclusion of the week, calculate what percentage of your time was devoted to each behavior. How do your results differ from those reported in Figure 5.2?

The importance of listening is even clearer when we consider how we use it in our personal and professional lives. Listening helps us build and maintain relationships and can even help us determine whether the person we are talking to is being deceitful (di Batista, 1997). Listening is also recognized as an essential skill for business success (Haigh, 2006). Because of effective listening, we are able to improve workplace relationships and be more productive (Nichols, 2006). Listening is even linked to successful communication within highly technical fields like medicine, in which improved listening skills on the part of doctors are associated with fewer malpractice claims from patients (Lenckus, 2005).

Four Types of Listening

Listening is classified into four main types: active listening, empathic listening, critical listening, and listening for enjoyment. **Active listening** is "involved listening with a purpose" (Barker, 1971). Active listening involves the steps of (1) listening carefully by using all available senses, (2) paraphrasing what is heard both mentally and verbally, (3) checking your understanding to ensure accuracy, and (4) providing feedback. Feedback consists of the listener's verbal and nonverbal responses to the speaker and the speaker's message. Feedback can be positive, whereby the speaker's message is confirmed, or negative, whereby the speaker's message is disconfirmed. Valued in conversation, small-group discussion, and even question-and-answer sessions in public speaking, active listening is a communication skill worth learning.

Empathic listening is a form of active listening in which you attempt to understand the other person. You engage in empathic listening by using both mindfulness,

active listening

Involved listening with a purpose.

empathic listening

Listening with a purpose and attempting to understand the other person.

critical listening

Listening that challenges the speaker's message by evaluating its accuracy, meaningfulness, and utility.

listening for enjoyment

Situations involving relaxing, fun, or emotionally stimulating information.

Listening for enjoyment is an easy way to relax.

which is being "fully engaged in the moment" (Wood, 2002), and empathy, which is the ability to perceive another person's worldview as if it were your own.

In **critical listening** you challenge the speaker's message by evaluating its accuracy, meaningfulness, and utility. Critical listening and critical thinking really go hand in hand: You cannot listen critically if you do not think critically. Skills in critical listening are especially important because we are constantly bombarded with commercials, telemarketing calls, and other persuasive messages. Later in the chapter we discuss several strategies you can use to listen and think critically.

Finally, **listening for enjoyment** involves seeking out situations involving relaxing, fun, or emotionally stimulating information. Whether you are listening to your favorite musical group or television show, or your friend telling a story, you continue listening because you enjoy it. Besides helping you relax, studies show that listening to enjoyable music can even reduce pain for hospital patients (A dose of music may ease the pain, 2000).

Barriers to Listening

Although you might agree that listening is important, you may not be properly prepared for effective listening. A survey conducted by a corporate training and development firm noted that 80% of corporate executives taking part in the survey rated listening as the most important skill in the workforce. Unfortunately, nearly 30% of those same executives said that listening was the

Listeners are sometimes distracted by noise and cannot listen to the speaker's message. Careful attention to the speaker allows listeners to avoid distractions.

most lacking communication skill among their employees (Salopek, 1999). In the section explaining the connection between listening and thinking we discussed several natural impediments to listening. In this section we explain barriers we create for ourselves in the listening process. Table 5.1 identifies noise, perceptions of others, and yourself as potential listening barriers.

TABLE 5.1 BARRIERS TO LISTENING

TYPE OF BARRIER	EXPLANATION AND EXAMPLE
NOISE	
Physical distractions	All the stimuli in the environment that keep you from focusing on the message. Example: loud music playing at a party
Mental distractions	The wandering of the mind when it is supposed to be focusing on something. Example: thinking about a lunch date while listening to a teacher
Factual distractions	Focusing so intently on the details that you miss the main point. Example: listening to all details of a conversation but forgetting the main idea
Semantic distractions	Overresponding to an emotion-laden word or concept. Example: not listening to a teacher when she mentions "Marxist theory"
PERCEPTION OF OTHERS	
Status	Devoting attention based on the social standing, rank, or perceived value of another. Example: not listening to a freshman in a group activity
Stereotypes	Treating individuals as if they are the same as others in a given category. Example: assuming all older people have similar opinions
Sights and sounds	Letting appearances or voice qualities affect your listening. Example: not listening to a person with a screechy voice
YOURSELF	
Egocentrism	Excessive self-focus, or seeing yourself as the central concern in every conversation. Example: redirecting conversations to your own problems
Defensiveness	Acting threatened and feeling like you must defend what you have said or done. Example: assuming others' comments are veiled criticisms of you
Experiential superiority	Looking down on others as if their experience with life is not as good as yours. Example: not listening to those with less experience
Personal bias	Letting your own predispositions, or strongly held beliefs, interfere with your ability to interpret information correctly. Example: assuming that people are generally truthful (or deceitful)
Pseudolistening	Pretending to listen but letting your mind or attention wander to something else. Example: daydreaming while your professor is lecturing

View the video "Senior Seminar" on the *Online Learning Center,* and analyze how various barriers to effective listening were present in the group interaction.

Gender Differences in Listening

Have you ever had a conversation with a person of the opposite sex and thought afterwards that they just did not listen well? If so, you are not alone. Debra Tannen, a linguistics professor and acclaimed author of the book *You Just Don't Understand: Women and Men in Conversation*, suggests that men and women have very distinct communication styles that influence everything from how they use vocal inflections to how they listen. For example, Tannen (2001) suggests that men tend to be more instrumental or task-oriented when communicating whereas women tend to be more relationally oriented. Although there are many similarities between men and women, Table 5.2 lists some of the more commonly observed differences relevant to listening.

TABLE 5.2 LISTENING DIFFERENCES BETWEEN MEN AND WOMEN

	WOMEN	MEN
PURPOSE FOR LISTENING	Listen to understand the other person's emotions and to find common interests	Listen in order to take action and solve problems
LISTENING PREFERENCES	Like complex information that requires careful evaluation	Like short, concise, unambiguous, and error-free communication
LISTENING AWARENESS	Are highly perceptive to how well the other person understands	Often fail to recognize when others do not understand
NONVERBAL LISTENING BEHAVIORS	Tend to be attentive and to have sustained eye contact with the other person	Tend to be less attentive and to use glances to monitor reactions; use eye contact to indicate liking
INTERRUPTIVE BEHAVIORS	Interrupt less often, with interruptions usually signaling agreement and support	Interrupt more often, with interruptions often used to switch topics

SOURCE: Tannen (2001); Watson, Lazarus, & Thomas (1999); and Weisfield & Stack (2002).

So far in this chapter, we have emphasized the importance of listening while at the same time pointing out both natural and self-taught barriers to effective listening. Faced with this knowledge, you might wonder how any of us can hope to

How Can You Become a Better Listener?

become effective listeners. After all, the potential barriers are many. Fortunately, each of us can take several steps to overcome these barriers to good listening. In this section we highlight how you can become a better listener by listening critically and using verbal and nonverbal communication effectively.

Listen and Think Critically

Critical listening and critical thinking go hand in hand: You cannot listen critically without also thinking critically. We have already noted that critical listening is a form of active listening in which you carefully analyze the accuracy, meaningfulness, and utility of a speaker's message. Similarly, **critical thinking** involves analyzing the speaker, the situation, and the speaker's ideas to make critical judgments about the message being presented. Although we discuss critical thinking in terms of its relationship to critical listening, you also use critical thinking when reading, watching television, or analyzing the ingredients of a tasty meal.

critical thinking

Analyzing the speaker, the situation, and the speaker's ideas to make critical judgments about the message being presented.

One way to think critically is to analyze the communication situation, or the context in which communication is occurring. One of our students recently attended a job interview for a position requiring "excellent public-speaking skills." As a communication major she was excited about this job prospect. At the interview she found herself surrounded by nearly 50 other applicants. During a presentation she learned that the company sold "natural" products like filtered water, organic toothpaste, and even chemical-free moist wipes for babies. Through a little critical thinking and listening, she quickly figured out that the company was actually a type of pyramid scheme and the "interview" was an attempt to get her to purchase bulk quantities of the products and then "market" those products to her friends and family. The people explaining the products were indeed experts, but her analysis of the situation told her that this job was not the one for her.

The second strategy for engaging in critical listening and thinking is to carefully analyze the speaker's ideas. Table 5.3 lists the general skills you should develop to do this effectively. As you can see, the first skill is to identify supporting material. When analyzing the message, a good starting point is to determine whether the speaker is using evidence from other sources to support main points. Does the speaker identify the source(s)? Are the sources recognizable as qualified experts on the topic? Do the sources have any potential bias that would diminish their credibility? We view these questions as essential for effective critical listening, especially given the frequent use of Internet sources by speakers. Our experience is that not only are many Internet sources of poor quality but some even intentionally distort information.

Third, you need to determine whether speakers are describing things that they have seen themselves or presenting conclusions that they have drawn themselves, or are reporting the descriptions and conclusions of others. The distinctions between these concepts involve the differences between first-person and third-person

TABLE 5.3 ANALYZING THE SPEAKER'S IDEAS	
STRATEGY	EXPLANATION
Identify support	Evaluate the process by which the speaker discovered information or gained knowledge, as well as specific elements of the message content.
Evaluate arguments	Analyze the reasoning process underlying key points made in a speech or statement for use of emotional, logical, and personal proof.

observations and inferences. To recognize these differences you should do the following:

1. *Distinguish between observations and inferences.* Observations are descriptions based on phenomena that can be sensed—seen, heard, tasted, smelled, or felt. Inferences are generalizations from or about information you have received through your senses. You might observe that a number of people who are homeless live in your community. Based on that observation, you might infer that your community does not have enough affordable housing. Observations are more likely to be agreed upon by observers; inferences vary widely in terms of agreement between individuals (Brooks & Heath, 1989).

2. *Distinguish between first-person and second-person observations.* A **first-person observation** is based on something that was personally sensed; a **second-person observation** is a report of what another person observed. First-person observations are typically more accurate because they are direct accounts rather than inferences drawn from others' accounts.

A final skill in critical listening is to analyze the credibility of the speaker. **Source credibility** is the extent to which the speaker is perceived as competent to make the claims he or she is making. If you wanted to know what procedures were required to study in Europe for a semester, who would give you the best information? Would you be more likely to trust your roommate, who heard about foreign exchange programs during freshman orientation; your adviser, who had an exchange student a few years back; or the director of international programs on your campus? If your car ran poorly, would you trust your neighbor's advice or that of an auto mechanic? The choice seems obvious in these situations. When assessing the credibility of a speaker, you should determine whether the speaker has qualifications, whether the speaker has experience, and whether the speaker has any evident bias or ulterior motive for taking a certain position.

As you can see, critical listeners must evaluate several aspects of the communication situation, the speaker's message, and even the speaker's credibility. Critical thinking and listening are skills that each of us can develop with practice. The next time you hear a classmate present information, a teacher lecture on a concept, or a friend discuss options for evening entertainment, you have a perfect opportunity to practice critical thinking and listening. As with any skill, diligent practice now will allow those skills to become automatic in the future.

first-person observation

Observations based on something that you personally have sensed.

second-person observation

A report of what another person observed.

source credibility

The extent to which the speaker is perceived as competent to make the claims he or she is making.

As a college student you have multiple opportunities to practice effective listening skills. Select one of your classes in which the teacher lectures for at least part of the class period. During that time make note of the main points for the lecture as well as any supporting material used to bolster the main point (teachers tend to rely on examples as supporting material). Were there any main points that did not have supporting material? If you find such instances, ask your teacher to provide an example to illustrate what he or she is talking about.

Use Verbal Communication Effectively

The notion of verbal components of listening may seem strange to you. You may reason that if you are engaged in listening, you cannot also be speaking. However, transactional communication assumes that you are simultaneously a sender and a receiver. That is, you can make verbal responses even as you are deeply involved in listening. To determine your current competence in this area, consider the skills you regularly practice:

1. *Invite additional comments.* Suggest that the speaker add more details or give additional information. Phrases such as "Go on," "What else?" "How did you feel about that?" and "Did anything else occur?" encourage the speaker to continue to share ideas and information.

2. *Ask questions.* One method of inviting the speaker to continue is to ask direct questions, requesting more in-depth details, definitions, or clarification.

3. *Identify areas of agreement or common experience.* Briefly relate similar past experiences, or briefly explain a similar point of view that you hold. Sharing ideas, attitudes, values, and beliefs is the basis of communication. In addition, such comments demonstrate your understanding.

4. *Vary verbal responses.* Use a variety of responses, such as "Yes," "I see," "Go on," and "Right" instead of relying on one standard, unaltered response, such as "Yes," "Yes," "Yes."

5. *Provide clear verbal responses.* Use specific and concrete words and phrases in your feedback to the speaker. Misunderstandings can occur if you do not provide easily understood responses.

6. *Use descriptive, nonevaluative responses.* Better to say "Your statistics are from an organization that is biased against gun control" (descriptive) than to say "Your speech was a bunch of lies" (evaluative). Trivializing or joking about serious disclosures suggests a negative evaluation of the speaker. Similarly, derogatory remarks are seen as offensive. Acting superior to the speaker by stating that you believe you have a more advanced understanding suggests an evaluative tone.

7. *Provide affirmative and affirming statements.* Comments such as "Yes," "I see," "I understand," and "I know" provide affirmation. Offering praise and specific positive statements demonstrates concern.

8. *Avoid complete silence.* The lack of any response suggests that you are not listening to the speaker. The "silent treatment" induced by sleepiness or lack

of interest may result in defensiveness or anger on the part of the speaker. Appropriate verbal feedback demonstrates your active listening.

9. *Allow the other person the opportunity of a complete hearing.* When you discuss common feelings or experiences, avoid dominating the conversation. Allow the other person to go into depth and detail; give him or her the option of changing the topic under discussion; and let him or her talk without being interrupted.

Use Nonverbal Communication Effectively

Although you demonstrate active listening through verbal skills, the majority of your active-listening ability is shown through nonverbal communication. The following nonverbal skills are essential to your ability to demonstrate active listening. As you listen to another person, have a friend observe you to determine if you are practicing these skills.

1. *Demonstrate bodily responsiveness.* Use movement and gestures to show your awareness of the speaker's message. Shaking your head in disbelief, checking the measurements of an object by indicating the size with your hands, and moving toward a person who is disclosing negative information are appropriate bodily responses.

2. *Lean forward.* By leaning toward the speaker, you demonstrate interest in the speaker. A forward lean suggests responsiveness as well as interest. In addition, leaning places you in a physical state of readiness to listen to the speaker.

3. *Use direct body orientation.* Do not angle yourself away from the speaker; instead, sit or stand so that you are directly facing him or her. A parallel body position allows the greatest possibility for observing and listening to the speaker's verbal and nonverbal messages. When you stand or sit at an angle to the speaker, you may be creating the impression that you are attempting to get away or that you are moving away from the speaker. An angled position also blocks your vision and allows you to be distracted by other stimuli in the environment.

4. *Maintain relaxed but alert posture.* Your posture should not be tense or "proper," but neither should it be so relaxed that you appear to be resting. Slouching suggests unresponsiveness; a tense body position suggests nervousness or discomfort; and a relaxed position accompanied by crossed arms and legs, a backward lean in a chair, and a confident facial expression suggests arrogance. Your posture should suggest to others that you are interested and that you are comfortable talking with them.

5. *Establish an open body position.* Sit or stand with your body open to the other person. Crossing your arms or legs may be more comfortable, but that posture frequently suggests that you are closed off psychologically as well as physically. In order to maximize your nonverbal message to the other person that you are "open" to him or her, you should sit or stand without crossing your arms or legs.

6. *Use positive, responsive facial expressions and head movement.* Your face and head will be the speaker's primary focus. The speaker will be observing you, and your facial expressions and head movement will be the key. You can

demonstrate your interest by nodding your head to show interest or agreement. You can use positive and responsive facial expressions, such as smiling and raising your eyebrows.

7. *Establish direct eye contact.* The speaker will be watching your eyes for interest. One of the first signs of a lack of interest is the tendency to be distracted by other stimuli in the environment. For example, an instructor who continually glances out the door of her office, a roommate who sneaks peeks at the television program that is on, or a business executive who regularly looks at his watch is, while appearing to listen, indicating lack of interest. Try to focus on and direct your gaze at the speaker. When you begin to look around the room, you may find any number of other stimuli to distract your attention from the speaker and the message.

8. *Sit or stand close to the speaker.* Establishing close proximity to the speaker has two benefits. First, you put yourself in a position that allows you to hear the other person and that minimizes distracting noises, sights, and other stimuli. Second, you demonstrate your concern or your positive feelings for the speaker. You probably do not stand or sit close to people you do not like or respect, or with whom you do not have common experiences. Close physical proximity enables active listening.

9. *Be vocally responsive.* Change your pitch, rate, inflection, and volume as you respond to the speaker. Making appropriate changes and choices shows that you are actually listening, in contrast to responding in a standard, patterned manner that suggests you are only appearing to listen. The stereotypic picture of a husband and wife at the breakfast table, with the husband, hidden behind a newspaper, responding, "Yes, yes, yes" in a monotone while the wife tells him that their son has shaved his head, she is running off with the mail carrier, and the house is on fire provides a familiar example of the appearance of listening while one is actually oblivious to the speaker's message.

10. *Provide supportive utterances.* Sometimes you can demonstrate more concern through nonverbal sounds such as "Mmm," "Mmm-hmm," and "Uh-huh" than you can by stating "Yes, I understand." You can easily provide supportive utterances while others are talking or when they pause. You are suggesting to them that you are listening but do not want to interrupt with a verbalization of your own at this particular time. Such sounds encourage the speaker to continue without interruption.

Check Your Understanding

When we listen to others, we are actually engaging in a specialized form of the perception process you read about in chapter 2. Because listening is a specialized form of perceiving, you should engage in perception checking to ensure that your perceptions match what the speaker intends. In the context of listening, rather than calling this perception checking, we might refer to it as checking your understanding. You can check your understanding by practicing these skills:

1. *Ask questions for clarification.* Before testing your understanding of the speaker's message, make sure you have a clear idea of what he is saying. Begin by asking questions to gain more information. For specific factual information

you may use closed questions (such as "yes-no" questions), and for more general information you may ask open-ended questions (questions pertaining to what, when, where, how, and why). Once you have gained sufficient information, you can ask the speaker to check your understanding against what he intended.

2. *Paraphrase the speaker's message.* Using "I statements," you attempt to paraphrase what you think the speaker was saying so that she can determine whether your understanding matches what she intended.

3. *Paraphrase the speaker's intent.* Using "I statements," you attempt to paraphrase what you interpret as the intent or motivation of the speaker. After hearing your assumptions about his intent, the speaker may talk with you more to refine your understanding.

4. *Identify areas of confusion.* If there are specific aspects of the message that you are still confused about, mention those to the speaker while you are expressing your initial understanding of the message.

5. *Invite clarification and correction.* Asking the speaker to correct your interpretation of the message will invite additional explanation. The ensuing dialogue will help you and the speaker to more effectively share meaning.

6. *Go back to the beginning.* As necessary, return to the first step in this process to check your new understanding of the speaker's message, intent, and so on. Good listening is a process without clear beginning and ending points, so you should check your understanding at each stage in the process.

Effective Listening in Different Situations

Listening in the Workplace

As our nation has shifted from an industrial-based economy to an information-based economy, effective listening has become recognized as an essential skill for workers. Statistics from the U.S. Bureau of Labor Statistics show that by 2014 just under 80% of the workforce in the United States will be employed in service-oriented industries like education, health care, retail sales, and state and local government (Berman, 2005). These jobs all have one thing in common—they require employee–customer interaction in which listening skills translate into revenue.

To become a more effective listener in professional situations, you need to apply several of the suggestions mentioned previously. Jennifer Salopek (1999), the president of a corporate training firm, suggests that you do the following:

1. Be aware of when you are not listening.
2. Monitor your nonverbal behaviors to determine whether you are giving appropriate feedback to the speaker.
3. Hear people out and minimize interruptions.
4. Learn to ask nonaggressive questions to elicit more information from the speaker.
5. Summarize what the person said, and check to make sure you understand correctly.

In addition to these suggestions, Bob Gunn (2001), president of a consulting firm for many Fortune 500 companies, notes the importance of empathic listening in professional situations:

> Feelings are to the quality of hearing as our sense of smell is to the enjoyment of a great meal or our sense of touch is to the expression of love. You are listening deeply when you become "lost in the words" and find yourself experiencing deep feelings of joy, gratitude, surprise, curiosity, warmth, closeness, wonder, beauty, or appreciation. You are hearing at a more profound level. The stronger the feeling, the more profound the understanding. And the more profound the understanding, the clearer the subsequent course of action. (p. 12)

Gunn's point is that effective listeners must understand not only what their customers are saying but also what they are feeling. Those who do this effectively are able to build stronger relationships with customers and clients.

Listening in the Classroom

Take a moment to think about how often, as a student, you find yourself listening to a lecture. If you were to estimate how much of your time is spent listening to lectures, how much would it be? If you said "a lot," you would not be alone. Researchers have estimated that college students spend at least 10 hours per week attending lectures (Anderson & Armbruster, 1986). If you take a typical 15 credit/hour load, that 10 hours per week translates into about 80% of your time in class being spent listening to lectures (Armbruster, 2000). The prominence of listening in students' lives led Vinson and Johnson (1990, p. 116) to coin the phrase **"lecture listening"**—the ability to listen to, mentally process, and recall lecture information.

lecture listening

The ability to listen to, mentally process, and recall lecture information.

What constitutes effective lecture listening? Although a variety of answers have been offered, educational researcher Michael Gilbert (1988) provides the following general suggestions:

1. *Find areas of interest in what you are listening to.* Constantly look for how you can use the information.
2. *Remain open.* Avoid the temptation to focus only on the lecturer's delivery; withhold evaluative judgments until the lecture has finished; recognize your emotional triggers and avoid letting them distract you.
3. *Work at listening.* Capitalize on your mind's ability to think faster than the lecturer can talk. Mentally summarize and review what has been said, mentally organize information, and find connections to what you already know or are currently learning.
4. *Avoid letting distractions distract.* Monitor your attention and recognize when it is waning. If you are becoming distracted, refocus your attention on the lecturer.
5. *Listen for and note main ideas.* Focus on the central themes of what is being presented, and make notes about those themes. Effective notes outlining the main ideas of a lecture can, in some cases, be more useful than pages of notes containing unorganized details.

lecture cues

Verbal or nonverbal signals that stress points or indicate transitions between ideas during a lecture.

In addition to Gilbert's suggestions, communication researcher Dan O'Hair and colleagues (1988) recommend that you practice flexibility in listening. By practicing your listening skills while watching information-packed documentaries or while

Lecture listening is a common communication behavior for students.

attending public presentations on campus, you will not only become a more effective lecture listener but will also learn valuable information!

A final lecture listening strategy, one that we view as essential, is to take effective notes. Our own research has found that effective note taking during lectures can increase scores on exams by more than 20%—a difference between receiving a C and an A (Titsworth & Kiewra, 1998). Unfortunately, students typically do not record enough notes during a lecture. Research generally shows that less than 40% of the information in a lecture makes it into students' notes. In short, most students are unable to capitalize on the benefits of note taking simply because their notes are incomplete.

Now that you understand why note taking is so important, how can you become a more effective note taker? Most universities have study skills centers where you can find information on different note-taking formats. Although the exact format for note taking might vary from one person to another, the objective is the same. In your notes your goal should be to record both the outline of the lecture—called organizational points—and the details supporting those points. The most effective way to ensure that you record all of these points is to listen for **lecture cues**—verbal or nonverbal signals that stress points or indicate transitions between ideas during a lecture. Table 5.4 summarizes various types of lecture cues commonly used by teachers. While taking notes you should listen and watch for these types of cues.

TABLE 5.4   COMMON LECTURE CUES USED BY TEACHERS

Type of Cue	Example	Main Uses
Written cues		
Outlines	Outline of lecture on transparency or PowerPoint slide	Indicate main and subordinate ideas
Words/phrases	Term written on the chalkboard	Stress important terms and accompanying definitions
Verbal importance cues	"Now, *and this will be on the exam next week,* we will explore . . ."	Stress important concepts deemed essential for recall/understanding
Semantic cues	"Here is an *example* [*definition, explanation, conclusion, implication,* or *illustration*] of uncertainty reduction theory in action . . ."	Signal common types of details that make up the lecture content
Organizational cues	"The *third thing* I want to discuss today is . . ."	Orally provide indications of main and subordinate points in a lecture
Nonverbal cues	Holding up two fingers when saying "I will discuss two concepts today . . ."	Can serve any of the functions of nonverbal behaviors discussed in the chapter on nonverbal communication

Our research has examined the importance of cues for students (Titsworth & Kiewra, 1998). We taught a group of students about organizational cues and had them listen for those cues and take notes during a videotaped lecture. Students in another group were not informed about organizational cues but viewed and took notes during the same lecture. Students who were taught about organizational cues recorded four times the number of organizational points and twice the number of details in their notes. These students were able to capitalize on their note-taking effectiveness; they received the equivalent of an A on a quiz about the lecture. Their counterparts, who were unaware of and did not listen for organizational cues, received the equivalent of a C. Our experiment looked at the effects of teaching students about organizational cues only. Imagine what could happen if these students had been taught about all types of lecture cues! Fortunately, you are now equipped with this information.

Listening to Media

Think about how much time you spend watching television; listening to the radio; reading magazines, newspapers, or books; reading and writing e-mail; chatting online; or just surfing the web. Many of us might avoid that question because the answer might frighten us. The American Academy of Pediatrics (2001) notes that children and adolescents spend more than 20 hours per week watching TV, which translates into approximately 3 hours per day. When including other forms of media, such as listening to music, playing video games, and using the Internet, this daily intake of media jumps to over 6½ hours per day, or over 42 hours per week. By the time you started your first college class (around the age of 18), you had viewed an estimated 200,000 acts of violence on TV alone. This intake of mediated messages does not diminish. By the time you reach age 70, it is estimated that you will have spent the equivalent of 7–10 years watching TV.

Given the quantity of mediated communication we are exposed to each day, we must become critical consumers of such information. Think how much money you would spend if you "bought in" to every commercial you saw, or think of how much time it would take for you to read every e-mail message you get (including "junk" e-mail). Simply put, good listening behaviors are essential because mediated communication is so prevalent.

One way to be an effective listener in a mediated culture is to have information literacy. **Information literacy** is defined by the American Library Association (2001) in the following way: "To be information literate an individual must recognize when information is needed and have the ability to locate, evaluate and use effectively the information needed." According to this definition, information-literate individuals are able to think critically, know when and how to find more information, and know how to evaluate information.

Mediated communication is not limited to advertising and television. In 2005 an estimated 1.1 billion people worldwide used the Internet (ClickZ, 2004). How do people use the Internet? Communication scholars at UCLA conducted a comprehensive study of various issues related to Internet use. They found that nearly 55% of Americans use the Internet for e-mail and that people feel the Internet increases their ability to stay in contact with others. Additionally, just over one quarter of Internet users indicated that they have online friends whom they would not have met through other means (UCLA Internet Report, 2000). The implication

information literacy

The ability to recognize when information is needed and to locate, evaluate, and effectively use the information needed.

Differences in Active Listening

The way individuals actively listen can vary from culture to culture. College students in Finland, for example, listen carefully and take notes but do not respond overtly while being addressed by the professor. In fact, they remain quite expressionless. In some Native American tribes and in some Hispanic groups, people avert their eyes when listening; but in groups such as northern whites and blacks, people tend to maintain eye contact while actively listening. How would you describe the norms of listening in your culture, community, or school?

of these data is that the Internet, once a form of mass communication, has become an important tool for interpersonal communication as well.

When communicating online with others, how can you be an effective listener? The principal problem with online communication—whether the mode is e-mail, chat rooms, listservs, or discussion groups—is that nonverbal communication is difficult. Recall that nonverbal communication provides significant clues about another person's emotions and feelings. Without the ability to see and hear the other person, how can you tell what that person is really thinking? To successfully listen for relational messages online, you must look for obvious clues such as **emoticons**—typographic symbols showing emotional meaning. Examples of emoticons include a "☺" at the end of a paragraph and ALL CAPITAL LETTERS to indicate "shouting." Because nonverbal communication is more difficult online, it is important to check your perceptions before responding to messages.

emoticons

Typographic symbols showing emotional meaning.

Listening in a Second Language

Many of the suggestions provided in this chapter are common for both native and ESL speakers. However, if you are a non-native speaker, some understanding of how to further develop your listening skills can speed your progress as an effective listener. Research suggests that second-language listening development requires two skills: vocabulary comprehension and metacognitive awareness (Vandergrift, 2006). Vocabulary comprehension is more than just memorizing lists of terms. Rather, vocabulary is strengthened by recognizing the sounds of words and associating those sounds with their meaning. Being immersed in a new culture will assist you in developing such connections, particularly if you seek out and engage in sustained conversations with others. You can also use television and other media to broaden your listening experiences and assist in vocabulary development.

In addition to developing your vocabulary, you should also try to develop your metacognitive skills. Metacognition is your ability to use "mental strategies" to assist in quickly determining the meaning of words. Learning to decipher words by drawing inferences on their meaning from the context and other words around them is one such strategy. Another example of metacognition is drawing parallels between English vocabulary and your native vocabulary. Through such strategies you will make quicker inferences about what new terms mean and will be able to listen more efficiently.

Of course, if you have difficulty listening because the other person is speaking rapidly or using words that you have not heard, you should feel comfortable telling the person. Adaptation to language differences is the responsibility of everyone involved in a communication situation, and you should not take on the entire challenge of trying to make the interaction succeed.

Although effective listening requires you to adapt your verbal, nonverbal and perception-checking skills to specific situations like the workplace, classroom, and mediated environments, you must also take care to enact ethical listening behaviors. To be an ethical listener, you should practice the following behaviors (adapted from Rehling, 2004):

How Can You Be an Ethical Listener?

1. *Recognize the sources of your own conversational habits.* Your family, school, and other life experiences have allowed you to develop certain habits that in some situations could be strengths and in others could represent areas for improvement. Recognizing those habits will allow you to more fully adapt to those with whom you are communicating.

2. *Monitor your communication to recognize when you are engaging in poor listening behaviors.* Perhaps the most important step to becoming an ethical listener is recognizing that you must work hard to be a good listener—a step that begins with an awareness of what you are doing in the situation.

3. *Apply general ethical principles to how you respond.* Planning your responses so that you are respectful to others is an example of how your own personal ethics can influence your listening behaviors.

4. *Adapt to others.* Recognize that other people also have unique communication styles and that you might need to adapt your listening behaviors so that you can fully understand what they are trying to say.

Chapter Review & Study Guide

SUMMARY

In this chapter you learned the following:

▶ Hearing is the physical act of receiving a sound. We hear all of the noises around us. Listening is the active process of receiving, paying attention to, assigning meaning to, and responding to sounds. Listening is an active process whereas hearing is reflexive.

▶ Understanding listening is important because effective listening behaviors are related to success in our personal relationships, our workplace productivity, and even our ability to think clearly.

▶ Listening is generally divided into active, empathic, critical, and enjoyment listening. Active listening, which is listening with a purpose, includes both empathic and critical listening. Empathic listening is when you are attempting to understand another person. For example, hearing your best friend complain about the behaviors of a significant other involves empathic listening. Critical listening requires evaluating a speaker's message for accuracy, meaningfulness, and usefulness. Listening to a salesperson's pitch requires careful critical listening behaviors. In addition to listening for pragmatic reasons, we also listen to things like music for enjoyment purposes.

▶ A variety of internal and external barriers prevent many of us from being effective listeners. One barrier is noise, which includes both physical distractions and internal distractions. Physical distractions are any audible noises in the communication environment. Internal distractions can include mental, factual, or semantic distractions. Perceptions of others and your own behaviors can also become barriers to effective listening.

▶ Critical thinking involves careful analysis of both the communication situation and the message of the speaker. Analyzing the situation requires that you carefully understand the communication situation in which you are involved. Analyzing the message involves evaluating the arguments and supporting material presented by the speaker, whether the speaker is presenting observations or inferences, and whether or not the speaker is credible.

▶ Verbal and nonverbal communication can be used to help you improve your listening behaviors. Asking questions, inviting additional comments, using descriptive responses, and providing affirming statements are all examples of effective verbal strategies. Being nonverbally responsive, using positive facial expressions, making direct eye contact, and providing positive vocal utterances are effective nonverbal strategies. Use of such strategies will encourage the speaker to continue speaking and providing you with information so that you can check your understanding.

▶ General verbal and nonverbal communication strategies can be adapted to specific listening situations including the workplace, classroom, and mediated environment.

▶ Ethical listening means that you should recognize and monitor your own communication style, apply general ethical principles to your responses, and adapt your communication style to others.

KEY TERMS

Go to the *Online Learning Center* at **www.mhhe.com/pearson3** to further your understanding of the following terminology.

Active listening	Hearing	Schema
Automatic attention	Information literacy	Second-person observation
Critical listening	Lecture cues	Selective attention
Critical thinking	Lecture listening	Short-term memory
Emoticon	Listening	Source credibility
Empathic listening	Listening for enjoyment	Working memory
First-person observation	Long-term memory	

STUDY QUESTIONS

1. Hearing is a _____ process, and listening is a _____ process.
   a. mental; physical
   b. mental; psychological
   c. physical; mental
   d. physical; physical

2. Which of the following statements is true?
   a. Personal and business relationships are not affected by listening.
   b. When communicating, college students spend over half of their lives listening.
   c. Listening constitutes only a small fraction of our communication activities.
   d. Listening does not contribute to recognizing deceit.

3. After your brain has sorted sound waves by importance, it processes the material in a part of your consciousness termed
   a. working memory
   b. selective attention
   c. long-term recall
   d. short-term memory

4. When you are listening and attempting to understand the other person's worldview, what type of listening are you utilizing?
   a. active
   b. empathic
   c. critical
   d. for enjoyment

5. If you are thinking about what happened last weekend at college while listening to your mom on the phone, you are exhibiting what type of barrier to listening?
   a. stereotypes
   b. egocentrism
   c. personal bias
   d. mental distraction

6. Which gender tends to listen in order to solve problems, is less attentive to nonverbal cues, and interrupts to switch topics?
   a. men
   b. women
   c. both genders
   d. neither gender

7. Critical thinking
   a. focuses solely on the details instead of the main point
   b. ignores the context in which communication is occurring
   c. is important when making judgments about the message being presented
   d. is only associated with listening

8. Asking questions to clarify information, paraphrasing messages, and identifying confusing areas are examples of
   a. barriers to listening
   b. listening for enjoyment
   c. techniques for checking your understanding of a message
   d. information literacy

9. Suggestions for lecture listening include
   a. focusing on the lecturer's delivery and avoiding summarizing and reviewing the information
   b. letting your attention stray in order to think creatively, listening for details, and ignoring lecture cues
   c. avoiding taking notes so you can focus on the lecture and the message delivery
   d. finding areas of interest to you, avoiding distractions, and listening for main ideas

10. The ability to locate, evaluate, and effectively use information is an important trait known as
    a. critical thinking
    b. information literacy
    c. hearing
    d. selective attention

Answers:
1. (c); 2. (b); 3. (a); 4. (b); 5. (d); 6. (a); 7. (c); 8. (c); 9. (d); 10. (b)

CRITICAL THINKING

1. Identify and define some barriers to listening that you have been aware of in your own experiences. Were you able to overcome the barriers?

2. Which of the verbal and nonverbal communication skills do you make use of in your conversa-tions? Which of them do others use when conversing with you? Are there any that you like or dislike more than others in either situation?

SELF-QUIZ

For further review, try the chapter self-quiz on the *Online Learning Center* at **www.mhhe.com/pearson3.**

REFERENCES

A dose of music may ease the pain. (2000, December). *Current Health, 27,* 2.

American Academy of Pediatrics. (2001, February). *Policy statement: Children, adolescents, and television.* Available at http://www.aap.org/policy/re0043.html.

American Library Association. (2001). *Report of the Presidential Committee on Information Literacy.* Available at http://www.ala.org/acrl/nili/ilit1st.html.

Anderson, T. H., & Armbruster, B. B. (1986). *The value of taking notes* (Reading Education Report No. 374). Champaign: University of Illinois at Urbana–Champaign, Center for the Study of Reading.

An ILA definition of listening. (1995). *ILA Listening Post, 53,* 1.

Armbruster, B. B. (2000). Taking notes from lectures. In R. Flippo & D. Caverly (Eds.), *Handbook of college reading and study strategy research* (pp. 175–199). Mahwah, NJ: Lawrence Erlbaum.

Barker, L. L. (1971). *Listening behavior.* Englewood Cliffs, NJ: Prentice-Hall.

Berman, J. M. (2005, November). Industry output and employment projections to 2014. *Monthly Labor Review,* 45–69.

Bochner, A. P., & Kelly, C. W. (1974). Interpersonal competence: Rationale, philosophy, and implementation of a conceptual framework. *Speech Teacher, 23,* 289.

Brooks, W. D., & Heath, R. W. (1989). *Speech communication* (6th ed.) Dubuque, IA: Wm. C. Brown.

Bureau of Labor Statistics. (2000, January 4). Bureau of Labor Statistics data. Available at http://146.192.4.24/cgibin/surveymost.

ClickZ. (2004, May 10). *Population explosion.* Available at http://www.clickz.com/stats/big_picture/geographics/article.php/5911_151151.

Di Batista, P. (1997). Deceivers' responses to challenges of their truthfulness: Difference between familiar lies and unfamiliar lies. *Communication Quarterly, 45,* 319–334.

Gilbert, M. B. (1988). Listening in school: I know you can hear me—but are you listening? *Journal of the International Listening Association, 2,* 121–132.

Gunn, B. (2001, February). Listening as feeling. *Strategic Finance, 82,* 12–15. Copyright 2001 by Institute of Management Accountants. Reproduced with permission of Institute of Management Accountants in the format Textbook via Copyright Clearance Center.

Haigh, G. (2006, September 22). Listen, don't just consult. *Times Educational Supplement,* p. 35.

Janusik, L. (2005). Conversational listening span: A proposed measure of conversational listening. *International Journal of Listening, 19,* 12–28.

Lenckus, D. (2005, November 28). Physician apologies, listening skills found to reduce medical malpractice claims. *Business Insurance,* p. 4.

Miller, G. A. (1994). The magical number seven, plus or minus two: Some limits on our capacity for processing information. *Psychology Review, 101,* 343–352.

O'Hair, M., O'Hair, D., & Wooden, S. (1988). Enhancement of listening skills as a prerequisite to improved study skills. *Journal of the International Listening Association, 2,* 113–120.

Nichols, M. (2006, September 15). Listen up for better sales. *Business Week Online,* p. 12.

Rankin, P. T. (1926). The measure of the ability to understand spoken language. *Dissertation Abstracts, 12,* 847.

Rehling, L. (2004). Improving teamwork through awareness of conversational styles. *Business Communication Quarterly, 67,* 475–482.

Salopek, J. (1999, September). Is anyone listening? Listening skills in the corporate setting. *Training & Development, 53,* 58–59.

Tannen, D. (2001). *You just don't understand: Women and men in conversations.* New York: HarperCollins.

Titsworth, B. S., & Kiewra, K. (1998, April). *By the numbers: The effects of organizational lecture cues on notetaking and achievement*. Paper presented at the American Educational Research Association Convention, San Diego.

UCLA Internet Report. (2000). *Surveying the digital future*. UCLA Center for Communication Policy. Available at http://www.ccp.ucla.edu.

Vandergrift, L. (2006). Second language listening: Listening ability or language proficiency? *Modern Language Journal, 90*, 6–18.

Vinson, L., & Johnson, C. (1990). The relationship between the use of hesitations and/or hedges and lecture listening: The role of perceived importance and a mediating variable. *Journal of the International Listening Association, 4*, 116–127.

Watson, K., Lazarus, C. J., & Todd, T. (1999). First-year medical students' listener preferences: A longitudinal study. *International Journal of Listening, 13*, 1–11.

Weinrauch, J., & Swanda, J. (1975). Examining the significance of listening: An exploratory study of contemporary management. *Journal of Business Communication, 13*, 25–32.

Weisfeld, C. C., & Stack, M. A. (2002). When I look into your eyes. *Psychology, Evolution and Gender, 4*, 125–147.

Werner, E. K. (1975). *A study of communication time*. Unpublished master's thesis, University of Maryland.

Wood, J. T. (2002). *Communication in our lives* (3rd ed). Belmont, CA: Wadsworth.

CHAPTER SIX

Interpersonal Communication

What will you learn?

When you have read and thought about this chapter, you will be able to:

1. Define interpersonal relationships and interpersonal communication.
2. Explain the importance of interpersonal relationships.
3. Describe the dark side of interpersonal relationships.
4. Explain the importance of friendships.
5. Name and explain the three stages in interpersonal relationships.
6. Identify some of the reasons people begin relationships.
7. Reveal ways to maintain positive relationships over time.
8. List some motivations for terminating relationships.
9. Name four essential interpersonal communication behaviors.

Interpersonal relationships can be complicated, and they sometimes require a lot of work. In this chapter you will learn about interpersonal relationships and interpersonal communication. A great deal of research has been conducted in this area of communication, and you may want to take an advanced course that focuses exclusively on interpersonal communication to learn more. For now we highlight some of the basic elements of interpersonal relationships and interpersonal communication. You will learn the stages of relational development, maintenance, and deterioration. You will also learn why people initiate relationships, maintain them, and end them. You will study such essential concepts as self-disclosing, using affectionate and supportive communication, influencing others, and developing a unique relationship. Although interpersonal communication is challenging, you will learn how to improve your communication in interpersonal relationships.

Not so long ago the term "friending" would have been considered just plain bad grammar. But today it has entered our vocabulary along with such websites as MySpace and Facebook. We live in a world where our social network is not necessarily confined to our family and those friends with whom we regularly spend time. Now that social network can consist of thousands of people from all over the world, thanks to online social networking.

Friending—social networking via the Internet—has many advantages. We can connect and communicate over long distances and at any time. We are able to discuss personal topics in the relative anonymity of cyberspace. And we can make social contacts without the messiness that sometimes characterizes face-to-face relationships. For example, if two Facebook "friends" have a disagreement, they can simply delete each other from their friends list. That delete button won't remove the person who lives next door or the "ex" who attends the same school.

Scholars are fascinated by the popularity of social networking websites. They see these websites as raising some important issues about friendship and interpersonal communication. For what reasons do people form their online relationships? How do people engage in interpersonal communication on what is actually a mass medium? How do individuals who are members of an online network make the transition to becoming true friends?

These questions about online social networking are equally interesting to pose regarding all of our interpersonal relationships. In this chapter you will learn about interpersonal communication by discovering why we join interpersonal relationships, how we communicate within those relationships, how relationships are maintained, and how to enrich them.

The Nature of Communication in Interpersonal Relationships

What Is Interpersonal Communication?

In the first chapter interpersonal communication was defined by the context, or the situation. In other words, interpersonal communication was defined as "the process of using messages to generate meaning between at least two people in a situation that allows mutual opportunities for both speaking and listening." When defined in this manner, interpersonal communication would include our interactions with strangers, with salespeople, and with waiters, as well as with our close friends, our lovers, and our family members. This definition is very broad.

Interpersonal communication may also be viewed as communication that occurs within interpersonal relationships (Miller & Steinberg, 1975). This idea suggests that interpersonal communication can be limited to those situations in which we have knowledge of the personal characteristics, qualities, or behaviors of the other person. Indeed, Miller and Steinberg assert that when we make guesses about the outcomes of conversations based on sociological or cultural information, we are communicating in a noninterpersonal way. When we make predictions based on more discriminating information about the other specific person, we are communicating interpersonally. When we communicate with others on the basis of general social interaction rules such as engaging in turn taking, making pleasantries, and discussing nonpersonal matters, we are engaging in impersonal or nonpersonal communication. When we communicate with others based on some knowledge of their uniqueness as individuals and a shared history, we are communicating interpersonally.

None of our interpersonal relationships are quite like any of our other interpersonal relationships. A friendship that you might have had in high school is not the same as your new friendships in college. Your relationship to your mother is not the same as your relationship to your father. Even if you have several intimate relationships with people, you will find that none of them is quite the same. On the one hand, our interpersonal relationships are mundane; on the other, they can also be the "sites for spiritual practice and mystical experience" (Crawford, 1996, p. 25).

Nonetheless, we have accumulated a great deal of knowledge on how to communicate more successfully in our interpersonal relationships (Julien et al., 2003). This chapter will explore that knowledge. We will consider those abilities that are essential in developing and developed relationships. But first, let us consider why we engage in interpersonal relationships.

What Are Interpersonal Relationships?

On the simplest level, relationships are associations or connections. Interpersonal relationships, however, are far more complex. **Interpersonal relationships** may be defined as associations between two people who are interdependent, who use some consistent patterns of interaction, and who have interacted for an extended period of time. Consider the different elements of this definition in more detail.

interpersonal relationships

Associations between two people who are interdependent, who use some consistent patterns of interaction, and who have interacted for an extended period of time.

- *Interpersonal relationships include two or more people.* Often, interpersonal relationships consist of just two people—a dating couple, a single parent and a child, a married couple, two close friends, or two co-workers. Interpersonal relationships can also involve more than two people—a family unit, a group of friends, or a social group.

- *Interpersonal relationships involve people who are interdependent.* Interdependence refers to people's being mutually dependent on each other and having an impact on each other. Friendship easily illustrates this concept. Your best friend, for example, may be dependent on you for acceptance and guidance. You, on the other hand, might require support and admiration. When individuals are independent of each other, or when dependence occurs only in one direction, we do not define the resulting association as an interpersonal relationship.

- *Individuals in interpersonal relationships use some consistent patterns of interaction.* These patterns may include behaviors generally understood across a variety of situations, as well as behaviors unique to the relationship. For example, a husband may always greet his wife with a kiss. This kiss is generally understood as a sign of warmth and affection. On the other hand, the husband may have unique nicknames for his wife that are not understood outside the relationship.

* *Individuals in interpersonal relationships generally have interacted for some time.* When you nod and smile at someone as you leave the classroom, when you meet a girlfriend's siblings for the first time, or when you place an order at a fast-food counter, you do not have an interpersonal relationship. Although participants use interpersonal communication to accomplish these activities, one-time interactions do not constitute interpersonal relationships. We should note, however, that interpersonal relationships might last for varying lengths of time—some are relatively short, and others continue for a lifetime.

MYTHS, METAPHORS, & MISUNDERSTANDINGS

In his book Relational Communication, *William Wilmot (1995) discusses various metaphors we have for relationships. For instance, relationships can be described as work, in that two people must negotiate and engage in a process of give-and-take; as a journey, in that people progress along a path as they move through a relationship; as a force, in that relationships are powerful, mystical, and perhaps even risky endeavors; and as a game, in that romance and perhaps friendship are viewed as a series of scripts from which individuals have to select the correct lines to win the contest. These metaphors have important implications for how people approach relationships. What do you think some of those implications are? What metaphor do you think best captures your own view of relationships?*

The Importance of Interpersonal Relationships

According to William Schutz (1976), we have three basic interpersonal needs that are satisfied through interaction with others:

1. The need for inclusion, or becoming involved with others
2. The need for affection, or holding fond or tender feeling toward another person
3. The need for control, or having the ability to influence others, our environment, and ourselves

Although we may be able to fulfill some of our physical, safety, and security needs through interactions with relative strangers, we can fulfill the other needs only through our interpersonal relationships.

The interdependent nature of interpersonal relationships suggests that people mutually satisfy their needs in this type of association. Interdependence suggests that one person is dependent on another to have some need fulfilled and that the other person (or persons) is dependent on the first to have the same or other needs fulfilled. For example, a child who is dependent on a parent may satisfy that parent's need for control. The parent, in turn, may supply the child's need for affection in hugging, kissing, or listening to the child.

Interpersonal relationships fulfill basic needs.

Complementary relationships—those in which each person supplies something the other person or persons lack—provide good examples of the manner in which we have our needs fulfilled in interpersonal relationships. A romantic involvement between a popular male and an intelligent female is an example of a complementary relationship, since the woman may find herself involved in the social events she desires and the man may find himself increasingly successful in his classes. Another example of a complementary relationship is a friendship between an introverted individual and an extroverted one. The introvert may teach her friend to be more self-reflective or to listen to others more carefully, while the extrovert might, in exchange, encourage her to be more outspoken or assertive.

Our needs also may be fulfilled in **symmetrical relationships**—those in which the participants mirror each other or are highly similar. A relationship between two intelligent individuals may reflect their need for intellectual stimulation. Two people of similar ancestry might marry in part to preserve their heritage.

Relationships are so important that we seek them out in electronic outlets as well as in face-to-face encounters. Consider the tragedy that occurred at Virginia Tech in April 2007. Thirty-two people lost their lives at the hands of a VT student. The news of the events in Blacksburg, Virginia, raced around the world through postings on the Internet.

Most interesting, from the standpoint of interpersonal relationships, are the thousands of blog entries that were written to reach out to other people. Grieving, normally conducted in face-to-face settings, occurred online. People shared their remorse and anger. They also said goodbye to friends and colleagues by posting responses on the blogs of those who they knew to have died.

Whether the other person or persons are similar to us or highly different, our needs are generally fulfilled through our relationships with them.

The Dark Side of Interpersonal Relationships

Interpersonal relationships are often pleasurable and positive experiences. However, we also know that they can be painful and negative. Spitzberg and Cupach (1998)

complementary relationships

Relationships in which each person supplies something the other person or persons lack.

symmetrical relationships

Relationships in which participants mirror each other or are highly similar.

Blogs and other online interactions were used to share information about the Virginia Tech tragedy, and they were used to mourn and grieve the loss of those who died.

have provided the most comprehensive treatment of the shadowy side of relationships. What are some of the qualities of negative relationships? Obsession that includes fatal attraction and jealousy certainly creates negative outcomes. Similarly, misunderstanding, gossip, conflict, and codependency can lead to harmful results. Abuse, which can include sexual, physical, mental, and emotional abuse, is truly harmful to individuals and destructive of relationships. Abusive relationships have probably always existed, but their presence seems more visible today as TV programs focus on the multiple kinds of abuse that occur in both marital and nonmarital relationships.

This chapter focuses primarily on positive interpersonal relationships and on how to improve interpersonal relationships. We will consider factors that seem to lead to more positive outcomes. However, note that interpersonal relationships can take a decidedly negative turn. In addition, some of the qualities that we associate with healthy relationships—self-disclosing, affectionate communication, mutual influence, and development of a unique relationship—can all become extreme and, therefore, unhealthy.

Too often textbooks speak exclusively about the positive aspects of interpersonal relationships. Readers are mistakenly led to believe that by practicing skills of openness and empathy and learning problem-solving and conflict resolution techniques, they will have successful and satisfying relationships. This unrealistic perspective leads to disillusionment when the person puts these ideas into action and does not find satisfying and successful interpersonal relationships. Effective communication, as you have been learning, is very challenging, and interpersonal communication may be the most challenging context of all.

Self-Disclosure in the Development of Interpersonal Relationships

self-disclosure

The process of making intentional revelations about yourself that others would be unlikely to know and that generally constitute private, sensitive, or confidential information.

One change that occurs as relationships become deeper and closer lies in the intentional revealing of personal information. **Self-disclosure** is the process of making intentional revelations about yourself that others would be unlikely to know and that generally constitute private, sensitive, or confidential information. Self-disclosure consists of information that is intentionally provided. Pearce and Sharp (1973) distinguish among self-disclosure, confession, and revelation. They define self-disclosure as voluntary, confession as forced or coerced information, and revelation as unintentional or inadvert communication.

Jourard (1964) suggests that self-disclosure makes one "transparent" to others, that disclosure helps others to see a person as a distinctive human being. Self-disclosure goes beyond self-description. More specifically, your position on abortion, your close relationship with your grandfather, your sexual history, your deepest fears, your proudest moments, and your problems with drugs or alcohol would be considered self-disclosure by most definitions. Self-disclosure is not always negative, but it is generally private information.

	Known to self	Not known to self
Known to others	I Open area	II Blind area
Not known to others	III Hidden area	IV Unknown area

Figure 6.1   Johari window
SOURCE: Luft, 1984.

Why Is Self-Disclosure Important?

Self-disclosure is important for three reasons: First, self-disclosure allows us to develop a greater understanding of ourselves. Consider the Johari window depicted in Figure 6.1. Joseph Luft and Harrington Ingham created this diagram to depict four kinds of information about a person. The open area (I) includes information that is known to you and to other people. Included would be your approximate height and weight, which are obvious to an observer. In addition, information that you freely disclose, such as your hometown, major, or age, is included in this quadrant. The blind area (II) consists of information that is known to others but unknown to you. Your personality characteristics that others perceive but that you do not recognize or acknowledge are included. The hidden area (III) includes information that you know about yourself but that others do not know. Any information that is hidden and that you do not self-disclose is included here. Finally, the unknown area (IV) comprises information that is unknown to you and to others. If you have not been diagnosed with a terminal disease, for instance, neither you nor others know when you will pass on.

The Johari window is not unchanging in size; rather, the quadrants can expand or contract. The Johari window may also have a different shape with different family members, friends, or acquaintances. For example, you might have a very large open area when you are considering the relationship between you and your closest friend. The hidden area may be very large when you consider the relationship among you and your classmates. As the size of one of the quadrants changes, so do all the others.

Self-disclosure allows you to develop a more positive attitude about yourself and others. Self-disclosure allows you to develop more meaningful relationships with others. Have you ever experienced a problem or faced a difficult situation? Most of us have, and we know that sharing our fears or telling others about our anguish provides comfort. For example, imagine that you committed a traffic violation and were caught. You might feel very guilty for doing the wrong thing, for having to pay a large fine, and for risking the loss of your driver's license. If you can find the courage to talk about your feelings to a friend, you might find that you are not alone, that almost everyone receives a traffic fine at one time or another.

Similarly, if you have recently experienced the loss of a family member, you may find that talking about your feelings and sharing your grief will lead to positive growth for you. Hastings (2000) found that self-disclosure is a powerful form of communication in grieving and in healing a fractured identity.

Through self-disclosure, relationships grow in depth and meaning. Partners in romantic relationships, for example, report greater feelings of security when self-disclosure between them is intentional and honest (Le Poire et al., 1997). When you self-disclose more to others, they will most likely disclose more to you. On the other hand, the inability to self-disclose can result in the end of a relationship. Without the opportunity for self-disclosure and active listening, relationships appear to be doomed to shallowness, superficiality, and termination.

At the same time, self-disclosure can be used inappropriately. Have you ever sat on an airplane next to a stranger who revealed highly personal information to you? Have you ever dated someone who insisted on sharing private information too early in the relationship? Have you ever had friends who told you negative information about themselves long before you knew virtually anything else about them? In the next section we will consider some of the findings about self-disclosure that may provide guidelines for your self-disclosing behavior.

What Factors Affect Appropriate Self-Disclosure?

Disclosure generally increases as relational intimacy increases. We do not provide our life story to people we have just met. Instead, in the developing relationship, we reveal an increasing amount of information. We might begin with positive information that is not highly intimate and then begin to share more personal information as we learn to trust the other person. In this way our disclosure tends to be incremental, or to increase over time.

Disclosure tends to be reciprocal. This conclusion is related to the previous one. When people offer us information about themselves, we tend to return the behavior in kind. Indeed, when people reciprocate self-disclosure, we tend to view them positively; when they do not, we tend to view them as incompetent (Cozby, 1972, 1973; Hosman & Tardy, 1980). Dindia, Fitzpatrick, and Kenny (1997) studied dyadic interaction between women and men and strangers and spouses. They concluded that in conversations, disclosure of highly intimate feelings was reciprocal. Reciprocity is also shown in nonverbal behaviors. Those who engaged in low-intimacy conditions also reciprocated by becoming less nonverbally pleasant and fluent as well as more verbally hostile. They also became more vocally anxious and less composed after their partners decreased intimacy.

Reciprocal disclosure generally does not occur in families. While parents have an expectation of self-disclosure from their children and adolescents, they do not perceive a need to reciprocate. A variety of factors affect adolescents' disclosures to their parents. Adolescents do not generally feel the need to disclose to their parents, and they are even more reluctant to disclose if their behavior is not sanctioned by their parents (Darling, Cumsille, Caldwell, & Dowdy, 2006; Smetana, Metzger, Gettman, & Campione-Barr, 2006). Grandparents may become the target of self-disclosures since they are sometimes seen as more empathetic and positive (Tam, Hewstone, Harwood, Voci, & Kenworthy, 2006).

Negative disclosure is directly related to the intimacy of the relationship; however, positive disclosure does not necessarily increase as the relationship becomes more intimate. What does this mean? As we become closer to another person, we are more likely to reveal negative information about ourselves. Positive information, on the other hand, flows through conversations from the earliest developmental stages throughout the lifetime of the relationship. Hence, negative information increases over time, but positive disclosure does not necessarily increase.

Disclosure may be avoided for a variety of reasons. Self-disclosure does not flow freely on all topics. Indeed, relational partners may avoid self-disclosure for reasons of self-protection, relationship protection, partner unresponsiveness, and social appropriateness. As Afifi and Guerrero observe, "Some things are better left unsaid" (1998, p. 231). At the same time, topics that are taboo under some conditions may be appropriate later, when conditions change (Roloff & Johnson, 2001).

People do not always avoid self-disclosure for noble reasons. College students who were in close relationships were asked if they disclosed their sexual histories before engaging in sex. While nearly all the students surveyed felt they were knowledgeable about safe sex, over 40% did not realize that revealing one's sexual history is a safe-sex practice. One-third of those who were sexually active had not disclosed their past sexual history with at least one partner prior to becoming sexually involved. And at least one-fifth of the sexually active students purposefully misrepresented their sexual history to their sex partners (Lucchetti, 1999).

Disclosure varies across cultures. Self-disclosure is not uniformly valued or disvalued around the world. For example, Chinese professionals view interpersonal communication differently in Chinese organizations and in American businesses. They view Chinese interactions to be characterized by blunt assertiveness, smooth amiability, and surface humility. They view American workplaces to be composed of sophisticated kindness, manipulative "stroking," and casual spontaneity (Wang & Chang, 1999). Koreans and Americans avoid making requests of others for different reasons. Koreans are concerned with avoiding negative evaluation from the hearer and avoiding hurting the other person's feelings, while Americans are more concerned with clarity (Kim & Bresnahan, 1994). These differences most likely transfer to differences in disclosures as well.

Disclosure varies by co-cultures. Males and females do not disclose to the same extent. Females intend to self-disclose more than do males, and, in fact, they do so. Males disclose more negative information than do females, while females disclose more honest information on the Internet than do males (Punyanunt-Carter, 2006). Males and females show some similar patterns in self-disclosure in that men use their male best friends and women use their female best friends equally as confidants.

Relational satisfaction and disclosure are curvilinearly related. Satisfaction is lowest with no disclosure and with excessive disclosure; it is highest when self-disclosure is provided at moderate levels. Consider your own personal relationships. Does this conclusion appear to be accurate?

The Importance of Friendships in Interpersonal Relationships

Friendship is important as it contributes to our well-being. People who have harmonious sibling relationships and same-gender friends report the highest levels of well-being (Sherman, Lansford, & Volling, 2006). While we celebrate romantic relationships, we do not similarly honor friendships. Rawlins (1992) notes that we ought to have a "friendship day" because our friendships are at least as important as our romantic relationships.

What does friendship mean? Friendships can be based on shared activities or on the level of information that we exchange with others. Young adolescents report that their friendships are based on shared activities, whereas emerging adults report that their friendships are based on self-disclosure (Radmacher & Azmitia, 2006). The communication of private information appears to gain in importance as people mature.

Friendships also change over time. Most people identify both family members and nonfamily members as friends. As people age, family members become more salient as friends (Pahl & Pevalin, 2005). For many older men, their only friend is their wife (Rawlins, 1922), though the same is not true for older women.

As you develop, your friendships are perceived to improve. Do friendships actually improve over time? While we cannot be sure, we do know that people *perceive* their friendships to be better over time (Way & Greene, 2006). Perhaps people come to understand the importance of friendship as they mature.

The quality of friendships is affected by other psychological predispositions. For example, individuals, attachment styles seem to predict friendships. People who are securely attached to others have lower levels of conflict with their friends and are able to rise above problems in their friendships. People who are avoidant, or not attached, experience higher levels of conflict and lower levels of companionship (Saferstein, Neimeyer, & Hagans, 2005).

Rawlins (1992) provides a six-stage model of how friendships develop. The first stage, role-limited interaction, includes an encounter in which individuals are polite and careful with their disclosures. Second, friendly relations occur when the two people determine that they have mutual interests or share other common ground. Third, moving toward friendship allows them to introduce a personal topic or to set up times to get together. Fourth, in nascent friendship they think of themselves as friends and begin to establish their own private ways of interacting. Fifth, the friends feel established in each other's lives, in what is termed a stabilized friendship. Finally, friendships may move to a waning friendship stage when the relationship diminishes. Not all friendships, however, reach this sixth stage.

Friendships are maintained differently depending on the intent of the relational partners. Rawlins (1992) notes that issues of romantic attraction must be negotiated early in a relationship. Guerrero and Chavez (2005) studied friends who both wanted the relationship to become romantic (mutual romance), friends neither of whom wanted the friendship to become romantic (platonic), and friends one of whom desired romance but felt that the partner did not (desiring or rejecting romance). They found that people in the mutual romance situation generally reported the most relationship maintenance behavior. People who were in the platonic or the rejecting-romance situations had fewer routine contacts and activities, were more likely to talk about other romantic situations, and were less flirtatious. People who were in the desiring-romance and mutual romance situations reported the most relationship talk. Clearly, friendships are dynamic and may lead to romantic relationships.

Friendships are not necessarily defined the same way in other cultures. People in collectivist cultures tend to have more intimate, but fewer, friendships. As people have more contact with others in the world, however, these patterns are showing signs of change. For example, Indonesian people, traditionally from a collectivisitic culture, now display extensive social contacts (French, Bae, Pidada, & Okhwa, 2006).

A new development, made possible by mediated communication, is friendships on the Internet. However, these friendships are perceived as less close and less supportive than are friendships that originate in face-to-face contact. Internet friends are also less likely to be engaged in joint activities (Mesch & Talmud, 2006).

Cross-Cultural Relationships

Because our culture is becoming increasingly diverse, the likelihood that you will be part of a cross-cultural friendship, or even romantic relationship, is far greater now than ever before. In many respects, cross-cultural relationships work like any other type of relationship—we enter into them for many of the same reasons; the processes of self-disclosure work the same; we even initiate and maintain them using many of the same skills.

One difference between same- and cross-cultural relationships is that we may feel more tentative in initiating a dialogue with a person from another culture. Perhaps this is because we are afraid of language barriers or accidentally saying something wrong. In other situations, such as when two people are assigned to a residence hall room as roommates, the relationship may be forced upon them. In either case, understanding how to develop a strong cross-cultural relationship is important. One approach to establishing such a relationship is to view it as a cooperative learning opportunity in which both participants work together to achieve a mutually shared understanding while learning about each other's cultures (Ronesi, 2003). In approaching the relationship in this way, try to do the following:

1. *Have meaningful personal interaction.* If you feel uncomfortable in the initial stages of interaction, you may be tempted to stick to very safe topics of conversation. Try to talk about some more personal and meaningful topics as well. For instance, what are the similarities and differences between your families? What religions do you practice? What are your hometowns like? What work experiences have you had? By talking about more personal topics like these, you will begin to learn about each other and start the self-disclosure cycle.

2. *Maintain equal status.* Research shows that when one person assumes a role of "leader" or "teacher," the relationship will have more trouble developing. Both members of the relationship should recognize that each has something unique to offer in terms of knowledge, creativity, openness, listening, and so on. Remembering to keep the new relationship focused on interpersonal closeness rather than task concerns can help prevent a perception of inequality in the early stages of the relationship.

3. *Find ways to build interdependence.* Any relationship will be stronger if both individuals bring something to the relationship. If each can find ways to help the other, interdependence will form, and the bond of the relationship will grow stronger.

4. *Respect individual differences.* People from different cultures are like anyone else; some are shy while others are outgoing; some are very cerebral while others are very practical; some like romantic comedies while others like action shows—the list goes on and on. You should not be surprised that individual differences will occasionally cause disagreement. Remember that such differences do not mean that you cannot make a cross-cultural relationship work; it may simply mean that you don't like certain personality characteristics. Just as with friends from your own culture, you occasionally have to overlook minor disagreement in light of the many other areas of agreement.

The Stages in Interpersonal Relationships

Communication and relationship development are symbiotic; that is, communication affects the growth of relationships, and the growth of relationships affects communicative behavior (Miller, 1976).

Relational Development

Knapp and Vangelisti (2000) identified 10 interaction stages of interpersonal relationships. Baxter (1983, 1984) and others have experimentally attempted to validate these stages. The model that Knapp and Vangelisti presented generally appears valid. Furthermore, this developmental model helps organize and explain relational changes. The first five stages cover **relational development**—the process by which relationships grow.

relational development

In Knapp's model the process by which relationships grow.

- *Stage 1: Initiating.* Is the short beginning period of an interaction. This stage involves first impressions, the sizing up of the other person, and attempts to find commonality.
- *Stage 2: Experimenting.* Occurs when the two people have clearly decided to find out more about each other, to quit scouting, and to start getting serious about each other. This stage includes sharing personal information at a safe level: what music, people, classes, professors, and food they like or dislike.
- *Stage 3: Intensifying.* Involves active participation, mutual concern, and an awareness that the relationship is developing because neither party has quit and both people are encouraging its development.
- *Stage 4: Integrating.* Means the two people start mirroring each other's behavior in manner, dress, and language. They merge their social circles, designate common property, and share interests and values.
- *Stage 5: Bonding.* Occurs when the two people commit to each other. They may exchange personal items as a symbol of commitment; they may participate in a public ritual that bonds them, as in the case of marriage; or they may vow to be friends for life and demonstrate that commitment by always being present at important points in each other's life.

Relational Maintenance

relational maintenance

In Knapp's model the process of keeping a relationship together.

Once individuals have bonded in a relationship, they enter a stage of **relational maintenance** in which they begin establishing strategies for keeping the relationship together. Although Altman and Taylor, as well as Knapp and Vangelisti, briefly considered relational maintenance, they did not do so in much detail. Wilmot (1980) suggests that relationships stabilize when the partners reach a basic level of agreement about what they want from the relationship. In addition, relationships can stabilize at any level of intimacy, and even "stabilized" relationships may have internal movement.

While the developmental model created by Altman and Taylor and extended by others would suggest that relational maintenance represents a plateau or leveling-off of the relationship, most evidence suggests that the maintenance phase is not best represented by a flat line. Instead, people become more intimate or closer at some periods and more distant and less close at other times. The maintenance phase of a relationship might be more appropriately depicted as a jagged, rather than a straight, line.

dialectic

The tension that exists between two conflicting or interacting forces, elements, or ideas.

contradictions

In dialectic theory the idea that each person in a relationship might have two opposing desires for maintaining the relationship.

Indeed, Baxter and her colleagues (Baxter, 1993; Baxter & Montgomery, 1996; Dindia & Baxter, 1987) and other researchers (Hause & Pearson, 1994; Lowrey-Hart & Pearson, 1997; Pawlowski, 1998) have developed and demonstrated the importance of dialectical theory in interpersonal relationships. **Dialectic** refers to the tension that exists between two conflicting or interacting forces, elements, or ideas. When dialectic theory is applied to interpersonal relationships, we acknowledge that relationships often incorporate contradictions or contrasts within them and that relationships are always in process. By **contradictions** we mean that each person might have two opposing desires for maintaining the relationship—you want to be with your partner, but you also have a need for space and time away from him or her. By

TABLE 6.1 BAXTER'S DIALECTIC TENSIONS	
INTEGRATION	SEPARATION
"Let's move in together."	"When we get married, I plan on keeping my maiden name and continuing in my career."
STABILITY	CHANGE
"I'm glad we've never moved."	"I'm feeling restless. I think it is time to plan a vacation!"
EXPRESSION	PRIVACY
"I did absolutely the dumbest thing last night. Let me tell you."	"I would rather not explain how I spent the weekend."

process we mean that relationships are always changing. Thus relational maintenance cannot be depicted as a flat line, but rather one that has peaks and valleys.

What are some of the primary dialectics identified by Baxter? Three emerged in the early work. The dialectic of integration/separation suggests the tension between wanting to be separate entities and wanting to be integrated with another person. The dialectic of stability/change suggests the tension between wanting events, conversations, and behavior to be the same and desiring change. The dialectic of expression/privacy suggests the tension between wanting to self-disclose and be completely open and wanting to be private and closed. Table 6.1 summarizes Baxter's primary dialectics.

Relational Deterioration

The last five stages identified by Knapp and Vangelisti (2000) occur during **relational deterioration**—the process by which relationships disintegrate.

relational deterioration

In Knapp's model the process by which relationships disintegrate.

- *Stage 1. Differentiating.* Occurs when the two partners start emphasizing their individual differences instead of their similarities. Rather than going to movies together, he plays basketball with his friends and she golfs with her friends. Some separate activities are healthy in a relationship, but in differentiation the pulling apart is to get away from each other.
- *Stage 2. Circumscribing.* Is characterized by decreased interaction, shorter times together, and less depth to sharing. The two people might go to public events together but do little together in private. Each person figuratively draws a circle around him- or herself, a circle that does not include the other person. The exchange of feelings, the demonstrations of commitment, and the obvious pairing are disappearing.
- *Stage 3. Stagnating.* Suggests a lack of activity, especially activity together. Interactions are minimal, functional, and only for convenience. The two people now find conversation and sharing awkward instead of stimulating. During this stage each individual may be finding an outlet elsewhere for developmental stages.
- *Stage 4. Avoiding.* Brings reluctance to interact, active avoidance, and even hostility. The two former partners are now getting in each other's way, each

Relational deterioration is marked by differentiating behavior.

seeing the other as an obstacle or a limitation. The amount of their talk may actually increase, but the content and intent are negative. Arguing, fighting, disagreeing, and flight mark their interactions.

- *Stage 5. Terminating.* Occurs when the two people are no longer seen by others or themselves as a pair. They increasingly dissociate, share nothing, claim common goods as individual property, and give back or get rid of the symbols of togetherness. Divorce, annulment, and dissolution are manifestations of this stage, as are people who no longer live together, former friends who have nothing to do with each other, and roommates who take separate and distant quarters.

Knapp and Vangelisti (2000) acknowledge that individuals do not progress in a linear way through the stages of development and deterioration (summarized in Table 6.2). They propose that people move within stages to maintain their equilibrium or stability. In other words, people might behave in a way that is more characteristic of one stage even though they are generally maintaining the interaction patterns of another stage.

In addition, communication skills can alter the relational trajectory. In relationships that are dysfunctional or deteriorating, communication can help to heal or remedy problems. In new relationships communication may stimulate relational development and growth. Aging relationships may be functional or dysfunctional. Communication skills allow us to subscribe to realistic hope in our relationships.

TABLE 6.2   AN OVERVIEW OF RELATIONAL DETERIORATION STAGES

Process	Stage	Representative Dialogue
	1. Differentiating	"I Just don't like big social gatherings."
		"Sometimes I don't understand you. This is one area where I'm certainly not like you at all."
	2. Circumscribing	"Did you have a good time on your trip?"
		"What time will dinner be ready?"
Coming Apart	3. Stagnating	"What's there to talk about?"
		"Right. I know what you're going to say, and you know what I'm going to say."
	4. Avoiding	"I'm so busy, I just don't know when I'll be able to see you."
		"If I'm not around when you try, you'll understand."
	5. Terminating	"I'm leaving you . . . and don't bother trying to contact me."
		"Don't worry."

SOURCE: Knapp and Vangelisti, 1996.

Finally, individuals do not move through each of these stages with everyone they meet. Research has shown that people base decisions to develop relationships on such factors as physical attractiveness, personal charisma, and communication behaviors (Friedman, Riggio, & Casella, 1988; Sabatelli & Rubin, 1986). In general, we are more likely to attempt to develop relationships with people who are attractive, emotionally expressive, extroverted, and spontaneous. In the next section we will consider some of the theories that suggest why we select some people with whom to relate and why we neglect, or even reject, other people.

Motivations for Initiating Relationships

Motivations for Initiating, Maintaining, and Terminating Relationships

What happens in initial interactions with people? While millions of people exist in this world, we have interpersonal relationships with a relatively small number of them. How do you determine which people you will select to be your friends, lovers, or family members? How are you attracted to them? Why do you cultivate relationships with them? How does communication figure into the equation?

First, **proximity**—the location, distance, or range between persons and things—is obvious but important. You are probably not going to have relationships with people from places you have never been. You are most likely to find others where you spend most of your time. For this reason a roommate can easily become a friend. Co-workers, too, often become friends (Sias & Cahill, 1998). People who attend the same religious services, belong to the same social clubs, or are members of the same gang are most likely to become friends. People who share a major or a dormitory, cafeteria, car pool, or part of the seating chart in a class are also likely candidates. To underline the potency of proximity, consider that changes in location (high school to college and college to job) often change relationship patterns.

Second, we select, from all the people we see, the ones we find high in **attractiveness,** which includes physical attractiveness, how desirable a person is to work with, and how much "social value" the person has for others (McCroskey & McCain, 1974). In other words, a person who is desirable to work with, who seems to have "social value" in that others also show interest in him or her, and who physically looks good to us is attractive (Pearson & Spitzberg, 1990). Attractiveness is not universal. The attractiveness and the importance of particular physical features vary from culture to culture (Hetsroni & Bloch, 1999) and from person to person. Because of perceptual differences, you will not be looking for the same person as everyone else.

proximity

The location, distance, or range between persons and things.

attractiveness

A concept that includes physical attractiveness, how desirable a person is to work with, and how much "social value" the person has for others.

TRY ◆ THIS

List the features of attractiveness of your best friend, your boyfriend or girlfriend, or your lover or spouse.

responsiveness

The idea that we tend to select our friends and loved ones from people who demonstrate positive interest in us.

Responsiveness, the idea that we tend to select our friends and loved ones from people who demonstrate positive interest in us, is another feature of attraction. Not everyone responds positively to us, but someone who does is likely to get our attention. Few characteristics are more attractive than someone who actively listens to us, thinks

We select friends
from among people
who are responsive
to us.

our jokes are funny, finds our vulnerabilities endearing, and sees our faults as amusing. In short, we practically never select our friends from among those who dislike us.

similarity

The idea that our
friends and loved ones
are usually people who
like or dislike the same
things we do.

Similarity, the idea that our friends and loved ones are usually people who like or dislike the same things we do, is another feature of attractiveness. People in interpersonal relationships often look, act, or think similarly. Whatever we consider most important is the similarity we seek, so some friends or people in loving relationships are bound by their interests, others by their ideology, and still others by their mutual likes and dislikes. A hard-core environmentalist is unlikely to be close personal friends with a developer, whereas the developer is likely to select friends from people in the same business, country club, and suburb. Thousands of people find their friends in the same circle where they work: clerical workers with clerical workers, managers with managers, and bosses with bosses. Similarity is a powerful source of attraction.

complementarity

The idea that we some-
times bond with peo-
ple whose strengths are
our weaknesses.

Complementarity is the idea that we sometimes bond with people whose strengths are our weaknesses. Whereas you may be slightly shy, your friend may be assertive. In situations that call for assertiveness, she may play that role for you. A math-loving engineer may find friendship with a people-loving communication major, who takes care of the engineer's social life while the engineer helps his friend with math courses. Having a friend or loved one who is too much like you can result in competitiveness that destroys the friendship.

Motivations for Maintaining Relationships

After you have gotten to know someone, why do you continue to relate to him or her? You may begin to relate to dozens of people, but you do not continue friendships, family relationships, or love relationships with everyone with whom you start a relationship. Consider the friends you had in elementary school or high school. Do you maintain any of those friendships now? Have you established an intimate relationship with someone but broken up with her or him? Do you have family members with whom you are close and others with whom you hardly speak? Let us consider some of the motivators that encourage continuing a relationship.

Although we initially develop a relationship on the basis of such factors as attractiveness and personal charisma, we maintain relationships for different reasons. Maintained relationships invite certain levels of predictability, or certainty (Perse & Rubin, 1989). Indeed, we attempt to create strategies that will provide us with additional personal information about our relational partners (Berger & Kellermann, 1989). We are also less concerned with partners' expressive traits (such as being extroverted and spontaneous) and more concerned with their ability to focus on us through empathic, caring, and concerned involvement (Davis & Oathout, 1987). Indeed, as relationships are maintained, partners not only become more empathic but also begin to mirror each other's behavior.

Co-cultural Differences

Motivations for maintaining relationships are not simple. Many co-cultural differences affect our maintenance behaviors. For example, women use more maintenance strategies than do men (Ragsdale, 1996). People with different ethnicities express different primary needs in their interpersonal relationships. According to Collier (1996), "Latinos emphasized relational support, Asian Americans emphasized a caring, positive exchange of ideas, African Americans emphasized respect and acceptance, and Anglo Americans emphasized recognizing the needs of the individual" (p. *i*). People from different generations view intergenerational communication differently (Harwood, McKee, & Lin, 2000). In addition, people display different levels of nonverbal involvement and intimacy with their romantic partners (Guerrero, 1996).

Satisfying Relationships

Couples can achieve satisfying and long-term relationships, however. Pearson (1996) looked at couples who had been happily married for more than 40 years. She found that many of these marriages were characterized by stubbornness ("This marriage will succeed no matter what"), distortion ("She is the most beautiful woman in the world"), unconditional acceptance (regardless of faults), and the continuous push and pull of autonomy or independence versus unity or interdependence. Maintaining positive, satisfying relationships is not easy, but the people who are the most satisfied with their relationships are probably those who have worked hardest at maintaining them. Communicatively, people in long-term and satisfied relationships are distinctive from those in short-term or unhappy relationships. Sillars, Shellen, McIntosh, and Pomegranate (1997) found that people in long-term and satisfied relationships are more likely to use joint rather than individual identity pronouns ("we" and "us" rather than "I" or "me").

Motivations for Terminating Relationships

Although our goal may be to maintain satisfying relationships, this outcome is not always possible. Relationships do not last. About half of all marriages end in divorce, and in second and third marriages, the failure rate is even higher. Why do interpersonal relationships end? What factors encourage people to seek the conclusion, rather than the continuation, of a relationship? We consider a few of these factors here.

TRY ◆ THIS

All of us have terminated relationships. Consider a relationship that you terminated within the last year or two. What factors caused you to terminate it?

hurtful messages

Messages that create
emotional pain or
upset.

Hurtful messages—messages that create emotional pain or upset—can end a relationship. Hurtful messages occur in most relationships, even those in which couples are very satisfied, and do not always end in disruption of the relationship. However, if hurtful messages become a pattern or are so intense that one partner cannot forget them, they can be disruptive. Why do some hurtful messages create significant relational problems while others do not? Duck and Pond (1989) suggest that the relational history, the closeness of the couple, and their satisfaction with the relationship all affect how people perceive and respond to their own interaction.

Hurtful messages may be more or less harmful to the relationship depending on the reaction of the second person. Vangelisti and Crumley (1998) determined that people responded in one of three ways: active verbal responses (for example, attacking the other, defending oneself, or asking for an explanation), acquiescent responses (for example, apologizing or crying), and invulnerable responses (for instance, laughing or ignoring the message). People who felt extremely hurt were more likely to use acquiescing responses than were those who were less hurt. People who were less hurt more often used invulnerability than did those who felt extremely hurt. They also found that relational satisfaction was positively related with active verbal responses.

**deceptive
communication**

The practice of deliber-
ately making some-
body believe things
that are not true.

Deceptive communication—the practice of deliberately making somebody believe things that are untrue—can also lead to relational dissatisfaction and termination. Probably, all relational partners engage in some level of deception from time to time. The "little white lie," the nonrevelation of the "whole truth," and the omission of some details are commonplace. However, deliberate and regular deception can lead to the destruction of trust and the end of the relationship.

NCA Ethics
Credo

We believe that truthfulness, accuracy, honesty, and reason are essential to the integrity of communication.

People may tell familiar lies (stories that are manufactured and that they tell again and again), or they may tell unfamiliar lies (untruths that are constructed on the spot). When they do so, they vary their behavior depending on whether they are telling familiar or unfamiliar lies by altering the length of their pauses, their eye gaze, and the amount of smiling and laughing in which they engage. Observers, however, cannot detect these alterations (di Battista, 1997). In short, we do not seem to be very accurate in determining deceptive behaviors.

aggressiveness

Assertion of one's rights
at the expense of oth-
ers and care about
one's own needs but
no one else's.

Aggressiveness occurs when people stand up for their rights at the expense of others and care about their own needs but no one else's. Aggressiveness might help you get your way a few times, but ultimately, others will avoid you and let their resentment show. People who engage in aggressive behavior may do so because of negative self-concepts or because they have learned this pattern of behavior growing up. Martin and Anderson (1997) show that both sons and daughters have patterns of verbal aggression that are similar to their mother's.

argumentativeness

The quality or state of
being argumentative;
synonymous with con-
tentiousness or com-
bativeness.

Aggressiveness is not the same as argumentativeness. **Argumentativeness,** defined as the quality or state of being argumentative, is synonymous with being contentious or combative. People who are argumentative are not verbally aggressive (Semic & Canary, 1997). Indeed, argumentative people may value argument as a normal social communicative activity. Argumentation varies across the life span (Schullery & Schullery, 2003). Argumentativeness patterns are shown to be similar between mothers and their children (Martin & Anderson, 1997).

Defensiveness occurs when a person feels attacked. Jack Gibb (1991) suggests that trust is essential to healthy relationships. But trust must be established between individuals, and not be based on roles, positions, or status. In other words, people should come to relationships without all of the trappings of the roles they play. Reducing defensiveness is essential to building trust.

defensiveness

Occurs when a person feels attacked.

Gibb distinguished between behaviors that encourage defensiveness and those that reduce defensiveness. He identified evaluation, control, neutrality, superiority, certainty, and strategy as promoting defensive behaviors in others:

- *Evaluation* occurs when an individual makes a judgment about another person or his or her behavior.
- *Control* suggests that the speaker does not allow the second person to join in the discussion of how a problem should be solved.
- *Neutrality* means that the originator of the message does not show concern for the second person.
- *Superiority* occurs when the first person treats the second as a person of lower status.
- *Certainty* denotes a lack of openness to alternative ideas.
- *Strategy* refers to the employment of manipulative and premeditative behavior.

Gibb then categorized the following behaviors as reducing defensiveness: description, problem orientation, empathy, equality, provisionalism, and spontaneity. People who use *description* report their observations rather than offering evaluative comments. People with a *problem orientation* do not act as though they have the solution, but are eager to discuss multiple ideas. *Empathy* implies concern for others, as shown through careful listening for both the content and the intent of the other's message. *Equality* means that the communicator demonstrates that he or she is neither superior nor inferior to the second person. *Provisionalism* suggests that the communicator does not communicate certainty or a total conviction, but is open to other ideas. *Spontaneity* implies naturalness and a lack of premeditation.

Gibb suggests that people replace those behaviors that create defensiveness with those that reduce it. Table 6.3 depicts the paired concepts. For example, rather than

TABLE 6.3   JACK GIBB'S CONTRIBUTION TO REDUCING DEFENSIVENESS

CREATE DEFENSIVENESS	REDUCE DEFENSIVENESS
Evaluation	Description
Control	Problem orientation
Neutrality	Empathy
Superiority	Equality
Certainty	Provisionalism
Strategy	Spontaneity

telling someone that he is late for a meeting and you do not appreciate waiting, you might note the time that he arrived and inquire empathically about his circumstances. Rather than being indifferent toward others and nonverbally suggesting that you are superior, you might make inquiries about them and provide messages expressing your multiple similarities.

◄ **SKILL** BUILDER ►

Rewrite the following statements in a way that would decrease defensiveness. Use the categories generated by Gibb. For example, you would replace evaluation with description.

1. *"What's wrong with you anyway?"*
2. *"Who's responsible for the mess in the library?"*
3. *"I don't really care what you do."*
4. *"We're not leaving here until I say we're leaving."*
5. *"We don't need to meet. I know how to solve the problem."*
6. *"I don't need your help."*

Essential Interpersonal Communication Behaviors

Many of the communication behaviors discussed in this text are important in interpersonal communication. You need to be aware of factors like perception, have a good self-concept, provide clear verbal and nonverbal cues to others, and be able to listen and empathize as others provide messages to you. Some additional communication behaviors are associated with effective interpersonal communication. In an interpersonal relationship you show affection and support, you influence others, and you develop the unique nature of the interpersonal relationship. In this section we consider these three interpersonal communication areas: affectionate communication; influence, which includes compliance-gaining and interpersonal dominance; and the development of the exclusive relationship.

Using Affectionate and Supportive Communication

Affection, the holding of fond or tender feelings toward another person, is essential in interpersonal relationships. You express your affectionate feelings for others in interpersonal relationships in a variety of ways. Often these expressions are nonverbal as you touch, hug, kiss, or caress another person. You also engage in verbal statements of affection such as "I care about you," "I really like being with you," or "I love you."

A number of variables affect the appropriateness of statements of affection. Therefore, affectionate communication may be viewed as risk-laden. Among the factors that you will consider when you choose to offer affectionate statements to a relational partner are your own and your partner's sex, the kind of relationship you have (platonic or romantic), the privacy and emotional intensity of the situation, and your predispositions (Floyd, 1997a, 1997b; Floyd & Morman, 1998, 2000). Telling another person that you love him or her may hold significantly different

Analyze the use of effective and supporting communication by watching the video clip titled "Opposites Attract" on the Online Learning Center.

meanings depending on your sex, your partner's sex, your past relationships, the degree of privacy of the situation in which you choose to share your feelings, and the other person's feelings about you.

Although generally positive, the expression of affection may not always be so. If the receiver of the affectionate message does not reciprocate, the sender may be embarrassed or feel that she or he has lost face. Floyd and Burgoon (1999) found that, indeed, expressions of liking do not always result in positive relational outcomes. Recall a time when you expressed affection toward another person and she or he did not return the same warmth. How did you feel? In general, when people have particular expectancies about communicative behavior and those expectancies are not met, both disruption and adaptation follow (LePoire & Yoshimura, 1999).

Supportive communication is also important in interpersonal communication. Support may include giving advice, expressing concern, and offering assistance. Although people generally respond well to supportive communication, the type of support preferred may vary as a result of the receiver's age (Caplan & Samter, 1999) and the support provider's goals (MacGeorge, 2001). In times of distress, comforting messages (suggesting a diversion, offering assistance, and expressing optimism, for example) encourage people to feel less upset. At the same time, the recipients of such messages may also feel demeaned. The distressed person is most likely to feel less upset when the comforting message is offered by a close friend rather than an acquaintance (Clark, Pierce, Hzu, Toosley, & Williams, 1998). Comfort, then, is viewed as most positive in close interpersonal relationships rather than in more distant ones.

Influencing Others

Later in this book we will discuss influencing others in public communication settings. For now, we consider the notion of influencing others in interpersonal settings. In general, influence is the power that a person has to affect other people's thinking or actions. In interpersonal communication, influence has been studied widely. One body of research has focused on compliance-gaining and compliance-resisting. **Compliance-gaining** may be defined as those attempts made by a source of messages to influence a target "to perform some desired behavior that the target otherwise might not perform" (Wilson, 1998, p. 273). Compliance-gaining occurs frequently in interpersonal communication. We ask a friend for advice, we ask a parent for financial assistance, or we encourage a relational partner to feel more committed. Children become more skillful at identifying situational and personal cues in possible compliance-gaining as they develop, with girls showing more sensitivity than boys (Marshall & Levy, 1998).

Compliance-resisting occurs when targets of influence messages refuse to comply with requests. When resisting requests, people often offer reasons for their refusal (Saeki & O'Keefe, 1994). People who are more sensitive to others and who are more adaptive are more likely to engage in further attempts to influence (Ifert & Roloff, 1997). Indeed, they may address some anticipated obstacles when they initiate their original request and they may adapt later attempts to influence by offering counterarguments.

For example, if you are asking a friend to borrow his car, you might consider some of the reasons he might refuse. He might state that he needs his car at the same time, that the last time you borrowed his car you returned it with no gas, or that the only time he ever hears from you is when you want something from him. In your initial message you might suggest to him that you believe you have been neglecting him and that you want to spend some time together and, in addition, that you have not been

compliance-gaining

Those attempts made by a source of messages to influence a target "to perform some desired behavior that the target otherwise might not perform."

compliance-resisting

The refusal of targets of influence messages to comply with requests.

as considerate as you could be with him. When he suggests that he needs his car at the same time that you do, you might offer to use his car at a different time.

Developing a Unique Relationship

Interpersonal relationships are defined by their uniqueness. In a sense relational couples create a "culture of two" (Betcher, 1987). They may have unique names for each other and shared experiences that others do not have with them, and they may develop distinctive patterns of interaction. Bruess and Pearson (1993) found that couples who created **personal idioms**—or unique forms of expression and language understood only by them—expressed high relational satisfaction. Did your parents have a unique name for you that no one else used? Do you have a way of referring to an event with an intimate that no one else understands? Do you have a way of expressing a thought, idea, or need to a friend that no one else can decipher? All of these are personal idioms.

Through playful interaction and the creation of **rituals**—formalized patterns of actions or words followed regularly—couples create a shared culture. Rituals may become so routine that we do not realize they are comprised in the fabric of a relationship. However, if a relational partner does not enact them, uneasiness often follows. For example, can you recall a time when your partner failed to call you, say "I love you," bring you flowers or a gift, or enact another regular behavior? Although the importance of the ritual was perhaps never verbalized, you probably felt hurt or neglected.

Bruess and Pearson (1997) suggest that the following rituals are important characteristics of long-term interpersonal relationships:

- *Couple-time rituals*—for example, exercising together or having dinner together every Saturday night
- *Idiosyncratic/symbolic rituals*—for example, calling each other by a special name or celebrating the anniversary of their first date
- *Daily routines and tasks*—for example, if living together, one partner always preparing the evening meal and the other always cleaning up afterward

personal idioms

Unique forms of expression and language understood only by individual couples.

rituals

Formalized patterns of actions or words followed regularly.

- *Intimacy rituals*—for example, giving each other a massage or, when apart, talking on the telephone before going to bed
- *Communication rituals*—for example, getting together for lunch every Friday afternoon or going out to a coffee bar with a significant other
- *Patterns, habits, and mannerisms*—for example, meeting her need to be complimented when going out for a fancy evening, and meeting his need to be reassured before family events
- *Spiritual rituals*—for example, attending services together or doing yoga together in the evening

The Possibilities for Improvement

Can you improve your communication in interpersonal relationships? Until relatively recently, many people felt that learning to relate more effectively to others was impossible. Today, however, most individuals feel such a possibility does exist. Are such changes easy? Generally, they are not. You should not expect that an introductory course in communication will solve all of your relational problems. Self-help books that promise instant success will probably result only in disillusionment. Courses on assertiveness training, relaxation techniques, and marital satisfaction provide only part of the answer. Improving relationships is a lifelong process that nobody perfects but that many people can pursue for their own benefit.

Bargaining

Often we engage in bargaining in our interpersonal relationships. **Bargaining** occurs when two or more parties attempt to reach an agreement on what each should give and receive in a transaction between them. Bargains may be explicit and formal, such as the kinds of agreements you reach with others to share tasks, to attend a particular event, or to behave in a specified way. Bargains may also be implicit and informal. For example, in exchange for receiving a compliment from him every day, you might agree not to relate embarrassing stories about your boyfriend. You may not even be aware of some of the unstated agreements you have with others with whom you communicate.

A study on interpersonal bargaining (Deusch & Kraus, 1962) identified three essential features of a bargaining situation:

1. All parties perceive the possibility of reaching an agreement in which each party would be better off, or no worse off, than if no agreement were reached.
2. All parties perceive more than one such agreement that could be reached.
3. Each party perceives the others as having conflicting preferences or opposed interests.

What are some examples of bargaining situations? You may want to go out with friends when your spouse would prefer a quiet evening at home. A woman might prefer to go hiking, whereas her husband is more eager to take a cruise. One person could use the word *forever* to mean a few days or weeks, whereas another assumes the word refers to a much longer period of time. In each of these instances, the disagreement can be resolved through bargaining.

bargaining

The process in which two or more parties attempt to reach an agreement on what each should give and receive in a transaction between them.

Thibaut and Kelley (1959) underlined the importance of bargaining in interpersonal communication:

> Whatever the gratifications achieved in dyads, however lofty or fine the motives satisfied may be, the relationship may be viewed as a trading or bargaining one. The basic assumption running throughout our analysis is that every individual voluntarily enters and stays in any relationship only as long as it is adequately satisfactory in terms of rewards and costs.

Learning Communication Skills

If you wish to improve your communication within your interpersonal relationships, you must commit yourself to learning a variety of communication skills. You must understand the importance of perceptual differences among people, the role of self-concept in communication, the nature of verbal language, and the role of nonverbal communication. You must be willing to share yourself through self-disclosure, and you must be willing to attempt to understand other people through careful and conscientious listening. In addition, you must recognize that even when you thoroughly understand these concepts and are able to implement them in your behavior, your interactions with others may not be successful. Communication is dependent on the interaction between two communicators, and one person cannot guarantee its success. Others may have conflicting goals, have different perspectives, or communicate incompetently.

Learning individual communication concepts and specific communication skills is essential to effective interaction. You also need to understand the impact of these skills. For example, you do not communicate at home the way you do in the classroom. Self-disclosure, which is especially appropriate and important within the family context, may be out of place in the classroom. Preparation and planning are important in an interview, but they may be seen as manipulative in a conversation between partners.

Maintaining Behavioral Flexibility

behavioral flexibility

The ability to alter behavior to adapt to new situations and to relate in new ways when necessary.

In addition to being improved by an understanding of communication concepts, skills, and settings, our interactions may be greatly enhanced by an underlying approach to communication behavior called **behavioral flexibility**—the ability to alter behavior to adapt to new situations and to relate in new ways when necessary (Pearson, 1983). Behavioral flexibility allows you to relax when you are with friends or to be your formal self while interviewing for a job. The key to behavioral flexibility may be self-monitoring, always being conscious of the effect of your words on the specific audience in a particular context.

TRY ◄ THIS

Define behavioral flexibility, and determine to what degree you exhibit this trait.

androgynous

Refers to persons who possess stereotypically female and male characteristics.

Flexibility is important in a variety of fields. For example, biologists and botanists have demonstrated that extinction of certain living things occurs because of an organism's inability to adapt to changes in the environment. Psychologists have suggested that women and men who are **androgynous**—who possess both stereotypically male and stereotypically female traits—are more successful in their interactions than are people who are unyieldingly masculine or absolutely feminine. Flexibility in gender roles is more useful than a static notion of what being a man or a woman means in our culture. For instance, if you are a single parent, you may be called on to behave in a loving and nurturing way to your child, regardless of your sex. If your goal is to be a successful manager in a large corporation, you may have to exhibit competitiveness, assertiveness, and a task orientation, regardless of your sex. As you move from interactions with co-workers to interactions with family and friends, you may need to change from traditionally "masculine" behaviors to those that have been considered "feminine."

Behavioral flexibility is especially important in interpersonal communication because relationships between people are in constant flux. For example, the family structure has gone through sharp changes in recent years. In addition, the United States has an increasingly older population. Changes in the labor force also require new skills and different ways of interacting with others. People travel more often and move more frequently. Four million unmarried couples cohabit (Singletary, 1999). As a result of these types of changes, people may interact differently today.

What kinds of changes can you expect in your own life that will affect your relationships with others? You may change your job 10 or more times. You may move your place of residence even more frequently. You probably will be married at least once, and possibly two or three times. You probably will have one child or more. You will experience loss of family members through death and dissolution of relationships. You may have a spouse whose needs conflict with your own. Other family members may view the world differently than you and challenge your perceptions. When your life appears to be most stable and calm, unexpected changes will occur.

How can behavioral flexibility assist you through life's changes? A flexible person draws on a large repertoire of behaviors. Such an individual is confident about sharing messages with others and about understanding the messages that others provide. The flexible person is able to self-disclose when appropriate but does not use this ability in inappropriate contexts. The flexible person can demonstrate listening skills but is not always the one who is listening. The flexible person can show concern for a child who needs assistance, can be assertive on the job, can be yielding when another person needs to exercise control, and can be independent when called on to stand alone. The flexible person does not predetermine one set of communication behaviors he or she will always enact. The flexible person is not dogmatic or narrow-minded in interactions with others.

To remember that changes are not always negative is important. In fact, considerable change is positive. For instance, when you graduate from college, the changes that occur are generally perceived as positive. When you enter into new relationships, you generally feel better about your life.

But even positive change can be stressful. Gail Sheehy, author of *Passages: Predictable Crises of Adult Life* (1976), wrote:

> We must be willing to change chairs if we want to grow. There is no permanent compatibility between a chair and a person. And there is no one right chair. What is right at one stage may be restricting at another or too soft.

TRY ◆ THIS

List the major changes you have made in your life, and determine how each has led to changes in your communication.

Chapter Review & Study Guide

SUMMARY

In this chapter you learned the following:

▶ Interpersonal communication is the process of using messages to generate meaning between at least two people in a situation that allows mutual opportunities for both speaking and listening.

▶ Interpersonal relationships provide one context in which people communicate with each other. Interpersonal relationships are associations between two or more people who are interdependent, who use some consistent patterns of interaction, and who have interacted for a period of time. Interpersonal relationships are established for a variety of reasons.

▶ Most interpersonal relationships are positive, but interpersonal relationships also have a dark side.

▶ Self-disclosure is the process of making intentional revelations about oneself that others would be unlikely to know and that generally constitutes private, sensitive, or confidential information.

▶ Most relationships go through definable stages of development, maintenance, and deterioration. Why do people initiate relationships?
  • Attraction and similarity are important.
  • Other factors include proximity, responsiveness, complementarity, and social exchange.

▶ Relationship maintenance is challenging.
  • Although some aspects of maintenance seem to generalize across most relationships, co-cultural differences affect our maintenance behaviors.
  • People can achieve satisfying relationships.

▶ Why do people terminate relationships? Hurtful messages, deceptive communication, and aggressiveness may have a destructive effect on interpersonal relationships.

▶ Although interpersonal communication behaviors cannot be prescribed, three communication behaviors are essential to competent interpersonal communication.
  • Affectionate communication includes the expression of fond or tender feelings toward another person.
  • One goal of interpersonal communicators is to influence others in their interpersonal relationships.
  • We develop our unique relationship through personal idioms and playful interactions.

▶ We can improve relationships through communication by developing behavioral flexibility.

KEY TERMS

Go to the *Online Learning Center* at **www.mhhe.com/pearson3** to further your understanding of the following terminology.

Aggressiveness	Compliance-resisting	Personal idioms
Androgynous	Contradictions	Proximity
Argumentativeness	Deceptive communication	Relational deterioration
Attractiveness	Defensiveness	Relational development
Bargaining	Dependence power	Relational maintenance
Behavioral flexibility	Dialectic	Responsiveness
Complementarity	Hurtful messages	Rituals
Complementary relationships	Interpersonal communication	Self-disclosure
Compliance-gaining	Interpersonal relationships	Similarity

STUDY QUESTIONS

1. Which is *not* an element of an interpersonal relationship?
   a. It includes two or more people.
   b. It involves people who are interdependent.
   c. Its patterns of interaction are inconsistent.
   d. Individuals in an interpersonal relationship have interacted for some time.
2. Interpersonal relationships are important because
   a. they fulfill our needs for inclusion, affection, and control
   b. physical, safety, and security needs cannot be met elsewhere
   c. dependence is vital
   d. we need to interact with people having similar interests
3. An extrovert being friends with an introvert demonstrates which type of relationship?
   a. symmetrical
   b. complementary
   c. negotiated
   d. no relationship
4. Obsession, jealousy, gossip, and mental abuse are examples of
   a. healthy interpersonal communication
   b. marital relationships
   c. the negative qualities and harmful effects of some interpersonal relationships
   d. positive problem-solving techniques
5. Which of the following statements regarding friendship is true?
   a. Friendships remain unvarying and unchanged over time.
   b. All friendships are maintained identically, regardless of relational partners' intent.
   c. The quality of friendship is affected by other psychological predispositions.

   d. For many older women, their only friend is their husband.
6. If two people in a relationship start to merge their social circles and purchase items together, they are exhibiting actions in the
   a. relational development stage
   b. relational maintenance stage
   c. relational deterioration stage
   d. relational dialectical stage
7. We may begin a relationship with someone based on how desirable that person is to work with in the classroom. This type of motivation refers to
   a. responsiveness
   b. similarity
   c. complementarity
   d. attractiveness
8. A motivation for terminating a relationship by deliberately making somebody believe untrue things is labeled
   a. deceptive communication
   b. aggressiveness
   c. argumentativeness
   d. defensiveness
9. Your childhood nickname and the pet name your significant other calls you are examples of
   a. compliance-gaining
   b. personal idioms
   c. rituals
   d. contradictions
10. Which of the following is very important in interpersonal communication, given that relationships between people are constantly changing?
   a. bargaining
   b. self-concept
   c. behavioral flexibility
   d. dialectic tensions

Answers:
1. (c); 2. (a); 3. (b); 4. (c); 5. (c); 6. (a); 7. (d); 8. (a); 9. (b); 10. (c)

CRITICAL THINKING

1. Consider a friendship you have or had. Explain that friendship in terms of the interpersonal relationship stages. Give examples that describe each stage.

2. How have you maintained your relationships with various people over time? If you have come close to terminating a relationship, how was it regained? Using terminology from the text, what was the reason for the near-termination?

SELF-QUIZ

For further review, try the chapter self-quiz on the *Online Learning Center* at **www.mhhe.com/pearson3**.

REFERENCES

Afifi, W. A., & Guerrero, L. K. (1998). Some things are better left unsaid II: Topic avoidance in friendships. *Communication Quarterly, 46*, 231–249.

Altman, I., & Taylor, D. A. (1973). *Social penetration: The development of interpersonal relationships*. New York: Holt, Rinehart & Winston.

Baxter, L. (1983). Relationship disengagement: An examination of the reversal hypothesis. *Western Journal of Speech Communication, 47*, 85–98.

Baxter, L. (1984). Trajectories of relationship disengagement. *Journal of Social and Personal Relationships, 1*, 29–48.

Baxter, L. (1993). The social side of personal relationships: A dialectical perspective. In S. Duck (Ed.), *Understanding relationship processes: Vol. 3. Social context and relationships* (pp. 139–165). Newbury Park, CA: Sage.

Baxter, L., & Montgomery, B. (1996). *Relating: Dialogues and dialects*. New York: Guilford Press.

Beaulieu, C. M. J. (2004). Intercultural study of personal space: A case study. *Journal of Applied Social Psychology, 34*, 794–805.

Berger, C. R., & Kellermann, K. (1989). Personal opacity and social information gathering. *Communication Research, 16*, 314–351.

Betcher, W. (1987). *Intimate play: Creating romance in everyday life*. New York: Viking Press.

Bruess, C. J. S., & Pearson, J. C. (1993). "Sweet Pea" and "Pussy Cat"? An examination of idiom use and marital satisfaction over the life cycle. *Journal of Social and Personal Relationships, 10*, 609–615.

Bruess, C. J. S., & Pearson, J. C. (1997). Interpersonal rituals in marriage and adult friendship. *Communication Monographs, 64*, 25–46.

Caplan, S. E., & Samter, W. (1999). The role of facework in younger and older adults' evaluations of social support messages. *Communication Quarterly, 47*, 245–264.

Clark, R. A, Pierce, K. F., Hsu, K., Toosley, A., & Williams, L. (1998). The impact of alternative approaches to comforting, closeness of relationship, and gender on multiple measures of effectiveness. *Communication Studies, 49*, 224–239.

Collier, M. J. (1996). Communication competence problematics in ethnic friendships. *Communication Monographs, 63*, 314–336.

Cozby, P. C. (1972). Self-disclosure, reciprocity, and liking. *Sociometry, 35*, 151–160.

Cozby, P. C. (1973). Self-disclosure: A literature review. *Psychological Bulletin, 79*, 73–91.

Crawford, L. (1996). Everyday Tao: Conversation and contemplation. *Communication Studies, 47*, 25–34.

Darling, N., Cumsille, P., Caldwell, L. L., & Dowdy, B. (2006). Predictors of adolescents' disclosure to parents and perceived parental knowledge: Between- and within-person differences. *Journal of Youth and Adolescence, 35*, 659–670.

Davis, M. H., & Oathout, H. A. (1987). Maintenance of satisfaction in romantic relationships: Empathy and relational competence. *Journal of Personality and Social Psychology, 53*, 397–498.

Deusch, M., & Kraus, R. M. (1962). Studies of interpersonal bargaining. *Journal of Conflict Resolution, 6*, 52.

di Battista, P. (1997). Deceivers' responses to challenges of their truthfulness: Difference between familiar lies and unfamiliar lies. *Communication Quarterly, 45*, 319–334.

Dindia, K., & Baxter, L. A. (1987). Strategies for maintaining and repairing marital relationships. *Journal of Social and Personal Relationships, 4*, 143–158.

Dindia, K., Fitzpatrick, M. A., & Kenny, D. A. (1997). Self-disclosure in spouse and stranger interaction. *Human Communication Research, 23*, 388–412.

Duck, S., & Pond, K. (1989). Friends, Romans, countrymen, lend me your retrospections: Rhetoric and reality in personal relationships. In C. Hendrick (Ed.), *Close relationships* (pp. 17–38). Newbury Park, CA: Sage.

Fitzpatrick, J., Liang, S., Feng, D., Crawford, D., Sorell, G. T., & Morgan-Fleming, B. (2006). Social values and self-disclosure: A comparison of Chinese native, Chinese resident (in U.S.) and North American spouses. *Journal of Comparative Family Studies, 37*, 113–127.

Floyd, K. (1997a). Affectionate communication in nonromantic relationships: Influences of communicator, relational, and contextual factors. *Western Journal of Communication, 61*, 279–298.

Floyd, K. (1997b). Communicating affection in dyadic relationships: An assessment of behavior and expectancies. *Communication Quarterly, 45*, 68–80.

Floyd, K., & Burgoon, J. K. (1999). Reacting to nonverbal expressions of liking: A test of interaction adaptation theory. *Communication Monographs, 66*, 219–239.

Floyd, K., & Morman, M. T. (1998). The measurement of affectionate communication. *Communication Quarterly, 46*, 144–162.

Floyd, K., & Morman, M. T. (2000). Reacting to the verbal expression of affection in same-sex interaction. *Southern Communication Journal, 65*, 287–299.

French, D. C., Bae, A., Pidada, S., & Okhwa, L. (2006). Friendships of Indonesian, South Korean, and U.S. college students. *Personal Relationships, 13*, 69–81.

Friedman, H. S., Riggio, J. R. E., & Casella, D. F. (1988). Nonverbal skill, personal charisma, and initial attraction. *Personality and Social Psychology Bulletin, 14*, 203–211.

Gibb, J. R. (1991). *Trust: A new vision of human relationships for business, education, family, and personal living* (2nd ed). North Hollywood, CA: Newcastle Publishing Co.

Guerrero, L. K. (1996). Attachment-style differences in intimacy and involvement: A test of the four- category model. *Communication Monographs, 63*, 269–292.

Guerrero, L. K., & Chavez, A. M. (2005). Relational maintenance in cross-sex friendships characterized by different types of romantic intent: An exploratory study. *Western Journal of Communication, 69*, 339–358.

Harwood, J., McKee, J., & Lin, M.-C. (2000). Younger and older adults' schematic representations of intergenerational communication. *Communication Monographs, 67*, 20–41.

Hastings, S. O. (2000). Self-disclosure and identity management by bereaved parents. *Communication Studies, 51*, 352–371.

Hause, K. S., & Pearson, J. C. (1994, November). *The ebb and flow of marriage: Relational dialectics over the family life cycle.* Paper presented at the meeting of the Speech Communication Association, New Orleans.

Hetsroni, A., & Bloch, L.-R. (1999). Choosing the right mate when everyone is watching: Cultural and sex differences in television dating games. *Communication Quarterly, 47*, 315–332.

Hosman, L. A., & Tardy, C. H. (1980). Self-disclosure and reciprocity in short- and long-term relationships: An experimental study of evaluational and attributional consequences. *Communication Quarterly, 28*, 20–29.

Ifert, D. E., & Roloff, M. E. (1997). Overcoming expressed obstacles to compliance: The role of sensitivity to the expressions of others and ability to modify self-presentation. *Communication Quarterly, 45*, 55–67.

Jourard, S. M. (1964). *The transparent self: Self-disclosure and well-being.* New York: Van Nostrand Reinhold.

Julien, D., Chartrand, E., Simard, M. C., Bouthillier, D., & Begin, J. (2003). Conflict, social support, and relationship quality: An observational study of heterosexual, gay male, and lesbian couples' communication. *Journal of Family Psychology, 17*, 419–428.

Kim, M.-S., & Bresnahan, M. (1994). A process model of request tactic evaluation. *Discourse Processes, 18*, 317–344.

Knapp, M. L., & Vangelisti, A. L. (2000). *Interpersonal communication and human relationships* (4th ed.) Boston: Allyn & Bacon.

LePoire, B. A., Haynes, J., Driscoll, J., Driver, B. N., Wheelis, T. F., Hyde, M. K., Prochaska, M., & Ramos, L. (1997). Attachment as a function of parental and partner approach-avoidance tendencies. *Human Communication Research, 23*, 413–441.

LePoire, B. A., & Yoshimura, S. M. (1999). The effects of expectancies and actual communication on nonverbal adaptation and communication outcomes: A test of interaction adaptation theory. *Communication Monographs, 66*, 1–30.

Le Roux, J. (2002). Effective educators are culturally competent communicators. *Intercultural Education, 13*, 37–48.

Lowrey-Hart, R., & Pearson, J. C. (1997, November). *There is a war inside of me between my blackness and your whiteness: Understanding the African American student experience in higher education through a relational dialectic perspective.* Paper presented at the meeting of the National Communication Association, Chicago.

Lucchetti, A. E. (1999). Deception in disclosing one's sexual history: Safe-sex avoidance or ignorance? *Communication Quarterly, 47*, 300–314.

MacGeorge, E. L. (2001). Support providers' interaction goals: The influence of attributions and emotions. *Communication Monographs, 68*, 72–97.

Mahon, N. (2006). A meta-analytic study of predictors for loneliness during adolescence. *Nursing Research, 55*, 308–315.

Marshall, L. J., & Levy, V. M., Jr. (1998). The development of children's perceptions of obstacles in compliance-gaining interactions. *Communication Studies, 49*, 342–357.

Martin, M. M., & Anderson, C. M. (1997). Aggressive communication traits: How similar are young adults and their parents in argumentativeness, assertiveness, and verbal aggressiveness. *Western Journal of Communication, 61*, 299–314.

McCroskey, J. C., & McCain, T. A. (1974). The measurement of interpersonal attraction. *Speech Monographs, 41*, 267–276.

Mesch, G., & Talmud, I. (2006). The quality of online and offline relationships: The role of multiplexity and duration of social relationships. *Information Society, 22*, 137–148.

Miller, G. R. (1976). *Explorations in interpersonal communication.* Beverly Hills, CA: Sage.

Miller, G. R., & Steinberg, M. (1975). *Between people: A new analysis of interpersonal communication.* Chicago: Science Research Associates.

Pahl, R., & Pevalin, D. J. (2005). Between family and friends: A longitudinal study of friendship choice. *British Journal of Sociology, 56,* 433–450.

Pawlowski, D. R. (1998). Dialectic tensions in marital partners' accounts of their relationships. *Communication Quarterly, 46,* 396–412.

Pearce, W. B., & Sharp, S. M. (1973). Self-disclosing communication. *Journal of Communication, 23,* 409–425.

Pearson, J. C. (1983). *Interpersonal communication: Clarity, confidence, concern.* Glenview, IL: Scott, Foresman.

Pearson, J. C. (1996). Forty-forever years? Primary relationships and senior citizens. In N. Vanzetti & S. Duck (Eds.), *A lifetime of relationships* (pp. 383–405). Pacific Grove, CA: Brooks/Cole.

Pearson, J. C., & Spitzberg, B. H. (1990). *Interpersonal communication: Concepts, components, and contexts.* Dubuque, IA: Wm. C. Brown.

Perse, E. M., & Rubin, R. B. (1989). Attribution in social and parasocial relationships. *Communication Research, 16,* 59–77.

Punyanunt-Carter, N. M. (2006). An analysis of college students' self-disclosure behaviors on the Internet. *College Student Journal, 40,* 329–331.

Radmacher, K., & Azmitia, M. (2006). Are there gendered pathways to intimacy in early adolescents' and emerging adults' friendships? *Journal of Adolescent Research, 21,* 415–448.

Ragsdale, J. D. (1996). Gender, satisfaction level, and the use of relational maintenance strategies in marriage. *Communication Monographs, 63,* 354–369.

Rawlins, W. (1992). *Friendship matters: Communication, dialectics, and the life course.* New York: Aldine de Gruyter.

Roloff, M. E., & Johnson, D. I. (2001). Reintroducing taboo topics: Antecedents and consequences of putting topics back on the table. *Communication Studies, 52,* 37–50.

Ronesi, L. M. (2003). Enhancing postsecondary intergroup relations at the university through student-run ESL instruction. *Journal of Language, Identity, and Education, 2,* 191–210.

Sabatelli, R. M., & Rubin, M. (1986). Nonverbal expressiveness and physical attractiveness as mediators of interpersonal perceptions. *Journal of Nonverbal Behavior, 10,* 120–133.

Saeki, M., & O'Keefe, B. (1994). Refusals and rejections: Designing messages to serve multiple goals. *Human Communication Research, 21,* 67–102.

Saferstein, J. A., Neimeyer, G. J., & Hagans, C. L. (2005). Attachment as a predictor of friendship qualities in college youth. *Social Behavior and Personality, 33,* 767–775.

Schullery, N. M., & Schullery, S. E. (2003). Relationship of argumentativeness to age and higher education. *Western Journal of Communication, 67,* 207–224.

Schutz, W. (1976). *The interpersonal underworld.* Palo Alto, CA: Science and Behavior Books.

Semic, B. A., & Canary, D. J. (1997). Trait argumentativeness, verbal aggressiveness, and minimally rational argument: An observational analysis of friendship discussions. *Communication Quarterly, 45,* 355–378.

Sheehy, G. (1976). *Passages: Predictable crises of adult life.* New York: Dutton.

Sherman, A. M., Lansford, J. E., & Volling, B. L. (2006). Sibling relationships and best friendships in young adulthood: Warmth, conflict, and well-being. *Personal Relationships, 13,* 151–165.

Sias, P. M., & Cahill, D. J. (1998). From coworkers to friends: The development of peer friendships in the workplace. *Western Journal of Communication, 62,* 273–299.

Sillars, A., Shellen, W., McIntosh, A., & Pomegranate, M. (1997). Relational characteristics of language: Elaboration and differentiation in marital conversations. *Western Journal of Communication, 61,* 403–422.

Singletary, M. (1999, February 21). The color of money. *The Washington Post,* pp. H1, H4.

Smetana, J. G., Metzger, A., Gettman, D. C., & Campione-Barr, N. (2006). Disclosure and secrecy in adolescent–parent relationships. *Child Development, 77,* 201–217.

Spitzberg, B. H., & Cupach, W. R. (1998). *The dark side of close relationships.* Mahwah, NJ: Lawrence Erlbaum.

Tam, T., Hewstone, M., Harwood, J., Voci, A., & Kenworthy, J. (2006). Intergroup contact and grandparent–grandchild communication: The effects of self-disclosure on implicit and explicit biases against older people. *Group Processes and Intergroup Relations, 9,* 413–429.

Thibaut, J. W., & Kelley, H. H. (1959). *The social psychology of groups.* New York: John Wiley.

Vangelisti, A. L., & Crumley, L. P. (1998). Reactions to messages that hurt: The influence of relational contexts. *Communication Monographs, 65,* 173–196.

Wang, S. H.-Y., & Chang, H.-C. (1999). Chinese professionals' perceptions of interpersonal communication in corporate America: A multidimensional scaling analysis. *Howard Journal of Communications, 10,* 297–315.

Way, N., & Greene, M. L. (2006). Trajectories of perceived friendship quality during adolescence: The patterns and contextual predictors. *Journal of Research on Adolescence, 16,* 293–320.

Wierzbicka, A. (2006). The concept of "dialogue" in cross-linguistic and cross-cultural perspective. *Discourse Studies, 8,* 675–703.

Wilmot, W. W. (1980). *Dyadic communication* (2nd ed.). Reading, MA: Addison-Wesley.

Wilmot, W. W. (1995). *Relational communication.* New York: McGraw-Hill.

Wilson, S. R. (1998). Introduction to the special issue on seeking and resisting compliance: The vitality of compliance-gaining research. *Communication Studies, 49,* 273–275.

CHAPTER SEVEN

Intercultural Communication

What will you learn?

When you have read and thought about this chapter, you will be able to:

1. Explain why you should study intercultural communication.
2. Distinguish between cultures and co-cultures.
3. Provide examples of co-cultural strategies.
4. Explain potential intercultural communication problems.
5. Identify broad cultural characteristics.
6. Practice strategies for improving communication with people from other cultures and co-cultures.

This chapter introduces you to communication between cultures and co-cultures. Being an effective communicator means interacting positively with people from various racial, ethnic, and cultural backgrounds. The goal of this chapter is to increase your confidence in your ability to communicate with people of other cultures and co-cultures. The chapter stresses the importance of communicating effectively in an ever-changing world. It explains cultures and co-cultures, reveals strategies used by co-cultures to interact with dominant cultures, identifies broad characteristics of several cultures, and provides strategies for improving intercultural communication. When you have completed this chapter, you should know more about people outside your own group, and you should feel more confident about communicating successfully with others.

"Harry and David, you are naturals. You are sand painters!" This praise from a Tibetan monk for two artists with developmental disabilities took place in a very unusual setting. Six monk-artists from Tibet had taken up a weeklong residency at the Passion Works Art Studio in Athens, Ohio. Passion Works sponsors collaborations between artists with and without disabilities, in the belief that creativity is an innate quality in all individuals and that art strengthens community ties.

Most of the monks did not speak English, but that did not stop them from collaborating closely with the Passion Works artists. The monks taught the artists with disabilities how to make mandalas, very detailed "paintings" using different-colored sand as the artistic medium. In turn, the Passion Works clients involved the monks in a project of painting pillowcases to make prayer flags, a traditional feature of the monks' Buddhist religion. Throughout the visit the residents and the visitors explored new forms of artwork and learned about their cultural similarities and differences. As one monk noted, "Though we didn't understand each others' language, painting and art was language enough to become friends" (www.passionworks.org).

The Tibetan monks shared one important similarity with the Passion Works artists. Both were accustomed to living as outsiders in their communities. People with disabilities are often disconnected from the larger community they live in, and Tibetan monks live sheltered in monasteries, feeling powerless and excluded under a government that many of them do not recognize as legitimate. For both sets of artists at the Passion Works Art Studio, art gave them a voice, a way to express themselves and connect with others.

This heartwarming story of the collaboration between the Passion Works artists and the Tibetan monks shows us that even in the face of seemingly huge obstacles—differing languages, differing cultural backgrounds, differing verbal and nonverbal abilities—humans can find a way to communicate and share. This chapter will help you understand strategies for communicating across cultures.

Why Is the Study of Intercultural Communication Important?

intercultural communication

The exchange of information between individuals who are unalike culturally.

Rogers and Steinfatt (1999) define **intercultural communication** as "the exchange of information between individuals who are unalike culturally." Not long ago, intercultural communication involved only missionaries, jet-setting business executives, foreign correspondents, and political figures. Now, however, developments in technology and shifts in demographics have created a world in which intercultural communication is common. Events on September 11, 2001, changed our perceptions of travel and of other cultures. Americans were surprised to find that they were hated; they soon discovered that they knew little about Islamic religion or about Afghanistan, Iraq, and Saudi Arabia. Intercultural communication is essential because of our increasing exposure to people of other cultures and co-cultures. More people are exposed to different global cultures through vacation travel, transnational jobs, international conflicts, military and humanitarian service, and the presence of immigrants, refugees, and new citizens.

More people are also exposed to different co-cultures—from ethnic groups, to neighborhood gangs, to partisan political groups, to gay and lesbian societies. Some of you will work and live every day with people different from yourself. Others of you will only occasionally encounter unfamiliar groups. But today chances are excellent that you will need to know the basics of intercultural communication presented in this chapter. The first reason, then, why you should study intercultural communication is that communication with people from other cultures and co-cultures is increasingly common.

A second reason to study intercultural communication is money. Today we sell our corn, wheat, and cars in Asia; and we buy coffee from Colombia, bananas from Costa Rica, and oil from Africa, the Middle East, and South America. Our clothing comes from China and Panama, our shoes are made in Mexico, and our cars may have been assembled in Germany, Hungary, or Canada. Business that was previously domestic is now global. The students of today will find themselves working with people from many different cultures because of our global economy.

A third reason to study intercultural communication is, simply, our curiosity about others. We are curious about people who don't look like us, sound like us, or live like us. We wonder why one woman always wears a long dress and veil, why someone would prefer polkas to rap, why a man wears a turban, and why some people do not eat meat. We are curious about arranged marriages, rituals like funerals and weddings, and sports like sumo wrestling, kick boxing, and cricket. We express disbelief that fanatics in an otherwise peace-loving religion promise heaven to suicidal followers as a reward for murdering innocent people. We do not understand religious fanatics and paramilitary groups in our own country who stockpile weapons to attack our own government. Intercultural communication includes better understanding of cultural and co-cultural friends and enemies.

A fourth reason to study intercultural communication is the convergence of technologies. For most of the twentieth century, intercultural activity required an expensive flight or phone call. Now people can cheaply communicate with each other around the world on the Internet. Phone, video, and audio merge into a system that can allow for sight and sound. Cell phones, pagers, and handheld computers bring communication technology to our fingertips. The new technologies have transformed interpersonal and face-to-face communication. We are now what Marshall McLuhan predicted: a global village.

A fifth reason to study intercultural communication is the influx of foreign-born immigrants, aliens, and refugees that has changed the face of America. In metropolitan Washington, DC, your waiter is from Colombia, South America; your cab driver is from Ethiopia; the porter is from the Sudan; the dry cleaner is from Korea; and the barber is a Vietnamese woman. The story is similar for Miami, New York City, Detroit, and Chicago. If not a melting pot, America is now (and always was) an exotic salad with many cultures contributing to its overall flavor. You can communicate better with people from other cultures if you know something about theirs.

Watch "The Right Kind of Care" video on the **Online Learning Center** *to see a realistic example of intercultural communication.*

What Are Cultures and Co-cultures?

culture

A unique combination of rituals, religious beliefs, ways of thinking, and ways of behaving that unify a group of people.

co-culture

A group that exists within a larger, dominant culture but differs from the dominant culture in some significant characteristic.

You have just learned that intercultural communication is the exchange of information between people of different cultures, but you may be uncertain about the definitions of culture and co-culture.

A **culture** is a unique combination of rituals (such as greeting and parting), religious beliefs, ways of thinking (such as the earth was created), and ways of behaving (such as women can marry at 14 years of age in Iran) that unify a group of people. Often we perceive cultural differences (see chapter 2 on perception) as emerging from nation-states (France, the Czech Republic), religious groups (Muslims, Buddhists, Amish), tribal groups (Kurds, Ibos, Potawatomi Nation), or even people united by a cause (Palestinians, the Taliban, al-Qaeda).

A **co-cultural group** exists within a larger, dominant culture but differs from the dominant culture in some significant characteristic. An Afghani who moves to America moves from a culture (Afghanistan) to a co-culture (an Afghani in America). An able-bodied, wealthy white male would quickly move from the dominant culture to a co-culture if he became handicapped in an automobile accident. Co-cultures are based on varied criteria: females because they are not equal to men in pay, power, or prestige; poor people because they are united in powerlessness; and gays because they lack rights and privileges. An individual can belong to many co-cultures. An American adolescent female immigrant from Panama who is a Roman Catholic earning minimum wage belongs to at least five co-cultures, but no one would say she is of the dominant culture in America.

Next we are going to explore some methods used by co-cultures to communicate with dominant cultures. An example would be a gay male who works in an office with a dominant culture of straight men and women. What choices does that person have in relating to other workers? The next section explains the goals of assimilation, accommodation, and separation.

The Goals of Co-cultural Communication

Some of the earlier studies of co-cultures focused on how little influence women had even when they were part of workforce teams. Kramarae (1981), for instance, called women a "muted group" because their ideas were undervalued, underestimated, and sometimes unheard. Like the "transparent man" in the musical *Chicago*—a person whom nobody noticed, addressed, or remembered—women were muted when their presence and voices were unheard or unheralded.

Co-cultures are often called "marginalized groups" because they live on the edges of the dominant culture; in other words, they exist on the margins. Who are the marginalized groups? Orbe (1996) calls them "nondominant groups" and categorizes them as "people of color, women, gays/lesbians/bisexuals, people with disabilities, lower/working class, and the young and the elderly." Who are the likely members of the dominant culture? Orbe quotes Folb's (1994) list of the dominant as male, European American, heterosexual, able-bodied, youthful, middle/upper class, and/or Christian groups. Others dominant in our culture are the college-educated, people in the professions, home-owners, married couples, and people paid by the month instead of by the hour.

TRY ◆ THIS

Think of times when you were a marginalized, nondominant person trying to commu-nicate with someone from the dominant culture—for example, when you were a child trying to bargain with your parent, when you were an employee negotiating with your employer, when you were explaining an unpaid bill, or when you were appealing a grade. What strategies did you use to influence someone with an advantage over you?

Usually, marginalized, nondominant groups seek three possible goals in rela-tion to dominant groups: assimilation, accommodation, or separation. The **assimilation goal** means that the marginalized group attempts to fit in with the dominant group. They wear suits; you wear a suit. They don't have body piercing; you forgo the ear, lip, and eyebrow rings. They talk sports; you learn the names of the teams and players.

The **accommodation goal** means that the marginalized group manages to keep its co-cultural identity while striving for positive relationships with the dominant culture. For example, a woman brings her lesbian partner to the company picnic, makes no secret of the relationship at work, but does not flaunt her lesbianism to her heterosexual colleagues. A fundamentalist Christian woman never cuts her hair, always wears long dresses, and never wears makeup, but respects the right of co-workers to have their own religious beliefs without interference from her.

A third goal, **separation,** is achieved when the marginalized group relates as exclusively as possible with its own group and as little as possible with the domi-nant group. A number of very conservative religious groups like Hasidic Jews, the Amish, and black Muslims are examples. But marginalized individuals can live separate lives in the midst of the dominant culture by relentlessly focusing on work, studiously avoiding any but the most necessary interactions, and never socializing outside work with any colleagues.

The separation goal can be carried to an extreme with an "in your face" attitude about the nondomi-nant group's identity. Some skinheads are openly racist, some black and Hispanic groups are openly antiwhite, and some paramilitary groups are openly antigovernment. Queer Nation blatantly forces straight people to recognize the existence of gayness by outing prominent individuals. Such strate-gies are aggressive and confrontational and signal that the group does not want to be transparent.

assimilation goal

The marginalized group attempts to fit in with the dominant group.

accommodation goal

The marginalized group manages to keep co-cultural identity while striving for posi-tive relationships with the dominant culture.

separation goal

The marginalized group relates as exclusively as possible with its own group and as little as possible with the dominant group.

Co-cultural identity is maintained by distinctive clothing and other adornments.

◄ SKILL BUILDER ►

To what co-culture(s) do you belong? What strategies do you and others like you adopt in relating to the dominant culture? Think about verbal and nonverbal messages that your co-culture exchanges with those individuals outside your group.

What Are Some Intercultural Communication Problems?

Intercultural communication is subject to all the problems that can hamper effective interpersonal communication. Intercultural relationships are especially hindered by many of the perceptual distortions discussed in chapter 2, "Perception, Self, and Communication." How we select, organize, and interpret visual and message cues is even more important between cultures than among friends. Attribution and perceptual errors are more likely to occur between persons with many differences. Several additional problems may occur during intercultural interactions. Becoming aware of these issues can help you avoid them or reduce their effects. Keep in mind that although the barriers identified here can be problematic, they do not occur in every exchange.

Ethnocentrism

ethnocentrism

The belief that your own group or culture is superior to other groups or cultures.

The largest problem that occurs during intercultural communication is that people bring the prejudices of their culture to the interaction. **Ethnocentrism** is the belief that your own group or culture is superior to all other groups or cultures. You are ethnocentric if you see and judge the rest of the world only from your own culture's perspective. Some common examples include thinking that everyone should speak English, that people in the United States should not have to learn languages other than English, that the U.S. culture is better than Mexico's, or that the Asian custom of bowing is odd (Dodd, 1998). Each of us operates from an ethnocentric perspective, but problems arise when we interpret and evaluate other cultures in terms of our own. Generally, a lack of interaction with another culture fosters high levels of ethnocentrism and encourages the notion of cultural superiority. Ethnocentrism makes others feel defensive.

cultural relativism

The belief that another culture should be judged by its own context rather than measured against your culture.

In ethnocentrism you use your own culture as the measure that others are expected to meet; **cultural relativism** is the belief that another culture should be judged by its own context rather than measured against your culture. Saying that the Asian custom of bowing is odd overlooks the long history of bowing to one another as a sign of respect. To communicate effectively with people from different cultures, you need to accept people whose values and norms may be different from your own. An effective communicator avoids ethnocentrism and embraces cultural relativism.

Stereotyping

Ethnocentrism is not the only perceptual trap you can fall into in intercultural communication. Equally dangerous is the tendency to stereotype people in cultural and co-cultural groups. Rogers and Steinfatt (1999) define a stereotype as "a generalization about some group of people that oversimplifies their culture." The stereotype of a gay male is an effeminate fellow, but gay people are just as likely to be truckers, physicians, and athletes. Similarly, Jews are both wealthy and poor, Asians are both gifted at math and not, and black Americans are sometimes great athletes but sometimes not. Consider a former student who was ethnic Korean, whose last name was Schlumpberger (very German), and who had grown up in St. Paul, Minnesota. He could not speak Korean, had not been in the country since his birth, and grew up in a Caucasian family. So much for judging from appearances.

Why do people stereotype? Bruno (1999) observes, "The tribal drum beats in all societies, warning members of the tribe against the dangers of the others, those who are not members of the tribe, even those who are different within a society. The drum's messages result in different tribal behavior, from religious warfare in Northern Ireland and the Middle East, ethnic cleansing in Yugoslavia and Rwanda, to Neo-Nazi racial purification in Germany and America" (p. 855). Bruno notes that prejudice may be bold or subtle and can even occur among physicians against the disabled people they treat.

Allport (1958) originally observed that people are more likely to stereotype individuals and groups with whom they have little contact. For example, you might have a whole set of beliefs about Middle Eastern Muslim women, many of whom cover their bodies and faces and walk well behind their husbands. You may not realize that one of your neighbors is actually Muslim but does not follow some of the strict traditions of her religion.

Sometimes stereotyping occurs because people have had a negative or positive experience with a person from another culture or co-culture. In one investigation people stereotyped black people after only one observation of a negative behavior. In another, simply hearing about an alleged crime was sufficient to stereotype blacks (Henderson-King & Nisbett, 1996). Clearly, people are willing to stereotype with very little evidence.

Sexism is a stereotype that remains prevalent in most societies. One investigation examined the incidence, nature, and impact of everyday sexism as experienced by college women and men. The researchers found that women experienced one or two sexist incidents per week that had a strong negative impact. Included in these incidents were demeaning and degrading comments and behaviors as well as sexual objectification. The women experienced depression, anger, and lowered self-esteem because of these incidents. College men reported relatively fewer sexist incidents and less overall impact (Swim, Hyers, Cohen, & Ferguson, 2001).

How do people feel about receiving either negative or positive comments that reflect on their social group rather than on them as individuals? In general, people respond negatively to negative comments that are about them either as an individual or as a member of a social group. They also respond negatively when the comment was about them as a member of the social group, was positive, but reflected a stereotype. Participants in this study reported that even positive stereotypes caused increased anger and a desire to avoid or attack the speaker (Garcia, Miller, Smith, & Mackie, 2006).

What can an individual do who feels that another is stereotyping him or her? A study that tested the effectiveness of confrontation found that this strategy actually helps. While confrontations elicited negative emotions and evaluations toward the person doing the confronting, they also resulted in fewer stereotypic comments from the initial speaker. This may be due to the negative self-directed affect that was felt by the stereotyping speaker (Czopp, Monteith, & Mark, 2006).

What Are Some Characteristics of Different Cultures?

Accepting that your own culture is not superior to another person's culture is one way to improve intercultural communication. Another way is by understanding some of the values and norms of other cultures. For example, suppose you are an American teaching in Japan (a *collectivist* culture). Your students' first assignment is to give a speech before the class. After you give them the assignment, they automatically form groups, and each group selects a spokesperson to give the speech. In the United States (an *individualistic* culture), students would be unlikely to turn a public-speaking assignment into a small-group activity unless specifically directed to do so. If you don't know anything about the norms and customs of the Japanese culture, you might be totally baffled by your students' behavior.

In this section you will learn about five characteristics of cultures: individualistic versus collectivist cultures, uncertainty-accepting versus uncertainty-rejecting cultures, implicit-rule versus explicit-rule cultures, high-context versus low-context cultures, and M-time versus P-time cultures (see Figure 7.1). Keep in mind that the characteristics discussed here are general tendencies; they are not always true of a culture, and they are not true of everyone in a culture.

Individualistic Versus Collectivist Cultures

Much of what is known about individualistic and collectivist cultures comes from a study by Hofstede (1980) that involved more than 100,000 managers from 40 countries. Although neither China nor Africa was included, the study is a classic in its comprehensiveness.

Individualistic cultures value individual freedom, choice, uniqueness, and independence. These cultures place "I" before "we" and value competition over cooperation, private property over public or state-owned property, personal behavior over group behavior, and individual opinion over what anyone else might think. In an individualistic society people are likely to leave the family home or the geographic area in which they were raised to pursue their dreams; their loyalty to an organization has qualifications; they move from job to job; and they may leave churches that no longer meet their needs. Loyalty to other people has limits: Individualistic cultures have high rates of divorce and illegitimacy. According to the Hofstede (1980) study, the top-ranking individualistic cultures are the United States, Australia, Great Britain, Canada, and the Netherlands.

Collectivist cultures, on the other hand, value the group over the individual. These cultures place "we" before "I" and value commitment to family, tribe, and clan; their people tend to be loyal to spouse, employer, community, and country. Collectivist cultures value cooperation over competition, and group-defined social norms and duties over personal opinions (Coleman, 1998). An ancient Confucian saying captures the spirit of collectivist cultures: "If one wants to establish himself, he should help others to establish themselves first." The highest-ranking collectivist cultures are Venezuela, Pakistan, Peru, Taiwan, and Thailand (Hofstede, 1980).

Low-Context Versus High-Context Cultures

Edward Hall (1976, 1983) enriched our understanding of collectivist and individualistic cultures when he defined low-context and high-context systems of communication. In **low-context (LC) cultures,** found most frequently in individualistic countries like the United States and Scandinavia, communication tends to be centered

individualistic cultures

Cultures that value individual freedom, choice, uniqueness, and independence.

collectivist cultures

Cultures that value the group over the individual.

low-context (LC) cultures

Cultures like the United States and Scandinavia, in which communication tends to be centered on the source, with intentions stated overtly and with a direct verbal style.

Individualistic cultures vs. collectivist cultures

Individualistic cultures value individual freedom, choice, uniqueness, and independence, while collectivist cultures value the group, family, tribe, clan, and culture over the individual.

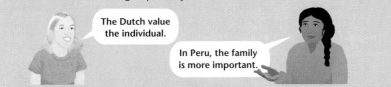

The Dutch value the individual.

In Peru, the family is more important.

Low-context cultures vs. high-context cultures

Low-context communication styles emphasize the source of communication, with intentions stated overtly. In high-context cultures much of the information about the source, intentions, and other information is understood but not explicitly stated.

I must state that North American and European cultures, including Norway, communicate with a direct verbal style.

In Argentina, some things we do not say. They are simply understood.

Uncertainty-accepting cultures vs. uncertainty-rejecting cultures

Uncertainty-accepting cultures are far more likely to tolerate ambiguity and diversity. Uncertainty-rejecting cultures have a more difficult time accepting these things.

Indian culture accepts uncertainty and ambiguity.

It's quite different in France.

Implicit-rule cultures vs. explicit-rule cultures

Implicit rules are implied rules for behavior in a culture and are "implicitly known" to all members of the culture. Explicit-rule cultures are more likely to openly discuss procedures for action and expectations for behavior.

In my culture, one should not question society's rules.

In the US, we can discuss behavioral expectations.

Monochronic cultures vs. polychronic cultures

Monochronic cultures view time as compartmentalized between task, personal, and social dimensions. Polychronic cultures view time as culturally based and relationally oriented.

It's been nice chatting, but I need to leave for my meeting.

We still have time to talk. Your meeting doesn't start for another 5 minutes!

View an animation of this illustration on the *Online Learning Center.*

Figure 7.1   Cultural differences.

on the source ("I"), with intentions stated overtly ("I want you to consider buying this . . .") and with a direct verbal style ("Get over here now!"). As Hall explained, "Most of the information must be in the transmitted message to make up for what is missing in the context" (1976, p. 101). Individual pride and self-esteem, personal autonomy and power, and individual ego-based emotions enter the picture in LC communication patterns (Ting-Toomey, 1997).

How do we characterize people in LC cultures? They are logical and linear. They believe that they control the environment, and they are generally present- and future-oriented. They rely on verbal messages rather than on nonverbal messages. They are competitive, and they prefer change over tradition.

As you consider these characteristics, note that challenging authorities and communicating openly and fully become values. Communication characteristics like argumentativeness, assertiveness, and disclosure are valued. If you consider the history of the United States and the ideals on which its government was based, elements of LC culture are abundant.

high-context (HC) cultures

Cultures like those of the Asian Pacific Rim and Central and South America, in which much of the meaning is "preprogrammed information" understood by the receiver and transmitted also by the setting in which the transaction occurs.

High-context (HC) cultures are more common in the Asian countries of the Pacific Rim, as well as Central and South America, where "only minimal information [is] in the transmitted message" (Hall, 1976, p. 111). Instead, in HC communication much of the meaning is "preprogrammed information" understood by the receiver and transmitted also by the setting in which the transaction occurs. Who is invited to the table, where people sit, and what everyone knows is supposed to occur ahead of time are important features in HC communication.

What are the characteristics of people in HC cultures? They are relational and intuitive. They feel harmony with nature and are cooperative. They are past-oriented, and they prefer traditions over change. Finally, they rely on nonverbal codes rather than verbal messages.

As communicators HC people are less verbally explicit than are LC people. Their long-term relationships allow more internalized understandings that do not require speech. At the same time, strong boundaries separate the "insider" from the "outsider."

Interestingly, all cultures have some concept of face, which reflects people's need for a sense of self-respect in a communication situation (Ting-Toomey, 1997).

Even Americans use the expression "He lost face." But the concept of face appears to be even more important in collectivist cultures, in which "we" looms larger than "I." Communicators "lose face" and "gain face" differently in different cultures. In the United States, for example, a teacher would definitely lose face if a student proved the teacher wrong in the classroom in front of the other students. Presidential contender Howard Dean "lost face" when he screamed an ending to a political rally of college-age volunteers after losing a primary vote in Iowa. Pundits portrayed him as "unpresidential" and called it Dean's "I have a scream" speech (Kurtz, 2004).

Cohen (1991) points out the importance of face in collectivist, HC cultures: "Given the importance of face, the members of collectivist cultures are highly sensitive to the effect of what they say on others" (p. 26). He adds, "Language is a social instrument—a device for preserving and promoting social interests as much as a means for transmitting information" (p. 26). Americans observe that people from HC cultures are almost excessive in their praise for their receivers, exuberant in their courtesy, and devoid of conflict, contradiction, and even directness; and they practically never say a direct "no" to even an unreasonable request.

Two caveats are in order. First, while we use low context and high context to describe entire cultures, a culture is never exclusively one context or the other. People who are low context are born and raised in Japan, Korea, and Malaysia every day. People who are high context are plentiful in the United States, Germany, and Sweden.

Second, high context and low context are sometimes useful to describe particular situations within larger cultures. For example, if you belong to a small religious congregation, you experience HC culture. A similar perspective is present when you are at a family gathering, at a party with friends, or playing intramural sports. You know the rules because you know the people.

You experience LC culture when you are in a new, public, or unknown place. Each time you go to an airport, a gas station, a large grocery store, or an all-sports mega store, you experience low context. The rules are generalized, codified, public, and external, but also accessible. They are not based on your idiosyncratic relationship with the people or place.

Uncertainty-Accepting Versus Uncertainty-Rejecting Cultures

Uncertainty-accepting cultures tolerate ambiguity, uncertainty, and diversity. Some of these cultures already have a mixture of ethnic groups, religions, and races. They are more likely to accept political refugees, immigrants, and new citizens from other places. They are less likely to have a rule for everything and more likely to tolerate general principles. Uncertainty-accepting cultures include the United States, Great Britain, Denmark, Sweden, Singapore, Hong Kong, Ireland, and India (Hofstede, 1980). Interestingly, Singapore is a country that is more tolerant of uncertainty and diversity but has many rules, including one prohibiting chewing gum. This oddity should serve as a reminder that these characteristics are generalizations and therefore are not found consistently in every culture.

Uncertainty-rejecting cultures have difficulty with ambiguity, uncertainty, and diversity. These cultures are more likely to have lots of rules, more likely to

uncertainty-accepting cultures

Cultures that tolerate ambiguity, uncertainty, and diversity.

uncertainty-rejecting cultures

Cultures that have difficulty with ambiguity, uncertainty, and diversity.

want to know exactly how to behave, and more likely to reject outsiders such as immigrants, refugees, and migrants who look and act differently than them. Among the most common uncertainty-rejecting cultures are Japan, France, Spain, Greece, Portugal, Belgium, Peru, Chile, Russia, China, and Argentina (Samovar, Porter, & Stefani, 1998).

This uncertainty-rejection can lead to communication problems. For example, an increasing number of Asian people now reside in the United States. Teachers who are conferring with Asian parents may find that their communicative style is different from that of European-Americans with whom they meet. Lee and Manning (2001) report that Asian parents do not start talking immediately in a teacher–parent conference. Instead, they rely on the teacher's tone of voice, gestures, facial expressions, posture, walk, and treatment of time and space to learn about how the teacher feels about their child. The nonverbal cues help the Asian parents reduce their uncertainty.

Implicit-Rule Versus Explicit-Rule Cultures

implicit-rule culture

A culture in which information and cultural rules are implied and already known to the participants.

explicit-rule culture

A culture in which information, policies, procedures, and expectations are explicit.

An **implicit-rule culture** is one in which information and cultural rules are implied and already known to the participants. For example, a traditional Arab woman knows that one of the rules of her culture is that she is to walk a few paces behind her husband. People from an implicit-rule culture tend to be more polite, less aggressive, and more accommodating. Implicit-rule cultures typically are found in the Middle East, Africa, and Latin America (Dodd, 1998).

An **explicit-rule culture** is one with explicit information, policies, procedures, and expectations. For example, in U.S. families parents often discuss beforehand with their small children how the children are to act during a visit from someone of importance. People from an explicit-rule culture tend to be more combative, less willing to please, and less concerned about offending others. Explicit-rule cultures typically are found in Northern and Western Europe and the United States (Dodd, 1998).

You might think about the difference between an implicit-rule culture and an explicit-rule culture in this way: In an implicit-rule culture the social rules are part of who and what you are. They are learned over time from others and are no more discussed than washing your hands or brushing your teeth are in America. In an explicit-rule country, rules are often developed, discussed, and negotiated as you go along.

M-Time Versus P-Time Cultures

M-time

The monochronic time schedule, which compartmentalizes time to meet personal needs, separates task and social dimensions, and points to the future.

The last intercultural characteristic we will consider here is another of Hall's (1983) concepts for differentiating among cultures of the world. **M-time,** or monochronic time schedule, compartmentalizes time to meet personal needs, separates task and social dimensions, and points to the future (Ting-Toomey, 1997). M-time is dominant in Canada, the United States, and Northern Europe.

These cultures see time as something that can be compartmentalized, wasted, or saved. Americans might schedule times to work out, to keep appointments, to go to meetings, and to take the family to a fast-food restaurant. Time is segmented, dedicated to work or social experiences (but usually not both), and plotted toward future events and activities. Within this scheme, getting to any appointment on time is treated with considerable importance.

If you travel to other parts of the world including most countries in Latin America and the Middle East, you will probably experience being an M-time person in a P-time world. You may feel psychologically stressed as others always seem to be late. On the other hand, you may note that they also focus only on you when you are conversing with them. They are not distracted by schedules or other commitments.

P-time, or polychronic time schedule, views time as "contextually based and relationally oriented" (Ting-Toomey, 1997, p. 395). For P-time cultures time is not saved or wasted; instead, time is only one factor in a much larger and more complicated context. Why halt a conversation with an old friend to hurry off to an appointment on a relatively unimportant issue?

Relationships in some contexts trump time considerations. P-time cultures orchestrate their relational and task obligations with the fluid movements of jazz, whereas M-time cultures treat life like a march in which people strive mainly to stay on schedule and be efficient, and value tasks over relationships. Typical P-time cultures are found in Latin America, the Middle East, Asia, France, Africa, and Greece. America is predominantly M-time because of the strong European influence, but some co-cultures within the United States exhibit P-time tendencies.

Businesspeople in P-time cultures do conduct business, but they do it very differently than those in M-time cultures. A businessperson might have a large waiting room outside of her or his office. Several people will be in that waiting room, and they use the space and time to meet with each other and to resolve issues. A great deal of business in M-time cultures is conducted in public rather than in a series of private meetings.

Table 7.1 summarizes the concepts we discussed in this section. Most of the information is adapted from Carley Dodd's (1998) book titled *Dynamics of Intercultural Communication.*

P-time

The polychronic time schedule, which views time as "contextually based and relationally oriented."

MYTHS, METAPHORS, & MISUNDERSTANDINGS

Diversity training has become a multimillion-dollar industry in the United States, with consultants numbering in the thousands. Training and related proactive efforts to address diverse workers and customers are often lumped under the umbrella of "managing" diversity. Kirby and Harter (2003) urge practitioners to consider the implications of using a "managerial" metaphor to understand and enact workforce diversity. What symbolic power is present in the metaphor of "managing" diversity? If metaphors can function to indirectly argue for a particular attitude toward a subject, what attitudes does the language of "managing" diversity imply? How might managerial language both enable and constrain organizational members' perceptions about working with a diverse workforce and customer base? Consider the implications of alternative metaphors: "respecting" diversity, "honoring" diversity, and "tolerating" diversity.

TABLE 7.1   SUMMARY OF CULTURAL CHARACTERISTICS

INDIVIDUALISTIC CULTURES TEND TO:	COLLECTIVIST CULTURES TEND TO:
Value individual freedom; place "I" before "we."	Value the group over the individual; place "we" before "I."
Value independence.	Value commitment to family, tribe, and clan.
Value directness and clarity.	Value cooperation over competition.
Examples: United States, Australia, Great Britain	*Examples:* Venezuela, Pakistan, Taiwan, Thailand

UNCERTAINTY-ACCEPTING CULTURES TEND TO:	UNCERTAINTY-REJECTING CULTURES TEND TO:
Be willing to take risks.	Be threatened by ideas and people from outside.
Avoid rules, seek flexibility, and reject hierarchy.	Establish formal rules for behavior; prefer stability, hierarchy, and structure.
Value individual opinion, general principles, and common sense.	Embrace written rules, regulation, and rituals.
Examples: United States, Great Britain, Denmark	*Examples:* Japan, France, Spain, Greece, Argentina

EXPLICIT-RULE CULTURES TEND TO:	IMPLICIT-RULE CULTURES TEND TO:
See cultural rules as explicit; explain and discuss procedures.	See cultural rules as already known to participants.
Separate person and issue.	See person and issue as one.
Be straightforward; people have to cope with embarrassment or insult.	Prefer "saving face" to soothe an insulted person.
Examples: Northern and Western Europe, United States	*Examples:* Middle East, Africa, Latin America

LOW-CONTEXT (LC) CULTURES TEND TO:	HIGH-CONTEXT (HC) CULTURES TEND TO:
See communication as centered on the source, "I."	See communication as centered on the receiver.
Employ a direct verbal style.	Load much of the meaning into the setting or context.
Load information into the transmitted message.	Avoid saying a direct "no" to a request.
Examples: United States, Western Europe, Scandinavia	*Examples:* Asian Pacific Rim, Central and South America

M-TIME CULTURES TEND TO:	P-TIME CULTURES TEND TO:
Compartmentalize time.	Factor in time as one element of a larger context.
Say that they can waste or save time.	Value social relationships and time considerations together.
Separate work and social time, task and relational time.	Orchestrate family and social responsibilities and task dimensions.
Examples: North America, Northern Europe	*Examples:* Latin America, Middle East, Asia, France, Africa

SOURCE: Dodd, 1998.

What Are Some Strategies for Improving Intercultural Communication?

Effective intercultural communication often takes considerable time, energy, and commitment. Although some people would like "10 easy steps" to effective intercultural communication, no foolproof plan is available. However, the strategies presented here should provide you with some ways to improve intercultural communication and avoid potential problems. Having some strategies in advance will prepare you for new situations with people from other cultures and co-cultures and will increase your confidence in your ability to communicate effectively with a variety of people.

1. *Conduct a personal self-assessment.* How do your own attitudes toward different cultures and co-cultures influence your communication with them? One of the first steps toward improving your intercultural communication skills is an honest assessment of your own communication style, beliefs, and prejudices.

2. *Practice supportive communication behaviors.* Supportive behaviors, such as empathy, encourage success in intercultural exchanges; defensive behaviors tend to hamper effectiveness.

3. *Develop sensitivity toward diversity.* One healthy communication perspective holds that you can learn something from all people. Diverse populations provide ample opportunity for learning. Take the time to learn about other cultures and co-cultures before a communication situation, but don't forget that you will also learn about others simply by taking a risk and talking to someone who is different from you. Challenge yourself. You may be surprised by what you learn.

4. *Avoid stereotypes.* Cultural generalizations go only so far; avoid making assumptions about another's culture, and get to know individuals for themselves.

5. *Avoid ethnocentrism.* You may know your own culture the best, but that familiarity does not make your culture superior to all others. You will learn more about the strengths and weaknesses of your own culture by learning more about other cultures.

We endorse freedom of expression, diversity of perspective, and tolerance of dissent to achieve the informed and responsible decision making fundamental to a civil society.

NCA Ethics
Credo

6. *Develop code sensitivity.* Code sensitivity refers to the ability to use the verbal and nonverbal language appropriate to the cultural or co-cultural norms of the individual with whom you are communicating. The more you know about another's culture, the better you will be at adapting.

7. *Seek shared codes.* A key ingredient in establishing shared codes is being open-minded about differences while you determine which communication style to adopt during intercultural communication.

Freedom of expres-
sion and a diversity
of perspective are
fundamental to a
civil society.

8. *Use and encourage descriptive feedback.* Effective feedback encourages adaptation and is crucial in intercultural communication. Both participants should
   be willing to accept feedback and exhibit supportive behaviors. Feedback
   should be immediate, honest, specific, and clear.

9. *Open communication channels.* Intercultural communication can be frustrating. One important strategy to follow during such interactions is to be
   patient as you seek mutual understanding.

10. *Manage conflicting beliefs and practices.* Think ahead about how you might
    handle minor and major differences, from everyday behavior to seriously
    different practices like punishments (beheading, stoning), realities (starva-
    tion, extreme poverty), and beliefs (male superiority, female subjugation).

 Of course, the most effective strategy for improving your intercultural
communication competence is practice. Fortunately, the increasing diversity
of our own culture means that intercultural communication practice can take
place with the people at the corner market, at your place of employment,
or even with the student sitting next to you in class. To learn from these many
instances of intercultural communication, you must learn to be reflexive. **Reflexivity**
means being self-aware and learning from interactions with the intent of improving future interactions. That is, you are able to assess the interaction, identify what
went well in the conversation and what could have been done better, and then
learn from those observations. Through reflexivity you will not only improve your
intercultural communication skills, but will also become a more effective communicator in nearly every situation.

Reflexivity

Being self-aware and
learning from interac-
tions with the intent of
improving future inter-
actions.

Chapter Review & Study Guide

SUMMARY

In this chapter you learned the following:

▶ The study of intercultural communication is important because:
- We are increasingly exposed to people of other cultures and co-cultures.
- We have an economic need to relate to others.
- We are curious about others.

▶ Co-cultures communicate with the dominant culture with different goals.
- The three goals of co-cultural communication with the dominant culture are separation, accommodation, and assimilation.

▶ Ethnocentrism and stereotyping result in communication problems in both intercultural and co-cultural interactions.

▶ Cultural barriers can be reduced by learning the norms and values of other cultures.

▶ Cultures can be characterized by variations such as:
- Individualistic versus collectivist cultures.
- Low-context versus high-context cultures.
- Uncertainty-accepting versus uncertainty-rejecting cultures.
- Implicit-rule versus explicit-rule cultures.
- M-time versus P-time cultures.

▶ You can strive to improve your own communication competence by:
- Conducting a personal self-assessment.
- Practicing supportive communication behaviors.
- Developing sensitivity toward diversity.
- Avoiding stereotypes.
- Avoiding ethnocentrism.
- Developing code sensitivity.
- Seeking shared codes.
- Using descriptive feedback.
- Opening communication channels.
- Managing conflicting beliefs and practices.

KEY TERMS

Go to the *Online Learning Center* at **www.mhhe.com/pearson3** to further your understanding of the following terminology.

Accommodation goal	Explicit-rule culture	M-time
Assimilation goal	High-context (HC) cultures	P-time
Co-culture	Implicit-rule culture	Reflexivity
Collectivist cultures	Individualistic cultures	Separation goal
Cultural relativism	Intercultural communication	Uncertainty-accepting cultures
Culture	Low-context (LC) cultures	Uncertainty-rejecting cultures
Ethnocentrism		

STUDY QUESTIONS

1. Which of the following statements is *not* true?
   a. The convergence of technologies has created a "global village."
   b. Communication with people from other cultures or co-cultures is becoming increasingly uncommon.
   c. The influx of foreign-born immigrants, aliens, and refugees has changed the face of America.
   d. Intercultural communication is vital because we are increasingly exposed to people from other cultures and co-cultures.

2. How does a culture differ from a co-culture?
   a. A co-cultural group does not differ from the dominant culture in significant characteristics.
   b. A co-cultural group exists within a larger culture, but some significant characteristics differ.

    c. A cultural group exists within a co-cultural group.

    d. They do not differ in any way.

3. When marginalized groups try to fit in with the dominant group, they are attempting to achieve

    a. accommodation

    b. separation

    c. distinction

    d. assimilation

4. When people bring prejudices of their culture to intercultural interactions, they are being

    a. ethnocentric

    b. stereotypical

    c. accommodating

    d. collectivist

5. When people stereotype, they

    a. judge another person's culture by its own context

    b. make a generalization about a group of people that oversimplifies their culture

    c. believe their own culture is superior to other cultures

    d. avoid making degrading comments with relation to sexual objectification

6. Cultures that are more concerned with individuality, competition, and private property are members of which type of culture?

    a. collectivist

    b. relativistic

    c. individualistic

    d. assimilated

7. People in which type of culture openly discuss behavioral expectations?

    a. uncertainty-accepting

    b. monochronic

    c. explicit-rule

    d. high-context

8. A culture in which communication is in a direct verbal style, with intentions stated explicitly, is termed

    a. low-context

    b. high-context

    c. collectivist

    d. monochronic

9. Those who schedule their days, are early for appointments, and plan for the future are probably members of a(n)

    a. M-time culture

    b. P-time culture

    c. uncertainty-accepting culture

    d. explicit-rule culture

10. If you are trying to improve your intercultural communication, you should do which of the following?

    a. Be ethnocentric.

    b. Avoid shared codes.

    c. Close communication channels.

    d. Conduct a personal self-assessment.

Answers:

1. (b); 2. (b); 3. (d); 4. (a); 5. (b); 6. (c); 7. (c); 8. (a); 9. (a); 10. (d)

CRITICAL THINKING

1. To which co-cultures do you belong? Describe some of the characteristics of them. Then examine how they are similar and how they differ.

2. Consider the cultural characteristics discussed in this chapter. Which cultures do you identify with most or prefer?

SELF-QUIZ

For further review, try the chapter self-quiz on the *Online Learning Center* at **www.mhhe.com/pearson3**.

REFERENCES

Allport, G. W. (1954/1958). *The nature of prejudice.* Cambridge, MA: Addison-Wesley/Garden City, NY: Doubleday.

Bruno, R. L. (1999). "Beating" the tribal drum: Rejecting disability stereotypes and preventing self-discrimination. *Disability and Society, 14,* 855–857.

Cohen, R. (1991). *Negotiating across cultures: Communication obstacles in international diplomacy.* Washington, DC: U.S. Institute of Peace.

Coleman, D. (1998, December 22). The group and self: New focus on a cultural rift. *The New York Times,* p. 40.

Czopp, A. M., Monteith, M. J., & Mark, A. Y. (2006). Standing up for a change: Reducing bias through interpersonal confrontation. *Journal of Personality and Social Psychology, 90,* 784–803.

Dodd, C. H. (1998). *Dynamics of intercultural communication* (5th ed.). New York: McGraw-Hill.

Folb, E. (1994). Who's got the room at the top? Issues of dominance and nondominance in intracultural communication. In L. A. Samovar & R. E. Porter (Eds.), *Intercultural communication: A reader* (pp. 119–127). Belmont, CA: Wadsworth.

Garcia, A. L., Miller, D. A., Smith, E. R., & Mackie, D. M. (2006). Thanks for the compliment? Emotional reactions to group-level versus individual-level compliments and insults. *Group Processes and Intergroup Relations, 9,* 307–324.

Hall, E. T. (1976). *Beyond culture.* New York: Doubleday.

Henderson-King, E., & Nisbett, R. E. (1996). Anti-black prejudice as a function of exposure to the negative behavior of a single black person. *Journal of Personality and Social Psychology, 71,* 654–664.

Hofstede, G. (1980). *Culture's consequences: International differences in work-related values.* Beverly Hills, CA: Sage.

Kirby, E., & Harter, L.M. (2003). Speaking the language of the bottom-line: The metaphor of "managing diversity." *Journal of Business Communication, 40,* 28–49.

Kramarae, C. (1981). *Women and men speaking.* Rowley, MA: Newbury House.

Kurtz, H. (2004, February 2–8). Win or lose, Dean's the story. *The Washington Post* (weekly edition), p. 10.

Lee, G.-L., & Manning, M. L. (2001). Treat Asian parents and families right. *Education Digest, 67,* 39–45.

Orbe, M. P. (1996). Laying the foundation for co-cultural communication theory: An inductive approach to studying "nondominant" communication strategies and the factors that influence them. *Communication Studies, 47,* 157–176.

Rogers, E. M., & Steinfatt, T. M. (1999). *Intercultural communication.* Prospect Heights, IL: Waveland Press.

Samovar, L. A., Porter, R. E., & Stefani, L. A. (1998). *Communication between cultures* (3rd ed.). Belmont, CA: Wadsworth.

Swim, J. K., Hyers, L. L., Cohen, L. L., & Ferguson, M. J. (2001). Everyday sexism: Evidence for its incidence, nature, and psychological impact from three daily diary studies. *Journal of Social Issues, 57,* 31–53.

Ting-Toomey, S. (1997). Managing intercultural conflicts effectively. In L. A. Samovar & R. E. Porter (Eds.), *Intercultural communication: A reader* (8th ed., pp. 392–404). Belmont, CA: Wadsworth.

CHAPTER EIGHT

Workplace Communication

What will you learn?

When you have read and thought about this chapter, you will be able to:

1. Explain various dimensions of workplace communication including different types of organizations and communication networks within organizations.
2. Create an effective résumé and cover letter.
3. Take steps to effectively prepare for employment interviews ranging from creating a self-inventory and personal network to planning for postinterview negotiations.
4. Enact skills relevant to workplace communication competence including immediacy, supportiveness, strategic ambiguity, and interaction management.
5. Engage in effective conflict management practices with others in your workplace.
6. Practice effective customer service behaviors.
7. Recognize and practice ethical workplace communication behaviors.

The very fabric of our social, cultural, and economic worlds is intertwined with various organizations including schools, clubs, places of worship, and the workplace. Our ability to communicate effectively and ethically within these various organizations determines, in large part, our opportunities for personal, social, and economic advancement. In this chapter you will learn about various skills related to workplace communication. Although we focus on the workplace, many of these skills are relevant to the many other organizations to which you belong.

Nearly three-fourths of the taxi drivers at the Minneapolis/ St. Paul airport face a dilemma each day. On the one hand, they want to provide good service to their customers and make enough money to support their families. On the other hand, if they are to follow the strictures of their religion, they feel they must refuse service to certain customers.

This dilemma arises from the fact that these cab drivers are immigrants from Somalia and adherents of Islam. They believe that transporting travelers who are obviously carrying alcohol violates their religion. Their refusal is not based on intoxication or the open containers; it is based on their interpretation of Islam's denouncement of alcohol consumption. The number of refusals has grown to more than 5000 a year (van Biema & Pickett, 2007). Needless to say, the actions of the taxi drivers have been a source of controversy.

At first, the airport administration tried to solve the problem by allowing cabs that prohibited alcohol to put a special-colored light on their roof. But this did not sit well with travelers. Some groups claimed that the travelers' rights were being violated and that such preferential treatment for the taxi drivers was not justified in publicly licensed transportation. The airport administration backpedaled from the roof light solution and now suspends drivers who refuse riders toting alcohol. The Muslim-American cab drivers have to decide whether to violate their religious beliefs or face the possibility of losing their livelihood.

Communication in the workplace involves more than learning how to be pleasant with customers, clients, and co-workers. As individuals with our own values and moral stances, we bring to the workplace certain assumptions and expectations, which may conflict with the assumptions and expectations of others in the workplace, as the cab drivers discovered. Communicating what you expect and what you value to others, and handling the potential conflicts that might arise, are vital skills to learn as you enter a new employment situation. In this chapter you will learn about communication in the workplace— how it works and what skills are needed to make the transition into a new organization and to manage conflict successfully and ethically.

What Is Workplace Communication?

Each of us belongs to several different organizations. For example, you may belong to one or more business organizations, perhaps as an employee, supervisor, or even investor. Because you are reading this book, you are most likely a college student and therefore are a member of an educational organization. You may also belong to a church, student clubs, and community service organizations, and, of course, we are all members of local, state, and national government organizations. In short, our workplace is one of many organizations to which we belong. Organizations exist because people's lives have become sufficiently complex that they must cooperate with one another. In other words, **organizations** are social collectives, or groups of people, in which activities are coordinated to achieve both individual and collective goals.

organizations

Social collectives, or groups of people, in which activities are coordinated to achieve both individual and collective goals.

MYTHS, METAPHORS, & MISUNDERSTANDINGS

Theorists who study workplace communication often rely on metaphors to describe organizational life. These metaphors can take on mythic, larger-than-life qualities. For instance, organizations can be compared to families, machines, and even living creatures. What do these metaphors suggest about communication in the workplace? What do they reveal about communication? How might some metaphors create potential misunderstandings? In small groups, develop a different metaphor for organizational life, and discuss its implications for understanding communication.

Being communicatively competent in the workplace involves understanding how the context of the organization influences communication processes and how the symbolic nature of communication differentiates it from other forms of organizational behavior. We define **organizational communication** as the ways in which groups of people both maintain structure and order through their symbolic interactions and allow individual actors the freedom to accomplish their goals. This definition recognizes that communication is the primary tool to influence organizations and gain access to organizational resources. To better understand key characteristics of workplace communication, you should recognize that there are different types of organizations and different types of communication networks within organizations.

organizational communication

The ways in which groups of people both maintain structure and order through their symbolic interactions and allow individual actors the freedom to accomplish their goals.

Types of Organizations

Talcott Parsons (1963) classified organizations into four primary types: economic, political, integration, and pattern maintenance. Although some organizations might overlap these categories, we usually can classify organizations according to their primary functions in society.

Organizations with an **economic orientation** tend to manufacture products and/or offer services for consumers. Most profit-oriented businesses like Target, Ford Motor Company, and even Tim's Family Bar-B-Que restaurant in Kansas City are oriented toward economic production. Because such organizations succeed or fail based on their ability to sell products to consumers, communication within these workplace settings must work to enhance productivity while at the same time persuade consumers of the value of their products.

economic orientation

Organizations that manufacture products and/or offer services for consumers.

Organizations with a **political orientation** generate and distribute power and control within society. Elected local, state, and federal officials; police and military forces; even financial institutions like the Federal Reserve Bank—all are examples of political organizations. Because political organizations must adhere to governing principles—the U.S. Constitution, for example—communication centers on the connection between practices and principles. For instance, the president must answer to Congress to justify the use of military force.

political orientation

Organizations that generate and distribute power and control within society.

Organizations with an **integration orientation** help to mediate and resolve discord among members of society. Our court system, public interest groups, and conflict management centers are all examples of integration-oriented organizations.

integration orientation

Organizations that help to mediate and resolve discord among members of society.

Complex organizations require members to perform specialized roles. Such specialization is often reflected by organizational structure.

One unique characteristic of communication within integrative organizations is the necessity of impartiality. A judge, for example, must not be biased in the way she or he talks to criminal defendants, and public interest groups must demonstrate that their objective benefits all of society and not just a few individuals.

Organizations with a **pattern-maintenance orientation** promote cultural and educational regularity and development within society. Organizations that function to teach individuals how to participate effectively in society, including families, schools, and religious groups, promote pattern maintenance. Communication within organizations focused on pattern maintenance emphasizes social support. Your family or your church, for instance, functions to provide you with personal and spiritual support. Even schools support individuals by helping them learn.

Communication Networks

Competent workplace communicators understand that the workplace comprises multiple communication networks. **Communication networks** are patterns of relationships through which information flows in an organization. Stohl (1995) describes communication networks as capturing "the tapestry of *relationships*—the complex web of *affiliations* among individuals and organizations as they are woven through the collaborative threads of communication" (p. 18). Communication networks emerge in organizations based on formal and informal communication (Stohl & Stohl, 2005).

Formal communication consists of messages that follow prescribed channels of communication throughout the organization. The most common way of depicting formal communication networks is with organizational charts like the one in Figure 8.1. Organizational charts provide clear guidelines as to who is responsible for a given task and which employees are responsible for others' performance. Figure 8.1 is a typical organizational chart for a bureaucratic structure. It shows, for instance, that Alexi reports to her boss, Cliff, and Julie reports to Sue.

Organizational charts demonstrate that communication can flow in several directions: downward, upward, and horizontally. **Downward communication** occurs whenever superiors initiate messages to subordinates. Ideally, downward communication should include such things as job instructions, job rationale, policy and procedures, performance feedback, and motivational appeals. Messages flowing from subordinates to superiors are labeled **upward communication.** Obviously, effective decision making depends on timely, accurate, and complete information traveling

pattern-maintenance orientation

Organizations that promote cultural and educational regularity and development within society.

communication networks

Patterns of relationships through which information flows in an organization.

formal communication

Messages that follow prescribed channels of communication throughout the organization.

downward communication

Messages flowing from superiors to subordinates.

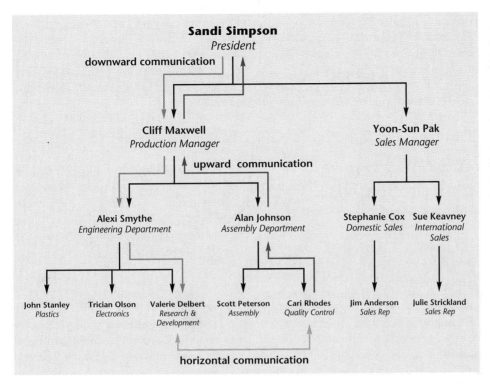

Figure 8.1 Formal communication flow.

upward from subordinates. Messages between members of an organization with equal power are labeled **horizontal communication.** Horizontal communication is important to organizational success when used to coordinate tasks, solve problems, share information, and resolve conflict. Horizontal communication receives much more attention in participatory organizational structures in which employees have more opportunity to formally participate in decision making (such as quality circles or autonomous work teams).

Informal communication is generally considered to be any interaction that does not generally follow the formal structure of the organization but emerges out of natural social interaction among organization members. Whereas formal communication consists of messages the organization recognizes as official, informal messages do not follow official lines. The concept of emergent organizational networks represents the informal, naturally occurring patterns of communication relationships in organizations (Susskind, Schwartz, Richards, & Johnson, 2005).

To hear people refer to informal interactions as grapevine communication is not uncommon. Information introduced into the grapevine travels quickly because messages are uninhibited by structural constraints. Although we publicly tend to discredit the grapevine, research has consistently shown that grapevine communication is amazingly accurate. Scholars have consistently reported 78–90% accuracy figures in their studies of grapevine communication in organizational settings (e.g., Caudron, 1998).

Competent workplace communicators take care in understanding the various communication networks within their organization. Much inefficiency can be avoided simply by following correct channels for communication. Moreover, effective workplace communicators understand the nature of both formal and informal communication. Managers who take time to develop and listen to sources of informal information are better equipped to understand employees' attitudes and concerns. When entering an organization, such as when you start your first job, asking other employees about communication practices is smart because you not only discover formal procedures but also make contact for informal sources of information.

How Should You Prepare Written Credentials?

Your written credentials should be designed to gain the attention of job interviewers. As you create your résumé and cover letter, remember that the purpose of employment interviews is to make decisions about the degree of fit between people and jobs. Collectively, your credentials should illustrate your ability to successfully do the job.

Résumés

Writing a résumé is a project that takes time and effort. You should view the process of compiling a résumé as an investment that pays off in numerous ways. The soul-searching involved in creating a résumé functions to focus your life accomplishments and future goals. A résumé puts you into employment databases and, if it is successful, lands you interviews. Résumés also serve employers in numerous ways. Résumés allow employers to predict the future performance of job candidates, simplify the hiring process, and serve as a reference source for the postinterview period (Henricks, 2000). To successfully create a résumé, you must consider style, content, and format.

Style

The style of a résumé involves the overall tone created by your linguistic and aesthetic choices. We recommend that the style of your résumé reflect your personality in a concise and professional way, be confident but not arrogant, and accurately highlight your credentials. Next, we provide several stylistic suggestions and illustrate them in the sample résumé provided in Figure 8.2.

First, writing résumés using complete sentences and the pronoun "I" is unnecessary. Descriptive clauses are sufficient as long as they are understandable. Many experts recommend beginning descriptive clauses with action verbs such as *planned, supervised,* and *conducted* (Henricks, 2000). These words catch employers' attention because they are concrete and indicate what you have done. Some commonly used action verbs are listed in Table 8.1. Should you use past- or present-tense verbs? The tense depends on whether you are currently performing the particular job duties. Use present-tense verbs for present employment and activities, and past-tense verbs for historical information.

Whenever possible, you should quantify information. The following examples illustrate how to quantify information to illustrate the scope of your accomplishments:

Managed a $30,000 budget for Lambda Chi Alpha.

Supervised 10 customer service representatives.

Increased sales by 200%.

Employers look for accomplishments like these because they are concrete, measurable, and significant.

140014 35st St South   701-236-8769
Omaha, NE 68048   bradshaws@umd.edu

Samantha Bradshaw

Objective   To obtain a position in Web design providing quality service to
                  non-profit organizations.

Experience   2003–Present   Ignus, Inc   Omaha, NE

Web Designer

- Plan and create Web sites.
- Scan, resize, and optimize all graphics.
- Attend sales meetings with clients and sales representatives.
- Suggest changes for sites of prospective clients.

2001–2003   Butler Machinery Company   Omaha, NE

Office Assistant

- Updated and maintained the machine inventory on
  company Web site.
- Performed miscellaneous office duties including typing,
  faxing, and mailing.
- Implemented training course for 20 new employees.

1999–2001   Mail Boxes Etc   Omaha, NE

Senior Sales Representative

- Packaged and shipped out packages for UPS, USPS, and
  FedEx.
- Sorted mail.
- Facilitated monetary transactions.
- Scanned pictures for company Web site.

Education   2001–2005   Creighton University   Omaha, NE

- B.A., Business Administration and Computer Science.
- Graduated Summa Cum Laude.
- GPA 3.85.

Skills   Proficient in HTML Language, Microsoft Access, Adobe
                  Photoshop, Microsoft Outlook, Fireworks, PhotoEditor,
                  Internet Explorer, C++ Language, Microsoft Excel, PowerPoint,
                  Word, Dreamweaver, and GoldMine Mktg.

Figure 8.2   Sample chronological résumé.

Be consistent. Whenever you make stylistic decisions, adhere to them. If you use bullets to present your job duties, use bullets throughout your résumé. If you put periods at the end of your bulleted descriptions, make sure you consistently use periods. If you indent one job title five spaces and underline, make sure all your job titles are indented five spaces and underlined.

TABLE 8.1   ACTION VERBS FOR RÉSUMÉS

Accomplished	Formulated	Ordered	Succeeded
Adapted	Generated	Participated	Supervised
Administered	Handled	Performed	Supplied
Analyzed	Headed	Persuaded	Supported
Balanced	Identified	Prepared	Tabulated
Disbursed	Managed	Revised	Uploaded
Examined	Modified	Searched	Verified
Executed	Notified	Selected	Volunteered
Explained	Obtained	Sponsored	Won
Filed	Offered	Streamlined	Wrote

Be concise. Remember that you do not have to put everything in a résumé. In fact, view your résumé as an appetizer. You can tell about the main course in the interview. Unless you have more than seven years of work experience, most experts agree that your résumé should not be longer than one page (Henricks, 2000).

Be neat. Given that employers have very limited time to spend reading your résumé, the overall impression it creates is important. Employers judge you and your capabilities based in part on the physical appearance of your résumé. Poorly proof-read, sloppy documents are difficult to ignore and will decrease your chances of securing an interview.

Content

The content of résumés for college students typically includes contact information as well as your objectives, education, experience, skills, and campus activities or community involvement. Without contact information the rest of your résumé is useless. On every résumé you send out, you must include complete information about how to contact you, including an e-mail address.

objective statement

An articulation of your goals.

An **objective statement**, or an articulation of your goals, is usually the first information on the résumé, just below your contact information. Objective statements are important because they allow you to tailor your credentials and goals to the needs of a particular organization and job description (Bennett, 2005). In addition to describing your personal goals, you should consider what the organization needs or what types of issues it faces when you are writing your objective statement. The following are examples of objective statements:

To apply programming skills in an environment with short deadlines and demanding customers.

To achieve consistent improvement in sales profitability of units under my supervision.

Employers also want to see your educational credentials. They do not necessarily believe that your college professors taught you everything you need to know to succeed at their company. Rather, your credentials show that you had the intellect to go to college, the determination to complete high school, and the capability of learning new things and finishing complex projects. In summarizing your education, you should include degrees awarded, completion dates (or anticipated completion dates), schools attended, majors and minors, and honors or scholarships. Employers always look at your education, but the further along you are in your career, the smaller the role your education plays on your résumé. Instead, experience becomes more important.

With few exceptions employers will focus much of their attention on your past jobs, whether you are a freshly minted college graduate or an experienced individual changing jobs or careers. Employers look at the types of jobs you have held, job tenure, job duties, and accomplishments. When describing your work experience, make sure you include a job title, the name of the organization, dates of employment, and a description of your major responsibilities and achievements. Remember to use action verbs (see Table 8.1) and to quantify accomplishments whenever possible.

Most résumés also include a skills section highlighting abilities ranging from the ability to use Microsoft Word to fluency in multiple languages. The skills section of your résumé should be tailored to the job description of the position for which you are applying.

Many college students end their résumé with a discussion of their campus activities and/or community involvement. When discussing membership in groups, do not stop at merely listing the group. Rather, indicate your level of involvement, including participation on committees and leadership positions. Involvement in campus and community organizations is important because involvement translates, in the mind of many employers, to workplace citizenship.

For help preparing business documents, explore the business documents templates on the Online Learning Center.

Format

Now that you are familiar with stylistic and content choices, you need to consider how to organize information on your résumé. College students typically rely on chronological, functional, and/or online formats.

The **chronological résumé,** which organizes your credentials over time, is what most people envision when they think of a résumé. A résumé based on time has long been the standard and, despite technological advances allowing for electronic résumés, continues to be the most widely accepted format (Henricks, 2000). The core concept of the chronological résumé is accomplishments over time. To refer to a résumé as "reverse chronological" would be more appropriate, because in describing your work experience (and education), you begin with your last or present job and continue back to past jobs. Figure 8.1 is an example of a chronological résumé.

Whereas the chronological format organizes your experience based on "when" you acquired it, the **functional résumé** organizes your experience by type of function performed. If you have had a variety of jobs (such as teaching, sales, and advertising), the functional résumé allows you to group jobs by the skills developed and duties performed. Graduating college students will use a functional résumé to group "professional experience" separately from "other work experience," which may include jobs that do not directly relate to your career goal but nonetheless illustrate your work ethic.

The impact of the Internet is evident in many facets of our lives, including our professional roles. For that reason you may need to have an online résumé, prepared in plain text (ASCII), hypertext markup language (HTML), or another format and posted on the web. Plain-text résumés have limited formatting options. For instance,

chronological résumé

A document that organizes your credentials over time.

functional résumé

A document that organizes your credentials by type of function performed.

Creating Electronic Résumés

You can create an electronic résumé by scanning your current résumé and converting it to a .pdf or .html file, or simply by creating these files from scratch. Files in .pdf format require a free computer program called Adobe Acrobat Reader to view. Files in .html formats are essentially web pages. Although nearly every computer has the necessary software to view .html files, the options for formatting the look of your résumé are more limited in .html files as compared with .pdf files. The following websites provide more information on creating electronic résumés:

www.eresumes.com
jobsmart.org/tools/resume
susanireland.com/eresumework.htm

you cannot center, bold, or italicize text. Résumés that use HTML formatting can include all sorts of fancy formatting. As more advanced technologies develop, other ways of transmitting résumés online will emerge. For more information on creating electronic résumés, we suggest that you consult several online sites that describe how to create an electronic résumé as identified in the accompanying e-note.

Cover Letters

cover letter

A short letter introducing you and your résumé to an interviewer.

A **cover letter** is a short letter introducing you and your résumé to an interviewer, and it typically accompanies your résumé. Cover letters are persuasive documents that function as an introduction, sales pitch, and overview of your qualifications as related to the job description. Cover letters are important because they help ensure that your résumé is read and help target your appeal for a particular job. As with any persuasive document, a cover letter has four main sections: (1) attention, (2) interest, (3) desire, and (4) action (Krizan, Merrier, & Jones, 2002).

After headings that contain your address and the interviewer's address, your cover letter should gain the attention of the reader. At this point you should specify the position for which you are applying, indicate how you heard about it, and provide a general overview of your qualifications. In the second paragraph you need to arouse the reader's interest and demonstrate your desire for the job. At this point you want to describe your major experiences and strengths as they relate to the job. If possible, mention one or two accomplishments that illustrate your proficiency and effectiveness. The main idea is to create interest and show how your skills and qualifications can be of value to the organization. You can refer the reader to the enclosed résumé for more detail on your qualifications and experience. In the third paragraph you need to suggest action. Restate your interest in the position or organization and your desire for a face-to-face meeting. Finally, express your appreciation for the reader's time and/or consideration.

When writing a résumé, you rarely use full sentences or poetic flair. A cover letter, however, provides an opportunity to demonstrate your writing skills. The design attributes of your cover letter should be consistent with your résumé, including typefaces, fonts, type sizes, line spacing, and paper choice. Figure 8.3 provides a conventional outline for generating a cover letter.

HEADING
Name
Address
City, State, Zip Code
Phone
e-mail address

INSIDE ADDRESS   **DATE**
Name, Title
Department, Organization
Address
City, State, Zip Code

SALUTATION:	Use title and last name if available (e.g., Dear Dr. Smith or Dear Ms. Jones). Do not use a first name unless you know the person well and are sure this is acceptable. If you do not have a name, use the title (e.g., Dear Employment Manager).
PARAGRAPH I:	Gain *attention* and state *purpose*—indicate the position or type of work for which you are applying. Mention how you heard about the opening or the organization. You may also want to provide a general overview of your qualifications for the position (functions as a preview statement for your letter).
PARAGRAPH II:	Arouse *interest* and demonstrate *desire*—summarize qualifications and describe enclosure. Here you want to describe your major strengths as they relate to the position you are seeking. If possible, mention one or two recent accomplishments that illustrate your proficiency and effectiveness. The main idea is to create interest and show how your skills and qualifications can be of value to the organization. Refer the reader to the enclosed résumé for more detail on your qualifications and experience.
PARAGRAPH III:	Suggest *action*. Restate your strong interest in the position or organization and your desire for a face-to-face meeting. Include a statement about how the reader may contact you. Finally, express your appreciation for the reader's time and/or consideration.

COMPLIMENTARY CLOSE (Sincerely yours,)

(Leave 3 blank lines)

NAME

POSTSCRIPT (Enclosure; Enc.)

Figure 8.3   Generic format for a cover letter.

Employment Interviews

Getting a job is work in itself. Self-knowledge and the ability to express what you believe to be true about yourself are essential in an interview. You should have a clear understanding of the career field in which you plan to spend your productive years, as well as some insight into the effects that current social

Asking and answering questions is the primary mode of communication in employment interviews.

and economic conditions may have on that field. Background information about the company or organization for which you would like to work and the position for which you are applying are also factors to consider before the interview. In this section you will learn about these issues including how to prepare for and participate in an interview as well as how to enact postinterview strategies.

Taking Self-Inventory

What do you really know about yourself? When was the last time you took inventory of your assets and liabilities? Could you express these qualities intelligently? Answers to these questions are essential when you are preparing for a job interview. One way of approaching this difficult task is to ask yourself what your friends, family, and co-workers would say about you. What words would they use to describe you, and why? What successes and failures would they attribute to you? Why do you need this self-assessment just to get a job? The answer is simply that you cannot talk intelligently about yourself if you do not know much about yourself.

In an employment interview no one speaks for you but you. No one knows your best features better than you do, and no one will benefit from your description of those assets more than you will. As an intelligent interviewee you must begin your preparation for a job search with a thorough assessment of your skills, interests, attributes, and achievements. Although not exclusive of other possible areas to explore, consider tallying the following:

- Your work and educational experiences
- Your motivations and goals
- Your strengths and weaknesses
- Your likes and dislikes
- Your skills
- Your roles in campus extracurricular activities
- Your professional experience, if any (including co-op programs and internships)
- Your interests and hobbies
- Your talents, aptitudes, and achievements
- What is important to you in a position and an organization

Be thorough in your analysis so that when you get ready to participate in a job interview, you will be able to define and describe the benefits you can bring to an organization. Ideally, you should then be able to summarize what you know about yourself in a single, detailed answer to the most commonly used first question in an employment interview: "Tell me about yourself."

On your journey to self-awareness, know that resources are available to help you. Most college campuses have career counseling centers dedicated to helping you better understand your passions and skills, as well as offering information about potential career paths. The Riley Guide at www.rileyguide.com has a good summary of career counseling sites available on the Internet.

TRY ◆ THIS

Several online career counseling sites provide numerous resources including interactive tests to give you an idea about possible career directions and articles dealing with various career issues. In his text Job-Hunting on the Internet, *Richard Bolles (1999) recommends John Holland's SDS (Self-Directed Search), which can be accessed at www.self-directed-search.com. Go to this link and complete the interactive career test.*

Creating a Network

Many people assume that the key to landing a good job is having a good résumé. Though partly true, this conventional wisdom is also incomplete: The key to finding great jobs is having a great network. A **network** is an intricate web of contacts and relationships designed to benefit the participants—including identifying leads and giving referrals (Bolles, 2000). People in your network, including family, friends, people you have met at social functions, and people you have worked and studied with, can assist you in identifying job leads and introducing you to yet others who can become a part of your network.

> **network**
>
> An intricate web of contacts and relationships designed to benefit the participants.

Because many college students have not yet had significant work experience, developing a network is critical to postcollege employment. Although some people are automatically part of our network—family and friends, for instance—we must cultivate others. Here are general strategies you can use to develop your network:

1. *Create an inventory of your network.* You should talk with people in your network who have significant work experience to make them aware that you are in the job market. They may give you leads or other contacts.

2. *Contact the career services office on your campus.* Most campuses offer several job fairs throughout the academic year or provide other networking opportunities. Taking advantage of these face-to-face meeting opportunities can be a very productive use of your time.

3. *Contact and join student chapters of professional organizations on your campus.* In communication, for instance, students often join clubs like the National Communication Association, the Association for Women in Communication, the Public Relations Society of America, or the Society for Professional Journalists. Campus chapters of these organizations provide very useful networking opportunities for members.

4. *Consider an internship.* If you are early in your academic career, an internship can provide valuable networking opportunities. Most colleges and universities offer options for students to earn course credit for internships—you should talk with your academic adviser about such options on your campus.

5. *Volunteer.* Simply taking the time to volunteer in your community can open many doors. Besides giving you the satisfaction that comes from helping others, your hard work and dedication will not go unnoticed by others.

Volunteering for a community organization will allow you to get to know many different types of people in your community, thus expanding your network.

6. *Take advantage of the Internet.* Joining professional discussion boards and posting your résumé online will allow you to be "visible" in the growing virtual cybercommunity. Using the Internet is perhaps the best and most practical way to establish a network in places around the country or even the world.

Searching for a Job

After you have reflected on your career interests and abilities, you can embark on the exciting, sometimes frustrating, journey of a job search. The U.S. job market has more than 16 million employers. How do you gain access to those employers who are hiring? According to Richard Bolles (2000) in *What Color Is Your Parachute?* the conventional job-hunting methods of networking, using placement offices on college campuses, and using employment agencies have the highest rates of success. Thanks to technological advances, we can now add another job-hunting method: electronic job banks. An aggressive job-hunting approach uses all available methods.

Information about job vacancies is readily available through classified ads, placement offices on college campuses, and employment agencies. Additionally, "job listings," also known as "job postings," are available online. Be warned, however, that online searches are most fruitful for those looking for computer-related jobs (Bolles, 1999). In fact, Bolles estimates that for individuals searching for non-computer-related jobs, only 3 out of 100 will find a job using online methods.

Investigating the Interviewer

To present yourself as a mature candidate for employment for any job, you will want to illustrate your knowledge of your chosen field, the effect of current social and economic conditions, and the trends in the field. You will want to keep current on all aspects of the career field because employers will view you more positively if you are conversant on these issues.

You should have a comprehensive understanding of the organization to which you are applying. You should be familiar with the current information on company officers, products or services offered, geographical locations, and potential mergers, acquisitions, and expansion plans.

It is important for you to be very familiar with the job description of the position for which you are applying. Nearly all organizations rely on official documents—job descriptions—to make business-related decisions, including hiring employees. A **job description** defines the job in terms of its content and scope. Although the format can vary, job descriptions may include information on job duties and responsibilities; the knowledge, skills, and abilities necessary to accomplish the duties; working conditions; relationships with co-workers, supervisors, and external stakeholders; and the extent of supervision required. To obtain a copy of the job description, you should contact the company's human resources department or the person managing the job search process. Besides providing you with information about the job expectations, the job description also serves as the legal cornerstone of interview questions and job-hiring practices.

job description

A document that defines the job in terms of its content and scope.

General Interviewing Strategies

Preplan

The best way for applicants to prepare for their role in job interviews is to know what employers seek in applicants and how they can find pertinent information. Remember, the major purpose of the interview is to obtain and synthesize information about the abilities of an individual and the requirements of the job. The best way to plan for a successful interview is to review the job description and information about the organization, familiarize yourself with current events affecting the particular industry and/or job, reflect on your experiences and skills as related to the job description, and prepare answers to important questions.

In preparing answers to potential interview questions, remember that questions are tailored to the job description at hand and seek to ascertain your abilities to accomplish job duties.

Practicing competent responses to potential questions is an important method of managing the anxiety that is normally experienced by interviewees. Mentally talk to yourself prior to the interview. Build your confidence by telling yourself that you have done all you can to prepare for the interview. You have anticipated questions and have prepared answers; you have learned about the company. You are ready for the interview.

Watch "Susan Elliott: Reporting for KTNT" on the *Online Learning Center* to see how to preplan for an interview.

Demonstrate Competence

During the interview you must present yourself as a potential asset to the organization. Doing so requires using verbal and nonverbal communication; specifically, you want to (1) create a good first impression, (2) speak with clarity, and (3) demonstrate interest.

Just as your written credentials should reflect a professional and competent image, so should you. One of the most obvious ways to create a good first impression is by the way you dress. The general rule is that you should match the style of dress of the interviewer. For professional positions, conservative dress is typically appropriate (dark suits, white shirts or blouses, standard ties for men, dark socks or neutral hose, dark shoes). Be sure to wear clothes that fit and are comfortable but not too casual. Be modest with your use of jewelry and cologne.

◄ SKILL BUILDER ►

Practice answering these typical job interview questions with a partner:

1. *Why would you like to work for us?*
2. *What do you know about our products or services?*
3. *How have your previous work positions prepared you for this position?*
4. *What do you think your previous supervisors would cite as your strengths? Weaknesses?*
5. *Describe a typical strategy that you would use in a customer service call.*
6. *What criteria do you use when assigning work to others?*
7. *How do you follow up on work assigned to others?*
8. *Which aspect of your education has prepared you most for this position?*
9. *Which course did you like most in college?*
10. *If you had your education to do over again, what would you do differently, and why?*
11. *Why did you choose _____ as your major?*
12. *What do you think is the greatest challenge facing this field today?*
13. *Which area of this field do you think will expand the most in the next few years?*

Arriving on time and introducing yourself in a courteous manner are also important to identity management. Allow the interviewer to take the lead. If an offer is made to shake hands, do so with a firm grip and a smile. Sit when asked to do so. Keep in mind, we are suggesting impression management techniques as a way to present yourself in a positive yet honest manner—not in a manipulative or dishonest manner.

Competent communicators speak with clarity. In one study of personnel interviewers' perceptions of applicants' communication skills, a lack of response clarity and poor grammar were among the most often cited communication inadequacies (Peterson, 1997). Yet 98% of respondents in Peterson's study, as well as other research (Ayres et al., 2001; Ralston & Kirkwood, 1999), indicated that such skills affect hiring decisions. Even if you have to pause

First impressions occur the instant an interview begins.

before responding, organize your answer and avoid slurring your words, using potentially offensive language, or using grammatically incorrect sentences. Many applicants do not convey clear messages because their sentences include vocalized pauses ("uhs," "ums"), verbal fillers ("you know"), and repetitive phrases ("things like that"). In sum, the employment interview is a context to practice the skills you have been learning about and developing in this course.

To be interpersonally effective in interviews, you must also demonstrate interest. One of the most important ways to do so is by maintaining strong eye contact with the interviewer. Several studies have indicated that eye contact is one of the most important indicators of interview success (Peterson, 1997; Young, Behnke, & Mann, 2004). Although you may be tempted to focus on responding to questions as the central interviewing skills, listening can demonstrate your interest and improve your responses. Also, use body language to show interest. Smile, nod, and give nonverbal feedback to the interviewer. Be sure to thank the interviewer for his or her time and consideration of you as a candidate.

Answer Questions Effectively and Ethically

Answering questions effectively is critical for interviewees. Research has shown that various strategies are associated with successfully answering questions (e.g., Tey, Ang, & Van Dyne, 2006). Four key guidelines emerge from that body of research: (1) offer relevant answers, (2) substantiate your claims with evidence, (3) provide accurate answers, and (4) be positive.

Your answers should be relevant to the question asked and to the job description. As an interviewee you should never evade questions; rather, you should respond to them thoroughly and directly. In discussing your skills and abilities, try to relate them to the specific position for which you are interviewing. Whenever possible, specify how and why you think you are well suited to this job. By so doing, you demonstrate your knowledge of the position and illustrate the transferability of your knowledge and skills to the job at hand.

Whatever claims you make about your experience, always provide support. Some interviewees give terse, underdeveloped responses, forcing the interviewer to probe endlessly. Do not just say, "I'm really organized." You need to substantiate this self-assertion with examples of when you have demonstrated organizational skills. Presenting claims without evidence can sound self-serving. If you offer evidence for your assertions, the objective facts and supporting examples will confirm your strengths.

All employers are searching for honest employees, so always provide accurate information. If an employer finds out you have misrepresented yourself during the interview by exaggerating or lying, everything you do and say will become suspect. Successful interviews feature candid conversation. If you are asked a question that you cannot answer, simply say so and do not act embarrassed. An interviewer will have more respect for an interviewee who admits to ignorance than for one who tries to fake an answer.

Accuracy should not be confused with confessing to every self-doubt or short-coming. In fact, be as positive as possible during interviews, as you are "selling" yourself to the employer. To volunteer some limitations or claim personal responsibility for past events is fine, especially in the context of challenges you have met or problems you have encountered. However, avoid being overly critical of others and yourself. You can highlight your strengths and downplay your weaknesses, but always be honest.

Ask Questions Effectively and Ethically

Any potential employer will recognize that you have questions about the job and/or organizational environment. After answering the interviewer's questions, you should be prepared to ask questions. This provides you with insight necessary to decide if you want this particular job, shows your interest in the job, and demonstrates communication skills.

Recognize that your questions make indirect statements about your priorities, ambitions, and level of commitment. Consequently, avoid overreliance on questions that focus on financial issues such as salary, vacation time, and benefits. Devise questions that elicit information about the company and/or job that you were unable to obtain through your research. Arrange questions so that the most important ones come first, because you may not get a chance to ask all of your prepared questions. Sample questions to ask employers are provided on the *Online Learning Center*.

MYTHS, METAPHORS, & MISUNDERSTANDINGS

Most interviewees approach the interview from a "performance" perspective in which they sell themselves to the organization or "try out" for a job. However, this approach fails to recognize that the potential employee must also assess whether the job and/or organization represents a good opportunity for personal and professional growth. How might the performance metaphor be re-envisioned to better capture the multidirectional persuasion that occurs in interview settings?

Be Prepared for Illegal Questions

Legally, employers must approach the hiring process with reference to the laws that govern employment. These laws are known as "equal employment opportunity (EEO) laws"; they are written and enacted by Congress and by individual state legislatures (Gutman, 2000). The purpose of such laws is to ensure that individuals are selected for employment without bias.

Employers should (1) describe the qualities and skills needed for the position they hope to fill, (2) construct questions that relate to those attributes, and (3) ask the same questions of all candidates for the position. These questions are known as "bona fide occupational qualification (BFOQ) questions." BFOQ questions should be about skills, training, education, work experience, physical attributes, and personality traits. With rare exceptions, questions should not be about age, gender, race, religion, physical appearance, disabilities, ethnic group, or citizenship.

Even with carefully planned BFOQ questions, employers will occasionally pose questions to interviewees that are intentionally or unintentionally illegal. For example, an employer might ask, "Are you married and do you have children?" when, in fact, he or she should really ask, "Is there anything that would prevent you from being able to travel frequently?" Often, illegal questions are unintentionally asked by untrained interviewers who are trying to be polite. In any circumstance you must carefully consider how to respond to the illegal question(s), using one or more of these strategies:

1. *Weigh the severity of the violation against your desire for the job.* If you really want the job, and the violation was minor, you may opt to provide a short answer or tactfully try to rephrase the question to avoid being forced to provide irrelevant information.

2. *Ask for clarification.* If you suspect that the illegal question is actually attempting to reference a BFOQ for the job, you can clarify what skills, knowledge, or attitudes the interviewer is attempting to assess.

3. *Be assertive.* You can tell the interviewer that the question is not related to the attributes specified in the job description or that the question, as phrased, asks for information that you do not have to provide. A less aggressive option is to politely decline to answer the question as phrased.

4. *Report the violation.* If the interviewer continues to ask illegal questions or is otherwise offensive, you might consider reporting the violation to a superior and/or to the federal Equal Employment Opportunity Commission (www.eeoc.gov) or a similar state agency.

The Postinterview Stage

Most interviews end with some plan for future action on the part of both the interviewee and interviewer. When the decision will be reached and how it will be communicated are usually specified by the interviewer. As an interviewee, make certain you carry out appropriate responsibilities, including writing to reconfirm your interest in the position and thanking the interviewer for his or her time. Additionally, you need to be prepared to deal with various interview outcomes.

A letter of appreciation is appropriate after an interview and should be sent within one or two days following the interview. If a company has been corresponding with you using e-mail, then you should send an e-mail thank-you letter. If you are still interested in the position, you should express that interest in the letter. If you are not interested in the position, a letter is still appropriate. In the latter case, in fairness to the employer, you should withdraw your candidacy.

After the employment interview you will hopefully receive a job offer. Making a final decision about accepting a job involves careful consideration of multiple pieces of information. Here are tips for conducting negotiations with your potential employer and making a final decision; for additional information visit www.collegegrad.com/offer/index.shtml.

1. *Wait for the appropriate time.* The interview is not the ideal place to discuss salary expectations and other points of negotiation. In the interview you have little bargaining power. Once the company makes an offer, you are "in demand" and have a better chance of negotiating various items.

2. *Know what you want in advance.* Once you have been offered the job, you should immediately be prepared to begin the negotiation process. Conduct research to determine common salary ranges for your type of position. Online salary databases like www.salary.com provide national and regional salary

profiles for different types of jobs. Depending on the type of position, you may also be able to negotiate moving expenses, start date, continuing education funding, and other types of benefits.

3. *Understand the implications of taking the job.* If the job involves moving, you may want to investigate the living expenses of the new community. Try using Sperling's Cost of Living Calculator, at www.bestplaces.net/col, to compare where you live now with the place you will relocate to if you accept the job.

4. *Get it in writing.* Be aware that a job offer and your acceptance of the job offer is a legally binding document. Take care to ensure that all negotiated items are included in the offer letter, and do not write an acceptance letter until you have a correct offer letter in hand.

5. *Be tactful in your response.* Regardless of whether you are accepting or declining the job offer, your official response should be professional. If you accept the position, your acceptance letter should thank the interviewer and formally state that you are accepting the position as described in the offer letter. If you decline the offer, you should state your reason(s) for not accepting the offer, explicitly decline the offer, and end on a pleasant note.

What Communication Skills Will You Need on the Job?

Previous sections of this chapter provided you with general information about organizations and taught you skills necessary for obtaining a job. This section emphasizes skills relevant to your role as an employee or organizational member. We begin by identifying several behaviors representing competent workplace communication and then discuss specific skills like conflict management and customer service effectiveness.

Competent Workplace Communication

Previous chapters stressed the importance of verbal and nonverbal communication, perception, and listening. Clearly, the ability to perceive accurately, use verbal and nonverbal symbols with precision, and listen carefully are skills that benefit workplace communicators. Let us consider four specific behaviors that are important in the workplace: immediacy, supportiveness, strategic ambiguity, and interaction management.

Immediacy

immediacy

Communication behaviors intended to create perceptions of psychological closeness with others.

When people engage in communication behaviors intended to create perceptions of psychological closeness with others, they are enacting **immediacy.** Immediacy can be both verbal and nonverbal. Smiling, reducing physical distance, and using animated gestures and facial expressions are all examples of nonverbally immediate behaviors whereas calling people by their first names, using "we" language, and telling stories are examples of verbal immediacy behaviors. Although much research exploring the positive effects of immediacy has taken place in classroom setting, Teven, McCroskey, and Richmond (2006) reason that immediacy also should influence workplace relationships between supervisors and subordinates. In their study they found that supervisors who are immediate are perceived as more trustworthy, higher in competence and goodwill, and more socially attractive. Moreover, employees working with immediate supervisors tend to be more motivated and willing to work hard. They conclude that organizations should devote greater attention to helping their managers learn to use immediacy because of its positive effect on workplace communication outcomes. Of course, as an entry-level employee you can also use immediacy behaviors to develop positive relationships with your co-workers and your supervisor.

Supportiveness

People engage in **supportive communication** when they listen with empathy, acknowledge the feelings of others, and engage in dialogue to help others maintain a sense of personal control. Of course, supportive communication is an important skill in any context, including workplace settings. Research reviewed by Hopkins (2001) suggests that supportive supervisor communication is one of the most significant factors influencing employee morale. To enhance your supportive communication skills, consider the following strategies adapted from Albrecht and Bach's (1997) discussion of supportive communication:

1. *Listen without judging.* Being judgmental while listening to a co-worker's explanation of a problem can cause you to lose focus of what she or he is really saying.
2. *Validate feelings.* Even if you disagree with something your co-workers say, validating their perceptions and feelings is an important step in building a trusting relationship.
3. *Provide both informational and relational messages.* Supportive communication involves both helping and healing messages. Providing a metaphorical "shoulder to cry on" is equally as important as providing suggestions and advice.
4. *Be confidential.* When co-workers share feelings and personal reflections with you, maintaining their trust and confidence is essential. Telling others or gossiping about the issue will destroy your credibility as a trustworthy co-worker.

Strategic Ambiguity

When learning to be competent communicators, we often assume that communication competence is associated with clarity. That is, we take for granted that to be a competent communicator is to be a clear communicator. Eisenberg (1984) disagrees with this assumption and points out that clarity is essential for competent communication only when clear communication is the objective of the communicator. Eisenberg argues that professional and workplace communication often features the **strategic use of ambiguity**—the purposeful use of symbols to allow multiple interpretations of messages. You have probably witnessed instances of strategic ambiguity on your college campus. At the beginning of each year, various student organizations undertake recruitment drives to gain new members. When presenting their organization, whether it be a student club or a Greek organization, members are often strategically ambiguous about some aspect of the organization. After all, recruiting would be difficult if we knew that there were really only a few members or that there is significant political infighting in the club. When you enter the workforce, you will encounter new examples of strategic ambiguity. During orientation, for example, you might learn about your new company's mission statement. Such mission statements are often strategically ambiguous so that all stakeholders (employees, managers, owners, and so on) can find relevant meaning in the statement.

supportive communication

Listening with empathy, acknowledging others' feelings, and engaging in dialogue to help others maintain a sense of personal control.

Watch "You Look Great" on the *Online Learning Center,* and analyze how Claire and Rachel enact supportive communication.

strategic ambiguity

The purposeful use of symbols to allow multiple interpretations of messages.

Of course, competent communicators must not only be skillful in recognizing the use of strategic ambiguity but also be able to use ambiguity when necessary.

Interaction Management

Workplace communication is somewhat different from other types of communication situations because conversations tend to flow between the technical jargon associated with the workplace setting and other topics brought up to relieve stress and pass time. Thus computer technicians might talk about megabytes and megapixels one minute and speculate on who will be voted off *Survivor* the next. Competent workplace communicators engage in **interaction management** to establish a smooth pattern of interaction that allows a clear flow between topics and ideas. Using pauses, changing pitch, carefully listening to topics being discussed, and responding appropriately are skills related to interaction management.

Cross-Cultural Skills

The changing nature of demographics means that the workplace is increasingly a cross-cultural setting. People who speak English as a second language are infused into all sectors of the workforce, filling nearly every type of position imaginable. If you speak English as a second language, you should emphasize these skills initially to aid your transition to the workplace. First, you should ask more questions to clarify instructions or expectations. Because you have both a new language and potentially a new set of technical terms to learn in your workplace, questioning is the most effective strategy for avoiding misunderstanding. In addition, you should pay careful attention to your co-workers. By observing them and asking questions if necessary, you can not only learn important vocabulary but also model interaction skills with customers or clients. Finally, keeping a journal of your daily activities is a good idea. The first few days and weeks may seem overwhelming, but you will learn a great deal. Keeping a journal can help you retain vocabulary, directions, and other important pieces of information more easily.

If you are a native speaker who works with a second-language speaker, you will also have to adapt your communication behaviors. You can help ease your co-worker's transition through some relatively easy steps. First, provide important directions in writing. Second-language speakers often find written directions easier to process because the pace of spoken language can be challenging. Written directions allow second-language speakers to process and reprocess important directions and policies. Second, take time to explain. You can help your co-worker(s) learn vocabulary and interaction skills more quickly if you take a few moments to explain how and why you communicate the way you do. Finally, be patient. Becoming impatient and frustrated will introduce new problems and make the situation worse for everyone. If you are patient, you will make the transition easier and will likely prevent problems from recurring.

Conflict Management Skills

Although the behavioral characteristics of competent communication are desirable in all communication situations, they will not ensure that your workplace communication is free from conflict. Workplace conflict can occur because of mundane issues such as one person playing a radio too loudly in her cubicle, or because of serious issues such as office politics pitting one faction of employees against

---

Interaction management

Establishing a smooth pattern of interaction that allows a clear flow between topics and ideas.

another. Indeed, conflict management skills are not just desirable but necessary for effective workplace communication.

People often view conflict negatively because they associate conflict with anger. However, conflict occurs anytime two or more people have goals that they perceive to be incompatible. When one employee wants to work late to finish a project and another wants to go home to be with his or her family, conflict could occur. In short, workplace conflict is a fact of life—the rule rather than the exception.

A variety of techniques can be used to manage conflict productively. Wilmot and Hocker (2005) suggest several approaches to managing conflict:

- *Avoidance*. With the avoidance style you deny the existence of conflict. Although avoidance can provide you with time to think through a situation, continued avoidance allows conflict to simmer and flare up with more intensity.

- *Competition*. With the competition style you view conflict as a "battle" and advance your own interests over those of others. Although the competitive style can be necessary when quick decisions must be made or when you are strongly committed to a position, this tactic can also be highly detrimental to the relationships between you and your co-workers.

- *Compromise*. With a compromising style you are willing to negotiate away some of your position as long as the other party in the conflict is willing to do the same. Compromise can be an effective strategy because it is a win-win proposition for both parties, but when used too often, it can become a sophisticated form of conflict avoidance.

- *Accommodation*. With the accommodating style you set aside your views and accept those of others. Accommodation can maintain harmony in relationships, but this strategy is problematic in many situations because tacit acceptance of others' views can stifle creative dialogue and decision making.

- *Collaboration*. A **collaborative style** involves thoughtful negotiation and reasoned compromise whereby both parties agree that the negotiated outcome is the best possible alternative under the circumstance. Although collaboration takes more time and effort to enact as a conflict management strategy, this approach typically results in the best possible outcome for all parties involved.

collaborative style

Thoughtful negotiation and reasoned compromise.

Customer Service Skills

We often hear that we now live in a "service economy" in which American companies increasingly make money by providing services. In this kind of business environment, one of the most important forms of external communication is that which occurs in providing service to organizational customers. Bitner, Booms, and Tetreault (1990) define the **customer service encounter** as "the moment of interaction between the customer and the firm" (p. 71). During this moment the organizational representative provides professional assistance in exchange for the customer's money or attention.

Customer service became a business buzzword during the 1990s, yet it means different things to different people. For some individuals, customer service means being friendly, shaking hands warmly, and initiating pleasant conversations with clients. For others, customer service means processing customers efficiently and quickly. Still others view customer service as involving listening intently to identify individual

customer service encounter

The moment of interaction between the customer and the firm.

needs and providing sufficient information and/or support to meet those needs. All perspectives are legitimate; however, we must remember that the customer is the ultimate judge of whether customer service interactions are satisfying.

MYTHS, METAPHORS, & MISUNDERSTANDINGS

A movement in the health care industry relabels "patients" as "customers" or "consumers." Similarly, some individuals believe that educators should view "students" as "customers." In small groups reflect on traditional provider–patient relationships and teacher–student relationships from the standpoint of customer service encounters. Discuss how communication patterns in such relationships might be different if viewed from a customer service standpoint. What are the advantages and disadvantages of the customer metaphor in health care and education? What potential "myths" of medicine and education are revealed through the customer metaphor? How might the customer metaphor both enable and constrain medicine and education?

Regardless of how employees understand the concept of customer service, most providers have the goal of influencing their customers' behaviors. An extensive body of research covers communication techniques for compliance gaining. In her book *Communicating with Customers: Service Approaches, Ethics, and Impact*, W. Z. Ford (1998) reviews compliance-gaining strategies used by customer service representatives. Her work is summarized in Table 8.2.

A wide range of occupations require interactions between employees and clients or customers. In many of these, the provision of service often involves some degree of emotional content (Waldron, 1994). Nurses interact with dying patients in a hospice, ministers counsel troubled parishioners, and social workers help physically abused women. Emotional communication also characterizes other less obvious occupations. Flight attendants must appear happy and attentive during international flights (Murphy, 2001) while bill collectors must remain stern and avoid any trace of sympathy in interactions (Rafeili & Sutton, 1990).

TABLE 8.2   COMPLIANCE-GAINING STRATEGIES USED BY CUSTOMER SERVICE REPRESENTATIVES

Promise: Promising a reward for compliance (e.g., "If you buy this car, I'll throw in a free stereo.")

Threat: Threatening to punish for noncompliance (e.g., "If you don't buy the car before the end of the week, I cannot guarantee the 6 percent interest rate.")

Pre-giving: Rewarding the customer before requesting compliance (e.g., "I will give you $50 just for test-driving this new car.")

Moral appeal: Implying that it is immoral not to comply (e.g., "Since you have small children, you should be looking at our larger models, with more safety features.")

Liking: Being friendly and helpful to get the customer in a good frame of mind to ensure compliance (e.g., "Good afternoon, my how you look nice today. How can I help you?")

SOURCE: Ford, 1998.

Arlie Hochschild was the first scholar to deal with this phenomenon in her book *The Managed Heart* (1983). She uses the term **emotional labor** to refer to jobs in which employees are expected to display certain feelings in order to satisfy organizational role expectations. Research has indicated that while emotional labor may be fiscally rewarding for the organization and the client, it can be dangerous for the service provider and lead to negative consequences such as burnout, job dissatisfaction, and turnover (Tracy, 2005).

emotional labor

Jobs in which employees are expected to display certain feelings in order to satisfy organizational role expectations.

What Ethical Dimensions Are Found in the Workplace?

Communicating in organizations is not an easy task. In fact, a pervasive part of organizational life is conflict—both destructive and productive. Conflict can destroy work relationships or create a needed impetus for organizational change and development. In this section we are concerned with the ethical dimensions of workplace communication. In particular, we focus our attention on aggressive communication and sexual harassment.

Aggressive Communication

Verbal aggressiveness is understood by communication scholars as an individual's communication that attacks the self-concepts of other people in order to inflict psychological pain (e.g., Infante, Riddle, Horvath, & Tulmin, 1992). Verbal aggression is on the rise in organizational settings, with a lot of aggression unrecognized by management. Workplace aggression includes all communication by which individuals attempt to harm others at work.

Neuman (1998) argues that workplace aggression occurs at three levels: (1) the withholding of cooperation, the spreading of rumors or gossip, consistent arguing,

Service-oriented jobs such as in restaurants and retail sales require the employee to engage in emotional labor—that is, to display certain feelings to satisfy expectations.

belligerency, and the use of offensive language; (2) intense arguments with supervisors, co-workers, and customers, and sabotage, verbal threats, and feelings of persecution; and (3) frequent displays of intense anger resulting in recurrent suicidal threats, physical fights, destruction of property, use of weapons, and the commission of murder, rape, and/or arson. Instances involving direct physical assaults constitute workplace violence; typically, this is a result of the escalation of workplace aggression.

Most of us are familiar with the term "going postal," originating from an incident in which a postal worker walked up to his boss, pulled a gun from a paper bag, and shot him (*Los Angeles Times*, July 18, 1995). Or perhaps we are familiar with the Fort Lauderdale man who opened fire on his former colleagues after being dismissed from his city job cleaning the beaches (*The New York Times*, February 10, 1996). Although mediated accounts of workplace violence typically focus on homicides, most workplace aggression involves less dramatic forms of verbal abuse. Studies of verbal aggression in the workplace suggest that 50% of workers admit to arguing and criticizing co-workers (Bennett & Lehman, 1996) and over 65% of managers report experiencing verbal aggression—including use of profanity, threats of retaliation, silent treatment, and the spreading of rumors—in response to negative performance evaluations (Geddes & Baron, 1997).

NCA Ethics Credo

We condemn communication that degrades individuals and humanity through distortion, intolerance, intimidation, coercion, hatred, and violence.

Cost cutting in the form of downsizing, layoffs, budget cuts, and pay freezes, as well as organizational change, engenders workplace aggression (Baron, 1999). Organizational communication research has detected negative effects of verbal aggression in workplace relationships (Coombs & Holladay, 2004). The psychological pain produced by verbal aggression includes embarrassment, feelings of inadequacy, humiliation, hopelessness, despair, and depression.

Sexual Harassment

Sexual harassment includes a set of behaviors that constitute workplace aggression. The 1991 Senate confirmation hearings for Supreme Court Justice Clarence Thomas made the issue of sexual harassment a topic of reflection and discussion in corporate boardrooms and schools and at family dinner tables. Accusations against Bill Clinton, then president of the United States, were lodged by Paula Jones, claiming that he sexually harassed her when he was governor of Arkansas. While sexual harassment has been a pervasive problem in the workplace for decades, these accusations against prominent public officials caused employees and employers alike to recognize the magnitude of the issue (Kreps, 1993).

What is sexual harassment? The Equal Employment Opportunity Communication (EEOC) defines **sexual harassment** as

sexual harassment

Unwelcome, unsolicited, repeated behavior of a sexual nature.

unwelcome sexual advances, requests for sexual favors, and other verbal or physical conduct of a sexual nature if (1) submission to the conduct is made a condition of employment, (2) submission to or rejection of the conduct is made the basis for an employment decision, or (3) the conduct seriously affects an employee's work performance or creates an intimidating, hostile, or offensive working environment.

Simply put, sexual harassment is unwelcome, unsolicited, repeated behavior of a sexual nature.

The EEOC definition of sexual harassment outlines two different, although sometimes overlapping, types of sexual harassment. The first type, termed **quid pro quo,** involves a situation in which an employee is offered a reward or is threatened with punishment based on his or her participation in a sexual activity. For example, a supervisor might tell her employee, "I will give you Friday off if you will meet me at my place tonight." The second type of sexual harassment creates a **hostile work environment,** or conditions in the workplace that are sexually offensive, intimidating, or hostile and that affect an individual's ability to perform his or her job. For example, if two males talk explicitly about the physical features of a female colleague in her presence, she asks them to stop, and they repeat the offense, sexual harassment has occurred.

A major obstacle to ending sexual harassment is the tendency of victims to avoid confronting the harasser. Most instances of sexual harassment are not confronted, exposed, or reported. Instead, the victim usually avoids the situation by taking time off, transferring to another area, or changing jobs. One of the primary reasons for avoidance is that the perpetrator is usually someone in the organization with authority and status—power over the victim—and the victim feels that exposure or confrontation will backfire.

Clearly, the EEOC's definition indicates that a wide range of communication behaviors can constitute sexual harassment, although many men and women see only serious offenses (for example, career benefits in exchange for sexual favors) as harassment. However, a person need not suffer severe psychological damage or extensive adverse work outcomes to be a victim of sexual harassment. Additionally, harassment is judged by its effects on the recipient, not by the intentions of the harasser. Because some people may regard any particular behavior as offensive, and others not, the courts use what is called the "reasonable person rule" to determine whether a reasonable person would find the behavior in question offensive. One limitation of this rule is evidence that men and women view sexual harassment differently (Solomon & Williams, 1997). In particular, sexual overtures that women typically view as insulting are viewed by men, in general, as flattering.

Sexual harassment is a serious and pervasive communication problem in modern organizational life, with both the targets of sexual harassment and those accused of sexual harassment (falsely or not) suffering personal and professional anguish. Note that even though a majority of sexual harassment cases involve women as victims, the EEOC guidelines apply equally to men.

quid pro quo sexual harassment

A situation in which an employee is offered a reward or is threatened with punishment based on his or her participation in a sexual activity.

hostile work environment sexual harassment

Conditions in the workplace that are sexually offensive, intimidating, or hostile and that affect an individual's ability to perform his or her job.

◄ SKILL BUILDER ►

Develop your skills at detecting sexual harassment in the workplace. Complete the interactive instruction program on sexual harassment sponsored by the New Jersey Chamber of Commerce (www.njchamber.com). The primary objective of this online tutorial is to help users better identify what behaviors in the workplace are considered sexual harassment so they can avoid and take action against any such behaviors. The tutorial is free, and at the end of the 30-minute session, users will receive a certificate of completion.

Chapter Review & Study Guide

SUMMARY

In this chapter you learned the following:

▶ Workplace communication takes place within the context of an organization. Such organizations are classified into four different types enacting these primary roles:
- Economic production organizations manufacture products or services.
- Political organizations generate and distribute power in society.
- Integrative organizations mediate and resolve conflict.
- Pattern-maintenance organizations promote cultural and educational regularity.

▶ Organizations have both informal networks and formal networks. Formal networks include downward, upward, and horizontal communication.

▶ Written credentials for employment interviews include résumés and cover letters.
- The résumé should be concise and stylistically reflect your personality in a professional way.
- The résumé should highlight your work experiences and other qualifications.
- The cover letter is a short statement introducing you and your résumé.
- The cover letter has four main sections: attention, interest, desire, and action.

▶ Effective strategies for preparing for a job interview include creating a self-inventory, creating networks, searching for a job, investigating the interviewer, being prepared to ask and answer questions, and conducting postinterview negotiations.

▶ Workplace communication competence involves general skills already covered in this text as well as four specialized skills: immediacy, supportiveness, strategic ambiguity, and interaction management.

▶ Conflict management skills include avoidance, competition, compromise, accommodation, and collaboration. Although each has advantages, the collaboration approach works best in many situations.

▶ Customer service interactions are essential aspects of contemporary work life. Customer service agents must learn to enact compliance-gaining skills and to engage in emotional labor.

▶ Unethical workplace communication can include aggressive communication and sexual harassment.
- Workplace aggression includes all communication by which individuals attempt to harm others.
- Sexual harassment is an extreme form of unethical communication involving an abuse of power.

KEY TERMS

Go to the *Online Learning Center* at **www.mhhe.com/pearson3** to further your understanding of the following terminology.

Chronological résumé
Communication networks
Cover letter
Downward communication
Economic orientation
Emotional labor
Formal communication
Functional résumé

Horizontal communication
Hostile work environment sexual harassment
Informal communication
Integration orientation
Job description
Objective statement
Organizations

Organizational communication
Pattern-maintenance orientation
Political orientation
Quid pro quo sexual harassment
Sexual harassment
Upward communication

STUDY QUESTIONS

1. An organization with this orientation generates and distributes power and control within society.
   a. economic
   b. pattern-maintenance
   c. political
   d. integration

2. Information flows in an organization through patterns of relationships known as
   a. communication networks
   b. organizational communication
   c. objective statements
   d. pattern-maintenance

3. When information is transferred between a worker and his or her boss formally, which type of communication has taken place?
   a. horizontal
   b. political
   c. societal
   d. upward

4. Which of the following is a true statement regarding written credentials?
   a. The objective statement is usually the last bit of information on the résumé.
   b. The cover letter is a document that organizes credentials by type of function performed.
   c. An effective résumé contains good style, content, and format.
   d. The only way to organize your résumé is chronologically.

5. When preparing for and taking part in an interview,
   a. you should dress a bit more casually than you expect the interviewer to dress
   b. you do not need to know the job description because the interviewer will tell you about the job's duties
   c. you should avoid using strong eye contact
   d. you should ask and answer questions effectively and ethically

6. By smiling, gesturing, and using facial expressions in the workplace to create perceptions of psychological closeness with others, you are enacting
   a. immediacy
   b. management
   c. ambiguity
   d. preparation

7. Which technique of conflict management is used to maintain relationship harmony but to stifle creative dialogue and decision making?
   a. compromise
   b. accommodation
   c. avoidance
   d. collaboration

8. Customer service representatives may use which of the following compliance-gaining strategies, in which the representative implies that it is immoral not to comply?
   a. promises
   b. threats
   c. pregiving
   d. moral appeals

9. Conflict in the workplace can be
   a. destructive
   b. productive
   c. neither a nor b
   d. both a and b

10. If your boss tells you that you can leave work early on Fridays if you go on a date with him or her, he or she is utilizing a type of sexual harassment called
    a. quid pro quo
    b. hostile work environment
    c. emotional labor
    d. nothing; it is not sexual harassment

Answers:

1. (c); 2. (a); 3. (d); 4. (c); 5. (d); 6. (a); 7. (b); 8. (d); 9. (d); 10. (a)

CRITICAL THINKING

1. Search online for some résumés. Based on the text, identify what the creator did correctly and what he or she could improve upon. Focus on the résumé's style, content, and format.

2. Think about some of your past jobs. In the workplace did people display immediacy, supportiveness, strategic ambiguity, or interaction management? What did they do to demonstrate these behaviors? What conflict management skills were utilized by your superiors? Were they successful?

SELF-QUIZ

For further review, try the chapter self-quiz on the *Online Learning Center* at **www.mhhe.com/pearson3.**

REFERENCES

Albrecht, T. L., & Bach, B. W. (1997). *Communication in complex organizations: A relational approach.* New York: Harcourt Brace.

Ayres, J., Wongprasert, T. K., Silva, J., Story, T., & Sawant, D. D. (2001). Effects of performance visualization on employment interviews. *Communication Quarterly, 49,* 160–172.

Baron, R. A. (1999). Social and personal determinants of workplace aggression: Evidence for the impact of perceived injustice and the type A behavior pattern. *Aggressive Behavior, 25,* 281–296.

Bennett, S. (2005). *The elements of résumé style: Essential rules and eye-opening advice for writing résumés and cover letters that work.* New York: AMACOM.

Bittner, M. J., Booms, B. H., & Tetreault, M. S. (1990). The service encounter: Diagnosing favorable and unfavorable incidents. *Journal of Marketing, 54,* 71–84.

Bolles, R. (1999). *Job-hunting on the Internet.* Berkeley, CA: Ten Speed Press.

Bolles, R. (2000). *What color is your parachute?* (30th ed.). Berkeley, CA: Ten Speed Press.

Caudron, S. (1998). They hear it through the grapevine. *Workforce, 77,* 25–27.

Coombs, T. W., & Holladay, S. J. (2004). Understanding the aggressive workplace: Development of the workplace tolerance questionnaire. *Communication Studies, 55,* 481–497.

Eisenberg, E. M. (1984). Ambiguity as strategy in organizational communication. *Communication Monographs, 51,* 227–242.

Ford, W. Z. (1998). *Communicating with customers: Service approaches, ethics, and impact.* Cresskill, NJ: Hampton Press.

Geddes, D., & Baron, R. (1997). Workplace aggression as a consequence of negative performance feedback. *Management Communications Quarterly, 10,* 433–454.

Gutman, A. (2000). *EEO law and personnel practices* (2nd ed.). Thousand Oaks, CA: Sage.

Henricks, M. (2000). *Kinko's guide to the winning résumé.* United States of America: Kinko's.

Hochschild, A. (1983). *The managed heart: Commercialization of human feeling.* Berkeley: University of California Press.

Hopkins, K. M. (2001). Manager intervention with troubled supervisors: Help and support at the top. *Management Communication Quarterly, 15,* 83–99.

Infante, D., Riddle, B., Horvath, G., & Tumlin, S. (1992). Verbal aggressiveness: Messages and reasons. *Communication Quarterly, 40,* 116–126.

Kreps, G. (1993). *Sexual harassment: Communication implications.* Cresskill, NJ: Hampton Press.

Krizan, A., Merrier, P., & Jones, C. (2002). *Business communication* (5th ed.). Cincinnati: South-Western College Publishing.

Murphy, A. (2001). The flight attendant dilemma: An analysis of communication and sensemaking during in-flight emergencies. *Journal of Applied Communication Research, 29,* 30–53.

Parsons, T. (1963). *Structure and process in modern societies.* New York: Free Press.

Rafeili, A., & Sutton, R. I. (1990). Busy stores and demanding customers: How do they affect the display of positive emotion? *Academy of Management Journal, 33,* 623–637.

Ralston, S. M., & Kirkwood, W. G. (1999). The trouble with applicant impression management. *Journal of Business and Technical Communication, 13*(2), 190–208.

Solomon, D., & Williams, A. (1997). Perceptions of social-sexual communication at work: The effects of message, situation, and observer characteristics on judgments of sexual harassment. *Journal of Applied Communication Research, 25,* 196–216.

Stohl, C. (1995). *Organizational communication: Connectedness in action.* Thousand Oaks, CA: Sage.

Stohl, M., & Stohl, C. (2005). Human rights, nation states, and NGOs: Structural holes and the emergence of global regimes. *Communication Monographs, 72,* 442–467.

Susskind, A. M., Schwartz, D. F., Richards, W. D., & Johnson, J. D., (2005). Evolution and diffusion of the Michigan State University tradition of organizational communication network research. *Communication Studies, 56,* 397–418.

Teven, J. J., McCroskey, J. C., & Richmond, V. P. (2006). Communication correlates of perceived Machiavellianism of supervisors: Communication orientations and outcomes. *Communication Quarterly, 54,* 127–142.

Tey, C., Ang, S., & Van Dyne, L. (2006). Personality, biographical characteristics, and job interview success: A longitudinal study of the mediating effects of inteviewing self-efficacy and the moderating effects of internal locus of causality. *Journal of Applied Psychology, 91,* 446–454.

Tracy, S. (2005). Locking up emotion: Moving beyond dissonance for understanding emotional labor discomfort. *Communication Monographs, 72,* 261–283.

Van Biema, D., & Pickett, K. (2007, January 29). Minnesota's teetotal taxis. *Time,* p. 30.

Wilmot, W. W., & Hocker, J. L. (2005). *Interpersonal conflict* (7th ed.). New York: McGraw-Hill.

Young, M. J., Behnke, R. R., & Mann, Y. M. (2004). Anxiety patterns in employment interviews. *Communication Reports, 17,* 49–57.

ADDITIONAL RESOURCES

Adams, B. (1999). *The complete résumé book for college students.* Holbrook, MA: Adams Media Corporation.

Allen, J. (2000). *The complete Q & A job interview book.* New York: John Wiley & Sons.

Graben, S. (2000). *The everything online job search book.* Holbrook, MA: Adams Media Corporation.

Lester, M.C. (1998). *Real life guide to starting your career: How to get the right job now!* Chapel Hill, NC: Pipeline Press/Associated Publishers Group.

Washington, T. (2000). *Interview power: Selling yourself face to face in the new millennium.* Bellevue, WA: Mount Vernon Press.

Yate, M. (2001). *Cover letters that knock 'em dead* (4th ed.). Holbrook, MA: Adams Media Corporation.

CHAPTER NINE

The Dynamics of Small-Group Communication

What will you learn?

When you have read and thought about this chapter, you will be able to:

1. Define small-group communication and state why it is important.
2. Recognize different types of groups.
3. Define leadership and explain its relevance to small-group communication.
4. Explain how culture develops in small groups.
5. Identify steps in the small-group decision-making process.
6. Discuss two examples of how technology can be used to facilitate small-group communication.
7. Utilize skills necessary for effective and ethical group communication.
8. Recognize strategies for ethically managing group conflict.

*S*mall groups permeate nearly all facets of our lives. Our families, our jobs, our courses, and our friends are all invigorated and driven by small groups of people. In this chapter we address several issues related to small-group communication. After discussing generally what small-group communication is, we turn to theories explaining concepts like leadership, group culture, and small-group decision making. The chapter concludes by discussing several processes related to small-group effectiveness: cohesiveness, use of technology, and skills used by ethical group communicators.

After Hurricane Katrina slammed into the Gulf Coast in August 2005, it left behind widespread devastation. But perhaps nowhere was this more evident than in the city of New Orleans, which became a virtual ghost town in some areas. Close to 80% of the city was flooded after the levies failed. Whole parishes became uninhabitable. Many city residents had to seek refuge in other towns and even other states, reducing the size of the city's population by 50%. The loss of life and property was of primary concern, of course, but New Orleans has suffered in other ways as well. Its social fabric began to tear apart, and its rich cultural heritage was in danger of being washed away with the flood waters.

New Orleans has long been a center of music. It is where jazz was born and where rock and roll was nurtured. Many famous musicians, such as Louis Armstrong, came from New Orleans. So it was not surprising that a group of musicians would take steps to help restore New Orleans following the Katrina tragedy. Led by singer and composer Harry Connick, Jr., and jazz greats Branford and Ellis Marsalis, a small group of artists forged a partnership with Habitat for Humanity to create a Musicians' Village in the Ninth Ward, one of the hardest-hit areas of the city and former home to many musicians.

The Musicians' Village project seeks to do more than create affordable housing for those who lost their homes and possessions. It also seeks to join neighbor to neighbor in personal relationships, to build a sense of community, and to provide a haven for the reemergence of the musical tradition that made New Orleans great.

Small groups of people can accomplish extraordinary things, as the dedicated group of musicians and house builders shows us. Groups are all around us; they are inescapable. We might even go so far as to say that groups are partly what make humans so . . . human. This chapter looks at the nature of groups—how communication works within groups, how leaders use their skills, and how group members can effectively and ethically contribute to solving problems.

Why Should You Learn About Small Groups?

Small groups are the basic building blocks of our society. Families, work teams, support groups, religious circles, and study groups are all examples of the groups on which our society is built. In fact, small groups are critical to our lives. In organizations, the higher up you go, the more time you will spend working in groups. For example, one report estimated that executives spend about *half* their time in business meetings (Cole, 1989). Membership in small groups is both common and important. Research has consistently documented teamwork as one of the most important communication skills for personal and professional success (Vice, 2001).

Small groups are important for five reasons (see Table 9.1). These reasons clarify why you will want to learn how to communicate effectively in small groups.

TABLE 9.1   WHY YOU SHOULD STUDY SMALL-GROUP COMMUNICATION

1. Humans need groups to meet needs they cannot meet as individuals.
2. Groups are everywhere.
3. Knowing how groups function and how to operate effectively in them is a highly valued skill.
4. Working effectively in groups requires training.
5. Small groups are a means of participating in the democratic process.

First, humans need groups; membership in groups meets needs that we cannot meet for ourselves. William Schutz (1958), a psychologist who studied group interaction, said that humans have needs for inclusion, affection, and control. The need for **inclusion**—the state of being involved with others—suggests that we need to belong to, or be included in, groups with others. As humans, we derive much of our identity, our beliefs about who we are, from the groups to which we belong. Starting with our immediate families and including such important groups as our church, mosque, or synagogue; interest groups; work teams; and social groups—all these help us define who we are. The need for **affection**—the emotion of caring for others and/or being cared for—means that we humans need to love and be loved, to know that we are important to others who value us as unique human beings. Finally, we have a need for **control**—the ability to influence our environment. We are better able to exercise such control if we work together in groups. One person cannot build a school, bridge, or new business. However, by working together in groups, we can accomplish these and other complex tasks. We need others to meet our needs.

inclusion

The state of being involved with others; a human need.

affection

The emotion of caring for others and/or being cared for.

control

The ability to influence our environment.

TRY ◆ THIS

Make a list of groups that you belong to. When making your list, identify at least one group you belong to for inclusion purposes, one group for affection purposes, and one group for control purposes. Do any of the groups you belong to meet all three of these needs?

Second, groups are everywhere. You will not be able to escape working in them. Think about all the groups to which you currently belong, including informal groups such as study groups or your "lunch bunch." Students typically belong to between 8 and 10 groups, but sometimes as many as 20 or more and rarely fewer than 2. Your presence in groups will not end upon graduation. Numerous companies have discovered how helpful groups can be and have installed groups at *all* levels.

The third reason is related to the second. Because group work is expected to increase in the future, particularly in business and industry, knowing how groups function and having the ability to operate effectively in them will be highly valued skills. A survey of college graduates showed that oral communication, problem-solving skills, and the ability to motivate and manage others were three of the top

American companies have come to realize how helpful groups can be in conducting their business.

four skills taught in college classes that were essential for workplace success—the fourth was written communication (Zekeri, 2004). So your future career success will likely depend on your ability to work well in teams and groups.

Fourth, being an effective group or team member cannot be left to chance. Just because you are placed on a team does not mean you know how to work effectively in that team. As helpful as groups can be to any organization, they often fail because group leaders have not thought through exactly what they want the groups to accomplish or because group members have not been trained in how to behave appropriately as part of a team (Vengel, 2006). Effective group participation cannot be taken for granted. Group members need training to understand the dynamics of small-group interaction, which is much more complex than dyadic (two-person) interaction.

Finally, groups can be an important way for Americans to participate in the democratic process; thus they have the potential to help us achieve our ideals as a society. Because we can accomplish so much more in groups than we can as individuals, group participation can be an important vehicle through which we create and govern our society. A lone voice "crying in the wilderness" may have little effect, but a group of people working hard for a cause in which they believe can lead to great changes. Furthermore, by talking in groups, we can become more confident in articulating our own beliefs, which, in turn, may lead us to be more vocal about our beliefs in a variety of contexts (Zorn, Rober, Broadfoot, & Weaver, 2006). For example, students who want to enact an honor code on their campus may face initial hesitation from peers. By talking in groups first, the students may be better able to find their voice to argue in favor of establishing an honor code.

Think, Pair, Share

Characteristics of Small Groups

Small-group communication includes a number of elements that make it both similar to and different from other communication activities. Take 10 minutes to think about each of the small-group communication characteristics listed below. Generate one example to illustrate each characteristic, and answer the question posed for each characteristic. After the 10 minutes are up, pair off with a partner and share your answers.

1. Small groups comprise individuals who (a) are mutually aware of each other as individuals and (b) are mutually aware of the collective nature of the group. Why do you think "mutual awareness" is so important to small groups?
2. Small-group interaction means that each person in the group can influence and be influenced by each other person in the group. Think of a small group you belong to. What are some ways that you have influenced that group? How have some of the group members influenced you? Do you think this "mutual influence" is important for small groups to be effective? Why or why not?
3. Small groups are interdependent—no member of the group can achieve the group's goal without other members of the group achieving the goal as well. Drawing on your own group experiences, what are some examples of interdependence?

TRY ◆ THIS

Watch the evening news on one of your local TV stations. While watching the news, make note of each civic or political group discussed. What was each group trying to achieve? Did some groups have the power to make decisions (such as political groups)? Did some groups advocate a certain position although they had no power to make decisions (such as community groups)?

What Is Small-Group Communication?

Small-group communication is the interaction among three to nine people who are working together to achieve an interdependent goal (Galanes & Adams, 2006). This definition implies several things:

- Groups must be small enough that members are mutually aware that the group is a collective entity. Groups typically contain between three and nine people but may be larger if members perceive the group as an entity.
- The substance that creates and holds the group together is the interaction between members.
- Group members are interdependent—they cannot achieve their goals without the help of other group members.

The definition of small-group communication just presented establishes *communication* as the essential process within a small group. Communication creates a group, shapes each group in unique ways, and maintains the group. As with other

small-group communication

Interaction among three to nine people working together to achieve an interdependent goal.

223

forms of human communication, small-group communication involves sending verbal and nonverbal signals that are perceived, interpreted, and responded to by other people. Group members pay attention to each other and coordinate their behavior in order to accomplish the group's assignment. Perfect understanding between the person sending the signal and those receiving the signal is never possible; in a group, members strive to have enough understanding to enable the group's purpose to be achieved.

The Types and Functions of Small Groups

Think for a moment about the different groups you belong to. You may regularly study with other students from your accounting class, you may belong to a club on campus, you may be assigned to participate in a student government group, and you likely have a group of friends with whom you socialize. What are the key differences between these groups? We identify four ways to categorize groups:

task-oriented groups

Also called secondary groups; groups formed for the purpose of completing tasks, such as solving problems or making decisions.

relationship-oriented groups

Also called primary groups; groups that are usually long-term and exist to meet our needs for inclusion and affection.

assigned groups

Groups that evolve out of a hierarchy whereby individuals are assigned membership to the group.

emergent groups

Groups resulting from environmental conditions leading to the formation of a cohesive group of individuals.

- **Task-oriented groups** (also called **secondary groups**) are formed for the purpose of completing tasks such as solving a problem or making a decision. A group of students studying for an exam are taking part in a task-oriented group.
- **Relationship-oriented groups** (also called **primary groups**) are usually long-term and exist to meet our needs for inclusion and affection. Your family is an example of a relationship-oriented group.
- **Assigned groups** evolve out of a hierarchy whereby individuals are appointed as members of the group. Being asked to serve on a student union advisory board is an example of an assigned group.
- **Emergent groups** are the results of environmental conditions leading to the formation of a cohesive group of individuals. A group of friends who meet at college is an example of an emergent group.

Classifying groups according to whether they are task-oriented, relationship-oriented, assigned, or emergent risks oversimplifying a more complex process. Because groups comprise people and are sustained through communication, they can go through several metamorphoses. As you probably can tell, primary or secondary groups are not pure. Members of primary groups, such as families, engage in work, make decisions, and must cooperate to complete tasks. Members of secondary groups forge strong personal bonds and provide each other with affection and recognition. In fact, some of the best secondary groups are those with strong primary characteristics, such that members feel appreciated and valued. Likewise, emergent groups can be institutionalized, and assigned groups can take on the characteristics of an emergent group.

Although understanding general characteristics of different types of groups is valuable, recognizing that groups are not static entities is equally important. We might belong to an assigned group formed for task purposes. As we interact with members of that group, a relationship-oriented social group may emerge. Just as our personal relationships can go through several turning points, our group membership is also constantly in flux.

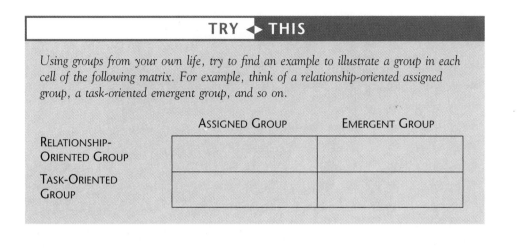

For most groups to work effectively, some structure is necessary. A primary task of the group leader is to provide necessary structure and direction for the group. In this section we explain what leadership is and examine several theories on the process of effective leadership.

The Role of Leadership in Small Groups

What Is Leadership?

Hackman and Johnson (2003) define **leadership** as a process of using communication to influence the behaviors and attitudes of others to meet group goals. Leadership, then, is enacted through communication and persuasion, not through physical force or coercion. Furthermore, only influence designed to benefit the group can be termed small-group leadership. One member persuading another to sabotage a group goal is not leadership according to this definition.

A leader is a person who influences the behavior and attitudes of others through communication. In small groups two types of leader are designated and emergent. A **designated leader** is someone who has been appointed or elected to a leadership position (such as a chair, team leader, coordinator, or facilitator). An **emergent leader** is someone who becomes an informal leader by exerting influence toward achievement of a group's goal but who does not hold the formal position or role of leader. Groups benefit from having a designated leader because designated leaders add stability and organization to the group's activities. An emergent leader can be any group member who helps the group meet its goals. Groups work best when all members contribute skills and leadership behaviors on behalf of the group.

How do leaders, designated or emergent, gain their ability to influence others? Wilmot and Hocker (2005) suggest that group leaders may gain interpersonal influence over groups through the use of **power**, which is the interpersonal influence that forms the basis for small-group leadership. According to Wilmot and Hocker's perspective, group leaders likely use one of three types of power:

- *Distributive power,* whereby the leader exerts influence over others.
- *Integrative power,* which highlights interdependence with another person or persons to achieve mutually agreed-upon goals.

leadership

A process of using communication to influence the behaviors and attitudes of others to meet group goals.

designated leader

Someone who has been appointed or elected to a leadership position.

emergent leader

Someone who becomes an informal leader by exerting influence toward achievement of a group's goal but who does not hold the formal position or role of leader.

power

Interpersonal influence that forms the basis for group leadership.

Leadership is about communication, not personality or luck.

- *Designated power*, which reflects the importance of relationships between people. Marriages, families, and groups often hold such power for us.

Wilmot and Hocker's perspective on power provides a general classification of how power functions. A classic study by French and Raven (1981) further helps to explain the concept of power by identifying specific sources of power used by leaders:

- *Reward power*—the ability to give followers what they want and need.
- *Punishment power*—the ability to withhold from followers what they want and need.
- *Coercion*—a form of punishment power that attempts to force compliance with hostile tactics.
- *Referent power*—power based on others' admiration and respect. Charisma is an extreme form of referent power that inspires strong loyalty and devotion from others.
- *Expert power*—when the other members value a person's knowledge or expertise.

All members of a group have the ability to influence other members. For instance, all members, not just the designated leader, can reward others, withhold rewards, or provide expertise potentially valuable to the group. In addition, a designated leader's influence usually stems from more than just legitimate power. Besides holding the title of leader, that person also has expertise, referent power, and so forth. In fact, if legitimate power is the leader's only source of influence, then someone else in the group with more broadly based power will probably emerge as a more influential informal leader. In short, all group members possess some sources of influence and can lead the group, even if they do not have the title of leader.

Theoretical Approaches to Group Leadership

Since Aristotle's time, people have been interested in what makes a good leader. Is leadership something you are born with? Can you learn to be a leader? In this section you will learn about three ways of thinking about effective leadership: leadership as style, leadership as communication competence, and leadership as planning. Although they are presented as separate perspectives, effective leaders learn to embrace key elements from each simultaneously.

Leadership Styles

Style approaches to studying leadership focus on the patterns of behavior leaders exhibit in groups. Considerable research has examined three major styles of designated leader: democratic, laissez-faire, and autocratic. **Democratic leaders** encourage members to participate in group decisions, even major ones: "What suggestions do you have for solving our problem?" **Laissez-faire leaders** take almost no initiative in structuring a group discussion; they are nonleaders whose typical response is "I don't care; whatever you want to do is fine with me." **Autocratic leaders** maintain strict control over their group, including making assignments and giving orders: "Here's how we'll solve the problem. First, you will . . ." Autocratic leaders ask fewer questions but answer more than democratic leaders; they make more attempts to coerce and fewer attempts to get others to participate (Foels, Driskell, Mullen, & Salas, 2000).

> Observe how Jay and Claire enact leadership behaviors in "Senior Seminar" on the *Online Learning Center* at www.mhhe.com/pearson3.

> **democratic leaders**
>
> Leaders who encourage members to participate in group decisions.

> **laissez-faire leaders**
>
> Leaders who take almost no initiative in structuring a group discussion.

> **autocratic leaders**
>
> Leaders who maintain strict control over their group.

TRY ◆ THIS

You have learned that there are different types of leadership style and that leaders base their ability to influence others on the exercise of power. What relationship do you think exists between leadership style and power? In the matrix below, check cells where you think the leadership style matches the base of power. Why do you think these relationships exist?

	DEMOCRATIC LEADER	AUTOCRATIC LEADER	LAISSEZ-FAIRE LEADER
REWARD POWER			
PUNISHMENT POWER			
LEGITIMATE POWER			
REFERENT POWER			
EXPERT POWER			

Groups vary in the amount of structure and control their members want and need, but research findings about style have been consistent (see Brown & Trevino, 2006). Most people in the United States prefer democratic groups and are more satisfied in democratically rather than autocratically led groups.

The style approaches imply a single leadership style good for all situations. However, most scholars believe that the style should match the needs of the situation.

For example, if you are in a group working on a class project and the deadline is tomorrow, a democratic leadership style might be ineffective because it takes longer to make decisions.

The Communication Competencies of Leaders

Communication scholars who adopt the communicative competencies approach have tried to focus on the communicative behaviors of leaders as they exercise interpersonal influence to accomplish group goals. They ask such questions as "What do effective leaders do?" The Communication Competency Model of Group Leadership, developed by Barge and Hirokawa (1989), is one of the most comprehensive models to address this question. This model assumes that leaders help a group achieve its goals through communication skills (competencies). Two competencies include the task and interpersonal, or relationship, distinctions discussed earlier. Leaders must be flexible to draw from a personal repertoire of such competencies. Some of the most important leader competencies are described briefly here:

- Effective leaders are able to clearly and appropriately communicate ideas to the group without dominating conversation.
- Effective leaders communicate a clear grasp of the task facing the group.
- Effective leaders are skilled at facilitating discussion.
- Effective leaders encourage open dialogue and do not force their own ideas on the group.
- Effective leaders place group needs over personal concerns.
- Effective leaders display respect for others during interaction.
- Effective leaders share in the successes and failures of the group.

The Planning Skills of Leaders

In addition to exhibiting an appropriate style and being a competent communicator, effective leaders must learn to plan. Although planning cannot prevent all problems from occurring, some up-front work can increase the likelihood of successful outcomes. Here are some tips for planning effective meetings:

1. *Know the task at hand.* Later in the chapter you will learn about the group problem-solving model. Effective leaders should understand the problem facing the group and take care to communicate that task to group members.

2. *Know the people.* As you will learn, individual group members will have different skills, motivations, frames of reference, and knowledge bases. Understanding how to draw on group members' strengths and manage interpersonal dynamics is a key role of the group leader.

3. *Collect information.* The group leader should attempt to become knowledgeable on all issues facing the group. If you are knowledgeable, you will know when discussions are off track.

4. *Distribute leadership.* In certain situations leadership should be distributed among all group members. The designated leader may need to delegate responsibility, especially when smaller tasks need to be assigned to individual group members. Distributed leadership, whereby all members share in leadership responsibilities, can result in highly productive group outcomes (Barge & Hirokawa, 1989).

GROUP AGENDA

DATE

I. *Approval of minutes from previous meeting(s).* The group facilitator should determine if there are any changes to the minutes and have group members vote to approve the minutes.

II. *Announcements.* Members of the group should make announcements relevant to the group but not necessarily tied to group business. For example, a group member might read a thank-you note from a person the group helped or might provide personal announcements that may be of interest to group members. Such announcements should be brief.

III. *Reports.* Individuals assigned to collect information or carry out tasks should report on their progress. If a report results in an action item—that is, something the group should discuss and vote on—the report should be included under new business. Reports in this segment of the meeting should be informative, but they do not necessarily require action at this time.

IV. *New business.* Items in this part of the agenda can include important discussions and/or action items. Discussions may or may not result in a vote, but action items should be voted on by the group.

V. *Old business.* Occasionally, action items and discussion from previous meetings may not be complete. In such cases those items should be listed under old business and approached in the same way as new business, with appropriate discussion and voting as necessary.

Figure 9.1   Standard group agenda template.

5. *Organize the discussion.* Although some types of group discussions may not need much organization—a short class discussion assigned by your teacher, for instance—most discussions need more structure. The group leader should plan an agenda for the discussion. The agenda should be adapted to the task at hand; however, a general template for the agenda is provided in Figure 9.1. As you can see, the typical agenda requires group members to agree on minutes from the past meeting to clear up any confusion or disagreement, make announcements, hear reports, consider new business, and reconsider old business as necessary.

Establishing Culture in Small Groups

When small groups are created, they immediately begin developing a unique group culture. Some group cultures are pleasant, whereas others are aggressive, hostile, and demeaning. In this section we will discuss the development of group norms, role structures enacted by group members, group cohesiveness, and how diversity affects group culture.

norms

Informal rules for group interaction created and sustained through communication.

The Development of Group Norms

The first time members meet as a group, they begin to establish the **norms**—informal rules for interaction created and sustained through communication—that will

Cultural Note

Cultural Differences in Small-Group Communication

- Conformity in small-group communication is more common in collectivist cultures (which value the group over the individual), such as Venezuela, Pakistan, Peru, and Taiwan.
- Competition and dissent are more common in individualistic cultures (which value freedom, choice, and independence), such as the United States, Australia, Great Britain, and Canada.
- A rigid hierarchy with a controlling group leader is preferred in uncertainty-rejecting cultures, such as India, Mexico, and the Philippines.
- Equality among group members, and use of first names, is preferred in uncertainty-accepting cultures, such as Israel, Australia, and New Zealand.
- Clear rules are expected in uncertainty-rejecting cultures, such as Japan and Greece.
- Flexible rules, high tolerance for ambiguity, and risk taking characterize uncertainty-accepting cultures, such as Great Britain.
- Ambiguity and saving face is important in collectivist cultures, such as China, Korea, and Japan.

Descriptions of various cultures are provided in more detail in chapter 7.

eventually guide the members' behaviors. George Homans (1950) called a norm "an idea in the minds of the members of a group, an idea that can be put in the form of a statement specifying what the members . . . ought to do, are expected to do, under given circumstances" (p. 73). At first, the full range of human behavior

The diversity of a group will influence group culture.

is available to members. For example, they may greet each other formally ("Ms.," "Dr.," "Professor," and so on), or they may speak informally and use first names. The initial pattern of behavior tends to set the tone for subsequent meetings and to establish the general norms that members will follow. The norms of any group tend to mirror the norms of the larger culture or co-culture in which the group exists. Such norms are also created and altered through communication between group members.

Most norms are not established directly. For example, if Ali comes late to a meeting and no one seems bothered, other members may get the message that coming to meetings on time is unnecessary. By saying nothing to Ali, the group, without consciously thinking about or formally "deciding," has begun to establish a norm that members need not be on time.

Norms often develop rapidly, without members consciously realizing what is occurring. They can be inferred by observing what members say and do. For example, repeated behaviors (such as members always sitting in the same seats) provide evidence of a norm. In addition, behaviors that are punished (such as one group member chastising another by saying, "It's about time you got here") indicate that a norm has been violated.

Members should pay attention to group norms to ensure that they are appropriate to the group task. As teachers we often observe students working in groups. As we walk around the classroom, groups seem to notice we are standing near them and quickly stop talking about the band playing at a local club and turn to the topic we asked them to discuss. As we walk away, discussion soon returns to music and fun. Such norms for playfulness, while important for relationship development, may begin to distract the group from assigned tasks. We certainly do not advocate "no fun time" in groups. In fact, we like to talk to our students about music and sports. Nevertheless, a norm that emphasizes all "fun time" and no "work time" can prevent the group from reaching its goal.

The Development of Roles for Group Members

Every group member enacts a unique **role,** which is a consistent pattern of interaction or behavior exhibited over time. In movies, characters enact roles to drive the story; in small groups, members enact roles to drive the interaction of the group. Whereas actors learn their roles from scripts, group members create their roles spontaneously during interactions with others and while drawing on their unique skills and attitudes. Just as an actor plays different roles in different scripts, individuals enact many diverse roles in the numerous groups to which they belong.

role

A consistent pattern of interaction or behavior exhibited over time.

The Types of Group Roles

Two major types of group roles are formal and informal. A **formal role** (sometimes called a **positional role**) is an assigned role based on an individual's position or title within a group. For example, Indira may be her service club's treasurer. As treasurer she is expected to perform certain duties, such as paying the club's bills, balancing the books, and making regular reports to the club about its financial status. These duties may even be specified in a job description for the position of treasurer. We also expect the person in a particular position to behave in certain ways. For example, what do you think Indira's fellow group members expect of her in addition to her assigned duties? Very likely they expect her to be well organized and to present her report clearly and concisely, without wandering into topics irrelevant to the treasury.

formal role

Also called positional role; an assigned role based on an individual's position or title within a group.

An **informal role** (sometimes called a **behavioral role**) is a role that is developed spontaneously within a group. The role of each group member is worked out by the interaction between the member and the rest of the group and continues to evolve as the group evolves. Informal roles strongly reflect members' personality characteristics, habits, and typical ways of interacting within a group. For example, Rich goofs around during fraternity meetings. He refuses to take anything seriously, cracks jokes that interrupt others, and calls members who work hard for the fraternity "overachievers." Rich's constant failure to take the group's job seriously has earned him the informal role of playboy in his group. In contrast, Jeff, one of the "overachievers," constantly reminds members about upcoming deadlines. His fraternity brothers have started calling him the group's timekeeper.

Behaviors That Define Roles

Roles enacted by group members comprise a set of behaviors that perform a function for the group. For formal roles the set of behaviors is often specified in writing. For informal roles the member performs the set of behaviors so regularly that others begin to expect it. Jeff's fraternity relies heavily on his timekeeping duties and would be lost (at least temporarily) if he did not perform them.

A number of classification schemes describe typical group functions that members' behaviors serve. One common scheme classifies behaviors by whether they perform task, maintenance, or self-centered functions. **Task functions** are behaviors that are directly relevant to the group's purpose and that affect the group's productivity; their purpose is to focus group members productively on their assignment. **Maintenance functions** are behaviors that focus on the interpersonal relationships among group members; they are aimed at supporting cooperative and harmonious relationships. Both task and maintenance functions are considered essential to effective group communication. On the other hand, **self-centered functions** are behaviors that serve the needs of the individual at the expense of the group. The person performing a self-centered behavior implies, "I don't care what the group needs or wants. *I* want . . ." He or she uses self-centered functions to manipulate other members for selfish goals that compete with group goals. Examples of statements that support task, maintenance, and self-centered functions are shown in Figure 9.2. The list is not exhaustive; many more functions could be added.

These behavioral functions combine to create a member's informal role, which is a comprehensive, general picture of how a particular member typically acts in a group. An example of how individual functions combine to create a role is shown in Figure 9.3. As you can see, information-giving and opinion-giving behaviors primarily characterize the information specialist role. The storyteller role comprises several behaviors including dramatizing, relieving tension, supporting, summarizing, and clarifying. Numerous other informal roles can be created through combinations of behaviors.

informal role

Also called a behavioral role; a role that is developed spontaneously within a group.

task functions

Behaviors that are directly relevant to the group's task and that affect the group's productivity.

maintenance functions

Behaviors that focus on the interpersonal relationships among group members.

self-centered functions

Behaviors that serve the needs of the individual at the expense of the group.

TRY ◆ THIS

Figure 9.3 illustrates how individual behavioral functions combine to create a role. How would you draw your own role in a group you belong to? Pick a group from your own life, and draw a pie diagram of behavioral functions of the group showing your role.

Task Functions and Statements

Initiating and orienting: "Let's make a list of what we still need to do."

Information giving: "Last year, the committee spent $150 on publicity."

Information seeking: "John, how many campus muggings were reported last year?"

Opinion giving: "I don't think the cost of parking stickers is the worst parking problem students have."

Clarifying: "Martina, are you saying that you couldn't support a proposal that increased student fees?"

Extending: "Another thing that Toby's proposal would let us do is . . ."

Evaluating: "One problem I see with Cindy's idea is . . ."

Summarizing: "So we've decided that we'll add two sections to the report, and Terrell and Candy will write them."

Coordinating: "If Carol interviews the mayor by Monday, then Jim and I can prepare a response by Tuesday's meeting."

Consensus testing: "We seem to be agreed that we prefer the second option."

Recording: "I think we decided at our last meeting. Let me check the minutes."

Maintenance (Relationship-Oriented) Functions and Statements

Establishing norms: "It doesn't help to call each other names. Let's stick to the issues."

Gatekeeping: "Pat, you look like you want to say something about the proposal."

Supporting: "I think Tara's point is well made, and we should look at it more closely."

Harmonizing: "Jared and Sally, I think there are areas where you are in agreement, and I would like to suggest a compromise that might work for you both."

Tension relieving: "We're getting tired and cranky. Let's take a 10-minute break."

Dramatizing: "That reminds me of a story about what happened last year when . . ."

Showing solidarity: "We've really done good work here!" or "We're all in this together."

Self-Centered Functions and Statements

Withdrawing: "Do whatever you want; I don't care," or not speaking at all.

Blocking: "I don't care if we've already voted; I want to discuss it again!"

Status and recognition seeking: "I have a lot more expertise than the rest of you, and I think we should do it the way I know works."

Figure 9.2 Examples of task, maintenance, and self-centered statements.

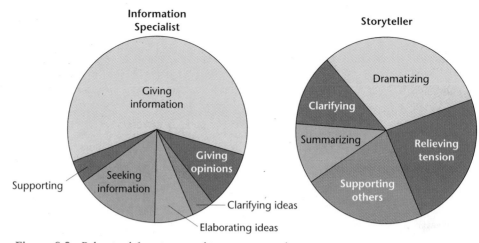

Figure 9.3 Behavioral functions combine to create roles.
SOURCE: Galanes and Brilhart, 1993.

Group Cohesiveness

Establishing a Cohesive Climate

group climate

The emotional tone or atmosphere members create within the group.

Another important element that helps shape a group's culture is the **group climate,** which is the emotional tone or atmosphere members create within the group. For example, you have probably attended a group meeting where the tension silenced everyone. That atmosphere of tension describes the group's climate. Three factors that contribute heavily to group climate are trust, cohesiveness, and supportiveness.

- *Trust* means that members believe they can rely on each other. Two types of trust relevant to groupwork are task trust and interpersonal trust. Task trust can be violated when group members do not contribute their share of the work (known as "hitchhikers"). Interpersonal trust means that others are working with the best interest of the group in mind rather than advancing hidden agendas.

- *Supportiveness* refers to an atmosphere of openness where members care about each other and create cohesiveness (Gibb, 1961). Examples of both supportive and defensive statements are found in Figure 9.4.

- *Cohesiveness* is the attachment members feel toward each other and the group. Highly cohesive groups are more open, handle disagreement more effectively, and typically perform better than noncohesive groups (Barker, 1991; Kelly & Duran, 1985).

Groupthink: An Unintended Outcome of Group Cohesiveness

groupthink

An unintended outcome of cohesion in which the desire for cohesion and agreement takes precedence over critical analysis and discussion.

Although cohesiveness is generally desirable for groups, dangers arise from too much cohesion. **Groupthink** happens when the desire for cohesion and agreement takes precedence over critical analysis and discussion. According to sociologist Irving Janis, groupthink can destroy effective decision making. Several historical decision-making blunders have been attributed to groupthink, including the failed Iranian

DEFENSIVE BEHAVIORS AND STATEMENTS

Evaluation:	Judging another person: "That's a completely ridiculous idea."
Control:	Dominating or insisting on your own way: "I've decided what we need to do."
Manipulating:	"Don't you think you should try it my way?"
Neutrality:	Not caring about how others feel: "It doesn't matter to me what you decide."
Superiority:	Pulling rank, maximizing status differences: "As group leader, I think we should . . ."
Certainty:	Being a "know-it-all": "You guys are completely off base. I know exactly how to handle this."

SUPPORTIVE BEHAVIORS AND STATEMENTS

Description:	Describing your own feelings without making those of others wrong: "I prefer the first option because . . ."
Problem orientation:	Searching for the best solution without predetermining what that should be: "We want to produce the best results, and that may mean some extra time from all of us."
Spontaneity:	Reacting honestly and openly: "Wow, that sounds like a great idea!"
Empathy:	Showing you care about the other members: "Jan, originally you were skeptical. How comfortable will you be if the group favors that option?"
Equality:	Minimizing status differences by treating members as equals: "I don't have all the answers. What do the rest of you think?"
Provisionalism:	Expressing opinions tentatively and being open to others' suggestions: "Maybe we should try a different approach . . ."

Figure 9.4 Examples of defensive and supportive statements.

hostage rescue mission, the space shuttle *Challenger* disaster, and the failure of American forces to foresee the attack on Pearl Harbor (Neck, 1996). Although groupthink may be difficult to detect when you are in a group, researchers have identified the following observable signs of groupthink:

- An illusion of invulnerability by the group
- An unquestioned belief in the morality of the group
- Collective efforts by group members to rationalize faulty decisions
- Stereotypic views of enemy leaders as evil, weak, or ineffective
- Self-censorship of alternative viewpoints
- A shared illusion that all group members think the same thing
- Direct pressure on group members expressing divergent opinions
- The emergence of "mind guards" to screen the group from information contradictory to the prevailing opinion

Although Janis's original description of groupthink suggests that these various characteristics lead to groupthink, and consequently result in bad decisions, recent studies suggest that Janis's groupthink characteristics actually occur after the group has already made the poor decision (Henningsen, Henningsen, Eden, DeKalb, & Cruz, 2006). Once groups make decisions, group members try to create and reinforce a consensus in support of the decision even in the face of evidence that the decision was poor. The desire for consensus then leads to all of the groupthink characteristics identified by Janis.

Groupthink is possible in nearly every group. To prevent groupthink from occurring, groups should seek all pertinent information, carefully assess the credibility of information relevant to the decision at hand, assign members to present counterarguments, and maintain a commitment to finding the best possible outcome as supported by the available evidence.

The Effect of Diversity on Group Culture

group culture

The socially negotiated system of rules that guide group behavior.

Group culture is the socially negotiated system of rules that guide group behavior. Group culture differs from national and ethnic cultures because a group culture is a relatively unstable and short-term phenomenon. That is, group cultures are constantly in flux and they disappear when the group dissolves. National and ethnic cultures change slowly and are relatively persistent. If you compare two groups from your own life, you can easily understand the concept of group culture. Your group of friends has implicit rules for behavior—inside jokes, slang, norms for touching, and shared objectives. Your group likely has a culture different from that of an assigned group of students you work with in one of your classes. Classroom groups are typically more formal, less cohesive, and more task-oriented.

within-group diversity

The presence of observable and/or implicit differences among group members.

Within-group diversity is the presence of observable and/or implicit differences between group members. We observe within-group diversity when group members differ based on visible characteristics. For example, to visually distinguish between males and females or between members of certain ethnic groups is easy. Group diversity can be implicit when members of a group have differing values, attitudes, and perspectives—personal characteristics that cannot be seen. Table 9.2 shows common examples of observable and implicit within-group diversity.

Differences between group members can have an impact on how they interact with one another and how effectively the group functions. To illustrate the effects of group diversity on group members' behaviors, here are several research findings on differences between how men and women interact in groups:

- In online discussion groups and other forms of computer-mediated communication, women tend to use more exclamation points as markers of friendliness—

TABLE 9.2   OBSERVABLE AND IMPLICIT WITHIN-GROUP DIVERSITY

	OBSERVABLE	IMPLICIT
DEFINITION	Within-group diversity based on physical characteristics that can be seen	Within-group diversity based on individuals' worldviews, perspectives, and other personality characteristics
EXAMPLE	Ethnicity, sex	Religious orientation, educational background

thus emphasizing the relational aspects of group communication (Waseleski, 2006).

- Female speakers tend to prefer standard (more formal) speech forms whereas male speakers tend to prefer vernacular (less formal) speech forms (Ladegaard & Dorthe, 2003).

- Although men are typically more influential in standard communication contexts, this difference diminishes in groups, especially when more than one woman is present. In such situations the influence of women is roughly equal to that of men (Carli, 2001).

- Recent research has observed no differences in perceived leadership ability regardless of whether the group is primarily task- or relationship-oriented; previous research had shown that women were better leaders in relationship-oriented groups (Won, 2006)

In addition to gender differences, cultural differences can also influence group dynamics. For instance, it is likely that work groups and even classroom groups will have at least one member for whom English is a second language. In such situations all group members should make sure that ESL members are fully included. Strategies for helping non-native speakers to feel included are (1) providing written information in advance of discussions, (2) asking someone in the group to take notes that can be copied and distributed to all group members, (3) viewing difference as a strength of the group, and (4) matching tasks to members' abilities. Particularly with the last suggestion, finding out the strengths of all group members is important. Second-language speakers often do not speak as often, but this does not mean that they do not have highly developed skills in other areas like computers, artwork, record keeping, and so on. Finding each member's strengths and using those to the group's advantage demonstrate effective and ethical leadership.

If you are a second-language speaker who is part of a group with mostly native speakers, you must practice being assertive. You should ask questions to clarify the activities of the group or points made during discussion. You should also let group members know about skills you have that could be useful to the group. Finally, try to recognize that in most situations group discussions are as much about relationship building as task accomplishment. Taking time to get to know other members of your group will not only help all of you build confidence in each other but will also potentially lead to meaningful friendships outside of class or the workplace.

Problem Solving and Decision Making

A primary task facing many groups is solving problems: Student clubs need to raise money, church groups need to plan activities, and social groups must find fun things to do. Group members must be both creative and critical to arrive at the best solutions to these problems. Groups are usually (but not always) better problem solvers than individuals, because several people can provide more information than one person. Groups also can supply more resources and collectively have a broader perspective. And group members can spot flaws in each other's reasoning. However, trade-offs occur. Group problem solving takes longer, and sometimes personality, procedural, or social problems make working as a team difficult for members. Group problem solving is superior under certain conditions, such as when multiple solutions are equally appropriate, decisions must be acceptable to all the members, and the group has ample time to meet (Vroom, 1973). Groups are particularly well suited for **conjunctive tasks,** for which no one member has all the necessary information but each member has some information to contribute. Individuals are often better at **disjunctive tasks,** which require little coordination and which can be completed by the most skilled member working alone (Smith, 1989). Group problem solving is usually more effective when the process is systematic and organized, because a group that does not have an overall plan for decision making is more likely to make a poor decision (Gouran & Hirokawa, 1986).

Effective Group Problem Solving

Groups using systematic procedures solve problems more effectively and have higher-quality discussions than do groups that do not use systematic procedures (Gouran, Brown, & Henry, 1978). Following a structured procedure often reminds discussants of something they forgot to do (such as analyze the problem thoroughly) in an earlier stage of problem solving and suggests logical priorities (Poole, 1983a, 1983b). An effective problem-solving process starts with an appropriate discussion question, includes an explicit discussion of the criteria the group will use to assess potential solutions, and follows a systematic problem-solving procedure.

Wording the Discussion Question

Problem-solving groups typically handle three basic types of discussion questions. Questions of *fact* deal with whether something is true or can be verified. Questions of *value* ask whether something is good or bad, better or worse. Cultural and individual values and beliefs are central to questions of value. Questions of *policy* ask what action should be taken. The key word *should* is either stated or implied in questions of policy. Examples of each type of question are presented in Figure 9.5.

Regardless of the type of discussion question guiding a problem-solving group, the leader must state the question appropriately. Well-stated questions are clear and measurable and focus on the problem rather than on a solution. First, the language and terminology should be concrete rather than abstract. If ambiguous terms such as *effective, good,* or *fair* are used, providing examples helps each group member have as close to the same meaning as possible. Figure 9.6 gives examples of how abstract terms can be made more concrete. Second, a well-stated discussion question helps group members know when the solution has been achieved. For example, a task force charged with "completing a report by May 15 on why membership has dropped from 100 to 50 members" knows exactly what to do by what deadline. Finally, a group should start its problem solving with a problem question rather than a solution question. Problem questions focus on the undesirable present state and imply that many solutions are possible. They do not bias a group toward one particular option. Solution questions, on the other hand, slant the group's discussion toward one particular option. They may inadvertently cause a group to ignore creative or unusual options because they blind members to some alternatives. Examples of problem and solution questions appear in Figure 9.7.

FACT

How has the divorce rate changed in the past 15 years?

How many Hispanic students graduate from high school each year?

What percentage of college students graduate in four years?

How often, on average, does a person speak each day?

What occupations earn the highest annual incomes?

VALUE

Why should people seek higher education?

How should Americans treat international students?

Does our legal system provide "justice for all"?

How should young people be educated about AIDS?

What is the value of standardized tests for college admission?

POLICY

What courses should students be required to take?

Should the state's drunk driving laws be changed?

What are the arguments for and against mandatory retirement?

Should the United States intervene in foreign disputes for humanitarian reasons?

What advantages should government provide for businesses willing to develop in high-risk areas of a city?

Figure 9.5   Examples of questions of fact, value, and policy.

Watch "Where There's Smoke" on the *Online Learning Center* at www. mhhe.com/pearson3, and determine what type(s) of questions are being addressed.

"I think Ms. Brown is **a good lawyer** because she is *very credible*. She *knows the law* and always *comes up with novel arguments* that her opposing lawyers can't counter."

"Our solution for the parking problem has to be **effective**. I mean, it has to *reduce parking complaints, eliminate the amount of driving around looking for a space that happens now, and not cost the university any money*."

"I think **weapons** should be made illegal. I mean, *guns* are really dangerous in the wrong hands, and you can't tell me that people need *semiautomatic assault rifles* to hunt with."

Figure 9.6   Making abstract concepts more concrete.

PROBLEM QUESTIONS	SOLUTION QUESTIONS
How can we reduce complaints about parking on campus?	How can we increase the number of parking spaces in the campus lots?
What can we do to increase attendance at our club's activities?	How can we improve publicity for our club's activities?
How can we make Ginny Avenue safer to cross?	How can we get the city council to reduce the speed limit on Ginny Avenue?

Figure 9.7   Problem questions versus solution questions.

Discussing Criteria

Criteria are the standards by which a group must judge potential solutions. For example, a solution's likely effectiveness ("Will it work?"), acceptability ("Will people vote for our proposal?"), and cost ("Does this option keep us within the budget?") are common criteria. Group members should discuss and agree on criteria before adopting a solution. Because criteria are based on the values of group members, two members, each using rational tools of decision making, can arrive at different conclusions. The more similar group members are in age, gender, ethnicity, background, attitudes, values, and beliefs, the easier they can agree on criteria.

Two kinds of criteria are common. Absolute criteria are those that must be met; the group has no leeway. Important criteria are those that should be met, but the group has some flexibility. Group members should give the highest priority to criteria that must be met. Ideas that do not meet absolute criteria should be rejected, and the rest should be ranked on how well they meet important criteria. Examples of absolute and important criteria are presented in Figure 9.8.

Identifying Alternatives

One of the most important jobs a leader has is to encourage group creativity. One procedure that encourages creativity is brainstorming, a technique that originated in the advertising industry to help develop imaginative advertising campaigns (Osborn, 1975). Group brainstorming is generally enhanced when groups are highly cohesive, when leaders are chosen democratically, and when group members have substantial knowledge related to the problem being addressed (Moore, 2000). In fact, Moore's research suggests that any two of these factors allow groups to outperform individuals when brainstorming.

Critical evaluation kills creativity, so the main rule of brainstorming is "no evaluation," at least during the brainstorming process. Evaluation of the ideas takes place *after* the group has exhausted its options.

Evaluating Alternatives

After group members have adequately brainstormed alternatives, the final task is to evaluate alternatives. At this stage in the discussion, criteria identified by the group

ABSOLUTE CRITERIA	IMPORTANT CRITERIA
(*Must* be met)	(*Should* be met)
• Must not cost more than $2 million	• Should be centrally located
• Must be wheelchair accessible	• Should have stage space for concerts
• Must include flexible space that can be arranged in different ways	• Should be attractive to all campus constituencies, including traditional and nontraditional students, faculty, and staff

Figure 9.8   Absolute criteria versus important criteria for a new student union.

in step two are used to judge the efficacy of each solution. Solutions failing to meet absolute criteria are quickly eliminated. Once the nonviable alternatives are eliminated, group members must evaluate each alternative based on remaining important criteria. Eventually, the group must determine which alternative best meets the set of important criteria identified in step two.

Beyond Problem Solving: Group Work in a New Era

In various places throughout the book, we have highlighted myths, metaphors, and misunderstandings. For small-group communication one of the most common myths is that groups function only to solve problems. Of course, groups serve multiple functions, sometimes simultaneously. In addition to helping us perform task functions like solving problems, groups also allow us to do the following:

1. *Make decisions*. Many groups exist to make decisions that are unrelated to specific problems. For example, student groups like fraternities and sororities make daily decisions such as planning social engagements, launching community outreach projects, and maintaining facilities. These decisions do not necessarily solve problems; rather, they sustain the day-to-day functions of the groups.

2. *Effect change*. Some groups want to influence society but do not have the power to make decisions. For example, several years ago the staff at one of our universities went on strike in an attempt to get better pay and benefits from the state. That group of employees had little power to make decisions—they could not force the state to provide a better offer. However, their actions as a group were meant to raise awareness and plead a case. They wanted to promote change even though they could not force change.

3. *Negotiate conflict*. Groups are often created to resolve conflict. In Los Angeles small groups were used to bring Latino-American and Armenian-American high school students together to resolve racial tensions. In fact, the National Communication Association in partnership with the Southern Poverty Law Center has used this strategy across the nation to promote intercultural understanding and to help resolve racial conflict.

4. *Foster creativity*. Groups help us achieve a level of creativity not possible when working alone. The idea that "two heads are better than one" is magnified in groups. People working together to identify creative ideas will likely be more successful than one person acting alone.

5. *Maintain ties between stakeholders*. A final function for small groups is to bring together stakeholders. **Stakeholders** are groups of people who have an interest in the actions of an organization. For example, most schools have parent–teacher organizations. The principal of a school might bring together selected teachers and parents to discuss issues facing the school so that open lines of communication between various stakeholders (parents, teachers, and administrators) can be maintained. Various organizations, including businesses, government agencies, and nonprofit organizations, use groups to establish and maintain communication between multiple groups of stakeholders.

stakeholders

Groups of people who have an interest in the actions of an organization.

As you can see, groups exist for many reasons. Although the heart of group activity may indeed be problem solving, not all groups exist solely for that purpose.

Technology and Group Communication Processes

Throughout this book we have explored how various forms of technology impact human communication. In small-group communication, technology can be used for facilitating communication as well as for sharing strategic information necessary for decision making. One form of group technology is decision support systems.

A **group decision support system (GDSS)** is an interactive network of computers with specialized software allowing users to generate solutions for unstructured problems (Sosik, Avolio, & Kahai, 1997). Although the exact nature of the GDSS environment can be tailored to specific situations, most GDSS-based group interactions are used to facilitate brainstorming and evaluation of alternatives. In a typical GDSS session members anonymously post ideas using a personal computer. Although postings are anonymous, each member of the group can see ideas posted by other members; ideas generated by one person may generate additional ideas by someone else. After a predetermined length of time for brainstorming, members can anonymously rank and/or rate each idea. The software summarizes the results of members' rankings and/or ratings. Most GDSSs also allow members to anonymously vote to indicate their choice for the best alternative. Some GDSSs also allow for anonymous text-based discussions using the computer.

Computers can be used to facilitate group communication.

group decision support system (GDSS)

An interactive network of computers with specialized software allowing users to generate solutions for unstructured problems.

The key characteristics of GDSSs are anonymity and efficiency. Because individuals' ideas are anonymous, discussions using GDSSs tend to result in better information sharing and critical analysis of ideas than face-to-face interactions (Lam & Schaubroek, 2000). In addition to being anonymous, GDSSs are also efficient. In reviewing more than 28 experimental studies comparing GDSS discussion groups to face-to-face groups, Hwang (1998) concluded that GDSSs resulted in significantly more ideas generated than traditional face-to-face groups. Thus, in the same amount of time, the efficiency of brainstorming is significantly improved by GDSS-based discussions. Aiken and Martin (1994) also suggest that GDSSs have the potential to reduce the likelihood of groupthink because alternative opinions can be presented anonymously.

With effort many of the GDSS advantages can be gained by setting up private chat rooms where users can log in anonymously. Online services like AOL and Yahoo! offer chat rooms as a free service. By using nonidentifiable nicknames, members of the group can post ideas for viewing by other group members. Entire discussions can take place in such chat rooms where each person remains anonymous.

While GDSS technology has many advantages for group decision making, some cautions are in order. First, the anonymity offered by GDSSs may take some of the emotion out of group discussions, thus making it more difficult for those with minority viewpoints to sway others in the group (McLeod, Baron, Weighner, & Yoon, 1997). Second, the effectiveness of any GDSS approach is dependent on the skill of the facilitator—a poor facilitator may actually hamper decision-making effectiveness, even with a GDSS system (Aakhus, 2001). Finally, true GDSS systems are very expensive and not practical for most college and university settings.

How Should You Communicate in Small Groups?

If you, as a group member, are responsible, with the other members, for the outcomes of the groups to which you belong, what can you do to help achieve productive outcomes? The ability to speak fluently and with polish is not essential, but the ability to speak clearly is. You will help fellow group members understand you better by organizing your comments during small-group discussions in the following ways:

1. *Relate your statements to preceding remarks.* Public speakers do not always have the opportunity to respond to remarks by others, but small-group members do. Your statement should not appear irrelevant. Clarify the relevance of your remark to the topic under discussion by linking your remark to the preceding remark. We recommend doing the following:

   - Briefly note the previous speaker's point that you want to address—for example, "I want to piggyback on Bill's comment by noting that we can meet our goal by . . ."

   - State your point clearly and concisely.

   - Summarize how your point adds to the comments made by others—for example, "So, I agree with Bill. We need to fund-raise, but we can't get so caught up in raising money that we forget about our goal of volunteering."

2. *Use conventional word arrangements.* When you speak, you should use clear, common language so people can understand you. Consider this comment: "I unequivocally recognize the meaningful contribution made by my colleague." While the language might impress some, a simple "I agree" would work just as well. We recommend the following to improve your verbal clarity during group discussions:

   - After connecting your idea to the discussion or previous speaker, state your point and then provide one piece of supporting information or additional explanation.

   - When done, ask if anyone needs you to clarify your point.

243

3. *Speak concisely.* The point here is simple: Don't be long-winded. The main advantage of small groups is their ability to approach a problem interactively. If you monopolize the discussion, that advantage of small-group communication may be diminished or lost completely. To learn to speak concisely, try the following:

   • Write down your idea before speaking. Those who are wordy during group discussions often spend much of their time trying to figure out what they want to say.

   • Try to talk for no more than one minute at a time. Of course, this time limit is arbitrary; however, one minute should be enough time to get an idea out for consideration, and you can always answer questions to clarify as needed.

4. *State one point at a time.* Sometimes this rule is violated appropriately, such as when a group member is presenting a report to the group. However, during give-and-take discussion, stating only one idea promotes efficiency and responsiveness. To ensure this practice, try the following strategies:

   • As a group, appoint a process observer to be in charge of keeping the group discussion moving along and preventing any member from bringing up more than one idea at a time. After using the process observer a few times, these behaviors become second nature.

   • If you have several ideas that vary in importance, provide some of the less important points to group members in written form for later reflection. Save discussion time for the most important ideas.

◀ **SKILL** BUILDER ▶

Practice your group communication skills while participating in class discussions. When your class is discussing a topic, make contributions by (1) connecting your comment to the previous person's statement, (2) using conventional word arrangements, (3) speaking concisely, and (4) stating only one point at a time.

Being an Ethical Group Member

The unique nature of small groups requires attention to special ethical concerns regarding the treatment of speech, people, and information. First, as noted in the NCA Credo of Ethics, discussed earlier in the book, the field of communication strongly supports the value of free speech. Many secondary groups are formed because several heads perform better than one, but that advantage will not be realized if group members are unwilling or afraid to speak freely in the group. An important ethical principle for small groups is that group members should be willing to share their unique perspectives. But they should also refrain from saying or doing things that prevent others from speaking freely. Members who are trustworthy and supportive are behaving ethically.

Second, group members must be honest and truthful. In a small group they should not intentionally deceive one another or manufacture information or evidence to persuade other members to adopt their point of view.

Third, group members must be thorough and unbiased when they evaluate information. Many decisions made in groups, from where to locate a mall to whether it is safe to launch a space shuttle in cold weather, affect people's lives. Such decisions will be only as good as the information on which they are based and the reasoning the members use to assess the information. Group members must consider *all* relevant information in an open-minded, unbiased way by using the best critical thinking skills they can; otherwise, tragedies can result.

Fourth, group members must behave with integrity. That is, they must be willing to place the good of the group ahead of their own goals. Some individuals cannot be team players because they are unable or unwilling to merge their personal agendas with those of the group. Groups are better off without such individuals. If you make a commitment to join a group, you should be the kind of team member who will benefit rather than harm the group. If you cannot in good conscience give a group your support, you should leave the group rather than pretend to support the group while sabotaging it.

Finally, group members must learn to manage **group conflict,** which is an expressed struggle between two or more members of a group (Galanes & Adams, 2007; Wilmot & Hocker, 2007). Although some conflict can actually help groups make better decisions because ideas are debated and tested more vigorously, too much conflict may result in decreased group cohesiveness and could actually cause the group to cease functioning. To manage conflict, group members must be ethical in the way they approach disagreement and be willing to listen to and compromise with others. Ethical disagreement happens when you express your disagreement openly, disagree with ideas rather than people, base your disagreement on evidence and reasoning, and react to disagreement positively rather than defensively (Galanes & Adams, 2007).

group conflict

An expressed struggle between two or more members of a group.

Chapter Review & Study Guide

SUMMARY

In this chapter you learned the following:

▶ Small-group communication is the interaction of a small group of people working together to achieve a common goal. Small-group communication is relevant to our lives because:
- Humans need groups to meet needs they cannot meet for themselves.
- Groups are everywhere.
- Group communication is a highly valued skill.
- Working effectively in groups requires training.

▶ Small groups can be classified as task related, relationship related, assigned, or emergent. Many groups can blur boundaries among these types of groups.

▶ Leadership is the process of using communication to influence the behaviors and attitudes of people to meet group goals. Various theories discuss how leadership affects small-group communication. The most effective leaders are able to adapt their leadership skills to the needs of the group. Additionally, all members of the group can potentially share leadership responsibilities.

▶ Group culture is created from several factors including within-group diversity, group norms, individuals' role structures, and group cohesiveness. Although group cohesiveness is generally viewed as a positive element of group culture, highly cohesive groups must take care to prevent groupthink from occurring.

▶ Group decision making involves four steps:
- Wording the discussion question.
- Discussing criteria for evaluating potential solutions.
- Brainstorming alternatives.
- Evaluating alternatives.

▶ Small-group communication can utilize technology to help facilitate communication and decision making.
- Computer networking, either traditional or peer-to-peer, allows members of a group to communicate electronically and share information.
- Group decision support systems use special software to facilitate brainstorming and decision making. Group members are able to anonymously present ideas to other members and are also able to anonymously rate and vote for specific alternatives.

▶ To effectively communicate in small groups, you must use clear language and make concise comments that are related to the comments of other group members. You should try to keep your comments limited to one issue at a time.

▶ Ethical behaviors in group contexts include allowing others to speak without fear, being honest and truthful, carefully evaluating alternatives, acting with integrity, and managing conflict ethically.

KEY TERMS

Go to the *Online Learning Center* at www.mhhe.com/**pearson3** to further your understanding of the following terminology.

Affection	Formal role	Maintenance functions
Assigned groups	Group climate	Norms
Autocratic leaders	Group conflict	Power
Conjunctive task	Group culture	Relationship-oriented groups
Control	Group decision support system	Role
Criteria	(GDSS)	Self-centered functions
Democratic leaders	Groupthink	Small-group communication
Designated leader	Inclusion	Stakeholders
Disjunctive tasks	Informal role	Task functions
Emergent groups	Laissez-faire leaders	Task-oriented groups
Emergent leader	Leadership	Within-group diversity

STUDY QUESTIONS

1. "Groups meet needs," "groups are everywhere," and "working effectively in groups requires training" are statements that explain
   a. types of small groups
   b. reasons for studying small-group communication
   c. ways of interacting in small groups
   d. methods of studying small-group communication

2. What is true of small groups?
   a. They are comprised of three to nine people.
   b. Members are interdependent.
   c. Group members work toward a common goal.
   d. All of the above.

3. Which type of group exists to meet our needs for inclusion and affection?
   a. task-oriented
   b. relationship-oriented
   c. assigned
   d. emergent

4. A process of using communication to influence the behaviors and attitudes of others to meet group goals and to benefit the group is termed
   a. groupthink
   b. inclusion
   c. leadership
   d. role

5. According to French and Raven, referent power is
   a. power based on others' admiration and respect
   b. the ability to give followers what they want and need
   c. when other members value a person's knowledge or expertise
   d. the ability to withhold from followers what they want and need

6. Informal rules for group interaction, the emotional tone created within a group, and group member roles are comprised in
   a. leadership skills
   b. brainstorming techniques
   c. maintenance functions
   d. a group's culture

7. Creating a discussion question, evaluating prospective solutions, and brainstorming and evaluating alternatives are steps in
   a. group conflict
   b. group diversity
   c. group decision making
   d. groupthink

8. Which of the following statements is true?
   a. Groups exist solely for problem solving.
   b. Effective leaders do not adapt their leadership skills to the needs of the group.
   c. Technology can be utilized to help facilitate communication within small groups.
   d. Groupthink is a helpful and effective method of decision making

9. When communicating with other group members, you should
   a. use technical language so you appear more credible
   b. state numerous points at a time
   c. be long-winded
   d. relate your remarks to previous statements

10. To manage group conflict ethically, members must
   a. be willing to listen to and compromise with others
   b. base their disagreements on feeling and intuition
   c. disagree with people rather than ideas
   d. defend their ideas and refuse to listen to others' ideas

Answers:
1. (b); 2. (d); 3. (b); 4. (c); 5. (a); 6. (d); 7. (c); 8. (c); 9. (d); 10. (a)

CRITICAL THINKING

1. Think of the groups to which you belong. Do they mesh with the text's definition of a small group? What are the groups' functions? What type of leader does each group have? What group norms are you expected to abide by?

2. When in the presence of a group, note the members' functions and related statements. Under which subcategory do the statements fall (refer to Figures 9.2 and 9.4)?

SELF-QUIZ

For further review, try the chapter self-quiz on the *Online Learning Center* at **www.mhhe.com/pearson3.**

REFERENCES

Aakhus, M. (2001). Technocratic and design stances toward communication expertise: How GDSS facilitators understand their work. *Journal of Applied Communication Research, 29,* 341–372.

Aiken, M., & Martin, J. (1994, September). Enhancing business communication with group decision support systems. *Bulletin of the Association for Business Communication, 57,* 24–27.

Barge, J. K., & Hirokawa, R. Y. (1989). Toward a communication competency model of group leadership. *Small Group Behavior, 20,* 167–189.

Barker, D. B. (1991, February). The behavioral analysis of interpersonal intimacy in group development. *Small Group Research, 22,* 76–91.

Brown, M. E., & Trevino, L. K. (2006). Socialized charismatic leadership, values congruence, and deviance in work groups. *Journal of Applied Psychology, 91,* 954–962.

Carli, L. L. (2001). Gender and social influence. *Journal of Social Issues, 57,* 725–742.

Cole, D. (1989, May). Meetings that make sense. *Psychology Today, 23,* 14.

Foels, R., Driskell, J. E., Mullen, B., & Salas, E. (2000). The effects of democratic leadership on group member satisfaction. *Small Group Research, 31,* 676–702.

French, J. R. P., & Raven, B. (1981). The bases of social power. In D. Cartwright & A. Zander (Eds.), *Group dynamics: Research and theory* (3rd ed.). New York: McGraw-Hill.

Galanes, G. J., & Adams, K. H. (2007). *Effective group discussion: Theory and practice.* New York: McGraw-Hill.

Gibb, J. R. (1961). Defensive communication. *Journal of Communication, 11,* 141–148.

Gouran, D. S., Brown, C., & Henry, D. R. (1978). Behavioral correlates of perceptions of quality in decision-making discussions. *Communication Monographs, 45,* 62.

Gouran, D. S., & Hirokawa, R. Y. (1986). Counteractive functions of communication in effective group decision-making. In R. Y. Hirokawa & M. S. Poole (Eds.), *Communication and group decision-making.* Beverly Hills, CA: Sage.

Hackman, M. Z., & Johnson, C. E. (2003). *Leadership: A communication perspective* (4th ed.) Prospect Heights, IL: Waveland Press.

Henningsen, D. D., Henningsen, M. L., Eden, J., & Cruz, M. G. (2006). Examining the symptoms of groupthink and retrospective sensemaking. *Small Group Research, 37,* 36–64.

Homans, G. C. (1950). *The human group.* New York: Harcourt Brace Jovanovich.

Hwang, M. (1998, February). Did task type matter in the use of decision room GDSS? A critical review and a meta-analysis. *Omega, 26,* 1–15.

Kelly, L., & Duran, R. L. (1985). Interaction and performance in small groups: A descriptive report. *International Journal of Small Group Research, 1,* 182–192.

Ladegaard, H. J., & Dorthe, B. (2003). Gender differences in your children's speech: The acquisition of sociolinguistic competence. *International Journal of Applied Linguistics, 13,* 222–233.

McLeod, P., Baron, R., Weighner, M., & Yoon, K. (1997). The eyes have it: Minority influence in face-to-face and computer-mediated group discussion. *Journal of Applied Psychology, 82,* 706–719.

Moore, R. (2000). Creativity of small groups and of persons working alone. *Journal of Social Psychology, 140,* 142–144.

Neck, C. (1996, November). Letterman or Leno: A groupthink analysis of successive decisions made by the National Broadcasting Company. *Journal of Managerial Psychology, 11,* 3–18.

Osborn, A. (1975). *Applied imagination.* New York: Scribner's.

Poole, M. S. (1983a). Decision development in small groups: II. A study of multiple sequences in decision making. *Communication Monographs, 50,* 224–225.

Poole, M. S. (1983b). Decision development in small groups: III. A multiple sequence model of group decision development. *Communication Monographs, 50,* 321–341.

Schutz, W. C. (1958). *FIRO: A three-dimensional theory of interpersonal behavior.* New York: Rinehart.

Smith, H. W. (1989). Group versus individual problem solving and type of problem solved. *Small Group Behavior, 20,* 357–366.

Sosik, J., Avolio, B., & Kahai, S. (1997). Effects of leadership style and anonymity on group potency and effectiveness in a group decision support system environment. *Journal of Applied Psychology, 82,* 90–104.

Vengel, A. (2006). Lead your team to victory: The dos and don'ts of effective group influence. *Contract Management, 46,* 69–70.

Vice, J. (2001). Developing communication and professional skills through analytical reports. *Business Communication Quarterly, 64,* 84–93.

Vroom, V. H. (1973). A new look at management decision-making. *Organizational Dynamics,* pp. 66–80.

Waseleski, C. (2006). Gender and the use of exclamation points in computer-mediated communication: An analysis of exclamation points posted to two electronic discussion lists. *Journal of Computer Mediated Communication, 11,* 1012–1024.

Wilmot, W. W., & Hocker, J. L. (2007). *Interpersonal Conflict* (7th ed.). New York: McGraw-Hill.

Won, H. L. (2006). Links between personalities and leadership perception in problem-solving groups. *The Social Science Journal, 43,* 659–672.

Zekeri, A. A. (2004). College curriculum competencies and skills former students found essential to their careers. *College Student Journal, 38,* 412–423.

Zorn, T. E., Roper, J., Broadfoot, K., & Weaver, C. K. (2006). Focus groups as sites of influential interaction: Building communicative self-efficacy and effecting attitudinal change in discussing controversial topics. *Journal of Applied Communication Research, 34,* 115–140.

CHAPTER TEN

Topic Selection and Audience Analysis

What will you learn?

When you have read and thought about this chapter, you will be able to:

1. Brainstorm for a topic appropriate for you and your audience.
2. Conduct a personal inventory for topics you know best.
3. Narrow a topic to save yourself time and to increase relevance.
4. Analyze your audience by demographics, interests, and concerns.
5. Recognize the challenge of changing an audience's existing positions.
6. Develop strategies for adapting you and your message to a specific audience.

*M*any speakers get stuck on this first step in creating a speech because they have too many choices and cannot settle on one choice. So this chapter focuses on how you can more quickly determine what topics are important to you and to your audience, how you can more rapidly narrow the focus so you do not waste time by exploring too broadly, and how you can analyze the audience to make sure that they will care about you and what you have to say. Your ability to inform or persuade an audience depends heavily on your skill in selecting an appropriate topic and in adapting that topic to the particular audience. Once you have mastered these skills for your classroom audience, you can apply them when you speak to other groups.

D oes public opinion determine what the media—newspapers, magazines, TV, radio, and blogs—cover? Or do the topics that the media cover shape public opinion? This is a question that media scholars have debated for decades. Many studies have lent some support to the second of these possibilities because of a theory known as agenda setting.

Agenda setting theory holds that the media highlight certain stories, which then lead the public to assign importance to the topics covered. In this way the stories more or less set the agenda of public opinion. Thus the war in Iraq, terrorism, global warming, star-crossed astronauts, and presidential campaigns are topics that have been on the minds of many people lately. If not, those people have probably watched or read very little news.

The media do, in fact, shape the choices that speakers make for their topics. A study by Thomas Christie (2006) compared the topics covered at the daily White House press briefings during two periods of time—a month when media coverage of war issues was high and a month when media coverage focused elsewhere. Christie found that war issues dominated the press briefings during the month that the media focused on the war, but in the month that the media focused on other issues, the war received very little mention in the press briefings. Christie concluded that, at least in part, the White House communication strategy shaped itself to reflect the hot topics in the media.

Do you think agenda setting is a good way to explain the relationship between the media and public opinion? Would the "hot topics" of the day influence your choices for speech topics? No matter what topic you select for a speech, you must take your audience into consideration. Sometimes that may require you to change your speech or even the topic itself. How much you need to adapt to an audience can be difficult to determine. In this chapter we will focus on how you should select topics while also understanding the nature of your audience. With every speech you will continue to grapple with the balance between personal views and audience adaptation.

How Do You Select a Topic?

Too often beginning speakers spend too much time dreaming up their topic. This chapter provides some shortcuts to rapid topic selection through brainstorming and personal inventories. Only a small amount of your speech preparation time should be dedicated to topic selection, because you should begin with subjects you already know.

Individual Brainstorming

brainstorming

A creative procedure for thinking of as many topics as you can in a limited time.

Brainstorming is thinking of as many topics as you can in a limited time so that you can select one topic that will be appropriate for you and your audience. Group brainstorming can be a useful technique for selecting a topic for group discussion; individual brainstorming can be an equally effective way to find a topic for your public speech. Indeed, this technique can help you generate many speech topics.

Most students find this method more productive than trying to think of just one topic for their speech.

You'll find individual brainstorming to be relatively quick and easy. First, give yourself a limited time—say, 5 minutes—and without trying to think of titles or even complete thoughts, write down as many potential topics as you can. When your time is up, you should have a rough list of possible ideas or topics for your speech. This step can be repeated if you want an even larger list. Second, select the *three* items from your list that are the most appealing to you as topics for your speech. Third, from those three topics choose the *one* that you think would be most appealing to both you and your audience.

Personal Inventories

Another way to find a topic for your presentation is to do a **personal inventory,** or an analysis of your own reading, viewing, and listening choices. You can learn much about yourself by reflecting on your own choices: I-Pod selections, chat room choices, video and audio downloads, and website selections. Examining your own choices will help you choose a topic that you already know something about.

Public speaking starts with the self—with what you know, have experienced, or are willing to learn. Self-analysis, through personal inventories, can help you uncover the areas in which you are qualified to speak.

While media use is one cue to your interests, you may also inventory the following:

- What you like best and least at work, about family life, about your community, and about our government, politics, and policies
- What causes take your time and energy: your religion, your political party, your position on important issues of our time, and so on
- What personal issues bother you and need to be brought to the attention of others: discrimination, environmental concerns, health issues, and so on

Let us look next at how you can select topics that emerged through brainstorming or personal inventories. Let us look first at your involvement in the topic and then at your knowledge of the topic.

personal inventory

An analysis of your own reading, viewing, and listening habits and behavior to discover topics of personal interest.

Your Topic's Importance

Once you have selected a possible topic, you should evaluate the topic to see if it is important both to you and to your audience, if you and the audience know enough about the topic, and if you are committed to the topic.

For example, you may love sports, know much about soccer, and even be an excellent player. But if the audience embraces American football and doesn't care to learn about a sport beloved by much of the rest of the world, then you face a difficult task: The audience does not consider your topic important.

Your Knowledge of the Topic

Once you have established that your topic is important to you and to your audience, you need to determine what you and your audience know about the subject. You are in the best position if you know more about the topic than they do. Also, you can add to what you know by talking to others, reading, and going to websites on the subject, as long as you correctly cite your sources. Let's say that you want to talk about the topic of national defense narrowed to service in the National Guard. Twice

Effective speakers know their subject.

deployed, you can speak with authority about military purpose and implementation, and your audience knows the topic is important. That condition is ideal for a presentation topic: You know much, and they know little, but they believe the topic to be important.

Your Commitment to the Topic

Even a topic that you know much about and that you and the audience believe to be important is not a good choice for a presentation unless you feel some passion about the subject. **Commitment** is a measure of how much time and effort you put into a cause. For example, you know that many children are waiting to be adopted; you deeply want more people to be concerned about heart disease and cancer because your relatives died from these diseases; or you want less government interference in our personal lives. You spend time and effort on what you care about, so those causes can guide you to an ideal topic for you and your audience.

Figure 10.1 provides some helpful pointers.

Topic Selection for ESL Speakers

Nearly every student finds topic selection to be one of the most challenging aspects of the speech preparation process. And for those who speak English as a second language, this step can be even more challenging because you may need to consider how to balance your personal knowledge and comfort with certain topics with what your audience will be able to relate to. In this section we provide various suggestions for non-native speakers to keep in mind when selecting a topic.

commitment

A measure of how much time and effort you put into a cause; your passion and concern about the topic.

1. *Draw on personal experience.* Depending on your culture you may or may not feel comfortable talking about your own personal experience. In America it is not only appropriate but potentially desirable to do so. Because the American culture is aligned toward respect for individuality, people's unique personal experiences are often viewed as important layers to an explanation or argument. Although you should use other types of support to document your speech, selecting a topic with which you have personal experience is wise.

2. *Review many examples.* To get a sense of what types of topics other students are likely to select, you should review as many example topics as possible. Using this textbook, resources from your instructor or library, and even an Internet search for "speech topics" can be a useful way to identify example topics. Although you should not feel bound to use one of the examples you find, you should try to get some sense of what types of topics are common.

1. Do not select a topic that is illegal to present. Most colleges and universities do not allow weapons and alcohol on campus or in classrooms.
2. Do not select an overused topic unless you have discovered a novel approach. Gun control, for example, is an old issue that invites a novel approach.
3. Do not select a topic that is trivial to the audience. You might love to talk about how toothpicks are made, but will your audience find the topic significant?

Figure 10.1 Tips for selecting topics.

You can then adapt your topic ideas to be consistent in scope, focus, and viewpoint if necessary.

3. *Consult with your instructor.* This individual is your most valuable resource in terms of topic selection. The best approach is to brainstorm three to five topic ideas and meet with your instructor to discuss advantages and disadvantages of each. You should also talk to him or her about how to appropriately narrow your topic.

4. *Remember that smaller is better.* If you find it difficult to read material quickly, you might benefit from selecting topics that are narrower in focus. Narrower topics will be easier to research and will likely be easier to organize.

How Do You Narrow Your Topic?

Even after determining importance, knowledge, and commitment, beginning presenters often select a topic that is too large for the time limits. Topics like selecting a lender, purchasing insurance, and overcoming an addiction may meet those three requirements, but they are too broad. They will produce hundreds of sources on the Internet, and they will give you more information than you can handle. If you take the time to carefully narrow a topic *before* you begin your search for additional information, you can save much time and even more frustration. Figure 10.2 shows one way to narrow your topic.

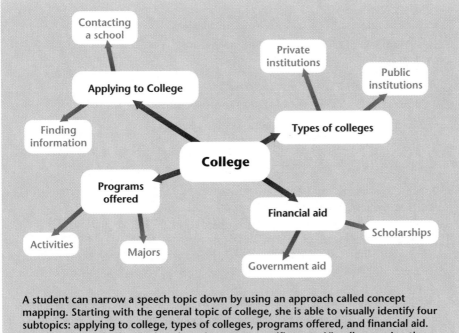

To see an example of a narrowed presentation topic, watch "Conveying the Central Idea" on the *Online Learning Center* at www.mhhe.com/pearson3.

A student can narrow a speech topic down by using an approach called concept mapping. Starting with the general topic of college, she is able to visually identify four subtopics: applying to college, types of colleges, programs offered, and financial aid. Each subtopic is further broken down into more specific areas. Visually mapping the topic-narrowing step in this way can help you see important dimensions of a particular topic area as well as connections between several dimensions of the topic.

Figure 10.2 Selecting and narrowing a topic.

Fitting Topic to Audience and Time

List three topics you think fit your interests and those of your audience. Select your top choice of the three. Pair with a classmate and see if you can cooperatively reduce the topic to a subject that can be communicated in 5 minutes or less.

An abstract category discovered through brainstorming or personal inventories can be narrowed by listing smaller categories directly related to that topic. The abstract topic "college," for example, might yield the following smaller categories directly related to it:

- Application process for state colleges
- Application process for out-of-state schools
- Where to apply for financial aid
- On-campus residence
- Programs of study

A slightly different approach to narrowing a topic involves taking a broad category, such as music, and listing as many smaller topics as you can that are at least loosely related to that topic:

- The development of country/western music
- The influence of rock music on our youth
- Rap artists
- Music therapy
- Why any good song sounds bad in an elevator
- Music education at the elementary school level
- The history of the mandolin
- Country singers who serve as role models

The list of more specific and concrete topics can be extended until you have a large number from which to choose.

How will you know if your topic is narrow enough? Things to consider include (1) the amount of information available on the narrowed topic, (2) the amount of information that can be conveyed within the time limits for the speech, and (3) whether the narrowed topic can be discussed with enough depth to keep audience members interested.

In this section on topic selection, you have learned what standards to apply to a topic. You need to determine the importance of the topic to you and your audience, your and the audience's knowledge about the topic, and your commitment to the topic. Once those three criteria are satisfied, you need to narrow or reduce your topic to one you can manage within the time limits established for the presentation. Still another approach is to look at the examples of successful topics in Table 10.1.

TABLE 10.1   POSSIBLE PRESENTATION TOPICS

What Is a Lobbyist?	Keeping Drugs out of Baseball
Protecting Yourself from Food-Borne Illnesses	Why the Poor Stay Poor
	CEO Compensation in Drug Companies
Why Tuition Keeps Rising	American Tobacco Sales to Other Nations

How Do You Analyze Your Audience?

Audience analysis is the collection and interpretation of audience characteristics through observation, inferences, questionnaires, or interviews. Why should you analyze your audience? Especially, why should you analyze an audience of classmates? Before we start talking about *how* to analyze an audience, we need to explain *why* we analyze an audience.

Suppose you are going to give an informative speech on the history of U.S. abortion law. Should you care that the audience consists of many persons whose religious beliefs prohibit abortion? In short, how will you know the major religious beliefs and interests of your audience unless you analyze the audience?

Audience analysis is similar to target marketing in advertising and public relations. Analysis can be as simple as "eyeballing" a group to estimate age, sex, and race or as complicated as polling people to discover their feelings on your topic. The information that follows is designed to make you more insightful about how you approach an audience and to invite you to think carefully about the people to whom you speak so that you can be as effective as possible.

audience analysis

The collection and interpretation of audience information obtained by observation, inferences, questionnaires, or interviews.

◄ SKILL BUILDER ►

Some people are much better than others at sizing up an audience. Check out your own skill at analyzing an audience by inferring audience characteristics. For example, what is the approximate range in age, what cultures or co-cultures are represented, how many commute, how many have traveled, and how many are actively involved with campus organizations? Perhaps your instructor will allow you to find out the accuracy of your inferences unless classmates might be uncomfortable revealing some of this information.

Four Levels of Audience Analysis

To begin, we will explore four levels of audience analysis. The categories are called *levels* because the first is relatively simple and the last is the most complex. The four levels begin with the distinction between captive and voluntary audiences.

Level 1: Captive and Voluntary Audiences

You need to decide how captive or voluntary your audience is because captive audiences take more convincing than voluntary audiences. How can you tell the difference?

Cultural Note

Seek Human Values

Some colleges have such diverse audiences that audience analysis seems impossible. Although challenging, an audience with a rich mix of races, religions, and languages invites the speaker to find topics that relate to us as human beings. All peoples of the world seek safety, security, food, shelter, and loving families. What values can you find in your audience that relate to your topic?

captive audience

An audience that has not chosen to hear a particular speaker or speech.

voluntary audience

A collection of people who choose to listen to a particular speaker or speech.

A **captive audience** did not choose to hear you or your speech. Your classmates are a largely captive audience for this reason. That means they are somewhat more difficult to inform or persuade than would be a **voluntary audience** of people who chose to hear you speak about a particular topic. The voluntary audience is easier to manage because they actually seek information or ideas. For the captive audience you and your topic are more or less accidental. But do not be discouraged about the classroom audience being largely captive because captive audiences have an upside: They often end up hearing and responding positively to a topic for which they never thought they had an interest. That is, they can be informed about a subject that they formerly found uninteresting, and they can be persuaded on topics they never would have listened to if they had a choice.

Level 2: Demographic Analysis

Another important step in the process of speech preparation is discovering the audience's demographic characteristics. The term *demographics* literally means

Does a teacher have a captive or a voluntary audience?

"the characteristics of the people." **Demographic analysis** is the collection and interpretation of data about the characteristics of people: name, age, sex, hometown, year in school, race, major subject, religion, and organizational affiliations. Demographic information can be important to public speakers by revealing the extent to which they will have to adapt themselves and their topics to an audience.

The groups to which your audience members belong can signal support for or hostility toward your topic. On a commuter campus pay attention to the bumper stickers. They can signal your audience's attitudes about gun control, abortion, and a host of other issues. Observe their accessories: Christian crosses, a Star of David, a Muslim head cover, sorority or fraternity letters, ethnic dress, VFW or American Legion or Rotary pin, a Harley-Davidson jacket, tell-tale tattoos—many signs revealing memberships that may also reflect attitudes about topics.

Public speakers usually rely heavily on demographic information. Politicians send personnel ahead to find out how many blue-collar workers, faithful party members, elderly people, union members, and hecklers they are likely to encounter. They consult opinion polls, population studies, and reliable persons in the area to discover the nature of a prospective audience. Conducting a demographic analysis of your class can serve a similar purpose—analysis will help you design a speech better adapted to your audience.

> **demographic analysis**
>
> The collection and interpretation of data about the characteristics of people.

Level 3: Audience and Topic Age and Interest

Topics, like people, live, change, and die—some have long and varied lives, while others pass quickly. Therefore you need to pay attention to the age and development of your subject matter and the age and development of your audience.

The age and development of your topic is your first concern. Some topics have endured for decades if not centuries:

- How much should government be allowed to intervene in our lives?
- How much or how little should government be allowed to tax and regulate?
- What can and should we do about the poor and marginalized in our society?
- What can and should we do about the privileged and overrewarded in our society?
- Should concern for the environment limit our exploration for oil?

These are just a few of the vexing problems that have been around for decades. Even young people have probably heard plenty about what they are supposed to believe about issues like gun control.

So what are you supposed to do about the age of issues and the age of audiences? Understand that more mature audiences, abundant in community colleges, have heard about many of these issues before, so they have to be viewed as more sophisticated on these topics. Younger audiences are less likely to have heard as much and are less likely to have hardened positions on the issues, so they can be treated differently. In fact, old, persistent issues need to be treated in new or novel ways, and not just a rehash of what the audience has heard repeatedly in the past. The effective presenter takes into account both the age of the issue and the age of the audience and skillfully adapts the topic to the particular audience for maximum effect.

Level 4: The Audience's Attitudes, Beliefs, and Values

attitude

A predisposition to respond favorably or unfavorably to a person, an object, an idea, or an event.

Another consideration in the process of speech preparation is to discern audience attitudes, beliefs, and values on an issue before giving the speech. An **attitude** is a predisposition to respond favorably or unfavorably to a person, an object, an idea, or an event. The attitudes of audience members can be assessed through questionnaires, by careful observation, or even by asking the right questions. If your audience comes from a place where many attitudes, beliefs, and values are shared, your audience analysis may be easy. For example, a speech about safe sex would be heard in some colleges with as much excitement as a speech on snails; however, at other colleges, the same speech could be grounds for dismissal. Attitudes toward politics, sex, religion, drugs, and even work vary in different geographic areas and co-cultures. Regardless of the purpose of your speech, the attitudes of audience members will make a difference in the appropriateness of your topic. Some examples of attitudes follow:

Antigovernment	Pro-business	Pro-conservation
Anti–gun control	Pro-green	Pro-technology
Antipollution	Pro-choice	Pro-diversity
Anti-immigration	Pro-life	Antirefugee
Pro–animal rights	Antitax	Pro–free trade

Everyone has attitudes about a variety of ideas, persons, and things. They are regarded as quite stable and often difficult to change. The effective public speaker learns as much as possible about audience attitudes before speaking to the group.

belief

A conviction; often thought to be more enduring than an attitude and less enduring than a value.

A **belief** is a conviction. Beliefs are usually considered more enduring than attitudes, but our attitudes often spring from our beliefs. Your belief in good eating habits may lead to a negative attitude toward overeating and obesity and to a positive attitude toward balanced meals and nutrition. Your audience's beliefs make a difference in how they respond to your speech. They may believe in upward mobility through higher education, in higher pay through hard work, or in social welfare. On the other hand, they may not believe in any of these ideas. Beliefs are like anchors to which our attitudes are attached. To discover the beliefs of an audience, you need to ask questions and to observe carefully. Some examples of beliefs follow:

Hard work pays off.	Good people will go to heaven.
Taxes are too high.	Work comes before play.
Anyone can get rich.	Government should be small.
Education pays.	

Knowing your audience's beliefs about your topic can be a valuable aid in informing and persuading them.

value

A deeply rooted belief that governs our attitude about something.

A **value** is a deeply rooted belief that governs our attitude about something. Both beliefs and attitudes can be traced to a value we hold. Learned from childhood through the family, religion, school, and many other sources, values are often so much a foundation for the rest of what we believe and know that they are not

E-Note

Ideas for Speeches

Check the websites of major television networks such as **www.cbs.com** to find top stories, in-depth stories, specialized items like "Eye on Politics," and information on CBS news productions, like *60 Minutes*.

questioned. Sometimes we remain unaware of our primary values until they clash. For example, a person might have an unquestioned belief that every individual has the right to be and do whatever he or she wishes—basic values of individuality and freedom—until it comes to homosexuality. Sexual orientation as an aspect of individual freedom may clash with the person's value of heterosexuality. Table 10.2 shows one method for ranking values.

The values held by your audience and the order in which the audience members rank these values can provide important clues about their attitudes and beliefs. Figure 10.3 shows one way to rank values. A speaker who addresses an audience without knowing the values of the audience members is taking a risk that can be avoided through careful audience analysis. The relationships among attitudes, beliefs, and values are illustrated in Figure 10.3.

Three Methods of Audience Analysis

This section examines three methods of analyzing an audience. The three methods are based on your observations of the audience, your inferences, and your questions and their answers.

Method 1: Observation

Effective public speakers must engage in active observation, using their senses (sight, hearing, smell, and touch) to build information about their audience. An effective

---

TABLE 10.2	RANKING VALUES

Rank-order five of the following values in their order of importance to you. If you can persuade some of your classmates, or the entire class, to do this as well, you will have information that will help you prepare your speech.

_____ Wisdom	_____ Wealth	_____ Fame
_____ A world at peace	_____ Security	_____ Health
_____ Freedom	_____ Fulfillment	_____ Love
_____ Equality		

How does your ranking compare to your classmates'? What other values might help you with your speech?

SOURCE: Heath, 1976.

Watch "Appealing to Motivations" on the *Online Learning Center* to see how presenters can adapt messages to audience members' attitudes, beliefs, and values.

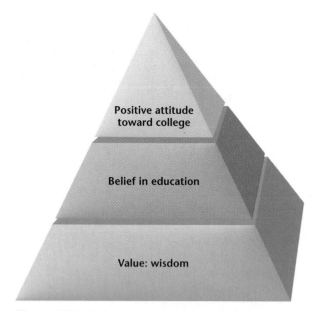

Figure 10.3   Relationships among attitudes, beliefs, and values.

lawyer selects an audience by questioning prospective jurors. The lawyer asks questions designed to discover prejudice, negative and positive attitudes, beliefs, and values. Later, as the witnesses testify, the lawyer observes jurors' verbal and nonverbal behavior and decides which arguments, evidence, and witnesses are influencing the jurors. People who speak on behalf of business associations, unions, political parties, colleges, and the underprivileged have usually spent years watching others and learning which approaches, arguments, and evidence are most likely to be accepted by an audience.

You can learn to observe your class. For every speech you give, you might listen to 20 or 25 given by others. You have a unique opportunity to discover your classmates' responses. Do they respond well to speakers who come on strong or to speakers who talk to them as equals? Do they like speeches about work, leisure, or ambition? Do they respond well to numbers and statistics, stories and examples, graphs and posters, or pictures and slides? As a listener in the classroom, you have a unique opportunity to observe your own and your classmates' responses to a variety of speakers.

Even though your audience may be more captive than most, you have an advantage over most public speakers. How many public speakers have an opportunity to hear every one of their listeners give a speech? Instead of sitting back like a passive observer, take advantage of the situation by listening actively, taking notes about each speaker's characteristics, and recording the audience's responses. You can analyze your audience continually by careful observation during each round of speeches.

Method 2: Inference

To draw an inference is to draw a tentative generalization based on some evidence. We draw an inference when we see someone dressed in rags and tentatively conclude that the person is homeless. Our inferences are often accurate—we infer from a man's wedding band that he is married, from the children tugging at his sleeve that he is a father, and from the woman holding his arm that she is his wife. We are basing these inferences on thin data, but they are probably correct. However, inferences can also be incorrect. The more evidence on which an inference is based, the more likely it is to be true.

You can base inferences on the observed characteristics of your audience, on demographic information, and on the information obtained from questionnaires. You can draw inferences either indirectly or directly. An indirect way to draw inferences is by observation. You might, for example, find that 85% of the students at a particular university hold part-time jobs (an observation). You might infer that the school is expensive, that financial aid is limited, or that the cost of area housing is high. You might also infer, from your limited information, that most of the students

The public speaker must consider different opinions among audience members that reflect different values.

in this school value their education, are exceptionally well motivated, or believe in saving money.

A more direct way to gather data on which to base inferences is to ask questions. You could, for example, ask either orally or in writing how many students in the class have part- or full-time jobs; how many are married, have families, and/or have grown children; how many plan to become wealthy; whether they were raised in an urban or a rural setting; and how many have strong religious ties. The answers to these questions provide valuable information about your audience.

Method 3: The Questionnaire

A more formal way to collect data on which you can base inferences is to ask your audience to fill out a **questionnaire** consisting of written questions developed to obtain demographic and attitudinal information. Demographic information can be easily gathered and summarized from questions similar to the following:

questionnaire

A set of written questions developed to obtain demographic and attitudinal information.

_____1. I am

    a. a first-year student

    b. a sophomore

    c. a junior

    d. a senior

_____2. I am

    a. 17–21 years old

    b. 22–35 years old

    c. 36–45 years old

    d. over 45

____3. I am

    a. single

    b. married

    c. divorced or separated

    d. widowed

____4. I have

    a. no children

    b. one child

    c. two children

    d. more than two children

The audience members do not have to identify themselves by name to provide this information. Keeping the questionnaires anonymous encourages honest answers and does not reduce the value of the information.

Attitudinal information can be collected in at least three ways. One way is to ask questions that place audience members in identifiable groups, as these questions do:

____5. I

    a. am active in organizations

    b. am not active in organizations

____6. I see myself as

    a. conservative

    b. liberal

    c. independent

____7. I see myself as

    a. strongly religious

    b. moderately religious

    c. unreligious

A second method of gaining attitudinal information is to ask people to rank values, such as hard work, higher education, high pay, and security. People's ranking of their values can provide additional information about their attitudes and beliefs.

The third method of collecting data about people's attitudes involves listing word concepts that reveal attitudes and then asking respondents to assess their attitudes toward these specific issues. One method is to use an attitudinal scale like the one in Table 10.3. The reactions to these and similar words or phrases can provide information that will help you approach your audience successfully. For example, if most persons in your audience are neutral to mildly favorable toward taxing tobacco, then your speech advocating tobacco taxes could be designed to move their attitudes from mildly favorable to strongly favorable. If the responses are negative, then you may have to work just to move your audience closer to a mildly disfavorable attitude or toward neutrality.

How Do You Adapt to the Audience?

Audience analysis yields information about your listeners that enables you to adapt yourself and your message to that audience. A speech is not imposed on a collection of listeners; a message is

TABLE 10.3   ATTITUDINAL SCALE

Next to each word or phrase, indicate your attitude toward it by writing in the appropriate number: (1) strongly favor, (2) mildly favor, (3) neutral, (4) mildly disfavor, or (5) strongly disfavor.

_____ a. Internet censorship

_____ b. Job security

_____ c. Gun control

_____ d. Minority groups

_____ e. Women's rights

_____ f. Alcohol consumption

_____ g. Military

_____ h. Recreational drugs

Compile data that indicate the attitudes within your class on one of these topics. What does this information tell you about how to approach your audience about this topic?

negotiated between a speaker and an audience and is designed to inform, entertain, inspire, teach, or persuade that audience. This negotiation is based on your analysis of your audience.

MYTHS, METAPHORS, & MISUNDERSTANDINGS

Speakers often misunderstand what it means to "adapt" a message to an audience, assuming that they must change their position on an issue because of audience members' perceptions. An important question to consider in adapting to an audience is "How do I adapt to an audience without letting the audience dictate my position?" The answer is that you analyze the audience not to discover your own position but to discover theirs—how much do they know about the topic? Finding out, for example, that an audience is likely to be utterly opposed to your position is not an indication that you should alter your position on the issue. Instead, you may have to adopt a more gradual approach to changing your listeners' minds than you would have liked.

Adapting Yourself

In public speaking you also have to adjust to information about the audience. Just as the college senior preparing for a job interview adapts to the interviewer in dress, manner, and language, the public speaker prepares for an audience by adapting to its expectations. How you look, how you behave, and what you say should be carefully tailored to your audience.

Adapting Your Verbal and Nonverbal Codes

The language you use in your speech, as well as your gestures, movements, and even facial expressions, should be adapted to your audience. Does your audience analysis indicate that your language should be conversational, formal, cynical, or technical? Does your analysis indicate that your listeners like numbers and statistics? Do your observations indicate that you should pace the stage or remain behind the lectern? Does your analysis indicate that you should not use taboo words in your speech lest you alienate your group, or does the audience like a little lively language?

Adapting Your Topic

Public speakers should be permitted to speak about any topic that fits the assignment. In the classroom, at least, you should select a topic that relates to you. Remember, you will be giving your speech to an audience of classmates; therefore the topic you select must be adapted to them. Audience analysis is a means of discovering the audience's position on the topic. From information based on observation, description, and inference, you have to decide how you are going to adapt your topic to this audience.

Audience analysis can tell you the challenges you face. If you want to speak in favor of physician-assisted suicide and your audience analysis indicates that the majority of your listeners are opposed to it, you need not conclude that the topic is inappropriate. You may, however, adapt to the members of your audience by starting with a position closer to theirs. Your initial step might be to make audience members feel less comfortable about their present position so that they are more prepared to hear your views.

Adapting Your Purpose

You should also adapt the purpose of your speech to your audience. Teachers often ask students to state the purpose of a speech—what do you want your audience to know, understand, or do? Thinking of your speech as one part of a series of informative talks your audience will hear about your topic may help. Your listeners have probably heard something about the topic before, and they are likely to hear about the topic again. Your particular presentation is just one of the audience's exposures to the topic.

Still, the immediate purpose of your speech is linked to a larger goal. The goal is the end you have in mind. Some examples of immediate purposes and long-range goals will illustrate the difference. The following is an example of the immediate purpose and long-range goal of an informative speech:

Immediate purpose: After listening to this speech, the audience should be able to identify three properties of printers.

Long-range goal: To increase the number of people who will read articles and books about printers.

The following is an example of the immediate purpose and long-range goal of a persuasive speech:

Immediate purpose: After my speech, the audience should be able to explain the low nutritional value of two popular junk foods.

Long-range goal: To dissuade the listeners from eating junk food.

You should note that an immediate purpose has four essential features. First, an immediate purpose is highly specific. Second, it includes the phrase *should be able to*. Third, it uses an action verb such as *state, identify, report, name, list, describe, explain, show,* or *reveal*. Fourth, it is stated from the viewpoint of the audience. You are writing the purpose as an audience objective. The more specific your immediate purpose, the better you will be able to determine whether you have accomplished that purpose.

Microtargeting: A New Kind of Audience Analysis

Until the 2004 presidential race, few people had heard of a new kind of audience analysis called **microtargeting,** a method of bringing national issues down to the individual level. The consulting firm contracted by the Republicans, TargetPoint Consulting, explains the reasoning behind microtargeting:

microtargeting

A method of bringing national issues down to the individual level.

> The control has switched from the seller to the buyer. Voters and consumers now have multiple sources for information and entertainment, and they control what they want and when they want it. The captive audience is gone. The empowered individual reigns.
>
> Most important: voters and consumers expect you to personally market and sell to them based on their unique wants, needs, biases and preferences. What was once exceptional is now expected, but until now, the data tools to give consumers what they want didn't exist. Now they do. (Microtargeting, 2006)

Among the very first people to publicize what was going on privately in the political campaign were two reporters for *The Washington Post,* who explained the concept after the Republicans succeeded in gaining the presidency for George W. Bush:

> Republican firms, including TargetPoint consultants and National Media Inc., delved into commercial databases that pinpointed consumer buying patterns and television-watching habits to unearth such information as Coors beer and bourbon drinkers skewing Republican, brandy and cognac drinkers tilting Democratic; college football TV viewers were more Republican than those who watch professional football; viewers of Fox News were overwhelmingly committed to vote for Bush; homes with telephone caller ID tended to be Republican; people interested in gambling, fashion and theater tended to be Democratic. (Edsall & Grimaldi, 2004)

The Wall Street Journal explained the technique before the November 2006 off-year elections as follows:

> The technique aims to identify potential supporters by collecting and analyzing the unprecedented amount of information now readily available—from census data to credit-card bills—to profile individual voters. Political strategists then tailor messages to entice those prospects to the polls, using the same methods marketers use to sell autos or aspirin to consumers. (Dreazen, 2006)

This new voter identification technique allowed the victorious Republicans to find Republicans in predominantly Democratic neighborhoods, to fashion messages that appealed directly to those individuals (antitax, pro-life, and so on), and to urge those voters to actually go to the voting booth ("Do you want those Democrats to raise your taxes by winning? You had better go vote").

You can use a form of microtargeting in your own presentations, including those in the classroom. Like the microtargeting firms, you can survey your class for information (usually anonymously) about political affiliations and positions on issues. Like the microtargeting professionals, you are likely to find that positions on issues tend to cluster: NASCAR fans are likely to be anti–gun control; pro-life advocates often embrace fundamentalist Christian beliefs; and antitax and pro-defense positions are often credited to Republicans. Like politicians you have an advantage if you know how your audience feels about a topic. You do not change your stance on the topic because of the audience, but you can and should adapt your message to account for the audience's positions on the issue.

Chapter Review & Study Guide

SUMMARY

In this chapter you learned the following:

▶ Two methods of topic selection are brainstorming and personal inventories.
- The topic needs to be important to you and your audience.
- The topic needs to be one that you know about and that your audience may want to know about.
- The topic needs to be one to which you are committed, to which you speak with passion and conviction.
- Once chosen, the topic needs to be narrowed to fit the time limits, the subject matter, and the audience.

▶ Four levels of audience analysis can help you determine topic appropriateness.
- Level 1 distinguishes between voluntary and captive audiences.
- Level 2, demographic analysis, evaluates the characteristics of audience members.
- Level 3, audience and topic age and interest, analyzes the audience's interest in and knowledge of a topic.
- Level 4 determines the audience's attitudes, beliefs, and values.

▶ Observation, inference, and questionnaires are three methods of audience analysis.
- Observation involves using your senses to interpret information about the specific audience.
- Inferences involve using data about the audience to draw tentative generalizations that can make the audience responses more predictable.
- Questionnaires garner demographic and attitudinal information about the audience.

▶ Presentations should be adapted to information about the audience gathered through audience analysis.
- You should adapt your own behavior to audience expectations.
- You should adapt your verbal and nonverbal codes to this audience.
- You should adapt your topic to this audience's knowledge and interest levels.
- You should adapt your purpose to what is possible with this audience.

▶ Microtargeting will help you learn how your audience feels about various issues and adapt your message if appropriate.

KEY TERMS

Go to the *Online Learning Center* at **www.mhhe.com/pearson3** to further your understanding of the following terminology.

Attitude
Audience analysis
Audience interest
Audience knowledge
Belief

Brainstorming
Captive audience
Commitment
Demographic analysis
Involvement

Microtargeting
Personal inventory
Questionnaire
Value
Voluntary audience

STUDY QUESTIONS

1. What is one basic element to keep in mind when selecting a topic for presentation?
   a. Take a lot of time in choosing a topic.
   b. Begin with a subject you already know.
   c. Select a topic you know nothing about.
   d. Choose a topic that does not affect you personally.

2. After choosing a topic, which of the following is necessary to do?
   a. Evaluate the importance of your topic.
   b. Determine how much you and your audience know about the topic.
   c. Realize your commitment to the topic.
   d. All of the above.

3. Why is it important to narrow your topic?
   a. To reduce the information load and meet time requirements.
   b. To reduce the depth of the topic.
   c. To reduce your interest in the topic.
   d. It is not important.

4. When you investigate the audience's demographics, interests, and concerns, you are
   a. brainstorming
   b. microtargeting
   c. analyzing the audience
   d. creating a captive audience

5. Which level of audience analysis includes collecting data about the characteristics of people?
   a. audience type
   b. audience interest in the topic
   c. audience's attitudes, beliefs, and values
   d. demographic analysis

6. A deeply rooted feeling that affects how we act toward an idea or concept is a(n)
   a. attitude
   b. belief
   c. value
   d. thought

7. A method of audience analysis that draws tentative generalizations based on some evidence is termed
   a. observation
   b. inference
   c. questionnaire
   d. survey

8. If you ask people to rank concepts in order of importance or if you ask questions that place individuals into identifiable groups, you are
   a. conducting a questionnaire
   b. brainstorming
   c. narrowing
   d. inferring

9. Which method of analysis involves making observations by using your senses in order to interpret information about the audience?
   a. involvement
   b. value
   c. inference
   d. observation

10. Which is *not* true regarding immediate purposes?
    a. They are highly specific.
    b. They include the phrase "should be able to."
    c. They use an action verb.
    d. They are stated from the viewpoint of the speaker.

Answers:

1. (b); 2. (d); 3. (a); 4. (c); 5. (d); 6. (c); 7. (b); 8. (a); 9. (d); 10. (d)

CRITICAL THINKING

1. Choose a broad topic, and then narrow the topic by creating your own concept map (see Figure 10.2). At what point do the topics become too specific to be discussed in depth?

2. If you are going to give a presentation to a room full of strangers, how might you quickly analyze your audience? What changes might you need to make in the presentation based on your rapid audience analysis?

SELF-QUIZ

For further review, try the chapter self-quiz on the *Online Learning Center* at **www.mhhe.com/pearson3**.

REFERENCES

Christie, T. B. (2006). Framing rationale for the Iraq war: The interaction of public support with mass media and public policy agendas. *International Communication Gazette, 68*, 519–532.

Dreazen, Y. J. (2006, October 31). Democrats, playing catch-up, tap database to woo potential voters. *The Wall Street Journal*, p. A1. Retrieved November 5, 2006, from Wall Street Journal Online.

Edsall, T. B., & Grimaldi, J. V. (2004, December 30). On November 2, GOP got more bang for its billion, analysis shows. *The Washington Post,* p. A1. Retrieved November 5, 2006, from Washington Post Online.

Microtargeting. (2006). Target Point. Retrieved November 5, 2006, from http://www.targetpointconsulting.com/MicroTargeting/default.aspx.

ADDITIONAL RESOURCES

You can find information on any topic by using Google or another search engine and appropriate words. Here are examples of a few sources on just two topic areas—health and politics.

HEALTH

www.cnn.com/HEALTH/   Information on diet, fitness, and parenting. Special feature: video clips.

www.webmd.com/   Health and medical news and information.

www.healthfinder.gov/   Health and human services from the U.S. government. Special feature: Leads to online publications.

www.dir.yahoo.com/Health/   Human health, diseases, medicine, sexual health, fitness, and nutrition.

POLITICS

www.cnn.com/POLITICS/   Cable News Network's political section, a middle-of-the-road, national perspective.

www.nytimes.com/pages/politics/index.html   News, opinions, and multimedia about political campaigns and elections from an East Coast, liberal perspective.

www.latimes.com/news/politics/   Political news and information on elected officials and candidates with an emphasis on West Coast and national government.

www.18-24bracket.com   A political news source from the perspective of young but highly perceptive reporters on the political front.

CHAPTER ELEVEN

Being Credible and Using Evidence

When you have read and thought about this chapter, you will be able to:

1. Define source credibility and explain why source credibility is important.
2. Identify four aspects of source credibility.
3. Effectively use personal experience, library resources, the Internet, and other people to gather evidence for your speeches.
4. Correctly use both internal and verbal citations to correctly attribute the sources of ideas and evidence.
5. Recognize seven different forms of supporting material that you can use in your speech.
6. Use ethical principles to present an honest and accurate image of yourself and the evidence that you use.

*E*ffective public presentations are an artfully crafted combination of you, your ideas, and the ideas and opinions of others. How you present yourself, your ideas, and your evidence will determine the credibility and confidence that audience members attribute to your speech. In this chapter you will learn about source credibility and the ways that you can increase your credibility by using strong evidence.

In the early stages of the 2004 presidential campaign, Howard Dean earned a great deal of credibility as a Democratic candidate. He was considered a frontrunner at the time. He made savvy use of the Internet, drew the interest of young voters, and took strong stances against the war in Iraq and in support of health care reform, appealing to his core Democratic constituency. But that credibility was shattered by one fateful speech on January 19.

That day Dean had come in a disappointing third in the Iowa caucus (a form of primary election), following late surges by two rivals. In the evening Dean addressed his supporters with his usual energy and enthusiasm, intending to rally his troops. Unfortunately, a faulty sound system forced Dean to shout into the microphone to be heard. And when he punctuated one forceful statement with a prolonged and loud "YEAHHHHHH!" what came to be known as the "Dean Scream" was born.

Dean's speech, and especially his yell, received more press coverage than the entire primary. CNN executives estimated that the scream was shown 630 times over a 4-day period following the speech. Remixes of the yell were immediately posted on the Internet (and can still be found there). Talk-show hosts made jokes about Dean, and even he joked about the clips on a late-night talk show. The blow to Dean's campaign was quick and decisive—his candidacy was essentially over by mid-February, just one month after the infamous scream.

Our credibility can hinge on the smallest things we do during a speech; just ask Howard Dean. Although most of us won't practice our primal scream on national television, we will make choices that have an impact on our credibility to an audience, such as how we dress, how we talk, and how we use stories and other supporting material in a speech. In this chapter you will learn about the interconnection between source credibility, supporting material, and effective, ethical communication.

Why Is Source Credibility Important?

Any speech starts with you. You are the messenger. Who and what you are makes all the difference. Audiences do not want to hear from someone they do not respect. And audiences will not listen to or retain information from someone who has not earned the right to talk about that subject.

An excellent question to remember as you launch your public-speaking experience is this one: Why are YOU telling us about this topic in this manner? Stated in this manner, the spotlight is on you: Who are you that we should listen to you? Stated like this—WHY are you telling us about this topic in this manner?—the focus shifts to your purpose. Nobody wants to listen to you blather about nothing. If you do not have something important to say, then you will be better off saying nothing. Stated like this—Why are you telling US about this topic in this manner?—the emphasis shifts to the audience. No matter who you may be, your speech will not be successful unless you have an audience receptive to your message. Stated like this—Why are you telling us about THIS TOPIC in this manner?—the focus moves to the message, to what you are going to speak about. Stated like this—Why are you telling us about this topic in THIS MANNER?—the emphasis is on how you organize and display your message.

If you just remember this question—WHY are YOU telling US about THIS TOPIC in THIS MANNER?—you are more likely to remember the important ingredients of the public-speaking process: purpose, source credibility, audience analysis, topic selection, and message organization and display (visual resources).

Watch both versions of the "Cell Phones" presentation on the Online Learning Center, *and compare the two in terms of source credibility.*

What Is Source Credibility?

More than 2,300 years ago Aristotle noted that a speaker's "character may almost be called the most effective means of persuasion he possesses." Since that time, scholars have continued to study the importance of the source, or speaker, because they correctly believe that *who* says something determines *who* will listen.

In the public-speaking classroom you are the source of the message. You need to be concerned about your **source credibility**—the audience's perception of your effectiveness as a speaker. You may feel that you do not have the same credibility as a high public official, a great authority on a topic, or an expert in a narrow field. Nonetheless, you can be a very credible source to your classmates, colleagues, or friends. Source credibility is not something a speaker possesses, like a suit of clothes. Instead, the audience determines credibility. Like beauty, credibility "is in the eye of the beholder" (Rosnow & Robinson, 1967).

A speaker's credibility depends in part on the speaker, him- or herself, the subject being discussed, the situation, and the audience. Have you served in the armed forces overseas? You may have earned the right to speak on national defense, the price of being in the National Guard, and the inside story of war. Have you grown up in another country? You may have earned the right to speak on another country's culture, food, or customs.

Similarly, you might be more credible to some audiences than to others—your classmates might find you credible but the local teamsters union might not. The personality characteristics of the audience members also affect their response to your message and to you as a source of that message (Wood & Kallgren, 1988). Some people are more inclined to respond positively to a speaker simply because he or she is attractive, whereas others focus on the content of the speech. Hacker, Zakahi, Giles, and McQuitty (2000) indicate that voters integrate a politician's persona with her or his position on issues, a blend of attractiveness and content.

How do you gain credibility with an audience? The answer is that you *earn* the right to speak,

source credibility

The audience's perception of your effectiveness as a speaker.

Rudy Giuliani gained fame for his leadership following the September 11, 2001, terrorist attacks in New York City. Past actions and behaviors allow speakers to establish credibility and earn the right to be heard.

through your experiences and accomplishments. As one person observed, "Before you express yourself, you need a self worth expressing." You may have earned the right to speak on a number of subjects. Have you worked in a fast-food restaurant? You may have earned the right to comment on the quality of fast food and service. Have you raised children? You may have earned the right to speak on the problems and pleasures of family life. What have you experienced, learned, or lived through that has earned you the right to speak?

TRY ◄ THIS

If you earn the right to speak through your life experiences and life learning, make a list of what you have done or learned that would invite others to see you as credible.

Four Aspects of Credibility

What do audience members perceive that signals speaker credibility? If individuals in the audience base credibility on judgments, what is the basis for those judgments? On what will your classmates be rating you when they judge your credibility? According to research, four of the most important aspects of credibility are competence, trustworthiness, dynamism, and common ground.

Competence

competence

The degree to which the speaker is perceived as skilled, reliable, experienced, qualified, authoritative, and informed; an aspect of credibility.

The first aspect of credibility is **competence**—the degree to which a speaker is perceived as skilled, qualified, experienced, authoritative, reliable, and informed. A speaker does not have to live up to all these adjectives; any one, or a few, might make the speaker credible. A machinist who displays her metalwork in a speech about junk sculpture as art is as credible as a biblical scholar who is demonstrating his ability to interpret scripture. They have different bases for their competence, but both can demonstrate competence in their areas of specialization.

Words, use of technology, and an air of authority convey your own competence as a speaker. What can you build into your speech that will help the audience perceive your competence? What experience have you had that is related to the subject? What training or knowledge do you have? How can you suggest to your audience that you have earned the right to speak about the subject? The most obvious way is to tell the audience of your expertise, but a creative speaker can think of dozens of ways to hint and suggest competence without being explicit and without seeming arrogant.

A speaker also signals competence by knowing the substance of the speech so well that he or she can deliver it without reading from note cards, without unplanned or vocalized pauses, and without mispronounced words. The speaker who knows the technical language in a specialized field and who can define the terms for the audience is signaling competence. The speaker who can translate complex ideas into language the audience can understand, who can find ways to illustrate ideas so that the audience can comprehend, and who is familiar with people who know about the subject signals competence.

Trustworthiness

The second aspect of credibility is **trustworthiness**—the degree to which a speaker is perceived as honest, fair, sincere, friendly, honorable, and kind. These perceptions are also earned. We judge people's honesty by their past behavior. Your classmates will judge your trustworthiness when you deliver your speech. How do you decide whether other speakers in your class are responsible, sincere, dependable, or just? What have you done to earn your audience's trust?

You may have to reveal to your audience why you are trustworthy. Have you held jobs that demanded honesty and responsibility? Have you been a cashier, a bank teller, or a supervisor? Have you given up anything to demonstrate you are sincere? The person who pays his or her own way through college ordinarily has to be very sincere about education. Being respectful of others' points of view can be a sign of fairness. What can you say or do that signals trustworthiness?

Here's what *not* to do: In an actual classroom incident, Hugo Ross (name changed to protect the guilty) was supposed to present the introductory portion of his presentation. Unfortunately, he forgot to do the assignment, but to save face he made up an introduction while five classmates presented theirs. Because Hugo was both creative and skilled, he delivered one of the best-sounding introductions of the day. Feeling guilty after the very positive response to his introduction, he confessed that he had made it up as the others spoke. Yes, he made up the statistics about how much junk food Americans eat during the Super Bowl, and he made up the material about how many American males die shortly after the event (allegedly from all the beer and brats). Hugo's violation of trust, not to mention his serious ethical lapse, made his audience suspicious every time he spoke. We assume our classmates and other presenters are telling the truth. When we find out they are not, we may not trust them again.

Dynamism

The third aspect of credibility is **dynamism**—the extent to which an audience perceives the speaker as bold, active, energetic, strong, empathic, and assertive. Audiences value behavior described by these adjectives. Perhaps when we consider their opposites—timid, tired, and meek—we can see why dynamism is attractive. People who exude energy and show the passion of their convictions impress others. Watch the television evangelists and note how they look and sound. You can learn to be dynamic. Evidence indicates that the audience's perception of your dynamism will enhance your credibility.

Dynamism is exhibited mainly by voice, movement, facial expressions, and gestures. A person who speaks forcefully and rapidly and with considerable vocal variety; a speaker who moves toward the audience, back behind the lectern, and over to the visual aid; and a speaker who uses facial expressions and gestures to make a point are all exhibiting dynamism. What can you do with your voice, movement, facial expressions, and gestures to show the audience you are a dynamic speaker?

trustworthiness

The degree to which the speaker is perceived as honest, fair, sincere, honorable, friendly, and kind; an aspect of credibility.

dynamism

The extent to which the speaker is perceived as bold, active, energetic, strong, empathic, and assertive; an aspect of credibility.

Emotion and passion on the part of the speaker influence the audience's perception of the speaker's dynamism.

Common Ground

Common ground is the sharing of values, beliefs, attitudes, and interests (Tuppen, 1974). You tell the audience explicitly how you agree with them. This kind of information sharing is not just demographic—sharing similarities about hometowns, family sizes, and so on—but ideological as well. That is, the speaker tells the audience which ideas he or she has in common with the audience.

For example, Jesse Jackson used common ground when he addressed more than 4,000 mostly white, rural southeastern Ohio college students and community members at a campus speech. He persuaded hundreds of students to register to vote by talking about how both the inner-city poor and the rural poor in their area share similar problems of illiteracy, illegitimate births, unemployment, drug dependency, bad schools, and poverty.

An informative speech may require a minimal amount of common ground. However, a persuasive speech requires that the speaker go beyond areas of complete agreement into areas in which the speaker is trying to make a case for acceptance of his or her point of view on the issue.

An example of a student speech in which the speaker used common ground was about dormitory food. The student knew most of the audience members had tasted it. She brought in a tray of dormitory food to remind them, and this established common ground. You do not have to be a national figure like Jesse Jackson to establish source credibility with an audience. Some speakers know so much that audiences listen; others are so dynamic that audiences listen; and still others inspire so much trust that audiences listen. You need to determine what you can do or say that will invite the audience to perceive you as credible.

◄ SKILL BUILDER ►

Because your credibility depends so heavily on how you are introduced, you should furnish an introduction of yourself when you speak to a group. Think of some topic that would be a good one for you, and then write an introduction for yourself that includes your name, your topic, and your qualifications (education, experience) for that topic.

Practical Advice on Increasing Credibility

Credibility depends on topics, audiences, and circumstances, and it may be different before, during, and after the speech. You may hold the speaker in high regard before the speech, but during the speech your perception of the speaker may diminish, and then after the speech your perception may move in a more positive direction because you decide that the message has merit.

Hundreds of studies of speaker credibility and related areas have revealed the following:

- High-credibility speakers can seek and change audience opinions more than low-credibility speakers (Karlins & Abelson, 1970; Rosnow & Robinson, 1967).
- Sometimes a **sleeper effect** occurs when source and message get separated in the listener's mind over time: a low-credibility speaker's message can gain

President Clinton and President Bush are quite different from each other. Yet each has speaking qualities that make his message highly credible to certain admirers.

influence while a high-credibility speaker's message can diminish over time (Hovland & Weis, 1967).

- Who introduces you as a speaker (preferably someone high in credibility) and how you are introduced (positive information or unintended negative information) can raise or lower your credibility (Thompson, 1967).
- Educational background can raise credibility. Andersen and Clevenger (1963) found that audiences perceived graduate students as more fair-minded, likable, and sincere than undergraduates.
- Harms (1961) found that judgments about a presenter's credibility can occur remarkably fast—in the first 10–15 seconds.
- Presenters perceived as high in status consistently earn higher credibility scores than presenters perceived as lower in status (Thompson, 1967).
- Disorganized speeches result in lower credibility (Sharp & McClung, 1966).
- Effective delivery skills—voice, gestures, movement—tend to raise credibility (Thompson, 1967).
- Nonfluencies such as unexpected or vocalized pauses ("mmm," "ahhh") can decrease a presenter's perceived credibility (Thompson, 1967).
- Your use of evidence, coupled with the audience's perception of the topic's importance and your competence as a speaker, interact to influence your credibility. Reinard and Myers (2005) found that although the use of any type of evidence increases your credibility, those effects are even greater when the audience perceive the topic to be important and you to be competent.
- In situations in which you are introduced to your audience, the timing and content of your introduction by another person is important. Mike Allen and colleagues (2002) found that highly credible speakers benefit from early identification whereas speakers with less initial credibility benefit from delayed identification of their qualifications in terms of perceived credibility. In other words, if you do not have automatic credibility based on qualifications, it may be best to delay letting the audience know your qualifications until after you have spoken.

How Should You Find and Use Information?

Although audience members look at several factors to determine your credibility, you have control over only some of those factors. For instance, you can practice your delivery to avoid nonfluencies, you can work to improve your gestures, and you can take care to create a well-organized speech. In addition, you can improve your own credibility by borrowing on the credibility of others. In this section you will learn how to conduct research and gather supporting material and how to evaluate those sources and use them effectively in your speeches. Research is critical to nearly every aspect of the speech-making process, as shown in Table 11.1.

What Information Sources Can You Use?

When preparing your presentation, you can use several different sources of information. We explain four of the most common: personal experience, written and visual resources, the Internet, and other people.

Personal Experience

personal experience

Use of your own life as a source of information.

The first place you should look for materials for the content of your speech is within yourself. Your **personal experience**—your own life as a source of information—is something about which you can speak with considerable authority. One student had been a "headhunter," a person who finds employees for employers willing to pay a premium for specific kinds of employees. This student gave a speech from his personal experience concerning what employers particularly value in employees. Another student had a brother who was autistic. In her informative speech she explained what autism is and how autistic children can grow up to be self-reliant and successful. Your special causes, jobs, and family can provide you with firsthand information that you can use in your speech.

TABLE 11.1   RESEARCH AND THE SPEECH PREPARATION PROCESS

Preparation Step	Benefit of Research
1. Selecting a topic	Research helps you discover and narrow topics.
2. Organizing ideas	Research helps you identify main and subordinate points.
3. Researching support materials	Research provides facts, examples, definitions, and other forms of support to give substance to your points.
4. Preparing an introduction and conclusion	Research may reveal interesting examples, stories, or quotes to begin or end the speech.
5. Practicing and delivering the speech	Because your speech is well researched, you will feel more confident and will seem more credible.

However, you should ask yourself critical questions about your personal experience before you use personal experience in your speech. Some of your experiences may be too personal or too intimate to share with strangers or even classmates. Others may be interesting but irrelevant to the topic of your speech. You can evaluate your personal experience as evidence, or as data on which proof may be based, by asking yourself the following questions:

1. Was your experience typical?
2. Was your experience so typical that it will bore an audience?
3. Was your experience so atypical that it was a chance occurrence?
4. Was your experience so personal and revealing that the audience may feel uncomfortable?
5. Was your experience one that this audience will appreciate or from which this audience can learn a lesson?
6. Does your experience really constitute proof or evidence of anything?

It is also important to consider the ethics of using your personal experience in a speech. Will your message harm others? Is the experience firsthand (your own) or someone else's? Experience that is not firsthand is probably questionable because information about others' experiences often becomes distorted as the message is passed from one person to another. Unless the experience is your own, you may find yourself passing along a falsehood.

 Students who speak English as a second language know well the various challenges when communicating with native speakers. To document some of these challenges, Australian scholar Jennifer Miller (2000) conducted a study exploring how ESL students develop a social identity in schools. Not surprisingly, Miller showed that while some ESL students achieve at high levels, others face stigmas associated with imperfect use of English.

When viewed from the perspective of source credibility and evidence, ESL students in public-speaking classes have unique advantages in terms of how to use their second language to enhance their credibility. Because non-native speakers have a wealth of knowledge about their own language as well as the unique customs and rituals associated with their culture, being a non-native speaker can provide valuable support for a speech. For example, if you are from the island nation of Sumatra, you could provide a unique perspective on how rising sea levels associated with global warming will displace indigenous populations; if you are from China, you could discuss how the world economy is causing Chinese culture to change; if you are from Latin America, you could discuss the impact of North American free trade in your country. In each case the native culture provides you with rich supporting material that will enhance the credibility of your presentation, all while adapting to your audience by speaking on a topic familiar to them. You might even provide a culturally driven twist on a topic also covered by a classmate. The point is this: Your culture is a potential wealth of information that will be perceived as highly credible supporting material if used effectively.

Library Resources

Modern libraries, like the ones found at most colleges and universities, are vastly different from the libraries used by students a mere 10 years ago. The rapid growth of information technology—computers, the Internet, electronic databases, and so on—has caused many libraries to transform themselves from being repositories of published information to being portals to digital information. So, rather than helping

Think, Pair, Share

The Ethical Use of Personal Experience

Take a moment to think about a "code of ethics" for speakers that explains when using personal experience is appropriate and inappropriate. If you were in charge, what "do's and don'ts" would you suggest about using personal experience? After jotting down some ideas, take a moment to share them with your discussion partner.

reference librarian

A librarian specifically trained to help you find sources of information.

you find a particular book or article, a **reference librarian**—someone specially trained to help you locate sources of information—is far more likely to teach you how to use one or more electronic databases. When most of your instructors were in school, the most important library skills involved understanding the difference between subject, author, and title indexing and knowing how to use the Library of Congress indexing system. Today those skills have been superseded by the need to understand how to access one of potentially thousands of databases to locate digital archives of articles and books.

Because each campus library works differently and has access to different databases, your instructors and your campus reference librarians can provide you with valuable information on how to use your school's library system. Here are some practical principles that you can adapt to your unique situation:

1. *Start at the center and work your way out.* This familiar saying applies when conducting research. First, the reference desk is the practical "center" of your library. Everything you need will start with a search of some type; the reference desk is there to help you conduct that search. You should start at the reference desk and ask for assistance if you are new to the university library. In addition to starting at the center of the library, you should begin by searching at the center of your topic. Following the principle that topics will be narrowed as you conduct research, start by researching the broad and typical elements of your topic. As you gain more information, you will be able to narrow your search to more specific (and possibly off-center) aspects of your topic.

2. *Understand that not all sources are equal.* Modern libraries offer access to many different types of sources ranging from books and academic journals to newspapers and trade magazines. Understanding what those different types of sources are is important because each will provide you with different types of information and each will likely be indexed in a different database. Table 11.2 identifies several different types of sources and suggests how you might use them as evidence. A key principle when conducting good research is that source variety is important—finding and using a variety of types of sources from this list is wise.

3. *Know your databases!* Having access to over 500 electronic databases at one university library is not uncommon. With so many options, figuring out which databases to use can seem daunting. Following the principle that you should start at the center, generalized databases like Academic Search Premier and Lexis-Nexis are excellent places to begin. The library computer catalog will also help you locate books and other resources in your library. Once you have located initial information, you may wish to consult more specific and specialized databases. For example, if you are doing a presentation about a

TABLE 11.2 TYPES OF SOURCES

SOURCE	USES
Fictional books	Some plots or characters can be used to illustrate points you are making in your speech.
Nonfiction books	Nonfiction books include historical, political, social, and scientific studies. Research reported in books tends to be very detailed but can also be somewhat out of date.
Academic journal articles	Academic journal articles tend to undergo blind peer reviews, which can help ensure high-quality information. Academic articles tend to report the results of very specific studies.
Government documents	The federal government produces publications ranging from compilations of congressional testimony to the results of million-dollar scientific studies. Many university libraries have a separate department for government documents.
Trade journal articles	Trade journals are targeted toward professionals in a particular profession or discipline. Trade journals tend to be practical but based on solid research.
Reference books	Your library reference department will have a number of reference books ranging from dictionaries and biographies to atlases. Depending on your speech topic, such sources can be very useful.
Encyclopedias	Encyclopedias are excellent places to learn about topics for which you know absolutely nothing. Encyclopedia entries provide short, easy-to-read explanations of the topic in question but tend to be dated and too general.
Magazine articles	Magazine articles provide timely information and tend to provide more in-depth coverage. The one disadvantage of magazine articles is that they are typically written by journalists with little or no expertise on the topics they write about.
Newspaper articles	Newspaper articles are among the timeliest sources of print information. Although they are up to date, they are written by journalists who may have little or no expertise on the topics they write about. They also tend to provide few details.
Web pages	Web pages are hard to describe because they come in so many variations. Later you will learn about how to locate effective websites. For now, understand that although websites provide easy access to current information, the quality of information on the web must always be verified.

medical topic, you may wish to consult MEDLINE. And if you are doing a persuasive speech, you may wish to consult the Opposing Viewpoints Resource Center to find "pro" and "con" articles on topics ranging from adoption to welfare reform. Remember that the reference librarian is trained to help you select and use the right databases for your topic.

4. *Recognize that good research requires reading, thinking, and more research.* Many students assume that their research task is over with one quick trip to the library. While the "one trip fits all" approach is appealing, it does not work

well. Once you have obtained initial research on your topic, the best thing you can do is to spend time reading those sources, revising your outline, and conducting more research to fill in gaps and find more specific information. Good research takes time, but the end result is outstanding evidence that is sure to impress.

Internet Resources

search engine

A program on the Internet that allows users to search for information.

The Internet has quickly been integrated into nearly every aspect of our lives, appearing on our cell phones, televisions, and even upscale refrigerators. As recently as the year 2000, norms for how to use the Internet were clear—most teachers "outlawed" the use of web pages as evidence in their classes because at that time the Internet was mostly a free-for-all for anyone with a thought. Now such norms would severely hamper solid research. Suffice it to say that the web is both a blessing and a curse. We have access to more information than ever, but filtering through the garbage can be overwhelming.

Locating Sources on the Web Although the web provides us with a valuable research tool, some care must be taken when searching it for information. Following are a few basic procedures for locating web materials:

1. *Use a search engine.* A **search engine** is a program on the Internet that is specially designed to help you search for information. Although search engines will locate thousands of sites that contain the word or phrase you are searching for, one criticism of search engines is that they return hundreds of irrelevant websites. An alternative to using a search engine is to use a virtual library, which provides links to websites that have been reviewed for relevance and

The Internet invites rapid information searches.

284

usability. The accompanying E-Note provides web addresses for several popular search engines and virtual libraries.

2. *Refine your search.* Many search engines give you two options for accessing information. One option is to click on one of the several topical categories displayed on the home page of the search engine site. By following progressively more specific subcategories, you can locate web sources on a relatively specific concept, person, object, hobby, and so on. The other option is to conduct a key-word/Boolean search. We recommend using the first option if you are still in the initial stages of selecting and narrowing a topic—the organized list of categories might help you in the process of topic selection. We recommend using the search option once you have identified and narrowed a topic. Figure 11.1 shows what the home page of Yahoo! looks like.

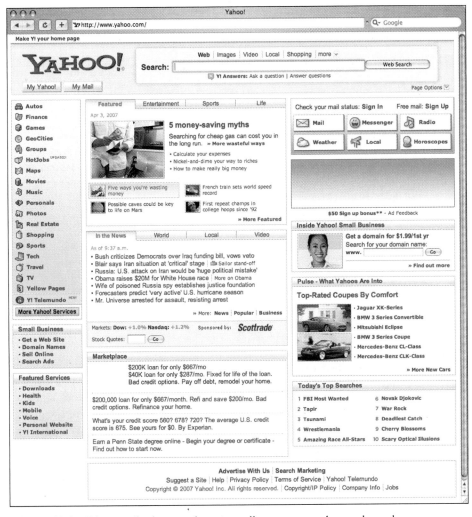

Figure 11.1   Yahoo! and other search engines allow you to use keyword searches or to browse topical categories. Both approaches can assist you in locating information and narrowing topics.

SOURCE: Yahoo! Inc., 2007.

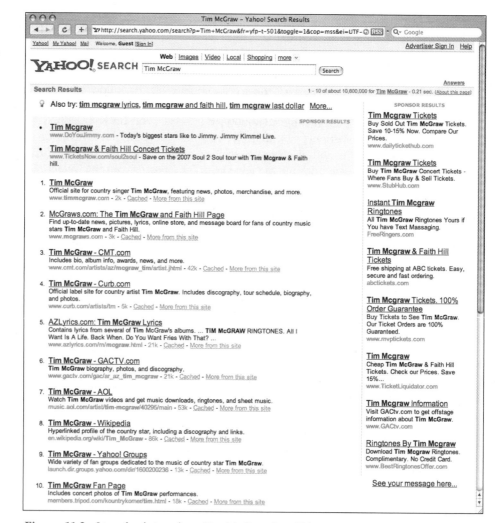

Figure 11.2   List of websites about Tim McGraw from Yahoo!
SOURCE: Yahoo! Inc., 2007.

Figure 11.2 shows how you can use the categories to find progressively more specific information—in this case about the popular singer Tim McGraw. Using the search feature to look for web pages on Tim McGraw will return a greater variety of sites, some of which may be relevant to your speech. Table 11.3 provides recommendations on how to more effectively narrow your searches.

3. *Evaluate carefully all sources of information found on the Internet*, especially when you locate the sources through a public domain search engine rather than your university library's home page. We provide suggestions for evaluating web sources and other types of information later in this chapter.

One additional point we like to make about the Internet is that people have different motives for creating web pages. Some websites are intended to be informative, others are intended to persuade, and still others are out to make money. You should understand that some websites are designed to conceal their true motive: A website

TABLE 11.3   TOOLS FOR NARROWING YOUR WEB SEARCH

WORD STEMMING

By default, browsers return any web page containing the word you asked it to search for. For example, if you want to search for the speech acronym *inform,* the search engine would return sites with the words *informative, information, informal, informing,* and so forth. To prevent this problem, type your search term with a single quote at the end.

Example: Inform'

PHRASE SEARCH

If you are looking for a phrase, put the phrase in quotation marks. For example, simply typing in *public speaking* would return all sites that contain the two words anywhere on the site. Placing the phrase in quote marks will return only sites using the phrase.

Example: "public speaking"

BOOLEAN OPERATORS

Boolean operators allow you to specify logical arguments for what you want returned in a list of matching websites. When multiple terms are typed in a search box (e.g., *tobacco addiction*), the default Boolean operator is to place *AND* between the terms. Returned websites will contain both tobacco and addiction somewhere on the page. Other Boolean operators include *NOT* (e.g., *PowerPoint NOT Microsoft*), which will return websites with the term before the operator but not sites with the term after the operator. You can also use the operator *OR* to find sites with one of two possible terms (e.g., *Coke OR Pepsi*).

PARENTHESES

Using parentheses allows you to nest Boolean search arguments. In the following example the search argument will look for websites containing the terms *media* and *violence* but not *television.*

Example: (media AND violence) NOT television

SOURCE: Adapted from Netscape's net search tips, at http://home.netscape.com/escapes/search/tips_0.html.

might look informative but actually tell only part of a story to persuade you to purchase a service or product. One way to understand the motive of websites is to pay attention to the server extension. Figure 11.3 explains the parts of a web address and the characteristics of web addresses with different server extensions. No single type of web address—based on the server extension—is necessarily better than another. Although knowledge of different types of web address can be valuable, all web resources require scrutiny.

◄ SKILL BUILDER ►

The University of California library has an excellent online exercise illustrating the importance of carefully evaluating web sources. The address of the exercise is www.lib.berkeley.edu/TeachingLib/Guides/Internet/Evaluate.html. Individually, in a group, or as a class, evaluate the various websites listed in the exercise. If you click on the "Tips and Tricks" links, the UC Berkeley librarians provide their own analyses of how effective the various sites are.

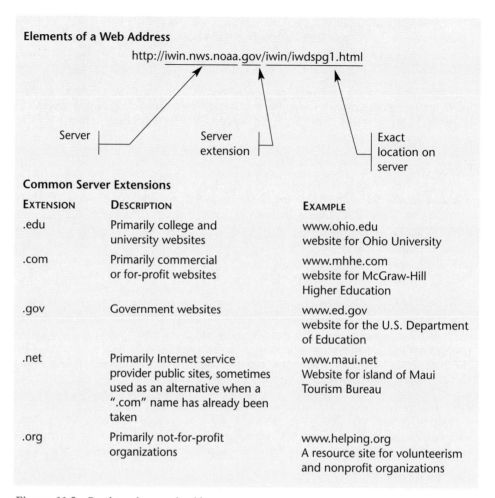

Elements of a Web Address

http://iwin.nws.noaa.gov/iwin/iwdspg1.html

Server

Server extension

Exact location on server

Common Server Extensions

EXTENSION	DESCRIPTION	EXAMPLE
.edu	Primarily college and university websites	www.ohio.edu website for Ohio University
.com	Primarily commercial or for-profit websites	www.mhhe.com website for McGraw-Hill Higher Education
.gov	Government websites	www.ed.gov website for the U.S. Department of Education
.net	Primarily Internet service provider public sites, sometimes used as an alternative when a ".com" name has already been taken	www.maui.net Website for island of Maui Tourism Bureau
.org	Primarily not-for-profit organizations	www.helping.org A resource site for volunteerism and nonprofit organizations

Figure 11.3   Breaking down web addresses.

People Resources

Speakers often overlook the most obvious sources of information—the people around them. You can get information for your speech from personal experience, written and visual resources, the Internet, *and* other people. The easiest way to secure information from other people is to ask them in an informational interview.

Finding People to Interview   As someone who needs information about a particular topic, your first step is to find the person or persons who can help you discover more information. Your instructor might have some suggestions about whom to approach. Among the easier and better sources of information are professors and administrators who are available on campus. They can be contacted during office hours or by appointment. Government officials, too, have an obligation to be responsive to your questions. Even big business and industrial concerns have public relations offices that can answer your questions. Your objective is to find someone, or a few people, who can provide you with the best information in the limited time you have to prepare your speech.

Conducting the Interview An interview can be an important and impressive source of information for your speech—if you conduct the interview properly. After you have carefully selected the person or persons you wish to interview, you need to observe these suggestions:

When interviewing experts, take careful notes so that you can accurately quote the person during your speech.

1. *On first contact with your interviewee or the interviewee's secretary, be honest about your purpose.* For example, you might say, "I want to interview Dr. Schwartz for 10 minutes about the plans for student aid for next year so that I can share that information with the 20 students in my public-speaking class." It is also wise to tell the interviewee how much time the interview will take.

2. *Prepare specific questions for the interview.* Think ahead of time about exactly what kind of information you will need to satisfy yourself and your audience. Conducting research prior to the interview is often advisable—you will be able to ask better questions. Keep your list of questions short enough to fit the time limit you have suggested to the interviewee.

3. *Be respectful toward the person you interview.* Remember that the person is doing you a favor. You do not need to question aggressively like Mike Wallace on *60 Minutes*. Instead, dress appropriately for the person's status, ask your questions politely, and thank your interviewee for granting you an interview.

4. *Tell the interviewee you are going to take notes so you can use the information in your speech.* If you are going to tape-record the interview, you need to ask the interviewee's permission, and you should be prepared to take notes in case the interviewee does not wish to be recorded. Even if you record the interview, it's a good idea to take notes as a backup in case something happens to the tape or tape recorder.

5. *When you quote the interviewee or paraphrase the person's ideas in your speech, use oral footnotes to indicate where you got the information.* Here's an example: "According to Dr. Fred Schwartz, the director of financial aid, the amount of student financial aid for next year will be slightly less than it was this year."

Sometimes the person you interview will be a good resource for additional information. For example, one of our students interviewed the director of disability services on our campus for her informative speech about learning disabilities. He not only answered her questions but also gave her an extensive packet of information on the topic. By picking the right source to interview, the student was able to obtain all of her research in one stop.

How Should You Cite Sources of Information Correctly?

bibliographic references

Complete citations that appear in the "references" or "works cited" section of your speech outline.

internal references

Brief notations indicating a bibliographic reference that contains the details you are using in your speech.

verbal citations

Oral explanations of who the source is, how recent the information is, and what the source's qualifications are.

Once you find source material, you must provide references for the source both on your outline and in your speech. **Bibliographic references** are complete citations that appear in the "references" or "works cited" section of your speech outline (or term paper). Your outline should also contain **internal references**, which are brief notations of which bibliographic reference contains the details you are using in your speech. Internal and bibliographic references help readers understand what sources were used to find specific details like statistics, quotations, and examples. Ask your instructor if a particular format should be used for references. The next chapter explains how you should prepare a bibliography for your outline using appropriate style guidelines.

In addition to citing sources in your outline, you must provide verbal citations during your presentation. Unlike the readers of a paper or speech outline, audience members are less concerned with page numbers and titles of articles. Rather, **verbal citations** tell listeners who the source is, how recent the information is, and what the source's qualifications are. The examples in Table 11.4 illustrate how to orally cite different types of sources. Of these sources, students have the most difficult time with web pages. Remember that the web address is only that—an address. Although the web address should be listed in the references or works cited page of your outline, giving the address during your presentation is seldom necessary. The exception would be if you wanted your audience to visit that particular website.

Tips for Effective Research

Learning how to conduct effective research is essential. The web has streamlined the diversity of information, but this ease necessitates a sound research strategy. In this section we address two issues. First, we explain why consulting various types of sources is essential. Second, we discuss key criteria you should use when evaluating sources.

The Importance of Source Variety

Not all sources tell you the same thing. On any given speech topic—global warming, for example—you can obtain information from each type of source: personal experience, visual and written sources, the Internet, and even personal interviews. Each type of source will yield different types of information. Personal experience might

TABLE 11.4	EXAMPLES OF VERBAL CITATIONS
TYPE OF SOURCE	EXAMPLE
Magazine article	"According to Fox Butterfield, a reporter for *The New York Times,* the crime rate declined in 2001."
Research study	"Elizabeth Graham, a communication researcher, found in a 1997 study that relationships go through different patterns after a divorce."
Web page	"The American Red Cross website, which I visited on October 25, 2001, stated that over 90 million dollars has been raised for the September 11 disaster relief efforts."

tell you how you contribute to global warming by driving your car or using electricity; magazine and newspaper articles might give general background on what global warming is; scientific journals might provide detailed statistics on how much the Earth is heating up; and web pages might describe groups committed to preventing warming. Our experience suggests that effective speakers consult all types of sources as they progress through the research process.

Criteria for Evaluating Sources

Merely finding sources does not ensure that you have effectively researched your speech. You must carefully evaluate the credibility and usefulness of each source. Bourhis, Adams, Titsworth, and Harter (2002) recommend that you use the following criteria when evaluating sources:

1. *Is the supporting material clear?* Sources should add clarity to your ideas rather than confusing the issue with jargon and overly technical explanations.

2. *Is the supporting material verifiable?* Listeners and readers should be able to verify the accuracy of your sources. Although verifying information in a book is easy—the book can be checked out and read—information obtained from a personal interview with the uncle of your sister's roommate is not.

3. *Is the source of the supporting material competent?* For each source you should be able to determine qualifications. If your source is a person, what expertise does the person have with the topic? If your source is an organization, what connection does the organization have to the issue?

4. *Is the source objective?* All sources—even news reports—have some sort of bias. The National Rifle Association has a bias against gun control; Greenpeace has a bias in favor of environmental issues; TV news programs have a bias toward vivid visual imagery. What biases do your sources have, and how might those biases affect the way they frame information?

5. *Is the supporting material relevant?* Loading your speech with irrelevant sources might make the speech seem well researched; however, critical listeners will see through this tactic. Include only sources that directly address the key points you want to make.

In addition to those suggestions, you should also look for materials that are timely and up-to-date. Some web pages might be old, or at least based on old information. Finding accurate information is necessary; finding up-to-date information adds even more credibility.

These criteria are not "yes or no" questions. Sources will meet some criteria well and fail others miserably. Your job as speaker is to weigh the benefits and drawbacks of each source and determine whether to include the source in your speech. Indeed, you have an ethical responsibility to carefully evaluate sources.

supporting materials

Information you can use to substantiate your arguments and to clarify your position.

What Supporting Materials Are Appropriate?

Now that you know where to look for information, the next step is locating **supporting materials,** information you can use to substantiate your arguments and to clarify your position. In this section you will examine examples, surveys, testimonial evidence, numbers and statistics, analogies, explanations, and definitions.

MYTHS, METAPHORS, & MISUNDERSTANDINGS

Evidence Is Proof

When researching a speech, inexperienced speakers often assume that the evidence they collect will act as proof supporting their claim. In fact, evidence becomes proof only when the audience accepts the accuracy of the evidence and the speaker's interpretation of what the evidence means. Because we strive for such proof in our speeches, speakers are encouraged to provide information supporting the accuracy of evidence as well as thorough explanations of what inferences should be drawn from evidence.

For further information see E. S. Inch & B. Warnick (2002), Critical thinking and communication: The use of reason in argument (4th ed.) (Boston: Allyn & Bacon).

Examples

examples

Specific instances used to illustrate your point.

Examples—specific instances used to illustrate your point—are among the most common supporting materials found in speeches. Sometimes a single example helps convince an audience; other times a relatively large number of examples may be necessary to achieve your purpose. For instance, the argument that a university gives admission priority to out-of-state students could be supported by showing the difference between the numbers of in-state and out-of-state students who are accepted, in relation to the number of students who applied in each group. Likewise, in a persuasive speech designed to motivate everyone to vote, you could present cases in which several more votes would have meant a major change in election results.

You should be careful when using examples. Sometimes an example may be so unusual that an audience will not accept the story as evidence or proof of anything. A student who refers to crime in his hometown as an example of the increasing crime problem is unconvincing if his hometown has considerably less crime than the audience is accustomed to. A good example must be plausible, typical, and related to the main point of the speech.

Two types of examples are factual and hypothetical: A *hypothetical* example cannot be verified, whereas a *factual* example can. The length of the example determines whether the example is brief or extended. The following is a brief factual example:

Watch "Using an Example" on the *Online Learning Center* to see how examples can be incorporated into presentations.

> According to the November 2001 issue of *Motor Trend*, "Volkswagen's incredible VW V-8 engine is the first new engine concept in decades" (p. 112).

Here is an extended hypothetical example:

> An example of a good excuse for a student missing class is that he or she has a serious auto accident on the way to class, ends up in the hospital, and has a signed medical statement from a physician to prove hospitalization for a week. A poor excuse for a student missing class is that the student, knowing beforehand when the final examination will be held, schedules a flight home for the day before the exam and wants an "excused absence."

The brief factual example is *verifiable*, meaning it can be supported by a source that the audience can check. The extended hypothetical example is not verifiable and is actually a composite of excuses.

Surveys

Another source of supporting materials commonly used in speeches is **surveys,** studies in which a limited number of questions are answered by a sample of the population to discover opinions on issues. Surveys are found most often in magazines or journals and are usually seen as more credible than an example or one person's experience because they synthesize the experience of hundreds or thousands of people. Public opinion polls fall into this category. One person's experience with alcohol can have an impact on an audience, but a survey indicating that one-third of all Americans abstain, one-third drink occasionally, and one-third drink regularly provides better support for an argument. As with personal experience, you should ask some important questions about the evidence found in surveys:

1. *How reliable is the source?* A report in a professional journal of sociology, psychology, or communication is likely to be more thorough and more valid than one found in a local newspaper.

2. *How broad was the sample used in the survey?* Did the survey include the entire nation, the region, the state, the city, the campus, or the class?

3. *Who was included in the survey?* Did everyone in the sample have an equally good chance of being selected, or were volunteers asked to respond to the questions?

4. *How representative was the survey sample?* For example, *Playboy's* readers may not be typical of the population in your state.

5. *Who performed the survey?* Was the survey firm nationally recognized, such as Lou Harris or Gallup, or did the local newspaper perform the survey? Did professionals such as professors, researchers, or management consultants administer the survey?

6. *Why was the survey done?* Was the survey performed for any self-serving purpose—for example, to attract more readers—or did the government conduct the study to help establish policy or legislation?

Testimonial Evidence

Testimonial evidence, a third kind of supporting material, is written or oral statements of others' experience used by a speaker to substantiate or clarify a point. One assumption behind testimonial evidence is that you are not alone in your beliefs, ideas, and arguments: Other people also support them. Another assumption is that the statements of others should help the audience accept your point of view. The three kinds of testimonial evidence you can use in your speeches are lay, expert, and celebrity.

Lay testimony is statements made by an ordinary person that substantiate or support what you say. In advertising, this kind of testimony shows ordinary people using or buying products and stating the fine qualities of those products. In a speech, lay testimony might be the words of your relatives, neighbors, or colleagues concerning an issue. Such testimony shows the audience that you and other ordinary people support the idea. Other examples of lay testimony are proclamations of faith by fundamentalist Christians at a church gathering and statements about the wonderful qualities of their college by alumni at a recruiting session.

Expert testimony is statements made by someone who has special knowledge or expertise about an issue or idea. In your speech you might quote a mechanic about problems with an automobile, an interior decorator about the aesthetic qualities of

surveys

Studies in which a limited number of questions are answered by a sample of the population to discover opinions on issues.

testimonial evidence

Written or oral statements of others' experience used by a speaker to substantiate or clarify a point.

lay testimony

Statements made by an ordinary person that substantiate or support what you say.

expert testimony

Statements made by someone who has special knowledge or expertise about an issue or idea.

fabrics, or a political pundit about the elections. The idea is to demonstrate that people with specialized experience or education support the positions you advocate in your speech.

Celebrity testimony is statements made by a public figure who is known to the audience. Celebrity testimony occurs in advertising when someone famous endorses a particular product. In your speech you might point out that a famous politician, a syndicated columnist, or a well-known entertainer endorses the position you advocate.

Although testimonial evidence may encourage your audience to adopt your ideas, you need to use such evidence with caution. An idea may have little credence even though many laypeople believe in it; an expert may be quoted on topics well outside his or her area of expertise; and a celebrity usually is paid for endorsing a product. To protect yourself and your audience, you should ask yourself the following questions before using testimonial evidence in your speeches:

1. Is the person you quote an expert whose opinions or conclusions are worthier than most other people's opinions?
2. Is the quotation about a subject in the person's area of expertise?
3. Is the person's statement based on extensive personal experience, professional study or research, or another form of firsthand proof?
4. Will your audience find the statement more believable because you got the quotation from this outside source?

Numbers and Statistics

A fourth kind of evidence useful for clarification or substantiation is numbers and statistics. Because numbers are easier to understand and digest when they appear in print, the public speaker has to simplify, explain, and translate their meaning in a speech. For example, instead of saying "There were 323,462 high school graduates," say "There were over 300,000 graduates." Other ways to simplify a number like 323,462 include writing the number on a chalkboard or poster and using a comparison, such as "Three hundred thousand high school graduates are equivalent to the entire population of Lancaster."

Statistics—numbers that summarize numerical information or compare quantities—are also difficult for audiences to interpret. For example, an audience will have difficulty interpreting a statement such as "Honda sales increased 47%." Instead, you could round off the figure to "nearly 50%," or you could reveal the number of sales this year and last year. You can also help the audience interpret the significance with a comparison such as "That is the biggest increase in sales experienced by any domestic or imported car dealer in our city this year."

You can greatly increase your effectiveness as a speaker if you illustrate your numbers by using visual resources, such as pie charts, line graphs, and bar graphs. You can help your audience by both saying and showing your figures. You also can help your audience visualize statistics by using visual imagery—for example, "That amount of money is greater than all the money in all our local banks," or "That many discarded tires would cover our city 6 feet deep in a single year."

Analogies

Another kind of supporting material used in public speeches is analogies. An **analogy** is a comparison of things in some respects, especially in position or function, that

---

celebrity testimony

Statements made by a public figure who is known to the audience.

statistics

Numbers that summarize numerical information or compare quantities.

To see how to effectively present statistics, watch "Using Statistics" on the *Online Learning Center*.

analogy

A comparison of things in some respects, especially in position or function, that are otherwise dissimilar.

Visual resources can help speakers explain the meaning of statistics and other supporting material. You will learn more about the use of visual resources in chapter 13.

are otherwise dissimilar. For instance, one government official said that trying to find Osama bin Laden in Afghanistan is like trying to find one particular rabbit in the state of West Virginia. Similarly, analogies can be used to show that ancient Roman society is analogous to American society and that a law applied in one state will work the same way in another.

An analogy also provides clarification, but it is not proof because the comparison inevitably breaks down. Therefore, a speaker who argues that American society will fail just as Roman society did can carry the comparison only so far because the form of government and the institutions in the two societies are quite different. Likewise, you can question the rabbit-in-West-Virginia analogy by pointing out the vast differences between the two things being compared. Nonetheless, analogies can be quite useful as a way to illustrate or clarify.

Explanations

Explanations are another important means of clarification and persuasion that you will often find in written and visual sources and in interviews. An **explanation** clarifies what something is or how it works. A discussion of psychology would offer explanations and answers, as well as their relation to the field—for example, "How does Freud explain our motivations?" "What is *catharsis*, and how is it related to aggression?" or "What do *id, ego,* and *superego* mean?"

explanation

A clarification of what something is or how it works.

A good explanation usually simplifies a concept or an idea by explaining the idea from the audience's point of view. William Safire, once a presidential speechwriter and now a syndicated columnist, provided an explanation in one of his columns about how the spelling of a word gets changed. He pointed out that experts who write dictionaries observe how writers and editors use the language. "When enough citations come in from cultivated writers, passed by trained copy editors," he quotes a lexicographer as saying, "the 'mistake' becomes the spelling" (Safire, 1980). You may find, too, that much of your informative speaking is explanation.

Definitions

definitions

Determinations of meaning through description, simplification, examples, analysis, comparison, explanation, or illustration.

Some of the most contentious arguments in our society center on **definitions,** or determinations of meaning through description, simplification, examples, analysis, comparison, explanation, or illustration. Experts and ordinary citizens have argued for years about definitions. For instance, when does art become pornography? Is withdrawal of life-support systems euthanasia or mercy? How you define a concept can make a considerable difference.

Definitions in a public speech are supposed to enlighten the audience by revealing what a term means. Sometimes you can use definitions that appear in standard reference works, such as dictionaries and encyclopedias, but simply trying to explain the word in language the audience will understand is often more effective. For example, suppose you use the term *subcutaneous hematoma* in your speech. *Subcutaneous hematoma* is jargon used by physicians to explain the blotch on your flesh, but you could explain the term in this way: "*Subcutaneous* means 'under the skin,' and *hematoma* means 'swelled with blood,' so the words mean 'blood swelling under the skin,' or what most of us call a 'bruise.'"

Ethical Considerations   Ethics and Source Credibility

As you have learned, credibility is a perceptual variable that is not based on external, objective measures of competence, trustworthiness, dynamism, and common ground. However, you retain an ethical obligation to project an honest image of yourself to your audience, to actually be the sort of person you purport to be. The well-known cliché that you can fool all of the people some of the time may be accurate, but an ethical communicator avoids "fooling" anyone.

To determine if you are behaving ethically, answer the following questions:

1. *Are your speech's immediate purpose and long-range goal sound?* Are you providing information or recommending change that would be determined worthy by current standards? Attempting to sell a substandard product or to encourage people to injure others would clearly not be sound; persuading people to accept new, more useful ideas and to be kinder to each other would be sound.

2. *Does your end justify your means?* This time-honored notion suggests that communicators can have ethical ends but may use unethical means of bringing the audience to a particular conclusion. You want them to join the armed forces, but should you use scare tactics to get them to join?

3. *Are you being honest with your audience?* Are you well informed about the subject instead of being a poseur who only pretends to know? Are you using good evidence and reasoning to convince your audience? Are your passions about the subject sincere?

Credibility does lie in the audience's perception of you, but you also have an ethical obligation to be the sort of person you project yourself to be. In addition, you must consider the influence of your message on the audience. Persuasive speeches, particularly, may lead to far-reaching changes in others' behaviors. Are the changes you are recommending consistent with standard ethical and moral guidelines? Have you thoroughly studied your topic so that you are convinced of the accuracy of the information you are presenting? Are you presenting the entire picture? Are you using valid and true arguments? In short, are you treating the listeners in the way you wish to be treated when someone else is speaking and you are the listener? The Golden Rule applies to the communication situation.

The Ethical Use of Supporting Material

Throughout this book we have emphasized various ethical requirements for communication that stem from the NCA Credo on Ethics. And, at various points in this chapter, we have pointed out ethical obligations faced by speakers when searching for and using supporting materials. Recall that the first point in the NCA Credo on Ethics states that accuracy and honesty are essential for ethical communication. In this final section we summarize the ethical obligations faced by speakers when working with supporting materials:

- *Speakers have an ethical obligation to find the best possible sources of information.* The Internet and full-text databases certainly provide us with easier research options; however, these tools do not necessarily improve the quality of our research. Importantly, the best sources of information are sometimes not available online or in full-text form. When you speak, your audience depends on you to present the best and most accurate information possible. As a result, many communication instructors emphasize the importance of using *quality* sources of information during a presentation. As we mentioned earlier in the chapter, selecting a variety of sources including print sources, Internet sources, and possibly even interviews can help improve the overall quality of sources that you base your presentation on.

- *Speakers have an ethical obligation to cite their sources of information.* Of course, one reason to cite sources of information is to avoid **plagiarism,** which is the intentional use of information from another source without crediting the source. All universities have specific codes of conduct that identify sanctions levied against those who are caught plagiarizing. Although we see relatively few cases of full plagiarism, we often see students mistakenly commit **incremental plagiarism,** which is the intentional or unintentional use of information from one or more sources without fully divulging how much information is directly quoted. We commonly see students use large chunks of information from web pages and other sources—many times this information is directly copied and pasted from the website. Failing to clearly identify what is directly quoted, even accidentally, is a form of plagiarism. Moreover, your instructor will likely evaluate your speech more favorably if you interpret the meaning of short quotations for the audience rather than overrelying on very large quotations.

- *Speakers have an ethical obligation to fairly and accurately represent sources.* How often have you heard politicians and other public figures complain that the media take their comments "out of context"? To avoid unfair and inaccurate representations of sources, whether they are newspaper articles, web pages, books, or even interviews, you must ensure that you fully understand the

plagiarism

The intentional use of information from another source without crediting the source.

incremental plagiarism

The intentional or unintentional use of information from one or more sources without fully divulging how much information is directly quoted.

two-sided argument

A source advocating one position presents an argument from the opposite viewpoint and then goes on to refute that argument.

points being made by the source. Remember, for example, that two-sided arguments are often used to present a point. A **two-sided argument** is one in which a source advocating one position presents an argument from the opposite viewpoint and then goes on to refute that viewpoint. To take an excerpt from a source in which the opposing argument is being presented for refutation and implying that the source was advocating the opposing argument is unethical. As a speaker you have liberty to disagree with points made by the sources you consult; you do not have the liberty to misrepresent those same sources.

Locating, understanding, and incorporating supporting material is one of the most important tasks you will undertake as a presenter of information and argument. As illustrated by Table 11.1, effective research literally impacts every step in the process of preparing and delivering a presentation. Taking care to effectively and ethically use your information will make you a better speaker and will garner the respect of your peers and teachers.

Chapter Review & Study Guide

SUMMARY

In this chapter you learned the following:

▶ Source credibility is the audience's perception of your effectiveness as a speaker. Source credibility is important because it helps the audience understand "why you are telling us about this topic in this manner."

- The WHY emphasizes the goal or the purpose of your presentation.
- The YOU emphasizes you as the speaker and why you have earned the right to speak.
- The US invites you to analyze the audience to determine their reason for listening to you.
- THIS TOPIC asks you to analyze the appropriateness of the subject you have selected.
- THIS MANNER requires you to consider the organization and other strategies that you selected for your presentation.

▶ Source credibility is created from the audience's perceptions of four dimensions of credibility.

- Audience perception of the speaker's competence.
- Audience perception of the speaker's trustworthiness.
- Audience perception of the speaker's dynamism.
- Audience perception of the speaker's common ground with the audience.

▶ Evidence for your speeches and other discussions come from various types of sources.

- Your personal experience can add to your credibility and clarify your personal knowledge; however, personal experience should be carefully evaluated before use.
- Library materials come in a variety of forms. The key to finding information in the library is knowing various databases to search.
- The Internet provides quick access to a variety of information, but that information must be carefully verified for accuracy.
- When using other persons, you should carefully plan interview questions to make your use of testimony more valid.

▶ Citations should be used to document your use of evidence. Bibliographic citations appear on your outline whereas verbal citations are presented orally during your speech.

▶ When looking for evidence, seven types of supporting material are typically used: examples, surveys, testimonials, numbers and statistics, analogies, explanations, and definitions.

▶ Speakers are obligated to follow ethical principles for establishing credibility and using evidence.

- You have an obligation to be true to yourself and have worthy purposes and goals. You should employ ethical means to achieve ethical ends.
- You have an obligation to use accurate information and to cite the sources of such information.

KEY TERMS

Go to the *Online Learning Center* at **www.mhhe.com/pearson3** to further your understanding of the following terminology.

Analogy	Explanation	Source credibility
Bibliographic references	Incremental plagiarism	Statistics
Celebrity testimony	Internal references	Supporting materials
Common ground	Lay testimony	Surveys
Competence	Personal experience	Testimonial evidence
Definitions	Plagiarism	Trustworthiness
Dynamism	Reference librarian	Two-sided argument
Examples	Search engine	Verbal citations
Expert testimony	Sleeper effect	

STUDY QUESTIONS

1. Which of the following statements regarding source credibility is *not* true?
   a. Source credibility is the audience's perception of the effectiveness of a speaker.
   b. Source credibility depends on the speaker, the subject discussed, the situation, and the audience.
   c. Source credibility is something a speaker possesses.
   d. The audience determines credibility.

2. Which aspect of source credibility is the degree to which a speaker is perceived as honest, friendly, and honorable?
   a. competence
   b. trustworthiness
   c. dynamism
   d. common ground

3. If a person speaks with vocal variety, moves toward the audience, or uses facial expressions and gestures, he or she is exhibiting which aspect of credibility?
   a. competence
   b. trustworthiness
   c. dynamism
   d. common ground

4. Which of the following results in higher credibility scores?
   a. disorganized speeches
   b. people perceived as low in status
   c. presence of nonfluencies
   d. effective delivery skills

5. Which of the following can be effectively utilized when gathering evidence for your speeches?
   a. personal experience
   b. library resources

   c. the Internet
   d. all of the above

6. Which type of source undergoes blind peer review to ensure high-quality information and contains specified studies?
   a. nonfiction books
   b. academic journal articles
   c. government documents
   d. trade journal articles

7. Brief notations in your outline that indicate a reference used in your speech are called _____ references, while _____ references are complete citations that appear in the "references" section of the speech outline.
   a. internal; bibliographic
   b. verbal; internal
   c. bibliographic; external
   d. external; verbal

8. When evaluating sources, you should ensure that the supporting material
   a. contains jargon and technical explanations
   b. comprises relevant and irrelevant information
   c. contains bias and is subjective
   d. is verifiable

9. Which type of supporting material includes written or oral statements of others' experiences?
   a. examples
   b. testimonial evidence
   c. numbers and statistics
   d. definitions

10. Information used to substantiate arguments and clarify a speaker's position is called
    a. competence
    b. sleeper effect
    c. supporting materials
    d. dynamism

Answers:
1. (c); 2. (b); 3. (c); 4. (d); 5. (d); 6. (b); 7. (a); 8. (d); 9. (b); 10. (c)

CRITICAL THINKING

1. As a speaker presenting to your class, what topics do you feel most credible speaking about? Why do you feel as such?

2. When watching the news or reading a newspaper, note whether the newscasters or writers cite their sources. Do they appear less credible if they do not mention where the information originated? Give examples.

SELF-QUIZ

For further review, try the chapter self-quiz on the *Online Learning Center* at **www.mhhe.com/pearson3.**

REFERENCES

Allen, M. (2002). Effect of timing of communicator identification and level of source credibility on attitude. *Communication Research Reports, 19,* 46–55.

Andersen, K., & Clevenger, T., Jr. (1963). A summary of experimental research in ethos. *Speech Monographs, 30,* 59–78.

Aristotle. (1941). Rhetoric. In R. McKeon (Ed.), *The basic works of Aristotle* (1, 1356a, ll. 12–14) (W. R. Roberts, Trans.). New York: Random House.

Bourhis, J., Adams, C., Titsworth, S., & Harter, L. (2002). *A style manual for communication studies.* New York: McGraw-Hill.

Dominick, J. R. (1996). *The dynamics of mass communication* (5th ed.). New York: McGraw-Hill.

Gregory, H. (1999). *Public speaking for college and career* (5th ed.). New York: McGraw-Hill.

Hacker, K. L., Zakahi, W. R., Giles, M. J., & McQuitty, S. (2000). Components of candidate images: Statistical analysis of the issue-persona dichotomy in the presidential campaign of 1996. *Communication Monographs, 67*(3), 227–238.

Harms, L. S. (1961). Listener judgments of status cues in speech. *Quarterly Journal of Speech, 47,* 168.

Hovland, C. I., & Weiss, W. (1967). The influence of source credibility on communicator effectiveness. In R. L. Rosnow & E. J. Robinson (Eds.), *Experiments in persuasion* (pp. 9–24). New York: Academic Press.

Karlins, M., & Abelson, H. (1970). *Persuasion.* New York: Springer.

Miller, J. M. (2000). Language use, identity, and social interaction: Migrant students in Australia, *Research on Language and Social Intention, 33,* 69–100.

Reinard, J., & Meyers, K. (2005, May). *Comparisons of models of persuasive effects of types of evidence introductions.* Paper presented at the International Communication Association Convention, New York.

Rosnow, R. L., & Robinson, E. J. (Eds.). (1967). *Experiments in persuasion.* New York: Academic Press.

Safire, W. (1980, November 30). When a mistake becomes correct, and vice versa. *Des Moines Sunday Register,* p. C3.

Sharp, H., Jr., & McClung, T. (1966). Effects of organization on the speaker's ethos. *Speech Monographs, 33,* 182–183.

Thompson, W. N. (1967). *Quantitative research in public address and communication.* New York: Random House.

Tuppen, C. J. (1974). Dimensions of communicator credibility: An oblique solution. *Speech Monographs, 41,* 253–260.

Wood, W., & Kallgren, C. A. (1988). Communicator attributes and persuasion: Recipients' access to attitude-relevant information in memory. *Personality and Social Psychology Bulletin, 14,* 172–182.

CHAPTER TWELVE

Organizing Your Presentation

What will you learn?

When you have read and thought about this chapter, you will be able to:

1. Deliver a purposeful introduction.
2. Devise creative openings for your presentation.
3. Apply the principles of outlining.
4. Choose an outline that best fits your topic.
5. Use transitions and signposts.
6. Deliver an appropriate conclusion.

In this chapter you will learn how to organize your presentation. You will examine the three main parts of a speech: introduction, body, and conclusion. You will learn the functions of each part and how to effectively organize the content. Understanding the parts of a speech, the functions of each part, and ways to organize the entire message is essential to becoming a successful presenter.

The annual **State of the Union address** presents any U.S. president with both a challenge and an opportunity. The president needs to put the best light on whatever actions were taken (or not taken) during the preceding year; at the same time, the chief executive can provide a glowing picture of whatever initiatives the administration intends to undertake in the coming year. The president and the White House speechwriters spend weeks on the speech. Perhaps the most difficult task is organizing the address—deciding which topics should be included and in what order.

President George W. Bush delivered his seventh State of the Union address before Congress on January 23, 2007, and he started off with a bang. He noted that he had the "high privilege" of being the first president to begin his address with "Madam Speaker," referring to the first female Speaker of the House, Nancy Pelosi. As his speech progressed, the president outlined policy initiatives ranging from health care, to immigration, to the global fight against AIDS. The war in Iraq also figured prominently in the speech.

But it was what President Bush did *not* include in his speech that drew some sharp criticism. Nowhere in the address was there any reference to the devastation caused by Hurricane Katrina just 15 months earlier, despite the fact that thousands of citizens in the Gulf Coast were still displaced and in desperate need of support from governmental agencies. Several critics faulted Bush for not giving priority to the Katrina recovery in his address to the nation.

How you organize a speech sends a signal to audience members. President Bush won points for his gracious introduction in which he acknowledged Nancy Pelosi's historic status in the House. But by the end of the speech, he left many people unhappy by failing to even mention the long-standing, devastating effects of Katrina. The president's State of the Union address illustrates how organizational choices affect the way an audience perceives a speech. This chapter will teach you about organization by discussing the key elements of a speech—the introduction, body, and conclusion—as well as how to outline your speech effectively.

The Introduction

Introduction

The first part of your presentation, where you fulfill the five functions of an introduction.

The **introduction** is the first part of your presentation, where you fulfill the five functions of an introduction. The introduction is important because audiences use it to "size up" a speaker. In the first few sentences, and certainly in the first few minutes of a speech, audience members decide whether to listen to you. They also decide whether your topic is important enough to hear. In those crucial early minutes, you can capture your audience's attention and keep their focus, or you can lose their attention—perhaps for the remainder of the presentation. This

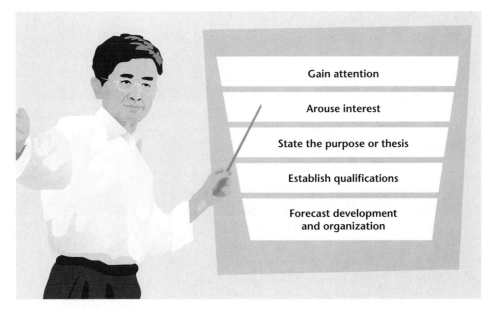

Figure 12.1   Functions of an introduction.

View an animation of this illustration on the *Online Learning Center.*

section of the chapter is devoted to helping you compose the best possible introduction, one that will grab your audience's attention and keep their minds on your topic.

The five functions of an introduction are illustrated in Figure 12.1. You do not need to fulfill these five functions in this order. Gaining audience attention often comes at the beginning, but maintaining attention is an important function throughout the speech. Forecasting the speech's organization often comes toward the end of an introduction, but even that function does not have to be last.

To assist you in composing an introduction for your public presentation, this section systematically explores the five functions and presents some examples.

TRY ◆ THIS

List the five functions of an introduction. Make sure the introduction of your speech includes these functions.

Gaining and Maintaining Audience Attention

The first function of an introduction is to gain and maintain attention. You gain and maintain the audience's attention by involving your audience in your topic. Here are some suggestions:

1. *Bring to the presentation the object or person about which you are going to speak.* A student speaking on health foods brings a tray full of health foods, which he shares with the audience after the speech; a student speaking on weightlifting brings her 250-pound friend to demonstrate the moves during the speech.

Ministers often invite the congregation to participate actively in the service.

See how to relate a story, cite a quotation, or arouse interest in your introduction by viewing clips on the *Online Learning Center.*

2. *Invite your audience to participate.* Ask questions and invite audience members to raise their hands and answer. Or have everyone stand up and perform the exercise that you are teaching them.

3. *Let your clothing relate to your presentation.* A nurse talking about the dangers of acute hepatitis wears a nurse's uniform; a construction worker dons a hard hat.

MYTHS, METAPHORS, & MISUNDERSTANDINGS

You can use metaphors to gain your audience's attention. For example, in Martin Luther King Jr.'s speech "I Have a Dream," he began by comparing the Emancipation Proclamation to a "great beacon light of hope" to African-Americans who had been "seared in the flames of withering injustice." He went on to describe the proclamation as a "joyous daybreak" that ended the "long night of captivity" (King, 1968). Such metaphors continue to inform racial rhetoric in our country. Pair off with another classmate and identify a speech topic and a related metaphor that could be used to gain the audience's attention.

4. *Exercise your audience's imagination.* Have the audience members close their eyes and imagine they are standing on a ski slope, standing before a judge on a driving-while-intoxicated charge, or slipping into a cool Minnesota lake when Miami and Houston are humid and steamy.

5. *Start with sight or sound.* One student gave a powerful presentation on motorcycle safety. He showed six slides as he talked about the importance

of wearing a helmet while driving a motorcycle. Only one item appeared in color on each slide: a crushed or battered helmet that had been worn by someone who lived through a motorcycle accident. His words spoke of safety; the battered helmets reinforced the message.

6. *Arouse audience curiosity.* Five hundred white people gathered to hear a presentation on diversity. The speaker was a Chinese man dressed in traditional Chinese attire. He started his presentation by saying nothing; he just slowly scanned his audience. The audience, accustomed to speakers who start by speaking, was mystified but exceedingly attentive. They were very curious about his quiet demeanor. Then he said, "Do you know how it feels to stand in front of a group this large and to see no one who looks like you?"

7. *Role-play.* A student invites an audience member to pretend to be a choking victim. The speaker then "saves" the victim by using the maneuver she is teaching the audience.

TRY ◆ THIS

See if you can determine how you decide that a presentation is organized. What are the verbal and nonverbal signs of organization? What words signal organization? What are the clues that tell you the speaker is organized? Can you use some of these techniques in your own presentation?

8. *Show a very short video.* A football player speaking on violence in that sport shows a short video of punt returns. He points out which players were deliberately trying to maim their opponents with face guards—as they have been taught to do.

9. *Present a brief quotation or have the audience read something you provided.* One enterprising student handed every class member an official-looking letter right before his speech. Each letter was a personalized summons to court for a moving violation that was detected by a police-owned spy camera at a busy intersection.

10. *State striking facts or statistics.* A student notes that 3,000 people died on September 11, 2001, at the hands of terrorists, and around 3,000 American soldiers had lost their lives in Iraq by November 2006. But, she continues, these numbers pale in comparison to the 23,000 Americans who died in a single battle, the Battle of Antietam, on April 17, 1862, in our own Civil War (Von Drehle, 2001).

11. *Self-disclose.* Tell audience members something about yourself—related to the topic—that they would not otherwise know: "I took hard drugs for six years"; "I was an eagle scout"; "I earn over $50,000 a year—legally."

12. *Tell a story, a narration.* A student tells this story: The little boy asked his grandfather if he was a hero because the grandson had heard that his grandpa fought in Vietnam when he was a young man. "No," said the old man, "I was not a hero, but I was in an entire battalion of heroes."

Think, Pair, Share

Create an Opening

Think first of some possible ways to start a speech that were not mentioned on pages 305–307. Then pair with a classmate and see if together you can think of three possible ways to start a speech that were not mentioned.

The preceding 12 suggestions for gaining and maintaining audience attention certainly are not the only possibilities, but they have all been used successfully by other students. Your introduction should not simply imitate what you read in this book; instead, think of ideas of your own that will work best for you and your audience.

Some words of caution about gaining and maintaining attention: No matter what method you use for gaining audience attention, avoid being overly dramatic. A student who pretended to cut himself and shot fake blood all over the front of the room got his teacher and his audience so upset that they could not listen to his presentation.

Always make sure your attention-getting strategy is related to your topic. Some speakers think every public speech must start with a joke. Starting with a joke is a big mistake if you are not good at telling jokes or if your audience is not interested in hearing them. Jokes can be used in the introduction of a speech if they are topically relevant, but they are just one of hundreds of ways a speaker can gain attention. Another overused device is writing something such as "S-E-X" on the chalkboard and then announcing your speech has nothing to do with sex but that you wanted to get the audience's attention. Again, the problem with this approach is that the attention-getting strategy has nothing to do with the topic. Finally, be wary of guests, animals, and PowerPoint because all three can eliminate you from the speaking situation: They will get all the attention, and they will become the presentation instead of you.

Arousing Audience Interest

The second function of an introduction is to arouse audience interest in the subject matter. The best way to arouse audience interest is to show clearly how the topic is related to the audience. A highly skilled speaker can adapt almost any topic to a given audience. Do you want to talk about collecting coins? Thousands of coins pass through each person's hands every year. Can you tell your audience how to spot a rare one? If you can arouse the audience's interest in currency, you will find it easier to encourage them to listen to your speech about the rare coins you have collected. Similarly, speeches about your life as a mother of four, a camp counselor, or the manager of a business can be linked to audience interests. The following good example relates the topic to the audience; these words are quoted from a student speech on drinking and driving:

> Do you know what the leading cause of death is for people who attend this college? Some of you might think it is a disease that causes the most deaths—cancer, heart attacks, or AIDS. No, the leading cause of death among students at this college is car accidents. Not just ordinary car accidents, but accidents in which the driver has been drinking.

The speaker related her topic to the audience by linking a national problem to her own college. She prepared the audience to receive more information and ideas about this common problem.

Stating the Purpose or Thesis

The third function of an introduction is to state the purpose or thesis of your speech. Why? Because informative speeches invite learning, and learning is more likely to occur if you reveal to the audience what you want them to know. Consider the difficulty of listening to a history professor who spends 50 minutes telling you every detail and date related to the Crusades. Observe how much more easily you can listen to a professor who begins the lecture by stating what you are supposed to learn: "I want you to understand why the Crusades began, who the main participants were, and when the Crusades occurred."

The following are two examples of statements of purpose or thesis:

> What I want you to remember from my speech is why our national debt is costing a billion dollars per day.

> You will learn in this presentation several methods of protecting your identity from crooks.

In speaking, as in teaching, audience members are more likely to learn and understand if your expectations are clear. That goal can be accomplished by stating the purpose in the introduction. Sometimes in a persuasive speech you may wish to delay revealing your purpose until you have set the stage for audience acceptance. Under most circumstances, though—and especially in informative speeches—you should reveal your purpose or thesis in your introduction.

Establishing Your Qualifications

The fourth function of an introduction is to describe any special qualifications you have to enhance your credibility. You can talk about your experience, your research, the experts you interviewed, and your own education and training in the subject. Although you should be wary about self-praise, you need not be reserved in stating why you can speak about the topic with authority. The following is an example of establishing credibility through self-disclosure:

> You can probably tell from my fingernails that my day job is repairing automobiles, a job I have held at the same dealership for over 12 years. I have repaired thousands of cars. That is why I want to tell you today why you and your insurance company have to pay such high prices for repair.

For more information on establishing source credibility, return to chapter 11 on this subject.

Forecasting Development and Organization

The fifth function of an introduction is to forecast the organization and development of the presentation. The forecast provides a preview of the main points you plan to cover. Audience members feel more comfortable when they know what to expect. You can help by revealing your plan for the speech. Are you going to discuss a problem and its solution? Are you going to make three main arguments with supporting materials? Let your audience know what you plan to do early in your speech. A forecast follows. Is it adequate in forecasting organization and development?

Today I plan to present three good reasons why race should be a factor in college admissions.

Sample Introduction That Fulfills the Five Functions

Below you will find Sarah Christianson's introduction to a persuasive speech on abortion titled "The Two Sides of Abortion." The margin notes indicate how the introduction fulfilled the functions.

Gains audience attention with controversial issue.

Relates topic to audience with active participation.

Arouses audience interest by introducing role of religion.

Relates topic to speaker. States the purpose of the presentation.

Reveals speaker qualifications.

Forecasts development and organization.

Relates topic to audience.

Imagine being in a situation where you were faced with the decision whether or not to have an abortion. How much would your religion, politics, and income influence your decision? By a show of hands, how many of you believe that religion is the major factor in abortion? How many of you think that your political views are a major factor? How many of you think that income would be a factor?

According to Cath4Choice.org retrieved on November 14, 2006, almost 70% of Roman Catholics believe that a woman who has an abortion for reasons other than to save her life can still be a good Catholic. As a young, female Catholic living in a society where abortion is one of many controversial topics facing women today, I believe that we as college students need to voice our opinion on this issue. My research shows that three outside forces influence a woman's decision to have an abortion—or not: Those three influences are religion, political view, and income.

Today we are going to discuss how religion affects a woman's decision, how political views can change her outlook, and how income limits her options. Males in the audience need to listen too, because they are the only reason that women need to make this important decision in their lives.

The Body

Most speakers begin composing their presentations with the body rather than the introduction because they need to know the content of the presentation to write an effective introduction.

The **body** of a presentation is the largest portion of the presentation in which you place your arguments and ideas, your evidence and examples, your proofs and illustrations, and your stories and testimonials. Since you usually do not have time to state in a presentation everything you know about a subject, you need to decide what information to include and what to exclude. Because the material you will use may not all be of equal importance, you need to decide placement—first, last, or in the middle. Selecting, prioritizing, and organizing are three skills that you will use in developing the body of your speech.

body

The largest part of the presentation, which contains the arguments, evidence, and main content.

Just as the introduction of a speech has certain functions to fulfill, so does the body. Following are the main functions of the body:

1. Increase what an audience knows about a topic (informative presentation).
2. Change an audience's attitudes or actions about a topic (persuasive presentation).
3. Present a limited number of arguments, stories, and/or ideas.
4. Provide support for your arguments and/or ideas.
5. Indicate the sources of your information, arguments, and supporting materials.

You already know something about organization. Every sentence you utter is organized. The words are arranged according to rules of syntax for the English language. Even when you are in conversation, you organize your speech. The first statement you make is often more general than that which follows. For instance, you might say, "I don't like DeMato for Congress," after which you might say why you don't like DeMato. You probably don't start by stating a specific fact, such as DeMato's voting record, her position on health care, or her torrid love life. Likewise, when we compose a speech, we tend to limit what we say, prioritize our points, and back them as necessary with support—all organized according to principles we have either subconsciously learned (as in the rules of syntax) or consciously studied (as in the rules of organization).

◄ SKILL BUILDER ►

On a separate sheet of paper, see if you can rearrange the following sentences into one well-organized paragraph. Figure out what principle of organization you used to establish the sentence order.

Divorce, teen pregnancy, drug use, and abortion are on the decline. College and health care are two exceptions. Houses keep getting bigger. People's health keeps improving. Almost everybody in America is better off than in our historical past. Crime rates are falling. The environment is cleaner.

SOURCE: Based on Easterbrook, G. (2004). The Progress Paradox: *How Life Gets Better While People Feel Worse*. New York: Random House as reviewed in Doherty, B. (2004, February 9–15). You Call This Fun? *The Washington Post National Weekly Edition*, p. 33.

The Principles of Outlining

An **outline** is a written plan that uses symbols, margins, and content to reveal the order, importance, and substance of your speech. An outline shows the sequence of your arguments or main points, indicates their relative importance, and states the content of your arguments, main points, and subpoints. The outline is a simplified, abstract version of your speech.

outline

A written plan that uses symbols, margins, and content to reveal the order, importance, and substance of a presentation.

Why should you learn how to outline? Here are three good reasons:

- Outlining is a skill that can be used to develop written compositions, to write notes in class, and to compose speeches.
- Outlining reinforces important skills like determining what is most important, what arguments and evidence will work best with this audience, and roughly how much time and effort will go into each part of your presentation.
- Outlining encourages you to speak conversationally because you do not have every word in front of you.

You will find that learning how to outline can provide you with a useful tool in your classes and at work. Outlining is versatile and easy to learn as long as you keep six principles of outlining in mind:

- *Principle 1: Link outline to purpose.* All the items of information in your outline should be directly related to your purpose and long-range goal. The

immediate purpose

What you expect to achieve on the day of your presentation.

long-range goal

What you expect to achieve by your message in the days, months, or years ahead.

immediate purpose is what you expect to achieve *on the day of your presentation.* You might want the audience to be able to distinguish between a row house and a townhouse, to rent a particular DVD, or to talk with others about a topic. All of these purposes can be achieved shortly after the audience hears about the idea. The **long-range goal** is what you expect to achieve by your message in the days, months, or years ahead. You may be talking about a candidate 2 months before the election, but you want your audience to vote a certain way at that future date. You may want to push people to be more tolerant toward persons of your race, gender, sexual preference, or religion, but tolerance is more likely to develop over time than instantly— so your goal is long-range.

- *Principle 2: Your outline is an abstract of the message you will deliver.* A simplification, the outline should be less than every word you speak but should include all important points and supporting materials. Some instructors say an outline should be about one-third the length of the actual presentation, if the message were in manuscript form. However, you should ask what your instructor expects in an outline, because some instructors like to see a very complete outline, whereas others prefer a brief outline. Nonetheless, the outline is not a manuscript but an abstract of the talk you intend to deliver, a plan that includes the important arguments or information you intend to present.

- *Principle 3: Each outline part is a single idea.* That is, the outline should consist of single units of information, usually in the form of complete sentences that express a single idea correctly presented below.

  I. Government regulation of handguns should be implemented to reduce the number of murders in this country.
    A. Half of the murders in the United States are committed by criminals using handguns.
    B. Half of the handgun deaths in the United States are caused by relatives, friends, or acquaintances of the victim.

main points

The most important points in a presentation; indicated by Roman numerals in an outline.

subpoints

The points in a presentation that support the main points; indicated by capital letters in an outline.

- *Principle 4: Your outline symbols signal importance.* In the example the **main points,** or most important points, are indicated with Roman numerals, such as I, II, III, IV, and V. The number of main points in a 5- to 10-minute message, or even a longer presentation, should be limited to the number you can reasonably cover, explain, or prove in the time permitted. Most 5-minute messages have from one to three main points. Even hour-long presentations must have a limited number of main points because most audiences are unable to remember more than seven main points.

  Subpoints, the points supporting the main points, or those of less importance, are indicated with capital letters, such as A, B, C, D, and E. Ordinarily, two subpoints under a main point are regarded as the minimum if any subpoints are to be presented. As with the main points, the number of subpoints should be limited; otherwise, the audience may lose sight of your main points. A good guideline is to present two or three of your best pieces of supporting material in support of each main point.

- *Principle 5: Your outline margins signal importance.* The larger the margin on the left, the less important the item is to your purpose. However, the margins are coordinated with the symbols explained previously; thus the main points have the same left margin, the subpoints have a slightly larger left margin, the sub-subpoints have a still larger left margin, and so on. A correct outline with the appropriate symbols and margins follows.

Why We Need Embryonic Stem Cell Research
by Amber Rasche

Introduction

I. As a person with diabetes in my family, I have been very concerned about the possibility of cures for this dreaded disease.

   A. Today I am going to talk with you about the importance of embryonic stem research in finding a cure.

   B. I hope you will care about this subject because none of us know who is going to suffer from this increasingly common disease.

   C. I will approach this subject by revealing how stem cell research became controversial, how the government slowed progress, and why you should agree with me that embryonic stem cell research needs to proceed.

Body

II. In the search for a cure, James Thomson in 1998 was the first biologist to isolate human embryonic stem cells.

   A. The goal of this research is to use stem cells to replace cells that have failed in the human body.

   B. Congress passed a bill in October 1998 prohibiting experimentation with embryonic stem cells except under very limited circumstances.

   C. Congress banned funding for any experimentation that would harm embryos.

   D. President Bush allowed research to continue on stem cells created before August 2001.

III. People favoring stem cell research demonstrate that the prohibition is unnecessarily keeping us from medical advances.

   A. Experts estimate that 400,000 embryos already exist in fertility clinics.

   B. Most of the existing embryos are discarded if they are not donated to science.

Conclusion

IV. Now that you have heard the history and the controversy surrounding cell research, I hope you will join me in keeping the government out of medical research so thousands of people with diseases like diabetes can have the hope of a cure in the near future.

- *Principle 6: Use parallel form.* **Parallel form** involves the consistent use of complete sentences, clauses, phrases, or words, but not a mixture of these. Hacker (1995), in her text on writing, says, "Readers expect items in a series to appear in parallel grammatical form" (p. 63). The same could be said of listeners. Most teachers prefer an outline consisting entirely of complete sentences because such an outline reveals more completely the speaker's message. An outline like the one on stem cell research is composed entirely of complete sentences; the form is parallel because no dependent clauses, phrases, or single words appear in the outline.

Marginal notes:

Speaker credibility: links speaker to topic.

Speaker announces topic.

Speaker relates topic to audience.

Speaker forecasts organization of presentation. Speaker states immediate persuasive purpose.

Principle 1: Outline links all major points to purpose.

Principle 2: Outline simplifies and reduces presentation to series of related sentences.

Principle 3: Each item in outline is one sentence.

Principle 4: Symbols (I, II, and A, B, etc.) indicate main and subordinate ideas.

Principle 5: Margins (far left for main points and indented for subordinate points) indicate importance.

Principle 6: Each item is in parallel form.

parallel form

The consistent use of complete sentences, clauses, phrases, or words in an outline.

The Rough Draft

Before you begin composing your outline, you can save time and energy by (1) selecting a topic that is appropriate for you, your audience, your purpose, and the situation; (2) finding arguments, examples, illustrations, quotations, stories, and other supporting materials from your experience, from written and visual resources, and from other people; and (3) narrowing your topic so that you can select the best materials from a large supply of available items.

rough draft

The preliminary organization of the outline of a presentation.

Once you have gathered materials consistent with your purpose, you can begin by developing a **rough draft** of your outline—a preliminary organization of the outline. The most efficient way to develop a rough draft is to choose a limited number of main points important for your purpose and your audience.

Next, you should see what materials you have from your experience, from written and visual resources, and from other people to support these main ideas. You need to find out if you have any materials that support your subpoints—facts, statistics, testimony, and examples. In short, you assemble your main points, your subpoints, and your sub-subpoints for your speech, always with your audience and purpose in mind. What arguments, illustrations, and supporting materials will be most likely to have an impact on the audience? Sometimes speakers get so involved in a topic that they select mainly those items that interest them. In public speaking you should select the items likely to have the maximum impact on the audience, not on you.

Composing an outline for a speech is a process. Even professional speechwriters may have to make important changes to their first draft. Some of the questions you need to consider as you revise your rough draft follow:

1. Are your main points consistent with your purpose?
2. Do your subpoints and sub-subpoints relate to your main points?
3. Are the items in your outline the best possible ones for this particular audience, for this topic, for you, for the purpose, and for the occasion?
4. Does your outline follow the principles of outlining?

Even after you have rewritten your rough draft, you would be wise to have another person—perhaps a classmate—examine your outline and provide an opinion about its content and correctness.

The next outline is an example of what a rough draft of a speech looks like:

Blogging
by Daniel Kalis

Introduction
My immediate purpose is to help my audience understand the origins, present practice, and the future of blogging.

Rough draft can have sentences, phrases, or just a word or two to indicate your overall plan for presentation.

Rough draft should be easy to change as you decide what to keep and what to discard based on what you can find about topic.

Rough draft is an early plan containing cues about what you want to say.

  I. What is blogging and what is its importance now and in the future?
    A. What is blogging?
    B. Why important?
 II. History
    A. Origin
      1. When?
      2. Who?
    B. Original uses
III. Present
    A. Reasons for popularity
    B. Complications
III. Future
    A. Trends
    B. Genres
 IV. Conclusion: Blogging is growing exponentially because of its many possibilities.

A rough draft of a speech does not necessarily follow parallel form, nor is it as complete as the sentence outline, which often develops out of the rough draft. Mostly, the rough draft provides an overview so that you can see how the parts of the speech—the main points and subpoints—fit together. When you are ready to finalize your outline, you have several options. The key-word and sentence outlines, are two possibilities.

 A great deal of research shows that ESL speakers benefit from preplanning strategies like preparing outlines before speaking or writing. Specifically, preparing outlines has been shown to improve language fluency while also increasing the depth and complexity of the ideas presented. In essence, outlines help you speak more clearly and develop more advanced ideas for your audience.

Outlines are effective as a final step in preparing a presentation because they help you formalize the ideas you want to present. Research reported by a researcher from the University of London suggests that for ESL speakers the use of concept mapping before constructing an outline may be beneficial (Ojima, 2006). Concept mapping involves the use of a visual flowchart to show relationships among key concepts related to your topic. Ojima found that the use of a concept map resulted in a better written product because students did not have to simultaneously brainstorm/formalize ideas while also concentrating on writing in a second language. Of course, concept mapping is a tool that could be beneficial for all students, not just nonnative speakers. By using concept mapping, you are more likely to consider how your ideas flow together—something that outlines tend to obscure.

The Sentence Outline

The sentence outline does not have all of the words that will occur in the delivered speech, but it does provide a complete guide to the content. A **sentence outline** consists entirely of complete sentences. It shows in sentence form your order of presentation; what kinds of arguments, supporting material, and evidence you plan to use; and where you plan to place them. A look at your outline indicates strengths and weaknesses. You might note, for instance, that you have insufficient information on one main point or a surplus of information on another.

In addition to the sentence outline itself, you may want to make notes on the functions being served by each part of your outline. For example, where are you trying to gain and maintain attention? Where are you trying to back up a major argument with supporting materials such as statistics, testimony, or specific instances? A sentence outline, along with side notes indicating functions, is a blueprint for your speech. The sentence outline can strengthen your speech performance by helping you present evidence or supporting materials that will make sense to audience members and will help you inform or persuade them.

The outline that follows is based on a student's speech. The immediate purpose of the speech is to recount the dangers of secondhand smoke. The long-term goal was to persuade the audience to support a statewide smoking ban. Notice that the outline consists entirely of sentences.

sentence outline

An outline consisting entirely of complete sentences.

Why We Need a Statewide Smoking Ban in Restaurants
by Jill Kertz

Introduction

I. More and more cities and states are considering smoking bans.
   A. How many of you do not like to eat in restaurants that permit smoking? [*Show of hands*]

B. Other cities in this state have implemented smoking bans in restaurants.

C. A statewide smoking ban in restaurants would benefit the general public.

Body

II. Our state needs a statewide ban on smoking.

   A. Smoke in restaurants annoys many customers.

   B. Secondhand smoke poses health risks to customers and employees.

      1. The American Cancer Society estimates 40,000 deaths from heart disease in nonsmokers from secondhand smoke.

      2. The American Cancer Society estimates 3,000 lung cancer deaths among nonsmokers from secondhand smoke.

   C. Some cities in this state and others nationwide have banned smoking in restaurants.

Conclusion

III. We need to enact a statewide ban on smoking in restaurants.

   A. A ban on smoking would benefit restaurant customers.

   B. A ban on smoking would benefit restaurant employees.

   C. A ban on smoking in restaurants would keep our state healthy.

The Key-Word Outline

Using a manuscript for your entire speech may invite you to become too dependent on the manuscript. Too much attention to notes reduces your eye contact and minimizes your attention to audience responses. Nonetheless, you can become very proficient at reading from a manuscript on which you have highlighted the important words, phrases, and quotations. A complete sentence outline may be superior to a manuscript in that it forces you to extemporize, to maintain eye contact, and to respond to audience feedback. Key words and phrases can also be underlined or highlighted on a sentence outline. An alternative method is simply to use a **key-word outline,** an outline consisting of important words or phrases to remind you of the content of the speech.

A key-word outline shrinks the ideas in a speech considerably more than does a sentence outline. A key-word outline ordinarily consists of important words and phrases, but it can also include statistics or quotations that are long or difficult to remember. The following outline came from a student's speech. Notice how the key-word format reduces the content to the bare essentials.

key-word outline

An outline consisting of important words or phrases to remind you of the content of the presentation.

The Youth Vote
by Amanda Peterson

Introduction

I. Politicians ignore youth vote

   A. Mostly 18- to 24-year-olds don't vote

   B. Statistics on voting

   C. Forecast of the reasons

Body

II. Youth apathetic to politics

   A. Sports & beer more interesting

   B. Don't know who represents them

III. Politics unappealing

   A. Partisanship

   B. Political scandals

A key-word outline fits easily on 3-by-5-inch or 4-by-6-inch note cards or on 8½-by-11-inch paper. If you choose note cards, the following suggestions may be useful:

1. Write instructions to yourself on your note cards. For instance, if you are supposed to write the title of your speech and your name on the chalk-board before your presentation begins, then you can write that instruction on the top of your first card.
2. Write on one side of the cards only. To use more cards with your key-word outline on one side only is better than to write front and back, which is more likely to result in confusion.
3. Number your note cards on the top so that they will be unlikely to get out of order. If you drop them, you can quickly reassemble them.
4. Write out items that might be difficult to remember. Extended quotations, difficult names, unfamiliar terms, and statistics are items you may want to include on your note cards to reduce the chances of error.
5. Practice delivering your presentation at least two times using your note cards. Effective delivery may be difficult to achieve if you have to fumble with unfamiliar cards.
6. Write clearly and legibly.

Figure 12.2   Tips for using note cards.

Conclusion
IV. What solution?
   A. More focus on youth
   B. More attention on campus

Figure 12.2 gives tips for using key-word note cards in your presentations.

Organizational Patterns

The body of a presentation can be outlined using a number of **organizational patterns,** arrangements of the contents of the message. Exactly which pattern of organization is most appropriate for your presentation depends in part on your purpose and on the nature of your material. For instance, if your purpose is to present a solution to a problem, your purpose lends itself well to the problem/solution organizational pattern. If your material focuses on something that occurred over time, then it might be most easily outlined within a time-sequence pattern.

In this section we will examine five organizational patterns. These five patterns are prototypes from which a skilled presenter can construct many others. Also, a number of organizational patterns may appear in the same message: An overall problem/solution organization may have within it a time-sequence pattern that explains the history of the problem.

The Time-Sequence Pattern

The **time-sequence pattern** is a method of organization in which the presenter explains a sequence of events in chronological order. Most frequently seen in informative presentations, this pattern can be used in presentations that consider

organizational patterns

Arrangements of the contents of a presentation.

time-sequence pattern

A method of organization in which the presenter explains a sequence of events in chronological order.

Cultural Note

Different Cultures Use Different Organizational Patterns

The dominant culture in North America embraces linear organizational patterns that move from a distinct beginning to a middle and end, that tend to state early and boldly who the speaker is and what the main point is, and that are rather detailed in structure with main points, subpoints, and even sub-subpoints. Do not assume that other cultures are the same. For example, in some Pacific Rim cultures, speakers start their presentations by putting themselves down instead of building up their credibility in an introduction; some Native American groups fill their messages with colorful imagery, metaphors, and illustrative stories instead of generating arguments and evidence; and some co-cultures, including African-Americans, hit on a recurring refrain with a pattern of organization that keeps circling back to a main point with many related narratives between each repetition. When addressing people from cultures different from your own, you should be aware of how they like to organize their messages.

the past, present, and future of an idea, an issue, a plan, or a project. This pattern is most useful for such topics as the following:

How the Salvation Army Began	The Future of Space Exploration
The Naming of a Team	The Development of Drugs for Treating HIV

Any topic that requires attention to events, incidents, or steps that take place over time is appropriate for this pattern of organization. Following is a brief outline of a composition organized in a time-sequence pattern:

What Is Buddhism?
by Jonathan Biersbach

Purpose: In this informative presentation I plan to reveal the past and present of this religion which is the fifth largest in the world but practically unknown to most Americans.

Introduction

Relates topic to self.

    I. I became interested in Buddhism in my travels in Southeast Asia where Buddhist temples are everywhere.

        A. In Bangkok I saw men in saffron robes, Buddhist monks, at every turn.

Relates topic to audience.

        B. So peaceful were they that I quickly became curious about how their religion worked.

Forecasts organization.

        C. I decided too that this religion would have some attractive qualities for Americans.

        D. Today I will share with you Buddhism's past and present so you will better understand the world's fifth largest religion.

Reveals purpose of presentation.

Body

    II. Gautama Buddha, Prince of the Shakyas, advanced his philosophy around the year 500 B.C.E.

Body consists of facts about Buddhism.

        A. His Four Noble Truths were actually intended as common medical practice, not as religious beliefs.

        B. His Four Noble Truths were followed by the Noble Eightfold Path.

C. After his death in 483 B.C.E., his philosophy spread throughout India and Asia and even to the Greeks by 180 B.C.E.

Conclusion

III. Buddhism has become a popular religion in the world.

    A. Only Christianity, Islam, Hindu, and traditional Chinese are larger.

    B. An estimated 350 million people now embrace Buddhism.

    C. You now know considerably more about this religion than do most Americans.

Summarizes content.
Brings in final facts and figures.

Ends by restating informative purpose.

A simpler example of a time-sequence pattern of organization is a recipe that depends on the combining of ingredients in the correct order.

The Cause/Effect Pattern

In using a **cause/effect pattern,** the presenter first explains the causes of an event, a problem, or an issue and then discusses its consequences, results, or effects. The presentation may be cause–effect, effect–cause, or even effect–effect. A presentation on inflation that uses the causal-sequence pattern might review the causes of inflation, such as low productivity, and review the effects of inflation, such as high unemployment and interest rates. The cause/effect pattern is often used in informative presentations that seek to explain an issue. This pattern differs from the problem/solution pattern in that the cause/effect pattern does not necessarily reveal what to do about a problem; instead, the organization allows for full explanation of an issue. An example of the cause/effect pattern follows:

cause/effect pattern

A method of organization in which the presenter first explains the causes of an event, a problem, or an issue and then discusses its consequences, results, or effects.

Drugs Plus Alcohol Equals Death
by Mark Potts

Purpose: This cause/effect informative presentation will explain how illegal drugs and legal alcohol often result in a lethal mix that leads to fights, abuse, and death.

Introduction

I. I do not personally take illegal drugs nor do I use alcohol, and I want you to know why.

    A. I know from my own research on the subject that these two ingredients can lead to tragedy.

    B. You too can be victimized by those who abuse alcohol and drugs, so you need to be aware of the problem.

    C. I am going to demonstrate how drugs and alcohol cause serious problems in the family and on the street.

Relates speaker to topic as researcher.

Relates topic to audience.

Reveals two-part organization.

Body

II. Drug and alcohol abuse are a major cause of family abuse.

    A. Half of spouse abuse cases and 38% of child abuse cases are linked to drugs and alcohol.

    B. Families sometimes strike back at the abuser with more physical and verbal abuse when defending themselves.

III. On the streets, drug and alcohol abuse lead to violent crimes.

    A. Almost half of all homicides and over half of all rape cases are related to drug and alcohol use.

    B. Drug peddling leads to gang wars and drug deal murders.

Relates causes and effects using facts and figures.

Conclusion

IV. Drug and alcohol abuse cause terrible problems inside the home and on the street, problems that you now know cause some of our most serious social ills.

Summarizes and repeats the purpose.

The cause/effect pattern of organization is a common pattern in fields as varied as medicine (tobacco causes cancer), economics (inflation causes recession), and religion (lack of faith results in damnation).

The Problem/Solution Pattern

The fourth pattern of organization, used most often in persuasive presentations, is the **problem/solution pattern,** in which the presenter describes a problem and proposes a solution. A message based on this pattern can be divided into two distinct parts, with an optional third part in which the presenter meets any anticipated objections to the proposed solution.

The problem/solution pattern can contain other patterns. For example, you might discuss the problem in time-sequence order, and you might discuss the solution using a topical-sequence pattern. Some examples of problem/solution topics follow:

Reducing Fat in Your Diet   Helping the Homeless

A New Way to Stop Smoking   Eliminating Nuclear Waste

Each example implies both a problem and a solution.

The problem/solution pattern of organization requires careful audience analysis because you have to decide how much time and effort to spend on each portion of the speech. Is the audience already familiar with the problem? If so, you might be able to discuss the problem briefly, with a few reminders to the audience of the problem's seriousness or importance. On the other hand, the problem may be so complex that both the problem and the solution cannot be covered in a single presentation. In that case you may have found a topic that requires both a problem presentation and a solution presentation. Your audience analysis is an important first step in determining the ratio of time devoted to the problem and to the solution.

A problem/solution speech in outline form looks like this:

The Benefits of Role-Playing Games
by Aaron Swenson

Purpose: This presentation will persuade the audience that role-playing games have a positive impact on practitioners.

Introduction

Relates topic to speaker.

Relates topic to audience.

Reveals organization and purpose.

I. I am a person who spends much time with role-playing games.
   A. By the time I complete this presentation I hope to teach more of you the delights of role games.
   B. I plan to tell you how these games evolved over time.
   C. I plan to show you what positive effects result from role games.

Body

Topical outline invites creative development of topic.

Places role games in historical context.

Relates ways that games bring positive results.

II. Role-playing games have been a major part of the "underground" youth culture since the 1980s.
   A. These role-playing games fire up young people's imaginations.
   B. These role-playing games require youth to "think outside the box."
   C. Over time these games have gone mainstream.
III. How do role-playing games aid individual development?
   A. While high school teaches conformity, role games encourage extensive use of the imagination.
   B. Role games introduce practitioners to complex rules and to extraordinary situations.
   C. Players have to imagine themselves as someone else.

    D. Players have to deal with fantasy-based situations like conquering demons and
        dragons.

Conclusion

IV. Role games have moved from underground to mainstream as they develop the imagi-
    nation with playing another, with complex rules, and with fantasy situations.
    A. I am a role-game addict.
    B. I hope you will consider becoming one as well.

Summarizes topic.

Builds speaker credibility.

States action purpose.

The problem/solution pattern has many applications in presentations on con-temporary problems and issues. The pattern can be used to discuss price-fixing, poverty, welfare, housing costs, the quality of goods, the quality of services, or the problems of being a student.

The Topical-Sequence Pattern

The **topical-sequence pattern,** used in both informative and persuasive presenta-tions, emphasizes the major reasons the audience should accept a point of view by addressing the advantages, disadvantages, qualities, and types of person, place, or thing. The topical-sequence pattern can be used to explain to audience members why you want them to adopt a certain point of view. This pattern is appropriate when you have three to five points to make, such as three reasons people should buy used cars, four of the main benefits of studying speech, or five characteristics of a good football player. This pattern of organization is among the most versatile. Here is the topical-sequence outline for a message informing audience members about ter-rorism and drugs.

topical-sequence pattern

A method of organiza-tion that emphasizes the major reasons an audience should accept a point of view by addressing the advan-tages, disadvantages, qualities, and types of person, place, or thing.

Solving the Literacy Problem
by Amy Trettel

Purpose: This informative speech will examine the problem of low literacy levels among children and suggest some possible solutions to the problem.

Introduction

  I. I worked last summer at a camp where I learned to my dismay that many grade-
    school-age children cannot read or write: They are illiterate Americans.
    A. Kids who can't read or write become a burden on you and on me because they
       may never succeed.
    B. Before this presentation is over I want you to know the size of this problem and
       some possible solutions.

Relates speaker to topic.

Relates topic to audience.

Reveals purpose and organization.

Body

  I. Young students read below proficiency level because they speak English as a second
    language, do not have parents who can help them, and do not have good schools to
    teach them.
    A. Forty percent of fourth-graders read below the basic level.
    B. Many students with literacy problems grow up in a home in which the parent or
       parents do not speak English.
    C. Many inner-city and rural schools lack books and teachers who can lift the veil of
       illiteracy.
 II. Solutions to the illiteracy problem in America are costly in time and money.
    A. Students who are learning to read and write require considerable time from the
       teachers.
    B. Reading programs before, after, and during school require funding that may need to
       be federal.

Overviews the problem.

Uses facts and figures as evidence of problem.

Offers three possible solutions.

C. Parents need to commit time and energy to reading and writing, or government needs to provide the help.

Conclusion

Summarizes and challenges audience.

III. I explored the problem of illiteracy among our youth in some detail before I proposed a three-part solution that could alleviate this problem in our country.

Transitions and Signposts

So far, you have examined organization in its broadest sense. To look at the presentation as a problem/solution or cause/effect pattern is like looking at a house's first floor and basement. We also need to look more closely at the design of the presentation by examining the elements that connect the parts of a speech—transitions and signposts.

transition

A bridge between sections of a presentation that helps the presenter move smoothly from one idea to another.

A **transition** is a bridge between sections of a message that helps a presenter move smoothly from one idea to another. Transitions also relax the audience momentarily. A typical transition is a brief flashback and a brief forecast that tells your audience when you are moving from one main point to another.

The most important transitions are between the introduction and the body, between the main points of the body, and between the body and the conclusion of the presentation. Other transitions can appear between the main heading and main points, between main points and subpoints, between subpoints and sub-subpoints, between examples, and between visual aids and the point being illustrated. Transitions can review, preview, or even be an internal summary, but they always explain the relationship between one idea and another. Transitions are the mortar between the building blocks of the speech. Without them cracks appear, and the structure is less solid. Table 12.1 gives examples of transitions.

signposts

Ways in which a presenter signals to an audience where the presentation is going.

Signposts are ways in which a presenter signals to an audience where the presentation is going. Signposts, as the name implies, are like road signs that tell a driver there is a curve, bump, or rough road ahead; they are a warning, a sign that the presenter is making a move. Whereas transitions are often a sentence or two, signposts can be as brief as a few words. Transitions review, state a relationship, and forecast; signposts merely point.

Beginning presenters often are admonished by their instructors for using signposts that are too blatant: "This is my introduction," "Here is my third main point," or "This is my conclusion." More experienced presenters choose more subtle but

---

TABLE 12.1   EXAMPLES OF TRANSITIONS

Transition from one main point to another: "Now that we have seen why computers are coming down in cost, let us look next at why software is so expensive."

Transition from a main point to a visual aid: "I have explained that higher education is becoming more and more expensive. This bar graph will show exactly how expensive it has become over the past 5 years."

Transition that includes a review, an internal summary, and a preview: "You have heard that suntanning ages the skin, and I have shown you the pictures of a Buddhist monk and a nighttime bartender who hardly ever exposed themselves to direct sunlight. Now I want to show you a picture of a 35-year-old woman who spent most of her life working in direct sunlight."

TABLE 12.2 EXAMPLES OF SIGNPOSTS	
"First, I will illustrate . . ."	"A second idea is . . ."
"Look at this bar graph . . ."	"Another reason for . . ."
"See what you think of this evidence . . ."	"Finally, we will . . ."

equally clear means of signposting: "Let me begin by showing you . . .," "A third reason for avoiding the sun is . . .," or "The best inference you can draw from what I have told you is . . ." Table 12.2 gives examples of signposts.

Transitions and signposts help presenters map a message for the audience. Transitions explain the relationships in the message by reflecting backward and forward. Signposts point more briefly to what the presenter is going to do at the moment. Both transitions and signposts help bind the message into a unified whole.

TRY ◆ THIS

How do you know when a speaker is drawing to a close? What signs, cues, or signals occur to prepare you for the end of a presentation? How will you indicate to an audience that your presentation is ending?

The Conclusion

Like the introduction, the **conclusion** fulfills functions. The conclusion finishes the presentation by fulfilling the four functions of an ending. The four functions of a conclusion need not occur in the order shown here, but they are all normally fulfilled in the last minutes of a presentation:

1. Forewarn the audience that you are about to finish.
2. Remind the audience of your central idea and the main points of your presentation.
3. Specify what the audience should think or do in response to your speech.
4. End the speech in a manner that makes audience members want to think and do as you recommend.

Let us examine these functions of a conclusion in greater detail.

The first function, the **brakelight function,** warns the audience that the end of the presentation is near. Can you tell when a song is about to end? Do you know when someone in a conversation is about to complete a story? Can you tell in a TV drama when the narrative is drawing to a close? The answer to these questions is usually yes because you get verbal and nonverbal signals that songs, stories, and dramas are about to end.

How do you use the brakelight function in a presentation? One student signaled the end of her speech by saying, "Five minutes is hardly time to consider all the complications of this issue. . . ." By stating that her time was up, she signaled her conclusion. Another said, "Thus men have the potential for much greater role flexibility

conclusion

The part that finishes the presentation by fulfilling the four functions of an ending.

brakelight function

A forewarning to the audience that the end of the presentation is near.

than our society encourages. . . ." The word *thus*, like *therefore*, signals the conclusion of a logical argument and indicates that the argument is drawing to a close.

The second function of a conclusion—reminding the audience of your central idea or the main points in your message—can be fulfilled by restating the main points, summarizing them briefly, or selecting the most important point for special treatment. Elizabeth Nnoko ended her persuasive speech on legalizing drug purchases from Canada by briefly summarizing her message:

> We have discussed the rising cost of prescription drugs, the problem with Medicare, myth and reality concerning importation of prescription drugs, and solutions that can be implemented to solve this issue.

The third function of a conclusion is to specify what you expect audience members to do as a result of your presentation. Do you want the audience to simply remember a few of your important points? Then tell them one last time the points you think are worth remembering. Do you want the audience to write down the argument they found most convincing, sign a petition, or talk to their friends? If so, you should state what you would regard as an appropriate response to your presentation. One student's presentation on unions concluded with the slogan "Buy the union label." Her ending statement specified what she expected of the audience.

The fourth function of a conclusion is to end the presentation in a manner that makes audience members want to think and do as you recommend. You can conclude with a rhetorical question: "Knowing what you know now, will you feel safe riding with a driver who has had a few drinks?"; a quotation: "As John F. Kennedy said, 'Forgive your enemies, but never forget their names'"; a literary passage: "We conclude with the words of Ralph Waldo Emerson, who said, 'It is one light which beams out a thousand stars; it is one soul which animates all men'"; or an action that demonstrates the point of the presentation: The speaker quickly assembles an electric motor for the class and shows that it works, the speaker twirls and does the splits in one graceful motion, or an experiment is completed as the mixture of baking soda and vinegar boils and smokes.

Some cautions about conclusions: In ending a presentation, as in initiating one, you need to avoid being overly dramatic. At one large college in the Midwest, the communication classes were taught on the third floor of the building. In one classroom a student was delivering a presentation about insanity. As the speech progressed, the class became increasingly aware that the young man delivering the presentation had a few problems. At first, he was difficult to understand: Words were run together, parts of sentences were incoherent, and pauses were too long. Near the end of the speech, the young man's eyes were rolling, and his jaw had fallen slack. At the very end of the presentation, he looked wildly at the audience, ran over to the open window, and jumped. The class was shocked. The instructor and students rushed to the window, expecting to see his shattered remains. Far below, on the ground, were 20 fraternity brothers holding a large firefighter's net, with the speaker waving happily from the center.

A better idea is to conclude your presentation with an inspirational statement, words that make audience members glad they spent the time and energy listening to you. One student delivered a single line at the end of his talk on using seatbelts that summarized his message and gave his audience something to remember: "It is not who is right in a traffic accident that really counts," he said, "it is who is left." That conclusion was clever, provided a brief summary, and was an intelligent and safe way to end a presentation.

Sample Conclusion That Fulfills the Four Functions

Following is the conclusion of a speech by Holly Scallen about safe sex. The side notes indicate how she fulfilled the functions of a conclusion.

I hope that everyone will leave today feeling a little more educated about safe sex. Both your parents and I will be able to sleep more peacefully tonight. If I was unable to answer your questions or you were too shy to ask, feel free to ask me later.

Brakelight function: Warns that end is near.

I have covered the basics: how to get pregnant, how to avoid pregnancy, what to do if you get a sexually transmitted disease (STD), and what to do if you or a loved one gets pregnant.

Reminds audience of main points.

I'm not preaching about what your morals say about premarital sex. I am simply giving advice to the college students who are sexually active or considering becoming active. I want everyone to look back at their college years with great memories, not reluctantly changing diapers or telling a loved one that you have a sexually transmitted disease.

Specifies what audience should do.

Our Wellness Center gives away condoms without cost. Take a handful for you and your friends. You do not want to be without one when you cannot control your hormones.

Ends in manner that urges recommended action.

The Bibliography

When you have completed your outline, you may be asked to provide a **bibliography,** a list of the sources you used in your presentation. The main idea behind a bibliography is to inform others of what sources you used for your speech and to enable them to check those sources for themselves. Each entry in your bibliography should be written according to a uniform style. Several accepted style manuals can answer your questions about the correct format for a bibliography: *The Publication Manual of the American Psychological Association* (APA), *The MLA Handbook*, and *The Chicago Manual of Style.* Since some teachers prefer MLA and others prefer APA, you should ask your instructor's preference. This textbook relies on the APA for its bibliography style; therefore, the examples below conform to APA guidelines.

bibliography
A list of sources used in a presentation.

Common sources of bibliographic material for student presentations are newspapers, magazines, journal articles, books, the Internet, and interviews. The correct forms for these sources are as follows:

Newspaper

Kolpack, J. (2006, November 15). More than the Dakota marker at stake. *The Forum*, p. D1.

Magazine

Drury, B. (2006, October). The doctors of mercy. *Men's Health, 21,* 180–187.

Journal

Vanesky, K., Docherty, C., Dapena, J., & Schrader, J. (2006). Ankle bracing can cause excessive knee external rotation torque. *Journal of Athletic Training, 41*(3), 239–244.

As you can see, the name of the author appears in reverse order so that the list can be easily alphabetized. Notice that the name of the author, the publication date, and the title of the article are followed by periods. Only the first words of the title and subtitle are capitalized. If a volume number is included in your entry, do not

Online Stylebooks for Footnotes and Bibliographies

www.apastyle.org. The American Psychological Association Online Manual provides a guide to the style used by National Communication Association publications.

www.columbia.edu/cu/cup/cgos/index/html. The Columbia Guide to Online Style is a comprehensive guide for citing or producing online documents. Guidelines are given for both humanities (Modern Language Association, or MLA) and social science (American Psychological Association, or APA) styles.

www.uvm.edu/~xli/reference/apa.html. This is a site from the University of Vermont that lists simplified guidelines for citing electronic sources.

write "p." or "pp." before the page numbers. When no volume number appears, you should include "p." for a single page or "pp." for more than one page.

Without an author the bibliographic entry changes slightly. The title of the article should appear first and the date should follow the title. The entry can then be alphabetized according to the first significant word in the article title.

Book

Rich, C. (2007). *Writing and reporting news.* Belmont, CA: Thomson Wadsworth.

Again, the authors' name is in reverse order for accurate alphabetization; the last author's name, date of publication, and book title are followed by periods. The place of publication is followed by a colon, and the name of the publisher is followed by a period. A bibliographic entry must specify the book pages if the entire book was not used.

For a book with two authors, use a comma and an ampersand (&) before the second surname. If a book has more than three authors, use commas to separate all the names and use an ampersand before the final surname.

Internet

Author, I. (date). Title of article. *Name of Periodical* [Electronic version], *xx*, pages. Retrieved (date) from (URL)

An example of a citation from a website would look like this:

Olson, D. (2006, November 15). Snowy season still gives chill. *Fargo Forum* [Electronic version], 3. Retrieved from http://www.in-forum.com/articles/ubdex,cfm

Bibliographic references to material taken from the Internet are fraught with difficulty because of unknown and possibly missing information. For instance, dates are often difficult to locate in online articles. If one is available, use the listed year of publication. Otherwise, you can use the date of the material's most recent update or, as a last resort, the precise date of your search.

The most important issue to keep in mind is that a reference is designed to enable someone else to locate the material you used in your presentation. Therefore, include as much information in your Internet reference as you can. If possible, conform the reference to the format above. Note that the italicized "*xx*" refers to a volume number when applicable. Also note that the reference does not end in a period because a period in the wrong place renders most Internet addresses unusable.

For more examples of Internet bibliographic entries, refer to the accompanying E-Note, which lists websites dealing with this subject.

Interview

Okigbo, C. (2006, September 18). [Personal interview].

Pamphlets, handbooks, and manuals may not have complete information about who wrote them, who published them, or when they were published. In that case you are expected to provide as much information as possible so that others can verify the source.

If you find sources you do not know how to place in bibliographic form, you can ask your bookstore or a librarian for *The Publication Manual of the American Psychological Association, The MLA Handbook,* or *The Chicago Manual of Style.* An excellent reference work designed for communication students is *A Style Manual for Communication Majors* (Bourhis, Adams, & Titsworth, 1999).

College composition texts also include the standard forms for footnote and bibliographic entries.

Chapter Review & Study Guide

SUMMARY

In this chapter you learned the following:

▶ An effective introduction fulfills five functions, which can occur in any order:
- It gains and maintains audience attention.
- It arouses audience interest in the topic.
- It states the purpose of the presentation.
- It describes the presenter's qualifications.
- It forecasts the organization and development of the presentation.

▶ An effective outline for a presentation follows six principles:
- It relates the information presented to the immediate purpose and long-range goal.
- It is an abstract of the message you will deliver.
- It expresses ideas in single units of information.
- It indicates the importance of items with rank-ordered symbols.
- It provides margins that indicate the importance of each entry visually.
- It states entries in parallel form (such as complete sentences, as in this list).

▶ The most frequently used patterns of organization in public presentations are:
- Time-sequence pattern, or chronology, with items presented serially over time.
- Topical-sequence pattern, with items listed as a limited number of qualities or characteristics.
- Problem/solution pattern, which poses a problem followed by a suggested solution.
- Cause/effect pattern, which posits a cause that results in some effect.

▶ Transitions and signposts link ideas and indicate direction to the audience.

▶ An effective conclusion fulfills certain functions:
- It forewarns listeners that the presentation is about to end.
- It reminds the audience of the central idea and main points of your presentation.
- It specifies what you expect from the audience as a result of the presentation.
- It ends the presentation in a manner that encourages the audience to think and act as you recommend.

▶ Often a bibliography, a list of sources, accompanies the complete outline.

KEY TERMS

Go to the *Online Learning Center* at **www.mhhe.com/pearson3** to further your understanding of the following terminology.

Bibliography	Key-word outline	Rough draft
Body	Long-range goal	Sentence outline
Brakelight function	Main points	Signposts
Cause/effect pattern	Organizational patterns	Subpoints
Conclusion	Outline	Time-sequence pattern
Immediate purpose	Parallel form	Topical-sequence pattern
Introduction	Problem/solution pattern	Transition

STUDY QUESTIONS

1. Which function of the introduction shows how the topic is related to the audience?
   a. gaining and maintaining audience attention
   b. arousing audience interest
   c. stating the purpose or thesis
   d. establishing speaker qualifications

2. Stating your purpose in the introduction
   a. is necessary because informative speeches do not invite learning, and this is your only opportunity to explain
   b. is unnecessary
   c. is necessary in both informative and persuasive speeches

d. is important because audience members are more likely to learn and understand if your expectations are clear

3. When developing the body of a speech, you must
   a. select, prioritize, and organize
   b. write your introduction first
   c. use as much information as possible
   d. utilize sources but not cite them

4. Which of the following statements is *not* true with regard to outlining?
   a. It uses symbols, margins, and content to reveal the order, importance, and substance of a presentation.
   b. All items of information in your outline do not need to be directly related to the speech's purpose and long-range goal.
   c. It encourages a conversational speaking tone because not every word is in front of you.
   d. Items should appear in parallel form.

5. Which type of outline consists mostly of important words or phrases but not complex information?
   a. main point
   b. sentence
   c. key-word
   d. cause/effect pattern

6. If you were giving a speech about the parking problem at your university with possible means to resolve it, which organizational pattern would be best?
   a. time-sequence
   b. cause/effect

   c. problem/solution
   d. topical

7. When a presenter explains a progression of events in chronological order, he or she is most likely using which organizational pattern?
   a. time-sequence
   b. cause/effect
   c. problem/solution
   d. topical

8. Which of the following help speakers move from one idea to another by reviewing, stating a relationship, and forecasting?
   a. transitions
   b. signposts
   c. subpoints
   d. goals

9. Reminding the audience of the speech's central idea and main points, specifying what is expected of audience members, and ending soundly are functions of the
   a. introduction
   b. transitions
   c. brakelight
   d. conclusion

10. A bibliography is
    a. a list of the sources used in a presentation
    b. written according to a uniform style such as APA or MLA
    c. used to inform others of what sources were used in the speech
    d. all of the above

Answers:
1. (b); 2. (d); 3. (a); 4. (b); 5. (c); 6. (c); 7. (a); 8. (a); 9. (d); 10. (d)

CRITICAL THINKING

1. Using the suggestions from the text, how would you begin your speech in order to gain the audience's attention if your speech topic was movies? Your university? Problems of the world such as war, famine, or poverty? Why did you choose these methods?

2. What happens on morning talk shows when the hosts wish to change subjects? Do they transition smoothly or simply announce the next topic? As a listener, which do you prefer?

SELF-QUIZ

For further review, try the chapter self-quiz on the *Online Learning Center* at **www.mhhe.com/pearson3**.

REFERENCES

Bourhis, J., Adams, C., & Titsworth, S. (1999). *A style manual for communication majors* (5th ed.). New York: McGraw-Hill.

Hacker, D. (1995). *A writer's reference* (3rd ed.). Boston: Bedford Books of St. Martin's Press.

King, M. L. (1968). *The peaceful warrior.* New York: Pocket Books.

Ojima, M. (2006). Concept mapping as pre-task planning: A case study of three Japanese ESL writers. *System, 34,* 566–585.

Von Drehle, D. (2001, September 17–23). Our Pearl Harbor. *The Washington Post* (National Weekly Edition), p. 6.

CHAPTER THIRTEEN

Delivery and Visual Resources

What will you learn?

When you have read and thought about this chapter, you will be able to:

1. State the advantages and disadvantages of each mode of delivery.
2. Name and explain each of the vocal aspects of delivery.
3. Name and explain each of the bodily aspects of delivery.
4. Understand when and why you should use visual resources in your speech.
5. Demonstrate the use of visual resources effectively and correctly in a speech.

M*any presentations with good content* never reach the listener because of poor delivery skills. This chapter explores the delivery of your presentation and the various visual aids you may use in your presentation. You will discover four modes of delivery and the various vocal and bodily aspects of delivery. The final section of the chapter examines some visual resources you can use in your speech—from chalkboards to electronic presentations—and explains how to use them. Read the chapter carefully so you can practice what you learn in successful presentations.

O
n May 17, 2004, students, faculty, and proud parents gathered for commencement at the University of Pennsylvania. The speaker, as is typical in such cases, embarked on a speech to inspire the students to use their gifts and talents to improve the lives of others. At one point he challenged them with questions: "What's the big idea? What's *your* big idea? What are you willing to spend your moral capital, your intellectual capital, your cash, your sweat equity in pursuing outside of the walls of the University of Pennsylvania?" He spoke movingly of the need to address significant "moral blind spots," ranging from racism and poverty to the spread of AIDS in Africa.

Planners for the commencement did not want a typical speaker; they wanted a "rock star" speaker with global recognition. Their choice was not the U.S. president or the secretary general of the United Nations or a foreign dignitary. They literally found a rock star—Bono, lead singer for U2. Imagine what it would be like to listen to someone with the natural instincts of a performer delivering an impassioned plea to stop needless death and discrimination. Think how Bono might have used his offbeat humor, musician's timing, and dramatic gestures to accentuate his message. When someone with Bono's skills delivers a message, audience members sit up and pay attention.

A convincing delivery and effective visual aids can make even an average speech sound great. Although we may not all have Bono's natural performing instincts, we can learn to present our message effectively and to use meaningful visual resources. In this chapter you will learn how to use eye contact, your voice, PowerPoint, and other resources to improve the presentation of your ideas.

What Is Delivery?

delivery

The presentation of a speech using your voice and body to communicate your message.

Delivery is the presentation of a speech using your voice and body to communicate your message. People have contradictory ideas about the importance of speech delivery. Some people think, "It's not what you say but how you say it that really counts." According to others, "What you say is more important than how you say it." Actually, what you say *and* how you say it are both important, but some researchers suggest that the influence of delivery on audience comprehension is overrated (Petrie, 1963). Those who challenge the importance of delivery do not say that delivery is unimportant; rather, in evaluating the relative importance of delivery and content, they see content as more important than delivery (Gundersen & Hopper, 1976). That said, the effective public speaker cannot ignore the importance of delivery.

What Are Four Modes of Delivery?

The four modes of delivery—extemporaneous, impromptu, manuscript, and memorized—vary in the amount of preparation required and their degree of spontaneity. Although the four modes are all possible choices, students of public speaking are least likely to use the manuscript and memorized modes. They may be asked to try the impromptu mode at times, but most speech assignments require the extemporaneous mode.

The Extemporaneous Mode

A presentation delivered in the **extemporaneous mode** is carefully prepared and practiced, but the presenter delivers the message conversationally without heavy dependence on notes. This mode is message- and audience-centered, with the speaker focused not on the notes but on the ideas being expressed. Considerable eye contact, freedom of movement and gesture, the language and voice of conversation, and the use of an outline or key-words to keep the speaker from reading or paying undue attention to the written script characterize this mode.

The word *extemporaneous* literally means "on the spur of the moment" in Latin; however, as practiced in the classroom, this mode of delivery only appears to be spontaneous. The speaker may choose different words as the speech is practiced and as she or he finally delivers the message, but the focus is on communicating the message to the audience.

You have seen this mode of delivery in the classroom, in some professors' lectures, sometimes in the pulpit, often in political and legal addresses, and usually in speeches by athletes, businesspeople, and community leaders who are experienced speakers. This mode is the one you will learn best in the classroom and the one that has the most utility outside the classroom.

extemporaneous mode

A carefully prepared and researched presentation delivered in a conversational style.

The Impromptu Mode

In the **impromptu mode** you deliver a presentation without notes, plans, or formal preparation and with spontaneity and conversational language. The word *impromptu* has Latin and French roots and means "in readiness."

You use the impromptu mode when you answer a question in class, when you say who you are, and when you give people directions on the street. You cannot say much in these situations unless you are "in readiness," that is, unless you know the answers. Ordinarily, this mode of delivery requires no practice and no careful choice of language. The impromptu mode encourages you to "think on your feet" without research, preparation, or practice.

impromptu mode

Delivery of a presentation without notes, plans, or formal preparation; characterized by spontaneity and conversational language.

The Manuscript Mode

As the name implies, in the **manuscript mode** you deliver a presentation from a script of the entire speech. The advantage of this mode is that the presenter knows exactly what to say. The disadvantages are that the written message invites a speaker to pay more attention to the script than to the audience, discourages eye contact, and prevents response to audience feedback.

Politicians, especially those who are likely to be quoted, as well as clergy and professors, sometimes use this mode of delivery, but students are rarely asked to use this mode except when reading an essay, poem, or short story to the class.

manuscript mode

Delivery of a presentation from a script of the entire speech.

The Memorized Mode

A presentation delivered in the **memorized mode** is committed to memory. This mode requires considerable practice and allows ample eye contact, movement, and gestures. However, this mode discourages the speaker from responding to feedback,

memorized mode

Delivering a presentation that has been committed to memory.

Think, Pair, Share

Match Mode to Situation

First think on your own of at least one situation in which each of the four modes of delivery would be most appropriate. Then pair with a classmate, compare notes, and see if you can think of more situations. Share your best ideas with the class.

from adapting to the audience during the speech, and from choosing words that might be appropriate at the moment. In other words, memorization removes spontaneity and increases the danger of forgetting. You have experienced this mode if you ever acted in a play and memorized your part. Politicians, athletes, and businesspeople who speak to the same kind of audience about the same subjects often end up memorizing their speeches. Even professors, when they teach a class for the third time in a week, may memorize the lesson for the day.

As a student in the communication classroom, you need to avoid overrehearsing your presentation to the point that you memorize the script. Most communication teachers and audiences respond negatively to speeches that sound memorized. As one person put it, "Any presentation that 'sounds memorized'—and most memorized presentations do—never lets the audience get beyond the impression that the speaker's words are not really his or her own, even if they are."

The mode you choose should be appropriate for the message, the audience, and the occasion. Students use the extemporaneous mode most often in learning public speaking because that mode teaches good preparation, adaptation to the audience, and focus on the message. Nonetheless, mode of delivery does not determine effectiveness. Comparing extemporaneous and memorized modes, two researchers concluded that the mode is not what makes the speaker effective. Instead, the speaker's ability is more important. Some speakers are more effective with extemporaneous speeches than with manuscripts, but some speakers use both modes with equal effectiveness (Hildebrandt & Stephens, 1963).

What Are the Vocal and Bodily Aspects of Delivery?

As you have already observed, delivery is how your voice and body affect the meaning of your presentation. They are important parts of the message you communicate to your audience.

Effective speech delivery has many benefits. Research indicates that effective delivery—the appropriate use of voice and body in public speaking—contributes to the credibility of the speaker (Bettinghaus, 1961). Indeed, student audiences characterize the poorest speakers by their voices and the physical aspects of delivery (Henrikson, 1944). Poor speakers are judged to be fidgety, nervous, and monotonous. They also maintain little eye contact and show little animation or facial expression (Gilkinson & Knower, 1941). Good delivery increases the audience's capacity to handle complex information (Vohs, 1964). Thus public speakers' credibility—the audience's evaluation of them as good or poor speakers—and their ability to convey complex information may be affected by the vocal and bodily aspects of delivery.

The Vocal Aspects of Presentation

Studying the vocal aspects of presentation is like studying music. The words of a presentation are like musical notes. As people speak, they create music. Just as different musicians can make the same notes sound quite different, public speakers can say words in different ways to get the audience to respond in various ways. The seven vocal aspects of presentation are pitch, rate, pauses, volume, enunciation, fluency, and vocal variety.

Pitch

Pitch is the highness or lowness of a speaker's voice—the voice's upward and downward movement, the melody produced by the voice. Pitch is what makes the difference between the "ohhh" you utter when you earn a poor grade in a class and the "ohhh" you utter when you see something or someone really attractive. The "ohhh" looks the same in print, but when the notes turn to music, the difference between the two expressions is vast. The pitch of your voice can make you sound either lively or listless. As a speaker you learn to avoid the two extremes: You avoid the lack of change in pitch that results in a monotone, and you avoid repeated changes in pitch that result in a singsong delivery. The best public speakers use the full range of their normal pitch.

Control of pitch does more than make a presentation sound pleasing. Changes in pitch can actually help an audience remember information (Woolbert, 1920). Voices perceived as "good" are characterized by a greater range of pitch, more upward and downward inflections, and more pitch shifts (Black, 1942). Certainly, one of the important features of pitch control is that pitch can alter the way an audience responds to the words. Presenters produce many subtle changes in meaning by changes in pitch. The speaker's pitch tells an audience whether the words are a statement or a question, whether the words mean what they say, and whether the speaker is expressing doubt, determination, irony, or surprise.

Presenters learn pitch control only through regular practice. An actor who is learning to deliver a line has to practice that line many times and in many ways before being sure that most people in the audience will understand the words as intended. The effective presenter rehearses a presentation before friends to discover whether the words are being understood as intended. You may sound angry when you do not intend to, adamant when you intend to sound doubtful, or frightened when you are only surprised. You are not always the best judge of how you sound to others, so you have to seek out and place some trust in other people's evaluations.

Rate

How fast should you speak when delivering a public presentation? Instructors often caution students to "slow down" because talking fast is a sign of anxiety or nervousness. Debaters speak very rapidly, but usually their opponents understand their message. What is the best way for you to deliver your speech?

Rate is the speed of delivery, or how fast you say your words. The normal rate for Americans is between 125 and 190 words per minute, but many variations occur. You need to remember that your rate of delivery depends on you—how fast you normally speak—and on the situation—few people talk fast at a funeral. Rate also depends on the audience and the subject matter. For example, children listening to a story understand better at slower rates, and complex materials may require more patient timing and more repetition. Most instructors like a presentation to sound conversational but not colloquial—not stilted and formal but not street talk either.

pitch

The highness or lowness of the speaker's voice.

rate

The speed at which speech is delivered, normally between 125 and 190 words per minute.

Pauses

pause

The absence of vocal sound used for dramatic effect, transition, or emphasis.

A third vocal characteristic of speech delivery is the **pause**—an absence of vocal sound used for dramatic effect, transition, or emphasis. Presentations are often a steady stream of words without silences, yet pauses can be used for dramatic effect and to get an audience to consider content. The speaker may begin a speech with rhetorical questions: "Have you had a cigarette today? Have you had two or three? Ten or eleven? Do you know what your habit is costing you in a year? A decade? A lifetime?" After each rhetorical question a pause allows audience members to answer the question mentally.

vocalized pauses

Breaks in fluency that negatively affect an audience's perception of the speaker's competence and dynamism.

On the other hand, **vocalized pauses** are breaks in fluency that negatively affect an audience's perception of the speaker's competence and dynamism. The "ahhhs" and "mmhhs" of the beginning speaker are disturbing and distracting. Unfortunately, even some experienced speakers have the habit of filling silences with vocalized pauses. One group teaches public speaking to laypersons by having members of the audience drop a marble into a can every time a speaker uses a vocalized pause. The resulting punishment—the clanging of the cans—breaks the habit. A more humane method might be to rehearse your presentation before a friend who signals you every time you vocalize a pause so that you vocalize less often when you deliver your speech to an audience. One speech instructor hit on the idea of rigging a light to the lectern so that every time a student speaker used a vocalized pause, the light went on for a moment. Try not to fear silence when you give your speech. Many audiences would prefer a little silence to vocalized pauses.

Volume

Volume is the relative loudness of your voice, but volume is more than just loudness. Variations in volume can convey emotion, importance, suspense, and

Electronic devices can enhance projection.

changes in meaning. You can use a stage whisper in front of an audience, just as you would whisper a secret to a friend. You can speak loudly and strongly on important points, letting your voice carry your conviction. Volume can change with the situation. For example, a pep rally may be filled with loud, virtually shouted speeches teeming with enthusiasm, whereas a eulogy may be delivered at a lower, respectful volume. An orchestra never plays so quietly that patrons cannot hear, but the musicians vary their volume. Similarly, a presenter who considers the voice an instrument learns how to speak softly, loudly, and in between to convey meaning.

Enunciation

Enunciation, the fifth vocal aspect of speech delivery, is the pronunciation and articulation of sounds and words. Because people's reading vocabulary is larger than their speaking vocabulary, they may use words in speeches they have rarely or never heard before. To deliver unfamiliar words is risky. One student in a communication class gave a speech about the human reproductive system. During the speech he managed to mispronounce nearly half the words used to describe the female anatomy. The speaker sounded incompetent to his audience. Rehearsing in front of friends, roommates, or family is a safer way to try out your vocabulary and pronunciation on an audience. Your objective should be to practice unfamiliar words until you are comfortable with them. Also be alert to the names of people you quote, introduce, or cite in your speech. Audiences are impressed when a student speaker correctly pronounces such names as Goethe, Monet, and de Chardin.

enunciation

The pronunciation and articulation of sounds and words.

Pronunciation is the act of correctly articulating words. The best way to avoid pronunciation errors is to look up unfamiliar words in a dictionary. Every dictionary has a pronunciation key. For instance, the entry for the word *belie* in the *Random House Dictionary of the English Language* looks like this:

pronunciation

The act of correctly articulating words.

> be-lie (bi lī′), v.t.,-lied, -ly-ing. 1. to show to be false; contradict: His trembling hands belied his calm voice . . .

The entry indicates that the word *belie* has two syllables. The pronunciation key states that the first *e* should be pronounced like the *i* in *if,* the *u* in *busy,* or the *ee* in *been.* The *i,* according to the pronunciation key, should be pronounced like the *ye* in *lye,* the *i* in *ice,* or the *ais* in *aisle.* The accent mark (′) indicates which syllable should receive heavier emphasis. You should learn how to use the pronunciation key in a dictionary, but if you still have some misgivings about how to pronounce a word, you should ask your instructor for assistance.

Articulation—the production of sounds—is another important part of enunciation. Examples of articulation problems are when you order "dry toast" (without butter) and get "rye toast" or when you asked for a "missing statement" and get a "mission statement." More dangerous articulation problems occur when your pharmacist hears your doctor say "Lunesta" (a sleeping pill) instead of "Neulasta" (a cancer therapy drug).

articulation

The production of sounds; a component of enunciation.

Poor articulation is a problem when it occurs in your own presentation. Problems occur because we often articulate carelessly. Among the common articulation problems are the dropping of final consonants and "-ing" sounds ("goin'," "comin'," and "leavin'"), the substitution of "fer" for "for," and the substitution of "ta" for "to." An important objective in public presentations, as in all communication, is to articulate accurately.

Fluency

The sixth vocal characteristic of delivery is **fluency**—the smoothness of the delivery, the flow of the words, and the absence of vocalized pauses. Fluency cannot be achieved by looking up words in a dictionary or by any other simple solution. Fluency is not even very noticeable. Listeners are more likely to notice errors than to notice the seemingly effortless flow of words in a well-delivered speech. Also, you can be too fluent. A speaker who seems too glib is sometimes considered dishonest. One study showed the importance of fluency: The audiences tended to perceive the speaker's fluency and smoothness of presentation as a main determinant of effectiveness (Hayworth, 1942).

To achieve fluency, public speakers must be confident about the content of their speeches. If speakers know what they are going to say and have practiced the words over and over, then they reduce disruptive repetition and vocalized pauses. If speakers master what they are going to say and focus on the overall rhythm of the speech, their fluency improves. Speakers must pace, build, and time the various parts of the speech so that they unite in a coherent whole.

◄ SKILL BUILDER ►

In private with a roommate, spouse, or friend, deliver part of your speech. Have the other person hit a metal spoon on a glass every time you utter a vocalized pause ("umm," "ahh") or filler words ("you know," "whatever"). The idea is to make you highly aware of nonfluencies and to encourage you to eliminate them from your speech.

Vocal Variety

The seventh vocal aspect of speech delivery—one that summarizes many of the others—is **vocal variety.** This term refers to voice quality, intonation patterns, inflections of pitch, and syllabic duration. Public presentations encourage vocal variety because studies show that variety improves effectiveness. One of the founders of the National Communication Association, Charles Woolbert, in a very early study of public reading, found that audiences retain more information when there are large variations in rate, force, pitch, and voice quality. More recently, George Glasgow studied an audience's comprehension of prose and poetry and found that comprehension decreased 10% when the presenter delivered material in a monotone. Another study showed that audience members understand more when listening to skilled speakers than when listening to unskilled speakers. They also recall more information both immediately after the speech and at a later date. The skilled speakers are more effective, whether the material is organized or disorganized, easy or difficult. Good vocalization was also found to include fewer but longer pauses, greater ranges of pitch, and more upward and downward inflections (Beighley, 1952; Black, 1942; Glasgow, 1952; Woolbert, 1920).

Delivery is not something that you read about; delivery is something that you do. Here are some tips for how to improve your vocal delivery:

1. Choose one aspect of vocal delivery and work on that aspect until you are confident enough to move to another. Do you speak in monotone? Work on vocal variety until you are confident enough to move on to eliminating nonfluencies.
2. Practice these skills in everyday life. With communication skills the world is your laboratory: Practice improving your skills even when conversing with friends.
3. Be determined and focused about improvement. You took years to become what you are today, and you will not change unless you are determined to improve.
4. Recognize that your ability to express yourself has positive payoffs in interviews, job performance, and human relations. Learn how to become an articulate person, someone who not only knows something but knows how to communicate that knowledge to others.

Figure 13.1   Tips for improving vocal delivery.

Take a look at the tips for improving vocal delivery in Figure 13.1 before moving on to the next section on the bodily aspects of presentation.

TRY ◆ THIS

Try reading a few paragraphs from a story or poem to your spouse, roommate, or friend to test yourself on vocal aspects of delivery. Let your listener give you an opinion and advice about your oral reading skills. What are your strengths? Your weaknesses? What can you do to improve on the weaknesses and take advantage of the strengths?

The Bodily Aspects of Presentation

The four bodily aspects of presentation are gestures, facial expressions, eye contact, and movement. These nonverbal indicators of meaning show how speakers relate to audiences, just as they show how individuals relate to each other. When you observe two persons busily engaged in conversation, you judge their interest in the conversation without hearing their words. Similarly, in public speaking the nonverbal bodily aspects of delivery reinforce what the speaker is saying. Kramer and Lewis (1931) showed that audience members who can see the speaker comprehend more of the speech than do audience members who cannot see the speaker. Apparently, the speaker's bodily movements convey enough meaning to enhance the audience's understanding of the message. Figure 13.2 illustrates effective delivery behaviors.

Gestures

Gestures are movements of the head, arms, and hands used to illustrate, emphasize, or signal ideas in a speech. People rarely worry about gestures in conversation, but

gestures

Movements of the head, arms, and hands to illustrate, emphasize, or signal ideas in a presentation.

Effective delivery will not make a poorly prepared speech good, but it can make a well-prepared speech great. Effective delivery encompasses a variety of behaviors, including variations in pitch and volume. Nonvocal aspects of effective delivery include gestures, facial expressions, eye contact, and movement.

Consistent eye contact

Facial expressions

Body movement

Use of gestures

View an animation of this illustration on the *Online Learning Center.*

Figure 13.2   Effective delivery behaviors.

when they give a speech in front of an audience, arms and hands seem to be bothersome. Perhaps people feel unnatural because public speaking is an unfamiliar situation. Do you remember the first time you drove a car, the first time you tried to swim, or the first time you kissed? The first time you give a speech, you might not feel any more natural than you did then. Nonetheless, physically or artistically skilled people make their actions look easy. A skilled golfer, a talented painter, and a graceful dancer all perform with seeming ease. Beginners make a performance look difficult. Apparently, we have to work diligently to make physical or artistic feats look easy.

What can you do to help yourself gesture naturally when you deliver your presentation? The answer lies in feelings and practice. When representatives from Mothers Against Drunk Driving (MADD) deliver speeches protesting lax laws on driving while intoxicated, they frequently present with sincerity and strong gestures. They also look very natural. The main reason for their natural delivery may be their feelings about the issue they are discussing. They are upset, and they show their emotion in their words and movements. They are mainly concerned with getting their message across. You can also deliver a speech more naturally by concentrating on getting the message across. Self-conscious attention to your gestures is often self-defeating—the gestures look studied, rehearsed, or slightly out of rhythm with your message. Selecting a topic you find involving can have the unexpected benefit of improving your delivery, especially if you concentrate on your audience and your message.

Hand gestures reinforce the verbal message.

1. Keep your hands out of your pockets and at your sides when not gesturing.
2. Do not lean on the lectern.
3. Gesture with the hand not holding your notes.
4. Make your gestures deliberate—big and broad enough so that they do not look accidental or timid.
5. Keep your gestures meaningful by using them sparingly and only when they reinforce something you are saying.
6. Practice your gestures just as you do the rest of your speech so that you become comfortable with the words and gestures.
7. Make your gestures appear natural and spontaneous.

Figure 13.3   Tips for gesturing effectively.

SOURCE: Gamble and Gamble, 2005

To see examples of effective delivery, watch "Using a Vivid Image" on the *Online Learning Center* at www.mhhe.com/pearson3.

Another way of learning to make appropriate gestures is to practice a speech in front of friends who are willing to make positive suggestions. Constructive criticism is also one of the benefits you can receive from your speech instructor and your classmates. Actors spend hours rehearsing lines and gestures so that they will look spontaneous and unrehearsed on stage. In time, and after many practice sessions, public speakers learn which arm, head, and hand movements seem to help and which seem to hinder their message. Through practice you too can learn to gesture naturally, in a way that reinforces, rather than detracts from, your message (see Figure 13.3).

Facial Expressions

Another physical aspect of delivery is facial expression. Your face is the most expressive part of your body. **Facial expressions** consist of the nonverbal cues expressed by the speaker's face. Eyebrows rise and fall; eyes twinkle, glare, and cry; lips pout or smile; cheeks can dimple or harden; and a chin can jut out in anger or recede in yielding. Some people's faces are a barometer of their feelings; others' faces seem to maintain the same appearance whether they are happy or sad or in pain. Because you do not ordinarily see your own face when you are speaking, you may not be fully aware of how you appear when you give a speech. In general, speakers are trying to maintain a warm and positive relationship with the audience, and they signal that intent by smiling as they would in conversation with someone they like. However, the topic, the speaker's intent, the situation, and the audience all help determine the appropriate facial expressions in a public speech. You can discover the appropriateness of your facial expressions by having friends, relatives, or classmates tell you how you look when practicing your speech. You can also observe how your instructors use facial expressions to communicate.

facial expressions

Any nonverbal cues expressed by the speaker's face.

Eye Contact

Another physical aspect of delivery important to the public speaker is eye contact. **Eye contact** refers to the extent to which the speaker looks directly at the audience. Too much eye contact—"staring down the audience"—is too much of a good thing, but too much gazing at notes—lack of eye contact—is poor delivery.

eye contact

The extent to which a speaker looks directly at the audience.

Audiences prefer maintenance of good eye contact (Cobin, 1962), and good eye contact improves source credibility (Beebe, 1974). Such conclusions are particularly important since individuals in other cultures may view eye contact differently. A presenter from another country may be viewed less positively by an American audience than she would be in her native country. Similarly, Americans need to recognize and appreciate cultural differences in eye contact as well as other nonverbal cues.

Eye contact is one of the ways people indicate to others how they feel about them. People are wary of others who do not look them in the eye during a conversation. Similarly, in public speaking, eye contact conveys your relationship with your audience. The public speaker who rarely or never looks at audience members may appear disinterested in them, and the audience may resent being ignored. The public speaker who looks over the heads of audience members or scans them so quickly that eye contact is not established may appear to be afraid of the audience. The proper relationship between audience and speaker is one of purposeful communication. You signal that sense of purpose by treating audience members as individuals with whom you wish to communicate—by looking at them for responses to your message.

How can you learn to maintain eye contact with your audience? One way is to know your speech so well that you have to glance only occasionally at your notes. The speaker who does not know the speech well is manuscript-bound. Delivering an extemporaneous speech from key-words or an outline is a way of encouraging yourself to keep an eye on the audience. One of the purposes of extemporaneous delivery is to enable you to adapt to your audience. That adaptation is not possible unless you are continually observing the audience's behavior to see if your listeners appear to understand your message.

Other ways of learning to use eye contact include scanning your entire audience and addressing various sections as you progress through your speech. Concentrating on the head nodders (not sleepers but affirmers) may also improve your eye contact. In almost every audience, some individuals overtly indicate whether your message is coming across. These individuals usually nod yes or no with their heads—thus the name *nodders*. Some speakers find that friendly faces and positive nodders improve their delivery.

MYTHS, METAPHORS, & MISUNDERSTANDINGS

Beginning speakers often assume that only one particular style of delivery is effective. Although we see many similarities in how political figures deliver speeches, most of us do not speak in front of audiences each day, nor do we have people helping us write our speeches. What counts as effective delivery changes from one audience to another and from one speaker to another. Effective speakers are aware of their own speaking style and understand the expectations of their audience so that they can adapt their delivery accordingly.

bodily movement

What the speaker does with his or her entire body during a presentation.

Movement

A fourth physical aspect of delivery is **bodily movement**—what the speaker does with his or her entire body during a presentation. Sometimes the situation limits movement. The presence of a fixed microphone, a lectern, a pulpit, or any other physical feature of the environment may limit your activity. The length of the speech can also make a difference. A short speech without movement is less difficult for both speaker and audience than is a very long speech.

Good movement is appropriate and purposeful. The "caged lion" who paces back and forth to work off anxiety is moving inappropriately and purposelessly in relation to the content of the presentation. You should move for a reason, such as walking a few steps when delivering a transition, thereby literally helping your audience to "follow you" to the next idea. Some speakers move forward on the points they regard as most important.

Because of the importance of eye contact, the speaker should always strive to face the audience, even when moving. Some other suggestions on movement relate to the use of visual aids. Speakers who write on the chalkboard during a speech have to turn their backs on the audience. Avoid turning your back by writing information on the board between classes, by preparing a poster, ahead of time, or by using an overhead projector.

You can learn through practice and observation. Watch your professors, teaching assistants, and fellow students when they deliver their speeches to determine what works for them. They may provide positive or negative examples. Similarly, you need to determine what works best for you when you practice your speech. The form in Table 13.1 can be used to evaluate nonverbal delivery.

TABLE 13.1 EVALUATION FORM FOR NONVERBAL ASPECTS OF DELIVERY

To summarize the material on vocal and bodily aspects of delivery, you should examine the sample evaluation form below. Use this scale to evaluate yourself and others on each of the following items: 1 = excellent, 2 = good, 3 = average, 4 = fair, 5 = weak.

VOCAL ASPECTS OF DELIVERY—THE VOICE

_____ Pitch: upward and downward inflections

_____ Rate: speed of delivery

_____ Pause: appropriate use of silence

_____ Volume: loudness of the voice

_____ Enunciation: articulation and pronunciation

_____ Fluency: smoothness of delivery

_____ Vocal variety: overall effect of all of the above

BODILY ASPECTS OF DELIVERY

_____ Gestures: use of arms and hands

_____ Facial expression: use of the face

_____ Eye contact: use of eyes

_____ Movement: use of legs and feet

Delivery Tips for Non-Native Speakers

If you are a student who speaks English as a second language, you may be particularly concerned about your delivery. After all, you must simultaneously try to remember what you want to say and try to select the appropriate words and pronounce them correctly. These concerns will differ greatly from one person to another depending on how comfortable you are with your topic and spoken English. Here are some suggestions for how to work on delivery issues that may be of unique concern to you:

1. *Recognize that you are not alone.* For most speakers the actual delivery of the speech is what causes the most anxiety. Even native speakers worry that they will forget what they intend to say or that they will say something incorrectly. If you have anxiety about delivery, your classmates will certainly empathize with you.

2. *Give yourself time.* Most of the other suggestions on this list require that you have some extra time to devote to improving your delivery. This means that you may need to begin working on your speeches much earlier in comparison to many of your classmates.

3. *Check pronunciation.* With several online pronunciation dictionaries, you can look up words and hear them pronounced. For new and unfamiliar words or words with many syllables, such resources can help you determine and practice correct pronunciation.

4. *Talk with your instructor about reasonable goals.* If you are still working on several pronunciation or grammar issues, you can use your public-speaking class as an opportunity to improve. With your instructor's help, identify a short list of items that you can work on over the course of the term. Your practice efforts will be more focused, and your instructor will have a clearer idea of what to concentrate on when giving feedback. If you do not set such objectives beforehand, both you and your instructor may have difficulty concentrating on specific and attainable areas for improvement.

5. *Understand that eye contact is important.* Especially if you come from a culture that does not emphasize eye contact, you should recognize that American audiences tend to weight this nonverbal delivery characteristic very heavily. To improve your eye contact, you should first get more comfortable maintaining eye contact during conversation. As your eye contact improves during one-on-one interactions, you can then work on better eye contact during speeches.

6. *Practice using audio or video recordings.* By listening to and/or watching yourself, you will be better able to isolate specific ways to improve your delivery. While observing a recording, make a list of two to four things you could do to improve your delivery, and then practice the speech, again focusing on those items.

How Can You Reduce Your Fear of Presenting?

We consider fear of presenting at this point because fear results in delivery problems. Effective presenters do not exhibit signs of anxiety. They do not shake, sweat, look at the floor, or appear afraid. If a speaker does appear on the verge of a nervous breakdown, the audience feels so sorry for him or her that they entirely miss the message.

Nearly everyone experiences some fear when presenting in front of an audience. In fact, more people fear public speaking than fear death (Wallechinshy, Wallace, & Wallace, 1997). Comedian Jerry Seinfeld once quipped that because of the widespread fear of public speaking, more people at a funeral would choose to be the person in the casket than the person speaking beside the casket. Beginning speakers often feel fear before and during their early presentations. Even experienced speakers sometimes feel fear when they face a new audience or a new situation. With fear being such a common occurrence, we need to look at some ways to reduce and control any fear of presenting.

The person who has studied this subject the most, James McCroskey (1997), calls fear of presenting **communication apprehension (CA),** defined as "an individual's level of fear or anxiety associated with either real or anticipated communication with another person or persons" (p. 78). Symptoms of CA include sleeplessness, worry, and reluctance before you present and "interfering, off-task thoughts" while you present (Greene, Rucker, Zauss, & Harris, 1988). Having "off-task thoughts" means losing focus on communicating your message to your audience, thinking instead about sweaty palms, shaking knees, and "cotton mouth," the feeling that your tongue is swollen and your mouth is as dry as the Sahara. One wit noted that public speakers suffer so often from wet palms and dry mouth that they should stick their hands in their mouth.

communication apprehension

An individual's level of fear or anxiety associated with either real or anticipated communication with another person or persons.

What else do we know about CA? The individuals with the most extreme levels of anxiety "show the largest improvement in perceived competence" (MacIntyre & MacDonald, 1998) when they take a public-speaking course. This large measure of improvement is, of course, a key reason for the shy, uncommunicative person to take the course. On the other hand, the person with very high CA still is unlikely to emerge as the star of the public-speaking classroom because others in the class already see themselves as fairly high in competence. Individuals with high CA may even set themselves up for lower grades in public speaking. Daly, Vangelisti, and Weber (1995) found that students high in anxiety exhibited "less audience adaptation, less concern for equipment likely to be available when the speech was presented, less concern about the tools available to aid in preparing the speech, more difficulty in coming up with information for speeches, and greater self-doubts about their capability as a speaker" (p. 394). So, even though a person with high CA might show the greatest improvement in perceived competence, that person still may have more doubts about his or her capability than do others and may not prepare successful performances.

Suggested Techniques for Reducing Your Fear

Fear of presenting is similar to other fears in life: You cannot overcome the fear unless you have a desire to do so. Fortunately, you can reduce fear in many ways, including the following:

skills approach

Reducing fear by systematically improving your presenting skills.

- The **skills approach** reduces fear by systematically improving your presenting skills. Rubin, Rubin, and Jordan (1997) demonstrated that taking a course in public speaking results in greater positive changes than those experienced by other students.

cognitive modification approach

Using positive thinking to bolster the beginning speaker's confidence.

visualization approach

Picturing yourself succeeding.

relaxation approach

Combining deep relaxation with fear-inducing thoughts.

- The **cognitive modification approach** bolsters the beginning speaker's confidence through positive thinking (see Motley, 1995). This technique invites you to substitute positive thoughts for negative ones. Changing the way you think about yourself and your performance ("I can do this assignment, and I can do it well") can actually improve your presentation (Robinson, 1997).

- The **visualization approach** involves picturing yourself succeeding (Ayres & Hopf, 1987). You already do this before almost every important event in your life (going on a first date, proposing, meeting the in-laws, interviewing for a job), so this approach is just a new application of a technique you have used before.

- The **relaxation approach** means combining deep relaxation with fear-inducing thoughts (Friedrich & Goss, 1984). Although you can do this by yourself, another person, such as a facilitator, usually provides the commands. The facilitator asks you to relax (actually lying down helps) and to think of a situation in which you are totally unstressed. The facilitator links your relaxed state to a word like "calm." After repeating this process, you start relaxing when you hear the word (you have been conditioned). The facilitator then walks you through whatever frightens you ("You are now walking to the front of the room") and says "calm" at the first signs of fright. This approach takes time, but the procedure does work for most people with high anxiety about presenting. See Figure 13.4 for an example of this relaxation technique.

To practice the relaxation techniques, do the following:

1. Sit in a comfortable chair or lie down in a comfortable place. As much as possible, rid the area of distracting noises. If possible, play relaxing music or a tape with the sounds of nature.
2. Begin with your face and neck, and tense the muscles. Then relax them. Tense again and hold the tensed position for 10 seconds. Relax again.
3. Tense your hands by clenching your fists. Relax. Tense again and hold for 10 seconds. Relax.
4. Tense your arms above your hands and to your shoulders. Relax. Tense again and hold for 10 seconds. Relax.
5. Tense your chest and stomach. Relax. Tense again and hold for 10 seconds. Relax.
6. Tense your feet by pulling the toes under. Relax. Tense again and hold for 10 seconds. Relax.
7. Tense your legs above the feet and up to the hips. Relax. Tense again and hold for 10 seconds. Relax.
8. Tense your entire body and hold for 10 seconds. Relax and breathe slowly.
9. Repeat the word *calm* to yourself. This will help you relate the word to the relaxed feeling you are now experiencing. In the future, when you feel anxious, the word *calm* should help you arrest the apprehension you experience.

Figure 13.4 Calming normal communication apprehension.
SOURCE: Gamble and Gamble, 2005

- The **self-managed approach** means that you reduce your fear of presenting with self-diagnosis and a variety of therapies. In other words, you attempt to uncover your fears and then decide what approach might reduce them. Dwyer (2000) points out that many therapies can reduce your fears, but no one therapy works for all people. You might decide that group therapy with a psychologist at the health service center would work best for you. Or you might decide that just taking a public-speaking course will help you overcome your fear of presenting.

self-managed approach

Reducing the fear of presenting with self-diagnosis and a variety of therapies.

What Are Visual Resources?

Do you learn best when you read something, when you watch something, or when you do something? Certainly, some skills are best learned by doing. Reading about how to insert streaming video into a PowerPoint presentation or watching another person perform the task is no substitute for trying to perform the task yourself. However, not everything lends itself to doing. You cannot "do" economics in the same way you can change a tire. Because so much of public speaking deals with issues and topics that cannot be performed, you must know the most effective methods of communicating in a public presentation.

To determine if people remember best through telling alone, through showing alone, or through both showing and telling, researchers measured retention 3 hours and 3 days after a communication attempt (Zayas-Boya, 1977–1978). The results follow:

METHOD	RETENTION 3 HOURS LATER	RETENTION 3 DAYS LATER
TELLING ALONE	70%	10%
SHOWING ALONE	72	20
SHOWING AND TELLING	85	65

Apparently, people retain information longer when they receive the message both through their eyes *and* through their ears. Audiences that remember a message because the visual resources helped their comprehension are more persuaded by the presentation than are audiences that do not see visual resources.

Students sometimes think that public-speaking instructors like them to use visual resources, but they will not use visual resources for public speaking outside the classroom. In fact, the use of visual resources is big business. Can you imagine an architect trying to explain to a board of directors how the new building will look without using models, drawings, and computer graphics? Can you envision a business presentation without PowerPoint? Can you sell most products without showing them? Apparently, the skillful use of visual resources is an expectation in the world of business and industry. The place to learn how to use visual resources is in the classroom.

What are **visual resources**? They are any items that can be seen by an audience for the purpose of reinforcing a message, from the way you dress, to words on the chalkboard, to items brought in to show what you are talking about. A student who wears a police uniform when talking about careers in law enforcement, one who provides a handout with an outline of her speech for the class, and yet another who brings in chemistry equipment are all using visual resources.

visual resources

Any items that can be seen by an audience for the purpose of reinforcing a message.

TRY ◄ THIS

Are you especially good at something that could enhance your presentation? Can you draw, sing, play an instrument, take photos, or create a PowerPoint presentation? Sometimes your own talents and abilities can greatly strengthen your presentation.

The Uses of Visual Resources

One of the main reasons for using visual resources has already been stated: People tend to learn and retain more when they both see and listen. The effective speaker knows when words alone will be insufficient to carry the message. Some messages are more effectively communicated through sight, touch, smell, and taste. Use visual resources when they reduce complexity for easier understanding (such as when you are explaining many or complex statistics or ideas) and when they support your message better than words (such as when you display a bar graph showing the increasing costs of home ownership). The use of visual resources demands that you become sensitive to what an audience will be unable to understand only through your words.

Visual resources are not appropriate for all speeches at all times. In fact, because they take preparation and planning, they may be impossible to use in many impromptu situations. Also, visual resources should not be used for their own sake. Having visual resources is no virtue unless they help the audience understand your message or unless they contribute in another way to your purpose.

Visual resources should be visible to the audience only when needed and should be removed from sight during the rest of the presentation. Otherwise, visual resources can become a distraction that steals the focus from you. See Figure 13.5 for additional tips on the use of visual resources.

Visual resources, like the facts in your speech, may require documentation. You should either show on the visual resource itself or tell the audience directly where you got the visual resource or the information on it.

---

1. Do not talk to your visual resources. Keep your eyes on your audience.
2. Display visual resources only when you are using them. Before or after they are discussed, they usually become a needless distraction to the audience.
3. Make sure everyone in the room can see your visual resources. Check the visibility of your visual resources before your speech, during practice. If the classroom is 25 feet deep, have a friend or family member determine if the visual resources can be read from 25 feet away. Above all, make sure you are not standing in front of your visual resources.
4. Leave visual resources in front of the audience long enough for complete assimilation. Few things are more irritating to an audience than to have half-read visual resources whipped away by a speaker.
5. Use a pointer or your inside arm for pointing to visual resources. The pointer keeps you from masking the visual, and using your inside arm helps you to avoid closing off your body from the audience.

Figure 13.5   Tips for using visual resources.

Types of Visual Resources

An effective presenter chooses carefully the visual resources that will reinforce the message. Following are various ways that presenters can render their messages more effective.

PowerPoint Presentations

Just as Googling is one of the most common ways to find information, PowerPoint is one of the most common means of presenting information and images. The upside of this Microsoft software is that PowerPoint offers great advantages to anyone making a presentation by providing text, images, video, sound, and graphics. The downside is that too often the slide show, with its dazzling technological features, becomes the presentation while the speaker stays hidden in the shadows, with barely a voice-over to indicate his or her presence. While you are learning public-speaking skills, you should use PowerPoint as a resource, not *the* source of the presentation, which should be you. See Figure 13.6 for some tips for using PowerPoint.

In a presentation on global warming, the speaker used this photo of a melting glacier from http://news.nationalgeographic.com/news/2004/12/.

Computer Graphics

Some of the tips in Figure 13.6 can serve you well when you use computer-generated graphics. Google and other Internet providers can furnish you with images of almost

Follow the suggestions below and watch "Using Internet Graphics" and "Presenting a PowerPoint Build" on the *Online Learning Center*.

1. Be very careful *not* to use too much text on each slide; lots of space with a simple background works best.
2. Leave slides in sight long enough for your audience to absorb their content (they will be visually and audibly upset if you pull a slide before they are ready).
3. Use the on-screen text as your notes instead of looking down and trying to read them in a semidarkened room (while mainly maintaining eye contact with your audience).
4. Use at least 36-point type for headings or titles and at least 24-point type for the remainder while avoiding all-caps because they are too bold.
5. Use the same colors throughout: light letters on dark background.
6. Use bullets, not numbers.
7. Vary your slides—some text, some images, some graphics—to keep your presentation lively and interesting.
8. Practice your presentation, preferably in the room in which you will present.
9. Have a backup plan in case of technological failure.

Figure 13.6   Tips for using PowerPoint.

anything. Go to Google and click on "Images," for example, and then type in what kind of images you seek. Type in the word "food," and you will get 2.2 million possible images that can be downloaded for your presentation. These days any student who knows her way around her computer's software can locate and reproduce photos, drawings, and art. Furthermore, she can create graphs from numbers and convert data into pie, line, or bar graphs. The latter can be blown up into very large images on a photocopier. Figure 13.7 shows examples of a bar graph, a pie chart, and a line graph, the kinds of graphics you can find on the Internet.

Video

Today everyone is a photographer and a videographer because cameras are everywhere, including in your phone. Not only that but you have easy access to video clips on the Internet. You can find movie "trailers" that illustrate your point, as well as video bits of everything from giggling babies to obedient dogs.

Photos and videos will enhance your presentation as long as you use them to reinforce and to illustrate, not to replace you as the main attraction. A student spiced up his informative presentation on the high cost of automobile repair by using a brief video in his introduction that showed a "before" view of his wrecked car, another brief video in the body of his presentation showing how a repair shop replaces a windshield, and a final brief video in his conclusion showing his newly repaired vehicle—with the bill for services rendered. Even though he used video to reinforce the main points of his presentation, he maintained eye contact with his audience and made sure that he was not a sideshow to the slide show.

Chalkboards and Slick Boards

Advantages

- These can be used to convey any statistic, fact, or detail that is difficult to communicate orally.
- These can be used to show words with which the audience is unfamiliar.
- These can be used to cue you, as in a key-word outline.

Disadvantages

- Writing on the board means your back is to the audience, so it's best to have the writing on the board before you speak.
- Unless you practice, you may find that writing on the board is difficult because you need to write large and legibly.

Cautions

- Bring your own slick board marker lest the ones at the board are dried out.
- Make sure that chalk is available lest you find none when you need it.
- Angle the chalk so it does not emit a cringe-inducing squeal on the board.

Posters

Advantages

- Posters can be prepared ahead of time to provide visual images or information.
- Posters can cue you about content without sacrificing eye contact.

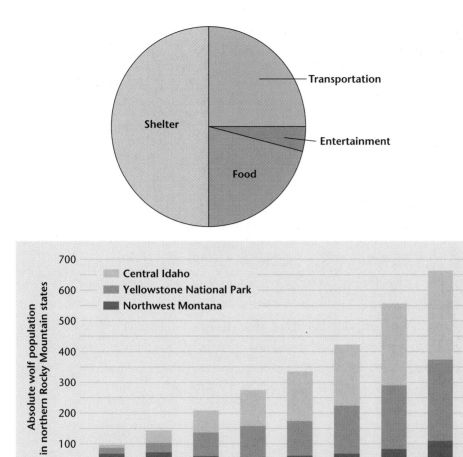

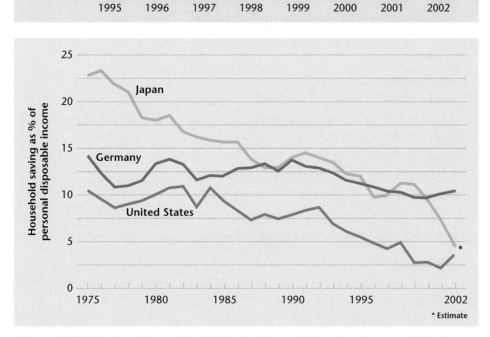

Figure 13.7   Pie charts, bar graphs, and line graphs can help your audience understand amounts, ratios, and proportions.

Disadvantages

* Few posters are big enough to be seen by all.
* Posters cannot and should not hold much text.

Cautions

* Keep your eyes on your audience, not on your poster.
* Keep messages and images simple and easy to convey.

Opaque and Overhead Projectors

Advantages

* Opaque projections can show objects enlarged on the screen.
* Overhead projections can show text or images on transparencies for all to see.
* Both can show text that you can use for cues instead of notes.
* Both allow for prior preparation or for use during a presentation.

Disadvantages

* Both work best with dim lights, which reduces eye contact with the audience.
* If you need the lights dimmed and brightened, you need a helper.

Cautions

* Have a backup plan because equipment can fail.

Handouts

Advantages

* An outline of your presentation provides notes for you and for the audience.
* An outline invites the audience to participate in your presentation.
* A handout can provide information too detailed to explain in a brief presentation.

Disadvantages

* The audience may read the handout instead of listening to you.
* Unless you print something important in your handout, the listeners trash the room with them.

Cautions

* Compose any handout carefully; spelling and grammar errors can reduce your credibility.

Blackboard and Other Electronic Connections

Advantages

* Your instructor can post your outline or handout for your audience to read or download.
* If your class has a chat room or discussion board, you can use those opportunities to analyze your audience or test for interest in your topic.

Disadvantages

- Your instructor may be the only person authorized to place items.
- Your instructor may not want to act as broker for every person who wants to post something for the class.

Cautions

- Be aware that some students ignore their electronic connections.
- Recognize that others may not have easy access to the system.

People and Other Living Things

Advantages

- A person or animal used as a visual resource can gain and maintain attention.
- A person or animal can provide an excellent example for your presentation.

Disadvantages

- People as visual aids are not completely controllable, and animals, snakes, and spiders are even less controllable.
- Your visual resource may detract from your presentation.

Cautions

- Be aware that universities and colleges may have rules about people (nonstudents) and animals on campus.

An oil worker could present wearing attire from his job to reinforce his credibility in an informative presentation on oil production.

You as a Visual Resource

Advantages

- You can dress in ways that reinforce your message, such as a uniform, a lab coat, or professional attire.
- You can wear pins, badges, T-shirts, hats, caps, and helmets that contribute to your message.

Disadvantages

- You might look great for your speech but ridiculous on campus.

Cautions

- Remember that your attire or lack thereof can detract from your purpose.

Some Final Cautions

- Recognize that many campuses have rules prohibiting alcohol, so using cans or bottles of beer or booze as a visual resource could be problematic.

1. Practice your presentation so that you can deliver your message with only occasional glances at your notes.
2. Keep your eyes on your audience so that you can sense whether you are communicating your message.
3. Use facial expressions, gestures, and movements to help communicate your message.
4. Use your voice like a musical instrument to keep the sounds interesting and to affect the audience's response.
5. Speak loudly enough for audience members to hear, slowly enough so that they can understand you, and smoothly enough so that they do not focus on your faults.
6. Use visual images to communicate material not easily understood through listening.
7. Make your writing on the chalkboard or on posters large enough for all to see and simple enough for all to understand.
8. Consider using photographs, drawings, live models, objects, slides, films, handouts, videos, and yourself to help communicate your message.
9. Sound conversational, look natural, and strive to communicate your message to your listeners.
10. Observe how your classmates, instructors, and other speakers deliver their presentations so that you can learn from them.

Figure 13.8   More tips for effective presentation.

- Be aware that few campuses allow firearms, even disassembled ones, as a visual resource for a classroom presentation.
- Note that health and safety regulations prohibit chemicals and living things that can sting, bite, or poison human beings.
- When in doubt about using a particular visual resource, check with your instructor.

Figure 13.8 lists some final tips for effective presentation.

Chapter Review & Study Guide

SUMMARY

In this chapter you learned the following:

▶ Four modes of delivery are:
- The extemporaneous mode, whereby the speech is carefully prepared but appears relatively spontaneous and conversational.
- The impromptu mode, which actually is spontaneous and without specific preparation.
- The manuscript mode, whereby the presenter uses a script throughout delivery.
- The memorized mode, which employs a script committed to memory.

▶ Vocal aspects of delivery include:
- Pitch—the highness or lowness of the presenter's voice.
- Rate—the speed of delivery.
- Pauses—the purposeful silence to invite thought or response.
- Volume—the loudness of the presenter's voice.
- Enunciation—the pronunciation and articulation of words.
- Fluency—the smoothness of delivery.
- Vocal variety—voice quality, intonation patterns, inflections, and syllabic duration.

▶ Bodily aspects of delivery include:
- Gestures—movement of the head, arms, and hands.
- Eye contact—sustained and meaningful attention to the eyes and faces of audience members.
- Facial expressions—the variety of messages the face can convey.
- Movement—the motion by the entire body but especially purposeful movement by the feet.

▶ A number of advantages, disadvantages, and cautions are associated with visual resources that reinforce the message, including:
- PowerPoint.
- Computer graphics.
- Video.
- Chalkboards.
- Slick boards.
- Posters.
- Opaque projectors.
- Overhead projectors.
- Handouts.
- Blackboard and other electronic connections.
- People and animals.
- Yourself.

KEY TERMS

Go to the *Online Learning Center* at **www.mhhe.com/pearson3** to further your understanding of the following terminology.

Articulation	Fluency	Relaxation approach
Bodily movement	Gestures	Self-managed approach
Communication apprehension	Impromptu mode	Skills approach
Cognitive modification approach	Manuscript mode	Visual resources
Delivery	Memorized mode	Visualization approach
Enunciation	Pause	Vocal variety
Extemporaneous mode	Pitch	Vocalized pauses
Eye contact	Pronunciation	
Facial expression	Rate	

STUDY QUESTIONS

1. Which mode of delivery encourages you to improvise and speak without previous research or preparation?
   a. extemporaneous
   b. impromptu
   c. manuscript
   d. memorized

2. A disadvantage of a presentation delivered in the memorized mode is
   a. the need to create carefully prepared notes
   b. a lack of practice
   c. a lack of eye contact
   d. the removal of spontaneity and the danger of forgetting

3. "Ummmms" or "aahhhhs" that disrupt a speaker's fluency are termed
   a. vocalized pauses
   b. enunciation
   c. articulation
   d. pitch

4. _____ is the highness or lowness of a speaker's voice, and _____ refers to the smoothness of delivery and flow of words.
   a. Volume; rate
   b. Pitch; fluency
   c. Rate; vocal variety
   d. Pitch; enunciation

5. Gestures are movements of the head, arms, and hands
   a. used to improve source credibility
   b. that appear rehearsed and out-of rhythm
   c. used to illustrate, emphasize, or signal ideas
   d. that convey a relationship with the audience

6. With regard to movement, the speaker should
   a. pace back and forth
   b. move without purpose
   c. move backwards when introducing an important point
   d. avoid turning his or her back to the audience

7. If you are nervous or anxious about giving your presentation, you may be experiencing
   a. gestures
   b. communication apprehension

c. cognitive modification
d. audience adaptation

8. Why are visual resources used?
   a. Speakers do not need to prepare as much because they can just read their PowerPoint.
   b. They are appropriate for all types of speeches.
   c. People tend to learn and retain more when they both see and listen.
   d. They are fun to watch.

9. When using PowerPoint, you should
   a. use a lot of text on each slide
   b. move the slides quickly because the audience will get bored
   c. vary your slides to keep the presentation interesting
   d. utilize all color combinations

10. Which visual resource can be used to show objects enlarged on a screen and can show text on transparencies but usually works best with the lights dimmed?
    a. opaque and overhead projectors
    b. posters
    c. video
    d. chalkboards

Answers:
1. (b); 2. (d); 3. (a); 4. (b); 5. (c); 6. (d); 7. (b); 8. (c); 9. (c); 10. (a)

CRITICAL THINKING

1. The next time you see your favorite late-night television host deliver the monologue, evaluate his or her delivery. Assess both vocal and bodily aspects of delivery.

2. In your classes, which types of visual resources do you benefit from the most? Which ones are not as useful?

SELF-QUIZ

For further review, try the chapter self-quiz on the *Online Learning Center* at **www.mhhe.com/pearson3**.

REFERENCES

Ayres, J., & Hopf, T. S. (1987). Visualization, systematic desensitization, and relational emotive therapy: A comparative evaluation. *Communication Education, 36,* 236–240.

Beebe, S. A. (1974). Eye contact: A nonverbal determinant of speaker credibility. *Speech Teacher, 23,* 21–25.

Beighley, K. C. (1952). An experimental study of the effect of four speech variables on listener comprehension. *Speech Monographs, 19,* 249–258.

Bettinghaus, E. (1961). The operation of congruity in an oral communication situation. *Speech Monographs, 28,* 131–142.

Black, J. W. (1942). A study of voice merit. *Quarterly Journal of Speech, 28,* 67–74.

Cobin, M. (1962). Response to eye contact. *Quarterly Journal of Speech, 48,* 415–418.

Daly, J. A., Vangelisti, A. L., Neel, H. L., & Cavanaugh, P. D. (1989). Pre-performance concerns associated with public speaking anxiety. *Communication Quarterly, 37,* 39–53.

Daly, J. A., Vangelisti, A. L., & Weber, D. J. (1995). Speech anxiety affects how people prepare speeches: A protocol analysis of the preparation processes of speakers. *Communication Monographs, 62,* 383–397.

Dwyer, K. K. (2000). The multidimensional model: Teaching students to self-manage high communication apprehension by self-selecting treatments. *Communication Education, 49,* 72–81.

Friedrich, G., & Goss, B. (1984). Systematic desensitization. In J. A. Daly & J. C. McCroskey (Eds.), *Avoiding communication: Shyness, reticence, and communication apprehension* (pp. 173–188). Beverly Hills, CA: Sage.

Gilkinson, H., & Knower, F. H. (1941). Individual differences among students of speech as revealed by psychological test—I. *Journal of Educational Psychology, 32,* 161–175.

Glasgow, G. M. (1952). A semantic index of vocal pitch. *Speech Monographs, 19,* 64–68.

Greene, J. O., Rucker, M. P., Zauss, E. S., & Harris, A. A. (1998). Communication anxiety and the acquisition of message-production skill. *Communication Education, 47,* 337–347.

Gundersen, D. G., & Hopper, R. (1976). Relationships between speech delivery and speech effectiveness. *Speech Monographs, 43,* 158–165.

Hayworth, D. (1942). A search for facts on the teaching of public speaking. *Quarterly Journal of Speech, 28,* 247–254.

Henrikson, E. H. (1944). An analysis of the characteristics of some "good" and "poor" speakers. *Speech Monographs, 11,* 120–124.

Hildebrandt, H. W., & Stephens, W. (1963). Manuscript and extemporaneous delivery in communicating information. *Speech Monographs, 30,* 369–372.

Kramer, E. J. J., & Lewis, T. R. (1931). Comparison of visual and nonvisual listening. *Journal of Communication, 1,* 16–20.

MacIntyre, P. D., & MacDonald, J. R. (1998). Public speaking anxiety: Perceived competence and audience congeniality. *Communication Education, 47,* 359–365.

McCroskey, J. C. (1997). Oral communication apprehension: A summary of recent theory and research. *Human Communication Research, 4,* 78–96.

Motley, M. T. (1995). *Overcoming your fear of public speaking: A proven method.* New York: McGraw-Hill Custom Series.

Petrie, C. R., Jr. (1963). Informative speaking: A summary and bibliography of related research. *Speech Monographs, 30,* 81.

Robinson, T. E., II (1997). Communication apprehension and the basic public speaking course: A national survey of in-class treatment techniques. *Communication Education, 46,* 188–197.

Rubin, R. B., Rubin, A. M., & Jordan, F. F. (1997). Effects of instruction on communication apprehension and communication competence. *Communication Education, 46,* 101–114.

Vohs, J. L. (1964). An empirical approach to the concept of attention. *Speech Monographs, 31,* 355–360.

Wallechinshy, D., Wallace, I., & Wallace, A. (1977). *The people's almanac presents the book of lists.* New York: Morrow.

Woolbert, C. (1920). The effects of various modes of public reading. *Journal of Applied Psychology, 4,* 162–185.

Zayas-Boya, E. P. (1977–1978). Instructional media in the total language picture. *International Journal of Instructional Media, 5,* 145–150.

ADDITIONAL RESOURCES

Edwards, M. (1992). "Now presenting . . ." (use of visual aids during sales presentations). *Sales & Marketing Management, 14,* 23–24.

Pierson, W. S. (1993). Talking through your eyes. *American Salesman, 10,* 21–24.

Pogatos, F. (Ed.). (1992). *Advances in nonverbal communication: Sociocultural, clinical, esthetic, and literary perspectives.* Philadelphia: Benjamin.

Rader, S. (1997). www.nvgc.vt.edu/support/fall97.html.

CHAPTER FOURTEEN

Informative Presentations

What will you learn?

When you have read and thought about this chapter, you will be able to:

1. Recognize the goals of informative presentations.
2. Identify topics appropriate for informative speaking.
3. Provide examples of immediate behavioral purposes for an informative presentation.
4. Define concepts related to informative speaking, such as information hunger, information relevance, extrinsic motivation, informative content, and information overload.
5. Use the skills of defining, describing, explaining, narrating, and demonstrating in an informative presentation.

The goal of informative presentations is to enhance an audience's knowledge and understanding of a topic. In this chapter you will learn how to choose topics for an informative speech and how to develop behavioral purposes for them. The chapter discusses techniques that will help you effectively present an informational speech to an audience. Effective informative speakers demonstrate certain skills that contribute to their effectiveness, so the chapter covers the skills of defining, describing, explaining, narrating, and demonstrating. Finally, the chapter includes an example of an informative presentation.

Career diplomat **David Firestein** was invited to deliver a speech on the 2004 presidential election at the Patrick Henry Library in Virginia. He could have chosen to give a straightforward review of the major events of the campaign, culminating in the defeat of Senator John Kerry and the re-election of President George W. Bush. But this was information that most people already knew. Firestein decided to take a different approach.

He analyzed why President Bush may have won the election by focusing on something unusual—country music. His speech examined the relative numbers, or density, of country music stations in "red states" (voting for Bush) as compared to "blue states" (voting for Kerry). Based on these statistics, Firestein concluded that the density of country music stations correlated strongly not only with which way the state voted but also with the margin of victory. In other words, those states with the most country music stations voted for Bush over Kerry and by wider margins than states with fewer country music stations.

Why would there be such a correlation? Firestein pointed to the lyrical messages in country music. According to his analysis, the top songs leading into the election emphasized traditional family values, patriotism, religion, and other themes similar to those in messages presented by the president and his supporters during the campaign. Firestein cleverly used information and analysis to show how country music could have helped Bush win the election. In this way he led his audience to think in new ways about the powerful influence of popular culture on American politics.

Informative speeches emphasize information. As a speaker your objective is to use information so that audience members will learn something new and perhaps think about the world in different ways. In this chapter you will learn skills for crafting such a speech.

How Do You Prepare an Informative Presentation?

To prepare an informative speech, you should ask yourself the following:

1. Why deliver the speech? That is, what is the intent, purpose, and goal of informative speaking?
2. What kinds of topics best lend themselves to informative speaking?
3. What are the immediate behavioral purposes of informative speaking, and how can you tell if you have fulfilled them?

What Is Your Goal?

The end product of informative speaking is to increase an audience's knowledge or understanding of a topic. You accomplish that goal by clarifying your topic in ways that retain the interest of your audience. To clarify a concept for an audience, the presenter assumes the audience does not understand the topic clearly until the speaker has an opportunity to explain the subject. Typically, most audience members have insufficient knowledge or understanding to master or comprehend the informative presentation topic. For example, food-borne bacteria have repeatedly caused illnesses that make audiences increasingly interested in information about food safety.

Clarifying a topic for an audience is a primary goal of an informative presentation, but a second concern is to make the topic interesting and significant to the audience. You arouse an audience's interest or curiosity about a topic by showing how the subject can be of importance, by relating stories of your own experiences with the subject, and by demonstrating gaps in your listeners' knowledge that they will want to fill. Early in the presentation you may reveal why the audience should know more

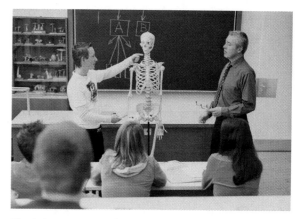

The informative speaker must arouse the interest of the audience and show the significance of the topic.

about our armed forces, student loans, or housing costs. How to make a topic palatable to the audience is a continuing concern of the informative speaker.

Besides being interesting, the informative presentation should meet the standard of significance. The significance of your message is its importance to the audience. The listeners, not the speaker, determine significance. For instance, a presentation on fathers who illegally withhold child support is more likely to be both interesting and significant to a roomful of struggling single mothers than to a roomful of sophomore fraternity men. A speech on the history of matches might lack interest and significance, and a speech on tax support for emerging nations might be high in significance but low in audience interest. Your task as an informative presenter is to adapt the topic to the audience so that they will find it informative, interesting, and significant.

TRY ◆ THIS

Many soft drink cans carry a warning to phenylketonurics, but very few people know what this warning means. Can you think of other words, concepts, or ideas that seem mysterious? Think of three for possible presentation topics.

What Topics Are Appropriate?

Chapter 10 already provided you with a general introduction to topic selection; here we will focus specifically on topics appropriate for the informative presentation.

The main intent of the presenter should be to be informative; that is, most of the content of the speech should focus on increasing audience knowledge and clarifying concepts. Many informative presentations reveal how to do something, what something is, or how something happens—speeches of exposition, definition and description, and demonstration, respectively. See the list of topics for a number of student-delivered informative speeches below.

What Is Stem Cell Research?

Emergency Life-Saving Techniques

New Technology for Diabetics

What Do Buddhists Believe?

Cures for Depression

This list of topics may give you some ideas for an informative presentation topic. Otherwise, refer back to chapter 10 for more ideas on how to find an appropriate topic for an informative presentation.

Your home culture can be an invaluable source for potential topics for your informative presentation. Besides the fact that you will feel more comfortable speaking on something with which you have experience, your classmates will likely be interested to learn how your culture is similar to and distinct from American culture. When trying to identify potential approaches, consider these possibilities: geography, religion, politics, the environment, music, theater, art, and sports. With these and other topics, you can easily show (and perhaps demonstrate) unique aspects of your culture and make comparisons to American culture.

What Is Your Purpose?

Two important questions for the informative speaker are these:

1. What do you want your audience to know or do as a result of your presentation?
2. How will you know if you are successful?

What Is a Behavioral Purpose?

Students learn better if they know exactly what the instructor expects them to learn. Similarly, an audience learns more from an informative presentation if the speaker states exactly what they are expected to know or do. The effects of an informative presentation, however, are unknown unless you make the effects behavioral; that is, your presentation should result in observable behavioral change. An instructor discovers whether students learned from a lecture by giving a quiz or having the students answer questions in class. In the same way, the informative speaker seeks to discover whether a message was effectively communicated by seeking overt feedback from the audience. The overt feedback you seek concerns the **immediate behavioral purposes** of your presentation—the actions expected from an audience during and immediately after a presentation.

The most common immediate behavioral purposes in an informative presentation encourage audience members to do the following:

1. *Describe objects, persons, or issues.* For example, after hearing a presentation, audience members can *describe* an English setter, a person with Down syndrome, or the Libertarian position on welfare.
2. *Distinguish between different things.* For example, after hearing a presentation, audience members can *distinguish* between fool's gold and real gold, between a counterfeit dollar and a real dollar, or between a conservative position and a liberal position.
3. *Compare items.* For example, after hearing a presentation, audience members can *compare* prices on automobiles with the same features and options, a poetic song and a sonnet, or diamonds for cut, clarity, and carats.
4. *Define words, objects, or concepts.* For example, after hearing a presentation, audience members can *define* what kerogen is, describe an English Tudor house, or explain the concept of macroeconomics.

immediate behavioral purposes

The actions expected from an audience during and immediately after a presentation.

5. *State what they have learned.* After hearing a presentation, audience members can tell you, or can write, the most important points of your speech or can tell others what you said.

6. *Show that they have learned.* For example, after watching a demonstration, audience members can do CPR, can show how to exercise correctly, or can assemble a small electric engine.

Have You Achieved Your Purpose?

The common behavioral purposes of an informative presentation are to describe, distinguish, compare, define, demonstrate, and state. How does a presenter know whether these behavioral purposes were accomplished? One method of discovering whether audience members learned anything from your presentation is to discover what they know both at the beginning and at the end of the speech. At the outset you can ask, "How many of you know about the routing number on your checks?" At the end of the presentation, you can ask the same question but call on someone to answer.

Similarly, you may ask your classmates to write down something or demonstrate that they understood your message. If you explained how to administer CPR, you could ask a volunteer to show that she understood the steps. Or, if your topic was to inform the class about nutrition, you could ask them to list the foods with the highest or lowest fat content. In each case you state the purpose in such a way that you can determine whether you accomplished your purpose. Figure 14.1 summarizes the steps you can use to determine whether you have met your goal as presenter.

Once you have decided on specific behavioral purposes for addressing an audience, you must select strategies for achieving those purposes. In other words, you must decide how to adapt your behavioral purposes and the materials of your presentation to your particular audience.

How Do You Effectively Present Information to an Audience?

Audience analysis (see chapter 10) can help you determine how much audience members already know and how much you will have to tell them. Then you have to decide how to generate information hunger, achieve information relevance, use extrinsic motivation, select content, and avoid information overload in your presentation.

Creating Information Hunger

An informative presentation is more effective if the presenter can generate **information hunger** in the audience—that is, if the presenter can create a need for information in the audience. Effective audience analysis reveals how you can create information hunger. Arousal of interest during the speech is related to how much the audience will comprehend (Petrie, 1963). You could use the following **rhetorical questions**—questions asked for effect, with no answer expected—to introduce an informative speech and to arouse audience interest: "Are you aware of the number of abused children in your hometown?" "Can you identify five warning signs of cancer?" or "Do you know how to get the best college education for your money?" Depending on the audience, these rhetorical questions could arouse interest.

information hunger

The audience's need for the information contained in the presentation.

rhetorical questions

Questions asked for effect, with no answer expected.

Giving an informative presentation is much like teaching a class. Your goal is to teach the audience about some fact, concept, process, or object. To determine whether you have met your goal as a presenter (or teacher), you must follow steps to assess whether your presentation achieved the desired behavioral outcome for your audience.

View an animation of this illustration on the *Online Learning Center*.

Step 1: Plan Objectives
The first step in planning your presentation should be to determine what objectives you want your audience to meet.

Step 2: Preassessment
The second step is to conduct a preassessment of your audience. Preassessment could take the form of asking a few classmates questions a few days before your presentation or even passing out a short quiz.

Step 3: Deliver Presentation
The third step is to actually teach or inform your audience. You plan your presentation so that it provides the best opportunity for your audience to meet the objectives you have set for them.

Step 4: Postassessment
The final step is post assessment. Like the preassessment, the postassessment could be informal—asking a few people questions after your presentation is completed—or more formal—handing out a quiz or survey.

Figure 14.1   Behavioral purposes for informative presentations.

Another method is to arouse the audience's curiosity. For example, you might state, "I have discovered a way to add 10 years to my life," "The adoption of the following plan will ensure lower taxes," or "I have a secret for achieving marital success." In addition, a brief quiz on your topic early in the speech arouses interest in finding the answers. Unusual clothing is likely to arouse interest in why you are so attired, and an object you created will likely inspire the audience to wonder how you made the object. Rhetorical questions and arousing curiosity are just a few of the many ways the presenter can generate information hunger.

Demonstrating Information Relevance

information relevance

The importance, novelty, and usefulness of the information to the audience.

A second factor relating an informative presentation to an audience is **information relevance**—the importance, novelty, and usefulness of the information to the audience. When selecting a topic for an informative presentation, the presenter should

Generating Information Hunger

Think first on your own of ways—besides asking rhetorical questions and arousing curiosity—that you could create information hunger in an audience. After writing down some ideas, share them with a classmate and see if the two of you can think of still others, the best of which can be shared with the class.

carefully consider the relevance of the topic to the particular audience. Skin cancer might be a better topic in the summer, when students are sunbathing, than in the winter, when they are studying for finals. A presentation on taxes could be awfully dull. A speech on how present tax laws cost audience members more than they cost the rich might be more relevant, and a speech on three ways to reduce personal taxes might be even more relevant. However, if your audience happens to be composed of 18- to 21-year-olds who have never paid taxes, none of the three topics might be relevant. Similarly, a speech on raising racehorses, writing a textbook, or living on a pension might be informative but not relevant because of the financial status, occupation, or age of the listeners. The informative presenter, then, should exercise some care in selecting a topic that interests the audience (Cofer, 1961).

People expose themselves first to information that is supportive or that fits in with what they already believe or know. Thus your intended listeners' predisposition toward a topic can determine whether they will hear your speech and then whether they will listen (Wheeless, 1974).

Revealing Extrinsic Motivation

A third factor in relating an informative presentation to an audience is **extrinsic motivation**—reasons outside the presentation itself for listening to the content of the presentation. An audience is more likely to listen to and comprehend a presentation if reasons exist outside the speech itself for concentrating on the content of the speech (Petrie & Carrel, 1976). A teacher who tells students to listen carefully because they will be tested at the end of the hour is using extrinsic motivation. A student can use extrinsic motivation at the beginning of a presentation by telling an audience, "Attention to this speech will alert you to ways you can increase energy and creativity," or "After hearing this speech, you will never purchase a poor-quality used car again."

Extrinsic motivation is related to the concept of information relevance. The audience member who would ordinarily lack interest in the topic of fashion might find that topic relevant when it is linked to learning the latest fashion trends. The audience member's interest in being cool is an extrinsic motivation for listening carefully to the presentation.

Any external reasons for listening need to be mentioned early in the presentation, before the message you want the audience to remember. A statement such as "You will need this background material for the report due at the end of this week" provides extrinsic motivation for the managers who hear this message from their employer. Similarly, in an informative presentation, you may be able to command more attention, comprehension, and action from audience members if they know some reasons outside the presentation itself for attending to your message.

extrinsic motivation

A method of making information relevant by providing the audience with reasons outside the presentation itself for listening to the content of the presentation.

To see how informative topics can be related to the interests of your audience, watch "Relating a Speech to the Listeners' Self-Interest" on the *Online Learning Center* at www.mhhe.com/pearson3.

◄ SKILL BUILDER ►

Either by yourself or with a partner, think or talk about how you would answer each of the following questions about your presentation:

1. *What can you do in your presentation to generate information hunger, to make your audience famished for more?*
2. *What can you do to make sure the audience knows the importance and usefulness of your topic?*
3. *What reasons outside the presentation itself (extrinsic motivation) does the audience have for listening to you?*

informative content

The main points and subpoints, illustrations, and examples used to clarify and inform.

Designing Informative Content

A fourth factor in relating an informative presentation to an audience is the selection of **informative content**—the main points and subpoints, illustrations, and examples used to clarify and inform. The following principles can guide you in selecting your speech content:

- *Audiences tend to remember and comprehend generalizations and main ideas better than details and specific facts* (Petrie, 1963). The usual advice to speakers—that content should be limited to a relatively small number of main points and generalizations—is well grounded. Specifically, public speakers are well advised to limit themselves to two to five main points. Audiences are unlikely to remember a larger number of main points.

- *Relatively simple words and concrete ideas are significantly easier to retain than are more complex materials* (Baird, 1974; Ernest, 1968). Long or unusual words may dazzle an audience into thinking you are intellectually gifted or verbally skilled, but they may also reduce audience understanding of the content. Keep the ideas and the words used to express those ideas at an appropriate level.

- *Humor can make a dull presentation more interesting to an audience, but humor does not seem to increase information retention.* The use of humor also improves the audience's perception of the character of the speaker and can increase a speaker's authoritativeness when a presentation is dull (Gruner, 1970).

- *Early remarks about how the presentation will meet the audience's needs can create anticipation and increase the chances that the audience will listen and understand* (Petrie, 1963). Whatever topic you select, you should tell audience members early

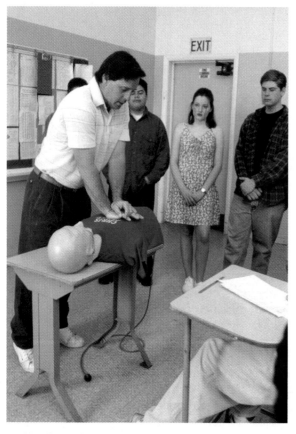

Having the audience practice what you preach greatly increases their comprehension.

in your presentation how the topic is related to them. Unless you relate the topic to their needs, they may choose not to listen.

- *Calling for overt audience response, or actual behavior, increases comprehension more than repetition does.* In a study of this subject, the overt responses invited were specific, "programmed" questions to which the appropriate overt responses were anticipated (Tucker, 1964). An informative presenter can ask for overt responses from audience members by having them perform the task being demonstrated (for example, two people dance after you explain the technique of the waltz); by having them stand, raise hands, or move chairs to indicate affirmative understanding of the speaker's statements (for example, "Raise your hand if you are familiar with local building codes"); or by having them write answers that will indicate understanding of the informative speech (for example, "List three ways to lower your blood pressure"). Having an audience go through an overt motion provides feedback to the speaker and can be rewarding and reinforcing for both presenter and listener.

Avoiding Information Overload

The informative speaker needs to be wary about the amount of information included in a presentation. The danger is **information overload**—providing much more information than the audience can absorb in amount, complexity, or both.

Information overload comes in two forms. One is *quantity:* The speaker tells more than audience members ever wanted to know about a subject, even when they are interested. The speaker tries to cram as much information as possible into the time allowed. Unfortunately, this cramming of information decreases understanding.

A second form of information overload is *complexity:* The speaker uses language or ideas that are beyond the capacity of the audience to understand. An engineer or a mathematician who unloads detailed formulas on the audience or a philosopher who soars into the ethereal heights of abstract ideas may leave the audience feeling frustrated and more confused than before the speech.

The solution to information overload is to speak on a limited number of main points with only the best supporting materials and to keep the message at a level the audience can understand.

information overload

Providing much more information than the audience can absorb in amount, complexity, or both.

Organizing Content

In an informative presentation, you can help the audience learn content by following these recommendations on how to organize your presentation:

1. Tell an audience what you are going to tell them (forecast), tell them, and tell them what you told them (Baird, 1974).
2. Use transitions and signposts to increase understanding (Petrie, 1963).
3. Tell your audience which points are most important.
4. Repeat important points for better understanding (Pence, 1954).

Audiences can more easily grasp information when they are invited to anticipate and to review the organization and content of your speech. That is why the body of your presentation is bracketed by a preview of what you are going to say and a summary/review of what you said.

When you have completed this section on how to effectively present your material, check your presentation against the checklist in Table 14.1.

TABLE 14.1   AN INFORMATIVE PRESENTATION CHECKLIST

_____1. Does your audience have some generalizations to remember from your details and specific facts?

_____2. Have you used simple words and concrete ideas to help your audience remember?

_____3. Can you comfortably use humor or wit in your presentation?

_____4. Have you told your listeners early in your presentation how your message will meet their needs?

_____5. Have you determined some way to involve the audience actively in your presentation?

_____6. Have you avoided information overload?

_____7. Have you used transitions, highlighted the most important points, included some repetition, and provided advance organizers?

To compare effective and less effective elements of informative presentation, watch both versions of the "Cell Phone" speech on the *Online Learning Center.*

Skills for an Informative Presentation

Public presenters who are highly effective at informative speaking demonstrate certain skills that contribute to their effectiveness. One of these skills is *defining*. Much of what an informative speaker does is reveal to an audience what certain terms, words, and concepts mean. Another skill is *describing*; the informative speaker often tells an audience how something appears: what it looks, sounds, feels, and even smells like. A third skill is *explaining*, or trying to say what something is in words the audience can understand. A fourth skill is *narrating*—an oral interpretation of a story, an event, or a description. A fifth skill is *demonstrating*, or showing an audience how to do something.

Defining

Definitions are not dull. In fact, they are often the issues we fight about in our society. For example, when does a collection of cells become a fetus? When does a fetus become a premature child? Or is a soul produced with the meeting of sperm and egg? Can marriage be between same-sex partners? If a baby boomer is someone born between 1946 and 1964, then what is someone who was born in 1985 called? Yes, we have serious battles over defining who is of retirement age (keeps getting older), who can go to war (fairly young), who can drink alcohol (often older than going to war), and what is a family (a gay couple with a child?).

We can define by using comparison and contrast, synonyms and antonyms, and even operational definition. A **comparison** shows the similarity between something well known and something less known. So, a student explained that tying a bow tie (unfamiliar to most) is the same as tying your shoelace (familiar to all), but since we are unaccustomed to tying a shoelace around our neck, the bow tie is challenging. A **contrast** clarifies by showing differences: "he was taller than you, fatter than you, and dumber than you."

A **synonym** defines by using a word close or similar in meaning to the one you are trying to define. A student speaking about depression used synonyms to help the

comparison

Shows the similarity between something well known and something less known.

contrast

Clarifies by showing differences.

synonym

Defines by using a word close or similar in meaning to the one you are trying to define.

listeners understand: "A depressed person feels demoralized, purposeless, isolated, and distanced from others." An **antonym** defines an idea by opposition. Hence, a student defined "a good used car" by what it is not: "Not full of dents, not high mileage, not worn on the seats, not using lots of oil, and not involved in a serious accident."

An **operational definition** defines by explaining a process. So, an operational definition of a cake is the sequence of actions depicted in a recipe. An operational definition of concrete is the formula-driven sequence of ingredients that correctly added over the correct time period results in concrete.

antonym

Defines an idea by opposition.

operational definition

Defines by explaining a process.

Describing

A second skill of the informative presenter is distinguishing between abstract and concrete words and between general and specific words. One of the best ways to make an informative speech interesting is by using language forcefully and effectively. You can do that best if you recognize certain differences among words.

For instance, some words refer generally to ideas, qualities, acts, or relationships: these are called **abstract words.** Examples of abstract words are *freedom* (an idea), *mysterious* (a quality), *altruism* (an act), and *parent-child* (a relationship). Other words are more specific, or **concrete,** because they refer to definite persons, places, objects, and acts, such as Dr. Bettsey L. Barhorst, the Eiffel Tower, and your economics textbook. Abstract words are useful in theorizing, summarizing, and discussing and are commonly used by educated persons discussing ideas. Concrete words are most useful in relating your personal experiences, direct observations, and feelings or attitudes. The important point about abstract and concrete language is to use the most appropriate words.

abstract words

Words or phrases that refer generally to ideas, qualities, acts, or relationships.

concrete words

Words that refer to definite persons, places, objects, and acts.

The most frequent error in informative presentations is the use of abstract terms where concrete words would be more forceful and clear. "I have really liked some courses of study here at Northern Virginia Community College," says a student to her classmates and adds, "but others I have disliked." This abstract, general statement has minimal impact. If speaking in concrete terms, the same student might say, "I have most enjoyed English, communication, and political science courses, and I have disliked courses in chemistry, mathematics, and physics." Descriptions in informative speeches should be specific, accurate, and detailed, rather than general and ambiguous.

Informative presenters should also attempt to use colorful **imagery**—words that appeal to the senses. A speaker describing a place might say that "the sun sets in an orange sky against the purple mountain," a victim of shock "appears lifeless, pallid, and clammy," or a manufactured meat "tastes like top-grade sirloin."

imagery

Use of words that appeal to the senses, that create pictures in the mind.

A valuable exercise for the informative speaker is to carefully review the rough draft of the presentation to discover abstract, general, ambiguous words that can be replaced by concrete ones.

TRY ◆ THIS

Think of something that you have explained to others many times at work or at home. Does your explanation get increasingly efficient with practice? Can you practice some of your explanations from your presentation on others before you address an audience so that your explanation will be easy to understand?

Explaining

explanation

A means of idea development that simplifies or clarifies an idea while arousing audience interest.

A third skill for the informative presenter is explaining an idea in words the audience can understand. An **explanation** is a means of idea development that simplifies or clarifies an idea while arousing audience interest.

An important step in explaining is analyzing, deconstructing, or dissecting something to enhance audience understanding. Unless you become skilled at dissecting a concept, your explanation may leave audience members more confused than they were before your presentation. You have to determine what you can do to make the concept more palatable to the audience. For example, a biology professor in an article about global warming (Harden & Eilperin, 2006) expressed the problem by explaining how animals and plants are migrating north or climbing higher—if they can—to survive:

> Wild species don't care who is in the White House. It is very obvious they are desperately trying to move to respond to the changing climate. Some are succeeding. But for the ones that are already at the mountain top or the poles, there is no place for them to go. They are the ones that are going extinct. (p. 19)

MYTHS, METAPHORS, & MISUNDERSTANDINGS

Students often see speakers as "conduits" of information, disseminating facts to an audience. Alternatively, you could think about speakers as "narrators" of public-speaking events. Audience members could be considered co-constructors of meaning about stories told. The introduction of the presentation could set the scene, including historical context. The organization of main points could be considered an unfolding plotline with heroes and villains, problems and solutions. In general, how does a narrative metaphor change, if at all, the way you would prepare for and deliver a public presentation?

Narrating

narrating

The oral presentation and interpretation of a story, a description, or an event; includes dramatic reading of prose or poetry.

To see how video can be used to enhance an informative presentation, watch "Playing Drums" on the *Online Learning Center*.

A fourth skill for informative speakers is **narrating**—the oral presentation and interpretation of a story, a description, or an event. In a presentation, narration includes the dramatic reading of some lines from a play, a poem, or another piece of literature; the voice-over on a series of slides or a silent film to illustrate a point in a speech; and even the reading of such information as a letter, a quotation, or a selection from a newspaper or magazine. The person who does the play-by-play account of a ball game is narrating, and so is the presenter who explains what a weaver is doing in an informative presentation on home crafts.

The person who uses narration in a presentation moves just a little closer to oral interpretation of literature, or even acting, because the narration is highlighted by being more dramatic than the surrounding words. Sections of your presentation that require this kind of special reading also require special practice. If you want a few lines of poetry in your presentation to have the desired impact, you will need to rehearse them.

Demonstrating

demonstrating

Showing the audience what you are explaining.

A fifth skill for informative speakers is **demonstrating**—showing the audience what you are explaining. Some topics are communicated best through words; other topics are best communicated by demonstrating. You can talk about CPR, the Heimlich maneuver, fashion trends, and weight lifting, and you can even read about these subjects. But nothing aids in the understanding of these topics better than seeing and doing CPR, practicing the Heimlich maneuver, seeing the latest fashion trends, or actually lifting some weights while learning about them.

An Example of an Informative Presentation

So far in this chapter, you have learned how to select a topic for your informative presentation; how to determine behavioral purposes and goals for the informative presentation; how to present information to an audience; how to organize the informative presentation; and how to define, describe, explain, narrate, and demonstrate the concepts in your presentation. Now let's look at the manuscript of an actual informative presentation delivered by a student.

Notice how the presenter gains and maintains the audience's attention, relates the topic to himself and to the audience, and forecasts the organization and development of the topic. Notice also how the presenter attempts to clarify the topic with examples high in audience interest; translates the ideas into language the audience can understand; and defines, describes, and explains. The marginal notes will help identify how the presenter is fulfilling the important functions of the introduction, body, and conclusion of an informative presentation.

The AK-47 by Alexei Victorovich

I am not a member of the National Rifle Association, not a member of the National Guard, and not even a veteran of any war, but I am a person who is interested in how weapons have shaped cultures and civilizations through the ages. I am a history major who likes to learn what shaped our past and influences our future. The book that aroused my interest was Jared Diamond's book titled *Guns, Germs, and Steel: The Fates of Human Societies*. In that book he shows among other things the role of weapons in human history. I read that book, and then decided to look more closely at a weapon often mentioned but rarely explained, a weapon that has had a profound influence on recent and current history—the AK-47. What I want you to know and understand today is what this weapon is, where it came from, and why we should know and care about its existence. When I have completed this presentation, I think you will be as impressed as I was about the destructive power of one weapon developed by one man who was just trying to protect his homeland from a powerful enemy.

Source credibility: Relates topic to presenter.

Announces topic.

Relates topic to audience.

States purpose forecasts content and organization.

Reveals intended audience response.

First, what is an AK-47? *Wikipedia* describes the AK-47 as a Russian-made assault rifle that was compact, light weight, and capable of selective firing. Unlike the auto-load rifles of the time, the AK-47 could be aimed, stopped, and started with multiple shells firing every time the trigger was depressed. Often called the *Kalashnikov AK-47* after its creator, the Russian website dedicated to this weapon correctly calls it "the most widespread weapon in the world. More than 50 armies of the world have in their arsenals firearms created by Kalashnikov. . . ." The inventor was Mikhail Kalashnikov, a Russian inventor who developed and standardized the assault rifle in 1947. That is why the weapon is called the AK-47, after the year of its invention. Now that you know who invented this weapon and where he is from, you should know why he invented this assault weapon.

Uses signpost.
Defines term.
Cites sources of information.

Uses direct quotation for support in the form of facts.

Uses transition.

Second, you should know why this Russian inventor, Mikhail Kalashnikov, invented the AK-47. Larry Kahaner, author of *AK-47: The Weapon That Changed the Face of War*, tells the story. In World War I, soldiers shot at each other for months from trenches with guns

Describes.

that shot a bullet with each pull of the trigger with frequent reloading necessary. In World War II, the Germans devised the *blitzkrieg* or "lightning war" in which they attacked one point in the enemy defenses, broke through, and invaded with waves of soldiers who thrust deep into the invaded territory.

Explains.

One of the places the Germans invaded was the town in Russia in which Mikhail Kalashnikov lived in September 1941. The Nazi soldiers killed 80% of the Russians who lived in Mikhail's home city of 80,000 people. Twenty-one-year-old Mikhail, wounded by enemy fire, took two days to reach medical help to mend his injured left shoulder. After that harrowing experience he had nightmares about his slaughtered comrades and, according to author Kahaner, "he became obsessed with creating a submachine gun that would drive the Germans from his homeland."

Uses narrative to reveal historical background.

Cites source and uses direct quote.

He sketched a prototype while recovering in the hospital, later developed that prototype in a metal shop, and then went to a technical school where he created a carbine. In 1947 he finally created the Avtomat Kalashnikova or automatic Kalashnikov or AK, a light-weight, durable submachine gun. He had created a weapon that would protect his country for decades, that would become the weapon of choice for many anti-Western armies, and that would arm terrorists around the world.

Defines term.

Forecasts in transition.

My third point is "Why should we care about this weapon?" Well, we worry about weapons of mass destruction, but nuclear weapons have not really destroyed humans yet. Atomic weapons twice fell on Japan with enough destructiveness to stop a war, but nuclear weapons have so far been used mainly to threaten destruction. The AK-47 and its relatives, on the other hand, have killed millions.

Uses signpost.

Uses contrast to clarify.

A December 2006 article in *The Washington Post Weekly Edition* revealed the following facts.

Cites source.

Reveals facts.

- In 1956 the Russians crushed the Hungarian revolt by using the AK-47 as the main armament to kill 50,000 Hungarians.
- In Vietnam American soldiers took AKs from enemy dead because the American-made M-16s jammed in combat.
- In the 1980s our CIA funneled $2 billion worth of Chinese-made AKs to Afghanistan to help the Afghans defeat the Russian occupiers.
- When America invaded Afghanistan after the World Trade Center was destroyed our soldiers found an enemy heavily armed with AKs.
- In Iraq Americans tried to arm the newly formed Iraqi army with American-made M-16s and M-4s only to find that the Iraqis insisted on AKs.
- The article quotes a senior advisor to the Coalitional Provisional Authority in Iraq as saying: "For better or worse, the AK-47 is the weapon of choice in that part of the world. It turns out that every Iraqi male above the age of 12 can take them apart and put them together blindfolded and is a pretty good shot."

Gives specific examples to support claim.

Uses direct quote from authoritative source.

For sixty years the AK-47 has reigned supreme on the battlefield, in urban warfare, and among terrorists around the world. Our fear of nuclear weapons is greater, but the AK-47 has been the unheralded weapon that has actually killed more people.

Signals ending.

I began this presentation by pointing out that I am a history major who was inspired by a book on how weapons shape cultures. I went from that large worldview to examine a specific weapon—the AK-47. While the world was trembling in fear of nuclear holocaust, a Russian man, wounded in battle, was only trying to protect his homeland. In so doing, he unleashed a weapon so efficient, effective, and powerful that it has wiped out more lives than any single weapon known to humankind. Most amazing is the fact that Mikhail Kalashnikov still lives. Eighty-five years old, author Kahaner describes him as "tiny, feeble,

Summarizes and reviews.

near deaf, his right hand losing control because of tremors." And what did this old man tell *The Guardian* in 2002? "I wish I had invented a lawnmower," he said. Mikhail's invention sixty years ago may be the most dramatic case of unintended consequences in world history.

Cites source.

Provides quote.

Annotated Bibliography

Diamond, J.(1999). *Guns, Germs, and Steel: The Fates of Human Societies*. New York: W. W. Norton & Company. The idea for the presentation came from this source. http://Kalshnikov.guns.ru The home page for a Russian website dedicated to history and details of Mikhail Kalashnikov and his invention, the AK-47. Retrieved December 9, 2006. http://en.wikpedia.org/wiki/AK-47. Retrieved December 9, 2006. The definitions came from this free web encyclopedia.

Kahaner, L. (2006, December 4–10), The weapon of mass destruction: Who needs nukes when there are so many AK-47s to go around? *The Washington Post Weekly Edition*, pp. 22–23. Much of the information for the presentation came from this source.

Annotated bibliography tells what each source revealed.

Chapter Review & Study Guide

SUMMARY

In this chapter you learned the following:

▶ Preliminary information that you need to know in informing others includes:
- The intent and goal of informative presentations.
- The kinds of topics that are most appropriate.
- The kinds of immediate behavioral purposes of informative presentations and how to determine if you have fulfilled them.

▶ Strategies for informing others include:
- Generating information hunger, an audience need for the information.
- Achieving information relevance by relating information to the audience.
- Using extrinsic motivation, reasons outside the presentation itself for understanding the presentation's content.

▶ Shaping the informative content requires:
- Limiting the number of main points.
- Limiting the number of generalizations.

- Selecting language the audience can understand.
- Using specifics to illustrate an abstract idea.
- Including humor or wit when appropriate.
- Revealing how the information meets audience needs.
- Avoiding information overload.
- Organizing content for greater understanding.

▶ Skills for informative presentations include:
- Defining meanings for an audience.
- Describing by using specific, concrete language.
- Explaining by clarifying and simplifying complex ideas.
- Narrating by using stories to illustrate your ideas.
- Demonstrating by showing a process or procedure to your audience.

KEY TERMS

Go to the *Online Learning Center* at **www.mhhe.com/pearson3** to further your understanding of the following terminology.

Abstract words	Explanation	Information relevance
Antonym	Extrinsic motivation	Informative content
Comparision	Imagery	Narrating
Concrete words	Immediate behavioral purposes	Operational definition
Contrast	Information hunger	Rhetorical questions
Demonstrating	Information overload	Synonym

STUDY QUESTIONS

1. The goal of informative presentations is to
   a. induce change in the audience
   b. discourage the audience from taking action
   c. increase an audience's knowledge or understanding of a topic
   d. identify a problem and determine a solution

2. How do you make an informational topic interesting to the audience?
   a. Relate your own experiences with the subject.
   b. Avoid telling stories of your own experiences with the subject.

   c. Maintain the gaps in your listeners' knowledge of your subject.
   d. Arousing interest is not important.

3. Which is *not* an appropriate topic for an informative presentation?
   a. CPR techniques
   b. animals and their positive effects on the elderly
   c. wedding traditions
   d. everyone should donate blood

4. If audiences are able to describe information or define words related to your topic during and after a presentation, you have successfully accomplished your
   a. demonstration
   b. immediate behavioral purposes
   c. imagery
   d. information overload

5. The first step in planning your presentation should be
   a. asking a few people questions after the presentation is complete
   b. teaching or informing your audience
   c. determining what objectives you want your audience to meet
   d. conducting a preassessment of the audience

6. Asking rhetorical questions and arousing curiosity are two ways a speaker can create
   a. behavioral purposes
   b. topics for informative speeches
   c. preassessments
   d. information hunger

7. When presenting information to an audience, a topic's importance, novelty, and usefulness is a key factor known as
   a. information relevance
   b. information hunger
   c. informative content
   d. information overload

8. Which of the following is *not* a guideline to follow when choosing the content of your presentation?
   a. Use relatively simple words because they are easier to understand.
   b. Tell the audience early in your presentation how the topic is related to them, so they will choose to listen.
   c. Develop as many main ideas and use as many details as possible to make the presentation interesting.
   d. Ask for overt responses from audience members to increase comprehension.

9. When organizing the content of your presentation, you should
   a. keep the topic a mystery until the body of the speech
   b. use transitions to increase understanding
   c. let the audience decide which points are the most important
   d. avoid repeating important points so the audience isn't bored

10. _____ simplify or clarify ideas while stimulating audience attention, and _____ is when you show the audience what you are explaining.
    a. Explanations; demonstrating
    b. Definitions; narrating
    c. Descriptions; demonstrating
    d. Narrations; defining

Answers:
1. (c); 2. (a); 3. (d); 4. (b); 5. (c); 6. (d); 7. (a); 8. (c); 9. (b); 10. (a)

CRITICAL THINKING

1. Think of stories you and your friends tell each other. How do they or you effectively create information hunger at the beginning of the story? Why are these methods successful?

2. Find a manuscript of an important speech (such as Martin Luther King Jr.'s "I Have a Dream" or Ronald Reagan's "Challenger" speech). On the manuscript, identify the important presentation functions being fulfilled. Did the speaker use transitions? Gain attention? Describe, explain, or define?

SELF-QUIZ

For further review, try the chapter self-quiz on the *Online Learning Center* at **www.mhhe.com/pearson3**.

REFERENCES

Baird, J. A. (1974). The effects of speech summaries upon audience comprehension of expository speeches of varying quality and complexity. *Central States Speech Journal, 25,* 119–127.

Cofer, N. C. (1961). *Verbal learning and verbal behavior.* New York: McGraw-Hill.

Ernest, C. (1968). Listening comprehension as a function of type of material and rate of presentation. *Speech Monographs, 35,* 154–158.

Gruner, C. R. (1970). The effect of humor in dull and interesting informative speeches. *Central States Speech Journal, 21,* 160–166.

Harden, B., & Eilperin, J. (2006, December 4–10). Wild species and ski resorts are on the move. *The Washington Post Weekly Edition,* p. 19.

Pence, O. L. (1954). Emotionally loaded argument: Its effectiveness in stimulating recall. *Quarterly Journal of Speech, 40,* 272–276.

Petrie, C. R., Jr. (1963). Informative speaking: A summary and bibliography of related research. *Speech Monographs, 30,* 79–91.

Petrie, C. R., Jr., & Carrel, S. D. (1976). The relationship of motivation, listening, capability, initial information, and verbal organizational ability to lecture comprehension and retention. *Speech Monographs, 43,* 187–194.

Tucker, C. D. (1964). An application of programmed learning to informative speech. *Speech Monographs, 31,* 142–152.

Wheeless, L. R. (1974). The effects of attitude, credibility, and homophily on selective exposure to information. *Speech Monographs, 41,* 329–338.

CHAPTER FIFTEEN

Persuasive Presentations

What will you learn?

When you have read and thought about this chapter, you will be able to:

1. Identify four action goals of persuasive speaking.
2. Distinguish between immediate behavioral purposes and ultimate goals.
3. Describe and utilize persuasive-speaking strategies.
4. Recall four ethical guidelines for persuasive speaking.
5. State and utilize some persuasive-speaking skills.
6. Use some strategies for resisting persuasive appeals.

*F*ew students think they will ever give a persuasive speech, but they admit that they are likely to be asked to introduce new products, convince others to use new methods, and talk with fellow workers about complying with policies and procedures. All of these efforts are simply variations of a persuasive presentation. In this chapter you will first learn what persuasion is. Then you will learn how to prepare a persuasive presentation, when to use some strategies of persuasion, and how persuasion can be perceived differently in various cultures and co-cultures. Because persuasion is perceived with suspicion in our culture, you will explore some ethical problems related to persuasion. Finally, you will learn some ways to protect yourself from unwanted persuasive efforts; in other words, you will learn some strategies for resisting persuasive appeals.

Laura Bush married George Bush only after an agreement that she would never, *ever* have to make a political speech on his behalf (Bruni, 2000). But however much she may have preferred a private life to a public one, she soon adapted herself to her husband's political lifestyle and delivered many speeches on his behalf in his march to the White House. As First Lady she became a capable spokeswoman for various causes, including breast cancer research, children's education, and literacy.

In her role as advocate for these causes, the First Lady has been called on to deliver many speeches. Consider, for example, a speech that she delivered in September 2006 at a White House Conference on Global Literacy, held at the New York Public Library. The purpose of her speech, given before an international audience, was to challenge every country to end illiteracy. How did she go about this?

She started with an anecdote about how she grew up with a love of reading that led her to be a teacher and librarian. She gave some startling statistics about the illiteracy affecting more than 800 million people worldwide. She then ticked off all the ways that investment in educating people pays off for a country: strengthened economies, healthy populations, and improved opportunities for citizens. It was a powerful, well-constructed speech. Clearly, Laura Bush had come a long way from the time of her initial "vow of silence."

Laura Bush's speech on illiteracy illustrates one of the approaches to persuasive speaking that you will learn about in this chapter. To be effective, a speech must be organized well. It must draw listeners in from the beginning. It must present arguments in a logical way. And it must be persuasive, especially if the object is to affect policy.

What Is a Persuasive Presentation?

persuasive presentation

A message designed to strategically induce change in an audience.

You will be expected to deliver at least one persuasive presentation in your class and, perhaps, many in your lifetime. A **persuasive presentation** is a message designed strategically to induce change in the audience. Your intention is to change the listeners in some way consistent with your purpose. Here are some examples of persuasive topics:

New Rules Needed for Drug Use Among Athletes

How to Succeed as a Single Mom

Managing Difficult People in the Workplace

Why Our Legislature Must Lower Tuition

You can generate possible topics by using brainstorming or concept mapping as described in chapter 10. Then make sure your topic relates to you (source credibility) and your audience (audience analysis), as well as being a topic of importance.

What Is Your Immediate Purpose and Ultimate Goal?

Your presentation should have an **immediate purpose**—a statement of what you intend to accomplish in this particular presentation. Given that a single presentation to a captive audience is unlikely to produce dramatic results, you need to be realistic about anticipated results. So, you might state, "My immediate purpose is to have my listeners write down the e-mail addresses of legislators so they can communicate with them about lowering our tuition."

You may also have an **ultimate goal**—a statement of purposes that could be achieved with continuing efforts to persuade. You know, for instance, that your one-shot persuasive effort to alert your listeners to steroids and designer drugs used by athletes is not going to produce a lot of action. But you also know that the more your audience hears about this issue from many sources, the more likely something will be done about it. You may be just one drop in a pond, but if enough raindrops fall the pond itself will change. Your ultimate goal could be stated like this: "My ultimate goal is to encourage my listeners to learn more about this issue over time so eventually new rules will keep performance-enhancing drugs out of the sports arena."

immediate purpose

A statement of what you intend to accomplish in this particular presentation.

ultimate goal

A statement of purposes that could be achieved with continuing attempts to persuade.

MYTHS, METAPHORS, & MISUNDERSTANDINGS

Most people misunderstand how persuasion works. For instance, some people think persuasion is the skillful manipulation of images to get people to do something they would not otherwise do. To them, persuasion is "seduction," getting their way with people by influencing them against their will. Actually, forcing people to think or behave as you wish is not persuasion but coercion. A related phenomenon involves tricking people or using fraudulent means to gain compliance; this is not persuasion but manipulation. Neither coercion nor manipulation is close to persuasion as portrayed in this text. Why? Because both coercion and manipulation bypass a person's ability to choose, to make a decision based on sound information and ideas.

Introducing Your Persuasive Presentation

The introduction for your persuasive presentation has many similarities to other introductions with one exception. The introduction seeks to gain and maintain attention (see chapter 12), relating the topic to the speaker (see chapter 11), and to forecast the organization and development of the presentation. Where the introduction differs from others is in relating the topic to the audience and in revealing the purpose of the presentation.

Shaping the Persuasive Purpose to the Listeners

In an informative presentation you state clearly at the outset what you want to accomplish. You tell the audience what you want them to learn from the very beginning. In a persuasive presentation you need to analyze your audience to determine when and how you are going to reveal your purpose. The reason for waiting to reveal your purpose is that the audience is likely to reject your message from the beginning unless you prepare the way. If you state in your first few words that you intend to change the audience's religion, political party, or position on abortion, you are likely to have them hostile from the beginning. To avoid rejection or hostility, you instead determine how much change you can ask for and decide what strategies you can use to gain the desired result.

Analyzing the Listeners

In chapter 10 you learned how to analyze an audience using everything from demographic analysis to surveys. Analyzing your audience is very important in persuasive presentations because you have to decide when you are going to reveal your purpose and how you are going to achieve that purpose.

You do not want to ask for too much change in your listeners because you are likely to get a **boomerang effect**—that is, the audience likes you and your message less after the presentation than they did before. To avoid that undesirable result, you must analyze your audience to decide when you should reveal your purpose. If you are not asking for much of a change, you may reveal your purpose in the introduction of the speech, or your introducer may even reveal the purpose for you. But if what you are asking the audience to think or do will take some preparation before they are likely to accept your purpose, then you should provide the reasons first and then reveal your action step toward the end of the presentation. Audience analysis is the key to when you reveal your purpose.

What Purposes Are Persuasive?

Two purposes of persuasive presentations are difficult to evaluate and measure; two others are challenging to present. You will need to consult with your instructor about which persuasive purposes are favored in your class.

The two persuasive purposes that are difficult to evaluate and measure are continuance and deterrence (Fotheringham, 1966). **Continuance** is encouraging the audience to keep doing what they are doing. Religious leaders often deliver messages encouraging their followers to keep the faith, to behave as their holy texts say. Managers often find themselves trying to motivate the people they manage to keep working to a high standard. Communication teachers sometimes are less convinced that this continuance purpose is a good thing because effectiveness is difficult to prove: The audience behaves the same way after the presentation as they did before, but is their continuing behavior related to the presentation?

Similarly, the persuasive purpose of **deterrence**—discouraging listeners from taking some action—is difficult to demonstrate. For instance, you deliver a presentation against some unhealthy habit—smoking, drinking, or using illegal drugs—to a group that does not smoke, drink, or use illegal drugs. How can anyone tell whether your presentation kept the listeners from those unhealthy habits? Again, some communication teachers invite this persuasive purpose; others do not.

On the other hand, very few communication teachers have difficulty with the two persuasive purposes of adoption and discontinuance. **Adoption** means that the listeners start a new behavior as a result of the persuasive presentation—for example, they start exercising, start eating healthy foods, and go on a diet. The persuader

boomerang effect

The audience likes you and your message less after your presentation than they did before.

continuance

Encouraging the audience to keep doing what they are doing.

deterrence

Discouraging listeners from taking some action.

adoption

The listeners start a new behavior as a result of the persuasive presentation.

has some proof of effectiveness if people in the audience state on a postpresentation questionnaire that they are going to take up some new behavior. Suppose a regional sales manager presents new and higher goals for the local sales representatives, and sales increase by 25% over the next 3 months. This is proof that the persuasive effort by the regional sales manager had the desired effect.

Discontinuance is a persuasive purpose rooted in convincing listeners to stop some current behavior—for example, to quit your gang, stop taking so much sick leave, or desist from drinking so much caffeine. Despite decades of discouraging them from eating too much, from exercising too little, and from smoking at all, Americans are the fattest people on earth, exercise way too little, and continue to die in large numbers from smoking cigarettes. Discontinuance and adoption are challenging persuasive purposes well worth your efforts in a presentation.

discontinuance

A persuasive purpose rooted in convincing listeners to stop some current behavior.

Why Should You Try to Persuade?

After reading that years of public service campaigns have failed to change Americans' eating, exercise, and smoking habits, you might wonder why anyone should expect you to be successful in a classroom presentation. The key factor is that face-to-face persuasive efforts are more effective than public service campaigns for at least two reasons.

One reason is that face-to-face communication is one of the most effective modes of communication. Consider the difference between a public service announcement on TV discouraging bulimia and a classroom presentation on the same subject by a classmate who confesses to bulimia and reveals to the class the awful, life-threatening effects of the disease. Which mode—a TV spot or the person herself—would have the most influence on you? Although you can see almost any entertainer on video, thousands of people show up for concerts because they want to see the entertainer in the flesh. The live concert has more soul than a video can provide. The same is true of classroom speeches: Actually experiencing someone's message in the flesh and in real time is a more powerful persuader than is a mediated message.

A second reason the classroom presentation is more effective is that the classroom has a captive audience. In other words, your classmates are not a voluntary audience that came to hear you in particular talk about your topic. Rather, many in the classroom audience have to listen to a speaker and message not of their choosing. The class ends up hearing from gang members, newly divorced individuals, persons on parole, successful business managers, top salespeople, single moms, and functional fathers. Credible presenters on many topics face an audience that often does not know what is going to be said until they hear the message. The unexpectedness of the experience increases the chances that you are going to be persuading at least some individuals in your audience.

To persuade others in school, at home, or at work, you must employ strategies chosen to work best on your listeners. The strategies described below will work only if you have correctly determined that your audience will respond positively to them. Here again, audience analysis is the key to effectiveness.

How Do You Persuade?

Using Argument to Persuade: Fact, Policy, and Value

argument

A proposition that asserts some course of action.

proposition of fact

An assertion that can be proved or disproved as consistent with reality.

proposition of policy

A proposal of a new rule.

proposition of value

A statement of what we should embrace as more important to our culture.

Listeners who know or like logic respond positively to arguments with evidence that constitutes proof. Lawyers and debaters are well versed in logical argument, and many educated people respond positively to this approach. An **argument** consists of a proposition that asserts some course of action. Ordinarily, the proposition concerns a question of fact, policy, or value. An example of a **proposition of fact**—an assertion that can be proved or disproved as consistent with reality—would be "The World Trade Center was destroyed by organized terrorists." To demonstrate the truth of this proposition, you would not have to prove that the World Trade Center was completely destroyed, but you would have to provide evidence that the destroyers were organized and that their goal was terrorism.

An example of a **proposition of policy**—a proposal of a new rule—would be "The USA should allow prescription drug trade with Canada." To demonstrate the merit of this proposition, you would provide evidence that such drug trade would reduce costs, increase efficiency, and satisfy the needs of customers. In other words, you would provide evidence that the policy should be adopted.

An example of a **proposition of value**—a statement of what we should embrace as more important to our culture—would be "Americans must put security over First Amendment freedoms." To demonstrate the merit of this proposition, you would provide evidence that airline searches, wiretapping, and profiling are more important than our right to protection against unreasonable searches, our expectation of privacy, and our right not to be singled out for negative treatment because of race or ethnicity. Why? Because those violations of rights keep us safe, and we want security more than we want freedoms.

What Is the Difference Between Evidence and Proof?

As anyone knows who watches *Law and Order* or any of the *CSI* spinoffs, evidence is what forensic scientists produce to convict felons. They bring out DNA, fingerprints, weapons, fiber samples, rape kits, and bloodstains as evidence that some perp committed a specific crime against a particular individual. In argumentation you are more likely to use other kinds of evidence like examples, surveys, testimonials, and numbers and statistics, as explained in chapter 11. The question is: Is your evidence proof to your listeners?

proof

Evidence that the receiver believes.

Proof is evidence that the receiver believes. In other words, you can listen to evidence without believing it, and if you do not believe the evidence, you are not going to accept the presenter's argument. Suppose a presenter is arguing that the listener should accept her policy proposition that "the USA should never use the death penalty." Her evidence is that the Bible says, "Thou shalt not kill," an idea that is elevated in importance because it happens to be a commandment that Moses brought down from the mountaintop on a tablet of stone. A person who believes that the Bible is without error and that we should obey every word will accept the commandment as proof. A person who does not accept the Bible as an authority or sees contradictions like the stoning of individuals to death for various offenses might not accept the commandment as proof. In other words, many things can constitute evidence, but only those items that the audience accepts constitute proof.

How Can You Test Evidence?

Your evidence must meet the **tests of evidence**—questions you can use to test the validity of the evidence in your presentations or in those of others:

1. *Is the evidence consistent with other known facts?* For instance, did the speaker look at a relatively large number of student co-ops to determine that student co-ops are successful? Have any student co-op bookstores failed?

2. *Would another observer draw the same conclusions?* Has anyone other than the speaker determined that other student co-ops are successful? What does the speaker mean by "success"?

3. *Does the evidence come from unbiased sources?* Does the vice-president for student affairs have anything to gain by favoring student co-op bookstores? Who made the claim that students will get better value for their used books? Who said other schools have established successful student co-ops?

4. *Is the source of the information qualified by education and/or experience to make a statement about the issue?* The vice-president may be well educated, but what does she know about co-op bookstores? What about the qualifications of the sources of the information on used books or successful co-ops?

5. *If the evidence is based on personal experience, how typical is that personal experience?* Personal experience that is typical, generalizable, realistic, and relevant can be good evidence.

6. *If statistics are used as evidence, are they from a reliable source; comparable with other known information; and current, applicable, and interpreted so that the audience can understand them?*

7. *If studies and surveys are used, are they authoritative, valid, reliable, objective, and generalizable?* A study done by persons who favor student co-op bookstores, for instance, would be questionable because the source of the study is biased.

8. *Are the speaker's inferences appropriate according to the data presented?* Does the presenter go too far beyond the evidence in concluding that students should establish their own co-op bookstore?

9. *Is important counterevidence overlooked?* Often, in our haste to make a positive case, we ignore or omit counterevidence. What evidence against student co-ops is left out?

10. *What is the presenter's credibility on the topic?* Has the speaker earned the right to speak on the topic through research, interviews, and a thorough examination of the issue? Does the speaker have experience related to the issue?

tests of evidence

Questions that can be used to test the validity of evidence.

Watch the "Sharks," "Stem Cell Research," and "Cow over Chemicals" video clips on the *Online Learning Center* to see examples of persuasive presentations.

The answers to these 10 questions are important. Evidence that meets these tests has met the requirements of good evidence.

 How we prepare and react to persuasive messages can vary from one culture to the next. For example, if you are from a high-context culture, you may prefer to be less direct when communicating. Alternatively, if you are from a highly individualistic culture, you may prefer to advance your own opinion without taking other viewpoints into consideration. When preparing your persuasive speech, you will likely need to blend some of the persuasive norms of your culture with the persuasive norms of American culture.

This chapter explains many of those Anglo-American norms. If you opt to use norms from your culture, you may need to provide some explanation for what you are doing. For example, African cultures tend to rely on stories to teach lessons or principles. If you use an extended story during your speech, you may need to be somewhat direct and tell audience members what they should learn from the story. While you should not abandon the norms for persuasion that you are familiar with, your persuasive messages may need additional explanation to be adapted to the expectations of your classmates.

Three Forms of Proof

From classical rhetoric you can derive three forms of proof. The first is called logical proof, or *logos* as the ancients called it: the use of argument and evidence to persuade (Reinhard, 1998). The second will be personal proof, or *ethos* concept. The third is emotional argument, or *pathos*. We will spend the most time on logical argument, the mode that is used most often and is, perhaps, the least understood.

The First Form of Proof: *Logos,* or Logical Proof

What Is the Structure of Argument?

Inductive argument provides enough specific instances for the listener to make an inferential leap to a generalization that summarizes the individual instances. For example, you might try to demonstrate that "low taxes are bad for our economy." Your specific instances might include the following:

Schools that are underfunded

Federal programs that are underfunded

Roads and highways that are neither repaired nor maintained

Social programs for the poor that are unfunded

Tuition that goes up because government support goes down

This series of individual instances can lead to an "inferential leap" to a generalization that low taxes are bad for our economy.

Another logical structure is **deductive argument,** which uses a general proposition applied to a specific instance to draw a conclusion. For example, from the major premise (generalization) "All drunk drivers are dangerous," you can move to a minor premise "Joann drives while drunk" to conclude that "Joann is dangerous." This particular logical structure is called a **syllogism** because it contains a major premise (a generalization) applied to a particular instance (a minor premise) that leads to a conclusion.

How Can You Rebut Arguments?

In class, at home, and in the workplace, others may rebut your arguments. **Rebuttal** involves arguing against someone else's position on an issue. If someone in your class gives a presentation with which you profoundly disagree, you may deliver a passionate persuasive presentation opposing that person's position on the issue. Here you will learn several ways to rebut arguments.

The weak points in any inductive argument are the clarity of the proposition, the quality of the individual instances, and the place where the inferential leap occurs. In

inductive argument

A logical structure that provides enough specific instances for the listener to make an inferential leap to a generalization that summarizes the individual instances.

deductive argument

A logical structure that uses a general proposition applied to a specific instance to draw a conclusion.

syllogism

A logical structure that contains a major premise (a generalization) applied to a particular instance (a minor premise) that leads to a conclusion.

rebuttal

Arguing against someone else's position on an issue.

the argument about local taxes, you could argue that it needs to state more clearly to what taxes the proposition refers. Does it refer to all taxes? To local or state taxes? To federal taxes only? The proposition is unclear. On the quality of the individual instances, does the presenter have any evidence that tuition goes up because taxes go down? Finally, how many instances do you have to have before you make the inferential leap?

In trying to persuade you that violent crime is on the rise, how many individual instances might be needed before you are convinced? The answer is that nobody really knows. All we know is that at some point you can quit providing individual instances because most of the audience agrees and the remainder never will. That is why you can always question the point at which the inferential leap occurred.

Likewise, deductive arguments are subject to rebuttal by questioning the major premise, the application of the minor premise, and the meaning of the conclusion. Are all drunk drivers dangerous? Perhaps the answer depends on how the state defines "drunk." Some states say a blood alcohol level of .08, some say .10, and others have some other limit. Apparently we cannot even agree on what percentage constitutes "drunkenness." Also, do we know what percentage Joann is carrying? She may or may not be drunk depending on the standard.

The point is that you can critically analyze both inductive and deductive arguments.

The Second Form of Proof:
Ethos, or Source Credibility

Chapter 11 focused on source credibility, so our discussion here will be brief. The fact is that you can persuade some listeners because you have earned the right to speak. You have competence, trustworthiness, and dynamism, or you share common ground. Your personal power or expertise, or your charisma or personality, can gain compliance. Popular preachers build mega-churches with thousands of worshipers who thrive on the minister's message. They are persuaded not just by proofs from the Bible but by the personal authority of the preacher. They believe him because of who he is. The pope and some politicians, entertainers, and community leaders have such credibility. In jury trials the lawyer who is most liked by the jury often wins regardless of the evidence because the jury believes the lawyer they like. But even in the classroom some presenters have more source credibility than others. For example, third-year students have more credibility than first-year students. The lesson here is that who and what you are can help you persuade others.

TRY ◆ THIS

What motivational appeals tend to work on you? Do you tend to do what others wish for you, or do the wishes of others cause you to rebel? Think carefully about what moves you to action. Do you think the same motivations that influence you also influence your audience?

The Third Form of Proof:
Pathos, or Emotional Proof

You may not be dazzled by a string of statistics that show how many people slide into bankruptcy each year, but you might get tears in your eyes about a local person—very much like yourself—who was so consumed by credit card debt that she and her family had to declare publicly that they would never be able to pay their debts.

Narrative—the telling of a story—is a powerful persuader. The world's holy books, such as the Koran and the Bible, and the teachings of Buddha are practically devoid of statistics but are full of stories and parables. We tell our children stories that teach them life lessons. In jury trials the person who wins often has the best story that accounts for all of the known facts in the case. You too can harness the power of the narrative by telling stories that support your proposition. A student whose persuasive purpose was to get Harley drivers to wear protective helmets had a simple strategy: He told three stories about motorcycle operators who wore helmets and lived. At the beginning of each story, he showed a single slide of that person's badly dented helmet. The visual image of the banged-up helmets and the stories of the three survivors made an indelible impression.

Although logical and emotional appeals are often seen as diametrically opposed concepts, most of our behavior and beliefs are based on a mixture of emotional and rational "reasons." A speaker may persuade an audience to accept his or her immediate behavioral purposes for emotional, rather than logical, reasons. A story about one person's bad experience with the campus bookstore may inspire many audience members to take their business to another store. The experience may have been a one-in-a-thousand situation, the episode may have been as much the customer's fault as the manager's, or such a bad experience may never have happened before. Such is the power of our emotions that they can persuade us to defy the law, fight another nation, or ignore evidence. As one writer stated:

> The creature man is best persuaded
> When heart, not mind, is inundated:
> Affect is what drives the will:
> Rationality keeps it still.*

The fear appeal is one of the most common appeals to emotion. Political ads remind us of the fear we felt in the wake of the 9/11 terrorist attacks, predict that an opponent will tax us to oblivion, and suggest that only one political party can protect us from our enemies. Financial gurus use fear to guide investments (bonds are losers, stocks are winners); businesses use fear to invite sales (prices go up this Wednesday); auto dealers use fear to close a sale (this one is the last of this model for this year). Fear appeals get us to brush our teeth, use deodorant, buy certain clothing, and wear certain perfumes and colognes.

Clearly, fear appeals work in advertising and in everyday life. As a speaker you can use fear appeals in an ethical manner if you do not exaggerate the threat and if you offer means of avoiding the fear. In other words, a presenter who arouses fear in an audience has an ethical obligation to provide reassurance as well. This sentence illustrates fear appeals and reassurances in a single thesis statement: "Not brushing your teeth can lead to gum disease and tooth loss, so listen to my tips on dental hygiene." A presentation that combines fear with reassurance results in greater shifts of opinion, and the audience holds the presenter in higher regard (Cope & Richardson, 1972).

---

*Karlins and Abelson, 1970

People Think Differently

The use of argument, evidence, and logic can be seen as a European-derived manner of thinking unendorsed either by non-European cultures or by North America's own co-cultures. Yook and Albert (1998), for example, found that Korean students as a group were significantly less likely to negotiate with a teacher over matters of grading and learning than were a group of American students. Foss and Griffin (1995) explain a feminist alternative to traditional persuasion in which the goal is not to attack and vanquish the opponent but to achieve understanding through "invitational rhetoric." Remember, different cultures and co-cultures may adopt quite different approaches to negotiating, arguing, and persuading.

Fear appeals are just one kind of emotional appeal commonly found in persuasive presentations. Other examples of possible emotional appeals are testimonials at funerals about the virtues of the deceased, appeals to loyalty and dedication at retirement ceremonies, appeals to patriotism in times of crisis, and appeals to justice in times of legal strife.

Organizing Your Persuasive Message

You already know some micro-organizational features of a persuasive presentation: You may not want to announce your purpose at the outset because you have to build toward acceptance by the end of the presentation. Here we consider some of the macro-organizational features: how you build, construct, or design your presentation to achieve your persuasive purpose.

In chapter 12 you learned that some organizational patterns are used more often in persuasive presentations: cause/effect, problem/solution, and topical-sequence. The topical-sequence pattern is especially useful in arguing advantages and disadvantages of some course of action.

The Monroe Motivated Sequence

To add to your repertoire of organizational patterns, let us consider a pattern of organization that presenters have used successfully for over three decades (Ehninger, 1970): the **Monroe Motivated Sequence.** Developed by a University of Iowa professor, Alan Monroe, this pattern of organization is popular for having five easy-to-follow steps:

- *Step 1: Attention.* You gain and maintain audience attention, and you determine a way to focus audience attention on the content of your presentation.

- *Step 2: Need.* Once you have the audience's attention, you show audience members how the speech is relevant to them. You arouse a need for the change you suggest in your persuasive presentation.

- *Step 3: Satisfaction.* Your speech either presents the information the audience needs or suggests a solution to their needs. You satisfy the audience by meeting their needs with your plan.

Monroe Motivated Sequence

A problem-solving format that encourages an audience to become concerned about an issue; especially appropriate for a persuasive presentation.

- *Step 4: Visualization.* You reinforce your idea in the audience's minds by getting audience members to *see* how your information or ideas will help them.
- *Step 5: Action.* Once the audience has visualized your idea, you plead for action. The audience might remember your main points in an informative presentation and state them to others, or the audience may go out and do what you ask in a persuasive presentation.

The Monroe Motivated Sequence is an appropriate organizational pattern for persuasive presentations, especially when the audience is reluctant to change or to accept a proposed action. See an illustration of the sequence in Figure 15.1.

Ethical Considerations

ethics

A set of principles of right conduct.

Ethics are a set of principles of right conduct. Many of our standards for ethical behavior are codified into law. We do not slander or libel someone who is an ordinary citizen. We do not start a panic that can endanger the lives of others. And we do not advocate the overthrow of our government.

Many principles of ethics are not matters of law, but violations of these unwritten rules do have consequences. No law exists against pointing out acne sufferers in the audience during your speech on dermatology or having your audience unknowingly eat cooked hamster meat, but audience members may find your methods so distasteful that they reject you and your persuasive message.

View an animation of this illustration on the *Online Learning Center.*

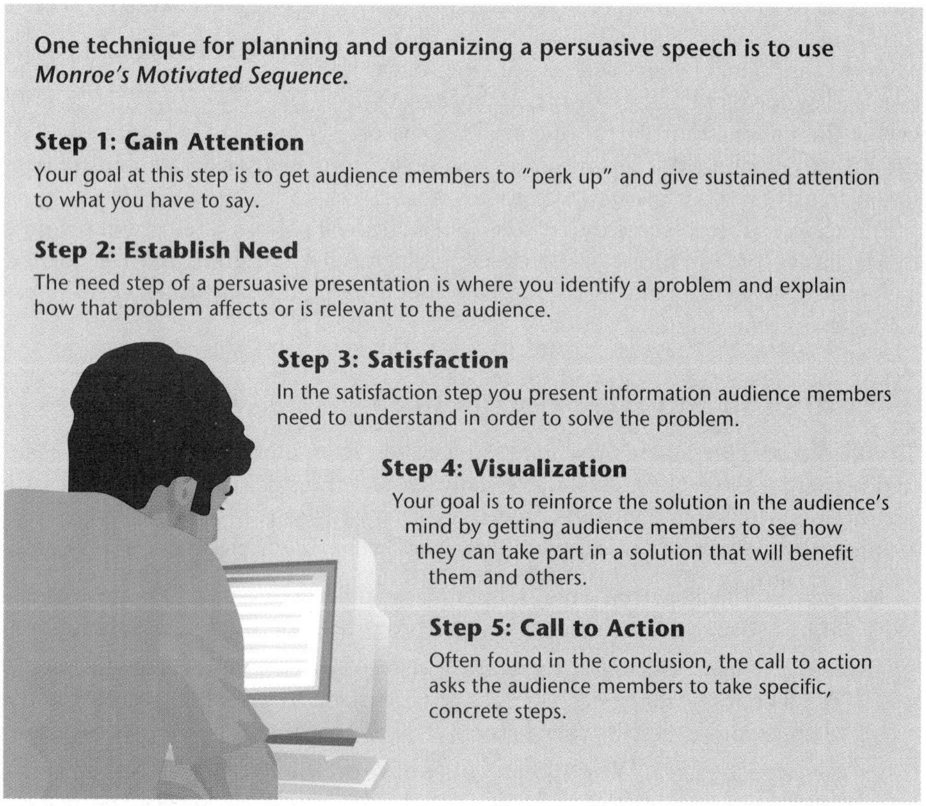

One technique for planning and organizing a persuasive speech is to use *Monroe's Motivated Sequence.*

Step 1: Gain Attention
Your goal at this step is to get audience members to "perk up" and give sustained attention to what you have to say.

Step 2: Establish Need
The need step of a persuasive presentation is where you identify a problem and explain how that problem affects or is relevant to the audience.

Step 3: Satisfaction
In the satisfaction step you present information audience members need to understand in order to solve the problem.

Step 4: Visualization
Your goal is to reinforce the solution in the audience's mind by getting audience members to see how they can take part in a solution that will benefit them and others.

Step 5: Call to Action
Often found in the conclusion, the call to action asks the audience members to take specific, concrete steps.

Figure 15.1   Monroe's Motivated Sequence.

The following are some of the generally accepted ethical standards that govern the preparation and delivery of a persuasive presenter.

1. *Accurately cite sources.* When you are preparing and delivering your speech, you should be very careful to gather and state your information accurately. Specifically, you should reveal from whom you received information. Making up quotations, attributing an idea to someone who never made the statement, omitting important qualifiers, quoting out of context, and distorting information are all examples of ethical violations.

2. *Respect sources of information.* Internet sources are sometimes the best available information and sometimes the worst. Show respect for your sources by revealing as completely as possible the credibility of your sources. This rule extends to respect for persons you interview. These people are willing to share information with you, so it behooves you to treat them and their information with respect, in person and in your presentation.

3. *Respect your audience.* Persuasion is a process that works most effectively with mutual respect between presenter and receiver. Attempts to trick the audience into believing something, lying to the audience, distorting the views of your opposition, or exaggerating claims for your own position are all ethically questionable acts. A presenter should speak truthfully and accurately; the best persuasive presenters can accurately portray the opposing arguments and still win with their own arguments and evidence. Audiences can be very hostile toward a person who has tricked

Professional persuaders tempt you to part with your money for their product.

393

Below is some final advice on what kind of arguments are most persuasive and where you should consider placing them for maximum effectiveness.

1. Place your best argument first or last but not in the middle (Janis & Feshbach, 1953).
2. Present one side of an issue if the audience is friendly, your position is the only one the audience is likely to hear, and you are seeking immediate change of opinion (Powell, 1965).
3. Present both sides of an issue to be perceived as open-minded and to reduce the effects of views the audience might hold opposing your point of view.
4. If your audience already knows an opposing point of view, refute those arguments before proceeding to your own view (Karlins & Abelson, 1970).
5. Be aware that novel arguments have more effect than familiar arguments (Sears & Freedman, 1965).

Figure 15.2   Tips for organizing your arguments.

them or who has lied, distorted, or exaggerated information simply to meet an immediate behavioral purpose or an ultimate goal.

4. *Respect your opponent.* Persuasive presentations invite rebuttal. Nearly always someone inside or outside your audience thinks your ideas or positions are wrong. A good rule of thumb is to respect your opponent, not only because he or she may be right but also because an effective persuasive presenter can take the best the opposition has to offer and still convince the audience he or she should be believed. The idea that you should respect your opponent means you should not indulge in name-calling or in bringing up past behaviors that are irrelevant to the issue. You should attack the other person's evidence, sources, or logic—not the person. Practical reasons for observing this rule of ethics include the following: Few of the issues about which people persuade are ever settled, you may find in time that your opponent's position is better in many respects than your own, and you will have to live with many issues not resolved in the manner you most desire.

You may get the impression from these four ethical guidelines that every persuasive speaker must be part angel. Not quite. The ethical rules for persuasive speaking allow for critical analysis of arguments and ideas, for profound differences of opinion, for the weighing of evidence and supporting materials, and for the swaying of the audience to your point of view. All of these strategies work best if you obey the ethical guidelines that call for the accurate citation of sources, respect for sources of information, respect for your audience, and respect for your opponent.

Figure 15.2 gives additional tips for organizing your arguments.

An Example of a Persuasive Presentation

Having discussed persuasion and ways to influence others, we turn now to an outline for an annotated persuasive presentation that illustrates many of the concepts introduced in the chapter. You should read the outline carefully for its strengths and its weaknesses. What methods does the presenter use to influence listeners? Do the arguments and evidence meet the tests discussed in this chapter? What could the presenter have done differently that would have made the message more appealing to you? The marginal notes should help you answer these questions.

Health Claims: Which Should You Believe and Obey?

Immediate purpose: To persuade my listeners to be skeptical of health claims and to adopt positive health practices supported by scientific evidence.

Ultimate goal: To have my listeners become critical thinkers about health claims so they can sort out which ones to practice for a healthier lifestyle.

Introduction

I. I am a senior in the premed program planning on a career in internal medicine.

   A. I have already been accepted at the School of Medicine to start working next year on the M.D. degree.

   B. I have spent the last three years learning in health and nutrition classes about the effects of diet and exercise on chronic diseases.

   C. All of you see, hear, and read about health claims, but you might wonder which, if any, should concern you.

   D. I will show you how contradictory these claims have become so you can discover the very few that are worth your time, effort, and obedience.

Body

II. You have a right to be confused about health claims because many health claims have been contradictory.

   A. In 2003 Vioxx was supposed to let people with arthritis "dance with the stars" until evidence showed that the drug was giving people heart attacks (2005, Loudon).

   B. Postmenopausal women were told in the 1990s that estrogen would delay Alzheimer's disease, prevent heart attacks, and stop incontinence, but by 2000 women were told to stop hormone supplements because they were causing cancer (2006, therubins.com).

   C. More recently, we were told that calcium and vitamin D would forestall osteoporosis until evidence showed that calcium made little difference except to form painful kidney stones (2006, NIH).

   D. The fish story is especially confusing because the health claims have changed back and forth several times.

      1. For years you were told eat fish for the omega-3 fatty acids (2006, AHA).

      2. Next, you were supposed to avoid fish because of mercury poisoning.

      3. But on March 13, 2006, *Newsweek* announced that the FDA says the benefits of eating fish outweigh the dangers.

III. Many if not most studies reported in the mass media do not meet the gold standard of scientific research.

   A. An ideal study uses a large, random sample in which a wide variety of subjects will be included.

   B. An ideal study is "double-blind": Neither the researcher nor the participants know who is receiving the tested medicine (2006, Research Methods).

   C. An ideal study is not sponsored by a company that might benefit from the results turning out a certain way.

IV. Only three health claims are worth observing so you can quit worrying about the rest.

   A. Exercise does prove to be good for the human body both for appearance and for health reasons (2005, Mayoclinic.com).

Source credibility: Links speaker to topic.

Gains attention.

Announces topic.

Reveals qualifications.

Relates topic to listeners.

Reveals purpose.

Forecasts organization and development.

States proposition.

Gives four specific pieces of evidence to support proposition.

Follows problem/ solution pattern of organization.

States problem: confusing health claims.

Gives oral footnote

States proposition supported by three charact-charistics of ideal study

Proposes action step: Presenter expects audience to follow only three pieces of health advice.

Cites sources throughout.

    B. Avoiding smoking, excessive drinking of alcohol, and illegal drugs is proven to promote healthful living (2006, Sciencedaily.com).

    C. Eating more fruits and vegetables, less red meat, and more fish lowers harmful fat in your diet (2005, Cancerresearchuk.org).

    D. Keeping your body weight to the recommended body mass index (BMI) tends to reduce risks that shorten life (2006, National Institutes of Health).

Conclusion

Summary/review of contents.

Immediate purpose fulfilled.

V. I have shown that health claims are contradictory, that they often do not meet the gold standard of scientific research, and that you can have a healthy life by following a few simple rules.

    A. You will worry less if you do not obey every health claim.

    B. You will live a longer and better life if you exercise, eat wisely, and avoid all those things your mother told you to avoid.

Bibliography

American Heart Association. (2006, November 25). *Fish, levels of mercury and omega-3 fatty acids.* Retrieved November 26, 2006, from http://www.americanheart.org/presenter.jhtml?identifier=3013797

Estrogen and Alzheimer's disease—part X. Retrieved November 27, 2006, from http://www.therubins.com/alzheim/alzestro9.htm

Exercise: 7 benefits of regular physical activity. (2005, July 26). Retrieved November 26, 2006, from http://www.mayoclinic.com/health/exercise/HQ01676

Healthy eating. (2005, October). Retrieved November 26, 2006, from http://www.info.cancerresearchuk.org/healthyliving/dietandhealthyeating/foodnutrientsandcancer/

Kantrowitz, B., & Kalb, C. (2006, March 13). *Food news blues: Fat is bad, but good fat is good.* Retrieved November 26, 2006, from http://www.msnbc.msn.com/id/11678153/site/newsweek/

Loudon, M. (2005, August 30). *The FDA exposed: An interview with Dr. David Graham, the Vioxx whistleblower.* Retrieved from NewsTarget.com.

Men who avoid certain risk factors in midlife may have longer, healthier life. (2006, November 19). Retrieved November 26, 2006, from http://www.sciencedaily.com/releases/2006/11/o61116121312.htm

National Heart, Lung and Blood Institute. (2006). *Calculate your BMI.* Retrieved on November 26, 2006, from http://www.nhlbisupport.com/bmi/

National Institutes of Health. (2006, February 15). *Calcium and vitamin D supplements offer modest bone improvements, no benefit for colorectal cancer.* Retrieved November 26, 2006, from http://www.nih.gov/news/pr/beb2006/nhlbi-15.htm

Research methods. Retrieved November 26, 2006, from http://www.webster.edu/~woolflm/statmethods.htm/

TRY ◆ THIS

How do you avoid telemarketers? What method of avoiding telemarketers do you find most satisfying? Do you feel guilty about any of your methods of avoidance?

How to Resist Persuasion

Listed below are some measures you can take to resist persuasion, not only in public presentations but also on the telephone, from salespeople, and in advertising:

1. *Remember: The best resistance is avoidance.* You do not have to watch or read advertising, go into stores where you do not intend to buy, listen to telemarketers, or watch half-hour television "infomercials."

2. *Be skeptical about all messages.* Persuaders who are seeking easy prey look for the uneducated, the desperate, the angry, the very young, the very old, and the unsuspecting. They avoid people who are educated, articulate, cautious, and careful. You should use your knowledge of argumentation, evidence, and proof to analyze claims.

3. *Check claims with other, unbiased sources.* A good rule is to verify any persuasive claims with at least two other sources of information. A politician tells you that lower taxes will be good for you. What do the editorials, the political commentators, and the opposition say about that plan? Consumer magazines, especially those that take no advertising, are less likely to be biased, as are news sources that embrace objectivity.

4. *Check out the credibility of the source.* Be suspicious if a salesperson will not reveal the phone numbers of satisfied customers, if a business is new or changes location often, and if a speaker has a questionable reputation for truth or reliability. Credible sources have people, institutions, and satisfied audiences who can vouch for them.

5. *Be cautious about accepting a persuasive appeal.* Most states have laws that allow even a signed contract to be rejected by the customer in the first 24 to 48 hours—in case you have second thoughts. Accepting claims on impulse is a dangerous practice that you can avoid by never making an important decision in the context of a sales pitch. Have you ever heard of a businessperson who refused to take the money the next day?

6. *Question the ethical basis of proposed actions.* Angry people are easy to turn to violence, desperate people willingly consider desperate measures, and frustrated people can easily become an unruly mob. You need to ask if the proposed action is self-serving, if the proposal pits one group against another, and if it will be good for you when viewed in retrospect.

7. *Use your knowledge and experience to analyze persuasive claims.* A claim that sounds too good to be true probably is. If you have a "gut feeling" that a claim seems wrong, you should find out why. You should use all you know about logic, evidence, and proof to see if the persuader is drawing a

Learn to be wary about good deals. Use your brain to protect yourself.

sound conclusion or making an inferential leap that is justified by the evidence. Finally, all evidence should be open to scrutiny.

8. *Use your own values as a check against fraudulent claims.* If someone is trying to get you to do something that runs counter to what you learned in your religion, in your home, about the law, or from your friends, you should be wary. Sales always enrich the seller but not always the buyer. You can choose to sacrifice, but you should not sacrifice unwittingly. Your values are good protection against those who would cheat you. You should ask yourself, "What would my parents, my friends, my neighbors, my professor, or my religion think of this decision?"

9. *Check what persuaders say against what they do.* You might add: Judge them more by what they do than by what they say. Talk may not be cheap, but words cost less than deeds, and the proof of what a person says is in his or her behavior. Many an "education governor" has cut the budget for education. You learn to trust people who do what they say; you learn to distrust those who say one thing and do another.

10. *Use your freedom of expression and freedom of choice as protection against unethical persuaders.* In the United States you can hear competing ideas, and the choice is yours. You can educate yourself about issues and ideas by reading, watching, and listening. Education and learning are powerful protection against persuaders who would take advantage of you. Use your freedoms to help defend yourself.

Now that you know 10 suggestions for resisting persuasion, you can practice the strategies for keeping others from manipulating your mind and picking your pockets.

Chapter Review & Study Guide

SUMMARY

In this chapter you learned the following:

▶ A persuasive presentation is a message designed strategically to induce change in the audience.

▶ A persuasive presentation has both immediate and ultimate goals.

▶ A persuasive presentation may have different features than other presentations:
  • The introduction may withhold the purpose.
  • The purpose may be revealed late.
  • The audience analysis indicates when to reveal the purpose.

▶ A persuasive presentation can have four different purposes:
  • Continuance and deterrence are action goals that are difficult to demonstrate because the audience exhibits no overt change.
  • Adoption and discontinuance are favored in persuasive presentations because the presenter expects overt change from the listeners.

▶ Face-to-face persuasive presentations are an effective means of changing a captive audience's mind.

▶ A persuasive presentation has the following characteristics:
  • It distinguishes among questions of fact, policy, and value.
  • It differentiates between evidence and proof.
  • It applies the tests of evidence.
  • It recognizes the difference between inductive and deductive arguments.
  • It uses logical argument, personal proof, and emotional argument appropriately.
  • It organizes and places best arguments to advantage.
  • It recognizes the five steps in the Monroe Motivated Sequence.

▶ A persuasive presentation should apply high ethical standards, the principles of right conduct.

▶ A number of strategies can be used to resist persuasion.

KEY TERMS

Go to the *Online Learning Center* at **www.mhhe.com/pearson3** to further your understanding of the following terminology.

Adoption	Ethics	Proposition of policy
Argument	Immediate purpose	Proposition of value
Boomerang effect	Inductive argument	Rebuttal
Continuance	Monroe Motivated Sequence	Syllogism
Deductive argument	Persuasive presentation	Tests of evidence
Deterrence	Proof	Ultimate goal
Discontinuance	Proposition of fact	

STUDY QUESTIONS

1. The intention of a persuasive presentation is to
   a. inform listeners of a certain topic
   b. change listeners in a way consistent with your purpose
   c. explain a concept
   d. describe an important issue

2. If an audience likes you and your message less after the presentation than they did before, what has taken place?

   a. logos
   b. believability
   c. boomerang effect
   d. continuance

3. When a presenter attempts to convince listeners to terminate a current behavior, what has taken place?
   a. discontinuance
   b. adoption

c. continuance

d. deterrence

4. If your evidence meets the tests of evidence, it will not

   a. come from unbiased sources

   b. be consistent with other well-known facts

   c. overlook counterevidence

   d. consist of authoritative, valid, and reliable surveys

5. When resisting persuasion from salespeople and advertisers, you should

   a. avoid using your own values as a check against fraudulent claims

   b. listen to all messages with an open mind

   c. accept the credibility of all sources

   d. question the ethical basis of proposed actions

6. Which type of argument uses a series of individual instances that lead to a generalization?

   a. deductive

   b. inductive

   c. rebuttal

   d. syllogism

7. A deductive argument can be rebutted by questioning the

   a. major premise

   b. clarity of the proposition

   c. quality of individual instances

   d. place where the inferential leap occurs

8. Which of the following statements regarding argument organization is true?

   a. Place your best argument in the middle.

   b. Present one side of an issue to reduce the effects of contrary arguments.

   c. Present one side of an issue when you are seeking immediate, temporary change of opinion.

   d. Familiar arguments have more effect than novel arguments.

9. In the Monroe Motivated Sequence, the visualization step involves

   a. gaining and maintaining audience attention

   b. presenting information or a solution to audience needs

   c. asking the audience to take specific steps

   d. reinforcing the solution by demonstrating how the solution will benefit the audience

10. Which is *not* an ethical standard to follow when preparing and delivering a persuasive presentation?

   a. Accurately cite sources.

   b. Respect sources of information by revealing their credibility.

   c. Respect your audience by speaking truthfully and accurately.

   d. Respect your opponent by attacking the other person's character instead of his or her evidence, sources, or logic.

Answers:

1. (b); 2. (c); 3. (a); 4. (c); 5. (d); 6. (b); 7. (a); 8. (c); 9. (d); 10. (d)

CRITICAL THINKING

1. When watching commercials, viewing print advertisements, or listening to a persuasive speaker, determine if the information presented meets the tests of evidence. Explain how this either strengthens or weakens the argument presented.

2. Which ethical standards of persuasive presentations do you think are most often violated? Provide examples.

SELF–QUIZ

For further review, try the chapter self-quiz on the *Online Learning Center* at **www.mhhe.com/pearson3**.

REFERENCES

Bruni, F. (2000, July 31). For Laura Bush, a direction that she never dreamed of. *The New York Times*.

Cope, F., & Richardson, D. (1972). The effects of measuring recommendations in a fear-arousing speech. *Speech Monographs, 39*, 148–150.

Ehninger, D. (1970). Argument as method: Its nature, its limitations, and its uses. *Speech Monographs, 37*, 101–110.

Ehninger, D., Gronbeck, B. E., & Monroe, A. H. (1984). *Principles of speech communication* (9th brief ed.). Glenview, IL: Scott, Foresman.

Foss, S. K., & Griffin, C. L. (1995). Beyond persuasion: A proposal for an invitational rhetoric. *Communication Monographs, 62*, 2–19.

Fotheringham, W. (1966). *Perspectives on persuasion*. Boston: Allyn & Bacon.

Janis, I. S., & Feshbach, S. (1953). Effects of fear-arousing communications. *Journal of Abnormal and Social Psychology, 48*, 78–92.

Karlins, M., & Abelson, H. I. (1970). *Persuasion: How opinions and attitudes are changed* (2nd ed.). New York: Springer.

Powell, F. A. (1965). The effects of anxiety-arousing messages when related to personal, familial, and impersonal referents. *Speech Monographs, 32*, 102–106.

Reinhard, J. C. (1988). The empirical study of the persuasive effects of evidence: The status after 50 years of research. *Human Communication Research, 15*, 3–59.

Sears, D., & Freedman, J. (1965). Effects of expected familiarity with arguments upon opinion change and selective exposure. *Journal of Personality and Social Psychology, 2*, 420–426.

glossary

A

abstract words 371
Words or phrases that refer generally to ideas, qualities, acts, or relationships.

accommodation goal 171
The marginalized group manages to keep co-cultural identity while striving for positive relationships with the dominant culture.

active listening 115
Involved listening with a purpose.

active perception 32
Perception in which your mind selects, organizes, and interprets that which you sense.

adaptors 91
Nonverbal movements that you might perform fully in private but only partially in public.

adoption 384
The listeners start a new behavior as a result of the persuasive presentation.

affect displays 91
Nonverbal movements of the face and body used to show emotion.

affection 221
The emotion of caring for others and/or being cared for.

aggressiveness 152
Assertion of one's rights at the expense of others and care about one's own needs but no one else's.

analogy 294
A comparison of things in some respects, especially in position or function, that are otherwise dissimilar.

androgynous 158
Refers to persons who possess stereotypically female and male characteristics.

antonym 371
Defines an idea by opposition.

argument 386
A proposition that asserts some course of action.

argumentativeness 152
The quality or state of being argumentative; synonymous with contentiousness or combativeness.

articulation 339
The production of sounds; a component of enunciation.

artifacts 99
Ornaments or adornments you display that hold communicative potential.

assigned groups 224
Groups that evolve out of a hierarchy whereby individuals are assigned membership to the group.

assimilation goal 171
The marginalized group attempts to fit in with the dominant group.

attitude 260
A predisposition to respond favorably or unfavorably to a person, an object, an idea, or an event.

attractiveness 149
A concept that includes physical attractiveness, how desirable a person is to work with, and how much "social value" the person has for others.

attribution 41
The assignment of meaning to people's behavior.

audience analysis 257
The collection and interpretation of audience information obtained by observation, inferences, questionnaires, or interviews.

autocratic leaders 227
Leaders who maintain strict control over their group.

automatic attention 112
The instinctive focus we give to stimuli signaling a change in our surroundings, stimuli that we deem important, or stimuli that we perceive to signal danger.

B

bargaining 157
The process in which two or more parties attempt to reach an agreement on what each should give and receive in a transaction between them.

behavioral flexibility   158
The ability to alter behavior to adapt to new situations and to relate in new ways when necessary.

belief   260
A conviction; often thought to be more enduring than an attitude and less enduring than a value.

bibliographic references   290
Complete citations that appear in the "references" or "works cited" section of your speech outline.

bibliography   325
A list of sources used in a presentation.

bodily movement   344
What the speaker does with his or her entire body during a presentation.

boomerang effect   384
The audience likes you and your message less after your presentation than they did before.

body   310
The largest part of the presentation, which contains the arguments, evidence, and main content.

brainstorming   252
A creative procedure for thinking of as many topics as you can in a limited time.

brakelight function   323
A forewarning to the audience that the end of the presentation is near.

C

captive audience   258
An audience that has not chosen to hear a particular speaker or speech.

cause/effect pattern   319
A method of organization in which the presenter first explains the causes of an event, a problem, or an issue and then discusses its consequences, results, or effects.

celebrity testimony   294
Statements made by a public figure who is known to the audience.

channel   12
The means by which a message moves from the source to the receiver of the message.

chronemics   94
Also called temporal communication; the way people organize and use time and the messages that are created because of their organization and use of it.

chronological résumé   195
A document that organizes your credentials over time.

cliché   71
An expression that has lost originality and force through overuse.

closure   38
The tendency to fill in missing information in order to complete an otherwise incomplete figure or statement.

co-culture   35, 170
(1) A group whose beliefs or behaviors distinguish it from the larger culture of which it is a part and with which it shares numerous similarities. (2)A group that exists within a larger, dominant culture but differs from the dominant culture in some significant characteristic.

code   13
A systematic arrangement of symbols used to create meanings in the mind of another person or persons.

cognitive modification approach   348
Using positive thinking to bolster the beginning speaker's confidence.

collaborative style   209
Thoughtful negotiation and reasoned compromise.

collectivist cultures   174
Cultures that value the group over the individual.

colloquialisms   71
Words and phrases used informally.

commitment   254
A measure of how much time and effort you put into a cause; your passion and concern about the topic.

common ground   278
Also known as co-orientation, the degree to which the speaker's values, beliefs, attitudes, and interests are shared with the audience; an aspect of credibility.

communication   10
The process of using messages to generate meaning.

communication competence   22
The ability to effectively exchange meaning through a common system of symbols, signs, or behavior.

communication networks   190
Patterns of relationships through which information flows in an organization.

communication apprehension   347
An individual's level of fear or anxiety associated with either real or anticipated communication with another person or persons.

comparison   370
Shows the similarity between something well known and something less known.

competence   276
The degree to which the speaker is perceived as skilled, reliable, experienced, qualified, authoritative, and informed; an aspect of credibility.

complementarity   150
The idea that we sometimes bond with people whose strengths are our weaknesses.

complementary relationships   139
Relationships in which each person supplies something the other person or persons lack.

complementation   87
Nonverbal and verbal codes add meaning to each other and expand the meaning of either message alone.

compliance-gaining   155
Those attempts made by a source of messages to influence a target "to perform some desired behavior that the target otherwise might not perform."

compliance-resisting   155
The refusal of targets of influence messages to comply with requests.

conclusion   323
The part that finishes the presentation by fulfilling the four functions of an ending.

concrete language   77
Words and statements that are specific rather than abstract or vague.

concrete words   371
Words that refer to definite persons, places, objects, and acts.

confirmation   50
Feedback in which others treat you in a manner consistent with who you believe you are.

conjunctive tasks   238
Group tasks for which no one member has all the necessary information but each member has some information to contribute.

connotative meaning   67
An individualized or personalized meaning of a word, which may be emotionally laden.

context   17
A set of circumstances or a situation.

continuance   384
Encouraging the audience to keep doing what they are doing.

contradiction   87
Verbal and nonverbal messages conflict.

contradictions   146
In dialectic theory the idea that each person in a relationship might have two opposing desires for maintaining the relationship.

contrast   370
Clarifies by showing differences.

control   221
The ability to influence our environment.

cover letter   196
A short letter introducing you and your résumé to an interviewer.

criteria   240
The standards by which a group must judge potential solutions.

critical listening   116
Listening that challenges the speaker's message by evaluating its accuracy, meaningfulness, and utility.

critical thinking   119
Analyzing the speaker, the situation, and the speaker's ideas to make critical judgments about the message being presented.

cultural competence   79
The ability of individuals and systems to respond respectfully and effectively to people of all cultures, classes, races, ethnic backgrounds, and religions in a manner that recognizes, affirms, and values the worth of individuals, families, and communities and protects and preserves the dignity of each.

cultural relativism   172
The belief that another culture should be judged by its own context rather than measured against your culture.

culture   34, 65, 170
(1) A system of shared beliefs, values, customs, behaviors, and artifacts that the members of a society use to cope with one another and with their world. (2) The socially transmitted behavior patterns, beliefs, attitudes, and values of a particular period, class, community, or population. (3) A unique combination of rituals, religious beliefs, ways of thinking, and ways of behaving that unify a group of people.

customer service encounter   209
The moment of interaction between the customer and the firm.

D

dating   78
Specifying when you made an observation, since everything changes over time.

deceptive communication 152
The practice of deliberately making somebody believe things that are not true.

decode 64
The process of assigning meaning to others' words in order to translate them into thoughts of your own.

decoding 13
The process of assigning meaning to the idea or thought in a code.

deductive argument 388
A logical structure that uses a general proposition applied to a specific instance to draw a conclusion.

defensiveness 153
Occurs when a person feels attacked.

definitions 296
Determinations of meaning through description, simplification, examples, analysis, comparison, explanation, or illustration.

delivery 334
The presentation of a speech by using your voice and body to communicate your message.

democratic leaders 227
Leaders who encourage members to participate in group decisions.

demographic analysis 259
The collection and interpretation of data about the characteristics of people.

demonstrating 372
Showing the audience what you are explaining.

denotative meaning 67
The agreed-upon meaning or dictionary meaning of a word.

descriptiveness 76
The practice of describing observed behavior or phenomena instead of offering personal reactions or judgments.

designated leader 225
Someone who has been appointed or elected to a leadership position.

deterrence 384
Discouraging listeners from taking some action.

dialectic 146
The tension that exists between two conflicting or interacting forces, elements, or ideas.

dialogue 15
The act of taking part in a conversation, discussion, or negotiation.

disconfirmation 50
Feedback in which others fail to respond to your notion of self by responding neutrally.

discontinuance 385
A persuasive purpose rooted in convincing listeners to stop some current behavior.

disjunctive tasks 238
Group tasks that require little coordination and that can be completed by the most skilled member working alone.

doublespeak 71
Any language that is purposefully constructed to disguise its actual meaning.

downward communication 190
Messages flowing from superiors to subordinates.

dyadic communication 19
Two-person communication.

dynamism 277
The extent to which the speaker is perceived as bold, active, energetic, strong, empathic, and assertive; an aspect of credibility.

E

economic orientation 189
Organizations that manufacture products and/or offer services for consumers.

emblems 90
Nonverbal movements that substitute for words and phrases.

emergent groups 224
Groups resulting from environmental conditions leading to the formation of a cohesive group of individuals.

emergent leader 225
Someone who becomes an informal leader by exerting influence toward achievement of a group's goal but who does not hold the formal position or role of leader.

emoticons 128
Typographic symbols showing emotional meaning.

emotional labor 211
Jobs in which employees are expected to display certain feelings in order to satisfy organizational role expectations.

empathic listening 115
Listening with a purpose and attempting to understand the other person.

emphasis 87
The use of nonverbal cues to strengthen verbal messages.

encode   65
The process of translating your thoughts into words.

encoding   13
The process of translating an idea or thought into a code.

enunciation   339
The pronunciation and articulation of sounds and words.

ethics   23, 392
(1) A set of moral principles or values. (2) A set of principles of right conduct.

ethnocentrism   172
The belief that your own group or culture is superior to other groups or cultures.

euphemism   71
A more polite, pleasant expression used instead of a socially unacceptable form.

examples   292
Specific instances used to illustrate your point.

expert testimony   293
Statements made by someone who has special knowledge or expertise about an issue or idea.

explanation   295, 372
(1) A clarification of what something is or how it works. (2) A means of idea development that simplifies or clarifies an idea while arousing audience interest.

explicit-rule culture   178
A culture in which information, policies, procedures, and expectations are explicit.

extemporaneous mode   335
A carefully prepared and researched presentation delivered in a conversational style.

extrinsic motivation   367
A method of making information relevant by providing the audience with reasons outside the presentation itself for listening to the content of the presentation.

eye contact   343
The extent to which a speaker looks directly at the audience.

F

face   54
The socially approved and presented identity of an individual.

facework   54
Verbal and nonverbal strategies that are used to present your own varying images to others and to help them maintain their own images.

facial expressions   343
Any nonverbal cues expressed by the speaker's face.

feedback   12
The receiver's verbal and nonverbal response to the source's message.

figure   38
The focal point of your attention.

first-person observation   120
Observations based on something that you personally have sensed.

fluency   340
The smoothness of delivery, the flow of words, and the absence of vocalized pauses.

formal communication   190
Messages that follow prescribed channels of communication throughout the organization.

formal role   231
Also called positional role; an assigned role based on an individual's position or title within a group.

frozen evaluation   78
An assessment of a concept that does not change over time.

functional résumé   195
A document that organizes your credentials by type of function performed.

fundamental attribution error   42
In judging other people, the tendency to attribute their successes to the situation and their failures to their personal characteristics.

G

gestures   341
Movements of the head, arms, and hands to illustrate, emphasize, or signal ideas in a presentation.

ground   38
The background against which your focused attention occurs.

group climate   234
The emotional tone or atmosphere members create within the group.

group conflict   245
An expressed struggle between two or more members of a group.

group culture   236
The socially negotiated system of rules that guide group behavior.

group decision support system (GDSS)   242
An interactive network of computers with specialized software allowing users to generate solutions for unstructured problems.

groupthink 234
An unintended outcome of cohesion in which the desire for cohesion and agreement takes precedence over critical analysis and discussion.

H

hearing 110
The act of receiving sound.

heterosexist language 73
Language that implies that everyone is heterosexual.

high self-monitors 54
Individuals who are highly aware of their identity management behavior.

high-context (HC) cultures 176
Cultures like those of the Asian Pacific Rim and Central and South America, in which much of the meaning is "preprogrammed information" understood by the receiver and transmitted also by the setting in which the transaction occurs.

horizontal communication 191
Messages between members of an organization with equal power.

hostile work environment sexual harassment 213
Conditions in the workplace that are sexually offensive, intimidating, or hostile and that affect an individual's ability to perform his or her job.

hurtful messages 152
Messages that create emotional pain or upset.

I

identity management 53
The control (or lack of control) of the communication of information through a performance.

illustrators 91
Nonverbal movements that accompany or reinforce verbal messages.

imagery 371
Use of words that appeal to the senses, that create pictures in the mind.

immediacy 206
Communication behaviors intended to create perceptions of psychological closeness with others.

immediate behavioral purposes 364
The actions expected from an audience during and immediately after a presentation.

immediate purpose 312, 383
(1) What you expect to achieve on the day of your presentation. (2) A statement of what you intend to accomplish in this particular presentation.

implicit-rule culture 178
A culture in which information and cultural rules are implied and already known to the participants.

impromptu mode 335
Delivery of a presentation without notes, plans, or formal preparation; characterized by spontaneity and conversational language.

inclusion 221
The state of being involved with others; a human need.

incremental plagiarism 297
The intentional or unintentional use of information from one or more sources without fully divulging how much information is directly quoted.

indexing 78
Identifying the uniqueness of objects, events, and people.

individualistic cultures 174
Cultures that value individual freedom, choice, uniqueness, and independence.

inductive argument 388
A logical structure that provides enough specific instances for the listener to make an inferential leap to a generalization that summarizes the individual instances.

inflection 97
The variety or changes in pitch.

informal communication 191
Any interaction that does not generally follow the formal structure of the organization but emerges out of natural social interaction among organization members.

informal role 232
Also called a behavioral role; a role that is developed spontaneously within a group.

information hunger 365
The audience's need for the information contained in the presentation.

information literacy 127
The ability to recognize when information is needed and to locate, evaluate, and effectively use the information needed.

information overload 369
Providing much more information than the audience can absorb in amount, complexity, or both.

information relevance 366
The importance, novelty, and usefulness of the information to the audience.

informative content   368
The main points and subpoints, illustrations, and examples used to clarify and inform.

integration orientation   189
Organizations that help to mediate and resolve discord among members of society.

interaction management   208
Establishing a smooth pattern of interaction that allows a clear flow between topics and ideas.

intercultural communication   168
The exchange of information between individuals who are unalike culturally.

internal references   290
Brief notations indicating a bibliographic reference that contains the details you are using in your speech.

interpersonal communication   19
The process of using messages to generate meaning between at least two people in a situation that allows mutual opportunities for both speaking and listening.

interpersonal relationships   137
Associations between two people who are interdependent, who use some consistent patterns of interaction, and who have interacted for an extended period of time.

interpretive perception   40
Perception that involves a blend of internal states and external stimuli.

intrapersonal communication   18
The process of using messages to generate meaning within the self.

introduction   304
The first part of your presentation, where you fulfill the five functions of an introduction.

J

jargon   73
The technical language developed by a professional group.

job description   201
A document that defines the job in terms of its content and scope.

K

key-word outline   316
An outline consisting of important words or phrases to remind you of the content of the presentation.

kinesics   89
The study of bodily movements, including posture, gestures, and facial expressions.

L

laissez-faire leaders   227
Leaders who take almost no initiative in structuring a group discussion.

language   64
A collection of symbols, letters, or words with arbitrary meanings that are governed by rules and used to communicate.

lay testimony   293
Statements made by an ordinary person that substantiate or support what you say.

leadership   225
A process of using communication to influence the behaviors and attitudes of others to meet group goals.

lecture cues   125
Verbal or nonverbal signals that stress points or indicate transitions between ideas during a lecture.

lecture listening   125
The ability to listen to, mentally process, and recall lecture information.

listening   111
The active process of receiving, constructing meaning from, and responding to spoken and/or nonverbal messages. It involves the ability to retain information, as well as to react empathically and/or appreciatively to spoken and/or nonverbal messages.

listening for enjoyment   116
Situations involving relaxing, fun, or emotionally stimulating information.

long-range goal   312
What you expect to achieve by your message in the days, months, or years ahead.

long-term memory   113
Our permanent storage place for information including but not limited to past experiences; language; values; knowledge; images of people; memories of sights, sounds, and smells; and even fantasies.

low self-monitors   54
Individuals who communicate with others with little attention to the responses to their messages.

low-context (LC) cultures   174
Cultures like the United States and Scandinavia, in which communication tends to be centered on the source, with intentions stated overtly and with a direct verbal style.

M

main points   312
The most important points in a presentation; indicated by Roman numerals in an outline.

maintenance functions   232
Behaviors that focus on the interpersonal relationships among group members.

manuscript mode   335
Delivery of a presentation from a script of the entire speech.

mass communication   20
The process of using messages to generate meanings in a mediated system, between a source and a large number of unseen receivers.

meaning   11
The understanding of the message.

memorized mode   335
Delivering a presentation that has been committed to memory.

message   12
The verbal or nonverbal form of the idea, thought, or feeling that one person (the source) wishes to communicate to another person or group of people (the receivers).

metaphors   22
A means to understanding and experiencing one thing in terms of another.

microtargeting   267
A method of bringing national issues down to the individual level.

Monroe Motivated Sequence   391
A problem-solving format that encourages an audience to become concerned about an issue; especially appropriate for a persuasive presentation.

M-time   178
The monochronic time schedule, which compartmentalizes time to meet personal needs, separates task and social dimensions, and points to the future.

N

narrating   372
The oral presentation and interpretation of a story, a description, or an event; includes dramatic reading of prose or poetry.

network   199
An intricate web of contacts and relationships designed to benefit the participants.

noise   14
Any interference in the encoding and decoding processes that reduces message clarity.

nonverbal codes   13, 89
(1) All symbols that are not words, including bodily movements, use of space and time, clothing and adornments, and sounds other than words. (2) Codes of communication consisting of symbols that are not words, including nonword vocalizations.

nonverbal communication   86
The process of using messages that are not words to generate meaning.

norms   229
Informal rules for group interaction created and sustained through communication.

O

objectics   99
Also called object language; the study of the human use of clothing and other artifacts as nonverbal codes.

objective statement   194
An articulation of your goals.

operational definition   77, 371
(1) A definition that identifies something by revealing how it works, how it is made, or what it consists of. (2) Defines by explaining a process.

organizational communication   189
The ways in which groups of people both maintain structure and order through their symbolic interactions and allow individual actors the freedom to accomplish their goals.

organizational patterns   317
Arrangements of the contents of a presentation.

organizations   189
Social collectives, or groups of people, in which activities are coordinated to achieve both individual and collective goals.

outline   311
A written plan that uses symbols, margins, and content to reveal the order, importance, and substance of a presentation.

P

paralinguistic features   97
The nonword sounds and nonword characteristics of language, such as pitch, volume, rate, and quality.

parallel form   313
The consistent use of complete sentences, clauses, phrases, or words in an outline.

paraphrasing   77
Restating another person's message by rephrasing the content or intent of the message.

pattern-maintenance orientation 190
Organizations that promote cultural and educational regularity and development within society.

pause 338
The absence of vocal sound used for dramatic effect, transition, or emphasis.

perception 32
The process of becoming aware of objects and events from the senses.

perceptual constancy 34
The idea that your past experiences lead you to see the world in a way that is difficult to change; your initial perceptions persist.

personal experience 280
Use of your own life as a source of information.

personal idioms 156
Unique forms of expression and language understood only by individual couples.

personal inventory 253
An analysis of your own reading, viewing, and listening habits and behavior to discover topics of personal interest.

persuasive presentation 382
A message designed to strategically induce change in an audience.

phatic communication 65
Communication that is used to establish a mood of sociability rather than to communicate information or ideas.

pitch 97, 337
The highness or lowness of the speaker's voice.

plagiarism 297
The intentional use of information from another source without crediting the source.

politeness 54
Our efforts to save face for others.

political orientation 189
Organizations that generate and distribute power and control within society.

power 225
Interpersonal influence that forms the basis for group leadership.

pragmatics 65
The study of language as it is used in a social context, including its effect on the communicators.

problem/solution pattern 320
A method of organization in which the presenter describes a problem and proposes a solution to that problem.

process 10
An activity, exchange, or set of behaviors that occurs over time.

profanity 72
Language that is disrespectful of things sacred.

pronunciation 339
The act of correctly articulating words.

proof 386
Evidence the receiver believes.

proposition of fact 386
An assertion that can be proved or disproved as consistent with reality.

proposition of policy 386
A proposal of a new rule.

proposition of value 386
A statement of what we should embrace as more important to our culture.

proxemics 93
The study of the human use of space and distance.

proximity 39, 149
(1) The principle that objects physically close to each other will be perceived as a unit or group. (2) The location, distance, or range between persons and things.

P-time 179
The polychronic time schedule, which views time as "contextually based and relationally oriented."

public communication 19
The process of using messages to generate meanings in a situation in which a single source transmits a message to a number of receivers.

Q

questionnaire 263
A set of written questions developed to obtain demographic and attitudinal information.

quid pro quo sexual harassment 213
A situation in which an employee is offered a reward or is threatened with punishment based on his or her participation in a sexual activity.

R

racist language 73
Language that insults a group because of its skin color or ethnicity.

rate 97, 337
(1) The pace of your speech. (2) The speed at which speech is delivered, normally between 125 and 190 words per minute.

rebuttal 388
Arguing against someone else's position on an issue.

receiver 12
A message target.

reference librarian 282
A librarian specifically trained to help you find sources of information.

reflexivity 182
Being self-aware and learning from interactions with the intent of improving future interactions.

regionalisms 73
Words and phrases specific to a particular region or part of the country.

regulation 87
Nonverbal codes are used to monitor and control interactions with others.

regulators 91
Nonverbal movements that control the flow or pace of communication.

rejection 50
Feedback in which others treat you in a manner that is inconsistent with your self-definition.

relational deterioration 147
In Knapp's model the process by which relationships disintegrate.

relational development 146
In Knapp's model the process by which relationships grow.

relational maintenance 146
In Knapp's model the process of keeping a relationship together.

relationship-oriented groups 224
Also called primary groups; groups that are usually long-term and exist to meet our needs for inclusion and affection.

relaxation approach 348
Combining deep relaxation with fear-inducing thoughts.

repetition 87
The same message is sent both verbally and nonverbally.

responsiveness 149
The idea that we tend to select our friends and loved ones from people who demonstrate positive interest in us.

rhetorical questions 365
Questions asked for effect, with no answer expected.

rituals 156
Formalized patterns of actions or words followed regularly.

role 34, 231
(1) The part an individual plays in a group; an individual's function or expected behavior. (2) A consistent pattern of interaction or behavior exhibited over time.

rough draft 314
The preliminary organization of the outline of a presentation.

S

Sapir-Whorf hypothesis 66
A theory that our perception of reality is determined by our thought processes and our thought processes are limited by our language and, therefore, that language shapes our reality.

schema 114
Organizational "filing systems" for thoughts held in long-term memory.

search engine 284
A program on the Internet that allows users to search for information.

second-person observation 120
A report of what another person observed.

selective attention 36, 112
(1) The tendency, when you expose yourself to information and ideas, to focus on certain cues and ignore others. (2) The sustained focus we give to stimuli we deem important.

selective exposure 36
The tendency to expose yourself to information that reinforces, rather than contradicts, your beliefs or opinions.

selective perception 37
The tendency to see, hear, and believe only what you want to see, hear, and believe.

selective retention 37
The tendency to remember better the things that reinforce your beliefs rather than those that oppose them.

self-actualization 48
According to Maslow, the fulfillment of one's potential as a person.

self-centered functions 232
Behaviors that serve the needs of the individual at the expense of the group.

self-disclosure   140
The process of making intentional revelations about yourself that others would be unlikely to know and that generally constitute private, sensitive, or confidential information.

self-esteem   51
The feeling you have about your self-concept; that is, how well you like and value yourself.

self-fulfilling prophecy   46
The idea that you behave and see yourself in ways that are consistent with how others see you.

self-image   50
The picture you have of yourself; the sort of person you believe you are.

self-managed approach   349
Reducing the fear of presenting with self-diagnosis and a variety of therapies.

self-serving bias   42
In assessing ourselves, the tendency to attribute our own successes to our personal qualities and our failures to the circumstances.

semantics   65
The study of the way humans use language to evoke meaning in others.

sentence outline   315
An outline consisting entirely of complete sentences.

separation goal   171
The marginalized group relates as exclusively as possible with its own group and as little as possible with the dominant group.

sexist language   73
Language that excludes individuals on the basis of gender.

sexual harassment   212
Unwelcome, unsolicited, repeated behavior of a sexual nature.

short-term memory   113
A temporary storage place for information.

signposts   322
Ways in which a presenter signals to an audience where the presentation is going.

similarity   39, 150
(1) The principle that elements are grouped together because they share attributes such as size, color, or shape. (2) The idea that our friends and loved ones are usually people who like or dislike the same things we do.

skills approach   347
Reducing fear by systematically improving your presenting skills.

slang   72
A specialized language of a group of people who share a common interest or belong to a similar co-culture.

sleeper effect   278
A change of audience opinion caused by the separation of the message content from its source over a period of time.

small-group communication   19, 223
(1) The process of using messages to generate meaning in a small group of people. (2) Interaction among three to nine people working together to achieve an interdependent goal.

source   12
A message initiator.

source credibility   120, 275
(1) The extent to which the speaker is perceived as competent to make the claims he or she is making. (2) The audience's perception of your effectiveness as a speaker.

stakeholders   241
Groups of people who have an interest in the actions of an organization.

statistics   294
Numbers that summarize numerical information or compare quantities.

strategic ambiguity   207
The purposeful use of symbols to allow multiple interpretations of messages.

subjective perception   33
Your uniquely constructed meaning attributed to sensed stimuli.

subpoints   312
The points in a presentation that support the main points; indicated by capital letters in an outline.

substitution   87
Nonverbal codes are used instead of verbal codes.

supporting materials   291
Information you can use to substantiate your arguments and to clarify your position.

supportive communication   207
Listening with empathy, acknowledging others' feelings, and engaging in dialogue to help others maintain a sense of personal control.

surveys   293
Studies in which a limited number of questions are answered by a sample of the population to discover opinions on issues.

syllogism   388
A logical structure that contains a major premise (a generalization) applied to a particular instance (a minor premise) that leads to a conclusion.

symbolic interactionism   46
The process in which the self develops through the messages and feedback received from others.

symmetrical relationships   139
Relationships in which participants mirror each other or are highly similar.

synonym   370
Defines by using a word close or similar in meaning to the one you are trying to define.

syntax   65
The way in which words are arranged to form phrases and sentences.

T

tactile communication   95
The use of touch in communication.

task functions   232
Behaviors that are directly relevant to the group's task and that affect the group's productivity.

task-oriented groups   224
Also called secondary groups; groups formed for the purpose of completing tasks, such as solving problems or making decisions.

testimonial evidence   293
Written or oral statements of others' experience used by a speaker to substantiate or clarify a point.

tests of evidence   387
Questions that can be used to test the validity of evidence.

time-sequence pattern   317
A method of organization in which the presenter explains a sequence of events in chronological order.

topical-sequence pattern   321
A method of organization that emphasizes the major reasons an audience should accept a point of view by addressing the advantages, disadvantages, qualities, and types of person, place, or thing.

transition   322
A bridge between sections of a presentation that helps the presenter move smoothly from one idea to another.

trustworthiness   277
The degree to which the speaker is perceived as honest, fair, sincere, honorable, friendly, and kind; an aspect of credibility.

two-sided argument   298
A source advocating one position presents an argument from the opposite viewpoint and then goes on to refute that argument.

U

ultimate goal   383
A statement of purposes that could be achieved with continuing attempts to persuade.

uncertainty-accepting cultures   177
Cultures that tolerate ambiguity, uncertainty, and diversity.

uncertainty-rejecting cultures   177
Cultures that have difficulty with ambiguity, uncertainty, and diversity.

upward communication   191
Messages flowing from subordinates to superiors.

V

value   260
A deeply rooted belief that governs our attitude about something.

verbal citations   290
Oral explanations of who the source is, how recent the information is, and what the source's qualifications are.

verbal codes   13
Symbols and their grammatical arrangement, such as languages.

visualization approach   348
Picturing yourself succeeding.

visual resources   349
Any items that can be seen by an audience for the purpose of reinforcing a message.

vocal cues   97
All of the oral aspects of sound except words themselves.

vocalized pauses   338
Breaks in fluency that negatively affect an audience's perception of the speaker's competence and dynamism.

vocal variety   340
Vocal quality, intonation patterns, inflections of pitch, and syllabic duration.

voluntary audience   258
A collection of people who choose to listen to a particular speaker or speech.

W

within-group diversity   236
The presence of observable and/or implicit differences among group members.

working memory   112
The part of our consciousness that interprets and assigns meaning to stimuli we pay attention to.

Credits

Chapter 1

PHOTOS: **2:** © Taxi/Getty Images; **11:** © Rhonda Sidney/The Image Works; **15:** © Bob Mahoney/The Image Works; **18:** © LWA-Sharie Kennedy/zefa/Corbis

QUOTATIONS: **23-24:** Nine commandments, NCA Credo, National Communication Association, Washington, DC. Reprinted by permission of NCA.

FIGURES: **48:** Figure 2.7, Maslow's hierarchy of needs, from A. Maslow & R. Lowery (Eds.) (1998). *Toward a psychology of being*, 3/e. Reprinted with permission of John Wiley & Sons, Inc.

Chapter 2

PHOTOS: **30:** © John Giustina/Iconica/Getty Images; **35:** © Aliza Averbach/Photo Researchers; **47:** © Sven Martson/The Image Works

QUOTATIONS: **35:** Levine, Susan (February 26, 2006). "Culturally sensitive medicine: Doctors learn to adapt to immigrant patients' ethnic and religious customs." *The Washington Post National Weekly Edition*, 23 (22), 31. © 2006, The Washington Post, reprinted with permission of Washington Post Writers Group. **47:** O'Connor, J. T. (1998). "A view from Mount Ritter: Two weeks in the Sierras changed my attitude toward life and what it takes to succeed," *Newsweek*, May 25, 1998, p. 17. (c) 1998 Newsweek, Inc. All rights reserved. Reprinted by permission. **49:** Susan Lang, "Contrast of U.S./Chinese memories shows impact of culture on 'self-concept'," *Cornell Chronicle* www.news.cornell.edu/Chronicle/ 01/6.28.01/memory-culture.html. Used by permission of

Cornell Chronicle and Cornell University.

TABLES: **55:** Table 2.1, Image Repair Strategies. The strategies, tactics, and key characteristics are from http://www.missouri.edu/commwlb/image_repair.html . The examples are the author's originals. Reprinted from *Public Relations Review* 1997:23, William Benoit, "Image repair discourse and crisis communication," p.179. Copyright 1997, with permission from Elsevier.

Chapter 3

PHOTOS: **62:** © image100/Corbis; **71:** © Bob Daemmrich Photo, Inc.; **72:** © David M. Grossman/The Image Works

FIGURES: **70:** Figure 3.2, The Ladder of Abstraction, concept adapted from Hayakawa, S.I. (1978). *Language in thought and action*. Harcourt Brace, publisher. Copyright controlled by Thomson Learning.

Chapter 4

PHOTOS: **84:** © Mike Watson Images/Corbis; **92:** © Paul Hawthorne/Getty Images; **96:** © AP/Wide World Photos; **99:** © M. Taghi/zefa/Corbis

QUOTATIONS: **94:** Hall (1963). "Proxemics: The study of man's spatial relations and boundaries. In Galdston (Ed.), *Man's image in medicine and anthropology*, pp. 422–445. Used by permission of International Universities Press, Inc.

Chapter 5

PHOTOS: **108:** © Bill Aron/PhotoEdit; **116:** (top) © Ken Wramton/Taxi/Getty Images, (bottom) © Image Source Pink/Getty

Images; **126:** © Sonda Dawes/The Image Works

QUOTATIONS: **125:** Gunn, B. (2001, February). "Listening as feeling," *Strategic Finance*, 82, 12–15. Copyright 2001 by Institute of Management Accountants. Reproduced with permission of Institute of Management Accountants in the format Textbook via Copyright Clearance Center.

Chapter 6

PHOTOS: **134:** © Myrleen Ferguson Cate/PhotoEdit; **139:** © Spencer Grant/PhotoEdit; **140:** MANNIE GARCIA/AFP/Getty Images; **148:** © Royalty-Free/Corbis; **150:** © Chuck Savage/Corbis

FIGURES: **141:** Figure 6.1, Johari window, from Joseph Luft (1984). *Group Processes: An Introduction to Group Dynamics*. NY: Mayfield Publishing Company. Copyright 1984, 1970, and 1969 by Joseph Luft. © The McGraw-Hill Companies, Inc. Used by permission.

TABLES: **148:** Table 6.2, An Overview of Stages, from Mark L. Knapp & Anita L.Vangelisti (1996). *Interpersonal Communication and Human Relationships*, 3/e. Boston: Allyn & Bacon. Copyright © 1996 by Pearson Education. Reprinted by permission of the publisher.

Chapter 7

PHOTOS: **166:** © Digital Vision/Getty Images; **171:** © AP/Wide World Photos; **182:** © Francis Dean/Dean Pictures/The Image Works

QUOTATIONS: **173:** Bruno (1999). "'Beating' the tribal drum: rejecting disability stereotypes and preventing self-discrimination." *Disability and Society*, 14, pp. 855–857. Reproduced by permission of the publisher (Taylor & Francis Ltd., http://www.informa world.com). **181:** NCA Ethics Credo, National Communication Association, Washington, DC. Reprinted by permission of NCA. *TABLES:* **180:** Table 7.1, Summary of Cultural Characteristics, Based on Carley Dodd (1998). *Dynamics of Intercultural Communication*, 4/e (McGraw-Hill). © 1998, The McGraw-Hill Companies, Inc. All rights reserved.

Chapter 8

PHOTOS: **186:** © Warren Morgan/Corbis; **190:** © Jim Pickerell/Stock Boston; **198:** © Bob Daemmrich/The Image Works; **202:** © DCA Productions/Taxi/Getty Images; **211:** © Dave Bartruff/Danita Delimont/Alamy *QUOTATIONS:* **204, 212:** NCA Ethics Credo, National Communication Association, Washington, DC. Reprinted by permission of NCA. *TABLES:* **210:** Table 8.2, Compliance-Gaining Strategies Used By Customer Service Representatives, from W.Z. Ford (1998). *Communicating with Customers: Service Approaches, Ethics, and Impact.* Cresskill, NJ: Hampton Press, 1998. Used by permission of Hampton Press.

Chapter 9

PHOTOS: **218:** © Sonda Dawes/The Image Works; **222:** © PM Images/Getty Images; **226:** © Jose Luis Pelaez, Inc./Corbis; **230:** © Bill Aron/-PhotoEdit; **242:** © Patrick Giardino/Corbis *FIGURES:* **234:** Figure 9.3, Behavior Functions Combine to Create Roles, from Gloria J. Galanes & John K. Brilhart (1993). *Communicating in Groups*, 2/e. Copyright © 1993 Times Mirror Higher Education Group, Inc. All rights reserved. Reprinted by

permission of The McGraw-Hill Companies.

Chapter 10

PHOTOS: **250:** © Peter Hvizdak/The Image Works; **254:** © Syracuse Newspapers/The Image Works; **258:** © Michael Newman/PhotoEdit; **263:** © Tim Sloan/AFP/Getty Images *QUOTATIONS:* **267:** (2006) Target-Point website http://beta.targetpoint. com/Modules/Main/default.aspx by permission of TargetPoint, 66 Canal Center Plaza No. 555, Alexandria, Virginia, 703-535-8508, fax-703-535-8517, info@targetpointconsulting. com. **267:** Edsall, T.B., & Grimaldi, J.V. (2004, December 30). "On November 2, GOP got more bang for its billion," Analysis, *Washington Post* (2004). Used by permission of Washington Post Writers Group. **267:** Dreazen, Yochi, J. (October 31, 2006). "Democrats, playing catch-up, tap database to woo potential voters," *Wall Street Journal*. Copyright © 2007 Dow Jones & Company, Inc. All Rights Reserved. *TABLES:* **261:** Table 10.2, Variability in Value System Priorities as Decision-Making Adaptation to Situational Differences, Robert Heath (1976). *Communication Monographs*, 43: p.325-333. © 1976 Speech Communication Association. Reproduced by permission of the publisher (Taylor & Francis Ltd., http://www.tandf.co.uk/journals), the author, and the National Communication Association.

Chapter 11

PHOTOS: **272:** © Jose Luis Pelaez, Inc./Corbis; **275:** © Richard A. Bloom/Corbis; **277:** © David Young-Wolff/PhotoEdit; **279:** (both) © Bob Daemmrich/The Image Works; **284:** © Bob Daemmrich/The Image Works; **289:** © Karen Preuss/The Image Works; **295:** © Syracuse Newspapers/The Image Works *FIGURES:* **285:** Figure 11.1, Home page for Yahoo! Reproduced with

permission of Yahoo! Inc. © 2007 by Yahoo! Inc. YAHOO! and the YAHOO! logo are trademarks of Yahoo! Inc. **286:** Figure 11.2, Yahoo! page showing results from Tim McGraw search. Reproduced with permission of Yahoo! Inc. © 2007 by Yahoo! Inc. YAHOO! and the YAHOO! logo are trademarks of Yahoo! Inc.

Chapter 12

PHOTOS: **302:** © Bob Daemmrich/The Image Works; **306:** © Frances Roberts/Alamy

Chapter 13

PHOTOS: **332:** © Purestock/Alamy; **338:** © Robert Brenner/PhotoEdit; **342:** © Najlah Feanny/Stock Boston; **351:** © Alexei Kalmykov/Reuters/Corbis; **355:** © John Boykin/PhotoEdit *QUOTATIONS:* **339:** Definition #1 of "belie" from *The Random House Dictionary of the English Language*. Copyright © by Random House, Inc. *FIGURES:* **343:** Figure 13.3, Tips for Gesturing Effectively, from Teri Kwal Gamble & Michael Gamble (2005). *Communication Works*, 8/e. Copyright © (2005) The McGraw-Hill Companies, Inc. Reprinted by permission. **348:** Figure 13.4, Calming Normal Communication Apprension, adapted from two exercises from Teri Kwal Gamble & Michael Gamble (2005). *Communication Works*, 8/e. Copyright © (2005) The McGraw-Hill Companies, Inc. Reprinted by permission.

Chapter 14

PHOTOS: **360:** © Kim Kulish/Corbis; **363:** © Matthias Tunger/Digital Vision; **368:** © Michael Newman/PhotoEdit

Chapter 15

PHOTOS: **380:** © Laurent Sazy/Atlas Press; **393:** © Robert Brenner/PhotoEdit; **397:** © Laura Dwight/PhotoEdit

index